Seven Contemporary Short Novels

Third Edition

Edited by Charles Clerc and Louis Leiter
University of the Pacific

HarperCollins*Publishers*

The second edition of *SEVEN CONTEMPORARY SHORT NOVELS* is still in print. Novels in that edition include Vonnegut, *Slaughterhouse-Five*; McCullers, *The Ballad of the Sad Café*; Roth, *Goodbye, Columbus*; Porter, *Noon Wine*; Bellow, *Seize the Day*; Steinbeck, *Of Mice and Men*; O'Connor, *The Violent Bear It Away*.

Printed in the United States of America.
97 98 99 12 11 10

Library of Congress Cataloging in Publication Data
Main entry under title:

Seven contemporary short novels.

Contents: Goodbye, Columbus / Philip Roth—The ballad of the sad café / Carson McCullers—Slaughterhouse-five / Kurt Vonnegut, Jr.—[etc.]
1. American fiction—20th century. I. Clerc, Charles. II. Leiter, Louis H.
PS659.S48 1982 808'.0427 81–21399
ISBN 0-673-15569-2

Acknowledgments

Goodbye, Columbus by Philip Roth from *Goodbye, Columbus*. Copyright © 1959 by Philip Roth. Reprinted by permission of the publisher Houghton Mifflin Company. • From *Collected Short Stories and the Novel, The Ballad of the Sad Café* by Carson McCullers. Reprinted by permission of Houghton Mifflin Company. • *Slaughterhouse-Five* by Kurt Vonnegut, Jr. Copyright © 1969 by Kurt Vonnegut, Jr. Reprinted by permission of the publisher, Delacorte Press/Seymour Lawrence. • From the "Introduction" by Ira C. Eaker, Lt. Gen. USAF (Ret.) to *The Destruction of Dresden* by David Irving. Copyright © 1963 by William Kimber & Co. Limited. Reprinted by permission of Holt, Rinehart and Winston, Publishers and William Kimber & Co. Limited. From the "Forward" by Air Marshal Sir Robert Saundby to *The Destruction of Dresden* by David Irving. Reprinted by permission of William Kimber & Co. Limited. • *'Leven Cent Cotton, Forty Cent Meat*. Words and Music by Bob Miller and Emma Dermer. Copyright 1929 by Triangle Music Publishing Co. © Copyright renewed 1956 by MCA MUSIC, A Division of MCA, Inc. Used by permission. All Rights Reserved. • Excerpt from "The Waking" by Theodore Roethke from the book *The Collected Poems of Theodore Roethke*. Copyright 1953 by Theodore Roethke. Reprinted by permission of Doubleday & Company, Inc. • *The Bluest Eye* by Toni Morrison. Copyright © 1970 by Toni Morrison. Reprinted by permission of Holt, Rinehart and Winston, Publishers. • *Being There*, copyright © 1970 by Jerzy Kosinski, is reprinted by permission of Harcourt Brace Jovanovich, Inc. • *Surfacing* by Margaret Atwood. Copyright © 1972 by Margaret Atwood. Reprinted by permission of Simon & Schuster, a Division of Gulf & Western Corporation. • *Seize the Day* by Saul Bellow. Copyright © 1956, 1974 by Saul Bellow. All rights reserved. Used by permission of Viking Penguin Inc.

Preface

The favorable reception of the second edition of *Seven Contemporary Short Novels* confirms our belief—as did the first edition—that a collection of this kind fulfills a real need among students and general readers alike. In this latest edition we present seven works meriting rank among other accomplished short novels of the world, past and present, of whatever national origin. Because of their high quality and assured stature, these short novels, three of which are new to this edition (and unavailable in any other collection), have much to offer in subject and theme, artistry and universality.

Some significant changes have been made in the third edition. To maintain our policy of printing contemporary works, we have included three novels published in the 1970s: *Surfacing* by the Canadian novelist and poet Margaret Atwood, *The Bluest Eye* by the Black-American writer Toni Morrison, and *Being There* by the Polish-American author Jerzy Kosinski.

Set on a Canadian island near the U.S. border, *Surfacing* is narrated by a young woman struggling toward self-discovery as she tries to reconcile a divided psyche. Aside from depicting the basic conflict of female and male principles, the novel also probes into such thematic subjects as alienation, communication, social relationships, sex, death, nature, and creation-destruction. *The Bluest Eye* is a powerful evocation of black experience, both brutal and tender in its treatment of victimization in a midwestern city in recent times. A yearning for blue eyes by a black child serves as a metaphor for the unfortunate pariahs of society. *Being There* is a trenchant and funny satire of our television age which, tongue-in-cheek, traces the skyrocketing national eminence of a virtually mindless cipher. He is launched in all seriousness from corridors of business and political power in New York and Washington. The questions and problems these novels address are as contemporary as daily newspaper headlines, and yet timeless in scope and far-reaching in application.

We have retained four novels: Kurt Vonnegut's *Slaughterhouse-Five*, Carson McCullers' *The Ballad of the Sad Café*, Philip Roth's *Goodbye, Columbus*, and Saul Bellow's *Seize the Day*. All seven novels have found wide critical acclaim for modernity of subject matter, brilliant sustained writing, and universality. As in our second edition, to emphasize the diversity of the novels, we have alternated women and men writers, urban and rural settings, varying themes and images of contemporary life. In technique they range from mimetic realism to parable to innovative science fiction. Their characters are black, white, Jewish, cosmopolitan northerners, backwoods southerners, and creatures from outer space. They represent the poor, the middle class, and the wealthy; their social surroundings extend from the primitive to the ordinary to the ultra-sophisticated, not to mention the galactic. The battle of the sexes figures prominently in each novel.

As in past editions, we refrain from tracing the history of the short novel. Nor do we attempt to define the short novel beyond saying simply that it is a type of fiction longer and more complex than a short story and more economical, if not necessarily less intricate than a novel. We are willing to settle for Vladimir Nabokov's felicitous observation that this genre goes about its business "by diminishing large things and enlarging small ones." So, whether novella, nouvelle, novelette, short novel, we mean simply a novel in which intrinsic brevity and artistic rightness are harmoniously fused.

Students and teachers will find useful the "Topics for Papers and Discussion" at the end of each short novel. In them such essential components of fiction as character, theme, plot, setting, narrative technique, symbolism, irony, style, and social significance are considered. The topics suggest the richness of each work and provide the student some direction and guidance for close textual analysis. Certain questions are better suited for discussion, others lend themselves more readily to written work, and all of them can be used profitably for individual enlightenment. We believe that the questions will provoke lively discussion and fruitful writing over a wide range of traditional and contemporary issues, as well as literary techniques. The brief up-to-date "Biographical Notes" at the end of the text serve at least cursorily to introduce the writer and to connect the anthologized novel to the body of the writer's work.

When our first edition appeared back in 1969, we stressed the enjoyment of reading and the experience of discovery that contemporary short novels provide. Now in 1982 we are pleased to be able to furnish students and general readers with a third new collection which we believe to be similarly rewarding. As works of art, these short novels can be studied and reread with increased appreciation, deepened pleasure, and enhanced understanding.

Charles Clerc and Louis Leiter

Contents

Goodbye, Columbus

PHILIP ROTH

"The heart is half a prophet."
Yiddish proverb

The first time I saw Brenda she asked me to hold her glasses. Then she stepped out to the edge of the diving board and looked foggily into the pool; it could have been drained, myopic Brenda would never have known it. She dove beautifully, and a moment later she was swimming back to the side of the pool, her head of short-clipped auburn hair held up, straight ahead of her, as though it were a rose on a long stem. She glided to the edge and then was beside me. "Thank you," she said, her eyes watery though not from the water. She extended a hand for her glasses but did not put them on until she turned and headed away. I watched her move off. Her hands suddenly appeared behind her. She caught the bottom of her suit between thumb and index finger and flicked what flesh had been showing back where it belonged. My blood jumped.

That night, before dinner, I called her.

"Who are you calling?" my Aunt Gladys asked.

"Some girl I met today."

"Doris introduced you?"

"Doris wouldn't introduce me to the guy who drains the pool, Aunt Gladys."

"Don't criticize all the time. A cousin's a cousin. How did you meet her?"

"I didn't really meet her. I saw her."

"Who is she?"

"Her last name is Patimkin."

"Patimkin I don't know," Aunt Gladys said, as if she knew

anybody who belonged to the Green Lane Country Club. "You're going to call her you don't know her?"

"Yes," I explained. "I'll introduce myself."

"Casanova," she said, and went back to preparing my uncle's dinner. None of us ate together: my Aunt Gladys ate at five o'clock, my cousin Susan at five-thirty, me at six, and my uncle at six-thirty. There is nothing to explain this beyond the fact that my aunt is crazy.

"Where's the suburban phone book?" I asked after pulling out all the books tucked under the telephone table.

"What?"

"The suburban phone book. I want to call Short Hills."

"That skinny book? What, I gotta clutter my house with that, I never use it?"

"Where is it?"

"Under the dresser where the leg came off."

"For God's sake," I said.

"Call information better. You'll go yanking around there, you'll mess up my drawers. Don't bother me, you see your uncle'll be home soon. I haven't even fed *you* yet."

"Aunt Gladys, suppose tonight we all eat together. It's hot, it'll be easier for you."

"Sure, I should serve four different meals at once. You eat pot roast, Susan with the cottage cheese, Max has steak. Friday night is his steak night, I wouldn't deny him. And I'm having a little cold chicken. I should jump up and down twenty different times? What am I, a workhorse?"

"Why don't we all have steak, or cold chicken—"

"Twenty years I'm running a house. Go call your girl friend."

But when I called, Brenda Patimkin wasn't home. She's having dinner at the club, a woman's voice told me. Will she be home after (my voice was two octaves higher than a choirboy's)? I don't know, the voice said, she may go driving golf balls. Who is this? I mumbled some words—nobody she wouldn't know I'll call back no message thank you sorry to bother . . . I hung up somewhere along in there. Then my aunt called me and I steeled myself for dinner.

She pushed the black whirring fan up to *High* and that way it managed to stir the cord that hung from the kitchen light.

"What kind of soda you want? I got ginger ale, plain seltzer, black raspberry, and a bottle cream soda I could open up."

"None, thank you."

"You want water?"

"I don't drink with my meals. Aunt Gladys, I've told you that every day for a year already—"

"Max could drink a whole case with his chopped liver only. He works hard all day. If you worked hard you'd drink more."

At the stove she heaped up a plate with pot roast, gravy, boiled potatoes, and peas and carrots. She put it in front of me and I could feel the heat of the food in my face. Then she cut two pieces of rye bread and put that next to me, on the table.

I forked a potato in half and ate it, while Aunt Gladys, who had seated herself across from me, watched. "You don't want bread," she said, "I wouldn't cut it it should go stale."

"I *want* bread," I said.

"You don't like with seeds, do you?"

I tore a piece of bread in half and ate it.

"How's the meat?" she said.

"Okay. Good."

"You'll fill yourself with potatoes and bread, the meat you'll leave over I'll have to throw it out."

Suddenly she leaped up from the chair. "Salt!" When she returned to the table she plunked a salt shaker down in front of me—pepper wasn't served in her home: she'd heard on Galen Drake that it was not absorbed by the body, and it was disturbing to Aunt Gladys to think that anything she served might pass through a gullet, stomach, and bowel just for the pleasure of the trip.

"You're going to pick the peas out is all? You tell me that, I wouldn't buy with the carrots."

"I love carrots," I said, "I love them." And to prove it, I dumped half of them down my throat and the other half onto my trousers.

"Pig," she said.

Though I am very fond of desserts, especially fruit, I chose not to have any. I wanted, this hot night, to avoid the conversation that revolved around my choosing fresh fruit over canned fruit, or canned fruit over fresh fruit; whichever I preferred, Aunt Gladys always had an abundance of the other jamming her refrigerator like stolen diamonds. "He wants canned peaches, I have a refrigerator full of grapes I have to get rid of . . ." Life was a throwing off for poor Aunt Gladys, her greatest joys were taking out the garbage, emptying her pantry, and making threadbare bundles for what she still referred to as the Poor Jews in Palestine. I only hope she dies with an empty refrigerator, otherwise she'll ruin eternity for everyone else, what with her Velveeta turning green, and her navel oranges growing fuzzy jackets down below.

My Uncle Max came home and while I dialed Brenda's number once again, I could hear soda bottles being popped open in the kitchen. The voice that answered this time was high, curt, and tired. "Hullo."

I launched into my speech. "Hello-Brenda-Brenda-you-don't-know - me - that - is - you - don't - know - my - name - but - I - held - your - glasses - for - you - this - afternoon - at - the - club . . . You - asked - me - to - I'm - not - a - member - my - cousin - Doris - is - Doris - Klugman - I - asked - who - you - were . . ." I breathed, gave her a chance to speak, and then went ahead and answered the silence on the other end. "Doris? She's the one who's always reading *War and Peace*. That's how I know it's the summer, when Doris is reading *War and Peace*." Brenda didn't laugh; right from the start she was a practical girl.

"What's your name?" she said.

"Neil Klugman. I held your glasses at the board, remember?"

She answered me with a question of her own, one, I'm sure, that is an embarrassment to both the homely and the fair. "What do you look like?"

"I'm . . . dark."

"Are you a Negro?"

"No," I said.

"What *do* you look like?"

"May I come see you tonight and show you?"

"That's nice," she laughed. "I'm playing tennis tonight."

"I thought you were driving golf balls."

"I drove them already."

"How about after tennis?"

"I'll be sweaty after," Brenda said.

It was not to warn me to clothespin my nose and run in the opposite direction; it was a fact, it apparently didn't bother Brenda, but she wanted it recorded.

"I don't mind," I said, and hoped by my tone to earn a niche somewhere between the squeamish and the grubby. "Can I pick you up?"

She did not answer a minute; I heard her muttering, "Doris Klugman, Doris Klugman . . ." Then she said, "Yes, Briarpath Hills, eight-fifteen."

"I'll be driving a—" I hung back with the year, "a tan Plymouth. So you'll know me. How will I know you?" I said with a sly, awful laugh.

"I'll be sweating," she said and hung up.

Once I'd driven out of Newark, past Irvington and the packed-in tangle of railroad crossings, switchmen shacks, lumberyards, Dairy Queens, and used-car lots, the night grew cooler. It was, in fact, as though the hundred and eighty feet that the suburbs rose in altitude above Newark brought one closer to heaven, for the sun itself became bigger, lower, and rounder, and soon I was driving past long lawns which seemed to be twirling water on themselves, and past houses where no one sat on stoops, where lights were on but no windows open, for those inside, refusing to share the very texture of life with those of us outside, regulated with a dial the amounts of moisture that were allowed access to their skin. It was only eight o'clock, and I did not want to be early, so I drove up and down the streets whose names were those of eastern colleges, as though the township, years ago, when things were named, had planned the destinies of the sons of its citizens. I thought of my Aunt Gladys and Uncle Max sharing a Mounds bar in the cindery darkness of their alley, on beach chairs, each cool breeze sweet to them as the promise of afterlife, and after a while I rolled onto the gravel roads of the small park where Brenda was playing tennis. Inside my glove compartment it was as though the map of *The City Streets of Newark* had metamorphosed into crickets, for those mile-long tarry streets did not exist for me any longer, and the night noises sounded loud as the blood whacking at my temples.

I parked the car under the black-green canopy of three oaks, and walked towards the sound of the tennis balls. I heard an exasperated voice say, "Deuce *again.*" It was Brenda and she sounded as though she was sweating considerably. I crackled slowly up the gravel and heard Brenda once more. "My ad," and then just as I rounded the path, catching a cuff full of burrs, I heard, "Game!" Her racket went spinning up in the air and she caught it neatly as I came into sight.

"Hello," I called.

"Hello, Neil. One more game," she called. Brenda's words seemed to infuriate her opponent, a pretty brown-haired girl, not quite so tall as Brenda, who stopped searching for the ball that had been driven past her, and gave both Brenda and myself a dirty look. In a moment

I learned the reason why: Brenda was ahead five games to four, and her cocksureness about there being just one game remaining aroused enough anger in her opponent for the two of us to share.

As it happened, Brenda finally won, though it took more games than she'd expected. The other girl, whose name sounded like Simp, seemed happy to end it at six all, but Brenda, shifting, running, up on her toes, would not stop, and finally all I could see moving in the darkness were her glasses, a glint of them, the clasp of her belt, her socks, her sneakers, and, on occasion, the ball. The darker it got the more savagely did Brenda rush the net, which seemed curious, for I had noticed that earlier, in the light, she had stayed back, and even when she had had to rush, after smashing back a lob, she didn't look entirely happy about being so close to her opponent's racket. Her passion for winning a point seemed outmatched by an even stronger passion for maintaining her beauty as it was. I suspected that the red print of a tennis ball on her cheek would pain her more than losing all the points in the world. Darkness pushed her in, however, and she stroked harder, and at last Simp seemed to be running on her ankles. When it was all over, Simp refused my offer of a ride home and indicated with a quality of speech borrowed from some old Katherine Hepburn movie that she could manage for herself; apparently her manor lay no further than the nearest briar patch. She did not like me and I her, though I worried it, I'm sure, more than she did.

"Who is *she?*"

"Laura Simpson Stolowitch."

"Why don't you call her Stolo?" I asked.

"Simp is her Bennington name. The ass."

"Is that where you go to school?" I asked.

She was pushing her shirt up against her skin to dry the perspiration. "No. I go to school in Boston."

I disliked her for the answer. Whenever anyone asks me where I went to school I come right out with it: Newark Colleges of Rutgers University. I may say it a bit too ringingly, too fast, too up-in-the-air, but I say it. For an instant Brenda reminded me of the pug-nosed little bastards from Montclair who come down to the library during vacations, and while I stamp out their books, they stand around tugging their elephantine scarves until they hang to their ankles, hinting all the while at "Boston" and "New Haven."

"Boston University?" I asked, looking off at the trees.

"Radcliffe."

We were still standing on the court, bounded on all sides by white lines. Around the bushes back of the court, fire-flies were cutting figure eights in the thorny-smelling air and then, as the night suddenly came all the way in, the leaves on the trees shone for an instant, as though they'd just been rained upon. Brenda walked off the court, with me a step behind her. Now I had grown accustomed to the dark, and as she ceased being merely a voice and turned into a sight again, some of my anger at her "Boston" remark floated off and I let myself appreciate her. Her hands did not twitch at her bottom, but the form revealed itself, covered or not, under the closeness of her khaki Bermudas. There were two wet triangles on the back of her tiny-collared white polo shirt, right where her wings would have been if she'd had a pair. She wore, to complete the picture, a tartan belt, white socks, and white tennis sneakers.

As she walked she zipped the cover on her racket.

"Are you anxious to get home?" I said.

"No."

"Let's sit here. It's pleasant."

"Okay."

We sat down on a bank of grass slanted enough for us to lean back without really leaning; from the angle it seemed as though we were preparing to watch some celestial event, the christening of a new star, the inflation to full size of a half-ballooned moon. Brenda zipped and unzipped the cover while she spoke; for the first time she seemed edgy. Her edginess coaxed mine back, and so we were ready now for what, magically, it seemed we might be able to get by without: a meeting.

"What does your cousin Doris look like?" she asked.

"She's dark—"

"Is she—"

"No," I said. "She has freckles and dark hair and she's very tall."

"Where does she go to school?"

"Northampton."

She did not answer and I don't know how much of what I meant she had understood.

"I guess I don't know her," she said after a moment. "Is she a new member?"

"I think so. They moved to Livingston only a couple of years ago."

"Oh."

No new star appeared, at least for the next five minutes.

"Did you remember me from holding your glasses?" I said.

"Now I do," she said. "Do you live in Livingston too?"

"No. Newark."

"We lived in Newark when I was a baby," she offered.

"Would you like to go home?" I was suddenly angry.

"No. Let's walk though."

Brenda kicked a stone and walked a step ahead of me.

"Why is it you rush the net only after dark?" I said.

She turned to me and smiled. "You noticed? Old Simp the Simpleton doesn't."

"Why do you?"

"I don't like to be up too close, unless I'm sure she won't return it."

"Why?"

"My nose."

"What?"

"I'm afraid of my nose. I had it bobbed."

"What?"

"I had my nose fixed."

"What was the matter with it?"

"It was bumpy."

"A lot?"

"No," she said, "I was pretty. Now I'm prettier. My brother's having his fixed in the fall."

"Does he want to be prettier?"

She didn't answer and walked ahead of me again.

"I don't mean to sound facetious. I mean why's he doing it?"

"He *wants* to . . . unless he becomes a gym teacher . . . but he won't," she said. "We all look like my father."

"Is he having his fixed?"

"Why are you so nasty?"

"I'm not. I'm sorry." My next question was prompted by a desire to sound interested and thereby regain civility; it didn't quite come out as I'd expected—I said it too loud. "How much does it cost?"

Brenda waited a moment but then she answered. "A thousand dollars. Unless you go to a butcher."

"Let me see if you got your money's worth."

She turned again; she stood next to a bench and put the racket down on it. "If I let you kiss me would you stop being nasty?"

We had to take about two too many steps to keep the approach from being awkward, but we pursued the impulse and kissed. I felt her hand on the back of my neck and so I tugged her towards me, too violently perhaps, and slid my own hands across the side of her body and around to her back. I felt the wet spots on her shoulder blades, and beneath them, I'm sure of it, a faint fluttering, as though something stirred so deep in her breasts, so far back it could make itself felt through her shirt. It was like the fluttering of wings, tiny wings no bigger than her breasts. The smallness of the wings did not bother me—it would not take an eagle to carry me up those lousy hundred and eighty feet that make summer nights so much cooler in Short Hills than they are in Newark.

2

The next day I held Brenda's glasses for her once again, this time not as momentary servant but as afternoon guest; or perhaps as both, which still was an improvement. She wore a black tank suit and went barefooted, and among the other women, with their Cuban heels and boned-up breasts, their knuckle-sized rings, their straw hats, which resembled immense wicker pizza plates and had been purchased, as I heard one deeply tanned woman rasp, "from the cutest little *shvartze* when we docked at Barbados," Brenda among them was elegantly simple, like a sailor's dream of a Polynesian maiden, albeit one with prescription sun glasses and the last name of Patimkin. She brought a little slurp of water with her when she crawled back towards the pool's edge, and at the edge she grabbed up with her hands and held my ankles, tightly and wet.

"Come in," she said up to me, squinting. "We'll play."

"Your glasses," I said.

"Oh break the goddam things. I hate them."

"Why don't you have your eyes fixed?"

"There you go again."

"I'm sorry," I said. "I'll give them to Doris."

Doris, in the surprise of the summer, had gotten past Prince Andrey's departure from his wife, and now sat brooding, not, it turned out, over the lonely fate of poor Princess Liza, but at the skin which she had lately discovered to be peeling off her shoulders.

"Would you watch Brenda's glasses?" I said.

"Yes." She fluffed little scales of translucent flesh into the air. "Damn it."

I handed her the glasses.

"Well, for God's sake," she said, "I'm not going to hold them. Put them down. *I'm* not her slave."

"You're a pain in the ass, you know that, Doris?" Sitting there, she looked a little like Laura Simpson Stolowitch, who was, in fact, walking somewhere off at the far end of the pool, avoiding Brenda and me because (I liked to think) of the defeat Brenda had handed her the night before; or maybe (I didn't like to think) because of the strangeness of my presence. Regardless, Doris had to bear the weight of my indictment of both Simp and herself.

"Thank you," she said. "After I invite you up for the day."

"That was yesterday."

"What about last year?"

"That's right, your mother told you last year too—invite Esther's boy so when he writes his parents they won't complain we don't look after him. Every summer I get my day."

"You should have gone with them. That's not our fault. You're not our charge," and when she said it, I could just tell it was something she'd heard at home, or received in a letter one Monday mail, after she'd returned to Northampton from Stowe, or Dartmouth, or perhaps from that weekend when she'd taken a shower with her boyfriend in Lowell House.

"Tell your father not to worry. Uncle Aaron, the sport. I'll take care of myself," and I ran on back to the pool, ran into a dive, in fact, and came up like a dolphin beside Brenda, whose legs I slid upon with my own.

"How's Doris?" she said.

"Peeling," I said. "She's going to have her skin fixed."

"*Stop* it," she said, and dove down beneath us till I felt her clamping her hands on the soles of my feet. I pulled back and then down too, and then, at the bottom, no more than six inches above the wiggling black lines that divided the pool into lanes for races, we bubbled a kiss into each other's lips. She was smiling there, at *me,* down at the bottom of the swimming pool of the Green Lane Country Club. Way above us, legs shimmied in the water and a pair of fins skimmed greenly by: my cousin Doris could peel away to nothing for all I cared, my Aunt Gladys have twenty feedings every night, my father and mother could roast away their asthma down in the furnace of Arizona, those penniless deserters—I didn't care for anything but Brenda. I went to pull her towards me just as she started fluttering up; my hand hooked on to the front of her suit and the cloth pulled away from her. Her breasts swam towards me like two pink-nosed fish and she let me hold them. Then, in a moment, it was the sun who kissed us both, and we were out of the water, too pleased with each other to smile. Brenda shook the wetness of her hair onto my face and with the drops that touched me I felt she had made a promise to me about the summer, and, I hoped, beyond.

"Do you want your sun glasses?"

"You're close enough to see," she said. We were under a big blue umbrella, side-by-side on two chaise longues, whose plastic covers sizzled against our suits and flesh; I turned my head to look at Brenda and smelled that pleasant little burning odor in the skin of my shoulders. I turned back up to the sun, as did she, and as we talked, and it grew hotter and brighter, the colors splintered under my closed eyelids.

"This is all very fast," she said.

"Nothing's happened," I said softly.

"No. I guess not. I sort of feel something has."

"In eighteen hours?"

"Yes. I feel . . . pursued," she said after a moment.

"*You* invited *me,* Brenda."

"Why do you always sound a little nasty to me?"

"Did I sound nasty? I don't mean to. Truly."

"You do! *You* invited *me,* Brenda. So what?" she said. "That isn't what I mean anyway."

"I'm sorry."

"Stop apologizing. You're so automatic about it, you don't even mean it."

"Now you're being nasty to me," I said.

"No. Just stating the facts. Let's not argue. I like you." She turned her head and looked as though she too paused a second to smell the summer on her own flesh. "I like the way you look." She saved it from embarrassing me with that factual tone of hers.

"Why?" I said.

"Where did you get those fine shoulders? Do you play something?"

"No," I said. "I just grew up and they came with me."

"I like your body. It's fine."

"I'm glad," I said.

"You like mine, don't you?"

"No," I said.

"Then it's denied you," she said.

I brushed her hair flat against her ear with the back of my hand and then we were silent a while.

"Brenda," I said, "you haven't asked me anything about me."

"How you feel? Do you want me to ask you how you feel?"

"Yes," I said, accepting the back door she gave me, though probably not for the same reasons she had offered it.

"How *do* you feel?"

"I want to swim."

"Okay," she said.

We spent the rest of the afternoon in the water. There were eight of those long lines painted down the length of the pool and by the end of the day I think we had parked for a while in every lane, close enough to the dark stripes to reach out and touch them. We came back to the chairs now and then and sang hesitant, clever, nervous, gentle dithyrambs about how we were beginning to feel towards one another. Actually we did not have the feelings we said we had until we spoke them—at least I didn't; to phrase them was to invent them and own them. We whipped our strangeness and newness into a froth that resembled love, and we dared not play too long with it, talk too much of it, or it would flatten and fizzle away. So we moved back and forth from chairs to water, from talk to silence, and considering my unshakable edginess with Brenda, and the high walls of ego that rose, buttresses and all, between her and her knowledge of herself, we managed pretty well.

At about four o'clock, at the bottom of the pool, Brenda suddenly wrenched away from me and shot up to the surface. I shot up after her.

"What's the matter?" I said.

First she whipped the hair off her forehead. Then she pointed a hand down towards the base of the pool. "My brother," she said, coughing some water free inside her.

And suddenly, like a crew-cut Proteus rising from the sea, Ron Patimkin emerged from the lower depths we'd just inhabited and his immensity was before us.

"Hey, Bren," he said, and pushed a palm flat into the water so that a small hurricane beat up against Brenda and me.

"What are you so happy about?" she said.

"The Yankees took two."

"Are we going to have Mickey Mantle for dinner?" she said.

"When the Yankees win," she said to me, treading so easily she seemed to have turned the chlorine to marble beneath her, "we set an extra place for Mickey Mantle."

"You want to race?" Ron asked.

"No, Ronald. Go race alone."

Nobody had as yet said a word about me. I treaded unobtrusively as I could, as a third party, unintroduced, will step back and say nothing, awaiting the amenities. I was tired, however, from the afternoon's sport, and wished to hell brother and sister would not tease and chat much longer. Fortunately Brenda introduced me. "Ronald, this is Neil Klugman. This is my brother, Ronald Patimkin."

Of all things there in the fifteen feet water, Ron reached out his hand to shake. I returned the shake, not quite as monumentally as he apparently expected; my chin slipped an inch into the water and all at once I was exhausted.

"Want to race?" Ron asked me good-naturedly.

"Go ahead, Neil, race with him. I want to call home and tell them you're coming to dinner."

"Am I? I'll have to call my aunt. You didn't say anything. My clothes—"

"We dine *au naturel.*"

"What?" Ronald said.

"Swim, baby," Brenda said to him and it ached me some when she kissed him on the face.

I begged out of the race, saying I had to make a phone call myself, and once upon the tiled blue border of the pool, looked back to see Ron taking the length in sleek, immense strokes. He gave one the feeling that after swimming the length of the pool a half dozen times he would have earned the right to drink its contents; I imagined he had, like my Uncle Max, a colossal thirst and a gigantic bladder.

Aunt Gladys did not seem relieved when I told her she'd have only three feedings to prepare that night. "Fancy-shmancy" was all she said to me on the phone.

We did not eat in the kitchen; rather, the six of us—Brenda, myself, Ron, Mr. and Mrs. Patimkin, and Brenda's little sister, Julie—sat around the dining room table, while the maid, Carlota, a Navaho-faced Negro who had little holes in her ears but no earrings, served us the meal. I was seated next to Brenda, who was dressed in what was *au naturel* for her: Bermudas, the close ones, white polo shirt, tennis sneakers and white socks. Across from me was Julie, ten, round-faced, bright, who before dinner, while the other little girls on the street had been playing with jacks and boys and each other, had been on the back lawn putting golf balls with her father. Mr. Patimkin reminded me of my father, except that when he spoke he did not surround each syllable with a wheeze. He was tall, strong, ungrammatical, and a ferocious eater. When he attacked his salad—after drenching it in bottled French dressing—the veins swelled under the heavy skin of his forearm. He ate three helpings of salad, Ron had four, Brenda and Julie had two, and only Mrs. Patimkin and I had one each. I did not like Mrs. Patimkin, though she was certainly the handsomest of all of us at the table. She was disastrously polite to me, and with her purple eyes, her dark hair, and large, persuasive frame, she gave me the feeling of some captive beauty, some wild princess, who has been tamed and made the servant to the king's daughter—who was Brenda.

Outside, through the wide picture window, I could see the back lawn with its twin oak trees. I say oaks, though fancifully, one might call them sporting-goods trees. Beneath their branches, like fruit dropped from their limbs, were two irons, a golf ball, a tennis can, a baseball bat, basketball, a first-baseman's glove, and what was apparently a riding crop. Further back, near the scrubs that bounded the Patimkin property and in front of the small basketball court, a square red blanket, with a white O stitched in the center, looked to be on fire against the green grass. A breeze must have blown outside, for the net on the basket moved; inside we ate in the steady coolness of air by Westinghouse. It was a pleasure, except that eating among those Brobdingnags, I felt for quite a while as though four inches had been clipped from my shoulders, three inches from my height, and for good measure, someone had removed my ribs and my chest had settled meekly in towards my back.

There was not much dinner conversation; eating was heavy and methodical and serious, and it would be just as well to record all that was said in one swoop, rather than indicate the sentences lost in the passing of food, the words gurgled into mouthfuls, the syntax chopped and forgotten in heapings, spillings, and gorgings.

To Ron: When's Harriet calling?

Ron: Five o'clock.

Julie: It *was* five o'clock.

Ron: Their time.

Julie: Why is it that it's earlier in Milwaukee? Suppose you took a plane back and forth all day. You'd never get older.

Brenda: That's right, sweetheart.

Mrs. P.: What do you give the child misinformation for? Is that why she goes to school?

Brenda: I don't know why she goes to school.

Mr. P. (lovingly): College girl.

Ron: Where's Carlota? Carlota!

Mrs. P.: Carlota, give Ronald more.

Carlota (calling): More what?

Ron: Everything.

Mr. P.: Me too.

Mrs. P.: They'll have to *roll* you on the links.

Mr. P. (pulling his shirt up and slapping his black, curved belly): What are you talking about? Look at that?

Ron (yanking his T-shirt up): Look at *this*.

Brenda (to me): Would you care to bare your middle?

Me (the choir boy again): No.

Mrs. P.: That's right, Neil.

Me: Yes. Thank you.

Carlota (over my shoulder, like an unsummoned spirit): Would *you* like more?

Me: No.

Mr. P.: He eats like a bird.

Julie: Certain birds eat a lot.

Brenda: Which ones?

Mrs. P.: Let's not talk about animals at the dinner table. Brenda, why do you encourage her?

Ron: Where's Carlota, I gotta play tonight.

Mr. P.: Tape your wrist, don't forget.

Mrs. P.: Where do you live, Bill?

Brenda: Neil.

Mrs. P.: Didn't I say Neil?

Julie: You said "Where do you live, *Bill?*"

Mrs. P.: I must have been thinking of something else.

Ron: I hate tape. How the hell can I play in tape?

Julie: Don't curse.

Mrs. P.: That's right.

Mr. P.: What is Mantle batting now?

Julie: Three twenty-eight.

Ron: Three twenty-five.

Julie: Eight!

Ron: Five, jerk! He got three for four in the second game.

Julie: Four for four.
Ron: That was an error, Minoso should have had it.
Julie: I didn't think so.
Brenda (to me): See?
Mrs. P.: See what?
Brenda: I was talking to Bill.
Julie: Neil.
Mr. P.: Shut up and eat.
Mrs. P.: A little less talking, young lady.
Julie: I didn't say anything.
Brenda: She was talking to me, sweetie.
Mr. P.: What's this *she* business. Is that how you call your mother? What's dessert?

The phone rings, and though we are awaiting dessert, the meal seems at a formal end, for Ron breaks for his room, Julie shouts "Harriet!" and Mr. Patimkin is not wholly successful in stifling a belch, though the failure even more than the effort ingratiates him to me. Mrs. Patimkin is directing Carlota not to mix the milk silverware and the meat silverware again, and Carlota is eating a peach while she listens; under the table I feel Brenda's fingers tease my calf. I am full.

We sat under the biggest of the oak trees while out on the basketball court Mr. Patimkin played five and two with Julie. In the driveway Ron was racing the motor of the Volkswagen. "Will somebody *please* move the Chrysler out from behind me?" he called angrily. "I'm late as it is."

"Excuse me," Brenda said, getting up.

"I think I'm behind the Chrysler," I said.

"Let's go," she said.

We backed the cars out so that Ron could hasten on to his game. Then we reparked them and went back to watching Mr. Patimkin and Julie.

"I like your sister," I said.

"So do I," she said. "I wonder what she'll turn out to be."

"Like you," I said.

"I don't know," she said. "Better probably." And then she added, "or maybe worse. How can you tell? My father's nice to her, but I'll give her another three years with my mother . . . Bill," she said, musingly.

"I didn't mind that," I said. "She's very beautiful, your mother."

"I can't even think of her as my mother. She hates me. Other girls, when they pack in September, at least their mothers help them. Not mine. She'll be busy sharpening pencils for Julie's pencil box while I'm carrying my trunk around upstairs. And it's so obvious why. It's practically a case study."

"Why?"

"She's jealous. It's so corny I'm ashamed to say it. Do you know my mother had the best back-hand in New Jersey? Really, she was the best tennis player in the state, man or woman. You ought to see the pictures of her when she was a girl. She was so healthy-looking. But not chubby or anything. She was soulful, truly. I love her in those pictures. Sometimes I say to her how beautiful the pictures are. I even asked to have one blown up so I could have it at school. 'We have other things to do with our money, young lady, than spend it on old photographs.' Money! My father's up to here with it, but whenever I buy a coat you should hear her. 'You don't have to go to Bonwit's, young lady, Ohrbach's has the strongest fabrics of any of them.' Who *wants* a strong fabric! Finally I get what I want, but not till she's had a chance to aggravate me. Money is a waste for her. She doesn't even know how to enjoy it. She still thinks we live in Newark."

"But you get what you want," I said.

"Yes. Him," and she pointed out to Mr. Patimkin who had just swished his third straight set shot through the basket to the disgruntlement, apparently, of Julie, who stamped so hard at the ground that she raised a little dust storm around her perfect young legs.

"He's not too smart but he's sweet at least. He doesn't treat my brother the way she treats me. Thank God, for that. Oh, I'm tired of talking about them. Since my freshman year I think every conversation I've ever had has always wound up about my parents and how awful it is. It's universal. The only trouble is they don't know it."

From the way Julie and Mr. Patimkin were laughing now, out on the court, no problem could ever have seemed less universal; but, of course, it was universal for Brenda, more than that, cosmic—it made every cashmere sweater a battle with her mother, and her life, which, I was certain, consisted to a large part of cornering the market on fabrics that felt soft to the skin, took on the quality of a Hundred Years' War . . .

I did not intend to allow myself such unfaithful thoughts, to line up with Mrs. Patimkin while I sat beside Brenda, but I could not shake from my elephant's brain that she-still-thinks-we-live-in-Newark remark. I did not speak, however, fearful that my tone would shatter our post-dinner ease and intimacy. It had been so simple to be intimate with water pounding and securing all our pores, and later, with the sun heating them and drugging our senses, but now, in the shade and the open, cool and clothed on her own grounds, I did not want to voice a word that would lift the cover and reveal that hideous emotion I always felt for her, and is the underside of love. It will not always *stay* the underside—but I am skipping ahead.

Suddenly, little Julie was upon us. "Want to play?" she said to me. "Daddy's tired."

"C'mon," Mr. Patimkin called. "Finish for me."

I hesitated—I hadn't held a basketball since high school—but Julie was dragging at my hand, and Brenda said, "Go ahead."

Mr. Patimkin tossed the ball towards me while I wasn't looking and it bounced off my chest, leaving a round dust spot, like the shadow of a moon, on my shirt. I laughed, insanely.

"Can't you catch?" Julie said.

Like her sister, she seemed to have a knack for asking practical, infuriating questions.

"Yes."

"Your turn," she said. "Daddy's behind forty-seven to thirty-nine. Two hundred wins."

For an instant, as I placed my toes in the little groove that over the years had been nicked into a foul line, I had one of those instantaneous waking dreams that plague me from time to time, and send, my friends tell me, deadly cataracts over my eyes: the sun had sunk, crickets had come and gone, the leaves had blackened, and still Julie and I stood alone on the lawn, tossing the ball at the basket; "Five hundred wins," she called, and then when she beat me to five hundred she called, "Now *you* have to reach it," and I did, and the night lengthened, and she called, "*Eight* hundred wins," and we played on and then it was eleven hundred that won and we played on and it never was morning.

"Shoot," Mr. Patimkin said. "You're me."

That puzzled me, but I took my set shot and, of course, missed. With the Lord's blessing and a soft breeze, I made the lay-up.

"You have forty-one. I go," Julie said.

Mr. Patimkin sat on the grass at the far end of the court. He took his shirt off, and in his undershirt, and his whole day's growth of beard, looked like a trucker. Brenda's old nose fitted him well. There was a bump in it, all right; up at the bridge it seemed as though a small eight-sided diamond had been squeezed in under the skin. I knew Mr. Patimkin would never bother to have that stone cut from his face, and yet, with joy and pride, no doubt, had paid to have Brenda's diamond removed and dropped down some toilet in Fifth Avenue Hospital.

Julie missed her set shot, and I admit to a slight, gay, flutter of heart.

"Put a little spin on it," Mr. Patimkin told her.

"Can I take it again?" Julie asked me.

"Yes." What with paternal directions from the sidelines and my own grudging graciousness on the court, there did not seem much of a chance for me to catch up. And I wanted to, suddenly, I wanted to win, to run little Julie into the ground. Brenda was back on one elbow, under the tree, chewing on a leaf, watching. And up in the house, at the kitchen window, I could see that the curtain had swished back—the sun too low now to glare off electrical appliances—and Mrs. Patimkin was looking steadily out at the game. And then Carlota appeared on the back steps, eating a peach and holding a pail of garbage in her free hand. She stopped to watch too.

It was my turn again. I missed the set shot and laughingly turned to Julie and said, "Can I take it again?"

"No!"

So I learned how the game was played. Over the years Mr. Patimkin had taught his daughters that free throws were theirs for the asking; he could afford to. However, with the strange eyes of Short Hills upon me, matrons, servants, and providers, I somehow felt I couldn't. But I had to and I did.

"Thanks a lot, Neil," Julie said when the game was ended—at 100—and the crickets had come.

"You're welcome."

Under the trees, Brenda smiled. "Did you let her win?"

"I think so," I said. "I'm not sure."

There was something in my voice that prompted Brenda to say, comfortingly, "Even Ron lets her win."

"It's all nice for Julie," I said.

3

The next morning I found a parking space on Washington Street directly across from the library. Since I was twenty minutes early I decided to stroll in the park rather than cross over to work; I didn't particularly care to join my colleagues, who I knew would be sipping early morning coffee in the binding room, smelling still of all the orange crush they'd drunk that weekend at Asbury Park. I sat on a bench and looked out towards Broad Street and the morning traffic. The Lackawanna commuter trains were rumbling in a few blocks to the north and I could hear them, I thought—the sunny green cars, old and clean, with windows that opened all the way. Some mornings, with time to kill before work, I would walk down to the tracks and watch the open windows roll in, on their sills the elbows of tropical suits and the edges of briefcases, the properties of businessmen arriving in town from Maplewood, the Oranges, and the suburbs beyond.

The park, bordered by Washington Street on the west and Broad on the east, was empty and shady and smelled of trees, night, and dog leavings; and there was a faint damp smell too, indicating that the huge rhino of a water cleaner had passed by already, soaking and whisking the downtown streets. Down Washington Street, behind me, was the Newark Museum—I could see it without even looking: two oriental vases in front like spittoons for a rajah, and next to it the little annex to which we had traveled on special buses as schoolchildren. The annex was a brick building, old and vine-covered, and always reminded me of New Jersey's link with the beginning of the country, with George Washington, who had trained his scrappy army—a little bronze tablet informed us children—in the very park where I now sat. At the far end of the park, beyond the Museum, was the bank building where I had gone to college. It had been converted some years before into an extension of Rutgers University; in fact, in what once had been the bank president's waiting room I had taken a course called Contemporary Moral Issues. Though it was summer now, and I was out of college three years, it was not hard for me to remember the other students, my friends, who had worked evenings in Bamberger's and Kresge's and had used the commissions they'd earned pushing ladies' out-of-season shoes to pay their laboratory fees. And then I looked out to Broad Street again. Jammed between a grimy-windowed bookstore and a cheesy luncheonette was the marquee of a tiny art theater—how many years had passed since I'd stood beneath that marquee, lying about the year of my birth so as to see Hedy Lamarr swim naked in *Ecstasy;* and then, having slipped the ticket taker an extra quarter, what disappointment I had felt at the frugality of her Slavic charm . . . Sitting there in the park, I felt a deep knowledge of Newark, an attachment so rooted that it could not help but branch out into affection.

Suddenly it was nine o'clock and everything was scurrying. Wobbly-heeled girls revolved through the doors of the telephone building across the way, traffic honked desperately, policeman barked, whistled, and waved motorists to and fro. Over at St. Vincent's Church the huge dark portals swung back and those bleary-eyes that had risen early for Mass now blinked at the light. Then the worshipers had stepped off the church steps and were racing down the streets towards desks, filing cabinets, secretaries, bosses, and—if the Lord had seen fit to remove a mite of harshness from their lives—to the comfort of air-conditioners pumping at their windows. I got up and crossed over to the library, wondering if Brenda was awake yet.

The pale cement lions stood unconvincing guard on the library steps, suffering their usual combination of elephantiasis and arteriosclerosis, and I was prepared to pay them as little attention as I had for the past eight months were it not for a small colored boy who stood in front of one of them. The lion had lost all of its toes the summer before to a safari of juvenile delinquents, and now a new tormentor stood before him, sagging a little in his knees, and growling. He would growl, low and long, drop back, wait, then growl again. Then he would straighten up, and, shaking his head, he would say to the lion, "Man, you's a coward . . ." Then, once again, he'd growl.

The day began the same as any other. From behind the desk on the main floor, I watched the hot high-breasted teen-age girls walk twitchingly up the wide flight of marble stairs that led to the main reading room. The stairs were an imitation of a staircase somewhere in Versailles, though in their toreador pants and sweaters these young daughters of Italian leatherworkers, Polish brewery hands, and Jewish furriers were hardly duchesses. They were not Brenda either, and any lust that sparked inside me through the dreary day was academic and time-passing. I looked at my watch occasionally, thought of Brenda, and waited for lunch and then for after lunch, when I would take over the Information Desk upstairs and John McKee, who was only twenty-one but wore elastic bands around his sleeves, would march starchily down the stairs to work assiduously at stamping books in and out. John McRubberbands was in his last year at Newark State Teachers College where he was studying at the Dewey Decimal System in preparation for his lifework. The library was not going to be my lifework, I knew it. Yet, there had been some talk—from Mr. Scapello, an old eunuch who had learned somehow to disguise his voice as a man's—that when I returned from my summer vacation I would be put in charge of the Reference Room, a position that had been empty ever since that morning when Martha Winney had fallen off a high stool in the Encyclopedia Room and shattered all those frail bones that come together to form what in a woman half her age we would call the hips.

I had strange fellows at the library and, in truth, there were many hours when I never quite knew how I'd gotten there or why I stayed. But I did stay and after a while waited patiently for that day when I would go into the men's room on the main floor for a cigarette and, studying myself as I expelled smoke into the mirror, would see that at some moment during the morning I had gone pale, and that under my skin, as under McKee's and Scapello's and Miss Winney's, there was a thin cushion of air separating the blood from the flesh. Someone had pumped it there while I was stamping out a book, and so life from now on would be not a throwing off, as it was for Aunt Gladys, and not a gathering in, as it was for Brenda, but a bouncing off, a numbness. I began to fear this, and yet, in my muscleless devotion to my work, seemed edging towards it, silently, as Miss Winney used to edge up to the *Britannica*. Her stool was empty now and awaited me.

Just before lunch the lion tamer came wide-eyed into the library. He stood still for a moment, only his fingers moving, as though he were counting the number of marble stairs before him. Then he walked creepily about on the marble floor, snickering at the clink of his taps and the way his little noise swelled up to the vaulted ceiling. Otto, the guard at the door, told him to make less noise with his shoes, but that did not seem to bother the little boy. He clacked on his tiptoes, high, secretively, delighted at the opportunity Otto had given him to practice this posture. He tiptoed up to me.

"Hey," he said, "where's the heart section?"

"The what?" I said.

"The heart section. Ain't you got no heart section?"

He had the thickest sort of southern Negro dialect and the only word that came clear to me was the one that sounded like heart.

"How do you spell it?" I said.

"*Heart.* Man, pictures. Drawing books. Where you got them?"

"You mean art books? Reproductions?"

He took my polysyllabic word for it. "Yea, they's them."

"In a couple places," I told him. "Which artist are you interested in?"

The boy's eyes narrowed so that his whole face seemed black. He started backing away, as he had from the lion. "All of them . . ." he mumbled.

"That's okay," I said. "You go look at whichever ones you want. The next flight up. Follow the arrow to where it says Stack Three. You remember that? Stack Three. Ask somebody upstairs."

He did not move; he seemed to be taking my curiosity about his taste as a kind of poll-tax investigation. "Go ahead," I said, slashing my face with a smile, "right up there . . ."

And like a shot he was scuffling and tapping up towards the heart section.

After lunch I came back to the in-and-out desk and there was John McKee, waiting, in his pale blue slacks, his black shoes, his barber-cloth shirt with the elastic bands, and a great knit tie, green, wrapped into a Windsor knot, that was huge and jumped when he talked. His breath smelled of hair oil and his hair of breath and when he spoke, spittle cobwebbed the corners of his mouth. I did not like him and at times had the urge to yank back on his armbands and slingshoot him out past Otto and the lions into the street.

"Has a little Negro boy passed the desk? With a thick accent? He's been hiding in the art books all morning. You know what those boys *do* in there."

"I saw him come in, John."

"So did I. Has he gone *out* though."

"I haven't noticed. I guess so."

"Those are *very* expensive books."

"Don't be so nervous, John. People are supposed to touch them."

"There is touching," John said sententiously, "and there is touching. Someone should check on him. I was afraid to leave the desk here. You know the way they treat the housing projects we give them."

"*You* give them?"

"The city. Have you seen what they do at Seth Boyden? They threw *beer* bottles, those big ones, on the *lawn.* They're taking over the city."

"Just the Negro sections."

"It's easy to laugh, you don't live near them. I'm going to call Mr. Scapello's office to check the Art Section. Where did he ever find out about art?"

"You'll give Mr. Scapello an ulcer, so soon after his egg-and-pepper sandwich. I'll check, I have to go upstairs anyway."

"You know what they do in there," John warned me.

"Don't worry, Johnny, *they're* the ones who'll get warts on their dirty little hands."

"Ha ha. Those books happen to cost—"

So that Mr. Scapello would not descend upon the boy with his chalky fingers, I walked up the three flights to Stack Three, past the receiving room where rheumy-eyed Jimmy Boylen, our fifty-one-year-old boy, unloaded books from a cart; past the reading room, where bums off Mulberry Street slept over *Popular Mechanics;* past the smoking corridor where damp-browed summer students from the law school relaxed, some smoking, others trying to rub the colored dye from their tort texts off their fingertips; and finally, past the periodical room, where a few ancient ladies who'd been motored down from Upper Montclair now huddled in their chairs, pince-nezing over yellowed, fraying society pages in old old copies of the Newark *News.* Up on Stack Three I found the boy. He was seated on the glass-brick floor holding an open book in his lap, a book, in fact, that was bigger than his lap and had to be propped up by his knees. By the light of the window behind him I could see the hundreds of spaces between the hundreds of tiny black corkscrews that were his hair. He was very black and shiny, and the flesh of his lips did not so much appear to be a different color as it looked to be unfinished and awaiting another coat. The lips were parted, the eyes wide, and even the ears seemed to have a heightened receptivity. He looked ecstatic—until he saw me, that is. For all he knew I was John McKee.

"That's okay," I said before he could even move, "I'm just passing through. You read."

"Ain't nothing *to* read. They's pictures."

"Fine." I fished around the lowest shelves a moment, playing at work.

"Hey, mister," the boy said after a minute, "where is this?"

"Where is what?"

"Where is these pictures? These people, man, they sure does look cool. They ain't no yelling or shouting here, you could just see it."

He lifted the book so I could see. It was an expensive large-sized edition of Gauguin reproductions. The page he had been looking at showed an 8 1/2 x 11 print, in color, of three native women standing knee-high in a rose-colored stream. It *was* a silent picture, he was right.

"That's Tahiti. That's an island in the Pacific Ocean."

"That ain't no place you could go, is it? Like a ree-*sort?"*

"You could go there, I suppose. It's very far. People live there . . ."

"Hey, *look,* look here at this one." He flipped back to a page where a young brown-skinned maid was leaning forward on her knees, as though to dry her hair. "Man," the boy said, "that's the fuckin life." The euphoria of his diction would have earned him eternal banishment from the Newark Public Library and its branches had John or Mr. Scapello—or, God forbid, the hospitalized Miss Winney—come to investigate.

"Who took these pictures?" he asked me.

"Gauguin. He didn't take them, he painted them. Paul Gauguin. He was a Frenchman."

"Is he a white man or a colored man?"

"He's white."

"Man," the boy smiled, chuckled almost, "I knew that. He don't *take* pictures like no colored men would. He's a good picture taker . . . *Look, look,* look here at this one. Ain't that the fuckin *life?"*

I agreed it was and left.

Later I sent Jimmy Boylen hopping down the stairs to tell McKee that everything was all right. The rest of the day was uneventful. I sat at the Information Desk thinking about Brenda and reminding myself that that evening I would have to get gas before I started up to Short Hills, which I could see now, in my mind's eye, at dusk, rose-colored, like a Gauguin stream.

When I pulled up to the Patimkin house that night, everybody but Julie was waiting for me on the front porch: Mr. and Mrs., Ron, and Brenda, wearing a dress. I had not seen her in a dress before and for an instant she did not look like the same girl. But that was only half the surprise. So many of those Lincolnesque college girls turn out to be limbed for shorts alone. Not Brenda. She looked, in a dress, as though she'd gone through life so attired, as though she'd never worn shorts, or bathing suits, or pajamas, or anything but that pale linen dress. I walked rather bouncingly up the lawn, past the huge weeping willow, towards the waiting Patimkins, wishing all the while that I'd had my car washed. Before I'd even reached them, Ron stepped forward and shook my hand, vigorously, as though he hadn't seen me since the Diaspora. Mrs. Patimkin smiled and Mr. Patimkin grunted something and continued twitching his wrists before him, then raising an imaginary golf club and driving a ghost of a golf ball up and away towards the Orange Mountains, that are called Orange, I'm convinced, because in that various suburban light that's the *only* color they do not come dressed in.

"We'll be right back," Brenda said to me. "You have to sit with Julie. Carlota's off."

"Okay," I said.

"We're taking Ron to the airport."

"Okay."

"Julie doesn't want to go. She says Ron pushed her in the pool this afternoon. We've been waiting for you, so we don't miss Ron's plane. Okay?"

"Okay."

Mr. and Mrs. Patimkin and Ron moved off, and I flashed Brenda just the hint of a glare. She reached out and took my hand a moment.

"How do you like me?" she said.

"You're great to baby-sit for. Am I allowed all the milk and cake I want?"

"Don't be angry, baby. We'll be right back." Then she waited a moment, and when I failed to deflate the pout from my mouth, she gave *me* a glare, no hints about it. "I *meant* how do you like me in a dress!" Then she ran off towards the Chrysler, trotting in her high heels like a colt.

When I walked into the house, I slammed the screen door behind me.

"Close the other door too," a little voice shouted. "The air-conditioning."

I closed the other door, obediently.

"Neil?" Julie called.

"Yes."

"Hi. Want to play five and two?"

"No."

"Why not?"

I did not answer.

"I'm in the television room," she called.

"Good."

"Are you supposed to stay with me?"

"Yes."

She appeared unexpectedly through the dining room. "Want to read a book report I wrote?"

"Not now."

"What do you want to do?" she said.

"Nothing, honey. Why don't you watch TV?"

"All right," she said disgustedly, and kicked her way back to the television room.

For a while I remained in the hall, bitten with the urge to slide quietly out of the house, into my car, and back to Newark, where I might even sit in the alley and break candy with my own. I felt like Carlota; no, not even as comfortable as that. At last I left the hall and began to stroll in and out of rooms on the first floor. Next to the living room was the study, a small knotty-pine room jammed with cater-cornered leather chairs and a complete set of *Information Please Almanacs.* On the wall hung three colored photo-paintings; they were the kind which, regardless of the subjects, be they vital or infirm, old or youthful, are characterized by bud-cheeks, wet lips, pearly teeth, and shiny, metallized hair. The subjects in this case were Ron, Brenda, and Julie at about ages fourteen, thirteen, and two. Brenda had long auburn hair, her diamond-studded nose, and no glasses; all combined to make her look a regal thirteen-year-old who'd just gotten smoke in her eyes. Ron was rounder and his hairline was lower, but that love of spherical objects and lined courts twinkled in his boyish eyes. Poor little Julie was lost in the photo-painter's Platonic idea of childhood; her tiny humanity was smothered somewhere back of gobs of pink and white.

There were other pictures about, smaller ones, taken with a Brownie Reflex before photo-paintings had become fashionable. There was a tiny picture of Brenda on a horse; another of Ron in bar mitzvah suit, *yamalkah,* and *tallas;* and two pictures framed together —one of a beautiful, faded woman, who must have been, from the eyes, Mrs. Patimkin's mother, and the other of Mrs. Patimkin herself, her hair in a halo, her eyes joyous and not those of a slowly aging mother with a quick and lovely daughter.

I walked through the archway into the dining room and stood a moment looking out at the sporting goods tree. From the television room that winged off the dining room, I could hear Julie listening to *This Is Your Life.* The kitchen, which winged off the other side, was empty, and apparently, with Carlota off, the Patimkins had had dinner at the club. Mr. and Mrs. Patimkin's bedroom was in the middle of the house, down the hall, next to Julie's, and for a moment I wanted to see what size bed those giants slept in—I imagined it wide and deep as a swimming pool—but I postponed my investigation while Julie was in the house, and instead opened the door in the kitchen that led down to the basement.

The basement had a different kind of coolness from the house, and it had a smell, which was something the upstairs was totally without. It felt cavernous down there, but in a comforting way, like the simulated caves children make for themselves on rainy days, in hall closets, under blankets, or in between the legs of dining room tables. I flipped on the light at the foot of the stairs and was not surprised at the pine paneling, the bamboo furniture, the ping-pong table, and the mirrored bar that was stocked with every kind and size of glass, ice bucket, decanter, mixer, swizzle stick, shot glass, pretzel bowl—all the bacchanalian paraphernalia, plentiful, orderly, and untouched, as it can be only in the bar of a wealthy man who never entertains drinking people, who himself does not drink, who, in fact, gets a fishy look from his wife when every several months he takes a shot of schnapps before dinner. I went behind the bar where there was an aluminum sink that had not seen a dirty glass, I'm sure, since Ron's bar mitzvah party, and would not see another, probably, until one of the Patimkin children was married or engaged. I would have poured myself a drink—just as a wicked wage for being forced into servantry—but I was uneasy about breaking the label on a bottle of whiskey. You had to break a label to get a drink. On the shelf back of the bar were two dozen bottles—twenty-three to be exact—of Jack Daniels, each with a little booklet tied to its collared neck informing patrons how patrician of them it was to drink the stuff. And over the Jack Daniels were more photos: there was a blown-up newspaper photo of Ron palming a basketball in one hand like a raisin; under the picture it said, "*Center,* Ronald Patimkin, Millburn High School, 6′4″, 217 pounds." And there was another picture of Brenda on a horse, and next to that, a velvet mounting board with ribbons and medals clipped to it: Essex County Horse Show 1949, Union County Horse Show 1950, Garden State Fair 1952, Morristown Horse Show 1953, and so on—all for Brenda, for jumping and running or galloping or whatever else young girls receive ribbons for. In the entire house I hadn't seen one picture of Mr. Patimkin.

The rest of the basement, back of the wide pine-paneled room, was gray cement walls and linoleum floor and contained innumerable electrical appliances, including a freezer big enough to house a family of Eskimos. Beside the freezer, incongruously, was a tall old refrigerator; its ancient presence was a reminder to me of the Patimkin roots in Newark. This same refrigerator had once stood in the kitchen of an apartment in some four-family house, probably in the same neighborhood where I had lived all my life, first with my parents and then, when the two of them went wheezing off to Arizona, with my aunt and uncle. After Pearl Harbor the refrigerator had made the move up to Short Hills; Patimkin Kitchen and Bathroom Sinks had gone to war: no new barracks was complete until it had a squad of Patimkin sinks lined up in its latrine.

I opened the door of the old refrigerator; it was not empty. No longer did it hold butter, eggs, herring in cream sauce, ginger ale, tuna fish salad, an occasional corsage—rather it was heaped with fruit, shelves swelled with it, every color, every texture, and hidden within, every kind of pit. There were greengage plums, black plums, red plums, apricots, nectarines, peaches, long horns of grapes, black, yellow, red, and cherries, cherries flowing out of boxes and staining everything scarlet. And there were melons—cantaloupes and honeydews—and on the top shelf, half of a huge watermelon, a thin sheet of wax paper clinging to its bare red face like a wet lip. Oh Patimkin! Fruit grew in their refrigerator and sporting goods dropped from their trees!

I grabbed a handful of cherries and then a nectarine, and I bit right down to its pit.

"You better wash that or you'll get diarrhea."

Julie was standing behind me in the pine-paneled room. She was wearing *her* Bermudas and *her* white polo shirt which was unlike Brenda's only in that it had a little dietary history of its own.

"What?" I said.

"They're not washed yet," Julie said, and in such a way that it seemed to place the refrigerator itself out-of-bounds, if only for me.

"That's all right," I said, and devoured the nectarine and put the pit in my pocket and stepped out of the refrigerator room, all in one second. I still didn't know what to do with the cherries. "I was just looking around," I said.

Julie didn't answer.

"Where's Ron going?" I asked, dropping the cherries into my pocket, among my keys and change.

"Milwaukee."

"For long?"

"To see Harriet. They're in love."

We looked at each other for longer than I could bear. "Harriet?" I asked.

"Yes."

Julie was looking at me as though she were trying to look behind me, and then I realized that I was standing with my hands out of sight. I brought them around to the front, and, I swear it, she did peek to see if they were empty.

We confronted one another again; she seemed to have a threat in her face.

Then she spoke. "Want to play ping-pong?"

"God, yes," I said, and made for the table with two long, bounding steps. "You can serve."

Julie smiled and we began to play.

I have no excuses to offer for what happened next. I began to win and I liked it.

"Can I take that one over?" Julie said. "I hurt my finger yesterday and it just hurt when I served."

"No."

I continued to win.

"That wasn't fair, Neil. My shoelace came untied. Can I take it—"

"No."

We played, I ferociously.

"Neil, you leaned over the table. That's illegal—"

"I didn't lean and it's not illegal."

I felt the cherries hopping among my nickels and pennies.

"Neil, you gypped me out of a point. You have nineteen and I have eleven—"

"Twenty and *ten,*" I said. "Serve!"

She did and I smashed my return past her—it zoomed off the table and skittered into the refrigerator room.

"You're a cheater!" she screamed at me. "You cheat!" Her jaw was trembling as though she carried a weight on top of her pretty head. *"I hate* you!" And she threw her racket across the room and it clanged off the bar, just as, outside, I heard the Chrysler crushing gravel in the driveway.

"The game isn't over," I said to her.

"You cheat! And you were stealing fruit!" she said, and ran away before I had my chance to win.

Later that night, Brenda and I made love, our first time. We were sitting on the sofa in the television room and for some ten minutes had not spoken a word to each other. Julie had long since gone to a weepy bed, and though no one had said anything to me about her crying, I did not know if the child had mentioned my fistful of cherries, which, some time before, I had flushed down the toilet.

The television set was on and though the sound was off and the house quiet, the gray pictures still wiggled at the far end of the room. Brenda was quiet and her dress circled her legs, which were tucked back beneath her. We sat there for some while and did not speak. Then she went into the kitchen and when she came back she said that it sounded as though everyone was asleep. We sat a while longer, watching the soundless bodies on the screen eating a silent dinner in someone's silent restaurant. When I began to unbutton her dress she resisted me, and I like to think it was because she knew how lovely she looked in it. But she looked lovely, my Brenda, anyway, and we folded it carefully and held each other close and soon there we were, Brenda falling, slowly but with a smile, and me rising.

How can I describe loving Brenda? It was so sweet, as though I'd finally scored that twenty-first point.

When I got home I dialed Brenda's number, but not before my aunt heard and rose from her bed.

"Who are you calling at this hour? The doctor?"

"No."

"What kind phone calls, one o'clock at night?"

"Shhh!" I said.

"He tells *me* shhh. Phone calls one o'clock at night, we haven't got a big enough bill," and then she dragged herself back into the bed, where with a martyr's heart and bleary eyes she had resisted the downward tug of sleep until she'd heard my key in the door.

Brenda answered the phone.

"Neil?" she said.

"Yes," I whispered. "You didn't get out of bed, did you?"

"No," she said, "the phone is next to the bed."

"Good. How is it in bed?"

"Good. Are you in bed?"

"Yes," I lied, and tried to right myself by dragging the phone by its cord as close as I could to my bedroom.

"I'm in bed with you," she said.

"That's right," I said, "and I'm with you."

"I have the shades down, so it's dark and I don't see you."

"I don't see you either."

"That was so nice, Neil."

"Yes. Go to sleep, sweet, I'm here," and we hung up without goodbyes. In the morning, as planned, I called again, but I could hardly hear Brenda or myself for that matter, for Aunt Gladys and Uncle Max were going on a Workmen's Circle picnic in the afternoon, and there was some trouble about grape juice that had dripped all night from a jug in the refrigerator and by morning had leaked out onto the floor. Brenda was still in bed and so could play our game with some success, but I had to pull down all the shades of my senses to imagine myself beside her. I could only pray our nights and mornings would come, and soon enough they did.

4

Over the next week and a half there seemed to be only two people in my life: Brenda and the little colored kid who liked Gauguin. Every morning before the library opened, the boy was waiting; sometimes he seated himself on the lion's back, sometimes under his belly, sometimes he just stood around throwing pebbles at his mane. Then he would come inside, tap around the main floor until Otto stared him up on tiptoes, and finally headed up the long marble stairs that led to Tahiti. He did not always stay to lunch time, but one very hot day he was there when I arrived in the morning and went through the door behind me when I left at night. The next morning, it was, that he did not show up, and as though in his place, a very old man appeared, white, smelling of Life Savers, his nose and jowls showing erupted veins beneath them. "Could you tell me where I'd find the art section?"

"Stack Three," I said.

In a few minutes, he returned with a big brown-covered book in his hand. He placed it on my desk, withdrew his card from a long moneyless billfold and waited for me to stamp out the book.

"Do you want to take this book *out?*" I said.

He smiled.

I took his card and jammed the metal edge into the machine; but I did not stamp down. "Just a minute," I said. I took a clipboard from under the desk and flipped through a few pages, upon which were games of battleship and tick-tack-toe that I'd been playing through the week with myself. "I'm afraid there's a hold on this book."

"A what?"

"A hold. Someone's called up and asked that we hold it for them. Can I take your name and address and drop a card when it's free . . ."

And so I was able, not without flushing once or twice, to get the book back in the stacks. When the colored kid showed up later in the day, it was just where he'd left it the afternoon before.

As for Brenda, I saw her every evening and when there was not a night game that kept Mr. Patimkin awake and in the TV room, or a Hadassah card party that sent Mrs. Patimkin out of the house and brought her in at unpredictable hours, we made love before the silent screen. One muggy, low-skied night Brenda took me swimming at the club. We were the only ones in the pool, and all the chairs, the cabañas, the lights, the diving boards, the very water seemed to exist only for our pleasure. She wore a blue suit that looked purple in the lights and down beneath the water it flashed sometimes green, sometimes black. Late in the evening a breeze came up off the golf course and we wrapped ourselves in one huge towel, pulled two chaise longues together, and despite the bartender, who was doing considerable pacing back and forth by the bar window, which overlooked the pool, we rested side by side on the chairs. Finally the bar light itself flipped off, and then, in a snap, the lights around the pool went down and out. My heart must have beat faster, or something, for Brenda seemed to guess my sudden doubt—*we should go,* I thought.

She said: "That's okay."

It was very dark, the sky was low and starless, and it took a while for me to see, once again, the diving board a shade lighter than the night, and to distinguish the water from the chairs that surrounded the far side of the pool.

I pushed the straps of her bathing suit down but she said no and rolled an inch away from me, and for the first time in the two weeks I'd known her she asked me a question about me.

"Where are your parents?" she said.

"Tucson," I said. "Why?"

"My mother asked me."

I could see the life guard's chair now, white almost.

"Why are you still here? Why aren't you with them?" she asked.

"I'm not a child any more, Brenda," I said, more sharply than I'd intended. "I just can't go wherever my parents are."

"But then why do you stay with your aunt and uncle?"

"They're not my parents."

"They're better?"

"No. Worse. I don't *know* why I stay with them."

"Why?" she said.

"Why don't I know?"

"Why do you stay? You do know, don't you?"

"My job, I suppose. It's convenient from there, and it's cheap, and it pleases my parents. My aunt's all right really . . . Do I really have to explain to your mother why I live where I do?"

"It's not for my mother. I want to know. I wondered why you weren't with your parents, that's all."

"Are you cold?" I asked.

"No."

"Do you want to go home?"

"No, not unless you do. Don't you feel well, Neil?"

"I feel all right," and to let her know that I was still me, I held her to me, though that moment I was without desire.

"Neil?"

"What?"

"What about the library?"

"Who wants to know that?"

"My father," she laughed.

"And you?"

She did not answer a moment. "And me," she said finally.

"Well, what about it? Do I like it? It's okay. I sold shoes once and like the library better. After the Army they tried me for a couple months at Uncle Aaron's real estate company—Doris' father—and I like the library better than that . . ."

"How did you get a job *there?*"

"I worked there for a little while when I was in college, then when I quit Uncle Aaron's, oh, I don't know . . ."

"What did you take in college?"

"At Newark Colleges of Rutgers University I majored in philosophy. I am twenty-three years old. I—"

"Why do you sound nasty again?"

"Do I?"

"Yes."

I didn't say I was sorry.

"Are you planning on making a career of the library?"

"Bren, I'm not planning anything. I haven't planned a thing in three years. At least for the year I've been out of the Army. In the Army I used to plan to go away weekends. I'm—I'm not a planner." After all the truth I'd suddenly given her, I shouldn't have ruined it for myself with that final lie. I added, "I'm a liver."

"I'm a pancreas," she said.

"I'm a —"

And she kissed the absurd game away; she wanted to be serious.

"Do you love me, Neil?"

I did not answer.

"I'll sleep with you whether you do or not, so tell me the truth."

"That was pretty crude."

"Don't be prissy," she said.

"No, I mean a crude thing to say about me."

"I don't understand," she said, and she didn't, and that she didn't pained me; I allowed myself the minor subterfuge, however, of forgiving Brenda her obtuseness. "Do you?" she said.

"No."

"I want you to."

"What about the library?"

"What about it?" she said.

Was it obtuseness again? I thought not—and it wasn't, for Brenda said, "When you love me, there'll be nothing to worry about."

"Then of course I'll love you." I smiled.

"I know you will," she said. "Why don't you go in the water, and I'll wait for you and close my eyes, and when you come back you'll surprise me with the wet. Go ahead."

"You like games, don't you?"

"Go ahead. I'll close my eyes."

I walked down to the edge of the pool and dove in. The water felt colder than it had earlier, and when I broke through and was headed blindly down I felt a touch of panic. At the top again, I started to swim the length of the pool and then turned at the end and started back, but suddenly I was sure that when I left the water Brenda would be gone. I'd be alone in this damn place. I started for the side and pulled myself up and ran to the chairs and Brenda was there and I kissed her.

"God," she shivered, "you didn't stay long."

"I know."

"My turn," she said, and then she was up and a second later I heard a little crack of water and then nothing. Nothing for quite a while.

"Bren," I called softly, "are you all right?" but no one answered.

I found her glasses on the chair beside me and held them in my hands. "Brenda?"

Nothing.

"Brenda?"

"No fair calling," she said and gave me her drenched self. "Your turn," she said.

This time I stayed below the water for a long while and when I surfaced again my lungs were ready to pop. I threw my head back for air and above me saw the sky, low like a hand pushing down, and I began to swim as though to move out from under its pressure. I wanted to get back to Brenda, for I worried once again—and there was no evidence, was there?—that if I stayed away too long she would not be there when I returned. I wished that I had carried her glasses away with me, so she would have to wait for me to lead her back home. I was having crazy thoughts, I knew, and yet they did not seem uncalled for in the darkness and strangeness of that place. Oh how I wanted to call out to her from the pool, but I knew she would not answer and I forced myself to swim the length a third time, and then a fourth, but midway through the fifth I felt a weird fright again, had momentary thoughts of my own extinction, and that time when I came back I held her tighter than either of us expected.

"Let go, let go," she laughed, "my turn—"

"But Brenda—"

But Brenda was gone and this time it seemed as though she'd never come back. I settled back and waited for the sun to dawn over the ninth hole, prayed it would if only for the comfort of its light, and when Brenda finally returned to me I would not let her go, and her cold wetness crept into me somehow and made me shiver. "That's it, Brenda. Please, no more games," I said and then when I spoke again I held her so tightly I almost dug my body into hers, "I love you," I said, "I do."

So the summer went on. I saw Brenda every evening: we went swimming, we went for walks, we went for rides, up through the mountains so far and so long that by the time we started back the fog had begun to emerge from the trees and push out into the road, and I would tighten my hands on the wheel and Brenda would put on her glasses and watch the white line for me. And we would eat—a few nights after my discovery of the fruit refrigerator Brenda led me to it herself. We would fill huge soup bowls with cherries, and in serving dishes for roast beef we would heap slices of watermelon. Then we would go up and out the back doorway of the basement and onto the back lawn and sit under the sporting-goods tree, the light from the TV room the only brightness we had out there. All we would hear for a while were just the two of us spitting pits. "I wish they would take root overnight and in the morning there'd just be watermelons and cherries."

"If they took root in this yard, sweetie, they'd grow refrigerators and Westinghouse Preferred. I'm not being nasty," I'd add quickly, and Brenda would laugh, and say she felt like a greengage plum, and I would disappear down into the basement and the cherry bowl would now be a greengage plum bowl, and then a nectarine bowl, and then a peach bowl, until, I have to admit it, I cracked my frail bowel, and would have to spend the following night, sadly, on the wagon. And then too we went out for corned beef sandwiches, pizza, beer and shrimp, ice cream sodas, and hamburgers. We went to the Lions Club Fair one night and Brenda won a Lions Club ashtray by shooting three baskets in a row. And when Ron came home from Milwaukee we went from time to time to see him play basketball in the semi-pro summer league, and it was those evenings that I felt a stranger with Brenda, for she knew all the players' names, and though for the most part they were gawky-limbed and dull, there was one named Luther Ferrari who was neither, and whom Brenda had dated for a whole year in high school. He was Ron's closest friend and I remembered his name from the Newark *News:* he was one of the great Ferrari brothers, All State all of them in at least two sports. It was Ferrari who called Brenda Buck, a nickname which apparently went back to her ribbon-winning days. Like Ron, Ferrari was exceedingly polite, as though it was some affliction of those over six feet three; he was gentlemanly towards me and gentle towards Brenda, and after a while I balked when the suggestion was made that we go to see Ron play. And then one night we discovered that at eleven o'clock the cashier of the Hilltop Theatre went home and the manager disappeared into his office, and so that summer we saw the last quarter of at least fifteen movies, and then when we were driving home

—driving Brenda home, that is—we would try to reconstruct the beginnings of the films. Our favorite last quarter of a movie was *Ma and Pa Kettle in the City,* our favorite fruit, greengage plums, and our favorite, our only, people, each other. Of course we ran into others from time to time, some of Brenda's friends, and occasionally, one or two of mine. One night in August we even went to a bar out on Route 6 with Laura Simpson Stolowitch and her fiancé, but it was a dreary evening. Brenda and I seemed untrained in talking to others, and so we danced a great deal, which we realized was one thing we'd never done before. Laura's boyfriend drank stingers pompously and Simp —Brenda wanted me to call her Stolo but I didn't—Simp drank a tepid combination of something like ginger ale and soda. Whenever we returned to the table, Simp would be talking about "the dance" and her fiancé about "the film," until finally Brenda asked him "Which film?" and then we danced till closing time. And when we went back to Brenda's we filled a bowl with cherries which we carried into the TV room and ate sloppily for a while; and later, on the sofa, we loved each other and when I moved from the darkened room to the bathroom I could always feel cherry pits against my bare soles. At home, undressing for the second time that night, I would find red marks on the undersides of my feet.

And how did her parents take all of this? Mrs. Patimkin continued to smile at me and Mr. Patimkin continued to think I ate like a bird. When invited to dinner I would, for his benefit, eat twice what I wanted, but the truth seemed to be that after he'd characterized my appetite that first time, he never really bothered to look again. I might have eaten ten times my normal amount, have finally killed myself with food, he would still have considered me not a man but a sparrow. No one seemed distressed by my presence, though Julie had cooled considerably; consequently, when Brenda suggested to her father that at the end of August I spend a week of my vacation at the Patimkin house, he pondered a moment, decided on the five iron, made his approach shot, and said yes. And when she passed on to her mother the decision of Patimkin Sink, there wasn't much Mrs. Patimkin could do. So, through Brenda's craftiness, I was invited.

On that Friday morning that was to be my last day of work, my Aunt Gladys saw me packing my bag and she asked where I was going. I told her. She did not answer and I thought I saw awe in those red-rimmed hysterical eyes—I had come a long way since that day she'd said to me on the phone, "Fancy-shmancy."

"How long you going, I should know how to shop I wouldn't buy too much. You'll leave me with a refrigerator full of milk it'll go bad it'll stink up the refrigerator—"

"A week," I said.

"A *week?*" she said. "They got room for a week?"

"Aunt Gladys, they don't live over the store."

"I lived over a store I wasn't ashamed. Thank God we always had a roof. We never went begging in the streets," she told me as I packed the Bermudas I'd just bought, "and your cousin Susan we'll put through college, Uncle Max should live and be well. We didn't send her away to camp for August, she doesn't have shoes when she wants them, sweaters she doesn't have a drawerful—"

"I didn't say anything, Aunt Gladys."

"You don't get enough to eat here? You leave over sometimes I show your Uncle Max your plate it's a shame. A child in Europe could make a four-course meal from what you leave over."

"Aunt Gladys." I went over to her. "I get everything I want here. I'm just taking a vacation. Don't I deserve a vacation?"

She held herself to me and I could feel her trembling. "I told your mother I would take care of her Neil she shouldn't worry. And now you go running—"

I put my arms around her and kissed her on the top of her head. "C'mon," I said, "you're being silly. I'm not running away. I'm just going away for a week, on a vacation."

"You'll leave their telephone number God forbid you should get sick."

"Okay."

"Millburn they live?"

"Short Hills. I'll leave the number."

"Since when do Jewish people live in Short Hills? They couldn't be real Jews believe me."

"They're real Jews," I said.

"I'll see it I'll believe it." She wiped her eyes with the corner of her apron, just as I was zipping up the sides of the suitcase. "Don't close the bag yet. I'll make a little package with some fruit in it, you'll take with you."

"Okay, Aunt Gladys," and on the way to work that morning I ate the orange and the two peaches that she'd put in a bag for me.

A few hours later Mr. Scapello informed me that when I returned from my vacation after Labor Day, I would be hoisted up onto

Martha Winney's stool. He himself, he said, had made the same move some twelve years ago, and so it appeared that if I could manage to maintain my balance I might someday be Mr. Scapello. I would also get an eight-dollar increase in salary which was five dollars more than the increase Mr. Scapello had received years before. He shook my hand and then started back up the long flight of marble stairs, his behind barging against his suit jacket like a hoop. No sooner had he left my side than I smelled spearmint and looked up to see the old man with veiny nose and jowls.

"Hello, young man," he said pleasantly. "Is the book back?"

"What book?"

"The Gauguin. I was shopping and I thought I'd stop by to ask. I haven't gotten the card yet. It's two weeks already."

"No," I said, and as I spoke I saw that Mr. Scapello had stopped midway up the stairs and turned as though he'd forgotten to tell me something. "Look," I said to the old man, "it should be back any day." I said it with a finality that bordered on rudeness, and I alarmed myself, for suddenly I saw what would happen: the old man making a fuss, Mr. Scapello gliding down the stairs, Mr. Scapello scampering up to the stacks, Scapello scandalized, Scapello profuse, Scapello presiding at the ascension of John McKee to Miss Winney's stool. I turned to the old man, "Why don't you leave your phone number and I'll try to get a hold of it this afternoon—" but my attempt at concern and courtesy came too late, and the man growled some words about public servants, a letter to the Mayor, snotty kids, and left the library, thank God, only a second before Mr. Scapello returned to my desk to remind me that everyone was chipping in for a present for Miss Winney and that if I liked I should leave a half dollar on his desk during the day.

After lunch the colored kid came in. When he headed past the desk for the stairs, I called over to him. "Come here," I said. "Where are you going?"

"The heart section."

"What book are you reading?"

"That Mr. Go-again's book. Look, man, I ain't doing nothing wrong. I didn't do *no* writing in *any*thing. You could search me—"

"I know you didn't. Listen, if you like that book so much why don't you please take it home? Do you have a library card?"

"No sir, I didn't take *nothing*."

"No, a library card is what we give to you so you can take books home. Then you won't have to come down here every day. Do you go to school?"

"Yes, sir. Miller Street School. But this here's summertime. It's okay I'm not in school. I ain't *supposed* to be in school."

"I know. As long as you go to school you can *have* a library card. You could take the book home."

"What you keep telling me take that book home for? At home somebody dee-*stroy* it."

"You could hide it someplace, in a desk—"

"Man," he said, squinting at me, "why don't you want me to come round here?"

"I didn't say you shouldn't."

"I *likes* to come here. I likes them stairs."

"I like them too," I said. "But the trouble is that someday somebody's going to take that book out."

He smiled. "Don't you worry," he said to me. "Ain't nobody done that yet," and he tapped off to the stairs and Stack Three.

Did I perspire that day! It was the coolest of the summer, but when I left work in the evening my shirt was sticking to my back. In the car I opened my bag, and while the rush-hour traffic flowed down Washington Street, I huddled in the back and changed into a clean shirt so that when I reached Short Hills I'd look as though I was deserving of an interlude in the suburbs. But driving up Central Avenue I could not keep my mind on my vacation, or for that matter on my driving: to the distress of pedestrians and motorists, I ground gears, overshot cross-walks, hesitated at green and red lights alike. I kept thinking that while I was on vacation that jowly bastard would return to the library, that the colored kid's book would disappear, that my new job would be taken away from me, that, in fact my old job—but then why should I worry about all that: the library wasn't going to be *my* life.

5

"Ron's getting married!" Julie screamed at me when I came through the door. "Ron's getting married!"

"Now?" I said.

"Labor Day! He's marrying Harriet, he's marrying Harriet." She began to sing it like a jump-rope song, nasal and rhythmic. "I'm going to be a sister-in-law!"

"Hi," Brenda said, "I'm going to be a sister-in-law."

"So I hear. When did it happen?"

"This afternoon he told us. They spoke long distance for forty minutes last night. She's flying here next week, and there's going to be a *huge* wedding. My parents are flittering all over the place. They've got to arrange everything in about a day or two. And my father's taking Ron in the business—but he's going to have to start at two hundred a week and then work himself up. That'll take till October."

"I thought he was going to be a gym teacher."

"He was. But now he has responsibilities . . ."

And at dinner Ron expanded on the subject of responsibilities and the future.

"We're going to have a boy," he said, to his mother's delight, "and when he's about six months old I'm going to sit him down with a basketball in front of him, and a football, and a baseball, and then whichever one he reaches for, that's the one we're going to concentrate on."

"Suppose he doesn't reach for any of them," Brenda said.

"Don't be funny, young lady," Mrs. Patimkin said.

"I'm going to be an aunt," Julie sang, and she stuck her tongue out at Brenda.

"When is Harriet coming?" Mr. Patimkin breathed through a mouthful of potatoes.

"A week from yesterday."

"Can she sleep in my room?" Julie cried. "*Can* she?"

"No, the guest room—" Mrs. Patimkin began, but then she remembered me—with a crushing side glance from those purple eyes, and said, "Of course."

Well, I did eat like a bird. After dinner my bag was carried—by me—up to the guest room which was across from Ron's room and right down the hall from Brenda. Brenda came along to show me the way.

"Let me see your bed, Bren."

"Later," she said.

"Can we? Up here?"

"I think so," she said. "Ron sleeps like a log."

"Can I stay the night?"

"I don't know."

"I could get up early and come back in here. We'll set the alarm."

"It'll wake everybody up."

"I'll remember to get up. I can do it."

"I better not stay up here with you too long," she said. "My mother'll have a fit. I think she's nervous about your being here."

"So am I. I hardly know them. Do you think I should really stay a whole week?"

"A whole week? Once Harriet gets here it'll be so chaotic you can probably stay two months."

"You think so?"

"Yes."

"Do you want me to?"

"Yes," she said, and went down the stairs so as to ease her mother's conscience.

I unpacked my bag and dropped my clothes into a drawer that was empty except for a packet of dress shields and a high school yearbook. In the middle of my unpacking, Ron came clunking up the stairs.

"Hi," he called into my room.

"Congratulations," I called back. I should have realized that any word of ceremony would provoke a handshake from Ron; he interrupted whatever it was he was about to do in his room, and came into mine.

"Thanks." He pumped me. "Thanks."

Then he sat down on my bed and watched me as I finished unpacking. I have one shirt with a Brooks Brothers label and I let it linger on the bed a while; the Arrows I heaped in the drawer. Ron sat there rubbing his forearm and grinning. After a while I was thoroughly unsettled by the silence.

"Well," I said, "that's something."

He agreed, to *what* I don't know.

"How does it feel?" I asked, after another longer silence.

"Better. Ferrari smacked it under the boards."

"Oh. Good," I said. "How does getting married feel?"

"Ah, okay, I guess."

I leaned against the bureau and counted stitches in the carpet.

Ron finally risked a journey into language. "Do you know anything about music?" he asked.

"Something, yes."

"You can listen to my phonograph if you want."

"Thanks, Ron. I didn't know you were interested in music."

"Sure. I got all the Andre Kostelanetz records ever made. You like Mantovani? I got all of him too. I like semiclassical a lot. You can hear my Columbus record if you want . . ." he dwindled off. Finally he shook my hand and left.

Downstairs I could hear Julie singing. "I'm going to be an a-a-aunt," and Mrs. Patimkin saying to her, "No, honey, you're going to be a sister-in-law. Sing that, sweetheart," but Julie continued to sing, "I'm going to be an a-a-aunt," and then I heard Brenda's voice joining hers, singing, "We're going to be an a-a-aunt," and then Julie joined that, and finally Mrs. Patimkin called to Mr. Patimkin, "Will you make her stop encouraging her . . ." and soon the duet ended.

And then I heard Mrs. Patimkin again. I couldn't make out the words but Brenda answered her. Their voices grew louder; finally I could hear perfectly. "I need a houseful of company at a time like this?" It was Mrs. Patimkin. "I asked you, Mother." "You asked your father. I'm the one you should have asked first. He doesn't know how much extra work this is for me . . ." "My God, Mother, you'd think we didn't have Carlota and Jenny." "Carlota and Jenny can't do everything. This is not the Salvation Army!" "What the hell does that mean?" "Watch your tongue, young lady. That may be very well for your college friends." "Oh, *stop* it, Mother!" "Don't raise your voice to me. When's the last time you lifted a finger to help around here?" "I'm not a slave . . . I'm a daughter." "You ought to learn what a day's work means." "Why?" Brenda said. *Why?*" "Because you're lazy," Mrs. Patimkin answered, "and you think the world owes you a living." "Whoever said *that?*" "You ought to earn some money and buy your own clothes." "Why? Good God, Mother, Daddy could live off the stocks alone, for God's sake. What are you complaining about?" "When's the last time you washed the dishes!" "Jesus Christ!" Brenda flared, "Carlota washes the dishes!" "Don't Jesus Christ me!" "Oh, Mother!" and Brenda was crying. "Why the hell are you like this!" "That's it," Mrs. Patimkin said "cry in front of your company . . ." "My *company* . . ." Brenda wept, "why don't you go yell at him too . . . why is everyone so nasty to me . . ."

From across the hall I heard Andre Kostelanetz let several thousand singing violins loose on "Night and Day." Ron's door was open and I saw he was stretched out, colossal, on his bed; he was singing along with the record. The words belonged to "Night and Day," but I didn't recognize Ron's tune. In a minute he picked up the phone and asked the operator for a Milwaukee number. While she connected him, he rolled over and turned up the volume on the record player, so that it would carry the nine hundred miles west.

I heard Julie downstairs. "Ha ha, Brenda's crying, ha ha, Brenda's crying."

And then Brenda was running up the stairs. "Your day'll come, you little bastard!" she called.

"*Brenda!*" Mrs. Patimkin called.

"*Mommy!*" Julie cried. "Brenda cursed at me!"

"What's going *on* here!" Mr. Patimkin shouted.

"You call *me,* Mrs. P?" Carlota shouted.

And Ron, in the other room, said, "Hello, Har, I told them . . ."

I sat down on my Brooks Brothers shirt and pronounced my own name out loud.

"Goddam her!" Brenda said to me as she paced up and down my room.

"Bren, do you think I should go—"

"Shhh . . ." She went to the door of my room and listened. "They're going visiting, thank God."

"Brenda—"

"Shhh . . . They've gone."

"Julie too?"

"Yes," she said. "Is Ron in his room? His door is closed."

"He went out."

"You can't hear anybody move around here. They all creep around in *sneakers.* Oh Neil."

"Bren, I asked you, maybe I should just stay through tomorrow and then go."

"Oh, it isn't you she's angry about."

"I'm not helping any."

"It's Ron, really. That he's getting married just has her flipped. And me. Now with that goody-good Harriet around she'll just forget I ever exist."

"Isn't that okay with you?"

She walked off to the window and looked outside. It was dark and cool; the trees rustled and flapped as though they were sheets that had been hung out to dry. Everything outside hinted at September, and for the first time I realized how close we were to Brenda's departure for school.

"Is it, Bren?" but she was not listening to me.

She walked across the room to a door at the far end of the room. She opened it.

"I thought that was a closet," I said.

"Come here."

She held the door back and we leaned into the darkness and could hear the strange wind hissing in the eaves of the house.

"What's in here?" I said.

"Money."

Brenda went into the room. When the puny sixty-watt bulb was twisted on, I saw that the place was full of old furniture—two wing chairs with hair-oil lines at the back, a sofa with a paunch in its middle, a bridge table, two bridge chairs with their stuffing showing, a mirror whose backing had peeled off, shadeless lamps, lampless shades, a coffee table with a cracked glass top, and a pile of rolled up shades.

"What is this?" I said.

"A storeroom. Our old furniture."

"How old?"

"From Newark," she said. "Come here." She was on her hands and knees in front of the sofa and was holding up its paunch to peek beneath.

"Brenda, what the hell are we doing here? You're getting filthy."

"It's not here."

"What?"

"The money. I told you."

I sat down on a wing chair, raising some dust. It had begun to rain outside, and we could smell the fall dampness coming through the vent that was outlined at the far end of the storeroom. Brenda got up from the floor and sat down on the sofa. Her knees and Bermudas were dirty and when she pushed her hair back she dirtied her forehead. There among the disarrangement and dirt I had the strange experience of seeing us, *both* of us, placed among disarrangement and dirt: we looked like a young couple who had just moved into a new apartment; we had suddenly taken stock of our furniture, finances, and future, and all we could feel any pleasure about was the clean smell of outside, which reminded us we were alive, but which, in a pinch, would not feed us.

"What money?" I said again.

"The hundred-dollar bills. From when I was a little girl . . ." and she breathed deeply. "When I was little and we'd just moved from

Newark, my father took me up here one day. He took me into this room and told me that if anything should ever happen to him, he wanted me to know where there was some money that I should have. He said it wasn't for anybody else but me, and that I should never tell anyone about it, not even Ron. Or my mother."

"How much was it?"

"Three hundred-dollar bills. I'd never seen them before. I was nine, around Julie's age. I don't think we'd been living here a month. I remember I used to come up here about once a week, when no one was home but Carlota, and crawl under the sofa and make sure it was still here. And it always was. He never mentioned it once again. Never."

"Where is it? Maybe someone stole it."

"I don't know, Neil. I suppose he took it back."

"When it was gone," I said, "my God, didn't you tell him? Maybe Carlota—"

"I never knew it was gone, until just now. I guess I stopped looking at one time or another . . . And then I forgot about it. Or just didn't think about it. I mean I always had enough, I didn't need this. I guess one day *he* figured I wouldn't need it."

Brenda paced up to the narrow, dust-covered window and drew her initials on it.

"Why did you want it now?" I said.

"I don't know . . ." she said and went over and twisted the bulb off.

I didn't move from the chair and Brenda, in her tight shorts and shirt, seemed naked standing there a few feet away. Then I saw her shoulders shaking. "I wanted to find it and tear it up in little pieces and put the goddam pieces in her purse! If it was there, I swear it, I would have done it."

"I wouldn't have let you, Bren."

"Wouldn't you have?"

"No."

"Make love to me, Neil. Right now."

"Where?"

"Do it! *Here.* On this cruddy cruddy cruddy sofa."

And I obeyed her.

The next morning Brenda made breakfast for the two of us. Ron had gone off to his first day of work—I'd heard him singing in the shower only an hour after I'd returned to my own room; in fact, I had still been awake when the Chrysler had pulled out of the garage, carrying boss and son down to the Patimkin works in Newark. Mrs. Patimkin wasn't home either; she had taken her car and had gone off to the Temple to talk to Rabbi Kranitz about the wedding. Julie was on the back lawn playing at helping Carlota hang the clothes.

"You know what I want to do this morning?" Brenda said. We were eating a grapefruit, sharing it rather sloppily, for Brenda couldn't find a paring knife, and so we'd decided to peel it down like an orange and eat the segments separately.

"What?" I said.

"Run," she said. "Do you ever run?"

"You mean on a track? God, yes. In high school we had to run a mile every month. So we wouldn't be Momma's boys. I think the bigger your lungs get the more you're supposed to hate your mother."

"I want to run," she said, "and I want you to run. Okay?"

"Oh, Brenda . . ."

But an hour later, after a breakfast that consisted of another grapefruit, which apparently is all a runner is supposed to eat in the morning, we had driven the Volkswagen over to the high school, behind which was a quarter-mile track. Some kids were playing with a dog out in the grassy center of the track, and at the far end, near the woods, a figure in white shorts with slits in the side, and no shirt, was twirling, twirling, and then flinging a shot put as far as he could. After it left his hand he did a little eagle-eyed tap dance while he watched it arch and bend and land in the distance.

"You know," Brenda said, "you look like me. Except bigger."

We were dressed similarly, sneakers, sweat socks, khaki Bermudas, and sweat shirts, but I had the feeling that Brenda was not talking about the accidents of our dress—if they were accidents. She meant, I was sure, that I was somehow beginning to look the way she wanted me to. Like herself.

"Let's see who's faster," she said, and then we started along the track. Within the first eighth of a mile the three little boys and their dog were following us. As we passed the corner where the shot putter was, he waved at us; Brenda called "Hi!" and I smiled, which, as you may or may not know, makes one engaged in serious running feel inordinately silly. At the quarter mile the kids dropped off and retired to the grass, the dog turned and started the other way, and I had a tiny knife in my side. Still I was abreast of Brenda, who as we started on the second lap, called "Hi!" once again to the lucky shot putter, who was reclining on the grass now, watching us, and rubbing his shot like a crystal ball. Ah, I thought, there's the sport.

"How about us throwing the shot put?" I panted.

"After," she said, and I saw beads of sweat clinging to the last strands of hair that shagged off her ear. When we approached the half mile Brenda suddenly swerved off the track onto the grass and tumbled down; her departure surprised me and I was still running.

"Hey, Bob Mathias," she called, "let's lie in the sun . . ."

But I acted as though I didn't hear her and though my heart pounded in my throat and my mouth was dry as a drought, I made my legs move, and swore I would not stop until I'd finished one more lap. As I passed the shot putter for the third time, I called "Hi!"

She was excited when I finally pulled up alongside of her. "You're good," she said. My hands were on my hips and I was looking at the ground and sucking air—rather, air was sucking me, I didn't have much to say about it.

"Uh-huh," I breathed.

"Let's do this every morning," she said. "We'll get up and have two grapefruit, and then you'll come out here and run. I'll time you. In two weeks you'll break four minutes, won't you, sweetie? I'll get Ron's stop watch." She was so excited—she'd slid over on the grass and was pushing my socks up against my wet ankles and calves. She bit my kneecap.

"Okay," I said.

"Then we'll go back and have a real breakfast."

"Okay."

"You drive back," she said, and suddenly she was up and running ahead of me, and then we were headed back in the car.

And the next morning, my mouth still edgy from the grapefruit segments, we were at the track. We had Ron's stop watch and a towel for me, for when I was finished.

"My legs are a little sore," I said.

"Do some exercises," Brenda said. "I'll do them with you." She heaped the towel on the grass and together we did deep knee bends, and sit-ups, and push-ups, and some high-knee raising in place. I felt overwhelmingly happy.

"I'm just going to run a half today, Bren. We'll see what I do . . ." and I heard Brenda click the watch, and then when I was on the far side of the track, the clouds trailing above me like my own white, fleecy tail, I saw that Brenda was on the ground, hugging her knees, and alternately checking the watch and looking out at me. We were the only ones there, and it all reminded me of one of those scenes in race-horse movies, where an old trainer like Walter Brennan and a young handsome man clock the beautiful girl's horse in the early Kentucky morning, to see if it really is the fastest two-year-old alive. There were differences all right—one being simply that at the quarter mile Brenda shouted out to me, "A minute and fourteen seconds," but it was pleasant and exciting and clean and when I was finished Brenda was standing up and waiting for me. Instead of a tape to break I had Brenda's sweet flesh to meet, and I did, and it was the first time she said that she loved me.

We ran—I ran—every morning, and by the end of the week I was running a 7:02 mile, and always at the end there was the little click of the watch and Brenda's arms.

At night, I would read in my pajamas, while Brenda, in her room, read, and we would wait for Ron to go to sleep. Some nights we had to wait longer than others, and I would hear the leaves swishing outside, for it had grown cooler at the end of August, and the air-conditioning was turned off at night and we were all allowed to open our windows. Finally Ron would be ready for bed. He would stomp around his room and then he would come to the door in his shorts and T-shirt and go into the bathroom where he would urinate loudly and brush his teeth. After he brushed his teeth I would go in to brush mine. We would pass in the hall and I would give him a hearty and sincere "Goodnight." Once in the bathroom, I would spend a moment admiring my tan in the mirror; behind me I could see Ron's jock straps hanging out to dry on the Hot and Cold knobs of the shower. Nobody ever questioned their tastefulness as adornment, and after a few nights I didn't even notice them.

While Ron brushed his teeth and I waited in my bed for my turn, I could hear the record player going in his room. Generally, after coming in from basketball, he would call Harriet—who was now only a few days away from us—and then would lock himself up with *Sports Illustrated* and Mantovani; however, when he emerged from his room for his evening toilet, it was not a Mantovani record I would hear playing, but something else, apparently what he'd once referred to as his Columbus record. I *imagined* that was what I heard, for I could not tell much from the last moments of sound. All I heard were bells moaning evenly and soft patriotic music behind them, and riding over it all, a deep kind of Edward R. Murrow gloomy voice: "*And so goodbye, Columbus,*" the voice intoned, ". . . *goodbye,*

Columbus . . . goodbye . . ." Then there would be silence and Ron would be back in his room; the light would switch off and in only a few minutes I would hear him rumbling down into that exhilarating, restorative, vitamin-packed sleep that I imagined athletes to enjoy.

One morning near sneaking-away time I had a dream and when I awakened from it, there was just enough dawn coming into the room for me to see the color of Brenda's hair. I touched her in her sleep, for the dream had unsettled me: it had taken place on a ship, an old sailing ship like those you see in pirate movies. With me on the ship was the little colored kid from the library— I was the captain and he my mate, and we were the only crew members. For a while it was a pleasant dream; we were anchored in the harbor of an island in the Pacific and it was very sunny. Up on the beach there were beautiful bare-skinned Negresses, and none of them moved; but suddenly *we* were moving, our ship, out of the harbor, and the Negresses moved slowly down to the shore and began to throw leis at us and say "Goodbye, Columbus . . . goodbye, Columbus . . . goodbye . . ." and though we did not want to go, the little boy and I, the boat was moving and there was nothing we could do about it, and he shouted at me that it was my fault and I shouted it was his for not having a library card, but we were wasting our breath, for we were further and further from the island, and soon the natives were nothing at all. Space was all out of proportion in the dream, and things were sized and squared in no way I'd ever seen before, and I think it was that more than anything else that steered me into consciousness. I did not want to leave Brenda's side that morning, and for a while I played with the little point at the nape of her neck, where she'd had her hair cut. I stayed longer than I should have, and when finally I returned to my room I almost ran into Ron who was preparing for his day at Patimkin Kitchen and Bathroom Sinks.

6

That morning was supposed to have been my last at the Patimkin house; however, when I began to throw my things into my bag late in the day, Brenda told me I could unpack—somehow she'd managed to inveigle another week out of her parents, and I would be able to stay right through till Labor Day, when Ron would be married; then, the following morning Brenda would be off to school and I would go back to work. So we would be with each other until the summer's last moment.

This should have made me overjoyed, but as Brenda trotted back down the stairs to accompany her family to the airport—where they were to pick up Harriet—I was not joyful but disturbed as I had been more and more with the thought that when Brenda went back to Radcliffe, that would be the end for me. I was convinced that even Miss Winney's stool was not high enough for me to see clear up to Boston. Nevertheless, I tossed my clothing back into the drawer and was able, finally, to tell myself that there'd been no hints of ending our affair from Brenda, and any suspicions I had, any uneasiness, was spawned in my own uncertain heart. Then I went into Ron's room to call my aunt.

"Hello?" she said.

"Aunt Gladys," I said, "how are you?"

"You're sick."

"No, I'm having a fine time. I wanted to call you, I'm going to stay another week."

"Why?"

"I told you. I'm having a good time. Mrs. Patimkin asked me to stay until Labor Day."

"You've got clean underwear?"

"I'm washing it at night. I'm okay, Aunt Gladys."

"By hand you can't get it clean."

"It's clean enough. Look, Aunt Gladys, I'm having a wonderful time."

"*Shmutz* he lives in and I shouldn't worry."

"How's Uncle Max?" I asked.

"What should he be? Uncle Max is Uncle Max. You, I don't like the way your voice sounds."

"Why? Do I sound like I've got on dirty underwear?"

"Smart guy. Someday you'll learn."

"What?"

"What do you mean *what?* You'll find out. You'll stay there too long you'll be too good for us."

"Never, sweetheart," I said.

"I'll see it I'll believe it."

"Is it cool in Newark, Aunt Gladys?"

"It's snowing," she said.

"Hasn't it been cool all week?"

"You sit around all day it's cool. For me it's not February, believe me."

"Okay, Aunt Gladys. Say hello to everybody."

"You got a letter from your mother."

"Good. I'll read it when I get home."

"You couldn't take a ride down you'll read it?"

"It'll wait. I'll drop them a note. Be a good girl," I said.

"What about your socks?"

"I go barefoot. Goodbye, honey." And I hung up.

Down in the kitchen Carlota was getting dinner ready. I was always amazed at how Carlota's work never seemed to get in the way of her life. She made household chores seem like illustrative gestures of whatever it was she was singing, even, if as now, it was "I Get a Kick out of You." She moved from the oven to the automatic dishwasher—she pushed buttons, turned dials, peeked in the glass-doored oven, and from time to time picked a big black grape out of a bunch that lay on the sink. She chewed and chewed, humming all the time, and then, with a deliberated casualness, shot the skin and the pit directly into the garbage disposal unit. I said hello to her as I went out the back door, and though she did not return the greeting, I felt a kinship with one who, like me, had been partially wooed and won on Patimkin fruit.

Out on the lawn I shot baskets for a while; then I picked up an iron and drove a cotton golf ball limply up into the sunlight; then I kicked a soccer ball towards the oak tree; then I tried shooting foul shots again. Nothing diverted me—I felt open-stomached, as though I hadn't eaten for months, and though I went back inside and came out with my own handful of grapes, the feeling continued, and I knew it had nothing to do with my caloric intake; it was only a rumor of the hollowness that would come when Brenda was away. The fact of her departure had, of course, been on my mind for a while, but overnight it had taken on a darker hue. Curiously, the darkness seemed to have something to do with Harriet, Ron's intended, and I thought for a time that it was simply the reality of Harriet's arrival that had dramatized the passing of time: we had been talking about it and now suddenly it was here—just as Brenda's departure would be here before we knew it.

But it was more than that: the union of Harriet and Ron reminded me that separation need not be a permanent state. People could marry each other, even if they were young! And yet Brenda and I had never mentioned marriage, except perhaps for that night at the pool when she'd said, "When you love me, everything will be all right." Well, I loved her, and she me, and things didn't seem all right at all. Or was I inventing troubles again? I supposed I should really have thought my lot improved considerably; yet, there on the lawn, the August sky seemed too beautiful and temporary to bear, and I wanted Brenda to marry me. Marriage, though, was not what I proposed to her when she drove the car up the driveway, alone, some fifteen minutes later. That proposal would have taken a kind of courage that I did not think I had. I did not feel myself prepared for any answer but "Hallelujah!" Any other kind of yes wouldn't have satisfied me, and any kind of no, even one masked behind the words, "Let's wait, sweetheart," would have been my end. So I imagine that's why I proposed the surrogate, which turned out finally to be far more daring than I knew it to be at the time.

"Harriet's plane is late, so I drove home," Brenda called.

"Where's everyone else?"

"They're going to wait for her and have dinner at the airport. I have to tell Carlota," and she went inside.

In a few minutes she appeared on the porch. She wore a yellow dress that cut a wide-bottomed U across her shoulders and neck, and showed where the tanned flesh began above her breasts. On the lawn she stepped out of her heels and walked barefoot over to where I was sitting under the oak tree.

"Women who wear high heels all the time get tipped ovaries," she said.

"Who told you that?"

"I don't remember. I like to think everything's ship-shape in there."

"Brenda, I want to ask you something . . ."

She yanked the blanket with the big O on it over to us and sat down.

"What?" she said.

"I know this is out of the blue, though really it's not . . . I want you to buy a diaphragm. To go to a doctor and get one."

She smiled. "Don't worry, sweetie, we're careful. Everything is okay."

"But that's the safest."

"We're safe. It'd be a waste."

"Why take chances?"

"But we *aren't*. How many things do you need."

"Honey, it isn't bulk I'm interested in. It's not even safety," I added.

"You just want me to own one, is that it? Like a walking stick, or a pith helmet—"

"Brenda, I want you to own one for . . . for the sake of pleasure."

"Pleasure? Whose? The doctor's?"

"Mine," I said.

She did not answer me, but rubbed her fingers along the ridge of her collarbone to wipe away the tiny globes of perspiration that had suddenly formed there.

"No, Neil, it's silly."

"Why?"

"Why? It just is."

"You know why it's silly, Brenda—because *I* asked you to do it?"

"That's sillier."

"If you asked *me* to buy a diaphragm we'd have to go straight to the Yellow Pages and find a gynecologist open on Saturday afternoon."

"I would never ask you to do that, baby."

"It's the truth," I said, though I was smiling. "It's the truth."

"It's not," she said, and got up and walked over to the basketball court, where she walked on the white lines that Mr. Patimkin had laid the day before.

"Come back here," I said.

"Neil, it's silly and I don't want to talk about it."

"Why are you being so selfish?"

"Selfish? You're the one who's being selfish. It's your pleasure . . ."

"That's right. My pleasure. Why not!"

"Don't raise your voice. Carlota."

"Then get the hell over here," I said.

She walked over to me, leaving white footprints on the grass. "I didn't think you were such a creature of the flesh," she said.

"Didn't you?" I said. "I'll tell you something that you ought to know. It's not even the pleasures of the flesh I'm talking about."

"Then frankly, I don't know *what* you're talking about. Why you're even bothering. Isn't what we use sufficient?"

"I'm bothering just because I want you to go to a doctor and get a diaphragm. That's all. No explanation. Just do it. Do it because I asked you to."

"You're not being reasonable—"

"Goddamit, Brenda!"

"Goddamit yourself!" she said and went up into the house.

I closed my eyes and leaned back and in fifteen minutes, or maybe less, I heard somebody stroking at the cotton golf ball. She had changed into shorts and a blouse and was still barefoot.

We didn't speak with each other, but I watched her bring the club back of her ear, and then swing through, her chin tilted up with the line of flight a regular golf ball would have taken.

"That's five hundred yards," I said.

She didn't answer but walked after the cotton ball and then readied for another swing.

"Brenda. Please come here."

She walked over, dragging the club over the grass.

"What?"

"I don't want to argue with you."

"Nor I with you," she said. "It was the first time."

"Was it such an awful thing for me to ask?"

She nodded.

"Bren, I know it was probably a surprise. It was for me. But we're not children."

"Neil, I just don't want to. It's not because you asked me to, either. I don't know where you get that from. That's not it."

"Then why is it?"

"Oh everything. I just don't feel *old* enough for all that equipment."

"What does age have to do with it?"

"I don't mean age. I just mean—well, *me*. I mean it's so conscious a thing to do."

"Of course it's conscious. That's exactly it. Don't you see? It would change us."

"It would change me."

"Us. Together."

"Neil, how do you think I'd feel lying to some doctor."

"You can go to Margaret Sanger, in New York. They don't ask any questions."

"You've done this before?"

"No," I said. "I just know. I read Mary McCarthy."

"That's exactly right. That's just what I'd feel like, somebody out of *her.*"

"Don't be dramatic," I said.

"You're the one who's being dramatic. You think there would be something affairish about it, then. Last summer I went with this whore who I sent out to buy—"

"Oh, Brenda, you're a selfish egotistical bitch! You're the one who's thinking about 'last summer,' about an end for us. In fact, that's the whole thing, isn't it—"

"That's right, I'm a bitch. I want this to end. That's why I ask you to stay another week, that's why I let you sleep with me in my own house. What's the *matter* with you! Why don't you and my mother take turns—one day she can plague me, the next you—"

"Stop it!"

"Go to hell, all of you!" Brenda said, and now she was crying and I knew when she ran off I would not see her, as I didn't, for the rest of the afternoon.

Harriet Ehrlich impressed me as a young lady singularly unconscious of a motive in others or herself. All was surfaces, and she seemed a perfect match for Ron, and too for the Patimkins. Mrs. Patimkin, in fact, did just as Brenda prophesied: Harriet appeared, and Brenda's mother lifted one wing and pulled the girl in towards the warm underpart of her body, where Brenda herself would have liked to nestle. Harriet was built like Brenda, although a little chestier, and she nodded her head insistently whenever anyone spoke. Sometimes she would even say the last few words of your sentence with you, though that was infrequent; for the most part she nodded and kept her hands folded. All evening, as the Patimkins planned where the newlyweds should live, what furniture they should buy, how soon they should have a baby—all through this I kept thinking that Harriet was wearing white gloves, but she wasn't.

Brenda and I did not exchange a word or a glance; we sat, listening, Brenda somewhat more impatient than me. Near the end Harriet began calling Mrs. Patimkin "Mother," and once, "Mother Patimkin," and that was when Brenda went to sleep. I stayed behind, mesmerized almost by the dissection, analysis, reconsideration, and finally, the embracing of the trivial. At last Mr. and Mrs. Patimkin tumbled off to bed, and Julie, who had fallen asleep on her chair, was carried into her room by Ron. That left us two non-Patimkins together.

"Ron tells me you have a very interesting job."

"I work in the library."

"I've always liked reading."

"That'll be nice, married to Ron."

"Ron likes music."

"Yes," I said. What had I *said?*

"You must get first crack at the best-sellers," she said.

"Sometimes." I said.

"Well," she said, flapping her hands on her knees, "I'm sure we'll all have a good time together. Ron and I hope you and Brenda will double with us soon."

"Not tonight." I smiled. "Soon. Will you excuse me?"

"Good night. I like Brenda very much."

"Thank you," I said as I started up the stairs.

I knocked gently on Brenda's door.

"I'm sleeping."

"Can I come in?" I asked.

Her door opened an inch and she said, "Ron will be up soon."

"We'll leave the door open. I only want to talk."

She let me in and I sat in the chair that faced the bed.

"How do you like your sister-in-law?"

"I've met her before."

"Brenda, you don't have to sound so damn terse."

She didn't answer and I just sat there yanking the string on the shade up and down.

"Are you still angry?" I asked at last.

"Yes."

"Don't be," I said. "You can forget about my suggestion. It's not worth it if this is what's going to happen."

"What did you expect to happen?"

"Nothing. I didn't think it would be so horrendous."

"That's because you can't understand my side."

"Perhaps."

"No perhaps about it."

"Okay," I said. "I just wish you'd realize what it is you're getting angry about. It's not my suggestion, Brenda."

"No? What is it?"

"It's me."

"Oh don't start that again, will you? I can't win, no matter what I say."

"Yes, you can," I said. "You have."

I walked out of her room, closing the door behind me for the night.

When I got downstairs the following morning there was a great deal of activity. In the living room I heard Mrs. Patimkin reading a list to Harriet while Julie ran in and out of rooms in search of a skate key. Carlota was vacuuming the carpet; every appliance in the kitchen was bubbling, twisting, and shaking. Brenda greeted me with a perfectly pleasant smile and in the dining room, where I walked to look out at the back lawn and the weather, she kissed me on the shoulder.

"Hello," she said.

"Hello."

"I have to go with Harriet this morning," Brenda told me. "So we can't run. Unless you want to go alone."

"No. I'll read or something. Where are you going?"

"We're going to New York. Shopping. She's going to buy a wedding dress. For after the wedding. To go away in."

"What are *you* going to buy?"

"A dress to be maid of honor in. If I go with Harriet then I can go to Bergdorf's without all that Ohrbach's business with my mother."

"Get me something, will you?" I said.

"Oh, Neil, are you going to bring that up again!"

"I was only *fooling*. I wasn't even thinking about that."

"Then why did you say it?"

"Oh Jesus!" I said, and went outside and drove my car down into Millburn Center where I had some eggs and coffee.

When I came back, Brenda was gone, and there were only Carlota, Mrs. Patimkin, and myself in the house. I tried to stay out of whichever rooms they were in, but finally Mrs. Patimkin and I wound up sitting opposite each other in the TV room. She was checking off names on a long sheet of paper she held; next to her, on the table, were two thin phone books which she consulted from time to time.

"No rest for the weary," she said to me.

I smiled hugely, embracing the proverb as though Mrs. Patimkin had just then coined it. "Yes. Of course," I said. "Would you like some help? Maybe I could help you check something."

"Oh, no," she said with a little head-shaking dismissal, "it's for Hadassah."

"Oh," I said.

I sat and watched her until she asked, "Is your mother in Hadassah?"

"I don't know if she is now. She was in Newark."

"Was she an active member?"

"I guess so, she was always planting trees in Israel for someone."

"Really?" Mrs. Patimkin said. "What's her name?"

"Esther Klugman. She's in Arizona now. Do they have Hadassah there?"

"Wherever there are Jewish women."

"Then I guess she is. She's with my father. They went there for their asthma. I'm staying with my aunt in Newark. She's not in Hadassah. My Aunt Sylvia is, though. Do you know her, Aaron Klugman and Sylvia? They belong to your club. They have a daughter, my cousin Doris—" I couldn't stop myself "—They live in Livingston. Maybe it isn't Hadassah my Aunt Sylvia belongs to. I think it's some TB organization. Or cancer. Muscular dystrophy, maybe. I know she's interested in *some* disease."

"That's very nice," Mrs. Patimkin said.

"Oh yes."

"They do very good work."

"I know."

Mrs. Patimkin, I thought, had begun to warm to me; she let the purple eyes stop peering and just look out at the world for a while without judging. "Are you interested in B'nai Brith?" she asked me. "Ron is joining, you know, as soon as he gets married."

"I think I'll wait till then," I said.

Petulantly, Mrs. Patimkin went back to her lists, and I realized it had been foolish of me to risk lightheartedness with her about Jewish affairs. "You're active in the Temple, aren't you?" I asked with all the interest I could muster.

"Yes," she said.

"What Temple do *you* belong to?" she asked in a moment.

"We used to belong to Hudson Street Synagogue. Since my parents left, I haven't had much contact."

I didn't know whether Mrs. Patimkin caught a false tone in my voice. Personally I thought I had managed my rueful confession pretty well, especially when I recalled the decade of paganism prior to my parents' departure. Regardless, Mrs. Patimkin asked immediately—and strategically it seemed—"We're all going to Temple Friday night. Why don't you come with us? I mean, are you orthodox or conservative?"

I considered. "Well, I haven't gone in a long time . . . I sort of switch . . ." I smiled. "I'm just Jewish," I said well-meaningly, but that too sent Mrs. Patimkin back to her Hadassah work. Desperately I tried to think of something that would convince her I wasn't an infidel. Finally I asked: "Do you know Martin Buber's work?"

"Buber . . . Buber," she said, looking at her Hadassah list. "Is he orthodox or conservative?" she asked.

". . . He's a philosopher."

"Is he *reformed?*" she asked, piqued either at my evasiveness or at the possibility that Buber attended Friday night services without a hat, and Mrs. Buber had only one set of dishes in her kitchen.

"Orthodox," I said faintly.

"That's very nice," she said.

"Yes."

"Isn't Hudson Street Synagogue orthodox?" she asked.

"I don't know."

"I thought you belonged."

"I was bar-mitzvahed there."

"And you don't know that it's orthodox?"

"Yes. I do. It is."

"Then *you* must be."

"Oh, yes, I am," I said. "What are you?" I popped, flushing.

"Orthodox. My husband is conservative," which meant, I took it, that he didn't care. "Brenda is nothing, as you probably know."

"Oh?" I said. "No, I didn't know that."

"She was the best Hebrew student I've ever seen," Mrs. Patimkin said, "but then, of course, she got too big for her britches."

Mrs. Patimkin looked at me, and I wondered whether courtesy demanded that I agree. "Oh, I don't know," I said at last, "I'd say Brenda is conservative. Maybe a little reformed . . ."

The phone rang, rescuing me, and I spoke a silent orthodox prayer to the Lord.

"Hello," Mrs. Patimkin said. ". . . no . . . I can *not,* I have all the Hadassah calls to make . . ."

I acted as though I were listening to the birds outside, though the closed windows let no natural noises in.

"Have Ronald drive them up . . . But we can't wait, not if we want it on time . . ."

Mrs. Patimkin glanced up at me; then she put one hand over the mouthpiece. "Would you ride down to Newark for me?"

I stood. "Yes. Surely."

"Dear?" she said back into the phone, "Neil will come for it . . . No, *Neil,* Brenda's friend . . . Yes . . . Goodbye.

"Mr. Patimkin has some silver patterns I have to see. Would you drive down to his place and pick them up?"

"Of course."

"Do you know where the shop is?"

"Yes."

"Here," she said, handing a key ring to me, "take the Volkswagen."

"My car is right outside."

"Take these," she said.

Patimkin Kitchen and Bathroom Sinks was in the heart of the Negro section of Newark. Years ago, at the time of the great immigration, it had been the Jewish section, and still one could see the little fish stores, the kosher delicatessens, the Turkish baths, where my grandparents had shopped and bathed at the beginning of the century. Even the smells had lingered: whitefish, corned beef, sour tomatoes—but now, on top of these, was the grander greasier smell of auto wrecking shops, the sour stink of a brewery, the burning odor from a leather factory; and on the streets, instead of Yiddish, one heard the shouts of Negro children playing at Willie Mays with a broom handle and half a rubber ball. The neighborhood had changed: the old Jews like my grandparents had struggled and died, and their offspring had struggled and prospered, and moved further and further west, towards the edge of Newark, then out of it, and up the slope of the Orange Mountains, until they had reached the crest and started down the other side, pouring into Gentile territory as the Scotch-Irish had poured through the Cumberland Gap. Now, in fact, the Negroes were making the same migration, following the steps of the Jews, and those who remained in the Third Ward lived the most squalid of lives and dreamed in their fetid mattresses of the piny smell of Georgia nights.

I wondered, for an instant only, if I would see the colored kid from the library on the streets here. I didn't, of course, though I was sure he lived in one of the scabby, peeling buildings out of which dogs, children, and aproned women moved continually. On the top floors, windows were open, and the very old, who could no longer creak down the long stairs to the street, sat where they had been put, in the screenless windows, their elbows resting on flufless pillows, and their heads tipping forward on their necks, watching the push of the young and the pregnant and the unemployed. Who would come after the Negroes? Who was left? No one, I thought, and someday these streets, where my grandmother drank hot tea from an old *jahrzeit* glass, would be empty and we would all of us have moved to the crest of the Orange Mountains, and wouldn't the dead stop kicking at the slats in their coffins then?

I pulled the Volkswagen up in front of a huge garage door that said across the front of it:

PATIMKIN KITCHEN AND BATHROOM SINKS
"Any Size—Any Shape"

Inside I could see a glass-enclosed office; it was in the center of an immense warehouse. Two trucks were being loaded in the rear, and Mr. Patimkin, when I saw him, had a cigar in his mouth and was shouting at someone. It was Ron, who was wearing a white T-shirt that said Ohio State Athletic Association across the front. Though he was taller than Mr. Patimkin, and almost as stout, his hands hung weakly at his sides like a small boy's; Mr. Patimkin's cigar locomoted in his mouth. Six Negroes were loading one of the trucks feverishly, tossing—my stomach dropped—sink bowls at one another.

Ron left Mr. Patimkin's side and went back to directing the men. He thrashed his arms about a good deal, and though on the whole he seemed rather confused, he didn't appear to be at all concerned about anybody dropping a sink. Suddenly I could see myself directing the Negroes—I would have an ulcer in an hour. I could almost hear the enamel surfaces shattering on the floor. And I could hear myself: "Watch it, you guys. Be careful, will you? *Whoops!* Oh, please be—*watch* it! Watch! Oh!" Suppose Mr. Patimkin should come up to me and say, "Okay, boy, you want to marry my daughter, let's see what you can do." Well, he would see: in a moment that floor would be a shattered mosaic, a crunchy path of enamel. "Klugman, what kind of worker are you? You work like you eat!" "That's right, that's right, I'm a sparrow, let me go." "Don't you even know how to load and unload?" "Mr. Patimkin, even breathing gives me trouble, sleep tires me out, let me go, let me go . . ."

Mr. Patimkin was headed back to the fish bowl to answer a ringing phone, and I wrenched myself free of my reverie and headed towards the office too. When I entered, Mr. Patimkin looked up from the phone with his eyes; the sticky cigar was in his free hand—he moved it at me, a greeting. From outside I heard Ron call in a high voice, "You can't all go to lunch at the same time. We haven't got all day!"

"Sit down," Mr. Patimkin shot at me, though when he went back to his conversation I saw there was only one chair in the office, his. People did not sit at Patimkin Sink—here you earned your money the hard way, standing up. I busied myself looking at the several calendars that hung from filing cabinets; they showed illustrations of women so dreamy, so fantastically thighed and uddered, that one could not think of them as pornographic. The artist who had drawn the calendar girls for "Lewis Construction Company," and "Earl's Truck and Auto Repair," and "Grossman and Son, Paper Box" had been painting some third sex I had never seen.

"Sure, sure, sure," Mr. Patimkin said into the phone. "Tomorrow, don't tell me tomorrow. Tomorrow the world could blow up."

At the other end someone spoke. Who was it? Lewis from the construction company? Earl from truck repair?

"I'm running a business, Grossman, not a charity."

So it was Grossman being browbeaten at the other end.

"Shit on that," Mr. Patimkin said. "You're not the only one in town, my good friend," and he winked at me.

Ah-ha, a conspiracy against Grossman. Me and Mr. Patimkin. I smiled as collusively as I knew how.

"All right then, we're here till five . . . No later."

He wrote something on a piece of paper. It was only a big X.

"My kid'll be here," he said. "Yea, he's in the business."

Whatever Grossman said on the other end, it made Mr. Patimkin laugh. Mr. Patimkin hung up without a goodbye.

He looked out the back to see how Ron was doing. "Four years in college he can't unload a truck."

I didn't know what to say but finally chose the truth. "I guess I couldn't either."

"You could learn. What am I, a genius? I learned. Hard work never killed anybody."

To that I agreed.

Mr. Patimkin looked at his cigar. "A man works hard he's got something. You don't get anywhere sitting on your behind, you know . . . The biggest men in the country worked hard, believe me. Even Rockefeller. Success don't come easy . . ." He did not say this so much as he mused it out while he surveyed his dominion. He was not a man enamored of words, and I had the feeling that what had tempted him into this barrage of universals was probably the combination of Ron's performance and my presence—me, the outsider who might one day be an insider. But did Mr. Patimkin ever consider that possibility? I did not know; I only knew that these few words he did speak could hardly transmit all the satisfaction and surprise he felt about the life he had managed to build for himself and his family.

He looked out at Ron again. "Look at him, if he played basketball like that they'd throw him the hell off the court." But he was smiling when he said it.

He walked over to the door. "Ronald, let them go to lunch."

Ron shouted back, "I thought I'd let some go now, and some later."

"Why?"

"Then somebody'll always be—"

"No fancy deals here," Mr. Patimkin shouted. "We all go to lunch at once."

Ron turned back. "All right, boys, lunch!"

His father smiled at me. "Smart boy? Huh?" He tapped his head. "That took brains, huh? He ain't got the stomach for business. He's an idealist," and then I think Mr. Patimkin suddenly realized who *I* was, and eagerly corrected himself so as not to offend. "That's all right, you know, if you're a schoolteacher, or like you, you know, a student or something like that. Here you need a little of the *gonif* in you. You know what that means? *Gonif?*"

"Thief," I said.

"You know more than my own kids. They're *goyim,* my kids, that's how much they understand." He watched the Negro loading gang walk past the office and shouted out to them, "You guys know how long an hour is? All right, you'll be back in an hour!"

Ron came into the office and of course shook my hand.

"Do you have that stuff for Mrs. Patimkin?" I asked.

"Ronald, get him the silver patterns." Ron turned away and Mr. Patimkin said, "When I got married we had forks and knives from the five and ten. This kid needs gold to eat off," but there was no anger; far from it.

I drove to the mountains in my own car that afternoon, and stood for a while at the wire fence watching the deer lightly prance, coyly feed, under the protection of signs that read DO NOT FEED THE

DEER, *By Order of South Mountain Reservation.* Alongside me at the fence were dozens of kids; they giggled and screamed when the deer licked the popcorn from their hands, and then were sad when their own excitement sent the young loping away towards the far end of the field where their tawny-skinned mothers stood regally watching the traffic curl up the mountain road. Young white-skinned mothers, hardly older than I, and in many instances younger, chatted in their convertibles behind me, and looked down from time to time to see what their children were about. I had seen them before, when Brenda and I had gone out for a bite in the afternoon, or had driven up here for lunch: in clotches of three and four they sat in the rustic hamburger joints that dotted the Reservation area while their children gobbled hamburgers and malteds and were given dimes to feed the jukebox. Though none of the little ones were old enough to read the song titles, almost all of them could holler out the words, and they did, while the mothers, a few of whom I recognized as high school mates of mine, compared suntans, supermarkets, and vacations. They looked immortal sitting there. Their hair would always stay the color they desired, their clothes the right texture and shade; in their homes they would have simple Swedish modern when that was fashionable, and if huge, ugly baroque ever came back, out would go the long, midget-legged marble coffee table and in would come Louis Quatorze. These were the goddesses, and if I were Paris I could not have been able to choose among them, so microscopic were the differences. Their fates had collapsed them into one. Only Brenda shone. Money and comfort would not erase her singleness—they hadn't yet, or had they? What was I loving, I wondered, and since I am not one to stick scalpels into myself, I wiggled my hand in the fence and allowed a tiny-nosed buck to lick my thoughts away.

When I returned to the Patimkin house, Brenda was in the living room looking more beautiful than I had ever seen her. She was modeling her new dress for Harriet and her mother. Even Mrs. Patimkin seemed softened by the sight of her; it looked as though some sedative had been injected into her, and so relaxed the Brenda-hating muscles around her eyes and mouth.

Brenda, without glasses, modeled in place; when she looked at me it was a kind of groggy, half-waking look I got, and though others might have interpreted it as sleepiness it sounded in my veins as lust. Mrs. Patimkin told her finally that she'd bought a very nice dress and I told her she looked lovely and Harriet told her she was very beautiful and that *she* ought to be the bride, and then there was an uncomfortable silence while all of us wondered who ought to be the groom.

Then when Mrs. Patimkin had led Harriet out to the kitchen, Brenda came up to me and said, "I *ought* to be the bride."

"You ought, sweetheart." I kissed her, and suddenly she was crying.

"What is it, honey?" I said.

"Let's go outside."

On the lawn, Brenda was no longer crying but her voice sounded very tired.

"Neil, I called Margaret Sanger Clinic," she said. "When I was in New York."

I didn't answer.

"Neil, they *did* ask if I was married. God, the woman sounded like my mother . . ."

"What did you say?"

"I said *no.*"

"What did she say?"

"I don't know. I hung up." She walked away and around the oak tree. When she appeared again she'd stepped out of her shoes and held one hand on the tree, as though it were a Maypole she were circling.

"You can call them back," I said.

She shook her head. "No, I can't. I don't even know why I called in the first place. We were shopping and I just walked away, looked up the number, and called."

"Then you can go to a doctor."

She shook again.

"Look, Bren," I said, rushing to her, "we'll go together, to a doctor. In New York—"

"I don't want to go to some dirty little office—"

"We won't. We'll go to the most posh gynecologist in New York. One who gets *Harper's Bazaar* for the reception room. How does that sound?"

She bit her lower lip.

"You'll come with me?" she asked.

"I'll come with you."

"To the office?"

"Sweetie, your husband wouldn't come to the office."

"No?"

"He'd be working."

"But you're not," she said.

"I'm on vacation," I said, but I had answered the wrong question. "Bren, I'll wait and when you're all done we'll buy a drink. We'll go out to dinner."

"Neil, I shouldn't have called Margaret Sanger—it's not right."

"It is, Brenda. It's the most right thing we can do." She walked away and I was exhausted from pleading. Somehow I felt I could have convinced her had I been a bit more crafty; and yet I did not want it to be craftiness that changed her mind. I was silent when she came back, and perhaps it was just that, my *not* saying anything, that prompted her finally to say, "I'll ask Mother Patimkin if she wants us to take Harriet too . . ."

7

I shall never forget the heat and mugginess of that afternoon we drove into New York. It was four days after the day she'd called Margaret Sanger—she put it off and put it off, but finally on Friday, three days before Ron's wedding and four before her departure, we were heading through the Lincoln Tunnel, which seemed longer and fumier than ever, like Hell with tiled walls. Finally we were in New York and smothered again by the thick day. I pulled around the policeman who directed traffic in his shirt sleeves and up onto the Port Authority roof to park the car.

"Do you have cab fare?" I said.

"Aren't you going to come with me?"

"I thought I'd wait in the bar. Here, downstairs."

"You can wait in Central Park. His office is right across the street."

"Bren, what's the diff—" But when I saw the look that invaded her eyes I gave up the air-conditioned bar to accompany her across the city. There was a sudden shower while our cab went crosstown, and when the rain stopped the streets were sticky and shiny, and below the pavement was the rumble of the subways, and in all it was like entering the ear of a lion.

The doctor's office was in the Squibb Building, which is across from Bergdorf Goodman's and so was a perfect place for Brenda to add to her wardrobe. For some reason we had never once considered her going to a doctor in Newark, perhaps because it was too close to home and might allow for possibilities of discovery. When Brenda got to the revolving door she looked back at me; her eyes were very watery, even with her glasses, and I did not say a word, afraid what a word, any word, might do. I kissed her hair and motioned that I would be across the street by the Plaza fountain, and then I watched her revolve through the doors. Out on the street the traffic moved slowly as though the humidity were a wall holding everything back. Even the fountain seemed to be bubbling boiling water on the people who sat at its edge, and in an instant I decided against crossing the street, and turned south on Fifth and began to walk the steaming pavement towards St. Patrick's. On the north steps a crowd was gathered; everyone was watching a model being photographed. She was wearing a lemon-colored dress and had her feet pointed like a ballerina, and as I passed into the church I heard some lady say, "If I ate cottage cheese *ten* times a day, I couldn't be that skinny."

It wasn't much cooler inside the church, though the stillness and the flicker of the candles made me think it was. I took a seat at the rear and while I couldn't bring myself to kneel, I did lean forward onto the back of the bench before me, and held my hands together and closed my eyes. I wondered if I looked like a Catholic, and in my wonderment I began to make a little speech to myself. Can I call the self-conscious words I spoke prayer? At any rate, I called my audience God. God, I said, I am twenty-three years old. I want to make the best of things. Now the doctor is about to wed Brenda to me, and I am not entirely certain this is all for the best. What is it I love, Lord? Why have I chosen? Who is Brenda? The race is to the swift. Should I have stopped to think?

I was getting no answers, but I went on. If we meet You at all, God, it's that we're carnal, and acquisitive, and thereby partake of You. I am carnal, and I know You approve, I just know it. But how carnal can I get? I am acquisitive. Where do I turn now in my acquisitiveness? Where do we meet? Which prize is You?

It was an ingenious meditation, and suddenly I felt ashamed. I got up and walked outside, and the noise of Fifth Avenue met me with an answer:

Which prize do you think, *schmuck?* Gold dinnerware, sporting-goods trees, nectarines, garbage disposals, bumpless noses, Patimkin Sink, Bonwit Teller—

But damn it, God, that *is* You!

And God only laughed, that clown.

On the steps around the fountain I sat in a small arc of a rainbow that the sun had shot through the spray of the water. And then I saw Brenda coming out of the Squibb Building. She carried nothing with her, like a woman who's only been window shopping, and for a moment I was glad that in the end she had disobeyed my desire.

As she crossed the street, though, that little levity passed, and then I was myself again.

She walked up before me and looked down at where I sat; when she inhaled she filled her entire body, and then let her breath out with a "Whew!"

"Where is it?" I said.

My answer, at first, was merely that victorious look of hers, the one she'd given Simp the night she'd beaten her, the one I'd gotten the morning I finished the third lap alone. At last she said, "I'm wearing it."

"Oh, Bren."

"He said shall I wrap it or will you take it with you?"

"Oh Brenda, I love you."

We slept together that night, and so nervous were we about our new toy that we performed like kindergartners, or (in the language of that country) like a lousy double-play combination. And then the next day we hardly saw one another at all, for with the last-minute wedding preparations came scurrying, telegramming, shouting, crying, rushing—in short, lunacy. Even the meals lost their Patimkin fullness, and were tortured out of Kraft cheese, stale onion rolls, dry salami, a little chopped liver, and fruit cocktail. It was hectic all weekend, and I tried as best I could to keep clear of the storm, at whose eye, Ron, clumsy and smiling, and Harriet, flittering and courteous, were being pulled closer and closer together. By Sunday night fatigue had arrested hysteria and all of the Patimkins, Brenda included, had gone off to an early sleep. When Ron went into the bathroom to brush his teeth I decided to go in and brush mine. While I stood over the sink he checked his supports for dampness; then he hung them on the shower knobs and asked me if I would like to listen to his records for a while. It was not out of boredom and loneliness that I accepted; rather a brief spark of lockerroom comradery had been struck there among the soap and the water and the tile, and I thought that perhaps Ron's invitation was prompted by a desire to spend his last moments as a Single Man with another Single Man. If I was right, then it was the first real attestation he'd given to my masculinity. How could I refuse?

I sat on the unused twin bed.

"You want to hear Mantovani?"

"Sure," I said.

"Who do you like better, him or Kostelanetz?"

"It's a toss-up."

Ron went to his cabinet. "Hey, how about the Columbus record? Brenda ever play it for you?"

"No. I don't think so."

He extracted a record from its case, and like a giant with a sea shell, placed it gingerly on the phonograph. Then he smiled at me and leaned back onto his bed. His arms were behind his head and his eyes fixed on the ceiling. "They give this to all the seniors. With the yearbook—" but he hushed as soon as the sound began. I watched Ron and listened to the record.

At first there was just a roll of drums, then silence, then another drum roll—and then softly, a marching song, the melody of which was very familiar. When the song ended, I heard the bells, soft, loud, then soft again. And finally there came a Voice, bowel-deep and historic, the kind one associates with documentaries about the rise of Fascism.

"The year, 1956. The season, fall. The place, Ohio State University . . ."

Blitzkrieg! Judgment Day! The Lord had lowered his baton, and the Ohio State Glee Club were lining out the Alma Mater as if their souls depended on it. After one desperate chorus, they fell, still screaming, into bottomless oblivion, and the Voice resumed:

"The leaves had begun to turn and redden on the trees. Smoky fires line Fraternity Row, as pledges rake the leaves and turn them to a misty haze. Old faces greet new ones, new faces meet old, and another year has begun . . ."

Music. Glee Club in great comeback. Then the Voice: "The place, the banks of the Olentangy. The event, Homecoming Game, 1956. The opponent, the ever dangerous Illini . . ."

Roar of crowd. New voice—Bill Stern: "Illini over the ball. The snap. Linday fading to pass, he finds a receiver, he passes long *long* down field—and IT'S INTERCEPTED BY NUMBER 43, HERB CLARK OF OHIO STATE! Clark evades one tackler, he evades another as he comes up to midfield. Now he's picking up blockers, he's down to the 45, the 40, the 35—"

And as Bill Stern egged on Clark, and Clark, Bill Stern, Ron, on his bed, with just a little body-english, eased Herb Clark over the goal.

"And it's the Buckeyes ahead now, 21 to 19. *What a game!*"

The Voice of History baritoned in again: "But the season was up and down, and by the time the first snow had covered the turf, it was the sound of dribbling and the cry *Up and In!* that echoed through the fieldhouse . . ."

Ron closed his eyes.

"The Minnesota game," a new, high voice announced, "and for some of our seniors, their last game for the red and white . . . The players are ready to come out on the floor and into the spot-light. There'll be a big hand of appreciation from this capacity crowd for some of the boys who won't be back next year. Here comes Larry Gardner, big Number 7, out onto the floor, Big Larry from Akron, Ohio . . ."

"Larry—" announced the P.A. system; "Larry," the crowd roared back.

"And here comes Ron Patimkin dribbling out. Ron, Number 11, from Short Hills, New Jersey. Big Ron's last game, and it'll be some time before Buckeye fans forget him . . ."

Big Ron tightened on his bed as the loudspeaker called his name; his ovation must have set the nets to trembling. Then the rest of the players were announced, and then basketball season was over, and it was Religious Emphasis Week, the Senior Prom (Billy May blaring at the gymnasium roof), Fraternity Skit Night, E. E. Cummings reading to students (verse, silence, applause); and then, finally, commencement:

"The campus is hushed this day of days. For several thousand young men and women it is a joyous yet a solemn occasion. And for their parents a day of laughter and a day of tears. It is a bright green day, it is June the seventh of the year one thousand nine hundred and fifty-seven and for these young Americans the most stirring day of their lives. For many this will be their last glimpse of the campus, of Columbus, for many many years. Life calls us, and anxiously if not nervously we walk out into the world and away from the pleasures of these ivied walls. But not from its memories. They will be the concomitant, if not the fundament, of our lives. We shall choose husbands and wives, we shall choose jobs and homes, we shall sire children and grandchildren, but we will not forget you, Ohio State. In the years ahead we will carry with us always memories of thee, Ohio State . . ."

Slowly, softly, the OSU band begins the Alma Mater, and then the bells chime that last hour. Soft, very soft, for it is spring.

There was goose flesh on Ron's veiny arms as the Voice continued. "We offer ourselves to you then, world, and come at you in search of Life. And to you, Ohio State, to you Columbus, we say thank you, thank you and goodbye. We will miss you, in the fall, in the winter, in the spring, but some day we shall return. Till then, goodbye, Ohio State, goodbye, red and white, goodbye, Columbus . . . goodbye, Columbus . . . goodbye . . ."

Ron's eyes were closed. The band was upending its last truckload of nostalgia, and I tiptoed from the room, in step with the 2163 members of the Class of '57.

I closed my door, but then opened it and looked back at Ron: he was still humming on his bed. Thee! I thought, my brother-in-law!

The wedding.

Let me begin with the relatives.

There was Mrs. Patimkin's side of the family: her sister Molly, a tiny buxom hen whose ankles swelled and ringed her shoes, and who would remember Ron's wedding if for no other reason than she'd martyred her feet in three-inch heels, and Molly's husband, the butter and egg man, Harry Grossbart, who had earned his fortune with barley and corn in the days of Prohibition. Now he was active in the Temple and whenever he saw Brenda he swatted her on the can; it was a kind of physical bootlegging that passed, I guess, for familial affection. Then there was Mrs. Patimkin's brother, Marty Kreiger, the Kosher Hot-Dog King, an immense man, as many stomachs as he had chins, and already, at fifty-five, with as many heart attacks as chins and stomachs combined. He had just come back from a health cure in the Catskills, where he said he'd eaten nothing but All-Bran and had won $1500 at gin rummy. When the photographer came by to take pictures, Marty put his hand on his wife's pancake breasts and said, "Hey, how about a picture of this!" His wife, Sylvia, was a frail, spindly woman with bones like a bird's. She had cried throughout the ceremony, and sobbed openly, in fact, when the rabbi had pronounced Ron and Harriet "man and wife in the eyes of God and the State of New Jersey." Later, at dinner, she had hardened enough to slap her husband's hand as it reached out for a cigar. However, when he reached across to hold her breast she just looked aghast and said nothing.

Also there were Mrs. Patimkin's twin sisters, Rose and Pearl, who both had white hair, the color of Lincoln convertibles, and nasal voices, and husbands who followed after them but talked only to each other, as though, in fact, sister had married sister, and husband had married husband. The husbands, named Earl Klein and Manny Kartzman, sat next to each other during the ceremony, then at dinner, and once, in fact, while the band was playing between courses, they rose, Klein and Kartzman, as though to dance, but instead walked to the far end of the hall where together they paced off the width of the floor. Earl, I learned later, was in the carpet business, and apparently he was trying to figure how much money he would make if the Hotel Pierre favored him with a sale.

On Mr. Patimkin's side there was only Leo, his half-brother. Leo was married to a woman named Bea whom nobody seemed to talk to. Bea kept hopping up and down during the meal and running over to the kiddie table to see if her little girl, Sharon, was being taken care of. "I told her not to take the kid. Get a baby-sitter, I said." Leo told me this while Brenda danced with Ron's best man, Ferrari. "She says what are we, millionaires? No, for Christ sake, but my brother's kids gets married, I can have a little celebration. No, we gotta *shlep* the kid with us. Aah, it gives her something to do! . . ." He looked around the hall. Up on the stage Harry Winters (né Weinberg) was leading his band in a medley from *My Fair Lady;* on the floor, all ages, all sizes, all shapes were dancing. Mr. Patimkin was dancing with Julie, whose dress had slipped down from her shoulders to reveal her soft small back, and long neck, like Brenda's. He danced in little squares and was making considerable effort not to step on Julie's toes. Harriet, who was, as everyone said, a beautiful bride, was dancing with her father. Ron danced with Harriet's mother, Brenda with Ferrari, and I had sat down for a while in the empty chair beside Leo so as not to get maneuvered into dancing with Mrs. Patimkin, which seemed to be the direction towards which things were moving.

"You're Brenda's boy friend? Huh?" Leo said.

I nodded—earlier in the evening I'd stopped giving blushing explanations. "You gotta deal there, boy," Leo said, "you don't louse it up."

"She's very beautiful," I said.

Leo poured himself a glass of champagne, and then waited as though he expected a head to form on it; when one didn't he filled the glass to the brim.

"Beautiful, not beautiful, what's the difference. I'm a practical man. I'm on the bottom, so I gotta be. You're Aly Khan you worry about marrying movie stars. I wasn't born yesterday . . . You know how old I was when I got married? Thirty-five years old. I don't know what the hell kind of hurry I was in." He drained his glass and refilled it. "I'll tell you something, one good thing happened to me in my whole life. Two maybe. Before I came back from overseas I got a letter from my wife—she wasn't my wife then. My mother-in-law found an apartment for us in Queens. Sixty-two fifty a month it cost. That's the last good thing that happened."

"What was the first?"

"What first?"

"You said *two* things," I said.

"I don't remember. I say two because my wife tells me I'm sarcastic and a cynic. That way maybe she won't think I'm such a wise guy."

I saw Brenda and Ferrari separate, and so excused myself and started for Brenda, but just then Mr. Patimkin separated from Julie and it looked as though the two men were going to switch partners. Instead the four of them stood on the dance floor and when I reached them they were laughing and Julie was saying, "What's so funny!" Ferrari said "Hi" to me and whisked Julie away, which sent her into peals of laughter.

Mr. Patimkin had one hand on Brenda's back and suddenly the other one was on mine. "You kids having a good time?" he said.

We were sort of swaying, the three of us, to "Get Me to the Church on Time."

Brenda kissed her father. "Yes," she said. "I'm so drunk my head doesn't even need my neck."

"It's a fine wedding, Mr. Patimkin."

"You want anything just ask me . . ." he said, a little drunken himself. "You're two good kids . . . How do you like that brother of yours getting married? . . . Huh? . . . Is that a girl or is that a girl?"

Brenda smiled, and though she apparently thought her father had spoken of her, I was sure he'd been referring to Harriet.

"You like weddings, Daddy?" Brenda said.

"I like my kids' weddings . . ." He slapped me on the back. "You two kids, you want anything? Go have a good time. Remember," he said to Brenda, "you're my honey . . ." Then he looked at me. "Whatever my Buck wants is good enough for me. There's no business too big it can't use another head."

I smiled though not directly at him, and beyond I could see Leo sopping up champagne and watching the three of us; when he caught my eye he made a sign with his hand, a circle with his thumb and forefinger, indicating, "That a boy, that a boy!"

After Mr. Patimkin departed, Brenda and I danced closely, and we only sat down when the waiters began to circulate with the main course. The head table was noisy, particularly at our end where the men were almost all teammates of Ron's, in one sport or another; they ate a fantastic number of rolls. Tank Feldman, Ron's roommate, who had flown in from Toledo, kept sending the waiter back for rolls, for celery, for olives, and always to the squealing delight of Gloria Feldman, his wife, a nervous, undernourished girl who continually looked down the front of her gown as though there were some sort of construction project going on under her clothes. Gloria and Tank, in fact, seemed to be self-appointed precinct captains at our end. They proposed toasts, burst into wild song, and continually referred to Brenda and me as "love birds." Brenda smiled at this with her eyeteeth and I brought up a cheery look from some fraudulent auricle of my heart.

And the night continued: we ate, we drank, we danced—Rose and Pearl did the Charleston with one another (while their husbands examined woodwork and chandeliers), and then I did the Charleston with none other than Gloria Feldman, who made coy, hideous faces at me all the time we danced. Near the end of the evening, Brenda, who'd been drinking champagne like her Uncle Leo, did a Rita Hayworth tango with herself, and Julie fell asleep on some ferns she'd whisked off the head table and made into a mattress at the far end of the hall. I felt a numbness creep into my hard palate, and by three o'clock people were dancing in their coats, shoeless ladies were wrapping hunks of wedding cake in napkins for their children's lunch, and finally Gloria Feldman made her way over to our end of the table and said, freshly, "Well, our little Radcliffe smarty, what have *you* been doing all summer?"

"Growing a penis."

Gloria smiled and left as quickly as she'd come, and Brenda without another word headed shakily away for the ladies' room and the rewards of overindulgence. No sooner had she left than Leo was beside me, a glass in one hand, a new bottle of champagne in the other.

"No sign of the bride and groom?" he said, leering. He'd lost most of his consonants by this time and was doing the best he could with long, wet vowels. "Well, you're next, kid, I see it in the cards . . .

You're nobody's sucker . . ." And he stabbed me in the side with the top of the bottle, spilling champagne onto the side of my rented tux. He straightened up, poured more onto his hand and glass, but then suddenly he stopped. He was looking into the lights which were hidden beneath a long bank of flowers that adorned the front of the table. He shook the bottle in his hand as though to make it fizz. "The son of a bitch who invented the fluorescent bulb should drop dead!" He set the bottle down and drank.

Up on the stage Harry Winters brought his musicians to a halt. The drummer stood up, stretched, and they all began to open up cases and put their instruments away. On the floor, relatives, friends, associates, were holding each other around the waists and the shoulders, and small children huddled around their parents' legs. A couple of kids ran in and out of the crowd, screaming at tag, until one was grabbed by an adult and slapped soundly on the behind. He began to cry, and couple by couple the floor emptied. Our table was a tangle of squashed everything; napkins, fruits, flowers; there were empty whisky bottles, droopy ferns, and dishes puddled with unfinished cherry jubilee, gone sticky with the hours. At the end of the table Mr. Patimkin was sitting next to his wife, holding her hand. Opposite them, on two bridge chairs that had been pulled up, sat Mr. and Mrs. Ehrlich. They spoke quietly and evenly, as though they had known each other for years and years. Everything had slowed down now, and from time to time people would come up to the Patimkins and Ehrlichs, wish them *mazel tov,* and then drag themselves and their families out into the September night, which was cool and windy, someone said, and reminded me that soon would come winter and snow.

"They never wear out, those things, you know that." Leo was pointing to the fluorescent lights that shone through the flowers. "They last for years. They could make a car like that if they wanted, that could never wear out. It would run on water in the summer and snow in the winter. But they wouldn't do it, the big boys . . . Look at me," Leo said, splashing his suit front with champagne, "I sell a good bulb. You can't get the kind of bulb I sell in the drugstores. It's a quality bulb. But I'm the little guy. I don't even own a car. His brother, and I don't even own an automobile. I take a train wherever I go. I'm the only guy I know who wears out three pairs of rubbers every winter. Most guys get new ones when they lose the old ones. I wear them out, like shoes. Look," he said, leaning into me, "I could sell a crappy bulb, it wouldn't break my heart. But it's not good business."

The Ehrlichs and Patimkins scraped back their chairs and headed away, all except Mr. Patimkin who came down the table towards Leo and me.

He slapped Leo on the back. "Well, how you doing, *shtarke?*"

"All right, Ben. All right . . ."

"You have a good time?"

"You had a nice affair, Ben, it must've cost a pretty penny, believe me . . ."

Mr. Patimkin laughed. 'When I make out my income tax I go to see Leo. He knows just how much money I spent . . . You need a ride home?" he asked me.

"No, thanks. I'm waiting for Brenda. We have my car."

"Good night," Mr. Patimkin said.

I watched him step down off the platform that held the head table, and then start towards the exit. Now the only people in the hall—the shambles of a hall—were myself, Leo, and his wife and child who slept, both of them, with their heads pillowed on a crumpled tablecloth at a table down on the floor before us. Brenda still wasn't around.

"When you got it," Leo said, rubbing his fingers together, "you can afford to talk like a big shot. Who needs a guy like me any more. Salesmen, you spit on them. You can go to the supermarket and buy anything. Where my wife shops you can buy sheets and pillowcases. Imagine, a grocery store! Me, I sell to gas stations, factories, small businesses, all up and down the east coast. Sure, you can sell a guy in a gas station a crappy bulb that'll burn out in a week. For inside the pumps I'm talking, it takes a certain kind of bulb. A utility bulb. All right, so you sell him a crappy bulb, and then a week later he puts in a new one, and while he's screwing it in he still remembers your name. Not me. I sell a quality bulb. It lasts a month, five weeks, before it even flickers, then it gives you another couple days, dim maybe, but so you shouldn't go blind. It hangs on, it's a quality bulb. Before it even burns out you notice it's getting darker, so you put a new one in. What people don't like is when one minute it's sunlight and the next dark. Let it glimmer a few days and they don't feel so bad. Nobody ever throws out my bulb—they figure they'll save them, can always use them in a pinch. Sometimes I say to a guy, you ever throw out a bulb you bought from Leo Patimkin? You gotta use psychology.

That's why I'm sending my kid to college. You don't know a little psychology these days, you're licked . . ."

He lifted an arm and pointed out to his wife; then he slumped down in his seat. "Aach!" he said, and drank off half a glass of champagne. "I'll tell you, I go as far as New London, Connecticut. That's as far as I'll go, and when I come home at night I stop first for a couple drinks. Martinis. Two I have, sometimes three. That seems fair, don't it? But to her a little sip or a bathtubful, it smells the same. She says it's bad for the kid if I come home smelling. The kid's a baby, for God's sake, she thinks that's the way I'm *supposed* to smell. A forty-eight-year-old man with a three-year-old kid! She'll give me a thrombosis that kid. My wife, she wants me to come home early and play with the kid before she goes to bed. Come home, she says, and *I'll* make you a drink. Hah! I spend all day sniffing gas, leaning under hoods with grimy *poilishehs* in New London, trying to force a lousy bulb into a socket—I'll screw it in myself, I tell them—and she thinks I want to come home and drink a martini from a jelly glass! How long are you going to stay in bars, she says. Till a Jewish girl is Miss Rheingold!

"Look," he went on after another drink, "I love my kid like Ben loves his Brenda. It's not that I don't want to play with her. But if I play with the kid and then at night get into bed with my wife, then she can't expect fancy things from me. It's one or the other. I'm no movie star."

Leo looked at his empty glass and put it on the table; he tilted the bottle up and drank the champagne like soda water. "How much do you think I make a week?" he said.

"I don't know."

"Take a guess."

"A hundred dollars."

"Sure, and tomorrow they're gonna let the lions out of the cage in Central Park. What do you think I make?"

"I can't tell."

"A cabdriver makes more than me. That's a fact. My wife's brother is a cabdriver, *he* lives in Kew Gardens. And he don't take no crap, no sir, not those cabbies. Last week it was raining one night and I said the hell with it, I'm taking a cab. I'd been all day in Newton, Mass. I don't usually go so far, but on the train in the morning I said to myself, stay on, go further, it'll be a change. And I know all the time I'm kidding myself. I wouldn't even make up the extra fare it cost me. But I stay on. And at night I still had a couple boxes with me, so when the guy pulls up at Grand Central there's like a genie inside me says get in. I even threw the bulbs in. Not even caring if they broke. And this cabbie says, Whatya want to do, buddy, rip the leather? Those are brand new seats I got. No, I said. Jesus Christ, he says, some goddam people. I get in and give him a Queens address which ought to shut him up, but no, all the way up the Drive he was Jesus Christing me. It's hot in the cab, so I open a window and *then* he turns around and says, Whatya want to do, give me a cold in the neck? I just got over a goddam cold . . ." Leo looked at me, bleary-eyed. "This city is crazy! If I had a little money I'd get out of here in a minute. I'd go to California. They don't need bulbs out there it's so light. I went to New Guinea during the war from San Francisco. *There,"* he burst, "there is the other good thing that happened to me, that night in San Francisco with this Hannah Schreiber. That's the both of them, you asked me I'm telling you—the apartment my mother-in-law got us, and this Hannah Schreiber. One night was all. I went to a B'nai Brith dance for servicemen in the basement of some big temple, and I met her. I wasn't married then, so don't make faces."

"I'm not."

"She had a nice little room by herself. She was going to school to be a teacher. Already I knew something was up because she let me feel inside her slip in the cab. Listen to me, I sound like I'm always in cabs. Maybe two other times in my life. To tell the truth I don't even enjoy it. All the time I'm riding I'm watching the meter. Even the pleasures I can't enjoy!"

"What about Hannah Schreiber?"

He smiled, flashing some gold in his mouth. "How do you like that name? She was only a girl, but she had an old lady's name. In the room she says to me she believes in oral love. I can still hear her: Leo Patimkin, I believe in oral love. I don't know what the hell she means. I figure she was one of those Christian Scientists or some cult or something. So I said, But what about for soldiers, guys going overseas who may get killed, God forbid." He shrugged his shoulders. "The smartest guy in the world I wasn't. But that's twenty years almost, I was still wet behind the ears. I'll tell you, every once in a while my wife—you know, she does for me what Hannah Schreiber did. I don't like to force her, she works hard. That to her is like a cab to me. I wouldn't force her. I can remember every time, I'll bet. Once after a Seder, my mother was still living, she should rest in peace. My wife was up to here with Mogen David. In fact, *twice* after

Seders. Aachhh! Everything good in my life I can count on my fingers! God forbid some one should leave me a million dollars, I wouldn't even have to take off my shoes. I got a whole other hand yet."

He pointed to the fluorescent bulbs with the nearly empty champagne bottle. "You call that a light? That's a light to *read* by? It's purple, for God's sake! Half the blind men in the world ruined themselves by those damn things. You know who's behind them? The optometrists! I'll tell you, if I could get a couple hundred for all my stock and the territory, I'd sell tomorrow. That's right, Leo A. Patimkin, one semester accounting, City College nights, will sell equipment, territory, good name. I'll buy two inches in the *Times.* The territory is from here to everywhere. I go where I want, my own boss, no one tells me what to do. You know the Bible? 'Let there be light—and there's Leo Patimkin!' That's my trademark, I'll sell that too. I tell them that slogan, the *poilishehs,* they think I'm making it up. What good is it to be smart unless you're in on the ground floor! I got more brains in my pinky than Ben got in his whole *head.* Why is it he's on top and I'm on the bottom! *Why!* Believe me, if you're born lucky, you're lucky!" And then he exploded into silence.

I had the feeling that he was going to cry, so I leaned over and whispered to him, "You better go home." He agreed, but I had to raise him out of his seat and steer him by one arm down to his wife and child. The little girl could not be awakened, and Leo and Bea asked me to watch her while they went out into the lobby to get their coats. When they returned, Leo seemed to have dragged himself back to the level of human communication. He shook my hand with real feeling. I was very touched.

"You'll go far," he said to me. "You're a smart boy, you'll play it safe. Don't louse things up."

"I won't."

"Next time we see you it'll be *your* wedding," and he winked at me. Bea stood alongside, muttering goodbye all the while he spoke. He shook my hand again and then picked the child out of her seat, and they turned towards the door. From the back, round-shouldered, burdened, child-carrying, they looked like people fleeing a captured city.

Brenda, I discovered, was asleep on a couch in the lobby. It was almost four o'clock and the two of us and the desk clerk were the only ones in the hotel lobby. At first I did not waken Brenda, for she was pale and wilted and I knew she had been sick. I sat beside her, smoothing her hair back off her ears. How would I ever come to know her, I wondered, for as she slept I felt I knew no more of her than what I could see in a photograph. I stirred her gently and in a half-sleep she walked beside me out to the car.

It was almost dawn when we came out of the Jersey side of the Lincoln Tunnel. I switched down to my parking lights, and drove on to the Turnpike, and there out before me I could see the swampy meadows that spread for miles and miles, watery, blotchy, smelly, like an oversight of God. I thought of that other oversight, Leo Patimkin, half-brother to Ben. In a few hours he would be on a train heading north, and as he passed Scarsdale and White Plains, he would belch and taste champagne and let the flavor linger in his mouth. Alongside him on the seat, like another passenger, would be cartons of bulbs. He would get off at New London, or maybe, inspired by the sight of his half-brother, he would stay on again, hoping for some new luck further north. For the world was Leo's territory, every city, every swamp, every road and highway. He could go on to Newfoundland if he wanted, Hudson Bay, and on up to Thule, and then slide down the other side of the globe and rap on frosted windows on the Russian steppes, if he wanted. But he wouldn't. Leo was forty-eight years old and he had learned. He pursued discomfort and sorrow, all right, but if you had a heartful by the time you reached New London, what new awfulness could you look forward to in Vladivostok?

The next day the wind was blowing the fall in and the branches of the weeping willow were fingering at the Patimkin front lawn. I drove Brenda to the train at noon, and she left me.

8

Autumn came quickly. It was cold and in Jersey the leaves turned and fell overnight. The following Saturday I took a ride up to see the deer, and did not even get out of the car, for it was too brisk to be standing at the wire fence, and so I watched the animals walk and run in the dimness of the late afternoon, and after a while everything, even the objects of nature, the trees, the clouds, the grass, the weeds, reminded me of Brenda, and I drove back down to Newark. Already we had sent our first letters and I had called her late one night, but in the mail and on the phone we had some difficulty discovering one another; we had not the style yet. That night I tried her again, and someone on her floor said she was out and would not be in till late.

Upon my return to the library I was questioned by Mr. Scapello about the Gauguin book. The jowly gentleman *had* sent a nasty letter about my discourtesy, and I was only able to extricate myself by offering a confused story in an indignant tone. In fact, I even managed to turn it around so that Mr. Scapello was apologizing to me as he led me up to my new post, there among the encyclopedias, the bibliographies, the indexes and guides. My bullying surprised me, and I wondered if some of it had not been learned from Mr. Patimkin that morning I'd heard him giving Grossman an earful on the phone. Perhaps I was more of a businessman than I thought. Maybe I could learn to become a Patimkin with ease . . .

Days passed slowly; I never did see the colored kid again, and when, one noon, I looked in the stacks, Gauguin was gone, apparently charged out finally by the jowly man. I wondered what it had been like that day the colored kid had discovered the book was gone. Had he cried? For some reason I imagined that he had blamed it on me, but then I realized that I was confusing the dream I'd had with reality. Chances were he had discovered someone else, Van Gogh, Vermeer . . . But no, they were not his kind of artists. What had probably happened was that he'd given up on the library and gone back to playing Willie Mays in the streets. He was better off, I thought. No sense carrying dreams of Tahiti in your head, if you can't afford the fare.

Let's see, what else did I do? I ate, I slept, I went to the movies, I sent broken-spined books to the bindery—I did everything I'd ever done before, but now each activity was surrounded by a fence, existed alone, and my life consisted of jumping from one fence to the next. There was no flow, for that had been Brenda.

And then Brenda wrote saying that she could be coming in for the Jewish holidays which were only a week away. I was so overjoyed I wanted to call Mr. and Mrs. Patimkin, just to tell them of my pleasure. However, when I got to the phone and had actually dialed the first two letters, I knew that at the other end there would be silence; if there was anything said, it would only be Mrs. Patimkin asking, "What is it you want?" Mr. Patimkin had probably forgotten my name.

That night, after dinner, I gave Aunt Gladys a kiss and told her she shouldn't work so hard.

"In less than a week it's Rosh Hashana and he thinks I should take a vacation. Ten people I'm having. What do you think, a chicken cleans itself? Thank God, the holidays come once a year, I'd be an old woman before my time."

But then it was only nine people Aunt Gladys was having, for only two days after her letter Brenda called.

"Oy Gut!" Aunt Gladys called. "Long *distance!*"

"Hello?" I said.

"Hello, sweetie?"

"Yes," I said.

"What *is* it?" Aunt Gladys tugged at my shirt. "What is it?"

"It's for me."

"Who?" Aunt Gladys said, pointing into the receiver.

"Brenda," I said.

"Yes?" Brenda said.

"Brenda?" Aunt Gladys said. "What does she call long distance, I almost had a heart attack."

"Because she's in Boston," I said. "Please, Aunt Gladys . . ."

And Aunt Gladys walked off, mumbling, "These kids . . ."

"Hello," I said again into the phone.

"Neil, how are you?"

"I love you."

"Neil, I have bad news. I can't come in this week."

"But, honey, it's the Jewish holidays."

"Sweet*heart,*" she laughed.

"Can't you say that, for an excuse?"

"I have a test Saturday, and a paper, and you know if I went home I wouldn't get anything done . . ."

"You would."

"Neil, I just *can't.* My Mother'd make me go to Temple, and I wouldn't even have enough time to see *you.*"

"Oh God, Brenda."

"Sweetie?"

"Yes?"

"Can't you come up here?" she asked.

"I'm working."

"The Jewish holidays," she said.

"Honey, I can't. Last year I didn't take them off, I can't all—"

"You can say you had a conversion."

"Besides, my aunt's having all the family for dinner, and you know what with my parents—"

"Come up, Neil."

"I can't just take two days off, Bren. I just got promoted and a raise—"

"The hell with the raise."

"Baby, it's my job."

"Forever?" she said.

"No."

"Then come. I've got a hotel room."

"For me?"

"For us."

"Can you do that?"

"No and yes. People do it."

"Brenda, you tempt me."

"Be tempted."

"I could take a train Wednesday right from work."

"You could stay till Sunday night."

"Bren, I can't. I still have to be back to work on Saturday."

"Don't you ever get a day *off?"* she said.

"Tuesdays," I said glumly.

"God."

"And Sunday," I added.

Brenda said something but I did not hear her, for Aunt Gladys called, "You talk all day long distance?"

"Quiet!" I shouted back to her.

"Neil, will you?"

"Damn it, yes," I said.

"Are you angry?"

"I don't think so. I'm going to come up."

"Till Sunday."

"We'll see."

"Don't feel upset, Neil. You sound upset. It is the Jewish holidays. I mean you *should* be off."

"That's right," I said. "I'm an orthodox Jew, for God's sake, I ought to take advantage of it."

"That's right," she said.

"Is there a train around six?"

"Every hour, I think."

"Then I'll be on the one that leaves at six."

"I'll be at the station," she said. "How will I know you?"

"I'll be disguised as an orthodox Jew."

"Me too," she said.

"Good night, love," I said.

Aunt Gladys cried when I told her I was going away for Rosh Hashana.

"And I was preparing a big meal," she said.

"You can still prepare it."

"What will I tell your mother?"

"I'll tell her, Aunt Gladys. Please. You have no right to get upset . . ."

"Someday you'll have a family you'll know what it's like."

"I have a family now."

"What's a matter," she said, blowing her nose, "That girl couldn't come home to see her family it's the holidays?"

"She's in school, she just can't—"

"If she loved her family she'd find time. We don't live six hundred years."

"She does love her family."

"Then one day a year you could break your heart and pay a visit."

"Aunt Gladys, you don't understand."

"Sure," she said, "when I'm twenty-three years old I'll understand everything."

I went to kiss her and she said, "Go away from me, go run to Boston . . ."

The next morning I discovered that Mr. Scapello didn't want me to leave on Rosh Hashana either, but I unnerved him, I think, by hinting that his coldness about my taking the two days off might just be so much veiled anti-Semitism, so on the whole he was easier to manage. At lunch time I took a walk down to Penn Station and picked up a train schedule to Boston. That was my bedtime reading for the next three nights.

She did not look like Brenda, at least for the first minute. And probably to her I did not look like me. But we kissed and held each other, and it was strange to feel the thickness of our coats between us.

"I'm letting my hair grow," she said in the cab, and that in fact was all she said. Not until I helped her out of the cab did I notice the thin gold band shining on her left hand.

She hung back, strolling casually about the lobby while I signed the register "Mr. and Mrs. Neil Klugman," and then in the room we kissed again.

"Your heart's pounding," I said to her.

"I know," she said.

"Are you nervous?"

"No."

"Have you done this before?" I said.

"I read Mary McCarthy."

She took off her coat and instead of putting it in the closet, she tossed it across the chair. I sat down on the bed; she didn't.

"What's the matter?"

Brenda took a deep breath and walked over to the window, and I thought that perhaps it would be best for me to ask nothing—for us to get used to each other's presence in quiet. I hung her coat and mine in the empty closet, and left the suitcases—mine and hers—standing by the bed.

Brenda was kneeling backwards in the chair, looking out the window as though out the window was where she'd rather be. I came up behind her and put my hands around her body and held her breasts, and when I felt the cool draft that swept under the sill, I realized how long it had been since that first warm night when I had put my arms around her and felt the tiny wings beating in her back. And then I realized why I'd really come to Boston—it had been long enough. It was time to stop kidding about marriage.

"Is something the matter?" I said.

"Yes."

It wasn't the answer I'd expected; I wanted no answer really, only to soothe her nervousness with my concern.

But I asked, "What is it? Why didn't you mention it on the phone?"

"It only happened today."

"School?"

"Home. They found out about us."

I turned her face up to mine. "That's okay. I told my aunt I was coming here too. What's the difference?"

"About the summer. About our sleeping together."

"Oh?"

"Yes."

". . . Ron?"

"No."

"That night, you mean, did Julie—"

"No," she said, "it wasn't *anybody.*"

"I don't get it."

Brenda got up and walked over to the bed where she sat down on the edge. I sat in the chair.

"My mother found the thing."

"The diaphragm?"

She nodded.

"When?" I asked.

"The other day, I guess." She walked to the bureau and opened her purse. "Here, you can read them in the order I got them." She tossed an envelope at me; it was dirty-edged and crumpled, as though it had been in and out of her pockets a good many times. "I got this one this morning," she said. "Special delivery."

I took out the letter and read:

PATIMKIN KITCHEN AND BATHROOM SINKS
"Any Size—Any Shape"

Dear Brenda—

Don't pay any Attention to your Mother's Letter when you get it. I love you honey if you want a coat I'll buy You a coat. You could always have anything you wanted. We have every faith in you so you won't be too upset by what your mother says in her Letter. Of course she is a little hystericall because of the shock and she has been Working so hard for Hadassah. She is a Woman and it is hard for her to understand some of the Shocks in life. Of course I can't say We weren't all surprised because from the beginning I was nice to him and Thought he would appreciate the nice vacation we supplied for him. Some People never turn out the way you hope and pray but I am willing to forgive and call Buy Gones, Buy Gones, You have always up till now been a good Buck and got good scholastic Grades and Ron has always been what we wanted a Good Boy, most important, and a Nice boy. This late in my life believe me I am not going to start hating my own flesh and blood. As for your mistake it takes Two to make a mistake and now that you will be away at school and from him and what you got involved in you will probably do all right I have every faith you will. You have to have faith in your children like in a

Business or any serious undertaking and there is nothing that is so bad that we can't forgive especially when Our own flesh and blood is involved. We have a nice close nitt family and why not???? Have a nice Holiday and in Temple I will say a Prayer for you as I do every year. On Monday I want you to go into Boston and buy a coat. Whatever you need because I know how Cold it gets up where you are . . . Give my regards to Linda and remember to bring her home with you on Thanksgiving like last year. You two had such a nice time. I have always never said bad things about any of your friends or Rons and that this should happen is only the exception that proves the rule. Have a Happy Holiday.

Your Father

And then it was signed "Ben Patimkin," but that was crossed out and written beneath "Your Father" were again, like an echo, the words, "Your Father."

"Who's Linda?" I asked.

"My roommate, last year." She tossed another envelope to me. "Here. I got this one in the afternoon. Air Mail."

The letter was from Brenda's mother. I started to read it and then put it down a moment. "You got this *after?*"

"Yes," she said. "When I got his I didn't know what was happening. Read hers."

I began again.

Dear Brenda:

I don't even know how to begin. I have been crying all morning and have had to skip my board meeting this afternoon because my eyes are so red. I never thought this would happen to a daughter of mine. I wonder if you know what I mean, if it is at least on your conscience, so I won't have to degrade either of us with a description. All I can say is that this morning when I was cleaning out the drawers and putting away your summer clothing I came upon something in your bottom drawer, *under* some sweaters which you probably remember leaving there. I cried the minute I saw it and I haven't stopped crying yet. Your father called a while ago and now he is driving home because he heard how upset I was on the phone.

I don't know what we ever did that you should reward us this way. We gave you a nice home and all the love and respect a child needs. I always was proud when you were a little girl that you could take care of yourself so well. You took care of Julie so beautifully it was a treat to see, when you were only fourteen years old. But you drifted away from your family, even though we sent you to the best schools and gave you the best money could buy. Why you should reward us this way is a question I'll carry with me to the grave.

About your friend I have no words. He is his parents' responsibility and I cannot imagine what kind of home life he had that he could act that way. Certainly that was a fine way to repay us for the hospitality we were nice enough to show to him, a perfect stranger. That the two of you should be carrying on like that in our very house I will never in my life be able to understand. Times certainly have changed since I was a girl that this kind of thing could go on. I keep asking myself if at least you didn't think of us while you were doing that. If not for me, how could you do this to your father? God forbid Julie should ever learn of this.

God only knows what you have been doing all these years we put our trust in you.

You have broken your parents' hearts and you should know that. This is some thank you for all we gave you.

Mother

She only signed "Mother" once, and that was in an extraordinarily miniscule hand, like a whisper.

"Brenda," I said.

"What?"

"Are you starting to cry?"

"No. I cried already."

"Don't start again."

"I'm trying not to, for God's sake."

"Okay . . . Brenda, can I ask you one question?"

"What?"

"Why did you leave it home?"

"Because I didn't plan on using it here, that's why."

"Suppose I'd come up. I mean I have come up, what about that?"

"I thought I'd come down first."

"So then couldn't you have carried it down then? Like a toothbrush?"

"Are you trying to be funny?"

"No. I'm just asking you why you left it home."

"I told you," Brenda said. "I thought I'd come home."

"But, Brenda, that doesn't make any sense. Suppose you did come home, and then you came back again. Wouldn't you have taken it with you then?"

"I don't *know.*"

"Don't get angry," I said.

"You're the one who's angry."

"I'm upset, I'm not angry."

"I'm upset then too."

I did not answer but walked to the window and looked out. The stars and moon were out, silver and hard, and from the window I could see over to the Harvard campus where lights burned and then seemed to flicker when the trees blew across them.

"Brenda . . ."

"What?"

"Knowing how your mother feels about you, wasn't it silly to leave it home? Risky?"

"What does how she feels about me have to do with it?"

"You can't trust her."

"Why can't I?"

"Don't you see. You *can't.*"

"Neil, she was only cleaning out the drawers."

"Didn't you know she would?"

"She never did before. Or maybe she did. Neil, I couldn't think of everything. We slept together night after night and nobody heard or noticed—"

"Brenda, why the hell are you willfully confusing things?"

"I'm not!"

"Okay," I said softly. "All right."

"It's you who's confusing things," Brenda said. "You act as though I wanted her to find it."

I didn't answer.

"Do you believe *that?*" she said, after neither of us had spoken for a full minute.

"I don't know."

"Oh, Neil, you're *crazy.*"

"What was crazier than leaving that damn thing around?"

"It was an oversight."

"Now it's an oversight, before it was deliberate."

"It was an oversight about the drawer. It wasn't an oversight about leaving it," she said.

"Brenda, sweetheart, wouldn't the safest, smartest, easiest, simplest thing have been to have taken it with you? Wouldn't it?"

"It didn't make any difference either way."

"Brenda, this is the most frustrating argument of my life!"

"You keep making it seem as though I *wanted* her to find it. Do you think I need this? Do you? I can't even go home any more."

"Is that so?"

"Yes!"

"No," I said. "You can go home—your father will be waiting with two coats and a half-dozen dresses."

"What about my mother?"

"It'll be the same with her."

"Don't be absurd. How can I face them!"

"Why can't you face them? Did you do anything wrong?"

"Neil, look at the reality of the thing, will you?"

"*Did* you do anything wrong?"

"Neil, *they* think it's wrong. They're my parents."

"But do you think it's wrong—"

"That doesn't *matter.*"

"It does to me, Brenda . . ."

"Neil, why are *you* confusing things? You keep accusing me of things."

"Damn it, Brenda, you're guilty of some things."

"What?"

"Of leaving that damn diaphragm there. How can you call it an oversight!"

"Oh, Neil, don't start any of that psychoanalytic crap!"

"Then why else did you do it? You wanted her to find it!"

"Why?"

"I don't know, Brenda, *why?"*

"Oh!" she said, and she picked up the pillow and threw it back on to the bed.

"What happens now, Bren?" I said.

"What does that mean?"

"Just that. What happens now?"

She rolled over on to the bed and buried her head in it.

"Don't start crying," I said.

"I'm *not.*"

I was still holding the letters and took Mr. Patimkin's from its envelope.

"Why does your father capitalize all these letters?"

She didn't answer.

"'As for your mistake,'" I read aloud to Brenda,"'it takes Two to make a mistake and now that you will be away at school and from him and what you got involved in you will probably do all right I have every faith you will. Your Father. Your Father.'"

She turned and looked at me; but silently.

"'I have always never said bad things about any of your friends or Rons and that this should happen is only the exception that proves the rule. Have a Happy Holiday.'" I stopped; in Brenda's face there was positively no threat of tears; she looked, suddenly, solid and decisive. "Well, what are you going to do?" I asked.

"Nothing."

"Who are you going to bring home Thanksgiving—Linda?" I said, "or me?"

"Who *can* I bring home, Neil?"

"I don't know, who can you?"

"Can I bring you home?"

"I don't know," I said, "can you?"

"Stop repeating the question!"

"I sure as hell can't give you the answer."

"Neil, be realistic. After this, can I bring you home? Can you see us all sitting around the table?"

"I can't if you can't, and I can if you can."

"Are you going to speak Zen, for God's sake!"

"Brenda, the choices aren't mine. You can bring Linda or me. You can go home or not go home. That's another choice. Then you don't even have to worry about choosing between me and Linda."

"Neil, you don't understand. They're still my parents. They did send me to the best schools, didn't they? They have given me everything I've wanted, haven't they?"

"Yes."

"Then how can I not go home? I *have* to go home."

"Why?"

"You don't understand. Your parents don't bother you any more. You're lucky."

"Oh, sure. I live with my crazy aunt, that's a real bargain."

"Families are different. You don't understand."

"Goddamit, I understand more than you think. I understand why the hell you left that thing lying around. Don't you? Can't you put two and two together?"

"Neil, what are you talking about! You're the one who doesn't understand. You're the one who from the very beginning was accusing me of things? Remember? Isn't it so? Why don't you have your eyes fixed? Why don't you have this fixed, that fixed? As if it were my fault that I *could* have them fixed. You kept acting as if I was going to run away from you every minute. And now you're doing it again, telling me I planted that thing on purpose."

"I loved you, Brenda, so I cared."

"I loved *you*. That's why I got that damn thing in the first place."

And then we heard the tense in which we'd spoken and we settled back into ourselves and silence.

A few minutes later I picked up my bag and put on my coat. I think Brenda was crying too when I went out the door.

Instead of grabbing a cab immediately, I walked down the street and out towards the Harvard Yard which I had never seen before. I entered one of the gates and then headed out along a path, under the tired autumn foliage and the dark sky. I wanted to be alone, in the dark; not because I wanted to think about anything, but rather because, for just a while, I wanted to think about nothing. I walked clear across the Yard and up a little hill and then I was standing in front of the Lamont Library, which, Brenda had once told me, had Patimkin Sinks in its rest rooms. From the light of the lamp on the path behind me I could see my reflection in the glass front of the building. Inside, it was dark and there were no students to be seen, no librarians. Suddenly, I wanted to set down my suitcase and pick up a rock and heave it right through the glass, but of course I didn't. I simply looked at myself in the mirror the light made of the window. I was only that substance, I thought, those limbs, that face that I saw in front of me. I looked, but the outside of me gave up little information about the inside of me. I wished I could scoot around to the other side of the window, faster than light or sound or Herb Clark on Homecoming Day, to get behind that image and catch whatever it was that looked through those eyes. What was it inside me that had turned pursuit and clutching into love, and then turned it inside out again? What was it that had turned winning into losing, and losing—who knows—into winning? I was sure I had loved Brenda, though standing there, I knew I couldn't any longer. And I knew it would be a long while before I made love to anyone the way I had made love to her. With anyone else, could I summon up such a passion? Whatever spawned my love for her, had that spawned such lust too? If she had only been slightly *not* Brenda . . . but then would I have loved her? I looked hard at the image of me, at that darkening of the glass, and then my gaze pushed through it, over the cool floor, to a broken wall of books, imperfectly shelved.

I did not look very much longer, but took a train that got me into Newark just as the sun was rising on the first day of the Jewish New Year. I was back in plenty of time for work.

TOPICS FOR PAPERS AND DISCUSSION

1. *The novel as social commentary.* From an insular love story oriented toward Jewish life, this novel expands outward to examine contemporary American society. What does it reveal of lower-class and upper-middle-class American Jewish life, and how does it radiate to our society in general? Explain the ways the novel reflects national absorption with any of the following: social status, financial gain, material acquisitions, suburbia, eating, mechanical conveniences, personal comfort, physical beauty and stylish apparel, work, education, sex, sports, and leisure time.

2. *The ambiguities of Neil Klugman.* What is Neil's background? He is an intelligent and sensitive narrator-participant, yet his character presents puzzling contradictions. Explain how he can be alternately genuine and hypocritical, firm and malleable, wise and foolish, mean and considerate, passive and competitive, arrogant and humble, dependent and independent. If Neil is unsettled, why is he also deeply attached to Newark? Why does he remain working at the library when he dislikes it? At the end he feels simultaneous gain and loss. Why? Is he left finally in a state of limbo?

3. *Interrelationships in the Patimkin family.* "The family is at the core of the Jewish social character," Frederick J. Hoffman has observed. Are the Patimkins exemplary? Mr. Patimkin writes, "We have a nice close nitt family. . . ." Is it closely knit? Judge whether the Patimkins are allies or foes, unified or disconnected. Analyze the letters from the mother and father to Brenda. Consider the Patimkin marriage, the parental and sibling relationships, and the Patimkin relatives. Also analyze the engagement and marriage of Ron and Harriet. Compare Neil's family, only one of whom, Aunt Gladys, actually appears.

4. *Physical settings.* Analyze the use of these major locations: (1) the home of Aunt Gladys in Newark, (2) the Patimkin residence in the suburb of

Short Hills, (3) the Newark Public Library, (4) the Pierre Hotel ballroom in Manhattan. Locate other settings and comment upon their thematic and symbolic function, particularly the Patimkin business in Newark and the Lamont Library at Harvard. What is the significance of the upward movement from Newark to Short Hills to the deer reserve in "the mountains"? How does the visitors' area of the reserve function symbolically as a summit?

5. *The Brenda-Neil relationship.* How does this novel escape from being a cliché of "love affair of society girl and boy from across the tracks"? Compare their ideas, values, and actions to show how they're alike and different. How is Neil made to seem servile, and how does he dominate? Why does Brenda use Neil as a weapon against her way of life, and paradoxically want to mold him in its image? Analyze her egotism and short-sightedness, her need for familial and monetary security, her avoidance of Jewishness and its traditions. Contrast her perceptiveness and her obtuseness, her masculinity and her femininity. At what level is her emotional maturity? Analyze the hotel room scene in which each affirms certain ties.

6. *Ethnic grouping.* In what ways are ethnic groups separated in the novel? How are they mixed? Does the novel make implicit distinctions among Jews who have maintained their religious and cultural traditions and those who have become virtually gentile? Is religion important in the novel? Establish gradations in the attitudes of whites toward blacks, ranging from animosity to kinship. Explain why the city of Newark is especially apt as a central locale. Also, why is it important that the library be a place open to all social classes and nationalities?

7. *Resonance of symbolism.* Explain how these objects connected with the Patimkins have symbolic meaning: the bounteous fruit, sports equipment, the old refrigerator, the old furniture stored in the attic, Brenda's glasses, Ron's Ohio State blanket, the "Goodbye, Columbus" record. Consider the following at the library: the lions, the stairs, the paintings of Gauguin. How is the wedding feast symbolic? What do names mean, for example, Klugman? How are the seasons of summer and fall symbolic? What is the significance of *Goodbye, Columbus* as a title, especially as it applies to Neil's dream about the ship and the black boy, his mate? In how many ways can the title be interpreted?

8. *The diaphragm perplex.* As a major symbol, what are the varied meanings of the diaphragm? How does it define the Neil-Brenda relationship? How does it function as objective correlative? Why does Neil insist that Brenda get a diaphragm, and why does she angrily refuse, then later relent? What is your interpretation of Brenda's act of leaving the diaphragm at home? Deliberate these possibilities: (1) she was forgetful and the result acccidental; (2) she was provident, but failed to anticipate the consequences; (3) it was an intentional ruthless act to

achieve a premeditated end. Which is more likely? Or is there some other explanation?

9. *The Roth brand of humor.* How is humor used? Make distinctions among satire, irony, and sarcasm. Who is being mocked by Roth, by Neil, by Brenda? In what ways does Roth reveal phony standards? Analyze the following examples of humor: Neil's answer about Doris: "Peeling . . . . She's going to have her skin fixed"; Neil's description of the "Goodbye, Columbus" record; his observation of the Patimkin library: "a complete set of *Information Please Almanacs";* Brenda's answer to Gloria about what she has been doing all summer: "Growing a penis"; Neil's thought outside St. Patrick's Church: "And God only laughed, that clown."

10. *The dialectic pattern of themes.* The novel contains numerous thematic polarities, which may be placed under three general headings: (1) *the social,* such as Jewishness and the loss or avoidance of Jewishness, social climbing and resistance to social climbing, wealth and poverty, outsiders and insiders; (2) *the psychological,* such as reality and illusion, the past and present, intellect and emotion, physical and aesthetic life, materialism and spirituality; and (3) *the romantic,* such as quest and seduction, the battle of the sexes, fulfillment and destruction. Analyze any of these dualities.

11. *Social mobility and immobility.* Reread the memorable paragraph in Part 6 beginning "Patimkin Kitchen and Bathroom Sinks was in the heart of the Negro section of Newark." Brenda says that her mother "still thinks we live in Newark." And Aunt Gladys asks, "Since when do Jewish people live in Short Hills?" Relate these and other pertinent passages to (in Irving Howe's words) "the moral and psychic consequences of the great transformation in American Jewish life." For all its depiction of the flux in urban and suburban areas, the novel also reveals social immobility. Where? Concentrate on specific evidence of movement and stasis in the novel.

12. *Techniques of "the double."* Analyze use of prototypes, replicas, and reflectors. How and to what ends are they used? The major "double" relationship obviously consists of Neil and the black boy who visits the library. Trace parallels between them. How do they both relate to "Tahiti"? Why is Neil so protective of the boy? Analyze the meaning of Brenda's remark to Neil: "You know, you look like me. Except bigger." Compare Ben and Ron, Brenda and Julie, Brenda and her mother, the Kleins and the Kartzmans at the wedding party.

13. *"Let there be light—and there's Leo Patimkin!"* Although he appears only in the wedding scene, Ben's half-brother is important. Why? A sad comic schlimazel, he is also a hero of sorts. How is he heroic? Carefully analyze his long, nearly nonstop speech. What does it reveal about him and his values? How is he different from the other Patimkins? Consider Leo's question about Ben and himself: "Why is it he's on top and I'm on

the bottom!" Weigh his statement: "I got more brains in my pinky than Ben got in his whole *head.*" Is Leo a failure? By what standards?

14. *The thematic meaning of athletics and competitiveness.* The Patimkins reflect America's passion for sports and physical fitness. Furthermore, they would seem to consecrate the adage, "A family that plays together stays together." But what does competition do to them? Why are athletics so important to them? How does Neil fare as an athlete? How do running and swimming function as thematic actions? Review Brenda's tennis match with Laura Simpson Stolowitch for what it reveals about the theme. Also consider the elder Patimkin's motives in letting Julie win at basketball and other games, and Neil's pleasure in beating her at Ping-Pong.

15. *"The American Dream" of success.* What is to account for Ben Patimkin's rise to wealth from impoverished beginnings? What are his attitudes toward work? Where does he place his values? Compare the positions of two Patimkin families (Ben's and Leo's) and two Klugman families (Uncle Aaron's and Uncle Max's). Is Neil aware of a disparity between dream and reality? In his experience with the dream world of the elite suburb, does Neil rise or fall? What is revealed about the attitudes of the black boy and Leo toward the American dream? Finally, in a larger sense, how does the novel reflect the dream and the reality of our nation?

The Ballad of the Sad Café

CARSON McCULLERS

The town itself is dreary; not much is there except the cotton mill, the two-room houses where the workers live, a few peach trees, a church with two colored windows, and a miserable main street only a hundred yards long. On Saturdays the tenants from the near-by farms come in for a day of talk and trade. Otherwise the town is lonesome, sad, and like a place that is far off and estranged from all other places in the world. The nearest train stop is Society City, and the Greyhound and White Bus Lines use the Forks Falls Road which is three miles away. The winters here are short and raw, the summers white with glare and fiery hot.

If you walk along the main street on an August afternoon there is nothing whatsoever to do. The largest building, in the very center of the town, is boarded up completely and leans so far to the right that it seems bound to collapse at any minute. The house is very old. There is about it a curious, cracked look that is very puzzling until you suddenly realize that at one time, and long ago, the right side of the front porch had been painted, and part of the wall—but the painting was left unfinished and one portion of the house is darker and dingier than the other. The building looks completely deserted. Nevertheless, on the second floor there is one window which is not boarded; sometimes in the late afternoon when the heat is at its worst a hand will slowly open the shutter and a face will look down on the town. It is a face like the terrible dim faces known in dreams—sexless and white, with two gray crossed eyes which are turned inward so sharply that they seem to be exchanging with each other one long and secret gaze of grief. The face lingers at the window for an hour or so, then the shutters are closed once more, and as likely as not there will not be another soul to be seen along the main street. These August afternoons—when your shift is finished there is absolutely nothing to do; you might as well walk down to the Forks Falls Road and listen to the chain gang.

However, here in this very town there was once a café. And this old boarded-up house was unlike any other place for many miles around. There were tables with cloths and paper napkins, colored streamers from the electric fans, great gatherings on Saturday nights. The owner of the place was Miss Amelia Evans. But the person most responsible for the success and gaiety of the place was a hunchback called Cousin Lymon. One other person had a part in the story of this café—he was the former husband of Miss Amelia, a terrible character who returned to the town after a long term in the penitentiary, caused ruin, and then went on his way again. The café has long since been closed, but it is still remembered.

The place was not always a café. Miss Amelia inherited the building from her father, and it was a store that carried mostly feed, guano, and staples such as meal and snuff. Miss Amelia was rich. In addition to the store she operated a still three miles back in the swamp, and ran out the best liquor in the county. She was a dark, tall woman with bones and muscles like a man. Her hair was cut short and brushed back from the forehead, and there was about her sunburned face a tense, haggard quality. She might have been a handsome woman if, even then, she was not slightly cross-eyed. There were those who would have courted her, but Miss Amelia cared nothing for the love of men and was a solitary person. Her marriage had been unlike any other marriage ever contracted in this county—it was a strange and dangerous marriage, lasting only for ten days, that left the whole town wondering and shocked. Except for this queer marriage, Miss Amelia had lived her life alone. Often she spent whole nights back in her shed in the swamp, dressed in overalls and gum boots, silently guarding the low fire of the still.

With all things which could be made by the hands Miss Amelia prospered. She sold chitterlins and sausage in the town near-by. On fine autumn days, she ground sorghum, and the syrup from her vats was dark golden and delicately flavored. She built the brick privy behind her store in only two weeks and was skilled in carpentering. It was only with people that Miss Amelia was not at ease. People, unless they are nilly-willy or very sick, cannot be taken into the hands and changed overnight to something more worthwhile and profitable. So that the only use that Miss Amelia had for other people was to make money out of them. And in this she succeeded. Mortgages on crops and property, a sawmill, money in the bank—she was the richest woman for miles around. She would have been rich as a congressman if it were not for her one great failing, and that was her passion for lawsuits and the courts. She would involve herself in long and bitter litigation over just a trifle. It was said that if Miss Amelia so much as stumbled over a rock in the road she would glance around instinctively as though looking for something to sue about it. Aside from these lawsuits she lived a steady life and every day was very much like the day that had gone before. With the exception of her ten-day marriage, nothing happened to change this until the spring of the year that Miss Amelia was thirty years old.

It was toward midnight on a soft quiet evening in April. The sky was the color of a blue swamp iris, the moon clear and bright. The crops that spring promised well and in the past weeks the mill had run a night shift. Down by the creek the square brick factory was yellow with light, and there was the faint, steady hum of the looms. It was such a night when it is good to hear from faraway, across the dark fields, the slow song of a Negro on his way to make love. Or when it is pleasant to sit quietly and pick a guitar, or simply to rest alone and think of nothing at all. The street that evening was deserted, but Miss Amelia's store was lighted and on the porch outside there were five people. One of these was Stumpy MacPhail, a foreman with a red face and dainty, purplish hands. On the top step were two boys in overalls, the Rainey twins—both of them lanky and slow, with white hair and sleepy green eyes. The other man was Henry Macy, a shy and timid person with gentle manners and nervous ways, who sat on the edge of the bottom step. Miss Amelia herself stood leaning against the side of the open door, her feet crossed in their big swamp boots, patiently untying knots in a rope she had come across. They had not talked for a long time.

One of the twins, who had been looking down the empty road, was the first to speak. 'I see something coming,' he said.

'A calf got loose,' said his brother.

The approaching figure was still too distant to be clearly seen. The moon made dim, twisted shadows of the blossoming peach trees along the side of the road. In the air the odor of blossoms and sweet spring grass mingled with the warm, sour smell of the near-by lagoon.

'No. It's somebody's youngun,' said Stumpy MacPhail.

Miss Amelia watched the road in silence. She had put down her rope and was fingering the straps of her overalls with her brown bony hand. She scowled, and a dark lock of hair fell down on her forehead. While they were waiting there, a dog from one of the houses down the road began a wild, hoarse howl that continued until a voice called out and hushed him. It was not until the figure was quite close, within the range of the yellow light from the porch, that they saw clearly what had come.

The man was a stranger, and it is rare that a stranger enters the town on foot at that hour. Besides, the man was a hunchback. He was scarcely more than four feet tall and he wore a ragged, dusty coat that reached only to his knees. His crooked little legs seemed too thin to carry the weight of his great warped chest and the hump that sat on his shoulders. He had a very large head, with deep-set blue eyes and a sharp little mouth. His face was both soft and sassy—at the moment his pale skin was yellowed by dust and there were lavender shadows beneath his eyes. He carried a lopsided old suitcase which was tied with a rope.

'Evening,' said the hunchback, and he was out of breath.

Miss Amelia and the men on the porch neither answered his greeting nor spoke. They only looked at him.

'I am hunting for Miss Amelia Evans.'

Miss Amelia pushed back her hair from her forehead and raised her chin. 'How come?'

'Because I am kin to her,' the hunchback said.

The twins and Stumpy MacPhail looked up at Miss Amelia.

'That's me,' she said. 'How do you mean "kin"?'

'Because——' the hunchback began. He looked uneasy, almost as though he was about to cry. He rested the suitcase on the bottom step, but did not take his hand from the handle. 'My mother was Fanny Jesup and she come from Cheehaw. She left Cheehaw some thirty years ago when she married her first husband. I remember hearing her tell how she had a half-sister named Martha. And back in Cheehaw today they tell me that was your mother.'

Miss Amelia listened with her head turned slightly aside. She ate her Sunday dinners by herself; her place was never crowded with a flock of relatives, and she claimed kin with no one. She had had a great-aunt who owned the livery stable in Cheehaw, but that aunt was now dead. Aside from her there was only one double first cousin who lived in a town twenty miles away, but this cousin and Miss Amelia did not get on so well, and when they chanced to pass each other they spat on the side of the road. Other people had tried very hard, from time to time, to work out some kind of far-fetched connection with Miss Amelia, but with absolutely no success.

The hunchback went into a long rigmarole, mentioning names and places that were unknown to the listeners on the porch and seemed to have nothing to do with the subject. 'So Fanny and Martha Jesup were half-sisters. And I am the son of Fanny's third husband. So that would make you and I——' He bent down and began to unfasten his suitcase. His hands were like dirty sparrow claws and they were trembling. The bag was full of all manner of junk—ragged clothes and odd rubbish that looked like parts out of a sewing machine, or something just as worthless. The hunchback scrambled among these belongings and brought out an old photograph. 'This is a picture of my mother and her half-sister.'

Miss Amelia did not speak. She was moving her jaw slowly from side to side, and you could tell from her face what she was thinking about. Stumpy MacPhail took the photograph and held it out toward the light. It was a picture of two pale, withered-up little children of about two and three years of age. The faces were tiny white blurs, and it might have been an old picture in anyone's album.

Stumpy MacPhail handed it back with no comment. 'Where you come from?' he asked.

The hunchback's voice was uncertain. 'I was traveling.'

Still Miss Amelia did not speak. She just stood leaning against the side of the door, and looked down at the hunchback. Henry Macy winked nervously and rubbed his hands together. Then quietly he left the bottom step and disappeared. He is a good soul, and the hunchback's situation had touched his heart. Therefore he did not want to wait and watch Miss Amelia chase this newcomer off her property and run him out of town. The hunchback stood with his bag open on the bottom step; he sniffled his nose, and his mouth quivered. Perhaps he began to feel his dismal predicament. Maybe he realized what a miserable thing it was to be a stranger in the town with a suitcase full of junk, and claiming kin with Miss Amelia. At any rate he sat down on the steps and suddenly began to cry.

It was not a common thing to have an unknown hunchback walk to the store at midnight and then sit down and cry. Miss Amelia rubbed back her hair from her forehead and the men looked at each other uncomfortably. All around the town was very quiet.

At last one of the twins said: 'I'll be damned if he ain't a regular Morris Finestein.'

Everyone nodded and agreed, for that is an expression having a certain special meaning. But the hunchback cried louder because he could not know what they were talking about. Morris Finestein was a person who had lived in the town years before. He was only a quick, skipping little Jew who cried if you called him Christ-killer, and ate light bread and canned salmon every day. A calamity had come over him and he had moved away to Society City. But since then if a man were prissy in any way, or if a man ever wept, he was known as a Morris Finestein.

'Well, he is afflicted,' said Stumpy MacPhail. 'There is some cause.'

Miss Amelia crossed the porch with two slow, gangling strides. She went down the steps and stood looking thoughtfully at the stranger. Gingerly, with one long brown forefinger, she touched the hump on his back. The hunchback still wept, but he was quieter now. The night was silent and the moon still shone with a soft, clear light—it was getting colder. Then Miss Amelia did a rare thing; she pulled out a bottle from her hip pocket and after polishing off the top with the palm of her hand she handed it to the hunchback to drink. Miss Amelia could seldom be persuaded to sell her liquor on credit, and for her to give so much as a drop away free was almost unknown.

'Drink,' she said. 'It will liven your gizzard.'

The hunchback stopped crying, neatly licked the tears from around his mouth, and did as he was told. When he was finished, Miss Amelia took a slow swallow, warmed and washed her mouth with it, and spat. Then she also drank. The twins and the foreman had their own bottle they had paid for.

'It is smooth liquor,' Stumpy MacPhail said. 'Miss Amelia, I have never known you to fail.'

The whisky they drank that evening (two big bottles of it) is important. Otherwise, it would be hard to account for what followed. Perhaps without it there would never have been a café. For the liquor of Miss Amelia has a special quality of its own. It is clean and sharp on the tongue, but once down a man it glows inside him for a long time afterward. And that is not all. It is known that if a message is written with lemon juice on a clean sheet of paper there will be no sign of it. But if the paper is held for a moment to the fire then the letters turn brown and the meaning becomes clear. Imagine that the whisky is the fire and that the message is that which is known only in the soul of a man—then the worth of Miss Amelia's liquor can be understood. Things that have gone unnoticed, thoughts that have been harbored far back in the dark mind, are suddenly recognized and comprehended. A spinner who has thought only of the loom, the dinner pail, the bed, and then the loom again—this spinner might drink some on a Sunday and come across a marsh lily. And in his palm he might hold this flower, examining the golden dainty cup, and in him suddenly might come a sweetness keen as pain. A weaver might look up suddenly and see for the first time the cold, weird radiance of midnight January sky, and a deep fright at his own smallness stop his heart. Such things as these, then, happen when a man has drunk Miss Amelia's liquor. He may suffer, or he may be spent with joy—but the experience has shown the truth; he has warmed his soul and seen the message hidden there.

They drank until it was past midnight, and the moon was clouded over so that the night was cold and dark. The hunchback still sat on the bottom steps, bent over miserably with his forehead resting on his knee. Miss Amelia stood with her hands in her pockets, one foot resting on the second step of the stairs. She had been silent for a long time. Her face had the expression often seen in slightly cross-eyed persons who are thinking deeply, a look that appears to be both very wise and very crazy. At last she said: 'I don't know your name.'

'I'm Lymon Willis,' said the hunchback.

'Well, come on in,' she said. 'Some supper was left in the stove and you can eat.'

Only a few times in her life had Miss Amelia invited anyone to eat with her, unless she were planning to trick them in some way, or make money out of them. So the men on the porch felt there was something wrong. Later, they said among themselves that she must have been drinking back in the swamp the better part of the afternoon. At any rate she left the porch, and Stumpy MacPhail and the twins went on off home. She bolted the front door and looked all around to see that her goods were in order. Then she went to the kitchen, which was at the back of the store. The hunchback followed her, dragging his suitcase, sniffing and wiping his nose on the sleeve of his dirty coat.

'Sit down,' said Miss Amelia. 'I'll just warm up what's here.'

It was a good meal they had together on that night. Miss Amelia was rich and she did not grudge herself food. There was fried chicken (the breast of which the hunchback took on his own plate), mashed rootabeggars, collard greens, and hot, pale golden, sweet potatoes. Miss Amelia ate slowly and with the relish of a farm hand. She sat with both elbows on the table, bent over the plate, her knees spread wide apart and her feet braced on the rungs of the chair. As for the hunchback, he gulped down his supper as though he had not smelled food in months. During the meal one tear crept down his dingy cheek—but it was just a little leftover tear and meant nothing at all. The lamp on the table was well-trimmed, burning blue at the edges of the wick, and casting a cheerful light in the kitchen. When Miss Amelia had eaten her supper she wiped her plate carefully with a slice of light bread, and then poured her own clear, sweet syrup over the bread. The hunchback did likewise—except that he was more finicky and asked for a new plate. Having finished, Miss Amelia tilted back her chair, tightened her fist, and felt the hard, supple muscles of her right arm beneath the clean, blue cloth of her shirtsleeves—an unconscious habit with her, at the close of a meal. Then she took the lamp from the table and jerked her head toward the staircase as an invitation for the hunchback to follow after her.

Above the store there were the three rooms where Miss Amelia had lived during all her life—two bedrooms with a large parlor in between. Few people had even seen these rooms, but it was generally known that they were well-furnished and extremely clean. And now Miss Amelia was taking up with her a dirty little hunchbacked stranger, come from God knows where. Miss Amelia walked slowly, two steps at a time, holding the lamp high. The hunchback hovered so close behind her that the swinging light made on the staircase wall one great, twisted shadow of the two of them. Soon the premises above the store were dark as the rest of the town.

The next morning was serene, with a sunrise of warm purple mixed with rose. In the fields around the town the furrows were newly plowed, and very early the tenants were at work setting out the young, deep green tobacco plants. The wild crows flew down close to the fields, making swift blue shadows on the earth. In town the people set out early with their dinner pails, and the windows of the mill were blinding gold in the sun. The air was fresh and the peach trees light as March clouds with their blossoms.

Miss Amelia came down at about dawn, as usual. She washed her head at the pump and very shortly set about her business. Later in the morning she saddled her mule and went to see about her property, planted with cotton, up near the Forks Falls Road. By noon, of course, everybody had heard about the hunchback who had come to the store in the middle of the night. But no one as yet had seen him. The day soon grew hot and the sky was a rich, midday blue.

Still no one had laid an eye on this strange guest. A few people remembered that Miss Amelia's mother had had a half-sister—but there was some difference of opinion as to whether she had died or had run off with a tobacco stringer. As for the hunchback's claim, everyone thought it was a trumped-up business. And the town, knowing Miss Amelia, decided that surely she had put him out of the house after feeding him. But toward evening, when the sky had whitened, and the shift was done, a woman claimed to have seen a crooked face at the window of one of the rooms up over the store. Miss Amelia herself said nothing. She clerked in the store for a while, argued for an hour with a farmer over a plow shaft, mended some chicken wire, locked up near sundown, and went to her rooms. The town was left puzzled and talkative.

The next day Miss Amelia did not open the store, but stayed locked up inside her premises and saw no one. Now this was the day that the rumor started—the rumor so terrible that the town and all the country about were stunned by it. The rumor was started by a weaver called Merlie Ryan. He is a man of not much account—sallow, shambling, and with no teeth in his head. He has the three-day malaria, which means that every third day the fever comes on him. So on two days he is dull and cross, but on the third day he livens up and sometimes has an idea or two, most of which are foolish. It was while Merlie Ryan was in his fever that he turned suddenly and said:

'I know what Miss Amelia done. She murdered that man for something in that suitcase.'

He said this in a calm voice, as a statement of fact. And within an hour the news had swept through the town. It was a fierce and sickly tale the town built up that day. In it were all the things which cause the heart to shiver—a hunchback, a midnight burial in the swamp, the dragging of Miss Amelia through the streets of the town on the way to prison, the squabbles over what would happen to her property—all told in hushed voices and repeated with some fresh and weird detail. It rained and women forgot to bring in the washing from the lines. One or two mortals, who were in debt to Miss Amelia, even put on Sunday clothes as though it were a holiday. People clustered together on the main street, talking and watching the store.

It would be untrue to say that all the town took part in this evil festival. There were a few sensible men who reasoned that Miss Amelia, being rich, would not go out of her way to murder a vagabond for a few trifles of junk. In the town there were even three good people, and they did not want this crime, not even for the sake of the interest and the great commotion it would entail; it gave them no pleasure to think of Miss Amelia holding to the bars of the penitentiary and being electrocuted in Atlanta. These good people judged Miss Amelia in a different way from what the others judged her. When a person is as contrary in every single respect as she was and when the sins of a person have amounted to such a point that they can hardly be remembered all at once—then this person plainly requires a special judgment. They remembered that Miss Amelia had been born dark and somewhat queer of face, raised motherless by her father who was a solitary man, that early in youth she had grown to be six feet two inches tall which in itself is not natural for a woman, and that her ways and habits of life were too peculiar ever to reason about. Above all, they remembered her puzzling marriage, which was the most unreasonable scandal ever to happen in this town.

So these good people felt toward her something near to pity. And when she was out on her wild business, such as rushing in a house to drag forth a sewing machine in payment for a debt, or getting herself worked up over some matter concerning the law—they had toward her a feeling which was a mixture of exasperation, a ridiculous little inside tickle, and a deep, unnamable sadness. But enough of the good people, for there were only three of them; the rest of the town was making a holiday of this fancied crime the whole of the afternoon.

Miss Amelia herself, for some strange reason, seemed unaware of all this. She spent most of her day upstairs. When down in the store, she prowled around peacefully, her hands deep in the pockets of her overalls and head bent so low that her chin was tucked inside the collar of her shirt. There was no bloodstain on her anywhere. Often she stopped and just stood somberly looking down at the cracks in the floor, twisting a lock of her short-cropped hair, and whispering something to herself. But most of the day was spent upstairs.

Dark came on. The rain that afternoon had chilled the air, so that the evening was bleak and gloomy as in wintertime. There were no stars in the sky, and a light, icy drizzle had set in. The lamps in the houses made mournful, wavering flickers when watched from the street. A wind had come up, not from the swamp side of the town but from the cold black pinewoods to the north.

The clocks in the town struck eight. Still nothing had happened. The bleak night, after the gruesome talk of the day, put a fear in some people, and they stayed home close to the fire. Others were gathered in groups together. Some eight or ten men had convened on the porch of Miss Amelia's store. They were silent and were indeed just waiting about. They themselves did not know what they were waiting for, but it was this: in times of tension, when some great action is impending, men gather and wait in this way. And after a time there will come a moment when all together they will act in unison, not from thought or from the will of any one man, but as though their instincts had merged together so that the decision belongs to no single one of them, but to the group as a whole. At such a time, no individual hesitates. And whether the matter will be settled peaceably, or whether the joint action will result in ransacking, violence, and crime, depends on destiny. So the men waited soberly on the porch of Miss Amelia's store, not one of them realizing what they would do, but knowing inwardly that they must wait, and that the time had almost come.

Now the door to the store was open. Inside it was bright and natural-looking. To the left was the counter where slabs of white meat, rock candy, and tobacco were kept. Behind this were shelves of salted white meat and meal. The right side of the store was mostly filled with farm implements and such. At the back of the store, to the left, was the door leading up the stairs, and it was open. And at the far right of the store there was another door which led to a little room that Miss Amelia called her office. This door was also open. And at eight o'clock that evening Miss Amelia could be seen there sitting before her rolltop desk, figuring with a fountain pen and some pieces of paper.

The office was cheerfully lighted, and Miss Amelia did not seem to notice the delegation on the porch. Everything around her was in great order, as usual. This office was a room well-known, in a dreadful way, throughout the country. It was there Miss Amelia transacted all business. On the desk was a carefully covered typewriter which she knew how to run, but used only for the most important documents. In the drawers were literally thousands of papers, all filed according to the alphabet. This office was also the place where Miss Amelia received sick people, for she enjoyed doctoring and did a great deal of it. Two whole shelves were crowded with bottles and various paraphernalia. Against the wall was a bench where the patients sat. She could sew up a wound with a burnt needle so that it would not turn green. For burns she had a cool, sweet syrup. For unlocated sickness there were any number of different medicines which she had brewed herself from unknown recipes. They wrenched loose the bowels very well, but they could not be given to small children, as they caused bad convulsions; for them she had an entirely separate draught, gentler and sweet-flavored. Yes, all in all, she was considered a good doctor. Her hands, though very large and bony, had a light touch about them. She possessed great imagination and used hundreds of different cures. In the face of the most dangerous and extraordinary treatment she did not hesitate, and no disease was so terrible but what she would undertake to cure it. In this there was one exception. If a patient came with a female complaint she could do nothing. Indeed at the mere mention of the words her face would slowly darken with shame, and she would stand there craning her neck against the collar of her shirt, or rubbing her swamp boots together, for all the world like a great, shamed, dumb-tongued child. But in other matters people trusted her. She charged no fees whatsoever and always had a raft of patients.

On this evening, Miss Amelia wrote with her fountain pen a good deal. But even so she could not be forever unaware of the group waiting out there on the dark porch, and watching her. From time to time she looked up and regarded them steadily. But she did not holler out to them to demand why they were loafing around her property like a sorry bunch of gabbies. Her face was proud and stern, as it always was when she sat at the desk of her office. After a time their peering in like that seemed to annoy her. She wiped her cheek with a red handkerchief, got up, and closed the office door.

Now to the group on the porch this gesture acted as a signal. The time had come. They had stood for a long while with the night raw and gloomy in the street behind them. They had waited long and just at that moment the instinct to act came on them. All at once, as though moved by one will, they walked into the store. At that moment the eight men looked very much alike—all wearing blue overalls, most of them with whitish hair, all pale of face, and all with a set, dreaming look in the eye. What they would have done next no one knows. But at that instant there was a noise at the head of the staircase. The men looked up and then stood dumb with shock. It was the hunchback, whom they had already murdered in their minds. Also, the creature was not at all as had been pictured to them—not a pitiful and dirty little chatterer, alone and beggared in this world. Indeed, he was like nothing any man among them had ever beheld until that time. The room was still as death.

The hunchback came down slowly with the proudness of one who owns every plank of the floor beneath his feet. In the past days he had greatly changed. For one thing he was clean beyond words. He still wore his little coat, but it was brushed off and neatly mended.

Beneath this was a fresh red and black checkered shirt belonging to Miss Amelia. He did not wear trousers such as ordinary men are meant to wear, but a pair of tight-fitting little knee-length breeches. On his skinny legs he wore black stockings, and his shoes were of a special kind, being queerly shaped, laced up over the ankles, and newly cleaned and polished with wax. Around his neck, so that his large, pale ears were almost completely covered, he wore a shawl of lime-green wool, the fringes of which almost touched the floor.

The hunchback walked down the store with his stiff little strut and then stood in the center of the group that had come inside. They cleared a space about him and stood looking with hands loose at their sides and eyes wide open. The hunchback himself got his bearings in an odd manner. He regarded each person steadily at his own eye-level, which was about belt line for an ordinary man. Then with shrewd deliberation he examined each man's lower regions—from the waist to the sole of the shoe. When he had satisfied himself he closed his eyes for a moment and shook his head, as though in his opinion what he had seen did not amount to much. Then with assurance, only to confirm himself, he tilted back his head and took in the halo of faces around him with one long, circling stare. There was a half-filled sack of guano on the left side of the store, and when he had found his bearings in this way, the hunchback sat down upon it. Cozily settled, with his little legs crossed, he took from his coat pocket a certain object.

Now it took some moments for the men in the store to regain their ease. Merlie Ryan, he of the three-day fever who had started the rumor that day, was the first to speak. He looked at the object which the hunchback was fondling, and said in a hushed voice:

'What is it you have there?'

Each man knew well what it was the hunchback was handling. For it was the snuffbox which had belonged to Miss Amelia's father. The snuffbox was of blue enamel with a dainty embellishment of wrought gold on the lid. The group knew it well and marveled. They glanced warily at the closed office door, and heard the low sound of Miss Amelia whistling to herself.

'Yes, what is it, Peanut?'

The hunchback looked up quickly and sharpened his mouth to speak. 'Why, this is a lay-low to catch meddlers.'

The hunchback reached in the box with his scrambly little fingers and ate something, but he offered no one around him a taste. It was not even proper snuff which he was taking, but a mixture of sugar and cocoa. This he took, though, as snuff, pocketing a little wad of it beneath his lower lip and licking down neatly into this with a flick of his tongue which made a frequent grimace come over his face.

'The very teeth in my head have always tasted sour to me,' he said in explanation. 'That is the reason why I take this kind of sweet snuff.'

The group still clustered around, feeling somewhat gawky and bewildered. This sensation never quite wore off, but it was soon tempered by another feeling—an air of intimacy in the room and a vague festivity. Now the names of the men of the group there on that evening were as follows: Hasty Malone, Robert Calvert Hale, Merlie Ryan, Reverend T. M. Willin, Rosser Cline, Rip Wellborn, Henry Ford Crimp, and Horace Wells. Except for Reverend Willin, they are all alike in many ways as has been said—all having taken pleasure from something or other, all having wept and suffered in some way, most of them tractable unless exasperated. Each of them worked in the mill, and lived with others in a two- or three-room house for which the rent was ten dollars or twelve dollars a month. All had been paid that afternoon, for it was Saturday. So, for the present, think of them as a whole.

The hunchback, however, was already sorting them out in his mind. Once comfortably settled he began to chat with everyone, asking questions such as if a man was married, how old he was, how much his wages came to in an average week, et cetera—picking his way along to inquiries which were downright intimate. Soon the group was joined by others in the town, Henry Macy, idlers who had sensed something extraordinary, women come to fetch their men who lingered on, and even one loose, towhead child who tiptoed into the store, stole a box of animal crackers, and made off very quietly. So the premises of Miss Amelia were soon crowded, and she herself had not yet opened her office door.

There is a type of person who has a quality about him that sets him apart from other and more ordinary human beings. Such a person has an instinct which is usually found only in small children, an instinct to establish immediate and vital contact between himself and all things in the world. Certainly the hunchback was of this type. He had only been in the store half an hour before an immediate contact had been established between him and each other individual. It was as though he had lived in the town for years, was a well-known character, and had been sitting and talking there on that guano sack for countless evenings. This, together with the fact that it was Saturday night, could account for the air of freedom and illicit gladness in the store. There was a tension, also, partly because of the oddity of the situation and because Miss Amelia was still closed off in her office and had not yet made her appearance.

She came out that evening at ten o'clock. And those who were expecting some drama at her entrance were disappointed. She opened the door and walked in with her slow, gangling swagger. There was a streak of ink on one side of her nose, and she had knotted the red handkerchief about her neck. She seemed to notice nothing unusual. Her gray, crossed eyes glanced over to the place where the hunchback was sitting, and for a moment lingered there. The rest of the crowd in her store she regarded with only a peaceable surprise.

'Does anyone want waiting on?' she asked quietly.

There were a number of customers, because it was Saturday night, and they all wanted liquor. Now Miss Amelia had dug up an aged barrel only three days past and had siphoned it into bottles back by the still. This night she took the money from the customers and counted it beneath the bright light. Such was the ordinary procedure. But after this what happened was not ordinary. Always before, it was necessary to go around to the dark back yard, and there she would hand out your bottle through the kitchen door. There was no feeling of joy in the transaction. After getting his liquor the customer walked off into the night. Or, if his wife would not have it in the home, he was allowed to come back around to the front porch of the store and guzzle there or in the street. Now, both the porch and the street before it were the property of Miss Amelia, and no mistake about it—but she did not regard them as her premises; the premises began at the front door and took in the entire inside of the building. There she had never allowed liquor to be opened or drunk by anyone but herself. Now for the first time she broke this rule. She went to the kitchen, with the hunchback close at her heels, and she brought back the bottles into the warm, bright store. More than that she furnished some glasses and opened two boxes of crackers so that they were there hospitably in a platter on the counter and anyone who wished could take one free.

She spoke to no one but the hunchback, and she only asked him in a somewhat harsh and husky voice: 'Cousin Lymon, will you have yours straight, or warmed in a pan with water on the stove?'

'If you please, Amelia,' the hunchback said. (And since what time had anyone presumed to address Miss Amelia by her bare name, without a title of respect?—Certainly not her bridegroom and her husband of ten days. In fact, not since the death of her father, who for some reason had always called her Little, had anyone dared to address her in such a familiar way.) 'If you please, I'll have it warmed.'

Now, this was the beginning of the café. It was as simple as that. Recall that the night was gloomy as in wintertime, and to have sat around the property outside would have made a sorry celebration. But inside there was company and a genial warmth. Someone had rattled up the stove in the rear, and those who bought bottles shared their liquor with friends. Several women were there and they had twists of licorice, a Nehi, or even a swallow of the whisky. The hunchback was still a novelty and his presence amused everyone. The bench in the office was brought in, together with several extra chairs. Other people leaned against the counter or made themselves comfortable on barrels and sacks. Nor did the opening of liquor on the premises cause any rambunctiousness, indecent giggles, or misbehavior whatsoever. On the contrary the company was polite even to the point of a certain timidness. For people in this town were then unused to gathering together for the sake of pleasure. They met to work in the mill. Or on Sunday there would be an all-day camp meeting—and though that is a pleasure, the intention of the whole affair is to sharpen your view of Hell and put into you a keen fear of the Lord Almighty. But the spirit of a café is altogether different. Even the richest, greediest old rascal will behave himself, insulting no one in a proper café. And poor people look about them gratefully and pinch up the salt in a dainty and modest manner. For the atmosphere of a proper café implies these qualities: fellowship, the satisfactions of the belly, and a certain gaiety and grace of behavior. This had never been told to the gathering in Miss Amelia's store that night. But they knew it of themselves, although never, of course, until that time had there been a café in the town.

Now, the cause of all this, Miss Amelia, stood most of the evening in the doorway leading to the kitchen. Outwardly she did not seem changed at all. But there were many who noticed her face. She watched all that went on, but most of the time her eyes were fastened lonesomely on the hunchback. He strutted about the store, eating from his snuffbox, and being at once sour and agreeable. Where Miss Amelia stood, the light from the chinks of the stove cast a glow, so that her brown, long face was somewhat brightened. She seemed to be looking inward. There was in her expression pain, perplexity, and uncertain joy. Her lips were not so firmly set as usual, and she swallowed often. Her skin had paled and her large empty hands were sweating. Her look that night, then, was the lonesome look of the lover.

This opening of the café came to an end at midnight. Everyone said good-bye to everyone else in a friendly fashion. Miss Amelia shut the front door of her premises, but forgot to bolt it. Soon everything —the main street with its three stores, the mill, the houses—all the town, in fact—was dark and silent. And so ended three days and nights in which had come an arrival of a stranger, an unholy holiday, and the start of the café.

Now time must pass. For the next four years are much alike. There are great changes, but these changes are brought about bit by bit, in simple steps which in themselves do not appear to be important. The hunchback continued to live with Miss Amelia. The café expanded in a gradual way. Miss Amelia began to sell her liquor by the drink, and some tables were brought into the store. There were customers every evening, and on Saturday a great crowd. Miss Amelia began to serve fried catfish suppers at fifteen cents a plate. The hunchback cajoled her into buying a fine mechanical piano. Within two years the place was a store no longer, but had been converted into a proper café, open every evening from six until twelve o'clock.

Each night the hunchback came down the stairs with the air of one who has a grand opinion of himself. He always smelled slightly of turnip greens, as Miss Amelia rubbed him night and morning with pot liquor to give him strength. She spoiled him to a point beyond reason, but nothing seemed to strengthen him; food only made his hump and his head grow larger while the rest of him remained weakly and deformed. Miss Amelia was the same in appearance. During the week she still wore swamp boots and overalls, but on Sunday she put on a dark red dress that hung on her in a most peculiar fashion. Her manners, however, and her way of life were greatly changed. She still loved a fierce lawsuit, but she was not so quick to cheat her fellow man and to exact cruel payments. Because the hunchback was so extremely sociable, she even went about a little—to revivals, to funerals, and so forth. Her doctoring was as successful as ever, her liquor even finer than before, if that were possible. The café itself proved profitable and was the only place of pleasure for many miles around.

So for the moment regard these years from random and disjointed views. See the hunchback marching in Miss Amelia's footsteps when on a red winter morning they set out for the pinewoods to hunt. See them working on her properties—with Cousin Lymon standing by and doing absolutely nothing, but quick to point out any laziness among the hands. On autumn afternoons they sat on the back steps chopping sugar cane. The glaring summer days they spent back in the swamp where the water cypress is a deep black green, where beneath the tangled swamp trees there is a drowsy gloom. When the path leads through a bog or a stretch of blackened water see Miss Amelia bend down to let Cousin Lymon scramble on her back—and see her wading forward with the hunchback settled on her shoulders, clinging to her ears or to her broad forehead. Occasionally Miss Amelia cranked up the Ford which she had bought and treated Cousin Lymon to a picture-show in Cheehaw, or to some distant fair or cockfight; the hunchback took a passionate delight in spectacles. Of course, they were in their café every morning, they would often sit for hours together by the fireplace in the parlor upstairs. For the hunchback was sickly at night and dreaded to lie looking into the dark. He had a deep fear of death. And Miss Amelia would not leave him by himself to suffer with this fright. It may even be reasoned that the growth of the café came about mainly on this account; it was a thing that brought him company and pleasure and that helped him through the night. So compose from such flashes an image of these years as a whole. And for a moment let it rest.

Now some explanation is due for all this behavior. The time has come to speak about love. For Miss Amelia loved Cousin Lymon. So much was clear to everyone. They lived in the same house together and were never seen apart. Therefore, according to Mrs. MacPhail, a warty-nosed old busybody who is continually moving her sticks of furniture from one part of the front room to another; according to her and to certain others, these two were living in sin. If they were related, they were only a cross between first and second cousins, and even that could in no way be proved. Now, of course, Miss Amelia was a powerful blunderbuss of a person, more than six feet tall—and Cousin Lymon a weakly little hunchback reaching only to her waist. But so much the better for Mrs. Stumpy MacPhail and her cronies, for they and their kind glory in conjunctions which are ill-matched and pitiful. So let them be. The good people thought that if those two had found some satisfaction of the flesh between themselves, then it was a matter concerning them and God alone. All sensible people agreed in their opinion about this conjecture—and their answer was a plain, flat *no*. What sort of thing, then, was this love?

First of all, love is a joint experience between two persons—but the fact that it is a joint experience does not mean that it is a similar experience to the two people involved. There are the lover and the beloved, but these two come from different countries. Often the beloved is only a stimulus for all the stored-up love which has lain quiet within the lover for a long time hitherto. And somehow every lover knows this. He feels in his soul that his love is a solitary thing. He comes to know a new, strange loneliness and it is this knowledge which makes him suffer. So there is only one thing for the lover to do. He must house his love within himself as best he can; he must create for himself a whole new inward world—a world intense and strange, complete in himself. Let it be added here that this lover about whom we speak need not necessarily be a young man saving for a wedding ring—this lover can be man, woman, child, or indeed any human creature on this earth.

Now, the beloved can also be of any description. The most outlandish people can be the stimulus for love. A man may be a doddering great-grandfather and still love only a strange girl he saw in the streets of Cheehaw one afternoon two decades past. The preacher may love a fallen woman. The beloved may be treacherous, greasy-headed, and given to evil habits. Yes, and the lover may see this as clearly as anyone else—but that does not affect the evolution of his love one whit. A most mediocre person can be the object of a love which is wild, extravagant, and beautiful as the poison lilies of the swamp. A good man may be the stimulus for a love both violent and debased, or a jabbering madman may bring about in the soul of someone a tender and simple idyll. Therefore, the value and quality of any love is determined solely by the lover himself.

It is for this reason that most of us would rather love than be loved. Almost everyone wants to be the lover. And the curt truth is that, in a deep secret way, the state of being beloved is intolerable to many. The beloved fears and hates the lover, and with the best of reasons. For the lover is forever trying to strip bare his beloved. The lover craves any possible relation with the beloved, even if this experience can cause him only pain.

It has been mentioned before that Miss Amelia was once married. And this curious episode might as well be accounted for at this point. Remember that it all happened long ago, and that it was Miss

Amelia's only personal contact, before the hunchback came to her, with this phenomenon—love.

The town then was the same as it is now, except there were two stores instead of three and the peach trees along the street were more crooked and smaller than they are now. Miss Amelia was nineteen years old at the time, and her father had been dead many months. There was in the town at that time a loom-fixer named Marvin Macy. He was the brother of Henry Macy, although to know them you would never guess that those two could be kin. For Marvin Macy was the handsomest man in this region—being six feet one inch tall, hard-muscled, and with slow gray eyes and curly hair. He was well off, made good wages, and had a gold watch which opened in the back to a picture of a waterfall. From the outward and worldly point of view Marvin Macy was a fortunate fellow; he needed to bow and scrape to no one and always got just what he wanted. But from a more serious and thoughtful viewpoint Marvin Macy was not a person to be envied, for he was an evil character. His reputation was as bad, if not worse, than that of any young man in the county. For years, when he was a boy, he had carried about with him the dried and salted ear of a man he had killed in a razor fight. He had chopped off the tails of squirrels in the pinewoods just to please his fancy, and in his left hip pocket he carried forbidden marijuana weed to tempt those who were discouraged and drawn toward death. Yet in spite of his well-known reputation he was the beloved of many females in this region—and there were at the time several young girls who were clean-haired and soft-eyed, with tender sweet little buttocks and charming ways. These gentle young girls he degraded and shamed. Then finally, at the age of twenty-two, this Marvin Macy chose Miss Amelia. That solitary, gangling, queer-eyed girl was the one he longed for. Nor did he want her because of her money, but solely out of love.

And love changed Marvin Macy. Before the time when he loved Miss Amelia it could be questioned if such a person had within him a heart and soul. Yet there is some explanation for the ugliness of his character, for Marvin Macy had had a hard beginning in this world. He was one of seven unwanted children whose parents could hardly be called parents at all; these parents were wild younguns who liked to fish and roam around the swamp. Their own children, and there was a new one almost every year, were only a nuisance to them. At night when they came home from the mill they would look at the children as though they did not know wherever they had come from.

If the children cried they were beaten, and the first thing they learned in this world was to seek the darkest corner of the room and try to hide themselves as best they could. They were as thin as little whitehaired ghosts, and they did not speak, not even to each other. Finally, they were abandoned by their parents altogether and left to the mercies of the town. It was a hard winter, with the mill closed down almost three months, and much misery everywhere. But this is not a town to let white orphans perish in the road before your eyes. So here is what came about: the eldest child, who was eight years old, walked into Cheehaw and disappeared—perhaps he took a freight train somewhere and went out into the world, nobody knows. Three other children were boarded out amongst the town, being sent around from one kitchen to another, and as they were delicate they died before Easter time. The last two children were Marvin Macy and Henry Macy, and they were taken into a home. There was a good woman in the town named Mrs. Mary Hale, and she took Marvin Macy and Henry Macy and loved them as her own. They were raised in her household and treated well.

But the hearts of small children are delicate organs. A cruel beginning in this world can twist them into curious shapes. The heart of a hurt child can shrink so that forever afterward it is hard and pitted as the seed of a peach. Or again, the heart of such a child may fester and swell until it is a misery to carry within the body, easily chafed and hurt by the most ordinary things. This last is what happened to Henry Macy, who so opposite to his brother, is the kindest and gentlest man in town. He lends his wages to those who are unfortunate, and in the old days he used to care for the children whose parents were at the café on Saturday night. But he is a shy man, and he has the look of one who has a swollen heart and suffers. Marvin Macy, however, grew to be bold and fearless and cruel. His heart turned tough as the horns of Satan, and until the time when he loved Miss Amelia he brought to his brother and the good woman who raised him nothing but shame and trouble.

But love reversed the character of Marvin Macy. For two years he loved Miss Amelia, but he did not declare himself. He would stand near the door of her premises, his cap in his hand, his eyes meek and longing and misty gray. He reformed himself completely. He was good to his brother and foster mother, and he saved his wages and learned thrift. Moreover, he reached out toward God. No longer did he lie around on the floor of the front porch all day Sunday, singing and playing his guitar; he attended church services and was present at all religious meetings. He learned good manners: he trained himself to rise and give his chair to a lady, and he quit swearing and fighting and using holy names in vain. So for two years he passed through this transformation and improved his character in every way. Then at the end of the two years he went one evening to Miss Amelia, carrying a bunch of swamp flowers, a sack of chitterlins, and a silver ring—that night Marvin Macy declared himself.

And Miss Amelia married him. Later everyone wondered why. Some said it was because she wanted to get herself some wedding presents. Others believed it came about through the nagging of Miss Amelia's great-aunt in Cheehaw, who was a terrible old woman. Anyway, she strode with great steps down the aisle of the church wearing her dead mother's bridal gown, which was of yellow satin and at least twelve inches too short for her. It was a winter afternoon and the clear sun shone through the ruby windows of the church and put a curious glow on the pair before the altar. As the marriage lines were read Miss Amelia kept making an odd gesture—she would rub the palm of her right hand down the side of her satin wedding gown. She was reaching for the pocket of her overalls, and being unable to find it her face became impatient, bored, and exasperated. At last when the lines were spoken and the marriage prayer was done Miss Amelia hurried out of the church, not taking the arm of her husband, but walking at least two paces ahead of him.

The church is no distance from the store so the bride and groom walked home. It is said that on the way Miss Amelia began to talk about some deal she had worked up with a farmer over a load of kindling wood. In fact, she treated her groom in exactly the same manner she would have used with some customer who had come into the store to buy a pint from her. But so far all had gone decently enough; the town was gratified, as people had seen what this love had done to Marvin Macy and hoped that it might also reform his bride. At least, they counted on the marriage to tone down Miss Amelia's temper, to put a bit of bride-fat on her, and to change her at last into a calculable woman.

They were wrong. The young boys who watched through the window on that night said that this is what actually happened: The bride and groom ate a grand supper prepared by Jeff, the old Negro who cooked for Miss Amelia. The bride took second servings of everything, but the groom picked with his food. Then the bride went about her ordinary business—reading the newspaper, finishing an inventory of the stock in the store, and so forth. The groom hung about in the doorway with a loose, foolish, blissful face and was not noticed. At eleven o'clock the bride took a lamp and went upstairs. The groom followed close behind her. So far all had gone decently enough, but what followed after was unholy.

Within half an hour Miss Amelia had stomped down the stairs in breeches and a khaki jacket. Her face had darkened so that it looked quite black. She slammed the kitchen door and gave it an ugly kick. Then she controlled herself. She poked up the fire, sat down, and put her feet up on the kitchen stove. She read the Farmer's Almanac, drank coffee, and had a smoke with her father's pipe. Her face was hard, stern, and had now whitened to its natural color. Sometimes she paused to jot down some information from the Almanac on a piece of paper. Toward dawn she went into her office and uncovered her typewriter, which she had recently bought and was only just learning how to run. That was the way in which she spent the whole of her wedding night. At daylight she went out to her yard as though nothing whatsoever had occurred and did some carpentering on a rabbit hutch which she had begun the week before and intended to sell somewhere.

A groom is in a sorry fix when he is unable to bring his well-beloved bride to bed with him, and when the whole town knows it. Marvin Macy came down that day still in his wedding finery, and with a sick face. God knows how he had spent the night. He moped about the yard, watching Miss Amelia, but keeping some distance away from her. Then toward noon an idea came to him and he went off in the direction of Society City. He returned with presents—an opal ring, a pink enamel doreen of the sort which was then in fashion, a silver bracelet with two hearts on it, and a box of candy which had cost two dollars and a half. Miss Amelia looked over these fine gifts and opened the box of candy, for she was hungry. The rest of the presents she judged shrewdly for a moment to sum up their value —then she put them in the counter out for sale. The night was spent in much the same manner as the preceding one—except that Miss Amelia brought her feather mattress to make a pallet by the kitchen stove, and she slept fairly well.

Things went on like this for three days. Miss Amelia went about her business as usual, and took great interest in some rumor that a bridge was to be built some ten miles down the road. Marvin Macy still followed her about around the premises, and it was plain from his face how he suffered. Then on the fourth day he did an extremely simple-minded thing: he went to Cheehaw and came back with a lawyer. Then in Miss Amelia's office he signed over to her the whole of his worldly goods, which was ten acres of timberland which he had bought with the money he had saved. She studied the paper sternly to make sure there was no possibility of a trick and filed it soberly in the drawer of her desk. That afternoon Marvin Macy took a quart bottle of whisky and went with it alone out in the swamp while the sun was still shining. Toward evening he came in drunk, went up to Miss Amelia with wet wide eyes, and put his hand on her shoulder. He was trying to tell her something, but before he could open his mouth she had swung once with her fist and hit his face so hard that he was thrown back against the wall and one of his front teeth was broken.

The rest of this affair can only be mentioned in bare outline. After this first blow Miss Amelia hit him whenever he came within arm's reach of her, and whenever he was drunk. At last she turned him off the premises altogether, and he was forced to suffer publicly. During the day he hung around just outside the boundary line of Miss Amelia's property and sometimes with a drawn crazy look he would fetch his rifle and sit there cleaning it, peering at Miss Amelia steadily. If she was afraid she did not show it, but her face was sterner than ever, and often she spat on the ground. His last foolish effort was to climb in the window of her store one night and to sit there in the dark, for no purpose whatsoever, until she came down the stairs next morning. For this Miss Amelia set off immediately to the courthouse in Cheehaw with some notion that she could get him locked in the penitentiary for trespassing. Marvin Macy left the town that day, and no one saw him go, or knew just where he went. On leaving he put a long curious letter, partly written in pencil and partly with ink, beneath Miss Amelia's door. It was a wild love letter—but in it were also included threats, and he swore that in his life he would get even with her. His marriage had lasted for ten days. And the town felt the special satisfaction that people feel when someone has been thoroughly done in by some scandalous and terrible means.

Miss Amelia was left with everything that Marvin Macy had ever owned—his timberwood, his gold watch, every one of his possessions. But she seemed to attach little value to them and that spring she cut up his Klansman's robe to cover her tobacco plants. So all that he had ever done was to make her richer and to bring her love. But, strange to say, she never spoke of him but with a terrible and spiteful bitterness. She never once referred to him by name but always mentioned him scornfully as 'that loom-fixer I was married to.'

And later, when horrifying rumors concerning Marvin Macy

reached the town, Miss Amelia was very pleased. For the true character of Marvin Macy finally revealed itself, once he had freed himself of his love. He became a criminal whose picture and whose name were in all the papers in the state. He robbed three filling stations and held up the A & P store of Society City with a sawed-off gun. He was suspected of the murder of Slit-Eyed Sam who was a noted highjacker. All these crimes were connected with the name of Marvin Macy, so that his evil became famous through many counties. Then finally the law captured him, drunk, on the floor of a tourist cabin, his guitar by his side, and fifty-seven dollars in his right shoe. He was tried, sentenced, and sent off to the penitentiary near Atlanta. Miss Amelia was deeply gratified.

Well, all this happened a long time ago, and it is the story of Miss Amelia's marriage. The town laughed a long time over this grotesque affair. But though the outward facts of this love are indeed sad and ridiculous, it must be remembered that the real story was that which took place in the soul of the lover himself. So who but God can be the final judge of this or any other love? On the very first night of the café there were several who suddenly thought of this broken bridegroom, locked in the gloomy penitentiary, many miles away. And in the years that followed, Marvin Macy was not altogether forgotten in this town. His name was never mentioned in the presence of Miss Amelia or the hunchback. But the memory of his passion and his crimes, and the thought of him trapped in his cell in the penitentiary, was like a troubling undertone beneath the happy love of Miss Amelia and the gaiety of the café. So do not forget this Marvin Macy, as he is to act a terrible part in the story which is yet to come.

During the four years in which the store became a café the rooms upstairs were not changed. This part of the premises remained exactly as it had been all of Miss Amelia's life, as it was in the time of her father, and most likely his father before him. The three rooms, it is already known, were immaculately clean. The smallest object had its exact place, and everything was wiped and dusted by Jeff, the servant of Miss Amelia, each morning. The front room belonged to Cousin Lymon—it was the room where Marvin Macy had stayed during the few nights he was allowed on the premises, and before that it was the bedroom of Miss Amelia's father. The room was furnished with a large chifforobe, a bureau covered with a stiff white linen cloth crocheted at the edges, and a marble-topped table. The bed was immense, an old fourposter made of carved, dark rosewood. On it were two feather mattresses, bolsters, and a number of handmade comforts. The bed was so high that beneath it were two wooden steps—no occupant had ever used these steps before, but Cousin Lymon drew them out each night and walked up in state. Beside the steps, but pushed modestly out of view, there was a china chamber-pot painted with pink roses. No rug covered the dark, polished floor and the curtains were of some white stuff, also crocheted at the edges.

On the other side of the parlor was Miss Amelia's bedroom, and it was smaller and very simple. The bed was narrow and made of pine. There was a bureau for her breeches, shirts, and Sunday dress, and she had hammered two nails in the closet wall on which to hang her swamp boots. There were no curtains, rugs, or ornaments of any kind.

The large middle room, the parlor, was elaborate. The rosewood sofa, upholstered in threadbare green silk, was before the fireplace. Marble-topped tables, two Singer sewing machines, a big vase of pampas grass—everything was rich and grand. The most important piece of furniture in the parlor was a big, glass-doored cabinet in which was kept a number of treasures and curios. Miss Amelia had added two objects to this collection—one was a large acorn from a water oak, the other a little velvet box holding two small, grayish stones. Sometimes when she had nothing much to do, Miss Amelia would take out this velvet box and stand by the window with the stones in the palm of her hand, looking down at them with a mixture of fascination, dubious respect, and fear. They were the kidney stones of Miss Amelia herself, and had been taken from her by the doctor in Cheehaw some years ago. It had been a terrible experience, from the first minute to the last, and all she had got out of it were those two little stones; she was bound to set great store by them, or else admit to a mighty sorry bargain. So she kept them and in the second year of Cousin Lymon's stay with her she had them set as ornaments in a watch chain which she gave to him. The other object she had added to the collection, the large acorn, was precious to her—but when she looked at it her face was always saddened and perplexed.

'Amelia, what does it signify?' Cousin Lymon asked her.

'Why, it's just an acorn,' she answered. 'Just an acorn I picked up on the afternoon Big Papa died.'

'How do you mean?' Cousin Lymon insisted.

'I mean it's just an acorn I spied on the ground that day. I picked it up and put it in my pocket. But I don't know why.'

'What a peculiar reason to keep it,' Cousin Lymon said. The talks of Miss Amelia and Cousin Lymon in the rooms upstairs, usually in the first few hours of the morning when the hunchback could not sleep, were many. As a rule, Miss Amelia was a silent woman, not letting her tongue run wild on any subject that happened to pop into her head. There were certain topics of conversation, however, in which she took pleasure. All these subjects had one point in common—they were interminable. She liked to contemplate problems which could be worked over for decades and still remain insoluble. Cousin Lymon, on the other hand, enjoyed talking on any subject whatsoever, as he was a great chatterer. Their approach to any conversation was altogether different. Miss Amelia always kept to the broad, rambling generalities of the matter, going on endlessly in a low, thoughtful voice and getting nowhere—while Cousin Lymon would interrupt her suddenly to pick up, magpie fashion, some detail which, even if unimportant, was at least concrete and bearing on some practical facet close at hand. Some of the favorite subjects of Miss Amelia were: the stars, the reason why Negroes are black, the best treatment for cancer, and so forth. Her father was also an interminable subject which was dear to her.

'Why, Law,' she would say to Lymon. 'Those days I slept. I'd go to bed just as the lamp was turned on and sleep—why, I'd sleep like I was drowned in warm axle grease. Then come daybreak Big Papa would walk in and put his hand down on my shoulder. " Get stirring, Little," he would say. Then later he would holler up the stairs from the kitchen when the stove was hot. "Fried grits," he would holler. "White meat and gravy. Ham and eggs." And I'd run down the stairs and dress by the hot stove while he was out washing at the pump. Then off we'd go to the still or maybe——'

'The grits we had this morning was poor,' Cousin Lymon said. 'Fried too quick so that the inside never heated.'

'And when Big Papa would run off the liquor in those days ——' The conversation would go on endlessly, with Miss Amelia's long legs stretched out before the hearth; for winter or summer there was always a fire in the grate, as Lymon was cold-natured. He sat in a low chair across from her, his feet not quite touching the floor and his torso usually well-wrapped in a blanket or the green wool shawl. Miss Amelia never mentioned her father to anyone else except Cousin Lymon.

That was one of the ways in which she showed her love for him. He had her confidence in the most delicate and vital matters. He alone knew where she kept the chart that showed where certain barrels of whisky were buried on a piece of property near by. He alone had access to her bank-book and the key to the cabinet of curios. He took money from the cash register, whole handfuls of it, and appreciated the loud jingle it made inside his pockets. He owned almost everything on the premises, for when he was cross Miss Amelia would prowl about and find him some present—so that now there was hardly anything left close at hand to give him. The only part of her life that she did not want Cousin Lymon to share with her was the memory of her ten-day marriage. Marvin Macy was the one subject that was never, at any time, discussed between the two of them.

So let the slow years pass and come to a Saturday evening six years after the time when Cousin Lymon came first to the town. It was August and the sky had burned above the town like a sheet of flame all day. Now the green twilight was near and there was a feeling of repose. The street was coated an inch deep with dry golden dust and the little children ran about half-naked, sneezed often, sweated, and were fretful. The mill had closed down at noon. People in the houses along the main street sat resting on their steps and the women had palmetto fans. At Miss Amelia's there was a sign at the front of the premises saying CAFÉ. The back porch was cool with latticed shadows and there Cousin Lymon sat turning the ice-cream freezer—often he unpacked the salt and ice and removed the dasher to lick a bit and see how the work was coming on. Jeff cooked in the kitchen. Early that morning Miss Amelia had put a notice on the wall of the front porch reading: Chicken Dinner—Twenty Cents Tonite. The café was already open and Miss Amelia had just finished a period of work in her office. All the eight tables were occupied and from the mechanical piano came a jingling tune.

In a corner near the door and sitting at a table with a child, was Henry Macy. He was drinking a glass of liquor, which was unusual for him, as liquor went easily to his head and made him cry or sing. His face was very pale and his left eye worked constantly in a nervous tic, as it was apt to do when he was agitated. He had come into the café sidewise and silent, and when he was greeted he did not speak. The child next to him belonged to Horace Wells, and he had been left at Miss Amelia's that morning to be doctored.

Miss Amelia came out from her office in good spirits. She attended to a few details in the kitchen and entered the café with the pope's nose of a hen between her fingers, as that was her favorite piece. She looked about the room, saw that in general all was well, and went over to the corner table by Henry Macy. She turned the chair around and sat straddling the back, as she only wanted to pass the time of day and was not yet ready for her supper. There was a bottle of Kroup Kure in the hip pocket of her overalls—a medicine made from whisky, rock candy, and a secret ingredient. Miss Amelia uncorked the bottle and put it to the mouth of the child. Then she turned to Henry Macy and, seeing the nervous winking of his left eye, she asked:

'What ails you?'

Henry Macy seemed on the point of saying something difficult, but, after a long look into the eyes of Miss Amelia, he swallowed and did not speak.

So Miss Amelia returned to her patient. Only the child's head showed above the table top. His face was very red, with the eyelids half-closed and the mouth partly open. He had a large, hard, swollen boil on his thigh, and had been brought to Miss Amelia so that it could be opened. But Miss Amelia used a special method with children; she did not like to see them hurt, struggling, and terrified. So she had kept the child around the premises all day, giving him licorice and frequent doses of the Kroup Kure, and toward evening she tied a napkin around his neck and let him eat his fill of the dinner. Now as he sat at the table his head wobbled slowly from side to side and sometimes as he breathed there came from him a little worn-out grunt.

There was a stir in the café and Miss Amelia looked around quickly. Cousin Lymon had come in. The hunchback strutted into the café as he did every night, and when he reached the exact center of the room he stopped short and looked shrewdly around him, summing up the people and making a quick pattern of the emotional material at hand that night. The hunchback was a great mischief-maker. He enjoyed any kind of to-do, and without saying a word he could set the people at each other in a way that was miraculous. It was due to him that the Rainey twins had quarreled over a jackknife two years past, and had not spoken one word to each other since. He was present at the big fight between Rip Wellborn and Robert Calvert Hale, and every other fight for that matter since he had come into the town. He nosed around everywhere, knew the intimate business of everybody, and trespassed every waking hour. Yet, queerly enough, in spite of this it was the hunchback who was most responsible for the great popularity of the café. Things were never so gay as when he was around. When he walked into the room there was always a quick feeling of tension, because with this busybody about there was never any telling what might descend on you, or what might suddenly be brought to happen in the room. People are never so free with themselves and so recklessly glad as when there is some possibility of commotion or calamity ahead. So when the hunchback marched into the café everyone looked around at him and there was a quick outburst of talking and a drawing of corks.

Lymon waved his hand to Stumpy MacPhail who was sitting with Merlie Ryan and Henry Ford Crimp. 'I walked to Rotten Lake today to fish,' he said. 'And on the way I stepped over what appeared at first to be a big fallen tree. But then as I stepped over I felt something stir and I taken this second look and there I was straddling this here alligator long as from the front door to the kitchen and thicker than a hog.'

The hunchback chattered on. Everyone looked at him from time to time, and some kept track of his chattering and others did not. There were times when every word he said was nothing but lying and bragging. Nothing he said tonight was true. He had lain in bed with a summer quinsy all day long, and had only got up in the late afternoon in order to turn the ice-cream freezer. Everybody knew this, yet he stood there in the middle of the café and held forth with such lies and boasting that it was enough to shrivel the ears.

Miss Amelia watched him with her hands in her pockets and her head turned to one side. There was a softness about her gray, queer eyes and she was smiling gently to herself. Occasionally she glanced from the hunchback to the other people in the café—and then her look was proud, and there was in it the hint of a threat, as though daring anyone to try to hold him to account for all his foolery. Jeff was bringing in the suppers, already served on the plates, and the new electric fans in the café made a pleasant stir of coolness in the air.

'The little youngun is asleep,' said Henry Macy finally.

Miss Amelia looked down at the patient beside her, and composed her face for the matter in hand. The child's chin was resting on the table edge and a trickle of spit or Kroup Kure had bubbled from the corner of his mouth. His eyes were quite closed, and a little family of gnats had clustered peacefully in the corners. Miss Amelia put her hand on his head and shook it roughly, but the patient did not awake. So Miss Amelia lifted the child from the table, being careful not to touch the sore part of his leg, and went into the office. Henry Macy followed after her and they closed the office door.

Cousin Lymon was bored that evening. There was not much going on, and in spite of the heat the customers in the café were good-humored. Henry Ford Crimp and Horace Wells sat at the middle table with their arms around each other, sniggering over some long joke—but when he approached them he could make nothing of it as he had missed the beginning of the story. The moonlight brightened the dusty road, and the dwarfed peach trees were black and motionless: there was no breeze. The drowsy buzz of swamp mosquitoes was like an echo of the silent night. The town seemed dark, except far down the road to the right there was the flicker of a lamp. Somewhere in the darkness a woman sang in a high wild voice and the tune had no start and no finish and was made up of only three notes which went on and on and on. The hunchback stood leaning against the banister of the porch, looking down the empty road as though hoping that someone would come along.

There were footsteps behind him, then a voice: 'Cousin Lymon, your dinner is set out upon the table.'

'My appetite is poor tonight,' said the hunchback, who had been eating sweet snuff all the day. 'There is a sourness in my mouth.'

'Just a pick,' said Miss Amelia. 'The breast, the liver, and the heart.'

Together they went back into the bright café, and sat down with Henry Macy. Their table was the largest one in the café, and on it there was a bouquet of swamp lilies in a Coca Cola bottle. Miss Amelia had finished with her patient and was satisfied with herself. From behind the closed office door there had come only a few sleepy whimpers, and before the patient could wake up and become terrified it was all over. The child was now slung across the shoulder of his father, sleeping deeply, his little arms dangling loose along his father's back, and his puffed-up face very red—they were leaving the café to go home.

Henry Macy was still silent. He ate carefully, making no noise when he swallowed, and was not a third as greedy as Cousin Lymon who had claimed to have no appetite and was now putting down helping after helping of the dinner. Occasionally Henry Macy looked across at Miss Amelia and again held his peace.

It was a typical Saturday night. An old couple who had come in from the country hesitated for a moment at the doorway, holding each other's hand, and finally decided to come inside. They had lived together so long, this old country couple, that they looked as similar as twins. They were brown, shriveled, and like two little walking peanuts. They left early, and by midnight most of the other customers were gone. Rosser Cline and Merlie Ryan still played checkers, and Stumpy MacPhail sat with a liquor bottle on his table (his wife would not allow it in the home) and carried on peaceable conversations with himself. Henry Macy had not yet gone away, and this was unusual, as he almost always went to bed soon after nightfall. Miss Amelia yawned sleepily, but Lymon was restless and she did not suggest that they close up for the night.

Finally, at one o'clock, Henry Macy looked up at the corner of the ceiling and said quietly to Miss Amelia: 'I got a letter today.'

Miss Amelia was not one to be impressed by this, because all sorts of business letters and catalogues came addressed to her.

'I got a letter from my brother,' said Henry Macy.

The hunchback, who had been goose-stepping about the café with his hands clasped behind his head, stopped suddenly. He was quick to sense any change in the atmosphere of a gathering. He glanced at each face in the room and waited.

Miss Amelia scowled and hardened her right fist. 'You are welcome to it,' she said.

'He is on parole. He is out of the penitentiary.'

The face of Miss Amelia was very dark, and she shivered although the night was warm. Stumpy MacPhail and Merlie Ryan pushed aside their checker game. The café was very quiet.

'Who?' asked Cousin Lymon. His large, pale ears seemed to grow on his head and stiffen. 'What?'

Miss Amelia slapped her hands palm down on the table. 'Because Marvin Macy is a——' But her voice hoarsened and after a few moments she only said: 'He belongs to be in that penitentiary the balance of his life.'

'What did he do?' asked Cousin Lymon.

There was a long pause, as no one knew exactly how to answer this. 'He robbed three filling stations,' said Stumpy MacPhail. But his words did not sound complete and there was a feeling of sins left unmentioned.

The hunchback was impatient. He could not bear to be left out of anything, even a great misery. The name Marvin Macy was unknown to him, but it tantalized him as did any mention of subjects which others knew about and of which he was ignorant—such as any reference to the old sawmill that had been torn down before he came, or a chance word about poor Morris Finestein, or the recollection of any event that had occurred before his time. Aside from this inborn curiosity, the hunchback took a great interest in robbers and crimes of all varieties. As he strutted around the table he was muttering the words 'released on parole' and 'penitentiary' to himself. But although he questioned insistently, he was unable to find anything, as nobody would dare to talk about Marvin Macy before Miss Amelia in the café.

'The letter did not say very much,' said Henry Macy. 'He did not say where he was going.'

'Humph!' said Miss Amelia, and her face was still hardened and very dark. 'He will never set his split hoof on my premises.'

She pushed back her chair from the table, and made ready to close the café. Thinking about Marvin Macy may have set her to brooding, for she hauled the cash register back to the kitchen and put it in a private place. Henry Macy went off down the dark road. But Henry Ford Crimp and Merlie Ryan lingered for a time on the front porch. Later Merlie Ryan was to make certain claims, to swear that on that night he had a vision of what was to come. But the town paid no attention, for that was just the sort of thing that Merlie Ryan would claim. Miss Amelia and Cousin Lymon talked for a time in the parlor. And when at last the hunchback thought that he could sleep she arranged the mosquito netting over his bed and waited until he had finished with his prayers. Then she put on her long nightgown, smoked two pipes, and only after a long time went to sleep.

That autumn was a happy time. The crops around the countryside were good, and over at the Forks Falls market the price of tobacco held firm that year. After the long hot summer the first cool days had a clean bright sweetness. Goldenrod grew along the dusty roads, and the sugar cane was ripe and purple. The bus came each day from Cheehaw to carry off a few of the younger children to the consolidated school to get an education. Boys hunted foxes in the pinewoods, winter quilts were aired out on the wash lines, and sweet potatoes bedded in the ground with straw against the colder months to come. In the evening, delicate shreds of smoke rose from the chimneys, and the moon was round and orange in the autumn sky. There is no stillness like the quiet of the first cold nights in the fall. Sometimes, late in the night when there was no wind, there could be heard in the town the thin wild whistle of the train that goes through Society City on its way far off to the North.

For Miss Amelia Evans this was a time of great activity. She was at work from dawn until sundown. She made a new and bigger condenser for her still, and in one week ran off enough liquor to souse the whole county. Her old mule was dizzy from grinding so much sorghum, and she scalded her Mason jars and put away pear preserves. She was looking forward greatly to the first frost, because she had traded for three tremendous hogs, and intended to make much barbecue, chitterlins, and sausage.

During these weeks there was a quality about Miss Amelia that many people noticed. She laughed often, with a deep ringing laugh, and her whistling had a sassy, tuneful trickery. She was forever trying out her strength, lifting up heavy objects, or poking her tough biceps with her finger. One day she sat down to her typewriter and wrote a story—a story in which there were foreigners, trap doors, and millions of dollars. Cousin Lymon was with her always, traipsing along behind her coat-tails, and when she watched him her face had a bright, soft look, and when she spoke his name there lingered in her voice the undertone of love.

The first cold spell came at last. When Miss Amelia awoke one morning there were frost flowers on the windowpanes, and rime had silvered the patches of grass in the yard. Miss Amelia built a roaring fire in the kitchen stove, then went out of doors to judge the day. The air was cold and sharp, the sky pale green and cloudless. Very shortly people began to come in from the country to find out what Miss Amelia thought of the weather; she decided to kill the biggest hog, and word got round the countryside. The hog was slaughtered and a low-oak fire started in the barbecue pit. There was the warm smell of pig blood and smoke in the back yard, the stamp of footsteps, the ring of voices in the winter air. Miss Amelia walked around giving orders and soon most of the work was done.

She had some particular business to do in Cheehaw that day, so after making sure that all was going well, she cranked up her car and got ready to leave. She asked Cousin Lymon to come with her, in fact, she asked him seven times, but he was loath to leave the commotion and wanted to remain. This seemed to trouble Miss Amelia, as she always liked to have him near to her, and was prone to be terribly homesick when she had to go any distance away. But after asking him seven times, she did not urge him any further. Before leaving she found a stick and drew a heavy line all around the barbecue pit, about two feet back from the edge, and told him not to trespass beyond that boundary. She left after dinner and intended to be back before dark.

Now, it is not so rare to have a truck or an automobile pass along the road and through the town on the way from Cheehaw to somewhere else. Every year the tax collector comes to argue with rich people such as Miss Amelia. And if somebody in the town, such as Merlie Ryan, takes a notion that he can connive to get a car on credit, or to pay down three dollars and have a fine electric icebox such as they advertise in the store windows of Cheehaw, then a city man will come out asking meddlesome questions, finding out all his troubles, and ruining his chances of buying anything on the installment plan. Sometimes, especially since they are working on the Forks Falls highway, the cars hauling the chain gang come through the town. And frequently people in automobiles get lost and stop to inquire how they can find the right road again. So, late that afternoon it was nothing unusual to have a truck pass the mill and stop in the middle of the road near the café of Miss Amelia. A man jumped down from the back of the truck, and the truck went on its way.

The man stood in the middle of the road and looked about him. He was a tall man, with brown curly hair, and slow-moving, deep-blue eyes. His lips were red and he smiled the lazy, half-mouthed smile of the braggart. The man wore a red shirt, and a wide belt of tooled leather; he carried a tin suitcase and a guitar. The first person in the town to see this newcomer was Cousin Lymon, who had heard the shifting of gears and come around to investigate. The hunchback stuck his head around the corner of the porch, but did not step out altogether into full view. He and the man stared at each other, and it was not the look of two strangers meeting for the first time and swiftly summing up each other. It was a peculiar stare they exchanged between them, like the look of two criminals who recognize each other. Then the man in the red shirt shrugged his left shoulder and turned away. The face of the hunchback was very pale as he watched the man go down the road, and after a few moments he began to follow along carefully, keeping many paces away.

It was immediately known throughout the town that Marvin Macy had come back again. First, he went to the mill, propped his elbows lazily on a window sill and looked inside. He liked to watch others hard at work, as do all born loafers. The mill was thrown into a sort of numb confusion. The dyers left the hot vats, the spinners and weavers forgot about their machines, and even Stumpy MacPhail, who was foreman, did not know exactly what to do. Marvin Macy still smiled his wet half-mouthed smiles, and when he saw his brother, his bragging expression did not change. After looking over the mill Marvin Macy went down the road to the house where he had been raised, and left his suitcase and guitar on the front porch. Then he walked around the millpond, looked over the church, the three stores, and the rest of the town. The hunchback trudged along quietly at some distance behind him, his hands in his pockets, and his little face still very pale.

It had grown late. The red winter sun was setting, and to the west the sky was deep gold and crimson. Ragged chimney swifts flew to their nests; lamps were lighted. Now and then there was the smell of smoke, and the warm rich odor of the barbecue slowly cooking in the pit behind the café. After making the rounds of the town Marvin Macy stopped before Miss Amelia's premises and read the sign above the porch. Then, not hesitating to trespass, he walked through the side yard. The mill whistle blew a thin, lonesome blast, and the day's shift was done. Soon there were others in Miss Amelia's back yard beside Marvin Macy—Henry Ford Crimp, Merlie Ryan, Stumpy MacPhail, and any number of children and people who stood around the edges of the property and looked on. Very little was said. Marvin Macy stood by himself on one side of the pit, and the rest of the people clustered together on the other side. Cousin Lymon stood somewhat apart from everyone, and he did not take his eyes from the face of Marvin Macy.

'Did you have a good time in the penitentiary?' asked Merlie Ryan, with a silly giggle.

Marvin Macy did not answer. He took from his hip pocket a large knife, opened it slowly, and honed the blade on the seat of his pants. Merlie Ryan grew suddenly very quiet and went to stand directly behind the broad back of Stumpy MacPhail.

Miss Amelia did not come home until almost dark. They heard the rattle of her automobile while she was still a long distance away, then the slam of the door and a bumping noise as though she were hauling something up the front steps of her premises. The sun had already set, and in the air there was the blue smoky glow of early winter evenings. Miss Amelia came down the back steps slowly, and the group in her yard waited very quietly. Few people in this world could stand up to Miss Amelia, and against Marvin Macy she had this special and bitter hate. Everyone waited to see her burst into a terrible holler, snatch up some dangerous object, and chase him altogether out of town. At first she did not see Marvin Macy, and her face had the relieved and dreamy expression that was natural to her when she reached home after having gone some distance away.

Miss Amelia must have seen Marvin Macy and Cousin Lymon at the same instant. She looked from one to the other, but it was not the wastrel from the penitentiary on whom she finally fixed her gaze of sick amazement. She, and everyone else, was looking at Cousin Lymon, and he was a sight to see.

The hunchback stood at the end of the pit, his pale face lighted by the soft glow from the smoldering oak fire. Cousin Lymon had a very peculiar accomplishment, which he used whenever he wished to ingratiate himself with someone. He would stand very still, and with just a little concentration, he could wiggle his large pale ears with marvelous quickness and ease. This trick he always used when he wanted to get something special out of Miss Amelia, and to her it was irresistible. Now as he stood there the hunchback's ears were wiggling furiously on his head, but it was not Miss Amelia at whom he was looking this time. The hunchback was smiling at Marvin Macy with an entreaty that was near to desperation. At first Marvin Macy paid no attention to him, and when he did finally glance at the hunchback it was without any appreciation whatsoever.

'What ails this Brokeback?' he asked with a rough jerk of his thumb.

No one answered. And Cousin Lymon, seeing that his accomplishment was getting him nowhere, added new efforts of persuasion. He fluttered his eyelids, so that they were like pale, trapped moths in his sockets. He scraped his feet around on the ground, waved his hands about, and finally began doing a little trotlike dance. In the last gloomy light of the winter afternoon he resembled the child of a swamphaunt.

Marvin Macy, alone of all the people in the yard, was unimpressed. 'Is the runt throwing a fit?' he asked, and when no one answered he stepped forward and gave Cousin Lymon a cuff on the side of his head. The hunchback staggered, then fell back on the ground. He sat where he had fallen, still looking up at Marvin Macy, and with great effort his ears managed one last forlorn little flap.

Now everyone turned to Miss Amelia to see what she would do. In all these years no one had so much as touched a hair of Cousin Lymon's head, although many had had the itch to do so. If anyone even spoke crossly to the hunchback, Miss Amelia would cut off this rash mortal's credit and find ways of making things go hard for him a long time afterward. So now if Miss Amelia had split open Marvin

Macy's head with the ax on the back porch no one would have been surprised. But she did nothing of the kind.

There were times when Miss Amelia seemed to go into a sort of trance. And the cause of these trances was usually known and understood. For Miss Amelia was a fine doctor, and did not grind up swamp roots and other untried ingredients and give them to the first patient who came along; whenever she invented a new medicine she always tried it out first on herself. She would swallow an enormous dose and spend the following day walking thoughtfully back and forth from the café to the brick privy. Often, when there was a sudden keen gripe, she would stand quite still, her queer eyes staring down at the ground and her fists clenched; she was trying to decide which organ was being worked upon, and what misery the new medicine might be most likely to cure. And now as she watched the hunchback and Marvin Macy, her face wore this same expression, tense with reckoning some inward pain, although she had taken no new medicine that day.

'That will learn you, Brokeback,' said Marvin Macy.

Henry Macy pushed back his limp whitish hair from his forehead and coughed nervously. Stumpy MacPhail and Merlie Ryan shuffled their feet, and the children and black people on the outskirts of the property made not a sound. Marvin Macy folded the knife he had been honing, and after looking about him fearlessly he swaggered out of the yard. The embers in the pit were turning to gray feathery ashes and it was now quite dark.

That was the way Marvin Macy came back from the penitentiary. Not a living soul in all the town was glad to see him. Even Mrs. Mary Hale, who was a good woman and had raised him with love and care —at the first sight of him even this old foster mother dropped the skillet she was holding and burst into tears. But nothing could faze that Marvin Macy. He sat on the back steps of the Hale house, lazily picking his guitar, and when the supper was ready, he pushed the children of the household out of the way and served himself a big meal, although there had been barely enough hoecakes and white meat to go round. After eating he settled himself in the best and warmest sleeping place in the front room and was untroubled by dreams.

Miss Amelia did not open the café that night. She locked the doors and all the windows very carefully, nothing was seen of her and Cousin Lymon, and a lamp burned in her room all the night long.

Marvin Macy brought with him bad fortune, right from the first, as could be expected. The next day the weather turned suddenly, and it became hot. Even in the early morning there was a sticky sultriness in the atmosphere, the wind carried the rotten smell of the swamp, and delicate shrill mosquitoes webbed the green millpond. It was unseasonable, worse than August, and much damage was done. For nearly everyone in the county who owned a hog had copied Miss Amelia and slaughtered the day before. And what sausage could keep in such weather as this? After a few days there was everywhere the smell of slowly spoiling meat, and an atmosphere of dreary waste. Worse yet, a family reunion near the Forks Falls highway ate pork roast and died, every one of them. It was plain that their hog had been infected—and who could tell whether the rest of the meat was safe or not? People were torn between the longing for the good taste of pork, and the fear of death. It was a time of waste and confusion.

The cause of all this, Marvin Macy, had no shame in him. He was seen everywhere. During work hours he loafed about the mill, looking in at the windows, and on Sundays he dressed in his red shirt and paraded up and down the road with his guitar. He was still handsome—with his brown hair, his red lips, and his broad strong shoulders; but the evil in him was now too famous for his good looks to get him anywhere. And this evil was not measured only by the actual sins he had committed. True, he had robbed those filling stations. And before that he had ruined the tenderest girls in the county, and laughed about it. Any number of wicked things could be listed against him, but quite apart from these crimes there was about him a secret meanness that clung to him almost like a smell. Another thing—he never sweated, not even in August, and that surely is a sign worth pondering over.

Now it seemed to the town that he was more dangerous than he had ever been before, as in the penitentiary in Atlanta he must have learned the method of laying charms. Otherwise how could his effect on Cousin Lymon be explained? For since first setting eyes on Marvin Macy the hunchback was possessed by an unnatural spirit. Every minute he wanted to be following along behind this jailbird, and he was full of silly schemes to attract attention to himself. Still Marvin Macy either treated him hatefully or failed to notice him at all. Sometimes the hunchback would give up, perch himself on the banister of the front porch much as a sick bird huddles on a telephone wire, and grieve publicly.

'But why?' Miss Amelia would ask, staring at him with her crossed, gray eyes, and her fists closed tight.

'Oh, Marvin Macy,' groaned the hunchback, and the sound of the name was enough to upset the rhythm of his sobs so that he hiccuped. 'He has been to Atlanta.'

Miss Amelia would shake her head and her face was dark and hardened. To begin with she had no patience with any traveling; those who had made the trip to Atlanta or traveled fifty miles from home to see the ocean—those restless people she despised. 'Going to Atlanta does no credit to him.'

'He has been to the penitentiary,' said the hunchback, miserable with longing.

How are you going to argue against such envies as these? In her perplexity Miss Amelia did not herself sound any too sure of what she was saying. 'Been to the penitentiary, Cousin Lymon? Why, a trip like that is no travel to brag about.'

During these weeks Miss Amelia was closely watched by everyone. She went about absent-mindedly, her face remote as though she had lapsed into one of her gripe trances. For some reason, after the day of Marvin Macy's arrival, she put aside her overalls and wore always the red dress she had before this time reserved for Sundays, funerals, and sessions of the court. Then as the weeks passed she began to take some steps to clear up the situation. But her efforts were hard to understand. If it hurt her to see Cousin Lymon follow Marvin Macy about the town, why did she not make the issues clear once and for all, and tell the hunchback that if he had dealings with Marvin Macy she would turn him off the premises? That would have been simple, and Cousin Lymon would have had to submit to her, or else face the sorry business of finding himself loose in the world. But Miss Amelia seemed to have lost her will; for the first time in her life she hesitated as to just what course to pursue. And, like most people in such a position of uncertainty, she did the worst thing possible—she began following several courses at once, all of them contrary to each other.

The café was opened every night as usual, and, strangely enough, when Marvin Macy came swaggering through the door, with the hunchback at his heels, she did not turn him out. She even gave him free drinks and smiled at him in a wild, crooked way. At the same time she set a terrible trap for him out in the swamp that surely would have killed him if he had got caught. She let Cousin Lymon invite him to Sunday dinner, and then tried to trip him up as he went down the steps. She began a great campaign of pleasure for Cousin Lymon—making exhausting trips to various spectacles being held in distant places, driving the automobile thirty miles to a Chautauqua, taking him to Forks Falls to watch a parade. All in all it was a distracting time for Miss Amelia. In the opinion of most people she was well on her way in the climb up fools' hill, and everyone waited to see how it would all turn out.

The weather turned cold again, the winter was upon the town, and night came before the last shift in the mill was done. Children kept on all their garments when they slept, and women raised the backs of their skirts to toast themselves dreamily at the fire. After it rained, the mud in the road made hard frozen ruts, there were faint flickers of lamplight from the windows of the houses, the peach trees were scrawny and bare. In the dark, silent nights of winter-time the café was the warm center point of the town, the lights shining so brightly that they could be seen a quarter of a mile away. The great iron stove at the back of the room roared, crackled, and turned red. Miss Amelia had made red curtains for the windows, and from a salesman who passed through the town she bought a great bunch of paper roses that looked very real.

But it was not only the warmth, the decorations, and the brightness, that made the café what it was. There is a deeper reason why the café was so precious to this town. And this deeper reason has to do with a certain pride that had not hitherto been known in these parts. To understand this new pride the cheapness of human life must be kept in mind. There were always plenty of people clustered around a mill—but it was seldom that every family had enough meal, garments, and fat back to go the rounds. Life could become one long dim scramble just to get the things needed to keep alive. And the confusing point is this: All useful things have a price, and are bought only with money, as that is the way the world is run. You know without having to reason about it the price of a bale of cotton, or a quart of molasses. But no value has been put on human life; it is given to us free and taken without being paid for. What is it worth? If you look around, at times the value may seem to be little or nothing at all. Often after you have sweated and tried and things are not better for you, there comes a feeling deep down in the soul that you are not worth much.

But the new pride that the café brought to this town had an effect on almost everyone, even the children. For in order to come to the café you did not have to buy the dinner, or a portion of liquor. There were cold bottled drinks for a nickel. And if you could not even afford that, Miss Amelia had a drink called Cherry Juice which sold for a penny a glass, and was pink-colored and very sweet. Almost everyone, with the exception of Reverend T. M. Willin, came to the café at least once during the week. Children love to sleep in houses other than their own, and to eat at a neighbor's table; on such occasions they behave themselves decently and are proud. The people in the town were likewise proud when sitting at the tables in the café. They washed before coming to Miss Amelia's, and scraped their feet very politely on the threshold as they entered the café. There, for a few hours at least, the deep bitter knowing that you are not worth much in this world could be laid low.

The café was a special benefit to bachelors, unfortunate people, and consumptives. And here it may be mentioned that there was some reason to suspect that Cousin Lymon was consumptive. The brightness of his gray eyes, his insistence, his talkativeness, and his cough—these were all signs. Besides, there is generally supposed to be some connection between a hunched spine and consumption. But whenever this subject had been mentioned to Miss Amelia she had become furious; she denied these symptoms with bitter vehemence, but on the sly she treated Cousin Lymon with hot chest plasters, Kroup Kure, and such. Now this winter the hunchback's cough was worse, and sometimes even on cold days he would break out in a heavy sweat. But this did not prevent him from following along after Marvin Macy.

Early every morning he left the premises and went to the back door of Mrs. Hale's house, and waited and waited—as Marvin Macy was a lazy sleeper. He would stand there and call out softly. His voice was just like the voices of children who squat patiently over those tiny little holes in the ground where doodlebugs are thought to live, poking the hole with a broom straw, and calling plaintively: 'Doodlebug, Doodlebug—fly away home. Mrs. Doodlebug, Mrs. Doodlebug. Come out, come out. Your house is on fire and all your children are burning up.' In just such a voice—at once sad, luring, and resigned—would the hunchback call Marvin Macy's name each morning. Then when Marvin Macy came out for the day, he would trail him about the town, and sometimes they would be gone for hours together out in the swamp.

And Miss Amelia continued to do the worst thing possible: that is, to try to follow several courses at once. When Cousin Lymon left the house she did not call him back, but only stood in the middle of the road and watched lonesomely until he was out of sight. Nearly every day Marvin Macy turned up with Cousin Lymon at dinnertime, and ate at her table. Miss Amelia opened the pear preserves, and the table was well-set with ham or chicken, great bowls of hominy grits, and winter peas. It is true that on one occasion Miss Amelia tried to poison Marvin Macy—but there was a mistake, the plates were confused, and it was she herself who got the poisoned dish. This she quickly realized by the slight bitterness of the food, and that day she ate no dinner. She sat tilted back in her chair, feeling her muscle, and looking at Marvin Macy.

Every night Marvin Macy came to the café and settled himself at the best and largest table, the one in the center of the room. Cousin Lymon brought him liquor, for which he did not pay a cent. Marvin Macy brushed the hunchback aside as if he were a swamp mosquito, and not only did he show no gratitude for these favors, but if the hunchback got in his way he would cuff him with the back of his hand, or say: 'Out of my way, Brokeback—I'll snatch you bald-headed.' When this happened Miss Amelia would come out from behind her counter and approach Marvin Macy very slowly, her fists clenched, her peculiar red dress hanging awkwardly around her bony knees. Marvin Macy would also clench his fists and they would walk slowly and meaningfully around each other. But, although everyone watched breathlessly, nothing ever came of it. The time for the fight was not yet ready.

There is one particular reason why this winter is remembered and still talked about. A great thing happened. People woke up on the second of January and found the whole world about them altogether changed. Little ignorant children looked out of the windows, and they were so puzzled that they began to cry. Old people harked back and could remember nothing in these parts to equal the phenomenon. For in the night it had snowed. In the dark hours after midnight the dim flakes started falling softly on the town. By dawn the ground was covered, and the strange snow banked the ruby windows of the church, and whitened the roofs of the houses. The snow gave the town a drawn, bleak look. The two-room houses near the mill were dirty, crooked, and seemed about to collapse, and somehow everything was dark and shrunken. But the snow itself—there was a beauty about it few people around here had ever known before. The snow was not white, as Northerners had pictured it to be; in the snow there were soft colors of blue and silver, the sky was a gentle shining gray. And the dreamy quietness of falling snow—when had the town been so silent?

People reacted to the snowfall in various ways. Miss Amelia, on looking out of her window, thoughtfully wiggled the toes of her bare foot, gathered close to her neck the collar of her nightgown. She stood there for some time, then commenced to draw the shutters and lock every window on the premises. She closed the place completely, lighted the lamps, and sat solemnly over her bowl of grits. The reason for this was not that Miss Amelia feared the snowfall. It was simply that she was unable to form an immediate opinion of this new event, and unless she knew exactly and definitely what she thought of a matter (which was nearly always the case) she preferred to ignore it. Snow had never fallen in this county in her lifetime, and she had never thought about it one way or the other. But if she admitted this snowfall she would have to come to some decision, and in those days there was enough distraction in her life as it was already. So she poked about the gloomy, lamplighted house and pretended that nothing had happened. Cousin Lymon, on the contrary, chased around in the wildest excitement, and when Miss Amelia turned her back to dish him some breakfast he slipped out of the door.

Marvin Macy laid claim to the snowfall. He said that he knew snow, had seen it in Atlanta, and from the way he walked about the town that day it was as though he owned every flake. He sneered at the little children who crept timidly out of the houses and scooped up handfuls of snow to taste. Reverend Willin hurried down the road with a furious face, as he was thinking deeply and trying to weave the snow into his Sunday sermon. Most people were humble and glad about this marvel; they spoke in hushed voices and said 'thank you' and 'please' more than was necessary. A few weak characters, of course, were demoralized and got drunk—but they were not numerous. To everyone this was an occasion and many counted their money and planned to go to the café that night.

Cousin Lymon followed Marvin Macy about all day, seconding his claim to the snow. He marveled that snow did not fall as does rain, and stared up at the dreamy, gently falling flakes until he stumbled from dizziness. And the pride he took on himself, basking in the glory of Marvin Macy—it was such that many people could not resist calling out to him: '"Oho," said the fly on the chariot wheel. "What a dust we do raise."'

Miss Amelia did not intend to serve a dinner. But when, at six o'clock, there was the sound of footsteps on the porch she opened the front door cautiously. It was Henry Ford Crimp, and though there was no food, she let him sit at a table and served him a drink. Others came. The evening was blue, bitter, and though the snow fell no longer there was a wind from the pine trees that swept up delicate flurries from the ground. Cousin Lymon did not come until after dark, with him Marvin Macy, and he carried his tin suitcase and his guitar.

'So you mean to travel?' said Miss Amelia quickly.

Marvin Macy warmed himself at the stove. Then he settled down at his table and carefully sharpened a little stick. He picked his teeth, frequently taking the stick out of his mouth to look at the end and wipe it on the sleeve of his coat. He did not bother to answer.

The hunchback looked at Miss Amelia, who was behind the counter. His face was not in the least beseeching; he seemed quite sure of himself. He folded his hands behind his back and perked up his ears confidently. His cheeks were red, his eyes shining, and his clothes were soggy wet. 'Marvin Macy is going to visit a spell with us,' he said.

Miss Amelia made no protest. She only came out from behind the counter and hovered over the stove, as though the news had made her suddenly cold. She did not warm her backside modestly, lifting her skirt only an inch or so, as do most women when in public. There was not a grain of modesty about Miss Amelia, and she frequently seemed to forget altogether that there were men in the room. Now as she stood warming herself, her red dress was pulled up quite high in the back so that a piece of her strong, hairy thigh could be seen by anyone who cared to look at it. Her head was turned to one side, and she had begun talking with herself, nodding and wrinkling her forehead, and there was the tone of accusation and reproach in her voice although the words were not plain. Meanwhile, the hunchback and Marvin Macy had gone upstairs—up to the parlor with the pampas grass and the two sewing machines, to the private rooms where Miss Amelia had lived the whole of her life. Down in the café you could hear them bumping around, unpacking Marvin Macy, and getting him settled.

That is the way Marvin Macy crowded into Miss Amelia's home. At first Cousin Lymon, who had given Marvin Macy his own room, slept on the sofa in the parlor. But the snowfall had a bad effect on him; he caught a cold that turned into a winter quinsy, so Miss Amelia gave up her bed to him. The sofa in the parlor was much too short for her, her feet lapped over the edges, and often she rolled off onto the floor. Perhaps it was this lack of sleep that clouded her wits; everything she tried to do against Marvin Macy rebounded on herself. She got caught in her own tricks, and found herself in many pitiful positions. But still she did not put Marvin Macy off the premises, as she was afraid that she would be left alone. Once you have lived with another, it is a great torture to have to live alone. The silence of a firelit room when suddenly the clock stops ticking, the nervous shadows in an empty house—it is better to take in your mortal enemy than face the terror of living alone.

The snow did not last. The sun came out and within two days the town was just as it had always been before. Miss Amelia did not open her house until every flake had melted. Then she had a big house cleaning and aired everything out in the sun. But before that, the very first thing she did on going out again into her yard, was to tie a rope to the largest branch of the chinaberry tree. At the end of the rope she tied a crocus sack tightly stuffed with sand. This was the punching bag she made for herself and from that day on she would box with it out in her yard every morning. Already she was a fine fighter—a little heavy on her feet, but knowing all manner of mean holds and squeezes to make up for this.

Miss Amelia, as has been mentioned, measured six feet two inches in height. Marvin Macy was one inch shorter. In weight they were about even—both of them weighing close to a hundred and sixty pounds. Marvin Macy had the advantage in slyness of movement, and in toughness of chest. In fact from the outward point of view the odds were altogether in his favor. Yet almost everybody in the town was betting on Miss Amelia; scarcely a person would put up money on Marvin Macy. The town remembered the great fight between Miss Amelia and a Fork Falls lawyer who had tried to cheat her. He had been a huge strapping fellow, but he was left three-quarters dead when she had finished with him. And it was not only her talent as a boxer that had impressed everyone—she could demoralize her enemy by making terrifying faces and fierce noises, so that even the spectators were sometimes cowed. She was brave, she practiced faithfully with her punching bag, and in this case she was clearly in the right. So people had confidence in her, and they waited. Of course there was no set date for this fight. There were just the signs that were too plain to be overlooked.

During these times the hunchback strutted around with a pleased little pinched-up face. In many delicate and clever ways he stirred up trouble between them. He was constantly plucking at Marvin Macy's trouser leg to draw attention to himself. Sometimes he followed in Miss Amelia's footsteps—but these days it was only in order to imitate her awkward long-legged walk; he crossed his eyes and aped her gestures in a way that made her appear to be a freak. There was something so terrible about this that even the silliest customers of the café, such as Merlie Ryan, did not laugh. Only Marvin Macy drew up the left corner of his mouth and chuckled. Miss Amelia, when this happened, would be divided between two emotions. She would look at the hunchback with a lost, dismal reproach—then turn toward Marvin Macy with her teeth clamped.

'Bust a gut!' she would say bitterly.

And Marvin Macy, most likely, would pick up the guitar from the floor beside his chair. His voice was wet and slimy, as he always had too much spit in his mouth. And the tunes he sang glided slowly from his throat like eels. His strong fingers picked the strings with dainty skill, and everything he sang both lured and exasperated. This was usually more than Miss Amelia could stand.

'Bust a gut!' she would repeat, in a shout.

But always Marvin Macy had the answer ready for her. He would cover the strings to silence the quivering left-over tones, and reply with slow, sure insolence.

'Everything you holler at me bounces back on yourself. Yah! Yah!'

Miss Amelia would have to stand there helpless, as no one has ever invented a way out of this trap. She could not shout out abuse that would bounce back on herself. He had the best of her, there was nothing she could do.

So things went on like this. What happened between the three of them during the nights in the rooms upstairs nobody knows. But the café became more and more crowded every night. A new table had to be brought in. Even the Hermit, the crazy man named Rainer Smith, who took to the swamp years ago, heard something of the situation and came one night to look in at the window and brood over the gathering in the bright café. And the climax each evening was the time when Miss Amelia and Marvin Macy doubled their fists, squared up, and glared at each other. Usually this did not happen after any especial argument, but it seemed to come about mysteriously, by means of some instinct on the part of both of them. At these times the café would become so quiet that you could hear the bouquet of paper roses rustling in the draft. And each night they held this fighting stance a little longer than the night before.

The fight took place on Ground Hog Day, which is the second of February. The weather was favorable, being neither rainy nor sunny, and with a neutral temperature. There were several signs that this was the appointed day, and by ten o'clock the news spread all over the county. Early in the morning Miss Amelia went out and cut down her punching bag. Marvin Macy sat on the back step with a tin can of hog fat between his knees and carefully greased his arms and his legs. A hawk with a bloody breast flew over the town and circled twice around the property of Miss Amelia. The tables in the café were moved out to the back porch, so that the whole big room was cleared for the fight. There was every sign. Both Miss Amelia and Marvin Macy ate four helpings of half-raw roast for dinner, and then lay down in the afternoon to store up strength. Marvin Macy rested in the big room upstairs, while Miss Amelia stretched herself out on the bench in her office. It was plain from her white stiff face what a torment it was for her to be lying still and doing nothing, but she lay there quiet as a corpse with her eyes closed and her hands crossed on her chest.

Cousin Lymon had a restless day, and his little face was drawn and tightened with excitement. He put himself up a lunch, and set out to find the ground hog—within an hour he returned, the lunch eaten, and said that the ground hog had seen his shadow and there was to be bad weather ahead. Then, as Miss Amelia and Marvin Macy were both resting to gather strength, and he was left to himself, it occurred to him that he might as well paint the front porch. The house had not been painted for years—in fact, God knows if it had ever been painted at all. Cousin Lymon scrambled around, and soon he had painted half the floor of the porch a gay bright green. It was a loblolly job, and he smeared himself all over. Typically enough he did not even finish the floor, but changed over to the walls, painting as high as he could reach and then standing on a crate to get up a foot higher. When the paint ran out, the right side of the floor was bright green and there was a jagged portion of wall that had been painted. Cousin Lymon left it at that.

There was something childish about his satisfaction with his painting. And in this respect a curious fact should be mentioned. No one in the town, not even Miss Amelia, had any idea how old the hunchback was. Some maintained that when he came to town he was about twelve years old, still a child—others were certain that he was well past forty. His eyes were blue and steady as a child's but there were lavender crêpy shadows beneath these blue eyes that hinted of age. It was impossible to guess his age by his hunched queer body. And even his teeth gave no clue—they were all still in his head (two were broken from cracking a pecan), but he had stained them with so much sweet snuff that it was impossible to decide whether they were old teeth or young teeth. When questioned directly about his age the hunchback professed to know absolutely nothing—he had no idea how long he had been on the earth, whether for ten years or a hundred! So his age remained a puzzle.

Cousin Lymon finished his painting at five-thirty o'clock in the afternoon. The day had turned colder and there was a wet taste in the air. The wind came up from the pinewoods, rattling windows, blowing an old newspaper down the road until at last it caught upon a thorn tree. People began to come in from the country; packed automobiles that bristled with the poked-out heads of children, wagons drawn by old mules who seemed to smile in a weary, sour way and plodded along with their tired eyes half-closed. Three young boys came from Society City. All three of them wore yellow rayon shirts and caps put on backward—they were as much alike as triplets, and could always be seen at cock fights and camp meetings. At six o'clock the mill whistle sounded the end of the day's shift and the crowd was complete. Naturally, among the newcomers there were some riffraff, unknown characters, and so forth—but even so the gathering was quiet. A hush was on the town and the faces of people were strange in the fading light. Darkness hovered softly; for a moment the sky was a pale clear yellow against which the gables of the church stood out in dark and bare outline, then the sky died slowly and the darkness gathered into night.

Seven is a popular number, and especially it was a favorite with Miss Amelia. Seven swallows of water for hiccups, seven runs around the millpond for cricks in the neck, seven doses of Amelia Miracle Mover as a worm cure—her treatment nearly always hinged on this number. It is a number of mingled possibilities, and all who love mystery and charms set store by it. So the fight was to take place at seven o'clock. This was known to everyone, not by announcement or words, but understood in the unquestioning way that rain is understood, or an evil odor from the swamp. So before seven o'clock everyone gathered gravely around the property of Miss Amelia. The cleverest got into the café itself and stood lining the walls of the room. Others crowded onto the front porch, or took a stand in the yard.

Miss Amelia and Marvin Macy had not yet shown themselves. Miss Amelia, after resting all afternoon on the office bench, had gone upstairs. On the other hand Cousin Lymon was at your elbow every minute, threading his way through the crowd, snapping his fingers nervously, and batting his eyes. At one minute to seven o'clock he squirmed his way into the café and climbed up on the counter. All was very quiet.

It must have been arranged in some manner beforehand. For just at the stroke of seven Miss Amelia showed herself at the head of the stairs. At the same instant Marvin Macy appeared in front of the café and the crowd made way for him silently. They walked toward each other with no haste, their fists already gripped, and their eyes like the eyes of dreamers. Miss Amelia had changed her red dress for her old overalls, and they were rolled up to the knees. She was barefooted and she had an iron strengthband around her right wrist. Marvin Macy had also rolled his trouser legs—he was naked to the waist and heavily greased; he wore the heavy shoes that had been issued him when he left the penitentiary. Stumpy MacPhail stepped forward from the crowd and slapped their hip pockets with the palm of his right hand to make sure there would be no sudden knives. Then they were alone in the cleared center of the bright café.

There was no signal, but they both struck out simultaneously. Both blows landed on the chin, so that the heads of Miss Amelia and Marvin Macy bobbed back and they were left a little groggy. For a few seconds after the first blows they merely shuffled their feet around on the bare floor, experimenting with various positions, and making mock fists. Then, like wildcats, they were suddenly on each other. There was the sounds of knocks, panting, and thumpings on the floor. They were so fast that it was hard to take in what was going on—but once Miss Amelia was hurled backward so that she staggered and almost fell, and another time Marvin Macy caught a knock on the shoulder that spun him around like a top. So the fight went on in this wild violent way with no sign of weakening on either side.

During a struggle like this, when the enemies are as quick and strong as these two, it is worth-while to turn from the confusion of the fight itself and observe the spectators. The people had flattened back as close as possible against the walls. Stumpy MacPhail was in a corner, crouched over and with his fists tight in sympathy, making strange noises. Poor Merlie Ryan had his mouth so wide open that a fly buzzed into it, and was swallowed before Merlie realized what had happened. And Cousin Lymon—he was worth watching. The hunchback still stood on the counter, so that he was raised up above everyone else in the café. He had his hands on his hips, his big head thrust forward, and his little legs bent so that the knees jutted outward. The excitement had made him break out in a rash, and his pale mouth shivered.

Perhaps it was half an hour before the course of the fight shifted. Hundreds of blows had been exchanged, and there was still a deadlock. Then suddenly Marvin Macy managed to catch hold of Miss Amelia's left arm and pinion it behind her back. She struggled and got a grasp around his waist; the real fight was now begun. Wrestling is the natural way of fighting in this county—as boxing is too quick and requires much thinking and concentration. And now that Miss Amelia and Marvin were locked in a hold together the crowd came out of its daze and pressed in closer. For a while the fighters grappled muscle to muscle, their hipbones braced against each other. Backward and forward, from side to side, they swayed in this way. Marvin Macy still had not sweated, but Miss Amelia's overalls were drenched and so much sweat had trickled down her legs that she left wet foot-prints on the floor. Now the test had come, and in these moments of terrible effort, it was Miss Amelia who was the stronger. Marvin Macy was greased and slippery, tricky to grasp, but she was stronger. Gradually she bent him over backward, and inch by inch she forced him to the floor. It was a terrible thing to watch and their deep hoarse breaths were the only sound in the café. At last she had him down, and straddled; her strong big hands were on his throat.

But at that instant, just as the fight was won, a cry sounded in the café that caused a shrill bright shiver to run down the spine. And what took place has been a mystery ever since. The whole town was there to testify what happened, but there were those who doubted their own eyesight. For the counter on which Cousin Lymon stood was at least twelve feet from the fighters in the center of the café. Yet at the instant Miss Amelia grasped the throat of Marvin Macy the hunchback sprang forward and sailed through the air as though he had grown hawk wings. He landed on the broad strong back of Miss Amelia and clutched at her neck with his clawed little fingers.

The rest is confusion. Miss Amelia was beaten before the crowd could come to their senses. Because of the hunchback the fight was won by Marvin Macy, and at the end Miss Amelia lay sprawled on the floor, her arms flung outward and motionless. Marvin Macy stood over her, his face somewhat popeyed, but smiling his old half-mouthed smile. And the hunchback, he had suddenly disappeared. Perhaps he was frightened about what he had done, or maybe he was so delighted that he wanted to glory with himself alone—at any rate he slipped out of the café and crawled under the back steps. Someone poured water on Miss Amelia, and after a time she got up slowly and dragged herself into her office. Through the open door the crowd could see her sitting at her desk, her head in the crook of her arm, and she was sobbing with the last of her grating, winded breath. Once she gathered her right fist together and knocked it three times on the top of her office desk, then her hand opened feebly and lay palm upward and still. Stumpy MacPhail stepped forward and closed the door.

The crowd was quiet, and one by one the people left the café. Mules were waked up and untied, automobiles cranked, and the three boys from Society City roamed off down the road on foot. This was not a fight to hash over and talk about afterward; people went home and pulled the covers up over their heads. The town was dark, except for the premises of Miss Amelia, but every room was lighted there the whole night long.

Marvin Macy and the hunchback must have left the town an hour or so before daylight. And before they went away this is what they did:

They unlocked the private cabinet of curios and took everything in it.

They broke the mechanical piano.

They carved terrible words on the café tables.

They found the watch that opened in the back to show a picture of a waterfall and took that also.

They poured a gallon of sorghum syrup all over the kitchen floor and smashed the jars of preserves.

They went out in the swamp and completely wrecked the still, ruining the big new condenser and the cooler, and setting fire to the shack itself.

They fixed a dish of Miss Amelia's favorite food, grits with sausage, seasoned it with enough poison to kill off the county, and placed this dish temptingly on the café counter.

They did everything ruinous they could think of without actually breaking into the office where Miss Amelia stayed the night. Then they went off together, the two of them.

That was how Miss Amelia was left alone in the town. The people would have helped her if they had known how, as people in this town will as often as not be kindly if they have a chance. Several housewives nosed around with brooms and offered to clear up the wreck. But Miss Amelia only looked at them with lost crossed eyes and shook her head. Stumpy MacPhail came in on the third day to buy a plug of Queenie tobacco, and Miss Amelia said the price was one dollar. Everything in the café had suddenly risen in price to be worth one dollar. And what sort of a café is that? Also, she changed very queerly as a doctor. In all the years before she had been much more popular than the Cheehaw doctor. She had never monkeyed with a patient's soul, taking away from him such real necessities as liquor, tobacco, and so forth. Once in a great while she might carefully warn a patient never to eat fried watermelon or some such dish it had never occurred to a person to want in the first place. Now all this wise doctoring was over. She told one-half of her patients that they were going to die outright, and to the remaining half she recommended cures so far-fetched and agonizing that no one in his right mind would consider them for a moment.

Miss Amelia let her hair grow ragged, and it was turning gray. Her face lengthened, and the great muscles of her body shrank until she was thin as old maids are thin when they go crazy. And those gray eyes—slowly day by day they were more crossed, and it was as though they sought each other out to exchange a little glance of grief and lonely recognition. She was not pleasant to listen to; her tongue had sharpened terribly.

When anyone mentioned the hunchback she would say only this: 'Ho! if I could lay hand to him I would rip out his gizzard and throw it to the cat!' But it was not so much the words that were terrible, but the voice in which they were said. Her voice had lost its old vigor; there was none of the ring of vengeance it used to have when she would mention 'that loom-fixer I was married to,' or some other enemy. Her voice was broken, soft, and sad as the wheezy whine of the church pump-organ.

For three years she sat out on the front steps every night, alone and silent, looking down the road and waiting. But the hunchback never returned. There were rumors that Marvin Macy used him to climb into windows and steal, and other rumors that Marvin Macy had sold him into a side show. But both these reports were traced back to Merlie Ryan. Nothing true was ever heard of him. It was in the fourth year that Miss Amelia hired a Cheehaw carpenter and had him board up the premises, and there in those closed rooms she has remained ever since.

Yes, the town is dreary. On August afternoons the road is empty, white with dust, and the sky above is bright as glass. Nothing moves—there are no children's voices, only the hum of the mill. The peach trees seem to grow more crooked every summer, and the leaves are dull gray and of a sickly delicacy. The house of Miss Amelia leans so much to the right that it is now only a question of time when it will collapse completely, and people are careful not to walk around the yard. There is no good liquor to be bought in the town; the nearest still is eight miles away, and the liquor is such that those who drink it grow warts on their livers the size of goobers, and dream themselves into a dangerous inward world. There is absolutely nothing to do in the town. Walk around the millpond, stand kicking at a rotten stump, figure out what you can do with the old wagon wheel by the side of the road near the church. The soul rots with boredom. You might as well go down to the Forks Falls highway and listen to the chain gang.

THE TWELVE MORTAL MEN

The Forks Falls highway is three miles from the town, and it is here the chain gang has been working. The road is of macadam, and the county decided to patch up the rough places and widen it at a certain dangerous place. The gang is made up of twelve men, all wearing black and white striped prison suits, and chained at the ankles. There is a guard, with a gun, his eyes drawn to red slits by the glare. The gang works all the day long, arriving huddled in the prison cart soon after daybreak, and being driven off again in the gray August twilight. All day there is the sound of the picks striking into the clay earth, hard sunlight, the smell of sweat. And every day there is music. One dark voice will start a phrase, half-sung, and like a question. And after a moment another voice will join in, soon the whole gang will be singing. The voices are dark in the golden glare, the music intricately blended, both somber and joyful. The music will swell until at last it seems that the sound does not come from the twelve men on the gang, but from the earth itself, or the wide sky. It is music that causes the heart to broaden and the listener to grow cold with ecstasy and fright. Then slowly the music will sink down until at last there remains one lonely voice, then a great hoarse breath, the sun, the sound of the picks in the silence.

And what kind of gang is this that can make such music? Just twelve mortal men, seven of them black and five of them white boys from this county. Just twelve mortal men who are together.

TOPICS FOR PAPERS AND DISCUSSION

1. *Amelia.* In what ways did Amelia's motherless childhood affect her relationship with men? Explain the significance of her father calling her "Little," and her finding an acorn when "Big Papa" died. Relate her nickname to the dwarf. Amelia inherited the store from Big Papa, but established the café because of Lymon. What does this development reveal psychologically? What light does her fantastic wedding and its aftermath throw on her emotional life? Why didn't she throw Marvin out of the café when he returned? Examine Amelia's various roles and the facets of her character. Lymon provokes and satisfies what unconscious impulses, desires, or needs of Amelia's personality?

2. *Characters as archetypes.* Read "Approaching the Unconscious" and "The Process of Individuation" in C. G. Jung's *Man and His Symbols* for help in understanding the characters psychologically, mythologically, and archetypally. What sense is to be made of Marvin as Amelia's "animus" (her psychological alter ego)? What caused the triumph of the negative aspect, and who is responsible? Show how the "trickster" (Lymon) functions as Amelia's "shadow" (repressed antisocial impulses, the "dark half of the personality"). Since the animus and shadow have a natural affinity for each other, what do they show us about Amelia's psyche?

3. *Minor characters.* Minor characters are used to fill out, give depth to, and play variations on the main ideas of the novel. How do Henry Macy, Merlie Ryan, Mary Hale, Stumpy MacPhail, and his wife define the town's relationship to Amelia? Examine the significance of the chain reaction when the town suspects her of murder. Consider also the minor characters' natural gravitation to the café, and their reactions to the impending fight and its aftermath. Enumerate the ways they are helpful in creating a believable atmosphere in which such extraordinary events

take place. Even though they may be one-dimensional, how do they help authenticate the three major characters?

4. *Grotesquerie.* One critic called the characters "metaphors and grotesques." Discuss the meaning of that phrase. How does the grotesque serve as metaphor? What thematic and artistic effects are achieved and what ends are served by the novel's use of the grotesque? Can the term *grotesquerie* be applied to the community and the environment as well? The danger involved in using the grotesque as a means of presenting and interpreting character is loss of verisimilitude. Does this loss take place? How? If not, why not? Define the particular qualities of the McCullers novel that prevent her characters from becoming mere freaks.

5. *The love theme.* Reread the passage one-third through the novel which begins, "First of all, love is a joint experience between two persons." Try first to clarify McCullers' concept of love. What does it include and exclude? Define what she means by love as it is worked out with her three principal characters. Then apply her concept to other relationships among the good and bad people. What modifications in her concept of love would be needed to include all relationships in the novel? The end necessitates what enlargement of the concept? Also, consider the relationship of betrayal as a thematic subject.

6. *Communication.* The principal characters and the citizens are remarkably silent, yet they communicate without words. How? Point out and examine compulsions, actions, gestures, glances, etc., and show what they communicate. When people do speak, what is the quality of their language? Compare Amelia's responses to Lymon's demands and to Marvin's playing and singing. Explain the connection between the thematic subjects of love and communication. Study the final section, "The Twelve Mortal Men," closely from this point of view to determine what major theme the "dark voices" communicate in their singing.

7. *A social novel.* What features make the novel a candidate for sociological interpretation? Consider the time and place, the class structure, the town government, homes, living conditions, educational facilities, and industry. Are the workers open to exploitation? Determine to what extent social conditions are the cause of the grotesqueries of character. What do the townspeople do for recreation? In what way do Amelia's store and still figure sociologically? Try to make a case for a sociological reading of the novel while preserving the rather special lyrical qualities of McCullers' work.

8. *Private need and communal responsibility.* The townspeople regard Amelia in a special way as a special being. How is her character molded by their needs and beliefs? Determine what community needs are answered by actions like healing, making whiskey, running a store and café. Ascertain the unconscious ritual needs that lie behind their

suspecting Amelia of murder, seeking out her presence, buying her goods, and on occasion engaging her in boxing and wrestling. What need is answered by their hesitation when Lymon throws himself on Amelia's back during the fight? Why does the town "cave in" when she shuts herself away?

9. *Isolation.* The town is isolated from the rest of the world, even from Society City; Amelia is set apart from the other characters; Marvin has been in prison; the members of the chain gang have been removed from society, and so on. How do isolation and individual loneliness relate to McCullers' vision of her world? What is the effect of various forms of love (and McCullers' love doctrine) on isolation and loneliness? Explain how isolation and loneliness are ameliorated by the individual, the chain gang, and the town. What, then, is significant of our final view of Miss Amelia?

10. *The store and café.* Psychologists have suggested that buildings may be symbols for human personality. Before the advent of Lymon, the store reveals what aspects of Amelia's personality? What of the community's? The changes that are undergone from store to café meet what needs of the community, and what psychological transformation takes place in Amelia? Consider the "unchanged" office and three rooms on the second floor. Examine the symbolic overtones of Lymon's painting the front porch green and the final condition of "the house of Miss Amelia." Consider thematic polarities like creation-destruction and prosperity-decay.

11. *The ballad form.* Look up the typical features of folk and literary ballads and compare them with the novel's form. Point out those characteristics of the ballad that help us understand the unique qualities of McCullers' story. Analyze her presentation of character, action, and idea; time, place, and scene. In what manner does she deviate from the technique and subject matter of the ballad, and to what ends? Comment on this assessment: "The style . . . transforms this eccentric tale into something as universal as the old ballads about love and dread, madness and revenge."

12. *Ritual combat.* Analyze the fight between Amelia and Marvin carefully for legendary and mythological associations. Consider the preparations, the symbolic involvement of the town and Society City, the townspeople's miming the fight, the bloody hawk, Lymon flying "through the air as though he had grown hawk wings," and one of the bystanders ritualistically closing the event. Explain McCullers' special use of the word "mystery" in this context, and her presentation of the fight so that the actual blows are minimized. What symbolic overtones involving combatants and citizens are suggested?

13. *Symbolism.* Assuming that the novel is densely symbolic, comment on the following: color (red and blue, black and white), numbers (it took

four days for Marvin to sign over his property to Amelia and four years for the store to become a café, the chain gang is three miles from town, Marvin returns after six years, twelve mortal men are chained together, etc.), clothing (as attitudes or aspects of character), food, whiskey, medicine, snuff box, kidney stones, acorn, hawk, white dust, paper roses, musical instruments (music, songs), weather (unseasonable heat, phenomenal snow), and landscape, such as the swamp.

14. *Myth and literature.* Myth in literature may serve therapeutic ends. In *Rites and Symbols of Initiation,* Mircea Eliade observes that myth, ritual, and "initiatory scenarios . . . are the expression of a psychodrama that answers a deep need in the human being. Everyone wants to experience certain perilous situations, to confront exceptional ordeals, to make his way into the Other World—and he experiences all this, on the level of his imaginative life, by reading fairy tales and by dreaming." With the novel in mind, respond to the validity of this statement, taking into account conscious and unconscious needs of people in general.

15. *"Twelve Mortal Men."* The final section concerning the chain gang might appear gratuitous or a mere lyrical flight. Yet how is it related to the main actions and themes? How does it comment on or serve as metaphor for the rest of the novel? Take the following into account: blacks and whites as prisoners suffering guilt, men linked together, music uniting three different areas, the last word of the novel. Discuss the hope this coda offers mankind. What do you make of the work being done on the symbolic road, patching "the rough places" and widening a "dangerous place," the "hard sunlight" and "golden glare," the special effect on the listener of the dark voices?

Slaughterhouse-Five

or, The Children's Crusade

A Duty-Dance with Death

KURT VONNEGUT, JR.

A fourth-generation German-American
now living in easy circumstances
on Cape Cod
(and smoking too much),
who, as an American infantry scout
hors de combat,
as a prisoner of war,
witnessed the fire-bombing
of Dresden, Germany,
"The Florence of the Elbe,"
a long time ago,
and survived to tell the tale.
This is a novel
somewhat in the telegraphic schizophrenic
manner of tales
of the planet Tralfamadore,
where the flying saucers
come from.
Peace.

For Mary O'Hare and Gerhard Müller

The cattle are lowing,
The Baby awakes.
But the little Lord Jesus
No crying He makes.

1

All this happened, more or less. The war parts, anyway, are pretty much true. One guy I knew really *was* shot in Dresden for taking a teapot that wasn't his. Another guy I knew really *did* threaten to have his personal enemies killed by hired gunmen after the war. And so on. I've changed all the names.

I really *did* go back to Dresden with Guggenheim money (God love it) in 1967. It looked a lot like Dayton, Ohio, more open spaces than Dayton has. There must be tons of human bone meal in the ground.

I went back there with an old war buddy, Bernard V. O'Hare, and we made friends with a cab driver, who took us to the slaughterhouse where we had been locked up at night as prisoners of war. His name was Gerhard Müller. He told us that he was a prisoner of the Americans for a while. We asked him how it was to live under Communism, and he said that it was terrible at first, because everybody had to work so hard, and because there wasn't much shelter or food or clothing. But things were much better now. He had a pleasant little apartment, and his daughter was getting an excellent education. His mother was incinerated in the Dresden fire-storm. So it goes.

He sent O'Hare a postcard at Christmastime, and here is what it said:

"I wish you and your family also as to your friend Merry Christmas and a happy New Year and I hope that we'll meet again in a world of peace and freedom in the taxi cab if the accident will."

I like that very much: "If the accident will."

I would hate to tell you what this lousy little book cost me in money and anxiety and time. When I got home from the Second World War twenty-three years ago, I thought it would be easy for me to write about the destruction of Dresden, since all I would have to do would be to report what I had seen. And I thought, too, that it would be a masterpiece or at least make me a lot of money, since the subject was so big.

But not many words about Dresden came from my mind then—not enough of them to make a book, anyway. And not many words come now, either, when I have become an old fart with his memories and his Pall Malls, with his sons full grown.

I think of how useless the Dresden part of my memory has been, and yet how tempting Dresden has been to write about, and I am reminded of the famous limerick:

There was a young man from Stamboul,
Who soliloquized thus to his tool:
"You took all my wealth
And you ruined my health,
And now you won't *pee,* you old fool."

And I'm reminded, too, of the song that goes:

My name is Yon Yonson,
I work in Wisconsin,
I work in a lumbermill there.
The people I meet when I walk down the street,
They say, "What's your name?"
And I say,
"My name is Yon Yonson,
I work in Wisconsin . . ."

And so on to infinity.

Over the years, people I've met have often asked me what I'm working on, and I've usually replied that the main thing was a book about Dresden.

I said that to Harrison Starr, the movie-maker, one time, and he raised his eyebrows and inquired, "Is it an anti-war book?"

"Yes," I said. "I guess."

"You know what I say to people when I hear they're writing anti-war books?"

"No. What *do* you say, Harrison Starr?"

"I say, 'Why don't you write an anti-*glacier* book instead?'"

What he meant, of course, was that there would always be wars, that they were as easy to stop as glaciers. I believe that, too.

And, even if wars didn't keep coming like glaciers, there would still be plain old death.

When I was somewhat younger, working on my famous Dresden book, I asked an old war buddy named Bernard V. O'Hare if I could come to see him. He was a district attorney in Pennsylvania. I was a writer on Cape Cod. We had been privates in the war, infantry scouts. We had never expected to make any money after the war, but we were doing quite well.

I had the Bell Telephone Company find him for me. They are wonderful that way. I have this disease late at night sometimes, involving alcohol and the telephone. I get drunk, and I drive my wife away with a breath like mustard gas and roses. And then, speaking gravely and elegantly into the telephone, I ask the telephone operators to connect me with this friend or that one, from whom I have not heard in years.

I got O'Hare on the line in this way. He is short and I am tall. We were Mutt and Jeff in the war. We were captured together in the war. I told him who I was on the telephone. He had no trouble believing it. He was up. He was reading. Everybody else in his house was asleep.

"Listen—" I said, "I'm writing this book about Dresden. I'd like some help remembering stuff. I wonder if I could come down and see you, and we could drink and talk and remember."

He was unenthusiastic. He said he couldn't remember much. He told me, though, to come ahead.

"I think the climax of the book will be the execution of poor old Edgar Derby," I said. "The irony is *so* great. A whole city gets burned down, and thousands and thousands of people are killed. And then this one American foot soldier is arrested in the ruins for taking a teapot. And he's given a regular trial, and then he's shot by a firing squad."

"Um," said O'Hare.

"Don't you think that's really where the climax should come?"

"I don't know anything about it," he said. "That's your trade, not mine."

As a trafficker in climaxes and thrills and characterization and wonderful dialogue and suspense and confrontations, I had outlined the Dresden story many times. The best outline I ever made, or anyway the prettiest one, was on the back of a roll of wallpaper.

I used my daughter's crayons, a different color for each main character. One end of the wallpaper was the beginning of the story, and the other end was the end, and then there was all that middle part, which was the middle. And the blue line met the red line and then the yellow line, and the yellow line stopped because the character represented by the yellow line was dead. And so on. The destruction of Dresden was represented by a vertical band of orange cross-hatching, and all the lines that were still alive passed through it, came out the other side.

The end, where all the lines stopped, was a beetfield on the Elbe, outside of Halle. The rain was coming down. The war in Europe had been over for a couple of weeks. We were formed in ranks, with Russian soldiers guarding us—Englishmen, Americans, Dutchmen, Belgians, Frenchmen, Canadians, South Africans, New Zealanders, Australians, thousands of us about to stop being prisoners of war.

And on the other side of the field were thousands of Russians and Poles and Yugoslavians and so on guarded by American soldiers. An exchange was made there in the rain—one for one. O'Hare and I climbed into the back of an American truck with a lot of others. O'Hare didn't have any souvenirs. Almost everybody else did. I had a ceremonial Luftwaffe saber, still do. The rabid little American I call Paul Lazzaro in this book had about a quart of diamonds and emeralds and rubies and so on. He had taken these from dead people in the cellars of Dresden. So it goes.

An idiotic Englishman, who had lost all his teeth somewhere, had his souvenir in a canvas bag. The bag was resting on my insteps. He would peek into the bag every now and then, and he would roll his eyes and swivel his scrawny neck, trying to catch people looking covetously at his bag. And he would bounce the bag on my insteps.

I thought this bouncing was accidental. But I was mistaken. He *had* to show somebody what was in the bag, and he had decided he could trust me. He caught my eye, winked, opened the bag. There was a plaster model of the Eiffel Tower in there. It was painted gold. It had a clock in it.

"There's a smashin' thing," he said.

And we were flown to a rest camp in France, where we were fed chocolate malted milkshakes and other rich foods until we were all covered with baby fat. Then we were sent home, and I married a pretty girl who was covered with baby fat, too.

And we had babies.

And they're all grown up now, and I'm an old fart with his memories and his Pall Malls. My name is Yon Yonson, I work in Wisconsin, I work in a lumbermill there.

Sometimes I try to call up old girl friends on the telephone late at night, after my wife has gone to bed. "Operator, I wonder if you could give me the number of a Mrs. So-and-So. I think she lives at such-and-such."

"I'm sorry, sir. There is no such listing."

"Thanks, Operator. Thanks just the same."

And I let the dog out, or I let him in, and we talk some. I let him know I like him, and he lets me know he likes me. He doesn't mind the smell of mustard gas and roses.

"You're all right, Sandy," I'll say to the dog. "You know that, Sandy? You're O.K."

Sometimes I'll turn on the radio and listen to a talk program from Boston or New York. I can't stand recorded music if I've been drinking a good deal.

Sooner or later I go to bed, and my wife asks me what time it is. She always has to know the time. Sometimes I don't know, and I say, "Search *me.*"

I think about my education sometimes. I went to the University of Chicago for a while after the Second World War. I was a student in the Department of Anthropology. At that time, they were teaching that there was absolutely no difference between anybody. They may be teaching that still.

Another thing they taught was that nobody was ridiculous or bad or disgusting. Shortly before my father died, he said to me, "You know—you never wrote a story with a villain in it."

I told him that was one of the things I learned in college after the war.

While I was studying to be an anthropologist, I was also working as a police reporter for the famous Chicago City News Bureau for twenty-eight dollars a week. One time they switched me from the night shift to the day shift, so I worked sixteen hours straight. We were supported by all the newspapers in town, and the AP and the UP and all that. And we would cover the courts and the police stations and the Fire Department and the Coast Guard out on Lake Michigan and all that. We were connected to the institutions that suppported us by means of pneumatic tubes which ran under the streets of Chicago.

Reporters would telephone in stories to writers wearing headphones, and the writers would stencil the stories on mimeograph sheets. The stories were mimeographed and stuffed into the brass and velvet cartridges which the pneumatic tubes ate. The very toughest reporters and writers were women who had taken over the jobs of men who'd gone to war.

And the first story I covered I had to dictate over the telephone to one of those beastly girls. It was about a young veteran who had taken a job running an old-fashioned elevator in an office building. The elevator door on the first floor was ornamental iron lace. Iron ivy snaked in and out of the holes. There was an iron twig with two iron lovebirds perched upon it.

This veteran decided to take his car into the basement, and he closed the door and started down, but his wedding ring was caught in all the ornaments. So he was hoisted into the air and the floor of the car went down, dropped out from under him, and the top of the car squashed him. So it goes.

So I phoned this in, and the woman who was going to cut the stencil asked me, "What did his wife say?"

"She doesn't know yet," I said. "It just happened."

"Call her up and get a statement."

"What?"

"Tell her you're Captain Finn of the Police Department. Say you have some sad news. Give her the news, and see what she says."

So I did. She said about what you would expect her to say. There was a baby. And so on.

When I got back to the office, the woman writer asked me, just for her own information, what the squashed guy had looked like when he was squashed.

I told her.

"Did it bother you?" she said. She was eating a Three Musketeers Candy Bar.

"Heck no, Nancy," I said. "I've seen lots worse than that in the war."

Even then I was supposedly writing a book about Dresden. It wasn't a famous air raid back then in America. Not many Americans knew how much worse it had been than Hiroshima, for instance. I didn't know that, either. There hadn't been much publicity.

I happened to tell a University of Chicago professor at a cocktail party about the raid as I had seen it, about the book I would write. He was a member of a thing called The Committee on Social Thought. And he told me about the concentration camps, and about how the Germans had made soap and candles out of the fat of dead Jews and so on.

All I could say was, "I know, I know. I *know.*"

World War Two had certainly made everybody very tough. And I became a public relations man for General Electric in Schenectady, New York, and a volunteer fireman in the village of Alplaus, where I bought my first home. My boss there was one of the toughest guys I ever hope to meet. He had been a lieutenant colonel in public relations in Baltimore. While I was in Schenectady he joined the Dutch Reformed Church, which is a very tough church, indeed.

He used to ask me sneeringly sometimes why I hadn't been an officer, as though I'd done something wrong.

My wife and I had lost our baby fat. Those were our scrawny years. We had a lot of scrawny veterans and their scrawny wives for friends. The nicest veterans in Schenectady, I thought, the kindest and funniest ones, the ones who hated war the most, were the ones who'd really fought.

I wrote the Air Force back then, asking for details about the raid on Dresden, who ordered it, how many planes did it, why they did it, what desirable results there had been and so on. I was answered by a man who, like myself, was in public relations. He said that he was sorry, but that the information was top secret still.

I read the letter out loud to my wife, and I said, "Secret? My God—from *whom?*"

We were United World Federalists back then. I don't know what we are now. Telephoners, I guess. We telephone a lot—or *I* do, anyway, late at night.

A couple of weeks after I telephoned my old war buddy, Bernard V. O'Hare, I really *did* go to see him. That must have been in 1964 or so—whatever the last year was for the New York World's Fair. *Eheu, fugaces labuntur anni.* My name is Yon Yonson. There was a young man from Stamboul.

I took two little girls with me, my daughter, Nanny, and her best friend, Allison Mitchell. They had never been off Cape Cod before. When we saw a river, we had to stop so they could stand by it and think about it for a while. They had never seen water in that long and narrow, unsalted form before. The river was the Hudson. There were carp in there and we saw them. They were as big as atomic submarines.

We saw waterfalls, too, streams jumping off cliffs into the valley of the Delaware. There were lots of things to stop and see—and then it was time to go, always time to go. The little girls were wearing white party dresses and black party shoes, so strangers would know at once how nice they were. "Time to go, girls," I'd say. And we would go.

And the sun went down, and we had supper in an Italian place, and then I knocked on the front door of the beautiful stone house of Bernard V. O'Hare. I was carrying a bottle of Irish whiskey like a dinner bell.

I met his nice wife, Mary, to whom I dedicate this book. I dedicate it to Gerhard Müller, the Dresden taxi driver, too. Mary O'Hare is a trained nurse, which is a lovely thing for a woman to be.

Mary admired the two little girls I'd brought, mixed them in with her own children, sent them all upstairs to play games and watch television. It was only after the children were gone that I sensed that Mary didn't like me or didn't like *something* about the night. She was polite but chilly.

"It's a nice cozy house you have here," I said, and it really was.

"I've fixed up a place where you can talk and not be bothered," she said.

"Good," I said, and I imagined two leather chairs near a fire in a paneled room, where two old soldiers could drink and talk. But she took us into the kitchen. She had put two straight-backed chairs at a kitchen table with a white porcelain top. That table top was screaming with reflected light from a two-hundred-watt bulb overhead. Mary had prepared an operating room. She put only one glass on it, which was for me. She explained that O'Hare couldn't drink the hard stuff since the war.

So we sat down. O'Hare was embarrassed, but he wouldn't tell me what was wrong. I couldn't imagine what it was about me that could burn up Mary so. I was a family man. I'd been married only once. I wasn't a drunk. I hadn't done her husband any dirt in the war.

She fixed herself a Coca-Cola, made a lot of noise banging the ice-cube tray in the stainless steel sink. Then she went into another part of the house. But she wouldn't sit still. She was moving all over the house, opening and shutting doors, even moving furniture around to work off anger.

I asked O'Hare what I'd said or done to make her act that way.

"It's all right," he said. "Don't worry about it. It doesn't have anything to do with you." That was kind of him. He was lying. It had everything to do with me.

So we tried to ignore Mary and remember the war. I took a couple of belts of the booze I'd brought. We would chuckle or grin sometimes, as though war stories were coming back, but neither one of us could remember anything good. O'Hare remembered one guy who got into a lot of wine in Dresden, before it was bombed, and we had to take him home in a wheelbarrow. It wasn't much to write a book about. I remembered two Russian soldiers who had looted a clock factory. They had a horse-drawn wagon full of clocks. They were happy and drunk. They were smoking huge cigarettes they had rolled in newspaper.

That was about *it* for memories, and Mary was still making noise. She finally came out in the kitchen again for another Coke. She took another tray of ice cubes from the refrigerator, banged it in the sink, even though there was already plenty of ice out.

Then she turned to me, let me see how angry she was, and that the anger was for me. She had been talking to herself, so what she said was a fragment of a much larger conversation. "You were just *babies* then!" she said.

"What?" I said.

"You were just babies in the war—like the ones upstairs!"

I nodded that this was true. We *had* been foolish virgins in the war, right at the end of childhood.

"But you're not going to write it that way, are you." This wasn't a question. It was an accusation.

"I—I don't know," I said.

"Well, *I* know," she said. "You'll pretend you were men instead of babies, and you'll be played in the movies by Frank Sinatra and John Wayne or some of those other glamorous, war-loving, dirty old men.

And war will look just wonderful, so we'll have a lot more of them. And they'll be fought by babies like the babies upstairs."

So then I understood. It was war that made her so angry. She didn't want her babies or anybody else's babies killed in wars. And she thought wars were partly encouraged by books and movies.

So I held up my right hand and I made her a promise: "Mary," I said, "I don't think this book of mine is ever going to be finished. I must have written five thousand pages by now, and thrown them all away. If I ever do finish it, though, I give you my word of honor: there won't be a part for Frank Sinatra or John Wayne.

"I tell you what," I said, "I'll call it 'The Children's Crusade.'"

She was my friend after that.

O'Hare and I gave up on remembering, went into the living room, talked about other things. We became curious about the real Children's Crusade, so O'Hare looked it up in a book he had, *Extraordinary Popular Delusions and the Madness of Crowds,* by Charles Mackay, LL. D. It was first published in London in 1841.

Mackay had a low opinion of *all* Crusades. The Children's Crusade struck him as only slightly more sordid than the ten Crusades for grown-ups. O'Hare read this handsome passage out loud:

History in her solemn page informs us that the crusaders were but ignorant and savage men, that their motives were those of bigotry unmitigated, and that their pathway was one of blood and tears. Romance, on the other hand, dilates upon their piety and heroism, and portrays, in her most glowing and impassioned hues, their virtue and magnanimity, the imperishable honor they acquired for themselves, and the great services they rendered to Christianity.

And then O'Hare read this: *Now what was the grand result of all these struggles? Europe expended millions of her treasures, and the blood of two million of her people; and a handful of quarrelsome knights retained possession of Palestine for about one hundred years!*

Mackay told us that the Children's Crusade started in 1213, when two monks got the idea of raising armies of children in Germany and France, and selling them in North Africa as slaves. Thirty thousand children volunteered, thinking they were going to Palestine. *They were no doubt idle and deserted children who generally swarm in great cities, nurtured on vice and daring,* said Mackay, *and ready for anything.*

Pope Innocent the Third thought they were going to Palestine, too, and he was thrilled. "These children are awake while we are asleep!" he said.

Most of the children were shipped out of Marseilles, and about half of them drowned in shipwrecks. The other half got to North Africa where they were sold.

Through a misunderstanding, some children reported for duty at Genoa, where no slave ships were waiting. They were fed and sheltered and questioned kindly by good people there—then given a little money and a lot of advice and sent back home.

"Hooray for the good people of Genoa," said Mary O'Hare.

I slept that night in one of the children's bedrooms. O'Hare had put a book for me on the bedside table. It was *Dresden, History, Stage and Gallery,* by Mary Endell. It was published in 1908, and its introduction began:

It is hoped that this little book will make itself useful. It attempts to give to an English-reading public a bird's-eye view of how Dresden came to look as it does, architecturally; of how it expanded musically, through the genius of a few men, to its present bloom; and it calls attention to certain permanent landmarks in art that make its Gallery the resort of those seeking lasting impressions.

I read some history further on:

Now, in 1760, Dresden underwent siege by the Prussians. On the fifteenth of July began the cannonade. The Picture-Gallery took fire. Many of the paintings had been transported to the Königstein, but some were seriously injured by splinters of bombshells,—notably Francia's "Baptism of Christ." Furthermore, the stately Kreuzkirche tower, from which the enemy's movements had been watched day and night, stood in flames. It later succumbed. In sturdy contrast with the pitiful fate of the Kreuzkirche, stood the Frauenkirche, from the curves of whose stone dome the Prussian bombs rebounded like rain. Friederich was obliged finally to give up the siege, because he learned of the fall of Glatz, the critical point of his new conquests. "We must be off to Silesia, so that we do not lose everything."

The devastation of Dresden was boundless. When Goethe as a young student visited the city, he still found sad ruins: "Von der Kuppel der Frauenkirche sah ich diese leidigen Trümmer zwischen die schöne städtische Ordnung hineingesät; da rühmte mir der Küster die Kunst des Baumeisters, welcher Kirche und Kuppel auf einen so unerwünschten Fall schon eingerichtet und bombenfest erbaut hatte.

Der gute Sakristan deutete mir alsdann auf Ruinene nach allen Seiten und sagte bedenklich lakonisch: Das hat der Feind gethan!"

The two little girls and I crossed the Delaware River where George Washington had crossed it, the next morning. We went to the New York World's Fair, saw what the past had been like, according to the Ford Motor Car Company and Walt Disney, saw what the future would be like, according to General Motors.

And I asked myself about the present: how wide it was, how deep it was, how much was mine to keep.

I taught creative writing in the famous Writers Workshop at the University of Iowa for a couple of years after that. I got into some perfectly beautiful trouble, got out of it again. I taught in the afternoons. In the mornings I wrote. I was not to be disturbed. I was working on my famous book about Dresden.

And somewhere in there a nice man named Seymour Lawrence gave me a three-book contract, and I said, "O.K., the first of the three will be my famous book about Dresden."

The friends of Seymour Lawrence call him "Sam." And I say to Sam now: "Sam—here's the book."

It is so short and jumbled and jangled, Sam, because there is nothing intelligent to say about a massacre. Everybody is supposed to be dead, to never say anything or want anything ever again. Everything is supposed to be very quiet after a massacre, and it always is, except for the birds.

And what do the birds say? All there is to say about a massacre, things like *"Poo-tee-weet?"*

I have told my sons that they are not under any circumstances to take part in massacres, and that the news of massacres of enemies is not to fill them with satisfaction or glee.

I have also told them not to work for companies which make massacre machinery, and to express contempt for people who think we need machinery like that.

As I've said: I recently went back to Dresden with my friend O'Hare. We had a million laughs in Hamburg and West Berlin and East Berlin and Vienna and Salzburg and Helsinki, and in Leningrad, too. It was very good for me, because I saw a lot of authentic backgrounds for made-up stories which I will write later on. One of them will be "Russian Baroque" and another will be "No Kissing" and another will be "Dollar Bar" and another will be "If the Accident Will," and so on.

And so on.

There was a Lufthansa plane that was supposed to fly from Philadelphia to Boston to Frankfurt. O'Hare was supposed to get on in Philadelphia and I was supposed to get on in Boston, and off we'd go. But Boston was socked in, so the plane flew straight to Frankfurt from Philadelphia. And I became a non-person in the Boston fog, and Lufthansa put me in a limousine with some other non-persons and sent us to a motel for a non-night.

The time would not pass. Somebody was playing with the clocks, and not only with the electric clocks, but the wind-up kind, too. The second hand on my watch would twitch once, and a year would pass, and then it would twitch again.

There was nothing I could do about it. As an Earthling, I had to believe whatever clocks said—and calendars.

I had two books with me, which I'd meant to read on the plane. One was *Words for the Wind,* by Theodore Roethke, and this is what I found in there:

I wake to sleep, and take my waking slow.
I feel my fate in what I cannot fear.
I learn by going where I have to go.

My other book was Erika Ostrovsky's *Céline and His Vision.* Céline was a brave French soldier in the First World War—until his skull was cracked. After that he couldn't sleep, and there were noises in his head. He became a doctor, and he treated poor people in the daytime, and he wrote grotesque novels all night. No art is possible without a dance with death, he wrote.

The truth is death, he wrote. *I've fought nicely against it as long as I could . . . danced with it, festooned it, waltzed it around . . . decorated it with streamers, titillated it . . .*

Time obsessed him. Miss Ostrovsky reminded me of the amazing scene in *Death on the Installment Plan* where Céline wants to stop the bustling of a street crowd. He screams on paper, *Make them stop . . . don't let them move anymore at all . . . There, make them freeze . . . once and for all! . . . So that they won't disappear anymore!*

I looked through the Gideon Bible in my motel room for tales of great destruction. *The sun was risen upon the Earth when Lot entered into Zo-ar,* I read. *Then the Lord rained upon Sodom and upon Gomorrah brimstone and fire from the Lord out of Heaven; and He overthrew those cities, and all the plain, and all the inhabitants of the cities, and that which grew upon the ground.*

So it goes.

Those were vile people in both those cities, as is well known. The world was better off without them.

And Lot's wife, of course, was told not to look back where all those people and their homes had been. But she *did* look back, and I love her for that, because it was so human.

So she was turned to a pillar of salt. So it goes.

People aren't supposed to look back. I'm certainly not going to do it anymore.

I've finished my war book now. The next one I write is going to be fun.

This one is a failure, and had to be, since it was written by a pillar of salt. It begins like this:

Listen:

Billy Pilgrim has come unstuck in time.

It ends like this:

Poo-tee-weet?

2

Listen:

Billy Pilgrim has come unstuck in time.

Billy has gone to sleep a senile widower and awakened on his wedding day. He has walked through a door in 1955 and come out another one in 1941. He has gone back through that door to find himself in 1963. He has seen his birth and death many times, he says, and pays random visits to all the events in between.

He says.

Billy is spastic in time, has no control over where he is going next, and the trips aren't necessarily fun. He is in a constant state of stage fright, he says, because he never knows what part of his life he is going to have to act in next.

Billy was born in 1922 in Ilium, New York, the only child of a barber there. He was a funny-looking child who became a funny-looking youth—tall and weak, and shaped like a bottle of Coca-Cola. He graduated from Ilium High School in the upper third of his class, and attended night sessions at the Ilium School of Optometry for one semester before being drafted for military service in the Second World War. His father died in a hunting accident during the war. So it goes.

Billy saw service with the infantry in Europe, and was taken prisoner by the Germans. After his honorable discharge from the Army in 1945, Billy again enrolled in the Ilium School of Optometry. During his senior year there, he became engaged to the daughter of the founder and owner of the school, and then suffered a mild nervous collapse.

He was treated in a veterans' hospital near Lake Placid, and was given shock treatments and released. He married his fiancée, finished his education, and was set up in business in Ilium by his father-in-law. Ilium is a particularly good city for optometrists because the General Forge and Foundry Company is there. Every employee is required to own a pair of safety glasses, and to wear them in areas where manufacturing is going on. GF&F has sixty-eight thousand employees in Ilium. That calls for a lot of lenses and a lot of frames.

Frames are where the money is.

Billy became rich. He had two children, Barbara and Robert. In time, his daughter Barbara married another optometrist, and Billy set him up in business. Billy's son Robert had a lot of trouble in high school, but then he joined the famous Green Berets. He straightened out, became a fine young man, and he fought in Vietnam.

Early in 1968, a group of optometrists, with Billy among them, chartered an airplane to fly them from Ilium to an international convention of optometrists in Montreal. The plane crashed on top of Sugarbush Mountain, in Vermont. Everybody was killed but Billy. So it goes.

While Billy was recuperating in a hospital in Vermont, his wife died accidentally of carbon-monoxide poisoning. So it goes.

When Billy finally got home to Ilium after the airplane crash, he was quiet for a while. He had a terrible scar across the top of his skull. He didn't resume practice. He had a housekeeper. His daughter came over almost every day.

And then, without any warning, Billy went to New York City, and got on an all-night radio program devoted to talk. He told about having come unstuck in time. He said, too, that he had been kidnapped by a flying saucer in 1967. The saucer was from the planet Tralfamadore, he said. He was taken to Tralfamadore, where he was displayed naked in a zoo, he said. He was mated there with a former Earthling movie star named Montana Wildhack.

Some night owls in Ilium heard Billy on the radio, and one of them called Billy's daughter Barbara. Barbara was upset. She and her husband went down to New York and brought Billy home. Billy insisted mildly that everything he had said on the radio was true. He said he had been kidnapped by the Tralfamadorians on the night of his daughter's wedding. He hadn't been missed, he said, because the Tralfamadorians had taken him through a time warp, so that he could be on Tralfamadore for years, and still be away from Earth for only a microsecond.

Another month went by without incident, and then Billy wrote a letter to the Ilium *News Leader,* which the paper published. It described the creatures from Tralfamadore.

The letter said that they were two feet high, and green, and shaped like plumber's friends. Their suction cups were on the ground, and their shafts, which were extremely flexible, usually pointed to the sky. At the top of each shaft was a little hand with a green eye in its palm. The creatures were friendly, and they could see in four dimensions. They pitied Earthlings for being able to see only three. They had many wonderful things to teach Earthlings, especially about time. Billy promised to tell what some of those wonderful things were in his next letter.

Billy was working on his second letter when the first letter was published. The second letter started out like this:

"The most important thing I learned on Tralfamadore was that when a person dies he only *appears* to die. He is still very much alive in the past, so it is very silly for people to cry at his funeral. All moments, past, present, and future, always have existed, always will exist. The Tralfamadorians can look at all the different moments just the way we can look at a stretch of the Rocky Mountains, for instance. They can see how permanent all the moments are, and they can look at any moment that interests them. It is just an illusion we have here on Earth that one moment follows another one, like beads on a string, and that once a moment is gone it is gone forever.

"When a Tralfamadorian sees a corpse, all he thinks is that the dead person is in bad condition in that particular moment, but that the same person is just fine in plenty of other moments. Now, when I myself hear that somebody is dead, I simply shrug and say what the Tralfamadorians say about dead people, which is 'So it goes.'"

And so on.

Billy was working on this letter in the basement rumpus room of his empty house. It was his housekeeper's day off. There was an old typewriter in the rumpus room. It was a beast. It weighed as much as a storage battery. Billy couldn't carry it very far very easily, which was why he was writing in the rumpus room instead of somewhere else.

The oil burner had quit. A mouse had eaten through the insulation of a wire leading to the thermostat. The temperature in the house was down to fifty degrees, but Billy hadn't noticed. He wasn't warmly dressed, either. He was barefoot, and still in his pajamas and a bathrobe, though it was late afternoon. His bare feet were blue and ivory.

The cockles of Billy's heart, at any rate, were glowing coals. What made them so hot was Billy's belief that he was going to comfort so many people with the truth about time. His door chimes upstairs had been ringing and ringing. It was his daughter Barbara up there, wanting in. Now she let herself in with a key, crossed the floor over his head, calling. "Father? Daddy, where are you?" And so on.

Billy didn't answer her, so she was nearly hysterical, expecting to find his corpse. And then she looked into the very last place there *was* to look—which was the rumpus room.

"Why didn't you answer me when I called?" Barbara wanted to know, standing there in the door of the rumpus room. She had the afternoon paper with her, the one in which Billy described his friends from Tralfamadore.

"I didn't *hear* you," said Billy.

The orchestration of the moment was this: Barbara was only twenty-one years old, but she thought her father was senile, even though he was only forty-six—senile because of damage to his brain in the airplane crash. She also thought that she was head of the family, since she had had to manage her mother's funeral, since she had to get a housekeeper for Billy, and all that. Also, Barbara and her husband were having to look after Billy's business interests, which were considerable, since Billy didn't seem to give a damn for business any more. All this responsibility at such an early age made her a bitchy flibbertigibbet. And Billy, meanwhile, was trying to hang onto his dignity, to persuade Barbara and everybody else that he was far from senile, that, on the contrary, he was devoting himself to a calling much higher than mere business.

He was doing nothing less now, he thought, than prescribing corrective lenses for Earthling souls. So many of those souls were lost and wretched, Billy believed, because they could not see as well as his little green friends on Tralfamadore.

"Don't lie to me, Father," said Barbara. "I know perfectly well you heard me when I called." This was a fairly pretty girl, except that she had legs like an Edwardian grand piano. Now she raised hell with him about the letter in the paper. She said he was making a laughing stock of himself and everybody associated with him.

"Father, Father, Father—" said Barbara, "what are we going to *do* with you? Are you going to force us to put you where your mother is?" Billy's mother was still alive. She was in bed in an old people's home called Pine Knoll on the edge of Ilium.

"What is it about my letter that makes you so mad?" Billy wanted to know.

"It's all just crazy. None of it's true!"

"It's all true." Billy's anger was not going to rise with hers. He never got mad at anything. He was wonderful that way.

"There is no such planet as Tralfamadore."

"It can't be detected from Earth, if that's what you mean," said Billy. "Earth can't be detected from Tralfamadore, as far as that goes. They're both very small. They're very far apart."

"Where did you get a crazy name like 'Tralfamadore?'"

"That's what the creatures who live there *call* it."

"Oh God," said Barbara, and she turned her back on him. She

celebrated frustration by clapping her hands. "May I ask you a simple question?"

"Of course."

"Why is it you never mentioned any of this before the airplane crash?"

"I didn't think the time was *ripe.*"

And so on. Billy says that he first came unstuck in time in 1944, long before his trip to Tralfamadore. The Tralfamadorians didn't have anything to do with his coming unstuck. They were simply able to give him insights into what was really going on.

Billy first came unstuck while World War Two was in progress. Billy was a chaplain's assistant in the war. A chaplain's assistant is customarily a figure of fun in the American Army. Billy was no exception. He was powerless to harm the enemy or to help his friends. In fact, he had no friends. He was a valet to a preacher, expected no promotions or medals, bore no arms, and had a meek faith in a loving Jesus which most soldiers found putrid.

While on maneuvers in South Carolina, Billy played hymns he knew from childhood, played them on a little black organ which was waterproof. It had thirty-nine keys and two stops—*vox humana* and *vox celeste.* Billy also had charge of a portable altar, an olive-drab attaché case with telescoping legs. It was lined with crimson plush, and nestled in that passionate plush were an anodized aluminum cross and a Bible.

The altar and the organ were made by a vacuum-cleaner company in Camden, New Jersey—and said so.

One time on maneuvers Billy was playing "A Mighty Fortress Is Our God," with music by Johann Sebastian Bach and words by Martin Luther. It was Sunday morning. Billy and his chaplain had gathered a congregation of about fifty soldiers on a Carolina hillside. An umpire appeared. There were umpires everywhere, men who said who was winning or losing the theoretical battle, who was alive and who was dead.

The umpire had comical news. The congregation had been theoretically spotted from the air by a theoretical enemy. They were all theoretically dead now. The theoretical corpses laughed and ate a hearty noontime meal.

Remembering this incident years later, Billy was struck by what a

Tralfamadorian adventure with death that had been, to be dead and to eat at the same time.

Toward the end of maneuvers, Billy was given an emergency furlough home because his father, a barber in Ilium, New York, was shot dead by a friend while they were out hunting deer. So it goes.

When Billy got back from his furlough, there were orders for him to go overseas. He was needed in the headquarters company of an infantry regiment fighting in Luxembourg. The regimental chaplain's assistant had been killed in action. So it goes.

When Billy joined the regiment, it was in the process of being destroyed by the Germans in the famous Battle of the Bulge. Billy never even got to meet the chaplain he was supposed to assist, was never even issued a steel helmet and combat boots. This was in December of 1944, during the last mighty German attack of the war.

Billy survived, but he was a dazed wanderer far behind the new German lines. Three other wanderers, not quite so dazed, allowed Billy to tag along. Two of them were scouts, and one was an antitank gunner. They were without food or maps. Avoiding Germans, they were delivering themselves into rural silences ever more profound. They ate snow.

They went Indian file. First came the scouts, clever, graceful, quiet. They had rifles. Next came the antitank gunner, clumsy and dense, warning Germans away with a Colt .45 automatic in one hand and a trench knife in the other.

Last came Billy Pilgrim, empty-handed, bleakly ready for death. Billy was preposterous—six feet and three inches tall, with a chest and shoulders like a box of kitchen matches. He had no helmet, no overcoat, no weapon, and no boots. On his feet were cheap, low-cut civilian shoes which he had bought for his father's funeral. Billy had lost a heel, which made him bob up-and-down, up-and-down. The involuntary dancing, up and down, up and down, made his hip joints sore.

Billy was wearing a thin field jacket, a shirt and trousers of scratchy wool, and long underwear that was soaked with sweat. He was the only one of the four who had a beard. It was a random, bristly beard, and some of the bristles were white, even though Billy was only twenty-one years old. He was also going bald. Wind and cold and violent exercise had turned his face crimson.

He didn't look like a soldier at all. He looked like a filthy flamingo.

And on the third day of wandering, somebody shot at the four from far away—shot four times as they crossed a narrow brick road. One shot was for the scouts. The next one was for the antitank gunner, whose name was Roland Weary.

The third bullet was for the filthy flamingo, who stopped dead center in the road when the lethal bee buzzed past his ear. Billy stood there politely, giving the marksman another chance. It was his addled understanding of the rules of warfare that the marksman *should* be given a second chance. The next shot missed Billy's kneecaps by inches, going end-on-end, from the sound of it.

Roland Weary and the scouts were safe in a ditch, and Weary growled at Billy, "Get out of the road, you dumb motherfucker." The last word was still a novelty in the speech of white people in 1944. It was fresh and astonishing to Billy, who had never fucked anybody —and it did its job. It woke him up and got him off the road.

"Saved your life again, you dumb bastard," Weary said to Billy in the ditch. He had been saving Billy's life for days, cursing him, kicking him, slapping him, making him move. It was absolutely necessary that cruelty be used, because Billy wouldn't do anything to save himself. Billy wanted to quit. He was cold, hungry, embarrassed, incompetent. He could scarcely distinguish between sleep and wakefulness now, on the third day, found no important differences, either, between walking and standing still.

He wished everybody would leave him alone. "You guys go on without me," he said again and again.

Weary was as new to war as Billy. He was a replacement, too. As a part of a gun crew, he had helped to fire one shot in anger—from a 57-millimeter antitank gun. The gun made a ripping sound like the opening of the zipper on the fly of God Almighty. The gun lapped up snow and vegetation with a blowtorch thirty feet long. The flame left a black arrow on the ground, showing the Germans exactly where the gun was hidden. The shot was a miss.

What had been missed was a Tiger tank. It swiveled its 88-millimeter snout around sniffingly, saw the arrow on the ground. It fired. It killed everybody on the gun crew but Weary. So it goes.

Roland Weary was only eighteen, was at the end of an unhappy childhood spent mostly in Pittsburgh, Pennsylvania. He had been unpopular in Pittsburgh. He had been unpopular because he was stupid and fat and mean, and smelled like bacon no matter how much he washed. He was always being ditched in Pittsburgh by people who did not want him with them.

It made Weary sick to be ditched. When Weary was ditched, he would find somebody who was even more unpopular than himself, and he would horse around with that person for a while, pretending to be friendly. And then he would find some pretext for beating the shit out of him.

It was a pattern. It was a crazy, sexy, murderous relationship Weary entered into with people he eventually beat up. He told them about his father's collection of guns and swords and torture instruments and leg irons and so on. Weary's father, who was a plumber, actually did collect such things, and his collection was insured for four thousand dollars. He wasn't alone. He belonged to a big club composed of people who collected things like that.

Weary's father once gave Weary's mother a Spanish thumbscrew in working condition—for a kitchen paperweight. Another time he gave her a table lamp whose base was a model one foot high of the famous "Iron Maiden of Nuremburg." The real Iron Maiden was a medieval torture instrument, a sort of boiler which was shaped like a woman on the outside—and lined with spikes. The front of the woman was composed of two hinged doors. The idea was to put a criminal inside and then close the doors slowly. There were two special spikes where his eyes would be. There was a drain in the bottom to let out all the blood.

So it goes.

Weary had told Billy Pilgrim about the Iron Maiden, about the drain in her bottom—and what that was for. He had talked to Billy about dum-dums. He told him about his father's Derringer pistol, which could be carried in a vest pocket, which was yet capable of making a hole in a man "which a bull bat could fly through without touching either wing."

Weary scornfully bet Billy one time that he didn't even know what a blood gutter was. Billy guessed that it was the drain in the bottom of the Iron Maiden, but that was wrong. A blood gutter, Billy learned, was the shallow groove in the side of the blade of a sword or bayonet.

Weary told Billy about neat tortures he'd read about or seen in the movies or heard on the radio—about other neat tortures he himself had invented. One of the inventions was sticking a dentist's drill into a guy's ear. He asked Billy what he thought the worst form of execution was. Billy had no opinion. The correct answer turned out to be this: "You stake a guy out on an anthill in the desert—see? He's facing upward, and you put honey all over his balls and pecker, and you cut off his eyelids so he has to stare at the sun till he dies." So it goes.

Now, lying in the ditch with Billy and the scouts after having been shot at, Weary made Billy take a very close look at his trench knife. It wasn't government issue. It was a present from his father. It had a ten-inch blade that was triangular in cross section. Its grip consisted of brass knuckles, was a chain of rings through which Weary slipped his stubby fingers. The rings weren't simple. They bristled with spikes.

Weary laid the spikes along Billy's cheek, roweled the cheek with savagely affectionate restraint. "How'd you like to be hit with this—hm? Hmmmmmmmmm?" he wanted to know.

"I wouldn't," said Billy.

"Know why the blade's triangular?"

"No."

"Makes a wound that won't close up."

"Oh."

"Makes a three-sided hole in a guy. You stick an ordinary knife in a guy—makes a slit. Right? A slit closes right up. Right?"

"Right."

"Shit. What do you know? What the hell they teach in college?"

"I wasn't there very long," said Billy, which was true. He had had only six months of college, and the college hadn't been a regular college, either. It had been the night school of the Ilium School of Optometry.

"Joe College," said Weary scathingly.

Billy shrugged.

"There's more to life than what you read in books," said Weary. "You'll find that out."

Billy made no reply to this, either, there in the ditch, since he didn't want the conversation to go on any longer than necessary. He was dimly tempted to say, though, that he knew a thing or two about gore. Billy, after all, had contemplated torture and hideous wounds at the beginning and the end of nearly every day of his childhood. Billy had an extremely gruesome crucifix hanging on the wall of his little bedroom in Ilium. A military surgeon would have admired the clinical fidelity of the artist's rendition of all Christ's wounds—the spear wound, the thorn wounds, the holes that were made by the iron spikes. Billy's Christ died horribly. He was pitiful.

So it goes.

Billy wasn't a Catholic, even though he grew up with a ghastly crucifix on the wall. His father had no religion. His mother was a substitute organist for several churches around town. She took Billy with her whenever she played, taught him to play a little, too. She said she was going to join a church as soon as she decided which one was right.

She never *did* decide. She did develop a terrific hankering for a crucifix, though. And she bought one from a Santa Fe gift shop during a trip the little family made out West during the Great Depression. Like so many Americans, she was trying to construct a life that made sense from things she found in gift shops.

And the crucifix went up on the wall of Billy Pilgrim.

The two scouts, loving the walnut stocks of their rifles in the ditch, whispered that it was time to move out again. Ten minutes had gone by without anybody's coming to see if they were hit or not, to finish them off. Whoever had shot was evidently far away and all alone.

And the four crawled out of the ditch without drawing any more fire. They crawled into a forest like the big, unlucky mammals they were. Then they stood up and began to walk quickly. The forest was dark and old. The pines were planted in ranks and files. There was no undergrowth. Four inches of unmarked snow blanketed the ground. The Americans had no choice but to leave trails in the snow as unambiguous as diagrams in a book on ballroom dancing—*step, slide, rest—step, slide, rest.*

"Close it up and keep it closed!" Roland Weary warned Billy Pilgrim as they moved out. Weary looked like Tweedledum or Tweedledee, all bundled up for battle. He was short and thick.

He had every piece of equipment he had ever been issued, every present he'd received from home: helmet, helmet liner, wool cap, scarf, gloves, cotton undershirt, woolen undershirt, wool shirt, sweater, blouse, jacket, overcoat, cotton underpants, woolen underpants, woolen trousers, cotton socks, woolen socks, combat boots, gas mask, canteen, mess kit, first-aid kit, trench knife, blanket, shelter-half, raincoat, bullet-proof Bible, a pamphlet entitled "Know Your Enemy," another pamphlet entitled "Why We Fight," and another pamphlet of German phrases rendered in English phonetics, which would enable Weary to ask Germans questions such as "Where is your headquarters?" and "How many howitzers have you?" or to tell them, "Surrender. Your situation is hopeless," and so on.

Weary had a block of balsa wood which was supposed to be a foxhole pillow. He had a prophylactic kit containing two tough condoms "For the Prevention of Disease Only!" He had a whistle he wasn't going to show anybody until he got promoted to corporal. He had a dirty picture of a woman attempting sexual intercourse with a Shetland pony. He had made Billy Pilgrim admire that picture several times.

The woman and the pony were posed before velvet draperies which were fringed with deedlee-balls. They were flanked by Doric columns. In front of one column was a potted palm. The picture that Weary had was a print of the first dirty photograph in history. The word *photography* was first used in 1839, and it was in that year, too, that Louis J. M. Daguerre revealed to the French Academy that an image formed on a silvered metal plate covered with a thin film of silver iodide could be developed in the presence of mercury vapor.

In 1841, only two years later, an assistant to Daguerre, André Le Fèvre, was arrested in the Tuileries Gardens for attempting to sell a gentleman a picture of the woman and the pony. That was where Weary bought his picture, too—in the Tuileries. Le Fèvre argued that the picture was fine art, and that his intention was to make Greek mythology come alive. He said the columns and the potted palm proved that.

When asked which myth he meant to represent, Le Fèvre replied that there were thousands of myths like that, with the woman a mortal and the pony a god.

He was sentenced to six months in prison. He died there of pneumonia. So it goes.

Billy and the scouts were skinny people. Roland Weary had fat to burn. He was a roaring furnace under all his layers of wool and straps and canvas. He had so much energy that he bustled back and forth between Billy and the scouts, delivering dumb messages which nobody had sent and which nobody was pleased to receive. He also began to suspect, since he was so much busier than anybody else, that he was the leader.

He was so hot and bundled up, in fact, that he had no sense of danger. His vision of the outside world was limited to what he could see through a narrow slit between the rim of his helmet and his scarf from home, which concealed his baby face from the bridge of his nose on down. He was so snug in there that he was able to pretend that he was safe at home, having survived the war, and that he was telling his parents and his sister a true war story—whereas the true war story was still going on.

Weary's version of the true war story went like this: There was a big German attack, and Weary and his antitank buddies fought like hell until everybody was killed but Weary. So it goes. And then Weary tied in with two scouts, and they became close friends immediately, and they decided to fight their way back to their own lines. They were going to travel fast. They were damned if they'd surrender. They shook hands all around. They called themselves "The Three Musketeers."

But then this damn college kid, who was so weak he shouldn't even have been in the army, asked if he could come along. He didn't even have a gun or a knife. He didn't even have a helmet or a cap. He couldn't even walk right—kept bobbing up-and-down, up-and-down, driving everybody crazy, giving their position away. He was pitiful. The Three Musketeers pushed and carried and dragged the college kid all the way back to their own lines, Weary's story went. They saved his God-damned hide for him.

In real life, Weary was retracing his steps, trying to find out what had happened to Billy. He had told the scouts to wait while he went back for the college bastard. He passed under a low branch now. It hit the top of his helmet with a *clonk*. Weary didn't hear it. Somewhere a big dog was barking. Weary didn't hear that, either. His war story was at a very exciting point. An officer was congratulating the Three Musketeers, telling them that he was going to put them in for Bronze Stars.

"Anything else I can do for you boys?" said the officer.

"Yes, sir," said one of the scouts. "We'd like to stick together for the rest of the war, sir. Is there some way you can fix it so nobody will ever break up the Three Musketeers?"

Billy Pilgrim had stopped in the forest. He was leaning against a tree with his eyes closed. His head was tilted back and his nostrils were flaring. He was like a poet in the Parthenon.

This was when Billy first came unstuck in time. His attention began to swing grandly through the full arc of his life, passing into death, which was violet light. There wasn't anybody else there, or any thing. There was just violet light—and a hum.

And then Billy swung into life again, going backwards until he was in pre-birth, which was red light and bubbling sounds. And then he swung into life again and stopped. He was a little boy taking a shower with his hairy father at the Ilium Y.M.C.A. He smelled chlorine from the swimming pool next door, heard the springboard boom.

Little Billy was terrified, because his father had said Billy was going to learn to swim by the method of sink-or-swim. His father was going to throw Billy into the deep end, and Billy was going to damn well swim.

It was like an execution. Billy was numb as his father carrried him from the shower room to the pool. His eyes were closed. When he opened his eyes, he was on the bottom of the pool, and there was beautiful music everywhere. He lost consciousness, but the music went on. He dimly sensed that somebody was rescuing him. Billy resented that.

From there he traveled in time to 1965. He was forty-one years old, and he was visiting his decrepit mother at Pine Knoll, an old people's home he had put her in only a month before. She had caught pneumonia, and wasn't expected to live. She did live, though, for years after that.

Her voice was nearly gone, so, in order to hear her, Billy had to put his ear right next to her papery lips. She evidently had something very important to say.

"How . . . ?" she began, and she stopped. She was too tired. She hoped that she wouldn't have to say the rest of the sentence, that Billy would finish it for her.

But Billy had no idea what was on her mind. "How *what,* Mother?" he prompted.

She swallowed hard, shed some tears. Then she gathered energy from all over her ruined body, even from her toes and fingertips. At last she had accumulated enough to whisper this complete sentence:

"How did I get so *old?*"

Billy's antique mother passed out, and Billy was led from the room by a pretty nurse. The body of an old man covered by a sheet was wheeled by just as Billy entered the corridor. The man had been a famous marathon runner in his day. So it goes. This was before Billy had his head broken in an airplane crash, by the way—before he became so vocal about flying saucers and traveling in time.

Billy sat down in a waiting room. He wasn't a widower yet. He sensed something hard under the cushion of his overstuffed chair. He dug it out, discovered that it was a book, *The Execution of Private Slovik,* by William Bradford Huie. It was a true account of the death before an American firing squad of Private Eddie D. Slovik, 36896415, the only American soldier to be shot for cowardice since the Civil War. So it goes.

Billy read the opinion of a staff judge advocate who reviewed Slovik's case, which ended like this: *He has directly challenged the authority of the government, and future discipline depends upon a resolute reply to this challenge. If the death penalty is ever to be imposed for desertion, it should be imposed in this case, not as a punitive measure nor as retribution, but to maintain that discipline upon which alone an army can succeed against the enemy. There was no recommendation for clemency in the case and none is here recommended.* So it goes.

Billy blinked in 1965, traveled in time to 1958. He was at a banquet in honor of a Little League team of which his son Robert was a member. The coach, who had never been married, was speaking. He was all choked up. "Honest to God," he was saying, "I'd consider it an honor just to be *water* boy for these kids."

Billy blinked in 1958, traveled in time to 1961. It was New Year's Eve, and Billy was disgracefully drunk at a party where everybody was in optometry or married to an optometrist.

Billy usually didn't drink much, because the war had ruined his stomach, but he certainly had a snootful now, and he was being unfaithful to his wife Valencia for the first and only time. He had somehow persuaded a woman to come into the laundry room of the house, and then sit up on the gas dryer, which was running.

The woman was very drunk herself, and she helped Billy get her girdle off. "What was it you wanted to talk about?" she said.

"It's all right," said Billy. He honestly thought it was all right. He couldn't remember the name of the woman.

"How come they call you Billy instead of William?"

"Business reasons," said Billy. That was true. His father-in-law, who owned the Ilium School of Optometry, who had set Billy up in practice, was a genius in his field. He told Billy to encourage people to call him Billy—because it would stick in their memories. It would also make him seem slightly magical, since there weren't any other grown Billys around. It also compelled people to think of him as a friend right away.

Somewhere in there was an awful scene, with people expressing disgust for Billy and the woman, and Billy found himself out in his automobile, trying to find the steering wheel.

The main thing now was to find the steering wheel. At first, Billy windmilled his arms, hoping to find it by luck. When that didn't work, he became methodical, working in such a way that the wheel could not possibly escape him. He placed himself hard against the left-hand door, searched every square inch of the area before him. When he failed to find the wheel, he moved over six inches, and searched again. Amazingly, he was eventually hard against the right-hand door, without having found the wheel. He concluded that somebody had stolen it. This angered him as he passed out.

He was in the back seat of his car, which was why he couldn't find the steering wheel.

Now somebody was shaking Billy awake. Billy still felt drunk, was still angered by the stolen steering wheel. He was back in World War Two again, behind the German lines. The person who was shaking him was Roland Weary. Weary had gathered the front of Billy's field jacket into his hands. He banged Billy against a tree, then pulled him away from it, flung him in the direction he was supposed to take under his own power.

Billy stopped, shook his head. "You go on," he said.

"What?"

"You guys go on without me. I'm all right."

"You're what?"

"I'm O.K."

"Jesus—I'd hate to see somebody *sick,*" said Weary, through five layers of humid scarf from home. Billy had never seen Weary's face. He had tried to imagine it one time, had imaged a toad in a fishbowl.

Weary kicked and shoved Billy for a quarter of a mile. The scouts were waiting between the banks of a frozen creek. They had heard the dog. They had heard men calling back and forth, too—calling like hunters who had a pretty good idea of where their quarry was.

The banks of the creek were high enough to allow the scouts to stand without being seen. Billy staggered down the bank ridiculously. After him came Weary, clanking and clinking and tinkling and hot.

"Here he is, boys," said Weary. "He don't want to live, but he's gonna live anyway. When he gets out of this, by God, he's gonna owe his life to the Three Musketeers." This was the first the scouts had heard that Weary thought of himself and them as the Three Musketeers.

Billy Pilgrim, there in the creekbed, thought he, Billy Pilgrim, was turning to steam painlessly. If everybody would leave him alone for just a little while, he thought, he wouldn't cause anybody any more trouble. He would turn to steam and float up among the treetops.

Somewhere the big dog barked again. With the help of fear and echoes and winter silences, that dog had a voice like a big bronze gong.

Roland Weary, eighteen years old, insinuated himself between the scouts, draped a heavy arm around the shoulder of each. "So what do the Three Musketeers do now?" he said.

Billy Pilgrim was having a delightful hallucination. He was wearing dry, warm, white sweatsocks, and he was skating on a ballroom floor. Thousands cheered. This wasn't time-travel. It had never happened, never would happen. It was the craziness of a dying young man with his shoes full of snow.

One scout hung his head, let spit fall from his lips. The other did the same. They studied the infinitesimal effects of spit on snow and history. They were small, graceful people. They had been behind German lines before many times—living like woods creatures, living from moment to moment in useful terror, thinking brainlessly with their spinal cords.

Now they twisted out from under Weary's loving arms. They told Weary that he and Billy had better find somebody to surrender to. The scouts weren't going to wait for them any more.

And they ditched Weary and Billy in the creekbed.

Billy Pilgrim went on skating, doing tricks in sweatsocks, tricks that most people would consider impossible—making turns, stopping on a dime and so on. The cheering went on, but its tone was altered as the hallucination gave way to time-travel.

Billy stopped skating, found himself at a lectern in a Chinese restaurant in Ilium, New York, on an early afternoon in the autumn of 1957. He was receiving a standing ovation from the Lions Club. He had just been elected President, and it was necessary that he speak. He was scared stiff, thought a ghastly mistake had been made. All those prosperous, solid men out there would discover now that they had elected a ludicrous waif. They would hear his reedy voice, the one he'd had in the war. He swallowed, knew that all he had for a voice box was a little whistle cut from a willow switch. Worse—he had nothing to say. The crowd quieted down. Everybody was pink and beaming.

Billy opened his mouth, and out came a deep, resonant tone. His voice was a gorgeous instrument. It told jokes which brought down the house. It grew serious, told jokes again, and ended on a note of humility. The explanation of the miracle was this: Billy had taken a course in public speaking.

And then he was back in the bed of the frozen creek again. Roland Weary was about to beat the living shit out of him.

Weary was filled with a tragic wrath. He had been ditched again. He stuffed his pistol into its holster. He slipped his knife into its scabbard. Its triangular blade and blood gutters on all three faces. And then he shook Billy hard, rattled his skeleton, slammed him against a bank.

Weary barked and whimpered through his layers of scarf from home. He spoke unintelligibly of the sacrifices he had made on Billy's behalf. He dilated upon the piety and heroism of "The Three Musketeers," portrayed, in the most glowing and impassioned hues, their virtue and magnanimity, the imperishable honor they acquired for themselves, and the great services they rendered to Christianity.

It was entirely Billy's fault that this fighting organization no longer existed, Weary felt, and Billy was going to pay. Weary socked Billy a good one on the side of his jaw, knocked Billy away from the bank and onto the snow-covered ice of the creek. Billy was down on all fours on the ice, and Weary kicked him in the ribs, rolled him over on his side. Billy tried to form himself into a ball.

"You shouldn't even *be* in the Army," said Weary.

Billy was involuntarily making convulsive sounds that were a lot like laughter. "You think it's funny, huh?" Weary inquired. He walked around to Billy's back. Billy's jacket and shirt and undershirt had been hauled up around his shoulders by the violence, so his back was naked. There, inches from the tips of Weary's combat boots, were the pitiful buttons of Billy's spine.

Weary drew back his right boot, aimed a kick at the spine, at the tube which had so many of Billy's important wires in it. Weary was going to break that tube.

But then Weary saw that he had an audience. Five German soldiers and a police dog on a leash were looking down into the bed of the creek. The soldiers' blue eyes were filled with a bleary civilian curiosity as to why one American would try to murder another one so far from home, and why the victim should laugh.

3

The Germans and the dog were engaged in a military operation which had an amusingly self-explanatory name, a human enterprise which is seldom described in detail, whose name alone, when reported as news or history, gives many war enthusiasts a sort of post-coital satisfaction. It is, in the imagination of combat's fans, the divinely listless loveplay that follows the orgasm of victory. It is called "mopping up."

The dog, who had sounded so ferocious in the winter distances, was a female German shepherd. She was shivering. Her tail was between her legs. She had been borrowed that morning from a farmer. She had never been to war before. She had no idea what game was being played. Her name was Princess.

Two of the Germans were boys in their early teens. Two were ramshackle old men—droolers as toothless as carp. They were irregulars, armed and clothed fragmentarily with junk taken from real soldiers who were newly dead. So it goes. They were farmers from just across the German border, not far away.

Their commander was a middle-aged corporal—red-eyed, scrawny, tough as dried beef, sick of war. He had been wounded four times—and patched up, and sent back to war. He was a very good soldier—about to quit, about to find somebody to surrender to. His bandy legs were thrust into golden cavalry boots which he had taken from a dead Hungarian colonel on the Russian front. So it goes.

Those boots were almost all he owned in this world. They were his home. An anecdote: One time a recruit was watching him bone and wax those golden boots, and he held one up to the recruit and said, "If you look in there deeply enough, you'll see Adam and Eve."

Billy Pilgrim had not heard this anecdote. But, lying on the black ice there, Billy stared into the patina of the corporal's boots, saw Adam and Eve in the golden depths. They were naked. They were so innocent, so vulnerable, so eager to behave decently. Billy Pilgrim loved them.

Next to the golden boots were a pair of feet which were swaddled in rags. They were crisscrossed by canvas straps, were shod with hinged wooden clogs. Billy looked up at the face that went with the clogs. It was the face of a blond angel, of a fifteen-year-old boy.

The boy was as beautiful as Eve.

Billy was helped to his feet by the lovely boy, by the heavenly androgyne. And the others came forward to dust the snow off Billy, and then they searched him for weapons. He didn't have any. The most dangerous thing they found on his person was a two-inch pencil stub.

Three inoffensive *bangs* came from far away. They came from German rifles. The two scouts who had ditched Billy and Weary had just been shot. They had been lying in ambush for Germans. They had been discovered and shot from behind. Now they were dying in the snow, feeling nothing, turning the snow to the color of raspberry sherbet. So it goes. So Roland Weary was the last of the Three Musketeers.

And Weary, bug-eyed with terror, was being disarmed. The corporal gave Weary's pistol to the pretty boy. He marveled at Weary's cruel trench knife, said in German that Weary would no doubt like to use the knife on him, to tear his face off with the spiked knuckles, to stick the blade into his belly or throat. He spoke no English, and Billy and Weary understood no German.

"Nice playthings you have," the corporal told Weary, and he handed the knife to an old man. "Isn't that a pretty thing? Hmmm?"

He tore open Weary's overcoat and blouse. Brass buttons flew like popcorn. The corporal reached into Weary's gaping bosom as though he meant to tear out his pounding heart, but he brought out Weary's bullet-proof Bible instead.

A bullet-proof Bible is a Bible small enough to be slipped into a soldier's breast pocket, over his heart. It is sheathed in steel.

The corporal found the dirty picture of the woman and the pony in Weary's hip pocket. "What a lucky pony, eh?" he said. "Hmmmm? Hmmmm? Don't you wish you were that pony?" He handed the picture to the other old man. "Spoils of war! It's yours, all yours, you lucky lad."

Then he made Weary sit down in the snow and take off his combat boots, which he gave to the beautiful boy. He gave Weary the boy's clogs. So Weary and Billy were both without decent military footwear now, and they had to walk for miles and miles, with Weary's clogs clacking, with Billy bobbing up-and-down, up-and-down, crashing into Weary from time to time.

"Excuse me," Billy would say, or "I beg your pardon."

They were brought at last to a stone cottage at a fork in the road. It was a collecting point for prisoners of war. Billy and Weary were taken inside, where it was warm and smoky. There was a fire sizzling and popping in the fireplace. The fuel was furniture. There were about twenty other Americans in there, sitting on the floor with their backs to the wall, staring into the flames—thinking whatever there was to think, which was zero.

Nobody talked. Nobody had any good war stories to tell.

Billy and Weary found places for themselves, and Billy went to sleep with his head on the shoulder of an unprotesting captain. The captain was a chaplain. He was a rabbi. He had been shot through the hand.

Billy traveled in time, opened his eyes, found himself staring into the glass eyes of a jade green mechanical owl. The owl was hanging upside down from a rod of stainless steel. The owl was Billy's optometer in his office in Ilium. An optometer is an instrument for measuring refractive errors in eyes—in order that corrective lenses may be prescribed.

Billy had fallen asleep while examining a female patient who was in a chair on the other side of the owl. He had fallen asleep at work before. It had been funny at first. Now Billy was starting to get worried about it, about his mind in general. He tried to remember how old he was, couldn't. He tried to remember what year it was. He couldn't remember that, either.

"Doctor—" said the patient tentatively.
"Hm?" he said.
"You're so quiet."
"Sorry."
"You were talking away there—and then you got so quiet."
"Um."
"You see something terrible?"
"Terrible?"
"Some disease in my eyes?"
"No, no," said Billy, wanting to doze again. "Your eyes are fine. You just need glasses for reading." He told her to go across the corridor—to see the wide selection of frames there.

When she was gone, Billy opened the drapes and was no wiser as to what was outside. The view was still blocked by a venetian blind, which he hoisted clatteringly. Bright sunlight came crashing in. There were thousands of parked automobiles out there, twinkling on a vast lake of blacktop. Billy's office was part of a suburban shopping center.

Right outside the window was Billy's own Cadillac El Dorado Coupe de Ville. He read the stickers on the bumper. "Visit Ausable Chasm," said one. "Support Your Police Department," said another. There was a third. "Impeach Earl Warren," it said. The stickers about the police and Earl Warren were gifts from Billy's father-in-law, a member of the John Birch Society. The date on the license plate was 1967, which would make Billy Pilgrim forty-four years old. He asked himself this: "Where have all the years gone?"

Billy turned his attention to his desk. There was an open copy of *The Review of Optometry* there. It was opened to an editorial, which Billy now read, his lips moving slightly.

What happens in 1968 will rule the fate of European optometrists for at least 50 years! Billy read. *With this warning, Jean Thiriart, Secretary of the National Union of Belgium Opticians, is pressing for formation of a "European Optometry Society." The alternatives, he says, will be the obtaining of professional status, or, by 1971, reduction to the role of spectacle-sellers.*

Billy Pilgrim tried hard to care.

A siren went off, scared the hell out of him. He was expecting World War Three at any time. The siren was simply announcing high noon. It was housed in a cupola atop a firehouse across the street from Billy's office.

Billy closed his eyes. When he opened them, he was back in World War Two again. His head was on the wounded rabbi's shoulder. A German was kicking his feet, telling him to wake up, that it was time to move on.

The Americans, with Billy among them, formed a fools' parade on the road outside.

There was a photographer present, a German war correspondent with a Leica. He took pictures of Billy's and Roland Weary's feet. The picture was widely published two days later as heartening evidence of how miserably equipped the American Army often was, despite its reputation for being rich.

The photographer wanted something more lively, though, a picture of an actual capture. So the guards staged one for him. They threw Billy into shrubbery. When Billy came out of the shrubbery, his face wreathed in goofy good will, they menaced him with their machine pistols, as though they were capturing him then.

Billy's smile as he came out of the shrubbery was at least as peculiar as Mona Lisa's, for he was simultaneously on foot in Germany in 1944 and riding his Cadillac in 1967. Germany dropped away, and 1967 became bright and clear, free of interference from any other time. Billy was on his way to a Lions Club luncheon meeting. It was a hot August, but Billy's car was air-conditioned. He was stopped by a signal in the middle of Ilium's black ghetto. The people who lived here hated it so much that they had burned down a lot of it a month before. It was all they had, and they'd wrecked it. The neighborhood reminded Billy of some of the towns he had seen in the war. The curbs and sidewalks were crushed in many places, showing where the National Guard tanks and half-tracks had been.

"Blood brother," said a message written in pink paint on the side of a shattered grocery store.

There was a tap on Billy's car window. A black man was out there. He wanted to talk about something. The light had changed. Billy did the simplest thing. He drove on.

Billy drove through a scene of even greater desolation. It looked like Dresden after it was fire-bombed—like the surface of the moon. The house where Billy had grown up used to be somewhere in what was so empty now. This was urban renewal. A new Ilium Government Center and a Pavilion of the Arts and a Peace Lagoon and high-rise apartment buildings were going up here soon.

That was all right with Billy Pilgrim.

The speaker at the Lions Club meeting was a major in the Marines. He said that Americans had no choice but to keep fighting in Vietnam until they achieved victory or until the Communists realized that they could not force their way of life on weak countries. The major had been there on two separate tours of duty. He told of many terrible and many wonderful things he had seen. He was in favor of increased bombings, of bombing North Vietnam back into the Stone Age, if it refused to see reason.

Billy was not moved to protest the bombing of North Vietnam, did not shudder about the hideous things he himself had seen bombing do. He was simply having lunch with the Lions Club, of which he was past president now.

Billy had a framed prayer on his office wall which expressed his method for keeping going, even though he was unenthusiastic about living. A lot of patients who saw the prayer on Billy's wall told him that it helped *them* to keep going, too. It went like this:

GOD GRANT ME
THE SERENITY TO ACCEPT
THE THINGS I CANNOT CHANGE,
COURAGE
TO CHANGE THE THINGS I CAN,
AND WISDOM ALWAYS
TO TELL THE
DIFFERENCE.

Among the things Billy Pilgrim could not change were the past, the present, and the future.

Now he was being introduced to the Marine major. The person who was performing the introduction was telling the major that Billy was a veteran, and that Billy had a son who was a sergeant in the Green Berets—in Vietnam.

The major told Billy that the Green Berets were doing a great job, and that he should be proud of his son.

"I *am.* I certainly *am,*" said Billy Pilgrim.

He went home for a nap after lunch. He was under doctor's orders to take a nap every day. The doctor hoped that this would relieve a complaint that Billy had: Every so often, for no apparent reason, Billy Pilgrim would find himself weeping. Nobody had ever caught Billy doing it. Only the doctor knew. It was an extremely quiet thing Billy did, and not very moist.

Billy owned a lovely Georgian home in Ilium. He was rich as Croesus, something he had never expected to be, not in a million years. He had five other optometrists working for him in the shopping plaza location, and netted over sixty thousand dollars a year. In addition, he owned a fifth of the new Holiday Inn out on Route 54, and half of three Tastee-Freeze stands. Tastee-Freeze was a sort of frozen custard. It gave all the pleasure that ice cream could give, without the stiffness and bitter coldness of ice cream.

Billy's home was empty. His daughter Barbara was about to get married, and she and his wife had gone downtown to pick out patterns for her crystal and silverware. There was a note saying so on the kitchen table. There were no servants. People just weren't interested in careers in domestic service anymore. There wasn't a dog, either.

There used to be a dog named Spot, but he died. So it goes. Billy had liked Spot a lot, and Spot had liked him.

Billy went up the carpeted stairway and into his and his wife's bedroom. The room had flowered wallpaper. There was a double bed with a clock-radio on a table beside it. Also on the table were controls for the electric blanket, and a switch to turn on a gentle vibrator which was bolted to the springs of the box mattress. The trade name of the vibrator was "Magic Fingers." The vibrator was the doctor's idea, too.

Billy took off his tri-focals and his coat and his necktie and his shoes, and he closed the venetian blinds and then the drapes, and he lay down on the outside of the coverlet. But sleep would not come. Tears came instead. They seeped. Billy turned on the Magic Fingers, and he was jiggled as he wept.

The doorchimes rang. Billy got off the bed and looked down through a window at the front doorstep, to see if somebody important had come to call. There was a crippled man down there, as spastic in space as Billy Pilgrim was in time. Convulsions made the man dance flappingly all the time, made him change his expressions, too, as though he was trying to imitate various famous movie stars.

Another cripple was ringing a doorbell across the street. He was on crutches. He had only one leg. He was so jammed between his crutches that his shoulders hid his ears.

Billy knew what the cripples were up to: They were selling subscriptions to magazines that would never come. People subscribed to them because the salesmen were so pitiful. Billy had heard about this racket from a speaker at the Lions Club two weeks before—a man from the Better Business Bureau. The man said that anybody who saw cripples working a neighborhood for magazine subscriptions should call the police.

Billy looked down the street, saw a new Buick Riviera parked about half a block away. There was a man in it, and Billy assumed correctly that he was the man who had hired the cripples to do this thing. Billy went on weeping as he contemplated the cripples and their boss. His doorchimes clanged hellishly.

He closed his eyes, and opened them again. He was still weeping, but he was back in Luxembourg again. He was marching with a lot of other prisoners. It was a winter wind that was bringing tears to his eyes.

Ever since Billy had been thrown into shrubbery for the sake of a picture, he had been seeing Saint Elmo's fire, a sort of electronic radiance around the heads of his companions and captors. It was in the treetops and on the rooftops of Luxembourg, too. It was beautiful.

Billy was marching with his hands on top of his head, and so were all the other Americans. Billy was bobbing up-and-down, up-and-down. Now he crashed into Roland Weary accidentally. "I beg your pardon," he said.

Weary's eyes were tearful also. Weary was crying because of

horrible pains in his feet. The hinged clogs were transforming his feet into blood puddings.

At each road intersection Billy's group was joined by more Americans with their hands on top of their haloed heads. Billy had smiles for them all. They were moving like water, downhill all the time, and they flowed at last to a main highway on a valley's floor. Through the valley flowed a Mississippi of humiliated Americans. Tens of thousands of Americans shuffled eastward, their hands clasped on top of their heads. They sighed and groaned.

Billy and his group joined the river of humiliation, and the late afternoon sun came out from the clouds. The Americans didn't have the road to themselves. The westbound lane boiled and boomed with vehicles which were rushing German reserves to the front. The reserves were violent, windburned, bristly men. They had teeth like piano keys.

They were festooned with machine-gun belts, smoked cigars and guzzled booze. They took wolfish bites from sausages, patted their horny palms with potato-masher grenades.

One soldier in black was having a drunk hero's picnic all by himself on top of a tank. He spit on the Americans. The spit hit Roland Weary's shoulder, gave Weary a *fourragère* of snot and blutwurst and tobacco juice and Schnapps.

Billy found the afternoon stingingly exciting. There was so much to see—dragon's teeth, killing machines, corpses with bare feet that were blue and ivory. So it goes.

Bobbing up-and-down, up-and-down, Billy beamed lovingly at a bright lavender farmhouse that had been spattered with machine-gun bullets. Standing in its cockeyed doorway was a German colonel. With him was his unpainted whore.

Billy crashed into Weary's shoulder, and Weary cried out sobbingly. "Walk right! Walk right!"

They were climbing a gentle rise now. When they reached the top, they weren't in Luxembourg any more. They were in Germany.

A motion-picture camera was set up at the border—to record the fabulous victory. Two civilians in bearskin coats were leaning on the camera when Billy and Weary came by. They had run out of film hours ago.

One of them singled out Billy's face for a moment, then focused at infinity again. There was a tiny plume of smoke at infinity. There was a battle there. People were dying there. So it goes.

And the sun went down, and Billy found himself bobbing in place in a railroad yard. There were rows and rows of boxcars waiting. They had brought reserves to the front. Now they were going to take prisoners into Germany's interior.

Flashlight beams danced crazily.

The Germans sorted out the prisoners according to rank. They put sergeants with sergeants, majors with majors, and so on. A squad of full colonels was halted near Billy. One of them had double pneumonia. He had a high fever and vertigo. As the railroad yard dipped and swooped around the colonel, he tried to hold himself steady by staring into Billy's eyes.

The colonel coughed and coughed, and then he said to Billy, "You one of my boys?" This was a man who had lost an entire regiment, about forty-five hundred men—a lot of them children, actually. Billy didn't reply. The question made no sense.

"What was your outfit?" said the colonel. He coughed and coughed. Every time he inhaled his lungs rattled like greasy paper bags.

Billy couldn't remember the outfit he was from.

"You from the Four-fifty-first?"

"Four-fifty-first what?" said Billy.

There was a silence. "Infantry regiment," said the colonel at last.

"Oh," said Billy Pilgrim.

There was another long silence, with the colonel dying and dying, drowning where he stood. And then he cried out wetly, "It's me, boys! It's Wild Bob!" That is what he had always wanted his troops to call him: "Wild Bob."

None of the people who could hear him were actually from his regiment, except for Roland Weary, and Weary wasn't listening. All Weary could think of was the agony in his own feet.

But the colonel imagined that he was addressing his beloved troops for the last time, and he told them that they had nothing to be ashamed of, that there were dead Germans all over the battlefield who wished to God that they had never heard of the Four-fifty-first. He said that after the war he was going to have a regimental reunion in his home town, which was Cody, Wyoming. He was going to barbecue whole steers.

He said all this while staring into Billy's eyes. He made the inside of poor Billy's skull echo with balderdash. "God be with you, boys!" he said, and that echoed and echoed. And then he said, "If you're ever in Cody, Wyoming, just ask for Wild Bob!"

I was there. So was my old war buddy, Bernard V. O'Hare.

Billy Pilgrim was packed into a boxcar with many other privates. He and Roland Weary were separated. Weary was packed into another car in the same train.

There were narrow ventilators at the corners of the car, under the eaves. Billy stood by one of these, and, as the crowd pressed against him, he climbed part way up a diagonal corner brace to make more room. This placed his eyes on a level with the ventilator, so he could see another train about ten yards away.

Germans were writing on the cars with blue chalk—the number of persons in each car, their rank, their nationality, the date on which they had been put aboard. Other Germans were securing the hasps on the car doors with wire and spikes and other trackside trash. Billy could hear somebody writing on his car, too, but he couldn't see who was doing it.

Most of the privates on Billy's car were very young—at the end of childhood. But crammed into the corner with Billy was a former hobo who was forty years old.

"I been hungrier than this," the hobo told Billy. "I been in worse places than this. This ain't so bad."

A man in a boxcar across the way called out through the ventilator that a man had just died in there. So it goes. There were four guards who heard him. They weren't excited by the news.

"Yo, yo," said one, nodding dreamily. "Yo, yo."

And the guards didn't open the car with the dead man in it. They opened the next car instead, and Billy Pilgrim was enchanted by what was in there. It was like heaven. There was candlelight, and there were bunks with quilts and blankets heaped on them. There was a cannonball stove with a steaming coffeepot on top. There was a table with a bottle of wine and a loaf of bread and a sausage on it. There were four bowls of soup.

There were pictures of castles and lakes and pretty girls on the walls. This was the rolling home of the railroad guards, men whose business it was to be forever guarding freight rolling from here to there. The four guards went inside and closed the door.

A little while later they came out smoking cigars, talking contentedly in the mellow lower register of the German language. One of them saw Billy's face at the ventilator. He wagged a finger at him in affectionate warning, telling him to be a good boy.

The Americans across the way told the guards again about the dead man on their car. The guards got a stretcher out of their own cozy car, opened the dead man's car and went inside. The dead man's car wasn't crowded at all. There were just six live colonels in there—and one dead one.

The Germans carried the corpse out. The corpse was Wild Bob. So it goes.

During the night, some of the locomotives began to tootle to one another, and then to move. The locomotive and the last car of each train were marked with a striped banner of orange and black, indicating that the train was not fair game for airplanes—that it was carrying prisoners of war.

The war was nearly over. The locomotives began to move east in late December. The war would end in May. German prisons everywhere were absolutely full, and there was no longer any food for the prisoners to eat, and no longer any fuel to keep them warm. And yet—here came more prisoners.

Billy Pilgrim's train, the longest train of all, did not move for two days.

"This ain't bad," the hobo told Billy on the second day. "This ain't nothing at all."

Billy looked out through the ventilator. The railroad yard was a desert now, except for a hospital train marked with red crosses—on a siding far, far away. Its locomotive whistled. The locomotive of Billy Pilgrim's train whistled back. They were saying, "Hello."

Even though Billy's train wasn't moving, its boxcars were kept locked tight. Nobody was to get off until the final destination. To the guards who walked up and down outside, each car became a single organism which ate and drank and excreted through its ventilators. It talked or sometimes yelled through its ventilators, too. In went water and loaves of blackbread and sausage and cheese, and out came shit and piss and language.

Human beings in there were excreting into steel helmets, which were passed to the people at the ventilators, who dumped them. Billy was a dumper. The human beings also passed canteens, which guards would fill with water. When food came in, the human beings were quiet and trusting and beautiful. They shared.

Human beings in there took turns standing or lying down. The legs of those who stood were like fence posts driven into a warm, squirming, farting, sighing earth. The queer earth was a mosaic of sleepers who nestled like spoons.

Now the train began to creep eastward.

Somewhere in there was Christmas. Billy Pilgrim nestled like a spoon with the hobo on Christmas night, and he fell asleep, and he traveled in time to 1967 again—to the night he was kidnapped by a flying saucer from Tralfamadore.

4

Billy Pilgrim could not sleep on his daughter's wedding night. He was forty-four. The wedding had taken place that afternoon in a gaily striped tent in Billy's backyard. The stripes were orange and black.

Billy and his wife, Valencia, nestled like spoons in their big double bed. They were jiggled by Magic Fingers. Valencia didn't need to be jiggled to sleep. Valencia was snoring like a bandsaw. The poor woman didn't have ovaries or a uterus any more. They had been removed by a surgeon—by one of Billy's partners in the new Holiday Inn.

There was a full moon.

Billy got out of bed in the moonlight. He felt spooky and luminous, felt as though he was wrapped in cool fur that was full of static electricity. He looked down at his bare feet. They were ivory and blue.

Billy now shuffled down his upstairs hallway, knowing he was about to be kidnapped by a flying saucer. The hallway was zebra-striped with darkness and moonlight. The moonlight came into the hallway through doorways of the empty rooms of Billy's two children, children no more. They were gone forever. Billy was guided by dread and the lack of dread. Dread told him when to stop. Lack of it told him when to move again. He stopped.

He went into his daughter's room. Her drawers were dumped. Her closet was empty. Heaped in the middle of the room were all the possessions she could not take on a honeymoon. She had a Princess telephone extension all her own—on her windowsill. Its tiny night light stared at Billy. And then it rang.

Billy answered. There was a drunk on the other end. Billy could almost smell his breath—mustard gas and roses. It was a wrong number. Billy hung up. There was a soft drink bottle on the windowsill. Its label boasted that it contained no nourishment whatsoever.

Billy Pilgrim padded downstairs on his blue and ivory feet. He went into the kitchen, where the moonlight called his attention to a half bottle of champagne on the kitchen table, all that was left from the reception in the tent. Somebody had stoppered it again. "Drink me," it seemed to say.

So Billy uncorked it with his thumbs. It didn't make a pop. The champagne was dead. So it goes.

Billy looked at the clock on the gas stove. He had an hour to kill before the saucer came. He went into the living room, swinging the bottle like a dinner bell, turned on the television. He came slightly unstuck in time, saw the late movie backwards, then forwards again. It was a movie about American bombers in the Second World War and the gallant men who flew them. Seen backwards by Billy, the story went like this:

American planes, full of holes and wounded men and corpses took off backwards from an airfield in England. Over France, a few German fighter planes flew at them backwards, sucked bullets and shell fragments from some of the planes and crewmen. They did the same for wrecked American bombers on the ground and those planes flew up backwards to join the formation.

The formation flew backwards over a German city that was in flames. The bombers opened their bomb bay doors, exerted a miraculous magnetism which shrunk the fires, gathered them into cylindrical steel containers, and lifted the containers into the bellies of the planes. The containers were stored neatly in racks. The Germans below had miraculous devices of their own, which were long steel tubes. They used them to suck more fragments from the crewmen and planes. But there were still a few wounded Americans, though, and some of the bombers were in bad repair. Over France, though, German fighters came up again, made everything and everybody as good as new.

When the bombers got back to their base, the steel cylinders were taken from the racks and shipped back to the United States of America, where factories were operating night and day, dismantling the cylinders, separating the dangerous contents into minerals. Touchingly, it was mainly women who did this work. The minerals were then shipped to specialists in remote areas. It was their business to put them into the ground, to hide them cleverly, so they would never hurt anybody ever again.

The American fliers turned in their uniforms, became high school kids. And Hitler turned into a baby, Billy Pilgrim supposed. That wasn't in the movie. Billy was extrapolating. Everybody turned into a baby, and all humanity, without exception, conspired biologically to produce two perfect people named Adam and Eve, he supposed.

Billy saw the war movies backwards then forwards—and then it was time to go out into his backyard to meet the flying saucer. Out he went, his blue and ivory feet crushing the wet salad of the lawn. He stopped, took a swig of the dead champagne. It was like 7-Up. He would not raise his eyes to the sky, though he knew there was a flying saucer from Tralfamadore up there. He would see it soon enough, inside and out, and he would see, too, where it came from soon enough—soon enough.

Overhead he heard the cry of what might have been a melodious owl, but it wasn't a melodious owl. It was a flying saucer from Tralfamadore, navigating in both space and time, therefore seeming to Billy Pilgrim to have come from nowhere all at once. Somewhere a big dog barked.

The saucer was one hundred feet in diameter, with portholes around its rim. The light from the portholes was a pulsing purple. The only noise it made was the owl song. It came down to hover over Billy, and to enclose him in a cylinder of pulsing purple light. Now there was the sound of a seeming kiss as an airtight hatch in the bottom of the saucer was opened. Down snaked a ladder that was outlined in pretty lights like a Ferris wheel.

Billy's will was paralyzed by a zap gun aimed at him from one of the portholes. It became imperative that he take hold of the bottom rung of the sinuous ladder, which he did. The rung was electrified, so that Billy's hands locked onto it hard. He was hauled into the airlock, and machinery closed the bottom door. Only then did the ladder, wound onto a reel in the airlock, let him go. Only then did Billy's brain start working again.

There were two peepholes inside the airlock—with yellow eyes pressed to them. There was a speaker on the wall. The Tralfamadorians had no voice boxes. They communicated telepathically. They were able to talk to Billy by means of a computer and a sort of electric organ which made every Earthling speech sound.

"Welcome aboard, Mr. Pilgrim," said the loudspeaker. "Any questions?"

Billy licked his lips, thought a while, inquired at last: "Why me?"

"That is a very *Earthling* question to ask, Mr. Pilgrim. Why *you?* Why *us* for that matter? Why *anything?* Because this moment simply *is.* Have you ever seen bugs trapped in amber?"

"Yes." Billy, in fact, had a paperweight in his office which was a blob of polished amber with three ladybugs embedded in it.

"Well, here we are, Mr. Pilgrim, trapped in the amber of this moment. There is no *why.*"

They introduced an anesthetic into Billy's atmosphere now, put him to sleep. They carried him to a cabin where he was strapped to a yellow Barca-Lounger which they had stolen from a Sears & Roebuck warehouse. The hold of the saucer was crammed with other stolen merchandise, which would be used to furnish Billy's artificial habitat in a zoo on Tralfamadore.

The terrific acceleration of the saucer as it left Earth twisted Billy's slumbering body, distorted his face, dislodged him in time, sent him back to the war.

When he regained consciousness, he wasn't on the flying saucer. He was in a boxcar crossing Germany again.

Some people were rising from the floor of the car, and others were lying down. Billy planned to lie down, too. It would be lovely to sleep. It was black in the car, and black outside the car, which seemed to be going about two miles an hour. The car never seemed to go any faster than that. It was a long time between clicks, between joints in the track. There would be a click, and then a year would go by, and then there would be another click.

The train often stopped to let really important trains bawl and hurtle by. Another thing it did was stop on sidings near prisons, leaving a few cars there. It was creeping across all of Germany, growing shorter all the time.

And Billy let himself down oh so gradually now, hanging onto the diagonal cross-brace in the corner in order to make himself seem nearly weightless to those he was joining on the floor. He knew it was important that he make himself nearly ghostlike when lying down. He had forgotten why, but a reminder soon came.

"Pilgrim—" said a person he was about to nestle with, "is that *you?"*

Billy didn't say anything, but nestled very politely, closed his eyes.

"God damn it," said the person. "That *is* you, isn't it?" He sat up and explored Billy rudely with his hands. "It's you, all right. Get the hell out of here."

Now Billy sat up, too—wretched, close to tears.

"Get out of here! I want to sleep!"

"Shut up," said somebody else.

"I'll shut up when Pilgrim gets away from here."

So Billy stood up again, clung to the cross-brace. "Where *can* I sleep?" he asked quietly.

"Not with me."

"Not with me, you son of a bitch," said somebody else. "You yell. You kick."

"I do?"

"You're God damn right you do. And whimper."

"I do?"

"Keep the hell away from here, Pilgrim."

And now there was an acrimonious madrigal, with parts sung in all quarters of the car. Nearly everybody, seemingly, had an atrocity story of something Billy Pilgrim had done to him in his sleep. Everybody told Billy Pilgrim to keep the hell away.

So Billy Pilgrim had to sleep standing up, or not sleep at all. And food had stopped coming in through the ventilators, and the days and nights were colder all the time.

On the eighth day, the forty-year-old hobo said to Billy, "This ain't bad. I can be comfortable anywhere."

"You can?" said Billy.

On the ninth day, the hobo died. So it goes. His last words were, "You think this is bad? This ain't bad."

There was something about death and the ninth day. There was a death on the ninth day in the car ahead of Billy's too. Roland Weary died—of gangrene that had started in his mangled feet. So it goes.

Weary, in his nearly continuous delirium, told again and again of the Three Musketeers, acknowledged that he was dying, gave many messages to be delivered to his family in Pittsburgh. Above all, he wanted to be avenged, so he said again and again the name of the person who had killed him. Everyone on the car learned the lesson well.

"Who killed me?" he would ask.

And everybody knew the answer, which was this: "Billy Pilgrim."

Listen—on the tenth night the peg was pulled out of the hasp on Billy's boxcar door, and the door was opened. Billy Pilgrim was lying at an angle on the corner-brace, self-crucified, holding himself there with a blue and ivory claw hooked over the sill of the ventilator. Billy coughed when the door was opened, and when he coughed he shit thin gruel. This was in accordance with the Third Law of Motion according to Sir Isaac Newton. This law tells us that for every action there is a reaction which is equal and opposite in direction.

This can be useful in rocketry.

The train had arrived on a siding by a prison which was originally constructed as an extermination camp for Russian prisoners of war.

The guards peeked inside Billy's car owlishly, cooed calmingly. They had never dealt with Americans before, but they surely understood this general sort of freight. They knew that it was essentially a liquid which could be induced to flow slowly toward cooing and light. It was nighttime.

The only light outside came from a single bulb which hung from a pole—high and far away. All was quiet outside, except for the guards, who cooed like doves. And the liquid began to flow. Gobs of it built up in the doorway, plopped to the ground.

Billy was the next-to-last human being to reach the door. The hobo was last. The hobo could not flow, could not plop. He wasn't liquid any more. He was stone. So it goes.

Billy didn't want to drop from the car to the ground. He sincerely believed that he would shatter like glass. So the guards helped him down, cooing still. They set him down facing the train. It was such a dinky train now.

There was a locomotive, a tender, and three little boxcars. The last boxcar was the railroad guards' heaven on wheels. Again—in that heaven on wheels—the table was set. Dinner was served.

At the base of the pole from which the light bulb hung were three seeming haystacks. The Americans were wheedled and teased over to those three stacks, which weren't hay after all. They were overcoats taken from prisoners who were dead. So it goes.

It was the guards' firmly expressed wish that every American without an overcoat should take one. The coats were cemented together with ice, so the guards used their bayonets as ice picks, pricking free collars and hems and sleeves and so on, then peeling off coats and handing them out at random. The coats were stiff and dome-shaped, having conformed to their piles.

The coat that Billy Pilgrim got had been crumpled and frozen in such a way, and was so small, that it appeared to be not a coat but a sort of large black, three-cornered hat. There were gummy stains on it, too, like crankcase drainings or old strawberry jam. There seemed to be a dead, furry animal frozen to it. The animal was in fact the coat's fur collar.

Billy glanced dully at the coats of his neighbors. Their coats all had brass buttons or tinsel or piping or numbers or stripes or eagles or moons or stars dangling from them. They were soldiers' coats. Billy was the only one who had a coat from a dead civilian. So it goes.

And Billy and the rest were encouraged to shuffle around their dinky train and into the prison camp. There wasn't anything warm or lively to attract them—merely long, low, narrow sheds by the thousands, with no lights inside.

Somewhere a dog barked. With the help of fear and echoes and winter silences, that dog had a voice like a big bronze gong.

Billy and the rest were wooed through gate after gate, and Billy saw his first Russian. The man was all alone in the night—a ragbag with a round, flat face that glowed like a radium dial.

Billy passed within a yard of him. There was barbed wire between them. The Russian did not wave or speak, but he looked directly into

Billy's soul with sweet hopefulness, as though Billy might have good news for him—news he might be too stupid to understand, but good news all the same.

Billy blacked out as he walked through gate after gate. He came to in what he thought might be a building on Tralfamadore. It was shrilly lit and lined with white tiles. It was on Earth, though. It was a delousing station through which all new prisoners had to pass.

Billy did as he was told, took off his clothes. That was the first thing they told him to do on Tralfamadore, too.

A German measured Billy's upper right arm with his thumb and forefinger, asked a companion what sort of an army would send a weakling like that to the front. They looked at the other American bodies now, pointed out a lot more that were nearly as bad as Billy's.

One of the best bodies belonged to the oldest American by far, a high school teacher from Indianapolis. His name was Edgar Derby. He hadn't been in Billy's boxcar. He'd been in Roland Weary's car, had cradled Weary's head while he died. So it goes. Derby was forty-four years old. He was so old he had a son who was a marine in the Pacific theater of war.

Derby had pulled political wires to get into the army at his age. The subject he had taught in Indianapolis was Contemporary Problems in Western Civilization. He also coached the tennis team, and took very good care of his body.

Derby's son would survive the war. Derby wouldn't. That good body of his would be filled with holes by a firing squad in Dresden in sixty-eight days. So it goes.

The worst American body wasn't Billy's. The worst body belonged to a car thief from Cicero, Illinois. His name was Paul Lazzaro. He was tiny, and not only were his bones and teeth rotten, but his skin was disgusting. Lazzaro was polka-dotted all over with dime-sized scars. He had had many plagues of boils.

Lazzaro, too, had been on Roland Weary's boxcar, and had given his word of honor to Weary that he would find some way to make Billy Pilgrim pay for Weary's death. He was looking around now, wondering which naked human being was Billy.

The naked Americans took their places under many showerheads along a white-tiled wall. There were no faucets they could control. They could only wait for whatever was coming. Their penises were shriveled and their balls were retracted. Reproduction was not the main business of the evening.

An unseen hand turned a master valve. Out of the showerheads gushed scalding rain. The rain was a blowtorch that did not warm. It jazzed and jangled Billy's skin without thawing the ice in the marrow of his long bones.

The Americans' clothes were meanwhile passing through poison gas. Body lice and bacteria and fleas were dying by the billions. So it goes.

And Billy zoomed back in time to his infancy. He was a baby who had just been bathed by his mother. Now his mother wrapped him in a towel, carried him into a rosy room that was filled with sunshine. She unwrapped him, laid him on the tickling towel, powdered him between his legs, joked with him, patted his little jelly belly. Her palm on his little jelly belly made potching sounds.

Billy gurgled and cooed.

And then Billy was a middle-aged optometrist again, playing hacker's golf this time—on a blazing summer Sunday morning. Billy never went to church any more. He was hacking with three other optometrists. Billy was on the green in seven strokes, and it was his turn to putt.

It was an eight-foot putt and he made it. He bent over to take the ball out of the cup, and the sun went behind a cloud. Billy was momentarily dizzy. When he recovered, he wasn't on the golf course any more. He was strapped to a yellow contour chair in a white chamber aboard a flying saucer, which was bound for Tralfamadore.

"Where am I?" said Billy Pilgrim.

"Trapped in another blob of amber, Mr. Pilgrim. We are where we have to be just now—three hundred million miles from Earth, bound for a time warp which will get us to Tralfamadore in hours rather than centuries."

"How—how did I get here?"

"It would take another Earthling to explain it to you. Earthlings are the great explainers, explaining why this event is structured as it is, telling how other events may be achieved or avoided. I am a Tralfamadorian, seeing all time as you might see a stretch of the Rocky Mountains. All time is all time. It does not change. It does not lend itself to warnings or explanations. It simply *is*. Take it moment by moment, and you will find that we are all, as I've said before, bugs in amber."

"You sound to me as though you don't believe in free will," said Billy Pilgrim.

"If I hadn't spent so much time studying Earthlings," said the Tralfamadorian, "I wouldn't have any idea what was meant by 'free will.' I've visited thirty-one inhabited planets in the universe, and I have studied reports on one hundred more. Only on Earth is there any talk of free will."

5

Billy Pilgrim says that the Universe does not look like a lot of bright little dots to the creatures from Tralfamadore. The creatures can see where each star has been and where it is going, so that the heavens are filled with rarefied, luminous spaghetti. And Tralfamadorians don't see human beings as two-legged creatures, either. They see them as great millepedes—"with babies' legs at one end and old people's legs at the other," says Billy Pilgrim.

Billy asked for something to read on the trip to Tralfamadore. His captors had five million Earthling books on microfilm, but no way to project them in Billy's cabin. They had only one actual book in English, which would be placed in a Tralfamadorian museum. It was *Valley of the Dolls,* by Jacqueline Susann.

Billy read it, thought it was pretty good in spots. The people in it certainly had their ups and downs, ups and downs. But Billy didn't want to read about the same ups and downs over and over again. He asked if there wasn't, please, some other reading matter around.

"Only Tralfamadorian novels, which I'm afraid you couldn't begin to understand," said the speaker on the wall.

"Let me look at one anyway."

So they sent him in several. They were little things. A dozen of them might have had the bulk of *Valley of the Dolls*—with all its ups and downs, ups and downs.

Billy couldn't read Tralfamadorian, of course, but he could at least see how the books were laid out—in brief clumps of symbols separated by stars. Billy commented that the clumps might be telegrams.

"Exactly," said the voice.

"They *are* telegrams?"

"There are no telegrams on Tralfamadore. But you're right: each clump of symbols is a brief, urgent message—describing a situation, a scene. We Tralfamadorians read them all at once, not one after the other. There isn't any particular relationship between all the messages, except that the author has chosen them carefully, so that, when seen all at once, they produce an image of life that is beautiful and surprising and deep. There is no beginning, no middle, no end, no suspense, no moral, no causes, no effects. What we love in our books are the depths of many marvelous moments seen all at one time."

Moments after that, the saucer entered a time warp, and Billy was flung back into his childhood. He was twelve years old, quaking as he stood with his mother and father on Bright Angel Point, at the rim of Grand Canyon. The little human family was staring at the floor of the canyon, one mile straight down.

"Well—" said Billy's father, manfully kicking a pebble into space, "there it *is.*" They had come to this famous place by automobile. They had had seven blowouts on the way.

"It was worth the trip," said Billy's mother raptly. "Oh, God—was it ever *worth* it."

Billy hated the canyon. He was sure that he was going to fall in. His mother touched him, and he wet his pants.

There were other tourists looking down into the canyon, too, and a ranger was there to answer questions. A Frenchman who had come all the way from France asked the ranger in broken English if many people committed suicide by jumping in.

"Yes, sir," said the ranger. "About three folks a year." So it goes.

And Billy took a very short trip through time, made a peewee jump of only ten days, so he was still twelve, still touring the West with his family. Now they were down in Carlsbad Caverns, and Billy was praying to God to get him out of there before the ceiling fell in.

A ranger was explaining that the Caverns had been discovered by a cowboy who saw a huge cloud of bats come out of a hole in the ground. And then he said that he was going to turn out all the lights, and that it would probably be the first time in the lives of most people there that they had ever been in darkness that was total.

Out went the lights. Billy didn't even know whether he was still alive or not. And then something ghostly floated in air to his left. It had numbers on it. His father had taken out his pocket watch. The watch had a radium dial.

Billy went from total dark to total light, found himself back in the war, back in the delousing station again. The shower was over. An unseen hand had turned the water off.

When Billy got his clothes back, they weren't any cleaner, but all the little animals that had been living in them were dead. So it goes. And his new overcoat was thawed out and limp now. It was much too small for Billy. It had a fur collar and a lining of crimson silk, and had apparently been made for an impresario about as big as an organ-grinder's monkey. It was full of bullet holes.

Billy Pilgrim dressed himself. He put on the little overcoat, too. It split up the back, and, at the shoulders, the sleeves came entirely free. So the coat became a fur-collared vest. It was meant to flare at its owner's waist, but the flaring took place at Billy's armpits. The Germans found him to be one of the most screamingly funny things they had seen in all of World War Two. They laughed and laughed.

And the Germans told everybody else to form in ranks of five, with Billy as their pivot. Then out of doors went the parade, and through gate after gate again. There were more starving Russians with faces like radium dials. The Americans were livelier than before. The jazzing with hot water had cheered them up. And they came to a shed where a corporal with only one arm and one eye wrote the name and serial number of each prisoner in a big, red ledger. Everybody was legally alive now. Before they got their names and numbers in the book, they were missing in action and probably dead.

So it goes.

As the Americans were waiting to move on, an altercation broke out in their rear-most rank. An American had muttered something which a guard did not like. The guard knew English, and he hauled the American out of ranks, knocked him down.

The American was astonished. He stood up shakily, spitting blood. He'd had two teeth knocked out. He had meant no harm by what he'd said, evidently, had no idea that the guard would hear and understand.

"Why me?" he asked the guard.

The guard shoved him back into ranks. "Vy you? Vy anybody?" he said.

When Billy Pilgrim's name was inscribed in the ledger of the prison camp, he was given a number, too, and an iron dogtag in which that number was stamped. A slave laborer from Poland had done the stamping. He was dead now. So it goes.

Billy was told to hang the tag around his neck along with his American dogtags, which he did. The tag was like a salt cracker, perforated down its middle so that a strong man could snap it in two with his bare hands. In case Billy died, which he didn't, half of the tag would mark his body and half would mark his grave.

After poor Edgar Derby, the high school teacher, was shot in Dresden later on, a doctor pronounced him dead and snapped his dogtag in two. So it goes.

Properly enrolled and tagged, the Americans were led through gate after gate again. In two days' time now their families would learn from the International Red Cross that they were alive.

Next to Billy was little Paul Lazzaro, who had promised to avenge Roland Weary. Lazzaro wasn't thinking about vengeance. He was thinking about his terrible bellyache. His stomach had shrunk to the size of a walnut. That dry, shriveled pouch was as sore as a boil.

Next to Lazzaro was poor, doomed old Edgar Derby, with his American and German dogs displayed like a necklace, on the outside of his clothes. He had expected to become a captain, a company commander, because of his wisdom and age. Now here he was on the Czechoslovakian border at midnight.

"Halt," said a guard.

The Americans halted. They stood there quietly in the cold. The sheds they were among were outwardly like thousands of other sheds they had passed. There was this difference, though: the sheds had tin chimneys, and out of the chimneys whirled constellations of sparks.

A guard knocked on a door.

The door was flung open from inside. Light leaped out through the door, escaped from prison at 186,000 miles per second. Out marched fifty middle-aged Englishmen. They were singing "Hail, Hail, the Gang's All Here" from the *Pirates of Penzance.*

These lusty, ruddy vocalists were among the first English-speaking prisoners to be taken in the Second World War. Now they were singing to nearly the last. They had not seen a woman or a child for four years or more. They hadn't seen any birds, either. Not even sparrows would come into the camp.

The Englishmen were officers. Each of them had attempted to escape from another prison at least once. Now they were here, dead-center in a sea of dying Russians.

They could tunnel all they pleased. They would inevitably surface within a rectangle of barbed wire, would find themselves greeted listlessly by dying Russians who spoke no English, who had no food or useful information or escape plans of their own. They could scheme all they pleased to hide aboard a vehicle or steal one, but no vehicle ever came into their compound. They could feign illness, if they liked, but that wouldn't earn them a trip anywhere, either. The only hospital in the camp was a six-bed affair in the British compound itself.

The Englishmen were clean and enthusiastic and decent and strong. They sang boomingly well. They had been singing together every night for years.

The Englishmen had also been lifting weights and chinning themselves for years. Their bellies were like washboards. The muscles of their calves and upper arms were like cannonballs. They were all masters of checkers and chess and bridge and cribbage and dominoes and anagrams and charades and Ping-Pong and billiards, as well.

They were among the wealthiest people in Europe, in terms of food. A clerical error early in the war, when food was still getting through to prisoners, had caused the Red Cross to ship them five hundred parcels every month instead of fifty. The Englishmen had hoarded these so cunningly that now, as the war was ending, they had three tons of sugar, one ton of coffee, eleven hundred pounds of chocolate, seven hundred pounds of tobacco, seventeen hundred pounds of tea, two tons of flour, one ton of canned beef, twelve hundred pounds of canned butter, sixteen hundred pounds of canned cheese, eight hundred pounds of powdered milk, and two tons of orange marmalade.

They kept all this in a room without windows. They had rat-proofed it by lining it with flattened tin cans.

They were adored by the Germans, who thought they were exactly what Englishmen ought to be. They made war look stylish and reasonable, and fun. So the Germans let them have four sheds, though one shed would have held them all. And, in exchange for coffee or chocolate or tobacco, the Germans gave them paint and lumber and nails and cloth for fixing things up.

The Englishmen had known for twelve hours that American guests were on their way. They had never had guests before, and they went to work like darling elves, sweeping, mopping, cooking, baking —making mattresses of straw and burlap bags, setting tables, putting party favors at each place.

Now they were singing their welcome to their guests in the winter night. Their clothes were aromatic with the feast they had been preparing. They were dressed half for battle, half for tennis or croquet. They were so elated by their own hospitality, and by all the goodies waiting inside, that they did not take a good look at their guests while they sang. And they imagined that they were singing to fellow officers fresh from the fray.

They wrestled the Americans toward the shed door affectionately, filling the night with manly blather and brotherly rodomontades. They called them "Yank," told them "Good show," promised them that "Jerry was on the run," and so on.

Billy Pilgrim wondered dimly who Jerry was.

Now he was indoors, next to an iron cookstove that was glowing cherry red. Dozens of teapots were boiling there. Some of them had whistles. And there was a witches' cauldron full of golden soup. The soup was thick. Primeval bubbles surfaced it with lethargical majesty as Billy Pilgrim stared.

There were long tables set for a banquet. At each place was a bowl made from a can that had once contained powdered milk. A smaller can was a cup. A taller, more slender can was a tumbler. Each tumbler was filled with warm milk.

At each place was a safety razor, a washcloth, a package of razorblades, a chocolate bar, two cigars, a bar of soap, ten cigarettes, a book of matches, a pencil, and a candle.

Only the candles and the soap were of German origin. They had a ghostly, opalescent similarity. The British had no way of knowing it, but the candles and the soap were made from the fat of rendered Jews and Gypsies and fairies and communists, and other enemies of the State.

So it goes.

The banquet hall was illuminated by candlelight. There were heaps of fresh-baked white bread on the tables, gobs of butter, pots of marmalade. There were platters of sliced beef from cans. Soup and scrambled eggs and hot marmalade pie were yet to come.

And, at the far end of the shed, Billy saw pink arches with azure draperies hanging between them, and an enormous clock, and two golden thrones, and a bucket and a mop. It was in this setting that the evening's entertainment would take place, a musical version of *Cinderella,* the most popular story ever told.

Billy Pilgrim was on fire, having stood too close to the glowing stove. The hem of his little coat was burning. It was a quiet, patient sort of fire—like the burning of punk.

Billy wondered if there was a telephone somewhere. He wanted to call his mother, to tell her he was alive and well.

There was silence now, as the Englishmen looked in astonishment at the frowsy creatures they had so lustily waltzed inside. One of the Englishmen saw that Billy was on fire. "You're on fire, lad!" he said, and he got Billy away from the stove and beat out the sparks with his hands.

When Billy made no comment on this, the Englishman asked him, "Can you talk? Can you hear?"

Billy nodded.

The Englishman touched him exploratorily here and there, filled with pity. "My God—what have they done to you, lad? This isn't a man. It's a broken kite."

"Are you really an American?" said the Englishman.

"Yes," said Billy.

"And your rank?"

"Private."

"What became of your boots, lad?"

"I don't remember."

"Is that coat a *joke?"*

"Sir?"

"Where did you get such a thing?"

Billy had to think hard about that. "They gave it to me," he said at last.

"Jerry gave it to you?"

"Who?"

"The Germans gave it to you?"

"Yes."

Billy didn't like the questions. They were fatiguing.

"Ohhhh—Yank, Yank, Yank—" said the Englishman, "that coat was an *insult.*"

"Sir?"

"It was a deliberate attempt to humiliate you. You mustn't let Jerry do things like that."

Billy Pilgrim swooned.

Billy came to on a chair facing the stage. He had somehow eaten, and now he was watching *Cinderella.* Some part of him had evidently been enjoying the performance for quite a while. Billy was laughing hard.

The women in the play were really men, of course. The clock had just struck midnight, and Cinderella was lamenting:

> "Goodness me, the clock has struck—
> Alackday, and fuck my luck."

Billy found the couplet so comical that he not only laughed—he shrieked. He went on shrieking until he was carried out of the shed and into another, where the hospital was. It was a six-bed hospital. There weren't any other patients in there.

Billy was put to bed and tied down, and given a shot of morphine. Another American volunteered to watch over him. This volunteer was Edgar Derby, the high school teacher who would be shot to death in Dresden. So it goes.

Derby sat on a three-legged stool. He was given a book to read. The book was *The Red Badge of Courage,* by Stephen Crane. Derby had read it before. Now he read it again while Billy Pilgrim entered a morphine paradise.

Under morphine, Billy had a dream of giraffes in a garden. The giraffes were following gravel paths, were pausing to munch sugar pears from treetops. Billy was a giraffe, too. He ate a pear. It was a hard one. It fought back against his grinding teeth. It snapped in juicy protest.

The giraffes accepted Billy as one of their own, as a harmless creature as preposterously specialized as themselves. Two approached him from opposite sides, leaned against him. They had long, muscular upper lips which they could shape like the bells of bugles. They kissed him with these. They were female giraffes —cream and lemon yellow. They had horns like doorknobs. The knobs were covered with velvet.

Why?

Night came to the garden of the giraffes, and Billy Pilgrim slept without dreaming for a while, and then he traveled in time. He woke up with his head under a blanket in a ward for nonviolent mental patients in a veterans' hospital near Lake Placid, New York. It was springtime in 1948, three years after the end of the war.

Billy uncovered his head. The windows of the ward were open. Birds were twittering outside. "Poo-tee-weet?" one asked him. The sun was high. There were twenty-nine other patients assigned to the ward, but they were all outdoors now, enjoying the day. They were free to come and go as they pleased, to go home, even, if they liked—and so was Billy Pilgrim. They had come here voluntarily, alarmed by the outside world.

Billy had committed himself in the middle of his final year at the Ilium School of Optometry. Nobody else suspected that he was going crazy. Everybody else thought he looked fine and was acting fine. Now he was in the hospital. The doctors agreed: He *was* going crazy.

They didn't think it had anything to do with the war. They were sure Billy was going to pieces because his father had thrown him into the deep end of the Y.M.C.A. swimming pool when he was a little boy, and had then taken him to the rim of the Grand Canyon.

The man assigned to the bed next to Billy's was a former infantry captain named Eliot Rosewater. Rosewater was sick and tired of being drunk all the time.

It was Rosewater who introduced Billy to science fiction, and in particular to the writings of Kilgore Trout. Rosewater had a tremendous collection of science-fiction paperbacks under his bed. He had brought them to the hospital in a steamer trunk. Those beloved, frumpish books gave off a smell that permeated the ward—like flannel pajamas that hadn't been changed for a month, or like Irish stew.

Kilgore Trout became Billy's favorite living author, and science fiction became the only sort of tales he could read.

Rosewater was twice as smart as Billy, but he and Billy were dealing with similar crises in similar ways. They had both found life meaningless, partly because of what they had seen in war. Rosewater, for instance, had shot a fourteen-year-old fireman, mistaking him for a German soldier. So it goes. And Billy had seen the greatest massacre in European history, which was the fire-bombing of Dresden. So it goes.

So they were trying to re-invent themselves and their universe. Science fiction was a big help.

Rosewater said an interesting thing to Billy one time about a book that wasn't science fiction. He said that everything there was to know about life was in *The Brothers Karamazov,* by Feodor Dostoevsky. "But that isn't *enough* any more," said Rosewater.

Another time Billy heard Rosewater say to a psychiatrist, "I think you guys are going to have to come up with a lot of wonderful *new* lies, or people just aren't going to want to go on living."

There was a still life on Billy's bedside table—two pills, an ashtray with three lipstick-stained cigarettes in it, one cigarette still burning, and a glass of water. The water was dead. So it goes. Air was trying to get out of that dead water. Bubbles were clinging to the walls of the glass, too weak to climb out.

The cigarettes belonged to Billy's chain-smoking mother. She had sought the ladies' room, which was off the ward for WACS and WAVES and SPARS and WAFS who had gone bananas. She would be back at any moment now.

Billy covered his head with his blanket again. He always covered his head when his mother came to see him in the mental ward—always got much sicker until she went away. It wasn't that she was ugly, or had bad breath or a bad personality. She was a perfectly nice, standard-issue, brown-haired, white woman with a high-school education.

She upset Billy simply by being his mother. She made him feel embarrassed and ungrateful and weak because she had gone to so much trouble to give him life, and to keep that life going, and Billy didn't really like life at all.

Billy heard Eliot Rosewater come in and lie down. Rosewater's bedsprings talked a lot about that. Rosewater was a big man, but not very powerful. He looked as though he might be made out of nose putty.

And then Billy's mother came back from the ladies' room, sat down on a chair between Billy's and Rosewater's bed. Rosewater greeted her with melodious warmth, asked how she was today. He seemed delighted to hear that she was fine. He was experimenting with being ardently sympathetic with everybody he met. He thought that might make the world a slightly more pleasant place to live in. He called Billy's mother "dear." He was experimenting with calling everybody "dear."

"Some day," she promised Rosewater, "I'm going to come in here, and Billy is going to uncover his head, and do you know what he's going to say?"

"What's he going to say, dear?"

"He's going to say, 'Hello, Mom,' and he's going to smile. He's going to say, 'Gee, it's good to see you, Mom. How have you been?'"

"Today could be the day."

"Every night I pray."

"That's a *good* thing to do."

"People would be surprised if they knew how much in this world was due to prayers."

"You never said a truer word, dear."

"Does your mother come to see you often?"

"My mother is dead," said Rosewater. So it goes.

"I'm sorry."

"At least she had a happy life as long as it lasted."

"That's a consolation, anyway."

"Yes."

"Billy's father is dead, you know," said Billy's mother. So it goes.

"A boy *needs* a father."

And on and on it went—that duet between the dumb, praying lady and the big, hollow man who was so full of loving echoes.

"He was at the top of his class when this happened," said Billy's mother.

"Maybe he was *working* too hard," said Rosewater. He held a book he wanted to read, but he was much too polite to read and talk, too, easy as it was to give Billy's mother satisfactory answers. The book was *Maniacs in the Fourth Dimension,* by Kilgore Trout. It was about people whose mental diseases couldn't be treated because the causes of the diseases were all in the fourth dimension, and three-dimensional Earthling doctors couldn't see those causes at all, or even imagine them.

One thing Trout said that Rosewater liked very much was that there really *were* vampires and werewolves and goblins and angels and so on, but that they were in the fourth dimension. So was William Blake, Rosewater's favorite poet, according to Trout. So were heaven and hell.

"He's engaged to a very rich girl," said Billy's mother.

"That's good," said Rosewater. "Money can be a great comfort sometimes."

"It really *can.*"

"Of course it can."

"It isn't much fun if you have to pinch every penny till it screams."

"It's nice to have a little breathing room."

"Her father owns the optometry school where Billy was going. He also owns six offices around our part of the state. He flies his own plane and has a summer place up on Lake George."

"That's a beautiful lake."

Billy fell asleep under his blanket. When he woke up again, he was tied to the bed in the hospital back in prison. He opened one eye, saw poor old Edgar Derby reading *The Red Badge of Courage* by candlelight.

Billy closed that one eye, saw in his memory of the future poor old Edgar Derby in front of a firing squad in the ruins of Dresden. There were only four men in that squad. Billy had heard that one man in each firing squad was customarily given a rifle loaded with blank cartridge. Billy didn't think there would be a blank cartridge issued in a squad that small, in a war that old.

Now the head Englishman came into the hospital to check on Billy. He was an infantry colonel captured at Dunkirk. It was he who had given Billy morphine. There wasn't a real doctor in the compound, so the doctoring was up to him. "How's the patient?" he asked Derby.

"Dead to the world."

"But not actually dead."

"No."

"How nice—to feel nothing, and still get full credit for being alive."

Derby now came to lugubrious attention.

"No, no—please—as you were. With only two men for each officer, and all the men sick, I think we can do without the usual pageantry between officers and men."

Derby remained standing. "You seem older than the rest," said the colonel.

Derby told him he was forty-five, which was two years older than the colonel. The colonel said that the other Americans had all shaved now, that Billy and Derby were the only two still with beards. And he said, "You know—we've had to imagine the war here, and we have imagined that it was being fought by aging men like ourselves. We had forgotten that wars were fought by babies. When I saw those freshly shaved faces, it was a shock. "'My God, my God—' I said to myself, 'It's the Children's Crusade.'"

The colonel asked old Derby how he had been captured, and Derby told a tale of being in a clump of trees with about a hundred other frightened soldiers. The battle had been going on for five days. The hundred had been driven into the trees by tanks.

Derby described the incredible artificial weather that Earthlings sometimes create for other Earthlings when they don't want those other Earthlings to inhabit Earth any more. Shells were bursting in the treetops with terrific bangs, he said, showering down knives and needles and razorblades. Little lumps of lead in copper jackets were crisscrossing the woods under the shellbursts, zipping along much faster than sound.

A lot of people were being wounded or killed. So it goes.

Then the shelling stopped, and a hidden German with a loud-speaker told the Americans to put their weapons down and come out of the woods with their hands on the top of their heads, or the shelling would start again. It wouldn't stop until everybody in there was dead.

So the Americans put their weapons down, and they came out of the woods with their hands on top of their heads, because they wanted to go on living, if they possibly could.

Billy traveled in time back to the veterans' hospital again. The blanket was over his head. It was quiet outside the blanket. "Is my mother gone?" said Billy.

"Yes."

Billy peeked out from under his blanket. His fiancée was out there now, sitting on the visitor's chair. Her name was Valencia Merble. Valencia was the daughter of the owner of the Ilium School of Optometry. She was rich. She was as big as a house because she couldn't stop eating. She was eating now. She was eating a Three Musketeers Candy Bar. She was wearing tri-focal lenses in harlequin frames, and the frames were trimmed with rhinestones. The glitter of the rhinestones was answered by the glitter of the diamond in her engagement ring. The diamond was insured for eighteen hundred dollars. Billy had found that diamond in Germany. It was booty of war.

Billy didn't want to marry ugly Valencia. She was one of the symptoms of his disease. He knew he was going crazy when he heard himself proposing marriage to her, when he begged her to take the diamond ring and be his companion for life.

Billy said, "Hello," to her, and she asked him if he wanted some candy, and he said, "No, thanks."

She asked him how he was, and he said, "Much better, thanks." She said that everybody at the Optometry School was sorry he was sick and hoped he would be well soon, and Billy said, "When you see 'em, tell 'em, 'Hello.'"

She promised she would.

She asked him if there was anything she could bring him from the outside, and he said, "No. I have just about everything I want."

"What about books?" said Valencia.

"I'm right next to one of the biggest private libraries in the world," said Billy, meaning Eliot Rosewater's collection of science fiction.

Rosewater was on the next bed, reading, and Billy drew him into the conversation, asked him what he was reading this time.

So Rosewater told him. It was *The Gospel from Outer Space,* by Kilgore Trout. It was about a visitor from outer space, shaped very much like a Tralfamadorian, by the way. The visitor from outer space made a serious study of Christianity, to learn, if he could, why Christians found it so easy to be cruel. He concluded that at least part of the trouble was slipshod storytelling in the New Testament. He supposed that the intent of the Gospels was to teach people, among other things, to be merciful, even to the lowest of the low.

But the Gospels actually taught this:

Before you kill somebody, make absolutely sure he isn't well connected. So it goes.

The flaw in the Christ stories, said the visitor from outer space, was that Christ, who didn't look like much, was actually the Son of the Most Powerful Being in the Universe. Readers understood that, so, when they came to the crucifixion, they naturally thought, and Rosewater read out loud again:

Oh, boy—they sure picked the wrong guy to lynch that *time!*

And that thought had a brother: *"There are* right people *to lynch."* Who? People not well connected. So it goes.

The visitor from outer space made a gift to Earth of a new Gospel. In it, Jesus really *was* a nobody, and a pain in the neck to a lot of people with better connections than he had. He still got to say all the lovely and puzzling things he said in the other Gospels.

So the people amused themselves one day by nailing him to a cross and planting the cross in the ground. There couldn't possibly be any repercussions, the lynchers thought. The reader would have to think that, too, since the new Gospel hammered home again and again what a nobody Jesus was.

And then, just before the nobody died, the heavens opened up, and there was thunder and lightning. The voice of God came crashing down. He told the people that he was adopting the bum as his son, giving him the full powers and privileges of The Son of the Creator of the Universe throughout all eternity. God said this: *From this moment on, He will punish horribly anybody who torments a bum who has no connections!*

Billy's fiancée had finished her Three Musketeers Candy Bar. Now she was eating a Milky Way.

"Forget books," said Rosewater, throwing that particular book under his bed. "The hell with 'em."

"That sounded like an interesting one," said Valencia.

"Jesus—if Kilgore Trout could only *write!*" Rosewater exclaimed. He had a point: Kilgore Trout's unpopularity was deserved. His prose was frightful. Only his ideas were good.

"I don't think Trout has ever been out of the country," Rosewater went on. "My God—he writes about Earthlings all the time, and they're all Americans. Practically nobody on Earth is an American."

"Where does he live?" Valencia asked.

"Nobody knows," Rosewater replied. "I'm the only person who ever heard of him, as far as I can tell. No two books have the same publisher, and every time I write him in care of a publisher, the letter comes back because the publisher has failed."

He changed the subject now, congratulated Valencia on her engagement ring.

"Thank you," she said, and held it out so Rosewater could get a close look. "Billy got that diamond in the war."

"That's the attractive thing about war," said Rosewater. "Absolutely everybody gets a little something."

With regard to the whereabouts of Kilgore Trout: he actually lived in Ilium, Billy's hometown, friendless and despised. Billy would meet him by and by.

"Billy—" said Valencia Merble.

"Hm?"

"You want to talk about our silver pattern?"

"Sure."

"I've got it narrowed down pretty much to either Royal Danish or Rambler Rose."

"Rambler Rose," said Billy.

"It isn't something we should *rush* into," she said. "I mean —whatever we decide on, that's what we're going to have to live with the rest of our lives."

Billy studied the pictures. "Royal Danish," he said at last.

"Colonial Moonlight is nice, too."

"Yes, it is," said Billy Pilgrim.

And Billy traveled in time to the zoo on Tralfamadore. He was forty-four years old, on display under a geodesic dome. He was reclining on the lounge chair which had been his cradle during his trip through space. He was naked. The Tralfamadorians were interested in his body—*all* of it. There were thousands of them outside, holding up their little hands so that their eyes could see him. Billy had been on Tralfamadore for six Earthling months now. He was used to the crowd.

Escape was out of the question. The atmosphere outside the dome was cyanide, and Earth was 446,120,000,000,000,000 miles away.

Billy was displayed there in the zoo in a simulated Earthling habitat. Most of the furnishings had been stolen from the Sears & Roebuck warehouse in Iowa City, Iowa. There was a color television set and a couch that could be converted into a bed. There were end tables with lamps and ashtrays on them by the couch. There was a home bar and two stools. There was a little pool table. There was wall-to-wall carpeting in federal gold, except in the kitchen and bathroom areas and over the iron manhole cover in the center of the floor. There were magazines arranged in a fan on the coffee table in front of the couch.

There was a stereophonic phonograph. The phonograph worked. The television didn't. There was a picture of one cowboy killing another one pasted to the television tube. So it goes.

There were no walls in the dome, no place for Billy to hide. The mint green bathroom fixtures were right out in the open. Billy got off his lounge chair now, went into the bathroom and took a leak. The crowd went wild.

Billy brushed his teeth on Tralfamadore, put in his partial denture, and went into his kitchen. His bottled-gas range and his refrigerator and his dishwasher were mint green, too. There was a picture painted on the door of the refrigerator. The refrigerator had come that way. It was a picture of a Gay Nineties couple on a bicycle built for two.

Billy looked at that picture now, tried to think something about the couple. Nothing came to him. There didn't seem to be *anything* to think about those two people.

Billy ate a good breakfast from cans. He washed his cup and plate and knife and fork and spoon and saucepan, put them away. Then he did exercises he had learned in the Army—straddle jumps, deep knee bends, sit-ups and push-ups. Most Tralfamadorians had no way of knowing Billy's body and face were not beautiful. They supposed that he was a splendid specimen. This had a pleasant effect on Billy, who began to enjoy his body for the first time.

He showered after his exercises and trimmed his toenails. He shaved, and sprayed deodorant under his arms, while a zoo guide on a raised platform outside explained what Billy was doing—and why. The guide was lecturing telepathically, simply standing there, sending out thought waves to the crowd. On the platform with him was the little keyboard instrument with which he would relay questions to Billy from the crowd.

Now the first question came—from the speaker on the television set: "Are you happy here?"

"About as happy as I was on Earth," said Billy Pilgrim, which was true.

There were five sexes on Tralfamadore, each of them performing a step necessary in the creation of a new individual. They looked identical to Billy—because their sex differences were all in the fourth dimension.

One of the biggest moral bombshells handed to Billy by the Tralfamadorians, incidentally, had to do with sex on Earth. They said their flying-saucer crews had identified no fewer than *seven* sexes on Earth, each essential to reproduction. Again: Billy couldn't possibly imagine what five of those seven sexes had to do with the making of a baby, since they were sexually active only in the fourth dimension.

The Tralfamadorians tried to give Billy clues that would help him imagine sex in the invisible dimension. They told him that there could be no Earthling babies without male homosexuals. There *could* be babies without female homosexuals. There couldn't be babies without women over sixty-five years old. There *could* be babies without men over sixty-five. There couldn't be babies without other babies who had lived an hour or less after birth. And so on.

It was gibberish to Billy.

There was a lot that Billy said that was gibberish to the Tralfamadorians, too. They couldn't imagine what time looked like to him. Billy had given up on explaining that. The guide outside had to explain as best he could.

The guide invited the crowd to imagine that they were looking across a desert at a mountain range on a day that was twinkling bright and clear. They could look at a peak or a bird or a cloud, at a stone right in front of them, or even down into a canyon behind them. But among them was this poor Earthling, and his head was encased in a steel sphere which he could never take off. There was only one eyehole through which he could look, and welded to that eyehole were six feet of pipe.

This was only the beginning of Billy's miseries in the metaphor. He was also strapped to a steel lattice which was bolted to a flatcar on rails, and there was no way he could turn his head or touch the pipe. The far end of the pipe rested on a bi-pod which was also bolted to the flatcar. All Billy could see was the little dot at the end of the pipe. He didn't know he was on a flatcar, didn't even know there was anything peculiar about his situation.

The flatcar sometimes crept, sometimes went extremely fast, often stopped—went uphill, downhill, around curves, along straightaways. Whatever poor Billy saw through the pipe, he had no choice but to say to himself, "That's life."

Billy expected the Tralfamadorians to be baffled and alarmed by all the wars and other forms of murder on Earth. He expected them to fear that the Earthling combination of ferocity and spectacular weaponry might eventually destroy part or maybe all of the innocent Universe. Science fiction had led him to expect that.

But the subject of war never came up until Billy brought it up himself. Somebody in the zoo crowd asked him through the lecturer what the most valuable thing he had learned on Tralfamadore was so far, and Billy replied, "How the inhabitants of a whole planet can live in peace! As you know, I am from a planet that has been engaged in senseless slaughter since the beginning of time. I myself have seen the bodies of schoolgirls who were boiled alive in a water tower by my own countrymen, who were proud of fighting pure evil at the time." This was true. Billy saw the boiled bodies in Dresden. "And I have lit my way in a prison at night with candles from the fat of human beings who were butchered by the brothers and fathers of those schoolgirls who were boiled. Earthlings must be the terrors of the Universe! If other planets aren't now in danger from Earth, they soon will be. So tell me the secret so I can take it back to Earth and save us all: How can a planet live at peace?"

Billy felt that he had spoken soaringly. He was baffled when he saw the Tralfamadorians close their little hands on their eyes. He knew from past experience what this meant: He was being stupid.

"Would—would you mind telling me—" he said to the guide, much deflated, "what was so stupid about that?"

"We know how the Universe ends—" said the guide, "and Earth has nothing to do with it, except that *it* gets wiped out, too."

"How—how *does* the Universe end?" said Billy.

"We blow it up, experimenting with new fuels for our flying

saucers. A Tralfamadorian test pilot presses a starter button, and the whole Universe disappears." So it goes.

"If you know this," said Billy, "isn't there some way you can prevent it? Can't you keep the pilot from *pressing* the button?"

"He has *always* pressed it, and he always *will.* We *always* let him and we always *will* let him. The moment is *structured* that way."

"So—" said Billy gropingly, "I suppose that the idea of preventing war on Earth is stupid, too."

"Of course."

"But you *do* have a peaceful planet here."

"Today we do. On other days we have wars as horrible as any you've ever seen or read about. There isn't anything we can do about them, so we simply don't look at them. We ignore them. We spend eternity looking at pleasant moments—like today at the zoo. Isn't this a nice moment?"

"Yes."

"That's one thing Earthlings might learn to do, if they tried hard enough: Ignore the awful times, and concentrate on the good ones."

"Um," said Billy Pilgrim.

Shortly after he went to sleep that night, Billy traveled in time to another moment which was quite nice, his wedding night with the former Valencia Merble. He had been out of the veterans' hospital for six months. He was all well. He had graduated from the Ilium School of Optometry—third in his class of forty-seven.

Now he was in bed with Valencia in a delightful studio apartment which was built on the end of a wharf on Cape Ann, Massachusetts. Across the water were the lights of Gloucester. Billy was on top of Valencia, making love to her. One result of this act would be the birth of Robert Pilgrim, who would become a problem in high school, but who would then straighten out as a member of the famous Green Berets.

Valencia wasn't a time-traveler, but she did have a lively imagination. While Billy was making love to her, she imagined that she was a famous woman in history. She was being Queen Elizabeth the First of England, and Billy was supposedly Christopher Columbus.

Billy made a noise like a small, rusty hinge. He had just emptied his seminal vesicles into Valencia, had contributed his share of the Green Beret. According to the Tralfamadorians, of course, the Green Beret would have seven parents in all.

Now he rolled off his huge wife, whose rapt expression did not change when he departed. He lay with the buttons of his spine along the edge of the mattress, folded his hands behind his head. He was rich now. He had been rewarded for marrying a girl nobody in his right mind would have married. His father-in-law had given him a new Buick Roadmaster, an all-electric home, and had made him manager of his most prosperous office, his Ilium office, where Billy could expect to make at least thirty thousand dollars a year. That was good. His father had been only a barber.

As his mother said, "The Pilgrims are coming up in the world."

The honeymoon was taking place in the bittersweet mysteries of Indian Summer in New England. The lovers' apartment had one romantic wall which was all French doors. They opened onto a balcony and the oily harbor beyond.

A green and orange dragger, black in the night, grumbled and drummed past their balcony, not thirty feet from their wedding bed. It was going to sea with only its running lights on. Its empty holds were resonant, made the song of the engines rich and loud. The wharf began to sing the same song, and then the honeymooners' headboard sang, too. And it continued to sing long after the dragger was gone.

"Thank you," said Valencia at last. The headboard was singing a mosquito song.

"You're welcome."

"It was nice."

"I'm glad."

Then she began to cry.

"What's the matter?"

"I'm so happy."

"Good."

"I never thought anybody would marry me."

"Um," said Billy Pilgrim.

"I'm going to lose weight for you," she said.

"What?"

"I'm going to go on a diet. I'm going to become beautiful for you."

"I like you just the way you are."

"Do you *really?*"

"Really," said Billy Pilgrim. He had already seen a lot of their marriage, thanks to time-travel, knew that it was going to be at least bearable all the way.

A great motor yacht named the *Scheherezade* now slid past the marriage bed. The song its engines sang was a very low organ note. All her lights were on.

Two beautiful people, a young man and a young woman in evening clothes, were at the rail in the stern, loving each other and their dreams and the wake. They were honeymooning, too. They were Lance Rumfoord, of Newport, Rhode Island, and his bride, the former Cynthia Landry, who had been a childhood sweetheart of John F. Kennedy in Hyannis Port, Massachusetts.

There was a slight coincidence here. Billy Pilgrim would later share a hospital room with Rumfoord's uncle, Professor Bertram Copeland Rumfoord of Harvard, official Historian of the United States Air Force.

When the beautiful people were past, Valencia questioned her funny-looking husband about war. It was a simple-minded thing for a female Earthling to do, to associate sex and glamor with war.

"Do you ever think about the war?" she said, laying a hand on his thigh.

"Sometimes," said Billy Pilgrim.

"I look at you sometimes," said Valencia, "and I get a funny feeling that you're just full of secrets."

"I'm not," said Billy. This was a lie, of course. He hadn't told anybody about all the time-traveling he'd done, about Tralfamadore and so on.

"You must have secrets about the war. Or, not secrets, I guess, but things you don't want to talk about."

"No."

"I'm *proud* you were a soldier. Do you know that?"

"Good."

"Was it awful?"

"Sometimes." A crazy thought now occurred to Billy. The truth of it startled him. It would make a good epitaph for Billy Pilgrim—and for me, too.

"Would you talk about the war now, if I *wanted* you to?" said Valencia. In a tiny cavity in her great body she was assembling the materials for a Green Beret.

"It would sound like a dream," said Billy. "Other people's dreams aren't very interesting, usually."

"I heard you tell Father one time about a German firing squad." She was referring to the execution of poor old Edgar Derby.

"Um."

"You had to bury him?"

"Yes."

"Did he see you with your shovels before he was shot?"

"Yes."

"Did he *say* anything?"

"No."

"Was he *scared?*"

"They had him doped up. He was sort of glassy-eyed."

"And they pinned a target to him?"

"A piece of paper," said Billy. He got out of bed, said, "Excuse me," went into the darkness of the bathroom to take a leak. He groped for the light, realized as he felt the rough walls that he had traveled back to 1944, to the prison hospital again.

The candle in the hospital had gone out. Poor old Edgar Derby had fallen asleep on the cot next to Billy's. Billy was out of bed, groping along a wall, trying to find a way out because he had to take a leak so badly.

He suddenly found a door, which opened, let him reel out into the prison night. Billy was loony with time-travel and morphine. He delivered himself to a barbed-wire fence which snagged him in a dozen places. Billy tried to back away from it, but the barbs wouldn't let go. So Billy did a silly little dance with the fence, taking a step this way, then that way, then returning to the beginning again.

A Russian, himself out in the night to take a leak, saw Billy dancing—from the other side of the fence. He came over to the curious scarecrow, tried to talk with it gently, asked it what country it was from. The scarecrow paid no atttention, went on dancing. So the Russian undid the snags one by one, and the scarecrow danced off into the night again without a word of thanks.

The Russian waved to him, and called after him in Russian, "Good-bye."

Billy took his pecker out, there in the prison night, and peed and peed on the ground. Then he put it away again, more or less, and contemplated a new problem: Where had he come from, and where should he go now?

Somewhere in the night there were cries of grief. With nothing better to do, Billy shuffled in their direction. He wondered what tragedy so many had found to lament out of doors.

Billy was approaching, without knowing it, the back of the latrine. It consisted of a one-rail fence with twelve buckets underneath it. The fence was sheltered on three sides by a screen of scrap lumber and flattened tin cans. The open side faced the black tarpaper wall of the shed where the feast had taken place.

Billy moved along the screen and reached a point where he could see a message freshly painted on the tarpaper wall. The words were written with the same pink paint which had brightened the set *for Cinderella.* Billy's perceptions were so unreliable that he saw the words as hanging in air, painted on a transparent curtain, perhaps. And there were lovely silver dots on the curtain, too. These were really nailheads holding the tarpaper to the shed. Billy could not imagine how the curtain was supported in nothingness, and he supposed that the magic curtain and the theatrical grief were part of some religious ceremony he knew nothing about.

Here is what the message said:

Billy looked inside the latrine. The wailing was coming from in there. The place was crammed with Americans who had taken their pants down. The welcome feast had made them as sick as volcanoes. The buckets were full or had been kicked over.

An American near Billy wailed that he had excreted everything but his brains. Moments later he said, "There they go, there they go." He meant his brains.

That was I. That was me. That was the author of this book.

Billy reeled away from his vision of Hell. He passed three Englishmen who were watching the excrement festival from a distance. They were catatonic with disgust.

"Button your pants!" said one as Billy went by.

So Billy buttoned his pants. He came to the door of the little hospital by accident. He went through the door, and found himself honeymooning again, going from the bathroom back to bed with his bride on Cape Ann.

"I missed you," said Valencia.

"I missed *you,*" said Billy Pilgrim.

Billy and Valencia went to sleep nestled like spoons, and Billy traveled in time back to the train ride he had taken in 1944—from maneuvers in South Carolina to his father's funeral in Ilium. He hadn't seen Europe or combat yet. This was still in the days of steam locomotives.

Billy had to change trains a lot. All the trains were slow. The coaches stunk of coal smoke and rationed tobacco and rationed booze and the farts of people eating wartime food. The upholstery of the iron seats was bristly, and Billy couldn't sleep much. He got to sleep soundly when he was only three hours from Ilium, with his legs splayed toward the entrance of the busy dining car.

The porter woke him up when the train reached Ilium. Billy staggered off with his duffel bag, and then he stood on the station platform next to the porter, trying to wake up.

"Have a good nap, did you?" said the porter.

"Yes," said Billy.

"Man," said the porter, "you sure had a hard-on."

At three in the morning on Billy's morphine night in prison, a new patient was carried into the hospital by two lusty Englishmen. He was tiny. He was Paul Lazzaro, the polka-dotted car thief from Cicero, Illinois. He had been caught stealing cigarettes from under the pillow of an Englishman. The Englishman, half asleep, had broken Lazzaro's right arm and knocked him unconscious.

The Englishman who had done this was helping to carry Lazzaro in now. He had fiery red hair and no eyebrows. He had been Cinderella's Blue Fairy Godmother in the play. Now he supported his half of Lazzaro with one hand while he closed the door behind himself with the other. "Doesn't weigh as much as a chicken," he said.

The Englishman with Lazzaro's feet was the colonel who had given Billy his knock-out shot.

The Blue Fairy Godmother was embarrassed, and angry, too. "If I'd known I was fighting a chicken," he said, "I wouldn't have fought so *hard.*"

"Um."

The Blue Fairy Godmother spoke frankly about how disgusting all the Americans were. "Weak, smelly, self-pitying—a pack of sniveling, dirty, thieving bastards," he said. "They're worse than the bleeding Russians."

"*Do* seem a scruffy lot," the colonel agreed.

A German major came in now. He considered the Englishmen as close friends. He visited them nearly every day, played games with them, lectured to them on German history, played their piano, gave them lessons in conversational German. He told them often that, if it weren't for their civilized company, he would go mad. His English was splendid.

He was apologetic about the Englishmen's having to put up with the American enlisted men. He promised them that they would not be inconvenienced for more than a day or two, that the Americans would soon be shipped to Dresden as contract labor. He had a monograph with him, published by the German Association of Prison Officials. It was a report on the behavior in Germany of American enlisted men as prisoners of war. It was written by a former American who had risen high in the German Ministry of Propaganda. His name was Howard W. Campbell, Jr. He would later hang himself while awaiting trial as a war criminal.

So it goes.

While the British colonel set Lazzaro's broken arm and mixed plaster for the cast, the German major translated out loud passages from Howard W. Campbell, Jr.'s monograph. Campbell had been a fairly well-known playwright at one time. His opening line was this one:

America is the wealthiest nation on Earth, but its people are mainly poor, and poor Americans are urged to hate themselves. To quote the American humorist Kin Hubbard, "It ain't no disgrace to be poor, but it might as well be." It is in fact a crime for an American to be poor, even though America is a nation of poor. Every other nation has folk traditions of men who were poor but extremely wise and virtuous, and therefore more estimable than anyone with power and gold. No such tales are told by the American poor. They mock themselves and glorify their betters. The meanest eating or drinking establishment, owned by a man who is himself poor, is very likely to have a sign on its wall asking this cruel question: "If you're so smart, why ain't you rich?" There will also be an American flag no larger than a child's hand —glued to a lollipop stick and flying from the cash register.

The author of the monograph, a native of Schenectady, New York, was said by some to have had the highest I.Q. of all the war criminals who were made to face a death by hanging. So it goes.

Americans, like human beings everywhere, believe many things that are obviously untrue, the monograph went on. *Their most destructive untruth is that it is very easy for any American to make money. They will not acknowledge how in fact hard money is to come by, and, therefore, those who have no money blame and blame and blame themselves. This inward blame has been a treasure for the rich and powerful, who have had to do less for their poor, publicly and privately, than any other ruling class since, say, Napoleonic times.*

Many novelties have come from America. The most startling of these, a thing without precedent, is a mass of undignified poor. They do not love one another because they do not love themselves. Once this is understood, the disagreeable behavior of American enlisted men in German prisons ceases to be a mystery.

Howard W. Campbell, Jr., now discussed the uniform of the American enlisted in World War Two: *Every other army in history, prosperous or not, has attempted to clothe even its lowliest soldiers so as to make them impressive to themselves and others as stylish experts in drinking and copulation and looting and sudden death. The American Army, however, sends its enlisted men out to fight and die in a modified business suit quite evidently made for another man, a sterilized but unpressed gift from a nose-holding charity which passes out clothing to drunks in the slums.*

When a dashingly-clad officer addresses such a frumpishly dressed bum, he scolds him, as an officer in any army must. But the officer's contempt is not, as in other armies, avuncular theatricality. It is a genuine expression of hatred for the poor, who have no one to blame for their misery but themselves.

A prison administrator dealing with captured American enlisted men for the first time should be warned: Expect no brotherly love, even between brothers. There will be no cohesion between the individuals. Each will be a sulky child who often wishes he were dead.

Campbell told what the German experience with captured American enlisted men had been. They were known everywhere to be the most self-pitying, least fraternal, and dirtiest of all prisoners of war, said Campbell. They were incapable of concerted action on their own behalf. They despised any leader from among their own number, refused to follow or even listen to him, on the grounds that he was no better than they were, that he should stop putting on airs.

And so on. Billy Pilgrim went to sleep, woke up as a widower in his empty home in Ilium. His daughter Barbara was reproaching him for writing ridiculous letters to the newspapers.

"Did you hear what I said?" Barbara inquired. It was 1968 again.

"Of course." He had been dozing.

"If you're going to act like a child, maybe we'll just have to *treat* you like a child."

"That isn't what happens next," said Billy.

"We'll *see* what happens next." Big Barbara now embraced herself. "It's awfully cold in here. Is the heat on?"

"The *heat?*"

"The furnace—the thing in the basement, the thing that makes hot air that comes out of these registers. I don't think it's working."

"Maybe not."

"Aren't you cold?"

"I hadn't noticed."

"Oh, my God, you *are* a child. If we leave you alone here, you'll freeze to death, you'll starve to death." And so on. It was very exciting for her, taking his dignity away in the name of love.

Barbara called the oil-burner man, and she made Billy go to bed, made him promise to stay under the electric blanket until the heat came on. She set the control of the blanket at the highest notch, which soon made Billy's bed hot enough to bake bread in.

When Barbara left, slamming the door behind her, Billy traveled in time to the zoo on Tralfamadore again. A mate had just been brought to him from Earth. She was Montana Wildhack, a motion picture star.

Montana was under heavy sedation. Tralfamadorians wearing gas masks brought her in, put her on Billy's yellow lounge chair; withdrew through his airlock. The vast crowd outside was delighted. All attendance records for the zoo were broken. Everybody on the planet wanted to see the Earthlings mate.

Montana was naked, and so was Billy, of course. He had a tremendous wang, incidentally. You never know who'll get one.

Now she fluttered her eyelids. Her lashes were like buggy whips. "Where *am* I?" she said.

"Everything is all right," said Billy gently. "Please don't be afraid."

Montana had been unconscious during her trip from Earth. The Tralfamadorians hadn't talked to her, hadn't shown themselves to her. The last thing she remembered was sunning herself by a swimming pool in Palm Springs, California. Montana was only twenty years old. Around her neck was a silver chain with a heart-shaped locket hanging from it—between her breasts.

Now she turned her head to see the myriads of Tralfamadorians outside the dome. They were applauding her by opening and closing their little green hands quickly.

Montana screamed and screamed.

All the little green hands closed tight, because Montana's terror was so unpleasant to see. The head zoo keeper ordered a crane operator, who was standing by, to drop a navy blue canopy over the dome, thus simulating Earthling night inside. Real night came to the zoo for only one Earthling hour of every sixty-two.

Billy switched on a floor lamp. The light from the single source threw the baroque detailing of Montana's body into sharp relief. Billy was reminded of fantastic architecture in Dresden, before it was bombed.

In time, Montana came to love and trust Billy Pilgrim. He did not touch her until she made it clear that she wanted him to. After she had been on Tralfamadore for what would have been an Earthling week, she asked him shyly if he wouldn't sleep with her. Which he did. It was heavenly.

And Billy traveled in time from that delightful bed to a bed in 1968. It was his bed in Ilium, and the electric blanket was turned up high. He was drenched in sweat, remembered groggily that his daughter had put him to bed, had told him to stay there until the oil burner was repaired.

Somebody was knocking on his bedroom door.

"Yes?" said Billy.

"Oil-burner man."

"Yes?"

"It's running good now. Heat's coming up."

"Good."

"Mouse ate through a wire from the thermostat."

"I'll be darned."

Billy sniffed. His hot bed smelled like a mushroom cellar. He had had a wet dream about Montana Wildhack.

On the morning after that wet dream, Billy decided to go back to work in his office in the shopping plaza. Business was booming as usual. His assistants were keeping up with it nicely. They were startled to see him. They had been told by his daughter that he might never practice again.

But Billy went into his examining room briskly, asked that the first patient be sent in. So they sent him one—a twelve-year-old boy who was accompanied by his widowed mother. They were strangers, new in town. Billy asked them a little about themselves, learned that the boy's father had been killed in Vietnam—in the famous five-day battle for Hill 875 near Dakto. So it goes.

While he examined the boy's eyes, Billy told him matter-of-factly about his adventures on Tralfamadore, assured the fatherless boy that his father was very much alive still in moments the boy would see again and again.

"Isn't that comforting?" Billy asked.

And somewhere in there, the boy's mother went out and told the receptionist that Billy was evidently going crazy. Billy was taken home. His daughter asked him again, "Father, Father, Father—what *are* we going to *do* with you?"

6

Listen:

Billy Pilgrim says he went to Dresden, Germany, on the day after his morphine night in the British compound in the center of the extermination camp for Russian prisoners of war. Billy woke up at dawn on that day in January. There were no windows in the little hospital, and the ghostly candles had gone out. So the only light came from pin-prick holes in the walls, and from a sketchy rectangle that outlined the imperfectly fitted door. Little Paul Lazzaro, with a broken arm, snored on one bed. Edgar Derby, the high school teacher who would eventually be shot, snored on another.

Billy sat up in bed. He had no idea what year it was or what planet he was on. Whatever the planet's name was, it was cold. But it wasn't the cold that had awakened Billy. It was animal magnetism which was making him shiver and itch. It gave him profound aches in his musculature, as though he had been exercising hard.

The animal magnetism was coming from behind him. If Billy had had to guess as to the source, he would have said that there was a vampire bat hanging upside down on the wall behind him.

Billy moved down toward the foot of his cot before turning to look at whatever it was. He didn't want the animal to drop into his face and maybe claw his eyes out or bite off his big nose. Then he turned. The source of the magnetism really did resemble a bat. It was Billy's impresario's coat with the fur collar. It was hanging from a nail.

Billy now backed toward it again, looking at it over his shoulder, feeling the magnetism increase. Then he faced it, kneeling on his cot, dared to touch it here and there. He was seeking the exact source of the radiations.

He found two small sources, two lumps an inch apart and hidden in the lining. One was shaped like a pea. The other was shaped like a tiny horseshoe. Billy received a message carried by the radiations. He was told not to find out what the lumps were. He was advised to be content with knowing that they could work miracles for him, provided he did not insist on learning their nature. That was all right with Billy Pilgrim. He was grateful. He was glad.

Billy dozed, awakened in the prison hospital again. The sun was high. Outside were Golgotha sounds of strong men digging holes for upright timbers in hard, hard ground. Englishmen were building themselves a new latrine. They had abandoned their old latrine to the Americans—and their theater, the place where the feast had been held, too.

Six Englishmen staggered through the hospital with a pool table on which several mattresses were piled. They were transferring it to living quarters attached to the hospital. They were followed by an Englishman dragging his mattress and carrying a dartboard.

The man with the dartboard was the Blue Fairy Godmother who had injured little Paul Lazzaro. He stopped by Lazzaro's bed, asked Lazzaro how he was.

Lazzaro told him he was going to have him killed after the war.

"Oh?"

"You made a big mistake," said Lazzaro. "Anybody touches me, he better *kill* me, or I'm gonna have *him* killed."

The Blue Fairy Godmother knew something about killing. He gave Lazzaro a careful smile. "There is still time for *me* to kill *you,*" he said, "if you really persuade me that it's the sensible thing to do."

"Why don't you go fuck yourself?"

"Don't think I haven't tried," the Blue Fairy Godmother answered.

The Blue Fairy Godmother left, amused and patronizing. When he was gone, Lazzaro promised Billy and poor old Edgar Derby that he was going to have revenge, and that revenge was sweet.

"It's the sweetest thing there is," said Lazzaro. "People fuck with me," he said, "and Jesus Christ are they ever fucking sorry. I laugh like hell. I don't care if it's a guy or a dame. If the President of the United States fucked around with me, I'd fix him good. You should have seen what I did to a dog one time."

"A dog?" said Billy.

"Son of a bitch bit me. So I got me some steak, and I got me the spring out of a clock. I cut that spring up in little pieces. I put points on the ends of the pieces. They were sharp as razor blades. I stuck 'em into the steak—way inside. And I went past where they had the dog tied up. He wanted to bite me again. I said to him, 'Come on, doggie—let's be friends. Let's not be enemies any more. I'm not mad.' He believed me."

"He *did?*"

"I threw him the steak. He swallowed it down in one big gulp. I waited around for ten minutes." Now Lazzaro's eyes twinkled. "Blood started coming out of his mouth. He started crying, and he rolled on the ground, as though the knives were on the outside of him instead of on the inside of him. Then he tried to bite out his own insides. I laughed, and I said to him, 'You got the right idea now. Tear your own guts out, boy. That's *me* in there with all those knives.'" So it goes.

"Anybody ever asks you what the sweetest thing in life is—" said Lazzaro, "it's revenge."

When Dresden was destroyed later on, incidentally, Lazzaro did not exult. He didn't have anything against the Germans, he said. Also, he said he liked to take his enemies one at a time. He was proud of never having hurt an innocent bystander. "Nobody ever got it from Lazzaro," he said, "who didn't have it coming."

Poor old Edgar Derby, the high school teacher, got into the conversation now. He asked Lazzaro if he planned to feed the Blue Fairy Godmother clock springs and steak.

"Shit," said Lazzaro.

"He's a pretty big man," said Derby, who, of course, was a pretty big man himself.

"Size don't mean a thing."

"You're going to *shoot* him?"

"I'm gonna *have* him shot," said Lazzaro. "He'll get home after the war. He'll be a big hero. The dames'll be climbing all over him. He'll settle down. A couple of years'll go by. And then one day there'll be a knock on his door. He'll answer the door, and there'll be a stranger out there. The stranger'll ask him if he's so-and-so. When he says he is, the stranger'll say, 'Paul Lazzaro sent me.' And he'll pull out a gun and shoot his pecker off. The stranger'll let him think a couple of seconds about who Paul Lazzaro is and what life's gonna be like without a pecker. Then he'll shoot him once in the guts and walk away." So it goes.

Lazzaro said that he could have anybody in the world killed for a thousand dollars plus traveling expenses. He had a list in his head, he said.

Derby asked him who all was on the list, and Lazzaro said, "Just make fucking sure *you* don't get on it. Just don't cross me, that's all." There was a silence, and then he added, "And don't cross my friends."

"You have *friends?*" Derby wanted to know.

"In the *war?*" said Lazzaro. "Yeah—I had a friend in the war. He's dead." So it goes.

"That's too bad."

Lazzaro's eyes were twinkling again. "Yeah. He was my buddy on the boxcar. His name was Roland Weary. He died in my arms." Now he pointed to Billy with his one mobile hand. "He died on account of this silly cocksucker here. So I promised him I'd have this silly cocksucker shot after the war."

Lazzaro erased with his hand anything Billy Pilgrim might be about to say. "Just forget about it, kid," he said. "Enjoy life while you can. Nothing's gonna happen for maybe five, ten, fifteen, twenty years. But lemme give you a piece of advice: Whenever the doorbell rings, have somebody else answer the door."

Billy Pilgrim says now that this really is the way he *is* going to die, too. As a time-traveler, he has seen his own death many times, has described it to a tape recorder. The tape is locked up with his will and some other valuables in his safe-deposit box at the Ilium Merchants National Bank and Trust, he says.

I, Billy Pilgrim, the tape begins, *will die, have died, and always will die on February thirteenth, 1976.*

At the time of his death, he says, he is in Chicago to address a large crowd on the subject of flying saucers and the true nature of time. His home is still in Ilium. He has had to cross three international boundaries in order to reach Chicago. The United States of America has been Balkanized, has been divided into twenty petty nations so that it will never again be a threat to world peace. Chicago has been hydrogen-bombed by angry Chinamen. So it goes. It is all brand new.

Billy is speaking before a capacity audience in a baseball park, which is covered by a geodesic dome. The flag of the country is behind him. It is a Hereford bull on a field of green. Billy predicts his own death within an hour. He laughs about it, invites the crowd to laugh with him. "It is high time I was dead," he says. "Many years ago," he said, "a certain man promised to have me killed. He is an old man now, living not far from here. He has read all the publicity associated with my appearance in your fair city. He is insane. Tonight he will keep his promise."

There are protests from the crowd.

Billy Pilgrim rebukes them. "If you protest, if you think that death is a terrible thing, then you have not understood a word I've said." Now he closes his speech as he closes every speech—with these words: "Farewell, hello, farewell, hello."

There are police around him as he leaves the stage. They are there to protect him from the crush of popularity. No threats on his life have been made since 1945. The police offer to stay with him. They are floridly willing to stand in a circle around him all night, with their zap guns drawn.

"No, no," says Billy serenely. "It is time for you to go home to your wives and children, and it is time for me to be dead for a little while—and then live again." At that moment, Billy's high forehead is in the cross hairs of a high-powered laser gun. It is aimed at him from the darkened press box. In the next moment, Billy Pilgrim is dead. So it goes.

So Billy experiences death for a while. It is simply violet light and a hum. There isn't anybody else there. Not even Billy Pilgrim is there.

Then he swings back into life again, all the way back to an hour after his life was threatened by Lazzaro—in 1945. He has been told to get out of his hospital bed and dress, that he is well. He and Lazzaro and poor old Edgar Derby are to join their fellows in the theater. There they will choose a leader for themselves by secret ballot in a free election.

Billy and Lazzaro and poor old Edgar Derby crossed the prison yard to the theater now. Billy was carrying his little coat as though it were a lady's muff. It was wrapped around and around his hands. He was the central clown in an unconscious travesty of that famous oil painting, "The Spirit of '76."

Edgar Derby was writing letters home in his head, telling his wife that he was alive and well, that she shouldn't worry, that the war was nearly over, that he would soon be home.

Lazzaro was talking to himself about people he was going to have killed after the war, and rackets he was going to work, and women he was going to make fuck him, whether they wanted to or not. If he had been a dog in a city, a policeman would have shot him and sent his head to a laboratory, to see if he had rabies. So it goes.

As they neared the theater, they came upon an Englishman who was hacking a groove in the Earth with the heel of his boot. He was marking the boundary between the American and English sections of the compound. Billy and Lazzaro and Derby didn't have to ask what the line meant. It was a familiar symbol from childhood.

The theater was paved with American bodies that nestled like spoons. Most of the Americans were in stupors or asleep. Their guts were fluttering, dry.

"Close the fucking door," somebody said to Billy. "Were you born in a barn?"

Billy closed it, took a hand from his muff, touched a stove. It was as cold as ice. The stage was still set for *Cinderella.* Azure curtains hung from arches which were shocking pink. There were golden thrones and the dummy clock, whose hands were set at midnight. Cinderella's slippers, which were airman's boots painted silver, were capsized side by side under a golden throne.

Billy and poor old Edgar Derby and Lazzaro had been in the hospital when the British passed out blankets and mattresses, so they had none. They had to improvise. The only space open to them was up on the stage, and they went up there, pulled the azure curtains down, made nests.

Billy, curled in his azure nest, found himself staring at Cinderella's silver boots under a throne. And then he remembered that his shoes were ruined, that he *needed* boots. He hated to get out of his nest, but he forced himself to do it. He crawled to the boots on all fours, sat, tried them on.

The boots fit perfectly. Billy Pilgrim was Cinderella, and Cinderella was Billy Pilgrim.

Somewhere in there was a lecture on personal hygiene by the head Englishman, and then a free election. At least half the Americans went on snoozing through it all. The Englishman got up on the stage, and he rapped on the arm of a throne with a swagger stick, called, "Lads, lads, lads—can I have your attention, please?" And so on.

What the Englishman said about survival was this: "If you stop taking pride in your appearance, you will very soon die." He said that he had seen several men die in the following way: "They ceased to stand up straight, then ceased to shave or wash, then ceased to get out of bed, then ceased to talk, then died. There is much to be said for it: it is evidently a very easy and painless way to go." So it goes.

The Englishman said that he, when captured, had made and kept the following vows to himself: To brush his teeth twice a day, to shave once a day, to wash his face and hands before every meal and after going to the latrine, to polish his shoes once a day, to exercise for at least half an hour each morning and then move his bowels, and to look into a mirror frequently, frankly evaluating his appearance, particularly with respect to posture.

Billy Pilgrim heard all this while lying in his nest. He looked not at the Englishman's face but his ankles.

"I *envy* you lads," said the Englishman.

Somebody laughed. Billy wondered what the joke was.

"You lads are leaving this afternoon for Dresden—a beautiful city, I'm told. You won't be cooped up like us. You'll be out where the life is, and the food is certain to be more plentiful than here. If I may inject a personal note: It has been five years now since I have seen a tree or flower or woman or child—or a dog or a cat or a place of entertainment, or a human being doing useful work of any kind.

"You needn't worry about bombs, by the way. Dresden is an open city. It is undefended, and contains no war industries or troop concentrations of any importance."

Somewhere in there, old Edgar Derby was elected head American. The Englishman called for nominations from the floor, and there weren't any. So he nominated Derby, praising him for his maturity and long experience in dealing with people. There were no further nominations, so the nominations were closed.

"All in favor?"

Two or three people said, "Aye."

Then poor old Derby made a speech. He thanked the Englishman for his good advice, said he meant to follow it exactly. He said he was sure that all the other Americans would do the same. He said that his primary responsibility now was to make damn well sure that everybody got home safely.

"Go take a flying fuck at a rolling doughnut," murmured Paul Lazzaro in his azure nest. "Go take a flying fuck at the moon."

The temperature climbed startlingly that day. The noontime was balmy. The Germans brought soup and bread in two-wheeled carts which were pulled by Russians. The Englishmen sent over real coffee and sugar and marmalade and cigarettes and cigars, and the doors of the theater were left open, so the warmth could get in.

The Americans began to feel much better. They were able to hold their food. And then it was time to go to Dresden. The Americans marched fairly stylishly out of the British compound. Billy Pilgrim again led the parade. He had silver boots now, and a muff, and a piece of azure curtain which he wore like a toga. Billy still had a beard. So did poor old Edgar Derby, who was beside him. Derby was imagining letters to home, his lips working tremulously:

Dear Margaret—We are leaving for Dresden today. Don't worry. It will never be bombed. It is an open city. There was an election at noon, and guess what? And so on.

They came to the prison railroad yard again. They had arrived on only two cars. They would depart far more comfortably on four. They saw the dead hobo again. He was frozen stiff in the weeds beside the track. He was in a fetal position, trying even in death to nestle like a spoon with others. There were no others now. He was nestling with thin air and cinders. Somebody had taken his boots. His bare feet were blue and ivory. It was all right, somehow, his being dead. So it goes.

The trip to Dresden was a lark. It took only two hours. Shriveled little bellies were full. Sunlight and mild air came in through the ventilators. There were plenty of smokes from the Englishmen.

The Americans arrived in Dresden at five in the afternoon. The boxcar doors were opened, and the doorways framed the loveliest city that most of the Americans had ever seen. The skyline was intricate and voluptuous and enchanted and absurd. It looked like a Sunday school picture of Heaven to Billy Pilgrim.

Somebody behind him in the boxcar said, "Oz." That was I. That was me. The only other city I'd ever seen was Indianapolis, Indiana.

Every other big city in Germany had been bombed and burned ferociously. Dresden had not suffered so much as a cracked windowpane. Sirens went off every day, screamed like hell, and people went down into cellars and listened to radios there. The planes were always bound for someplace else—Leipzig, Chemnitz, Plauen, places like that. So it goes.

Steam radiators still whistled cheerily in Dresden. Streetcars clanged. Telephones rang and were answered. Lights went on and off when switches were clicked. There were theaters and restaurants. There was a zoo. The principal enterprises of the city were medicine and food-processing and the making of cigarettes.

People were going home from work now in the late afternoon. They were tired.

Eight Dresdeners crossed the steel spaghetti of the railroad yard. They were wearing new uniforms. They had been sworn into the army the day before. They were boys and men past middle age, and two veterans who had been shot to pieces in Russia. Their assignment was to guard one hundred American prisoners of war, who would work as contract labor. A grandfather and his grandson were in the squad. The grandfather was an architect.

The eight were grim as they approached the boxcars containing their wards. They knew what sick and foolish soldiers they themselves appeared to be. One of them actually had an artificial leg, and carried not only a loaded rifle but a cane. Still—they were expected to earn obedience and respect from tall, cocky, murderous American infantrymen who had just come from all the killing at the front.

And then they saw bearded Billy Pilgrim in his blue toga and silver shoes, with his hands in a muff. He looked at least sixty years old. Next to Billy was little Paul Lazzaro with a broken arm. He was fizzing with rabies. Next to Lazzaro was the poor old high school teacher, Edgar Derby, mournfully pregnant with patriotism and middle age and imaginary wisdom. And so on.

The eight ridiculous Dresdeners ascertained that these hundred ridiculous creatures really *were* American fighting men fresh from the front. They smiled, and then they laughed. Their terror evaporated. There was nothing to be afraid of. Here were more crippled human beings, more fools like themselves. Here was light opera.

So out of the gate of the railroad yard and into the streets of Dresden marched the light opera. Billy Pilgrim was the star. He led the parade. Thousands of people were on the sidewalks, going home from work. They were watery and putty-colored, having eaten mostly potatoes during the past two years. They had expected no blessings beyond the mildness of the day. Suddenly—here was fun.

Billy did not meet many of the eyes that found him so entertaining. He was enchanted by the architecture of the city. Merry amoretti wove garlands above windows. Roguish fauns and naked nymphs peeked down at Billy from festooned cornices. Stone monkeys frisked among scrolls and seashells and bamboo.

Billy, with his memories of the future, knew that the city would be smashed to smithereens and then burned—in about thirty more days. He knew, too, that most of the people watching him would soon be dead. So it goes.

And Billy worked his hands in his muff as he marched. His fingertips, working there in the hot darkness of the muff, wanted to know what the two lumps in the lining of the little impresario's coat were. The fingertips got inside the lining. They palpated the lumps, the pea-shaped thing and the horseshoe-shaped thing. The parade had to halt by a busy corner. The traffic light was red.

There at the corner, in the front rank of pedestrians, was a surgeon who had been operating all day. He was a civilian, but his posture was military. He had served in two world wars. The sight of Billy offended him, especially after he learned from the guards that Billy was an American. It seemed to him that Billy was in abominable taste, supposed that Billy had gone to a lot of silly trouble to costume himself just so.

The surgeon spoke English, and he said to Billy, "I take it you find war a very comical thing."

Billy looked at him vaguely. Billy had lost track momentarily of where he was or how he had gotten there. He had no idea that people thought he was clowning. It was Fate, of course, which had costumed him—Fate, and a feeble will to survive.

"Did you expect us to *laugh?*" the surgeon asked him.

The surgeon was demanding some sort of satisfaction. Billy was mystified. Billy wanted to be friendly, to help, if he could, but his resources were meager. His fingers now held the two objects from the lining of the coat. Billy decided to show the surgeon what they were.

"You thought we would enjoy being *mocked?*" the surgeon said. "And do you feel *proud* to represent America as you do?"

Billy withdrew a hand from his muff, held it under the surgeon's nose. On his palm rested a two-carat diamond and a partial denture. The denture was an obscene little artifact—silver and pearl and tangerine. Billy smiled.

The parade pranced, staggered and reeled to the gate of the Dresden slaughterhouse, and then it went inside. The slaughterhouse wasn't a busy place any more. Almost all the hooved animals in Germany had been killed and eaten and excreted by human beings, mostly soldiers. So it goes.

The Americans were taken to the fifth building inside the gate. It was a one-story cement-block cube with sliding doors in front and back. It had been built as a shelter for pigs about to be butchered. Now it was going to serve as a home away from home for one hundred American prisoners of war. There were bunks in there, and two potbellied stoves and a water tap. Behind it was a latrine, which was a one-rail fence with buckets under it.

There was a big number over the door of the building. The number was *five.* Before the Americans could go inside, their only English-speaking guard told them to memorize their simple address, in case they got lost in the big city. Their address was this: "Schlachthof-fünf." *Schlachthof* meant *slaughterhouse. Fünf* was good old *five.*

7

Billy Pilgrim got onto a chartered airplane in Ilium twenty-five years after that. He knew it was going to crash, but he didn't want to make a fool of himself by saying so. It was supposed to carry Billy and twenty-eight other optometrists to a convention in Montreal.

His wife, Valencia, was outside, and his father-in-law, Lionel Merble, was strapped to the seat beside him.

Lionel Merble was a machine. Tralfamadorians, of course, say that every creature and plant in the Universe is a machine. It amuses them that so many Earthlings are offended by the idea of being machines.

Outside the plane, the machine named Valencia Merble Pilgrim was eating a Peter Paul Mound Bar and waving bye-bye.

The plane took off without incident. The moment was structured that way. There was a barbershop quartet on board. They were optometrists, too. They called themselves "The Febs," which was an acronym for "Four-eyed Bastards."

When the plane was safely aloft, the machine that was Billy's father-in-law asked the quartet to sing his favorite song. They knew what song he meant, and they sang it, and it went like this:

In my prison cell I sit,
With my britches full of shit,
And my balls are bouncing gently on the floor.
And I see the bloody snag
When she bit me in the bag.
Oh, I'll never fuck a Polack any more.

Billy's father-in-law laughed and laughed at that, and he begged the quartet to sing the other Polish song he liked so much. So they sang a song from the Pennsylvania coal mines that began:

Me and Mike, ve vork in mine.
Holy shit, ve have good time.
Vunce a veek ve get our pay.
Holy shit, no vork next day.

Speaking of people from Poland: Billy Pilgrim accidentally saw a Pole hanged in public, about three days after Billy got to Dresden. Billy just happened to be walking to work with some others shortly after sunrise, and they came to a gallows and a small crowd in front of a soccer stadium. The Pole was a farm laborer who was being hanged for having had sexual intercourse with a German woman. So it goes.

Billy, knowing the plane was going to crash pretty soon, closed his eyes, traveled in time back to 1944. He was back in the forest in Luxembourg again—with the Three Musketeers. Roland Weary was shaking him, bonking his head against a tree. "You guys go on without me," said Billy Pilgrim.

The barbershop quartet on the airplane was singing "Wait Till the Sun Shines, Nelly," when the plane smacked into the top of Sugarbush Mountain in Vermont. Everybody was killed but Billy and the copilot. So it goes.

The people who first got to the crash scene were young Austrian ski instructors from the famous ski resort below. They spoke to each other in German as they went from body to body. They wore black wind masks with two holes for their eyes and a red topknot. They looked like golliwogs, like white people pretending to be black for the laughs they could get.

Billy had a fractured skull, but he was still conscious. He didn't know where he was. His lips were working, and one of the golliwogs put his ear close to them to hear what might be his dying words.

Billy thought the golliwog had something to do with World War Two, and he whispered to him his address: "Schlachthof-fünf."

Billy was brought down Sugarbush Mountain on a toboggan. The golliwogs controlled it with ropes and yodeled melodiously for right-of-way. Near the bottom, the trail swooped around the pylons of a chair lift. Billy looked up at all the young people in bright elastic clothing and enormous boots and goggles, bombed out of their skulls with snow, swinging through the sky in yellow chairs. He supposed that they were part of an amazing new phase of World War Two. It was all right with him. Everything was pretty much all right with Billy.

He was taken to a small private hospital. A famous brain surgeon came up from Boston and operated on him for three hours. Billy was unconscious for two days after that, and he dreamed millions of things, some of them true. The true things were time-travel.

One of the true things was his first evening in the slaughterhouse. He and poor old Edgar Derby were pushing an empty two-wheeled cart down a dirt lane between empty pens for animals. They were going to a communal kitchen for supper for all. They were guarded by a sixteen-year-old German named Werner Gluck. The axles of the cart were greased with the fat of dead animals. So it goes.

The sun had just gone down, and its afterglow was back lighting the city, which formed low cliffs around the bucolic void to the idle stockyards. The city was blacked out because bombers might come, so Billy didn't get to see Dresden do one of the most cheerful things a city is capable of doing when the sun goes down, which is to wink its lights on one by one.

There was a broad river to reflect those lights, which would have made their nighttime winkings very pretty indeed. It was the Elbe.

Werner Gluck, the young guard, was a Dresden boy. He had never been in the slaughterhouse before, so he wasn't sure where the kitchen was. He was tall and weak like Billy, might have been a younger brother of his. They were, in fact, distant cousins, something they never found out. Gluck was armed with an incredibly heavy musket, a single-shot museum piece with an octagonal barrel and a smooth bore. He had fixed his bayonet. It was like a long knitting needle. It had no bloodgutters.

Gluck led the way to a building that he thought might contain the kitchen, and he opened the sliding door in its side. There wasn't a kitchen in there, though. There was a dressing room adjacent to a communal shower, and there was a lot of steam. In the steam were about thirty teen-age girls with no clothes on. They were German refugees from Breslau, which had been tremendously bombed. They had just arrived in Dresden, too. Dresden was jammed with refugees.

There those girls were with all their private parts bare, for anybody to see. And there in the doorway were Gluck and Derby and Pilgrim—the childish soldier and the poor old high school teacher and the clown in his toga and silver shoes—staring. The girls screamed. They covered themselves with their hands and turned their backs and so on, and made themselves utterly beautiful.

Werner Gluck, who had never seen a naked woman before, closed the door. Billy had never seen one, either. It was nothing new to Derby.

When the three fools found the communal kitchen, whose main job was to make lunch for workers in the slaughterhouse, everybody had gone home but one woman who had been waiting for them impatiently. She was a war widow. So it goes. She had her hat and coat on. She wanted to go home, too, even though there wasn't anybody there. Her white gloves were laid out side by side on the zinc counter top.

She had two big cans of soup for the Americans. It was simmering over low fires on the gas range. She had stacks of loaves of black bread, too.

She asked Gluck if he wasn't awfully young to be in the army. He admitted that he was.

She asked Edgar Derby if he wasn't awfully old to be in the army. He said he was.

She asked Billy Pilgrim what he was supposed to be. Billy said he didn't know. He was just trying to keep warm.

"All the real soldiers are dead," she said. It was true. So it goes.

Another true thing that Billy saw while he was unconscious in Vermont was the work that he and the others had to do in Dresden during the month before the city was destroyed. They washed windows and swept floors and cleaned lavatories and put jars into boxes and sealed cardboard boxes in a factory that made malt syrup. The syrup was enriched with vitamins and minerals. The syrup was for pregnant women.

The syrup tasted like thin honey laced with hickory smoke, and everybody who worked in the factory secretly spooned it all day long. They weren't pregnant, but they needed vitamins and minerals, too. Billy didn't spoon syrup on his first day at work, but lots of other Americans did.

Billy spooned it on his second day. There were spoons hidden all over the factory, on rafters, in drawers, behind radiators, and so on. They had been hidden in haste by persons who had been spooning syrup, who had heard somebody else coming. Spooning was a crime.

On his second day, Billy was cleaning behind a radiator, and he found a spoon. To his back was a vat of syrup that was cooling. The only other person who could see Billy and his spoon was poor old Edgar Derby, who was washing a window outside. The spoon was a tablespoon. Billy thrust it into the vat, turned it around and around, making a gooey lollipop. He thrust it into his mouth.

A moment went by, and then every cell in Billy's body shook him with ravenous gratitude and applause.

There were diffident raps on the factory window. Derby was out there, having seen all. He wanted some syrup, too.

So Billy made a lollipop for him. He opened the window. He stuck the lollipop into poor old Derby's gaping mouth. A moment passed, and then Derby burst into tears. Billy closed the window and hid the sticky spoon. Somebody was coming.

8

The Americans in the slaughterhouse had a very interesting visitor two days before Dresden was destroyed. He was Howard W. Campbell, Jr., an American who had become a Nazi. Campbell was the one who had written the monograph about the shabby behavior of American prisoners of war. He wasn't doing more research about prisoners now. He had come to the slaughterhouse to recruit men for a German military unit called "The Free American Corps." Campbell was the inventor and commander of the unit, which was supposed to fight only on the Russian front.

Campbell was an ordinary-looking man, but he was extravagantly costumed in a uniform of his own design. He wore a white ten-gallon hat and black cowboy boots decorated with swastikas and stars. He was sheathed in a blue body stocking which had yellow stripes running from his armpits to his ankles. His shoulder patch was a silhouette of Abraham Lincoln's profile on a field of pale green. He had a broad armband which was red, with a blue swastika in a circle of white.

He was explaining this armband now in the cement-block hog barn.

Billy Pilgrim had a boiling case of heartburn, since he had been spooning malt syrup all day long at work. The heartburn brought tears to his eyes, so that his image of Campbell was distorted by jiggling lenses of salt water.

"Blue is for the American sky," Campbell was saying. "White is for the race that pioneered the continent, drained the swamps and cleared the forests and built the roads and bridges. Red is for the blood of American patriots which was shed so gladly in years gone by."

Campbell's audience was sleepy. It had worked hard at the syrup factory, and then it had marched a long way home in the cold. It was skinny and hollow-eyed. Its skins were beginning to blossom with small sores. So were its mouths and throats and intestines. The malt syrup it spooned at the factory contained only a few of the vitamins and minerals every Earthling needs.

Campbell offered the Americans food now, steaks and mashed potatoes and gravy and mince pie, if they would join the Free American Corps. "Once the Russians are defeated," he went on, "you will be repatriated through Switzerland."

There was no response.

"You're going to have to fight the Communists sooner or later," said Campbell. "Why not get it over with now?"

And then it developed that Campbell was not going to go unanswered after all. Poor old Derby, the doomed high school teacher, lumbered to his feet for what was probably the finest moment in his life. There are almost no characters in this story, and almost no dramatic confrontations, because most of the people in it are so sick and so much the listless playthings of enormous forces. One of the main effects of war, after all, is that people are discouraged from being characters. But old Derby was a character now.

His stance was that of a punch-drunk fighter. His head was down. His fists were out front, waiting for information and battle plan. Derby raised his head, called Campbell a snake. He corrected that. He said that snakes couldn't help being snakes, and that Campbell, who *could* help being what he was, was something much lower than a snake or a rat—or even a blood-filled tick.

Campbell smiled.

Derby spoke movingly of the American form of government, with freedom and justice and opportunities and fair play for all. He said there wasn't a man there who wouldn't gladly die for those ideals.

He spoke of the brotherhood between the American and the Russian people, and how those two nations were going to crush the disease of Nazism, which wanted to infect the whole world.

The air-raid sirens of Dresden howled mournfully.

The Americans and their guards and Campbell took shelter in an echoing meat locker which was hollowed in living rock under the slaughterhouse. There was an iron staircase with iron doors at the top and bottom.

Down in the locker were a few cattle and sheep and pigs and horses hanging from iron hooks. So it goes. The locker had empty hooks for thousands more. It was naturally cool. There was no refrigeration. There was candlelight. The locker was whitewashed and smelled of carbolic acid. There were benches along a wall. The Americans went to these, brushing away flakes of whitewash before they sat down.

Howard W. Campbell, Jr., remained standing, like the guards. He talked to the guards in excellent German. He had written many popular German plays and poems in his time, and had married a famous German actress named Resi North. She was dead now, had been killed while entertaining troops in the Crimea. So it goes.

Nothing happened that night. It was the next night that about one hundred and thirty thousand people in Dresden would die. So it goes. Billy dozed in the meat locker. He found himself engaged again, word for word, gesture for gesture, in the argument with his daughter with which this tale began.

"Father," she said, "What are we going to *do* with you?" And so on. "You know who I could just kill?" she asked.

"*Who* could you kill?" said Billy.

"That Kilgore Trout."

Kilgore Trout was and is a science-fiction writer, of course. Billy has not only read dozens of books by Trout—he has also become Trout's friend, to the extent that anyone can become a friend of Trout, who is a bitter man.

Trout lives in a rented basement in Ilium, about two miles from Billy's nice white home. He himself has no idea how many novels he has written—possibly seventy-five of the things. Not one of them has made money. So Trout keeps body and soul together as a circulation man for the *Ilium Gazette,* manages newspaper delivery boys, bullies and flatters and cheats little kids.

Billy met him for the first time in 1964. Billy drove his Cadillac down a back alley in Ilium, and he found his way blocked by dozens of boys and their bicycles. A meeting was in progress. The boys were harangued by a man in a full beard. He was cowardly and dangerous, and obviously very good at his job. Trout was sixty-two years old back then. He was telling the kids to get off their dead butts and get their daily customers to subscribe to the fucking Sunday edition, too. He said that whoever sold the most Sunday subscriptions during the next two months would get a free trip for himself and his parents to Martha's fucking Vineyard for a week, all expenses paid.

And so on.

One of the newspaper boys was actually a newspaper *girl.* She was electrified.

Trout's paranoid face was terribly familiar to Billy, who had seen it on the jackets of so many books. But, coming upon that face suddenly in a home-town alley, Billy could not guess why the face was familiar. Billy thought maybe he had known this cracked messiah in Dresden somewhere. Trout certainly looked like a prisoner of war.

And then the newspaper girl held up her hand. "Mr. Trout—" she said, "if I win, can I take my sister, too?"

"Hell no," said Kilgore Trout. "You think money grows on *trees?"*

Trout, incidentally, had written a book about a money tree. It had twenty-dollar bills for leaves. Its flowers were government bonds. Its fruit was diamonds. It attracted human beings who killed each other around the roots and made very good fertilizer.

So it goes.

Billy Pilgrim parked his Cadillac in the alley, and waited for the meeting to end. When the meeting broke up, there was still one boy Trout had to deal with. The boy wanted to quit because the work was so hard and the hours were so long and the pay was so small. Trout was concerned, because, if the boy really quit, Trout would have to deliver the boy's route himself, until he could find another sucker.

"What are you?" Trout asked the boy scornfully. "Some kind of gutless wonder?"

This, too, was the title of a book by Trout, *The Gutless Wonder.* It was about a robot who had bad breath, who became popular after his halitosis was cured. But what made the story remarkable, since it was written in 1932, was that it predicted the widespread use of burning jellied gasoline on human beings.

It was dropped on them from airplanes. Robots did the dropping. They had no conscience, and no circuits which would allow them to imagine what was happening to the people on the ground.

Trout's leading robot looked like a human being, and could talk and dance and so on, and go out with girls. And nobody held it against him that he dropped jellied gasoline on people. But they found his halitosis unforgivable. But then he cleared that up, and he was welcomed to the human race.

Trout lost his argument with the boy who wanted to quit. He told the boy about all the millionaires who had carried newspapers as boys, and the boy replied: "Yeah—but I bet they quit after a week, it's *such* a royal screwing."

And the boy left his full newspaper bag at Trout's feet, with the customer book on top. It was up to Trout to deliver these papers. He didn't have a car. He didn't even have a bicycle, and he was scared to death of dogs.

Somewhere a big dog barked.

As Trout lugubriously slung the bag from his shoulder, Billy Pilgrim approached him. "Mr. Trout—?"

"Yes?"

"Are—are you *Kilgore* Trout?"

"Yes." Trout supposed that Billy had some complaint about the way his newspapers were being delivered. He did not think of himself as a writer for the simple reason that the world had never allowed him to think of himself in this way.

"The—the writer?" said Billy.

"The what?"

Billy was certain that he had made a mistake. "There's a writer named Kilgore Trout."

"There *is?*" Trout looked foolish and dazed.

"You never heard of him?"

Trout shook his head. "Nobody—nobody ever did."

Billy helped Trout deliver his papers, driving him from house to house in the Cadillac. Billy was the responsible one, finding the houses, checking them off. Trout's mind was blown. He had never met a fan before, and Billy was such an *avid* fan.

Trout told him that he had never seen a book of his advertised, reviewed, or on sale. "All these years," he said, "I've been opening the window and making love to the world."

"You must surely have gotten letters," said Billy. "I've felt like writing you letters many times."

Trout held up a single finger. "One."

"Was it *enthusiastic?*"

"It was *insane.* The writer said I should be President of the World."

It turned out that the person who had written this letter was Eliot Rosewater, Billy's friend in the veterans' hospital near Lake Placid. Billy told Trout about Rosewater.

"My God—I thought he was about fourteen years old," said Trout.

"A full grown man—a captain in the war."

" He *writes* like a fourteen-year-old," said Kilgore Trout.

Billy invited Trout to his eighteenth wedding anniversary which was only two days hence. Now the party was in progress.

Trout was in Billy's dining room, gobbling canapés. He was talking with a mouthful of Philadelphia cream cheese and salmon roe to an optometrist's wife. Everybody at the party was associated with optometry in some way, except Trout. And he alone was without glasses. He was making a great hit. Everybody was thrilled to have a real author at the party, even though they had never read his books.

Trout was talking to a Maggie White, who had given up being a dental assistant to become a homemaker for an optometrist. She was very pretty. The last book she had read was *Ivanhoe.*

Billy Pilgrim stood nearby, listening. He was palpating something in his pocket. It was a present he was about to give his wife, a white satin box containing a star sapphire cocktail ring. The ring was worth eight hundred dollars.

The adulation that Trout was receiving, mindless and illiterate as it was, affected Trout like marijuana. He was happy and loud and impudent.

"I'm afraid I don't read as much as I *ought* to," said Maggie.

"We're all afraid of something," Trout replied. "I'm afraid of cancer and rats and Doberman pinschers."

"I should know, but I don't, so I have to ask," said Maggie, "what's the most famous thing you ever wrote?"

"It was about a funeral for a great French chef."

"That sounds interesting."

"All the great chefs in the world are there. It's a beautiful ceremony." Trout was making this up as he went along. "Just before the casket is closed, the mourners sprinkle parsley and paprika on the deceased." So it goes.

"Did that really *happen?*" said Maggie White. She was a dull person, but a sensational invitation to make babies. Men looked at her and wanted to fill her up with babies right away. She hadn't had even one baby yet. She used birth control.

"Of course it happened," Trout told her. "If I wrote something that hadn't really happened, and I tried to sell it, I could go to jail. That's *fraud.*"

Maggie believed him. "I'd never thought about that before."

"Think about it now."

"It's like advertising. You have to tell the truth in advertising, or you get in trouble."

"Exactly. The same body of law applies."

"Do you think you might put *us* in a book sometime?"

"I put everything that happens to me in books."

"I guess I better be careful what I say."

"That's right. And I'm not the only one who's listening. God is listening, too. And on Judgment Day he's going to tell you all the things you said and did. If it turns out they're bad things instead of good things, that's too bad for you, because you'll burn forever and ever. The burning never stops hurting."

Poor Maggie turned gray. She believed *that,* too, and was petrified.

Kilgore Trout laughed uproariously. A salmon egg flew out of his mouth and landed in Maggie's cleavage.

Now an optometrist called for attention. He proposed a toast to Billy and Valencia, whose anniversary it was. According to plan, the barbershop quartet of optometrists, "The Febs," sang while people drank and Billy and Valencia put their arms around each other, just glowed. Everybody's eyes were shining. The song was "That Old Gang of Mine."

Gee, that song went, *but I'd give the world to see that old gang of mine.* And so on. A little later it said, *So long forever, old fellows and gals, so long forever old sweethearts and pals —God bless 'em—*And so on.

Unexpectedly, Billy Pilgrim found himself upset by the song and the occasion. He had never had an old gang, old sweethearts and pals, but he missed one anyway, as the quartet made slow, agonized experiments with chords—chords intentionally sour, sourer still, unbearably sour, and then a chord that was suffocatingly sweet, and then some sour ones again. Billy had powerful psychosomatic responses to the changing chords. His mouth filled with the taste of lemonade, and his face became grotesque, as though he really were being stretched on the torture engine called the *rack.*

He looked so peculiar that several people commented on it solicitously when the song was done. They thought he might have been having a heart attack, and Billy seemed to confirm this by going to a chair and sitting down haggardly.

There was silence.

"Oh my God," said Valencia, leaning over him, "Billy—are you all right?"

"Yes."

"You look so awful."

"Really—I'm O.K." And he was, too, except that he could find no explanation for why the song had affected him so grotesquely. He had supposed for years that he had no secrets from himself. Here was proof that he had a great big secret somewhere inside, and he could not imagine what it was.

People drifted away now, seeing the color return to Billy's cheeks, seeing him smile. Valencia stayed with him, and Kilgore Trout, who had been on the fringe of the crowd, came closer, interested, shrewd.

"You looked as though you'd seen a *ghost,*" said Valencia.

"No", said Billy. He hadn't seen anything but what was really before him—the faces of the four singers, those four ordinary men, cow-eyed and mindless and anguished as they went from sweetness to sourness to sweetness again.

"Can I make a guess?" said Kilgore Trout. "You saw through a *time window.*"

"A what?" said Valencia.

"He suddenly saw the past or the future. Am I right?"

"No," said Billy Pilgrim. He got up, put a hand into his pocket, found the box containing the ring in there. He took out the box, gave it absently to Valencia. He had meant to give it to her at the end of the song, while everybody was watching. Only Kilgore Trout was there to see.

"For me?" said Valencia.

"Yes."

"Oh my God," she said. Then she said it louder, so other people heard. They gathered around, and she opened it, and she almost screamed when she saw the sapphire with a star in it. "Oh, my God," she said. She gave Billy a big kiss. She said, "Thank you, thank you, thank you."

There was a lot of talk about what wonderful jewelry Billy had given to Valencia over the years. "My God—" said Maggie White, "she's already got the biggest diamond I ever saw outside of a movie." She was talking about the diamond Billy had brought back from the war.

The partial denture he had found inside his little impresario's coat, incidentally, was in his cufflinks box in his dresser drawer. Billy had a wonderful collection of cufflinks. It was the custom of the family to give him cufflinks on every Father's Day. He was wearing Father's Day cufflinks now. They had cost over one hundred dollars. They were made out of ancient Roman coins. He had one pair of cufflinks upstairs which were little roulette wheels that really worked. He had another pair which had a real thermometer in one and a real compass in the other.

Billy now moved above the party—outwardly normal. Kilgore Trout was shadowing him, keen to know what Billy had suspected or seen. Most of Trout's novels, after all, dealt with time warps and extrasensory perception and other unexpected things. Trout believed in things like that, was greedy to have their existence proved.

"You ever put a full-length mirror on the floor, and then have a dog stand on it?" Trout asked Billy.

"No."

"The dog will look down, and all of a sudden he'll realize there's nothing under him. He thinks he's standing on thin air. He'll jump a *mile.*"

"He *will?*"

"That's how *you* looked—as though you all of a sudden realized you were standing on thin air."

The barbershop quartet sang again. Billy was emotionally racked again. The experience was *definitely* associated with those four men and not what they sang.

Here is what they sang, while Billy was pulled apart inside:

> 'Leven cent cotton, forty cent meat,
> How in the world can a poor man eat?
> Pray for the sunshine, 'cause it will rain.
> Things gettin' worse, drivin' all insane;
> Built a nice barn, painted it brown;
> Lightnin' came along and burnt it down:
> No use talkin', any man's beat,
> With 'leven cent cotton and forty cent meat.
> 'Leven cent cotton, a car-load of tax,
> The load's too heavy for our poor backs . . .

And so on.

Billy fled upstairs in his nice white home.

Trout would have come upstairs with him if Billy hadn't told him not to. Then Billy went into the upstairs bathroom, which was dark.

He closed and locked the door. He left it dark, and gradually became aware that he was not alone. His son was in there.

"Dad—?" his son said in the dark. Robert, the future Green Beret, was seventeen then. Billy liked him, but didn't know him very well. Billy couldn't help suspecting that there wasn't much *to* know about Robert.

Billy flicked on the light. Robert was sitting on the toilet with his pajama bottoms around his ankles. He was wearing an electric guitar, slung around his neck on a strap. He had just bought the guitar that day. He couldn't play it yet and, in fact, never learned to play it. It was a nacreous pink.

"Hello, son," said Billy Pilgrim.

Billy went into his bedroom, even though there were guests to be entertained downstairs. He lay down on his bed, turned on the Magic Fingers. The mattress trembled, drove a dog out from under the bed. The dog was Spot. Good old Spot was still alive in those days. Spot lay down again in a corner.

Billy thought hard about the effect the quartet had had on him, and then found an association with an experience he had had long ago. He did not travel in time to the experience. He remembered it shimmeringly—as follows:

He was down in the meat locker on the night that Dresden was destroyed. There were sounds like giant footsteps above. Those were sticks of high-explosive bombs. The giants walked and walked. The meat locker was a very safe shelter. All that happened down there was an occasional shower of calcimine. The Americans and four of their guards and a few dressed carcasses were down there, and nobody else. The rest of the guards had, before the raid began, gone to the comforts of their own homes in Dresden. They were all being killed with their families.

So it goes.

The girls that Billy had seen naked were all being killed, too, in a much shallower shelter in another part of the stockyards.

So it goes.

A guard would go to the head of the stairs every so often to see what it was like outside, then he would come down and whisper to the other guards. There was a fire-storm out there. Dresden was one big flame. The one flame ate everything organic, everything that would burn.

It wasn't safe to come out of the shelter until noon the next day.

When the Americans and their guards did come out, the sky was black with smoke. The sun was an angry little pinhead. Dresden was like the moon now, nothing but minerals. The stones were hot. Everybody else in the neighborhood was dead.

So it goes.

The guards drew together instinctively, rolled their eyes. They experimented with one expression and then another, said nothing, though their mouths were often open. They looked like a silent film of a barbershop quartet.

"So long forever," they might have been singing, "old fellows and gals; So long forever, old sweethearts and pals—God bless 'em—"

"Tell me a story," Montana Wildhack said to Billy Pilgrim in the Tralfamadorian zoo one time. They were in bed side by side. They had privacy. The canopy covered the dome. Montana was six months pregnant now, big and rosy, lazily demanding small favors from Billy from time to time. She couldn't send Billy out for ice cream or strawberries, since the atmosphere outside the dome was cyanide, and the nearest strawberries and ice cream were millions of light years away.

She could send him to the refrigerator, which was decorated with the blank couple on the bicycle built for two—or, as now, she could wheedle, "Tell me a story, Billy boy."

"Dresden was destroyed on the night of February 13, 1945," Billy Pilgrim began. "We came out of our shelter the next day." He told Montana about the four guards who, in their astonishment and grief, resembled a barbershop quartet. He told her about the stockyards with all the fenceposts gone, with roofs and windows gone—told her about seeing little logs lying around. These were people who had been caught in the fire storm. So it goes.

Billy told her what had happened to the buildings that used to form cliffs around the stockyards. They had collapsed. Their wood had been consumed, and their stones had crashed down, had tumbled against one another until they locked at last in low and graceful curves.

"It was like the moon," said Billy Pilgrim.

The guards told the Americans to form in ranks of four, which they did. Then they had them march back to the hog barn which had been their home. Its walls still stood, but its windows and roof were gone, and there was nothing inside but ashes and dollops of melted glass. It was realized then that there was no food or water, and that the survivors, if they were going to continue to survive, were going to have to climb over curve after curve on the face of the moon.

Which they did.

The curves were smooth only when seen from a distance. The people climbing them learned that they were treacherous, jagged things—hot to the touch, often unstable—eager, should certain important rocks be disturbed, to tumble some more, to form lower, more solid curves.

Nobody talked much as the expedition crossed the moon. There was nothing appropriate to say. One thing was clear: Absolutely everybody in the city was supposed to be dead, regardless of what they were, and that anybody that moved in it represented a flaw in the design. There were to be no moon men at all.

American fighter planes came in under the smoke to see if anything was moving. They saw Billy and the rest moving down there. The planes sprayed them with machine-gun bullets, but the bullets missed. Then they saw some other people moving down by the riverside and they shot at them. They hit some of them. So it goes.

The idea was to hasten the end of the war.

Billy's story ended very curiously in a suburb untouched by fire and explosions. The guards and the Americans came at nightfall to an inn which was open for business. There was candlelight. There were fires in three fireplaces downstairs. There were empty tables and chairs waiting for anyone who might come, and empty beds with covers turned down upstairs.

There was a blind innkeeper and his sighted wife, who was the cook, and their two young daughters who worked as waitresses and maids. This family knew that Dresden was gone. Those with eyes had seen it burn and burn, understood that they were on the edge of a desert now. Still—they had opened for business, had polished the glasses and wound the clocks and stirred the fires, and waited and waited to see who would come.

There was no great flow of refugees from Dresden. The clocks ticked on, the fires crackled, the translucent candles dripped. And then there was a knock on the door, and in came four guards and one hundred American prisoners of war.

The innkeeper asked the guards if they had come from the city.

"Yes."

"Are there more people coming?"

And the guards said that, on the difficult route they had chosen, they had not seen another living soul.

The blind innkeeper said that the Americans could sleep in his stable that night, and he gave them soup and ersatz coffee and a little beer. Then he came out to the stable to listen to them bedding down in the straw.

"Good night, Americans," he said in German. "Sleep well."

9

Here is how Billy Pilgrim lost his wife, Valencia.

He was unconscious in the hospital in Vermont, after the airplane crashed on Sugarbush Mountain, and Valencia, having heard about the crash, was driving from Ilium to the hospital in the family Cadillac El Dorado Coupe de Ville. Valencia was hysterical, because she had been told frankly that Billy might die, or that, if he lived, he might be a vegetable.

Valencia adored Billy. She was crying and yelping so hard as she drove that she missed the correct turnoff from the throughway. She applied her power brakes, and a Mercedes slammed into her from behind. Nobody was hurt, thank God, because both drivers were wearing seat belts. Thank God, thank God. The Mercedes lost only a headlight. But the rear end of the Cadillac was a body-and-fender man's wet dream. The trunk and fenders were collapsed. The gaping trunk looked like the mouth of a village idiot who was explaining that he didn't know anything about anything. The fenders shrugged. The bumper was at a high port arms. "Reagan for President!" a sticker on the bumper said. The back window was veined with cracks. The exhaust system rested on the pavement.

The driver of the Mercedes got out and went to Valencia, to find out if she was all right. She blabbed hysterically about Billy and the airplane crash, and then she put her car in gear and crossed the median divider, leaving her exhaust system behind.

When she arrived at the hospital, people rushed to the windows to see what all the noise was. The Cadillac, with both mufflers gone, sounded like a heavy bomber coming in on a wing and a prayer. Valencia turned off the engine, but then she slumped against the steering wheel, and the horn brayed steadily. A doctor and a nurse ran out to find out what the trouble was. Poor Valencia was unconscious, overcome by carbon monoxide. She was a heavenly azure.

One hour later she was dead. So it goes.

Billy knew nothing about it. He dreamed on, and traveled in time and so forth. The hospital was so crowded that Billy couldn't have a room to himself. He shared a room with a Harvard history professor named Bertram Copeland Rumfoord. Rumfoord didn't have to look at Billy, because Billy was surrounded by white linen screens on rubber wheels. But Rumfoord could hear Billy talking to himself from time to time.

Rumfoord's left leg was in traction. He had broken it while skiing. He was seventy years old, but had the body and spirit of a man half that age. He had been honeymooning with his fifth wife when he broke his leg. Her name was Lily. Lily was twenty-three.

Just about the time poor Valencia was pronounced dead, Lily came into Billy's and Rumfoord's room with an armload of books. Rumfoord had sent her down to Boston to get them. He was working on a one-volume history of the United States Army Air Corps in World War Two. The books were about bombings and sky battles that had happened before Lily was even *born*.

"You guys go on without me," said Billy Pilgrim deliriously, as pretty little Lily came in. She had been an a-go-go girl when Rumfoord saw her and resolved to make her his own. She was a high school dropout. Her I.Q. was 103. "He *scares* me," she whispered to her husband about Billy Pilgrim.

"He bores the *hell* out of *me!*" Rumfoord replied boomingly. "All he does in his sleep is quit and surrender and apologize and ask to be left alone." Rumfoord was a retired brigadier general in the Air Force Reserve, the official Air Force Historian, a full professor, the author of twenty-six books, a multimillionaire since birth, and one of the great competitive sailors of all time. His most popular book was about sex and strenuous athletics for men over sixty-five. Now he quoted Theodore Roosevelt, whom he resembled a lot:

"'I could carve a better man out of a banana.'"

One of the things Rumfoord had told Lily to get in Boston was a copy of President Harry S. Truman's announcement to the world that an atomic bomb had been dropped on Hiroshima. She had a Xerox of it, and Rumfoord asked her if she had read it.

"No." She didn't read well, which was one of the reasons she had dropped out of high school.

Rumfoord ordered her to sit down and read the Truman statement now. He didn't know that she couldn't read much. He knew very little about her, except that she was one more public demonstration that he was a superman.

So Lily sat down and pretended to read the Truman thing, which went like this:

Sixteen hours ago an American airplane dropped one bomb on Hiroshima, an important Japanese Army base. That bomb had more power than 20,000 tons of T.N.T. It had more than two thousand times the blast power of the British "Grand Slam," which is the largest bomb ever yet used in the history of warfare.

The Japanese began the war from the air at Pearl Harbor. They have been repaid many-fold. And the end is not yet. With this bomb we have now added a new and revolutionary increase in destruction to supplement the growing power of our armed forces. In their present form these bombs are now in production, and even more powerful forms are in development.

It is an atomic bomb. It is a harnessing of the basic power of the universe. The force from which the sun draws its power has been loosed against those who brought war to the Far East.

Before 1939, it was the accepted belief of scientists that it was theoretically possible to release atomic energy. But nobody knew any practical method of doing it. By 1942, however, we knew that the Germans were working feverishly to find a way to add atomic energy to all the other engines of war with which they hoped to enslave the world. But they failed. We may be grateful to Providence that the Germans got the V-1's and V-2's late and in limited quantities and even more grateful that they did not get the atomic bomb at all.

The battle of the laboratories held fateful risks for us as well as the battles of the air, land, and sea, and we have now won the battle of the laboratories as we have won the other battles.

We are now prepared to obliterate more rapidly and completely every productive enterprise the Japanese have above ground in any city, said Harry Truman. *We shall destroy their docks, their factories, and their communications. Let there be no mistake; we shall completely destroy Japan's power to make war. It was to spare—*

And so on.

One of the books that Lily had brought Rumfoord was *The Destruction of Dresden,* by an Englishman named David Irving. It was an American edition, published by Holt, Rinehart and Winston in 1964. What Rumfoord wanted from it were portions of the forewords by his friends Ira C. Eaker, Lieutenant General, U.S.A.F., retired, and British Air Marshal Sir Robert Saundby, K.C.B., K.B.E., M.C., D.F.C., A.F.C.

I find it difficult to understand Englishmen or Americans who weep about enemy civilians who were killed but who have not shed a tear for our gallant crews lost in combat with a cruel enemy, wrote his friend General Eaker in part. *I think it would have been well for Mr. Irving to have remembered, when he was drawing the frightful picture of the civilians killed at Dresden, that V-1's and V-2's were at that very time falling on England, killing civilian men, women, and children indiscriminately, as they were designed and launched to do. It might be well to remember Buchenwald and Coventry, too.*

Eaker's foreword ended this way:

I deeply regret that British and U.S. bombers killed 135,000 people in the attack on Dresden, but I remember who started the last war and I regret even more the loss of more than 5,000,000 Allied lives in the necessary effort to completely defeat and utterly destroy nazism.

So it goes.

What Air Marshal Saundby said, among other things, was this:

That the bombing of Dresden was a great tragedy none can deny. That it was really a military necessity few, after reading this book, will believe. It was one of those terrible things that sometimes happen in wartime, brought about by an unfortunate combination of circumstances. Those who approved it were neither wicked nor cruel, though it may well be that they were too remote from the harsh realities of war to understand fully the appalling destructive power of air bombardment in the spring of 1945. The advocates of nuclear disarmament seem to believe that, if they could achieve their aim, war would become tolerable and decent. They would do well to read this book and ponder the fate of Dresden, where 135,000 people died as the result of an air attack with conventional weapons. On the night of March 9th, 1945, an air attack on Tokyo by American heavy bombers, using incendiary and high explosive bombs, caused the death of 83,793 people. The atom bomb dropped on Hiroshima killed 71,379 people.

So it goes.

"If you're ever in Cody, Wyoming," said Billy Pilgrim behind his white linen screens, "just ask for Wild Bob."

Lily Rumfoord shuddered, went on pretending to read the Harry Truman thing.

Billy's daughter Barbara came in later that day. She was all doped up, had the same glassy-eyed look that poor old Edgar Derby wore just before he was shot in Dresden. Doctors had given her pills so she could continue to function, even though her father was broken and her mother was dead.

So it goes.

She was accompanied by a doctor and a nurse. Her brother Robert was flying home from a battlefield in Vietnam. "Daddy—" she said tentatively. "Daddy—?"

But Billy was ten years away, back in 1958. He was examining the eyes of a young male Mongolian idiot in order to prescribe corrective lenses. The idiot's mother was there, acting as an interpreter.

"How many dots do you see?" Billy Pilgrim asked him.

And then Billy traveled in time to when he was sixteen years old, in the waiting room of a doctor. Billy had an infected thumb. There was only one other patient waiting—an old, old man. The old man was in agony because of gas. He farted tremendously, and then he belched.

"Excuse me," he said to Billy. Then he did it again. "Oh God—" he said, "I knew it was going to be bad getting old." He shook his head. "I didn't know it was going to be *this* bad."

Billy Pilgrim opened his eyes in the hospital in Vermont, did not know where he was. Watching him was his son Robert. Robert was wearing the uniform of the famous Green Berets. Robert's hair was short, was wheat-colored bristles. Robert was clean and neat. He was decorated with a Purple Heart and a Silver Star and a Bronze Star with two clusters.

This was a boy who had flunked out of high school, who had been an alcoholic at sixteen, who had run with a rotten bunch of kids, who had been arrested for tipping over hundreds of tombstones in a Catholic cemetery one time. He was all straightened out now. His posture was wonderful and his shoes were shined and his trousers were pressed, and he was a leader of men.

"Dad—?"

Billy Pilgrim closed his eyes again.

Billy had to miss his wife's funeral because he was still so sick. He was conscious, though, while Valencia was being put into the ground in Ilium. Billy hadn't said much since regaining consciousness, hadn't responded very elaborately to the news of Valencia's death and Robert's coming home from the war and so on—so it was generally believed that he was a vegetable. There was talk of performing an operation on him later, one which might improve the circulation of blood to his brain.

Actually, Billy's outward listlessness was a screen. The listlessness concealed a mind which was fizzing and flashing thrillingly. It was preparing letters and lectures about the flying saucers, the negligibility of death, and the true nature of time.

Professor Rumfoord said frightful things about Billy within Billy's hearing, confident that Billy no longer had any brain at all. "Why don't they let him *die?*" he asked Lily.

"I don't know," she said.

"That's not a human being anymore. Doctors are for human beings. They should turn him over to a veterinarian or a tree surgeon. *They'd* know what to do. Look at him! That's life, according to the medical profession. Isn't life wonderful?"

"I don't know," said Lily.

Rumfoord talked to Lily about the bombing of Dresden one time, and Billy heard it all. Rumfoord had a problem about Dresden. His one-volume history of the Army Air Force in World War Two was supposed to be a readable condensation of the twenty-seven-volume *Official History of the Army Air Force in World War Two.* The thing was, though, there was almost nothing in the twenty-seven volumes about the Dresden raid, even though it had been such a howling success. The extent of the success had been kept a secret for many years after the war—a secret from the American people. It was no secret from the Germans, of course, or from the Russians, who occupied Dresden after the war, who are in Dresden still.

"Americans have finally heard about Dresden," said Rumfoord, twenty-three years after the raid. "A lot of them know now how much worse it was than Hiroshima. So I've got to put something about it in my book. From the official Air Force standpoint, it'll all be new."

"Why would they keep it a secret so long?" said Lily.

"For fear that a lot of bleeding hearts," said Rumfoord, "might not think it was such a wonderful thing to do."

It was now that Billy Pilgrim spoke up intelligently. "I was there," he said.

It was difficult for Rumfoord to take Billy seriously, since Rumfoord had so long considered Billy a repulsive non-person who would be much better off dead. Now, with Billy speaking clearly and to the point, Rumfoord's ears wanted to treat the words as a foreign language that was not worth learning. "What did he say?" said Rumfoord.

Lily had to serve as an interpreter. "He said he was there," she explained.

"He was where?"

"I don't know," said Lily. "Where were you?" she asked Billy.

"Dresden," said Billy.

"Dresden," Lily told Rumfoord.

"He's simply echoing things we say," said Rumfoord.

"Oh," said Lily.

"He's got echolalia now."

"Oh."

Echolalia is a mental disease which makes people immediately repeat things that well people around them say. But Billy didn't really have it. Rumfoord simply insisted, for his own comfort, that Billy had it. Rumfoord was thinking in a military manner: that an inconvenient person, one whose death he wished for very much, for practical reasons, was suffering from a repulsive disease.

Rumfoord went on insisting for several hours that Billy had echolalia—told nurses and a doctor that Billy had echolalia now. Some experiments were performed on Billy. Doctors and nurses tried to get Billy to echo something, but Billy wouldn't make a sound for them.

"He isn't doing it now," said Rumfoord peevishly. "The minute you go away, he'll start doing it again."

Nobody took Rumfoord's diagnosis seriously. The staff thought Rumfoord was a hateful old man, conceited and cruel. He often said to them, in one way or another, that people who were weak deserved to die. Whereas the staff, of course, was devoted to the idea that weak people should be helped as much as possible, that nobody should die.

There in the hospital, Billy was having an adventure very common among people without power in time of war: He was trying to prove to a willfully deaf and blind enemy that he was interesting to hear and see. He kept silent until the lights went out at night, and then, when there had been a long period of silence containing nothing to echo, he said to Rumfoord, "I was in Dresden when it was bombed. I was a prisoner of war."

Rumfoord sighed impatiently.

"Word of honor," said Billy Pilgrim. "Do you believe me?"

"Must we talk about it now?" said Rumfoord. He had heard. He didn't believe.

"We don't ever have to talk about it," said Billy. "I just want you to know: I was there."

Nothing more was said about Dresden that night, and Billy closed his eyes, traveled in time to a May afternoon, two days after the end of the Second World War in Europe. Billy and five other American prisoners were riding in a coffin-shaped green wagon, which they had found abandoned, complete with two horses, in a suburb of Dresden. Now they were being drawn by the clop-clop-clopping horses down narrow lanes which had been cleared through the moonlike ruins. They were going back to the slaughterhouse for souvenirs of the war. Billy was reminded of the sounds of milkmen's horses early in the morning in Ilium, when he was a boy.

Billy sat in the back of the jiggling coffin. His head was tilted back and his nostrils were flaring. He was happy. He was warm. There was food in the wagon, and wine—and a camera, and a stamp collection, and a stuffed owl, and a mantel clock that ran on changes of barometric pressure. The Americans had gone into empty houses in the suburb where they had been imprisoned, and they had taken these and many other things.

The owners, hearing that the Russians were coming, killing and robbing and raping and burning, had fled.

But the Russians hadn't come yet, even two days after the war. It was peaceful in the ruins. Billy saw only one other person on the way to the slaughterhouse. It was an old man pushing a baby buggy. In the buggy were pots and cups and an umbrella frame, and other things he had found.

Billy stayed in the wagon when it reached the slaughterhouse, sunning himself. The others went looking for souvenirs. Later on in life, the Tralfamadorians would advise Billy to concentrate on the happy moments of his life, and to ignore the unhappy ones—to stare only at pretty things as eternity failed to go by. If this sort of selectivity had been possible for Billy, he might have chosen as his happiest moment his sun-drenched snooze in the back of the wagon.

Billy Pilgrim was armed as he snoozed. It was the first time he had been armed since basic training. His companions had insisted that he arm himself, since God only knew what sorts of killers might be in burrows on the face of the moon—wild dogs, packs of rats fattened on corpses, escaped maniacs and murderers, soldiers who would never quit killing until they themselves were killed.

Billy had a tremendous cavalry pistol in his belt. It was a relic of World War One. It had a ring in its butt. It was loaded with bullets the size of robins' eggs. Billy had found it in the bedside table in a house. That was one of the things about the end of the war: Absolutely anybody who wanted a weapon could have one. They were lying all around. Billy had a saber, too. It was a Luftwaffe ceremonial saber. Its hilt was stamped with a screaming eagle. The eagle was carrying a swastika and looking down. Billy found it stuck into a telephone pole. He had pulled it out of the pole as the wagon went by.

Now his snoozing became shallower as he heard a man and a woman speaking German in pitying tones. The speakers were commiserating with somebody lyrically. Before Billy opened his eyes, it seemed to him that the tones might have been those used by the friends of Jesus when they took His ruined body down from His cross. So it goes.

Billy opened his eyes. A middle-aged man and wife were crooning to the horses. They were noticing what the Americans had not noticed—that the horses' mouths were bleeding, gashed by the bits, that the horses' hooves were broken, so that every step meant agony, that the horses were insane with thirst. The Americans had treated their form of transportation as though it were no more sensitive than a six-cylinder Chevrolet.

These two horse pitiers moved back along the wagon to where they could gaze in patronizing reproach at Billy—at Billy Pilgrim, who was so long and weak, so ridiculous in his azure toga and silver shoes.

They weren't afraid of him. They weren't afraid of anything. They were doctors, both obstetricians. They had been delivering babies until the hospitals were all burned down. Now they were picnicking near where their apartment used to be.

The woman was softly beautiful, translucent from having eaten potatoes for so long. The man wore a business suit, necktie and all. Potatoes had made him gaunt. He was as tall as Billy, wore steel-rimmed tri-focals. This couple, so involved with babies, had never reproduced themselves, though they could have. This was an interesting comment on the whole idea of reproduction.

They had nine languages between them. They tried Polish on Billy Pilgrim first, since he was dressed so clownishly, since the wretched Poles were the involuntary clowns of the Second World War.

Billy asked them in English what it was they wanted, and they at once scolded him in English for the condition of the horses. They made Billy get out of the wagon and come look at the horses. When Billy saw the condition of his means of transportation, he burst into tears. He hadn't cried about anything else in the war.

Later on, as a middle-aged optometrist, he would weep quietly and privately sometimes, but never make loud *boo-hooing* noises.

Which is why the epigraph of this book is the quatrain from the famous Christmas carol. Billy cried very little, though he often saw things worth crying about, and in *that* respect, at least, he resembled the Christ of the carol:

The cattle are lowing,
The Baby awakes.
But the little Lord Jesus
No crying He makes.

Billy traveled in time back to the hospital in Vermont. Breakfast had been eaten and cleared away, and Professor Rumfoord was reluctantly becoming interested in Billy as a human being. Rumfoord questioned Billy gruffly, satisfied himself that Billy really had been in Dresden. He asked Billy what it had been like, and Billy told him about the horses and the couple picnicking on the moon.

The story ended this way: Billy and the doctors unharnessed the horses, but the horses wouldn't go anywhere. Their feet hurt too much. And then Russians came on motorcycles, and they arrested everybody but the horses.

Two days after that, Billy was turned over to the Americans, who shipped him home on a very slow freighter called the *Lucretia A. Mott.* Lucretia A. Mott was a famous American suffragette. She was dead. So it goes.

"It *had* to be done," Rumfoord told Billy, speaking of the destruction of Dresden.

"I know," said Billy.

"That's war."

"I know. I'm not complaining."

"It must have been hell on the ground."

"It was," said Billy Pilgrim.

"Pity the men who had to *do* it."

"I do."

"You must have had mixed feelings, there on the ground."

"It was all right," said Billy. "*Everything* is all right, and everybody has to do exactly what he does. I learned that on Tralfamadore."

Billy Pilgrim's daughter took him home later that day, put him to bed in his house, turned the Magic Fingers on. There was a practical nurse there. Billy wasn't supposed to work or even leave the house for a while, at least. He was under observation.

But Billy sneaked out while the nurse wasn't watching, and he drove to New York City, where he hoped to appear on television. He was going to tell the world about the lessons of Tralfamadore.

Billy Pilgrim checked into the Royalton Hotel on Forty-fourth Street in New York. He by chance was given a room which had once been the home of George Jean Nathan, the critic and editor. Nathan, according to the Earthling concept of time, had died back in 1958. According to the Tralfamadorian concept, of course, Nathan was still alive somewhere and always would be.

The room was small and simple, except that it was on the top floor, and had French doors which opened onto a terrace as large as the room. And beyond the parapet of the terrace was the air space over Forty-fourth Street. Billy now leaned over that parapet, looked down at all the people moving hither and yon. They were jerky little scissors. They were a lot of fun.

It was a chilly night, and Billy came indoors after a while, closed the French doors. Closing those doors reminded him of his honeymoon. There had been French doors on the Cape Ann love nest of his honeymoon, still were, always would be.

Billy turned on his television set, clicking its channel selector around and around. He was looking for programs on which he might be allowed to appear. But it was too early in the evening for programs that allowed people with peculiar opinions to speak out. It was only a little after eight o'clock, so all the shows were about silliness or murder. So it goes.

Billy left his room, went down the slow elevator, walked over to Times Square, looked into the window of a tawdry bookstore. In the window were hundreds of books about fucking and buggery and murder, and a street guide to New York City, and a model of the Statue of Liberty with a thermometer on it. Also in the window, speckled with soot and fly shit, were four paperback novels by Billy's friend, Kilgore Trout.

The news of the day, meanwhile, was being written in a ribbon of lights on a building to Billy's back. The window reflected the news. It was about power and sports and anger and death. So it goes.

Billy went into the bookstore.

A sign in there said that adults only were allowed in the back. There were peep shows in the back that showed movies of young women and men with no clothes on. It cost a quarter to look into a machine for one minute. There were still photographs of naked young people for sale back there, too. You could take those home. The stills were a lot more Tralfamadorian than the movies, since you could look at them whenever you wanted to, and they wouldn't change. Twenty years in the future, those girls would still be young, would still be smiling or smoldering or simply looking stupid, with their legs wide open. Some of them were eating lollipops or bananas. They would still be eating those. And the peckers of the young men would still be semierect, and their muscles would be bulging like cannonballs.

But Billy Pilgrim wasn't beguiled by the back of the store. He was thrilled by the Kilgore Trout novels in the front. The titles were all new to him, or he thought they were. Now he opened one. It seemed all right for him to do that. Everybody else in the store was pawing things. The name of the book was *The Big Board*. He got a few paragraphs into it, and then he realized that he *had* read it before —years ago, in the veterans' hospital. It was about an Earthling man and woman who were kidnapped by extra-terrestrials. They were put on display in a zoo on a planet called Zircon-212.

These fictitious people in the zoo had a big board supposedly showing stock market quotations and commodity prices along one wall of their habitat, and a news ticker, and a telephone that was supposedly connected to a brokerage on Earth. The creatures on Zircon-212 told their captives that they had invested a million dollars for them back on Earth, and that it was up to the captives to manage it so that they would be fabulously wealthy when they were returned to Earth.

The telephone and the big board and the ticker were all fakes, of course. They were simply stimulants to make the Earthlings perform vividly for the crowds at the zoo—to make them jump up and down and cheer, or gloat, or sulk, or tear their hair, to be scared shitless or to feel as contented as babies in their mothers' arms.

The Earthlings did very well on paper. That was part of the rigging, of course. And religion got mixed up in it, too. The news ticker reminded them that the President of the United States had declared National Prayer Week, and that everybody should pray. The Earthlings had had a bad week on the market before that. They had lost a small fortune in olive oil futures. So they gave praying a whirl.

It worked. Olive oil went up.

Another Kilgore Trout book there in the window was about a man who built a time machine so he could go back and see Jesus. It worked, and he saw Jesus when Jesus was only twelve years old. Jesus was learning the carpentry trade from his father.

Two Roman soldiers came into the shop with a mechanical drawing on papyrus of a device they wanted built by sunrise the next morning. It was a cross to be used in the execution of a rabble-rouser.

Jesus and his father built it. They were glad to have the work. And the rabble-rouser was executed on it.

So it goes.

The bookstore was run by seeming quintuplets, by five short, bald men chewing unlit cigars that were sopping wet. They never smiled, and each one had a stool to perch on. They were making money running a paper-and-celluloid whorehouse. They didn't have hard-ons. Neither did Billy Pilgrim. Everybody else did. It was a ridiculous store, all about love and babies.

The clerks occasionally told somebody to buy or get out, not to just look and look and look and paw and paw. Some of the people were looking at each other instead of the merchandise.

A clerk came up to Billy and told him the good stuff was in the back, that the books Billy was reading were window dressing. "That ain't what you want, for Christ's sake," he told Billy. "What you want's in *back.*"

So Billy moved a little farther back, but not as far as the part for adults only. He moved because of absentminded politeness, taking a Trout book with him—the one about Jesus and the time machine.

The time-traveler in the book went back to *Bible* times to find out one thing in particular: Whether or not Jesus had really died on the cross, or whether he had been taken down while still alive, whether he had really gone on living. The hero had a stethoscope along.

Billy skipped to the end of the book, where the hero mingled with the people who were taking Jesus down from the cross. The time-traveler was the first one up the ladder, dressed in clothes of the period, and he leaned close to Jesus so people couldn't see him use the stethoscope, and he listened.

There wasn't a sound inside the emaciated chest cavity. The Son of God was dead as a doornail.

So it goes.

The time-traveler, whose name was Lance Corwin, also got to measure the length of Jesus, but not to weigh him. Jesus was five feet and three and a half inches long.

Another clerk came up to Billy and asked him if he was going to buy the book or not, and Billy said that he wanted to buy it, please. He had his back to a rack of paperback books about oral-genital contacts from ancient Egypt to the present and so on, and the clerk supposed Billy was reading one of these. So he was startled when he saw what Billy's book was. He said, "Jesus Christ, where did you find this thing?" and so on, and he had to tell the other clerks about the pervert who wanted to buy the window dressing. The other clerks already knew about Billy. They had been watching him, too.

The cash register where Billy waited for his change was near a bin of old girly magazines. Billy looked at one out of the corner of his eye, and he saw this question on its cover: *What really became of Montana Wildhack?*

So Billy read it. He knew where Montana Wildhack *really* was, of course. She was back on Tralfamadore, taking care of the baby, but the magazine, which was called *Midnight Pussycats,* promised that she was wearing a cement overcoat under thirty fathoms of saltwater in San Pedro Bay.

So it goes.

Billy wanted to laugh. The magazine, which was published for lonesome men to jerk off to, ran the story so it could print pictures taken from blue movies which Montana had made as a teen-ager. Billy did not look closely at these. They were grainy things, soot and chalk. They could have been anybody.

Billy was again directed to the back of the store, and he went this time. A jaded sailor stepped away from a movie machine while the film was still running. Billy looked in, and there was Montana Wildhack alone on a bed, peeling a banana. The picture clicked off. Billy did not want to see what happened next, and a clerk importuned him to come over and see some really hot stuff they kept under the counter for connoisseurs.

Billy was mildly curious as to what could possibly have been kept hidden in such a place. The clerk leered and showed him. It was a photograph of a woman and a Shetland pony. They were attempting to have sexual intercourse between the Doric columns, in front of velvet draperies which were fringed with deedlee-balls.

Billy didn't get onto television in New York that night, but he *did* get onto a radio talk show. There was a radio station right next to Billy's hotel. He saw its call letters over the entrance of an office building, so he went in. He went up to the studio on an automatic elevator, and there were other people up there, waiting to go in. They were literary critics, and they thought Billy was one, too. They were going to discuss whether the novel was dead or not. So it goes.

Billy took his seat with the others around a golden oak table, with a microphone all his own. The master of ceremonies asked him his name and what paper he was from. Billy said he was from the *Ilium Gazette.*

He was nervous and happy. "If you're ever in Cody, Wyoming," he told himself, "just ask for Wild Bob."

Billy put his hand up at the very first part of the program, but he wasn't called on right away. Others got in ahead of him. One of them said that it would be a nice time to bury the novel, now that a Virginian, one hundred years after Appomattox, had written *Uncle Tom's Cabin.* Another one said that people couldn't read well enough anymore to turn print into exciting situations in their skulls, so that authors had to do what Norman Mailer did, which was to perform in public what he had written. The master of ceremonies asked people to say what they thought the function of the novel might be in modern society, and one critic said, "To provide touches of color in rooms with all-white walls." Another one said, "To describe blow-jobs artistically." Another one said, "To teach wives of junior executives what to buy next and how to act in a French restaurant."

And then Billy was allowed to speak. Off he went, in that beautifully trained voice of his, telling about the flying saucers and Montana Wildhack and so on.

He was gently expelled from the studio during a commercial. He went back to his hotel room, put a quarter into the Magic Fingers machine connected to his bed, and he went to sleep. He traveled in time back to Tralfamadore.

"Time-traveling again?" said Montana. It was artificial evening in the dome. She was breast-feeding their child.

"Hmm?" said Billy.

"You've been time-traveling again. I can always tell."

"Um."

"Where did you go this time? It wasn't the war. I can tell that, too."

"New York."

"The Big Apple."

"Hm?"

"That's what they used to call New York."

"Oh."

"You see any plays or movies?"

"No—I walked around Times Square some, bought a book by Kilgore Trout."

"Lucky *you.*" She did not share his enthusiasm for Kilgore Trout.

Billy mentioned casually that he had seen part of a blue movie she had made. Her response was no less casual. It was Tralfamadorian and guilt-free:

"Yes—" she said, "and I've heard about you in the war, about what a clown you were. And I've heard about the high-school teacher who was shot. He made a blue movie with a firing squad." She moved the baby from one breast to the other, because the moment was so structured that she *had* to do so.

There was a silence.

"They're playing with the clocks again," said Montana, rising, preparing to put the baby into its crib. She meant that their keepers were making the electric clocks in the dome go fast, then slow, then fast again, and watching the little Earthling family through peepholes.

There was a silver chain around Montana Wildhack's neck. Hanging from it, between her breasts, was a locket containing a photograph of her alcoholic mother—a grainy thing, soot and chalk. It could have been anybody. Engraved on the outside of the locket were these words:

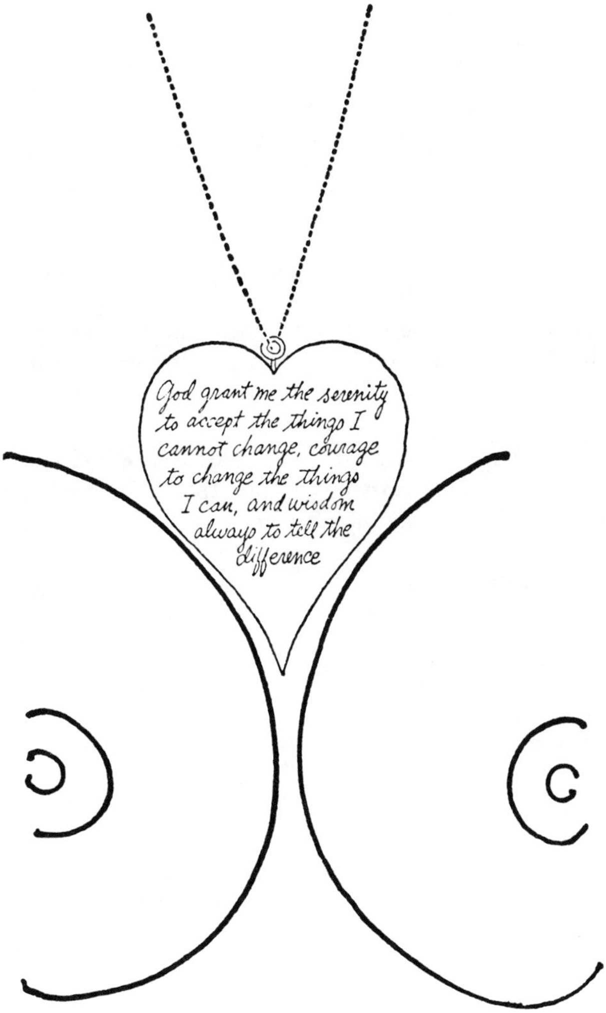

10

Robert Kennedy, whose summer home is eight miles from the home I live in all year round, was shot two nights ago. He died last night. So it goes.

Martin Luther King was shot a month ago. He died, too. So it goes.

And every day my Government gives me a count of corpses created by military science in Vietnam. So it goes.

My father died many years ago now—of natural causes. So it goes. He was a sweet man. He was a gun nut, too. He left me his guns. They rust.

On Tralfamadore, says Billy Pilgrim, there isn't much interest in Jesus Christ. The Earthling figure who is most engaging to the Tralfamadorian mind, he says, is Charles Darwin—who taught that those who die are meant to die, that corpses are improvements. So it goes.

The same general idea appears in *The Big Board* by Kilgore Trout. The flying saucer creatures who capture Trout's hero ask him about Darwin. They also ask him about golf.

If what Billy Pilgrim learned from the Tralfamadorians is true, that we will all live forever, no matter how dead we may sometimes seem to be, I am not overjoyed. Still—if I am going to spend eternity visiting this moment and that, I'm grateful that so many of those moments are nice.

One of the nicest ones in recent times was on my trip back to Dresden with my old war buddy, O'Hare.

We took a Hungarian Airlines plane from East Berlin. The pilot had a handlebar mustache. He looked like Adolph Menjou. He smoked a Cuban cigar while the plane was being fueled. When we took off, there was no talk of fastening seat belts.

When we were up in the air, a young steward served us rye bread and salami and butter and cheese and white wine. The folding tray in front of me would not open out. The steward went into the cockpit for a tool, came back with a beer-can opener. He used it to pry out the tray.

There were only six other passengers. They spoke many languages.

They were having nice times, too. East Germany was down below, and the lights were on. I imagined dropping bombs on those lights, those villages and cities and towns.

O'Hare and I had never expected to make any money—and here we were now, extremely well-to-do.

"If you're ever in Cody, Wyoming," I said to him lazily, "just ask for Wild Bob."

O'Hare had a little notebook with him, and printed in the back of it were postal rates and airline distances and the altitudes of famous mountains and other key facts about the world. He was looking up the population of Dresden, which wasn't in the notebook, when he came across this, which he gave me to read:

On an average, 324,000 new babies are born into the world every day. During that same day, 10,000 persons, on an average, will have starved to death or died from malnutrition. So it goes. *In addition, 123,000 persons will die for other reasons.* So it goes. *This leaves a net gain of about 191,000 each day in the world. The Population Reference Bureau predicts that the world's total population will double to 7,000,000,000 before the year 2000.*

"I suppose they will all want dignity," I said.

"I suppose," said O'Hare.

Billy Pilgrim was meanwhile traveling back to Dresden, too, but not in the present. He was going back there in 1945, two days after the city was destroyed. Now Billy and the rest were being marched into the ruins by their guards. I was there. O'Hare was there. We had spent the past two nights in the blind innkeeper's stable. Authorities had found us there. They told us what to do. We were to borrow picks and shovels and crowbars and wheelbarrows from our neighbors. We were to march with these implements to such and such a place in the ruins, ready to go to work.

There were barricades on the main roads leading into the ruins. Germans were stopped there. They were not permitted to explore the moon.

Prisoners of war from many lands came together that morning at such and such a place in Dresden. It had been decreed that here was where the digging for bodies was to begin. So the digging began.

Billy found himself paired as a digger with a Maori, who had been captured at Tobruk. The Maori was chocolate brown. He had whirlpools tattooed on his forehead and his cheeks. Billy and the Maori dug into the inert, unpromising gravel of the moon. The materials were loose, so there were constant little avalanches.

Many holes were dug at once. Nobody knew yet what there was to find. Most holes came to nothing—to pavement, or to boulders so huge they would not move. There was no machinery. Not even horses or mules or oxen could cross the moonscape.

And Billy and the Maori and others helping them with their particular hole came at last to a membrane of timbers laced over rocks which had wedged together to form an accidental dome. They made a hole in the membrane. There was darkness and space under there.

A German soldier with a flashlight went down into the darkness, was gone a long time. When he finally came back, he told a superior on the rim of the hole that there were dozens of bodies down there. They were sitting on benches. They were unmarked.

So it goes.

The superior said that the opening in the membrane should be enlarged, and that a ladder should be put in the hole so that the bodies could be carried out. Thus began the first corpse mine in Dresden.

There were hundreds of corpse mines operating by and by. They didn't smell bad at first, were wax museums. But then the bodies rotted and liquefied, and the stink was like roses and mustard gas.

So it goes.

The Maori Billy had worked with died of the dry heaves, after having been ordered to go down in that stink and work. He tore himself to pieces, throwing up and throwing up.

So it goes.

So a new technique was devised. Bodies weren't brought up any more. They were cremated by soldiers with flamethrowers right where they were. The soldiers stood outside the shelters, simply sent the fire in.

Somewhere in there the poor old high school teacher, Edgar Derby, was caught with a teapot he had taken from the catacombs. He was arrested for plundering. He was tried and shot.

So it goes.

And somewhere in there was springtime. The corpse mines were closed down. The soldiers all left to fight the Russians. In the suburbs, the women and children dug rifle pits. Billy and the rest of his group were locked up in the stable in the suburbs. And then, one morning, they got up to discover that the door was unlocked. World War Two in Europe was over.

Billy and the rest wandered out onto the shady street. The trees were leafing out. There was nothing going on out there, no traffic of any kind. There was only one vehicle, an abandoned wagon drawn by two horses. The wagon was green and coffin-shaped.

Birds were talking.

One bird said to Billy Pilgrim, *Poo-tee-weet?*"

TOPICS FOR PAPERS AND DISCUSSION

1. *Billy Pilgrim.* Seemingly Billy Pilgrim is outlandish and absurd, but in what sense may he be taken as heroic? Contrast the proclaimed heroics of nations and individuals with Billy's. Although he is said to be a "listless plaything of enormous forces," what needs or drives motivate Billy? Consider changes in his character as a result of the war. How and to what extent does Billy resemble any or all of the following: Everyman, Christ, noble fool, schizophrenic (consult R. D. Laing's *The Divided Self),* innocent initiate? What do Billy Pilgrim and Kurt Vonnegut have in common? (See Vonnegut's epigraph on the title page and his biographical note.)

2. *Time.* Billy "has come unstuck in time"—why? From the present time of the novel (1968), sort out various uses of time: the distant and recent past, the near and distant future. What is accomplished by this time-tripping? What details indicate that we are not to take this shuffling of chronological time as mere insanity? What is revealed of the narrator's character by his withholding scenes of the actual bombing until late in the novel? Assuming with modern scientists that time is not an undeviating entity, but that time warps and simultaneous spatial time actually exist, explain the relevance of time-shuffling to Vonnegut's central thematic concerns.

3. *Women and Billy.* What are the relationships of Valencia and Montana Wildhack to Billy? What differences and what similarities do you find in Billy with each as mate, as lover, as father of their children? Deduce Billy's attitudes toward his mother, his daughter Barbara, the drunken

woman at the New Year's Eve party, Maggie White, Lily Rumfoord, the Dresden women, and those in the initial chapter. Contrast the characterizations of these women.

4. *The functions of Tralfamadore and its philosophy.* What are Tralfamadore's views of time, free will, war, multisexes, death, and the fourth dimension? What do Billy and the reader learn from them? The Tralfamadorian way of life provides certain new perspectives for earthly events; what are they? In this connection, consider Derby's statement to the English colonel in Chapter 5: he "described the incredible artificial weather that Earthlings sometimes create for other Earthlings when they don't want those other Earthlings to inhabit Earth any more." What does Vonnegut's intention appear to be?

5. *Humor and satire.* In spite of its grim subjects (war and death), *Slaughterhouse-Five* is a very funny novel. How does Vonnegut's humor function, and what are the strengths and weaknesses of his satire? His work has been called profoundly moral. How then may one reconcile his playful wit with his fundamental seriousness? Can the authorial intrusions of Vonnegut himself into the story proper be considered comic? Explain. Vonnegut has remarked that the science-fiction passages are "just like the clowns in Shakespeare" who "lighten things up." Evaluate this statement, remembering that Shakespeare's clowns are often the wisest men of all.

6. *History and literary art.* Compare David Irving's historical account, *The Destruction of Dresden,* with the Dresden sections of the novel. What differences do you discover between the ways of history and literary art? Enumerate the advantages and disadvantages of the approach used by each author toward "the greatest massacre in European history." What, for instance, is gained by Vonnegut's skirting around or describing piecemeal what apparently ought to be the main event of the novel—the bombing and its aftermath? Consider understatement as a fictional technique.

7. *Death and rebirth.* How does Vonnegut's concern with death and rebirth function? Relate it to the Tralfamadorian notion of death. Death and resurrection is an archetype familiar to us in such events as the crucifixion and resurrection of Christ and other young gods. Billy nearly dies as a child (by drowning), as a young soldier (in World War II), as an older man (in a plane crash), but each time he is "reborn." Dresden is destroyed and reborn over "tons of human bone meal in the ground." Billy anticipates the time of his assassination and the time when he will "live again."

8. *"A new Gospel."* What is Vonnegut's interpretation of God's concern with the world? Discuss the presentation of religion by means of understatement, overstatement, irony, motif, and symbol. In *Rites and*

Symbols of Initiation, Mircea Eliade writes that with the loss of religious reality (he calls it "ritual reality"), initiatory patterns become "literary motifs" and deliver spiritual messages "directly to the imagination." Discuss this idea and the state of religion today. Vonnegut has said that he considers Alcoholics Anonymous to be a religion superior to others. Where is evidence of AA as religion in the novel? Discuss Billy as a "pilgrim," and the opening and closing uses of the Christmas carol of "the little Lord Jesus."

9. *Technology.* The novel is about machinery, material possessions, scientific instruments. "Magic Fingers" soothe, bombs obliterate. In this connection, consider optometry as a thematic metaphor. What is significant about Billy as an optometrist, and why does he virtually give up the profession? What are the implications of technology for the novel? What does it suggest about science, business, and "the work ethic" in America? Be sure to consider the technology of Tralfamadore and the Tralfamadorian penchant for viewing Billy and Montana in the geodesic dome.

10. *The interrelationship of story strands.* Vonnegut says that the novel is "jumbled and jangled," and seemingly the following four story strands militate against a unified structure of meaning: Vonnegut (autobiographical); Billy Pilgrim (domestic); Tralfamadore (science fiction); Dresden fire-bombing (war). Trace their relationships and show how the strands create a structure that is both unified and meaningful. Be sure to explain how each strand contributes to the novel's central thematic (moral, ethical, psychological) concerns.

11. *Identity crisis and fragmentation.* William Butler Yeats wrote that when civilizations decay, "Things fall apart; the center cannot hold." Recount evidence from the novel that the world, in Vonnegut's view, has become fragmented into multiple states of being and/or nonbeing. Do you detect the threat to the individual as loss of a cohesive self? Describe how Billy's alienation and disorientation are intended to reflect contemporary existence. What is his difficulty in defining "the self" before and after the war and plane crash? What evidence is there in the novel that the Tralfamadorian experience has helped him resolve the problem?

12. *Verbal motif as meaning. Slaughterhouse-Five* abounds in leitmotifs woven out of image, metaphor, and symbol, with each pattern of motif carrying some aspect of thematics. Consider these: so it goes, if the accident will, mustard gas and roses, nestling like spoons, Three Musketeers bars, black and orange (and blue, red, white, green) as colors, cripples, bugs in amber, blue and ivory feet, the barbershop quartet, androgynous figures, cellar (canyon, cavern, hell, locker, pool), etc. Analyze the technique of repetition for its thematic effectiveness. Discriminate between the most and least important.

13. *"Obscenity," "Immorality," and Censorship.* Discuss this proposition:

contrary to superficial evidence, the novel is not obscene or immoral (you may adopt the opposite point of view). *Slaughterhouse-Five* was prohibited from being taught in a small-town high school some years ago; the teacher who assigned it was arrested; copies of the book were actually burned because it was said to contain "obscene language" and "filth." What should one's attitude toward censorship be in a free society? Who should determine what is read and taught?

14. *Novel as potpourri.* Consider: a novel that appears on the surface to be a pastiche may achieve cohesiveness and unity (and thus approach the status of art) by thematic concerns touched on in every incongruous element. What ideas bind the following together? Bombs fly backwards; Christ makes a cross; a drunk is named Rosewater; Kilgore Trout is a kind of anagram; the Wearys collect torture instruments; an Englishman plays the Blue Fairy Godmother; we hear a bird sing *"Poo-tee-weet?"*, learn the history of a pornographic photo, see a dream of giraffes, etc. Also relate: drawings of a tombstone, a latrine sign, a locket; jokes, songs, allusions, poems, prayers. Explain how this pastiche becomes a work of art.

15. *Vonnegut's style.* Explain Vonnegut's reference to his narrative method as "telegraphic schizophrenic" and its similarity to the "manner of tales of the planet Tralfamadore" (as "brief clumps of symbols"). He has remarked that each section "should work, roughly as a poem works." Choose a section and submit it to a poetic analysis; try to determine if his intentions were realized. Consider such elements as image, metaphor, symbol, rhythm, tone, idea, dramatic tension, references to other parts of the novel. Describe the nature of his particular idiom; why has it become so popular with contemporary Americans, especially young people?

The Bluest Eye

Toni Morrison

To the two who gave me life
and the one who made me free

Here is the house. It is green and white. It has a red door. It is very pretty. Here is the family. Mother, Father, Dick, and Jane live in the green-and-white house. They are very happy. See Jane. She has a red dress. She wants to play. Who will play with Jane? See the cat. It goes meow-meow. Come and play. Come play with Jane. The kitten will not play. See Mother. Mother is very nice. Mother, will you play with Jane? Mother laughs. Laugh, Mother, laugh. See Father. He is big and strong. Father, will you play with Jane? Father is smiling. Smile, Father, smile. See the dog. Bowwow goes the dog. Do you want to play with Jane? See the dog run. Run, dog, run. Look, look. Here comes a friend. The friend will play with Jane. They will play a good game. Play, Jane, play.

Here is the house it is green and white it has a red door it is very pretty here is the family mother father dick and jane live in the green-and-white house they are very happy see jane she has a red dress she wants to play who will play with jane see the cat it goes meow-meow come and play come play with jane the kitten will not play see mother mother is very nice mother will you play with jane mother laughs laugh mother laugh see father he is big and strong father will you play with jane father is smiling smile father smile see the dog bowwow goes the dog do you want to play do you want to play with jane see the dog run run dog run look look here comes a friend the friend will play with jane they will play a good game play jane play

Hereisthehouseitisgreenandwhiteithasareddooritisveryprettyhereis the family mother father dick and jane live in the green and white house they are very happy see jane she has a red dress she wants to play who will playwithjaneseethecatitgoesmeowmeowcomeandplaycomeplaywith janethekittenwillnotplayseemothermotherisverynicemotherwillyou play with jane mother laughs laugh mother laugh seefather he is big and strongfatherwillyouplaywithjanefatherissmilingsmilefathersmilesee thedogbowwowgoesthedogdoyouwanttoplaydoyouwanttoplaywith janeseethedogrunrundogrunlooklookherecomesafriendthefriendwill playwithjanetheywillplayagoodgameplayjaneplayplayjaneplayplaypl

Quiet as it's kept, there were no marigolds in the fall of 1941. We thought, at the time, that it was because Pecola was having her father's baby that the marigolds did not grow. A little examination and much less melancholy would have proved to us that our seeds were not the only ones that did not sprout; nobody's did. Not even the gardens fronting the lake showed marigolds that year. But so deeply concerned were we with the health and safe delivery of Pecola's baby we could think of nothing but our own magic: if we planted the seeds, and said the right words over them, they would blossom, and everything would be all right.

It was a long time before my sister and I admitted to ourselves that no green was going to spring from our seeds. Once we knew, our guilt was relieved only by fights and mutual accusations about who was to blame. For years I thought my sister was right: it was my fault. I had planted them too far down in the earth. It never occurred to either of us that the earth itself might have been unyielding. We had dropped our seeds in our own little plot of black dirt just as Pecola's father had dropped his seeds in his own plot of black dirt. Our innocence and faith were no more productive than his lust or despair. What is clear now is that of all of that hope, fear, lust, love, and grief, nothing remains but Pecola and the unyielding earth. Cholly Breedlove is dead; our innocence too. The seeds shriveled and died; her baby too.

There is really nothing more to say—except why. But since why *is difficult to handle, one must take refuge in* how.

Autumn

Nuns go by as quiet as lust, and drunken men with sober eyes sing in the lobby of the Greek hotel. Rosemary Villanucci, our next-door friend who lives above her father's café, sits in a 1939 Buick eating bread and butter. She rolls down the window to tell my sister Frieda and me that we can't come in. We stare at her, wanting her bread, but more than that wanting to poke the arrogance out of her eyes and smash the pride of ownership that curls her chewing mouth. When she comes out of the car we will beat her up, make red marks on her white skin, and she will cry and ask us do we want her to pull her pants down. We will say no. We don't know what we should feel or do if she does, but whenever she asks us, we know she is offering us something precious and that our own pride must be asserted by refusing to accept.

School has started, and Frieda and I get new brown stockings and cod-liver oil. Grown-ups talk in tired, edgy voices about Zick's Coal Company and take us along in the evening to the railroad tracks where we fill burlap sacks with the tiny pieces of coal lying about. Later we walk home, glancing back to see the great carloads of slag being dumped, red hot and smoking, into the ravine that skirts the steel mill. The dying fire lights the sky with a dull orange glow. Frieda and I lag behind, staring at the patch of color surrounded by black. It is impossible not to feel a shiver when our feet leave the gravel path and sink into the dead grass in the field.

Our house is old, cold, and green. At night a kerosene lamp lights one large room. The others are braced in darkness, peopled by roaches and mice. Adults do not talk to us—they give us directions. They issue orders without providing information. When we trip and fall down they glance at us; if we cut or bruise ourselves, they ask us are we crazy. When we catch colds, they shake their heads in disgust at our lack of consideration. How, they ask us, do you expect anybody to get anything done if you all are sick? We cannot answer them. Our illness is treated with contempt, foul Black Draught, and castor oil that blunts our minds.

When, on a day after a trip to collect coal, I cough once, loudly, through bronchial tubes already packed tight with phlegm, my mother frowns. "Great Jesus. Get on in that bed. How many times do I have to tell you to wear something on your head? You must be the biggest fool in this town. Frieda? Get some rags and stuff that window."

Frieda restuffs the window. I trudge off to bed, full of guilt and self-pity. I lie down in my underwear, the metal in my black garters hurts my legs, but I do not take them off, for it is too cold to lie stockingless. It takes a long time for my body to heat its place in the bed. Once I have generated a silhouette of warmth, I dare not move, for there is a cold place one-half inch in any direction. No one speaks to me or asks how I feel. In an hour or two my mother comes. Her hands are large and rough, and when she rubs the Vicks salve on my chest, I am rigid with pain. She takes two fingers' full of it at a time, and massages my chest until I am faint. Just when I think I will tip over into a scream, she scoops out a little of the salve on her forefinger and puts it in my mouth, telling me to swallow. A hot flannel is wrapped about my neck and chest. I am covered up with heavy quilts and ordered to sweat, which I do—promptly.

Later I throw up, and my mother says, "What did you puke on the bed clothes for? Don't you have sense enough to hold your head out the bed? Now, look what you did. You think I got time for nothing but washing up your puke?"

The puke swaddles down the pillow onto the sheet—green-gray, with flecks of orange. It moves like the insides of an uncooked egg. Stubbornly clinging to its own mass, refusing to break up and be removed. How, I wonder, can it be so neat and nasty at the same time?

My mother's voice drones on. She is not talking to me. She is talking to the puke, but she is calling it my name: Claudia. She wipes it up as best she can and puts a scratchy towel over the large wet place. I lie down again. The rags have fallen from the window crack, and the air is cold. I dare not call her back and am reluctant to leave my warmth. My mother's anger humiliates me; her words chafe my cheeks, and I am crying. I do not know that she is not angry at me, but at my sickness. I believe she despises my weakness for letting the sickness "take holt." By and by I will not get sick; I will refuse to. But for now I am crying. I know I am making more snot, but I can't stop.

My sister comes in. Her eyes are full of sorrow. She sings to me: "When the deep purple falls over sleepy garden walls, someone thinks of me. . . ." I doze, thinking of plums, walls, and "someone."

But was it really like that? As painful as I remember? Only mildly. Or rather, it was a productive and fructifying pain. Love, thick and dark as Alaga syrup, eased up into that cracked window. I could smell it—taste it—sweet, musty, with an edge of wintergreen in its base—everywhere in that house. It stuck, along with my tongue, to the frosted windowpanes. It coated my chest, along with the salve, and when the flannel came undone in my sleep, the clear, sharp curves of air outlined its presence on my throat. And in the night, when my coughing was dry and tough, feet padded into the room, hands repinned the flannel, readjusted the quilt, and rested a moment on my forehead. So when I think of autumn, I think of somebody with hands who does not want me to die.

It was autumn too when Mr. Henry came. Our roomer. Our roomer. The words ballooned from the lips and hovered about our heads—silent, separate, and pleasantly mysterious. My mother was all ease and satisfaction in discussing his coming.

"You know him," she said to her friends. "Henry Washington. He's been living over there with Miss Della Jones on Thirteenth

Street. But she's too addled now to keep up. So he's looking for another place."

"Oh, yes." Her friends do not hide their curiosity. "I been wondering how long he was going to stay up there with her. They say she's real bad off. Don't know who he is half the time, and nobody else."

"Well, that old crazy nigger she married up with didn't help her head none."

"Did you hear what he told folks when he left her?"

"Uh-uh. What?"

"Well, he run off with that trifling Peggy—from Elyria. You know."

"One of Old Slack Bessie's girls?"

"That's the one. Well, somebody asked him why he left a nice good church woman like Della for that heifer. You know Della always did keep a good house. And he said the honest-to-God real reason was he couldn't take no more of that violet water Della Jones used. Said he wanted a woman to smell like a woman. Said Della was just too clean for him."

"Old dog. Ain't that nasty!"

"You telling me. What kind of reasoning is that?"

"No kind. Some men just dogs."

"Is that what give her them strokes?"

"Must have helped. But you know, none of them girls wasn't too bright. Remember that grinning Hattie? She wasn't never right. And their Auntie Julia is still trotting up and down Sixteenth Street talking to herself."

"Didn't she get put away?"

"Naw. County wouldn't take her. Said she wasn't harming anybody."

"Well, she's harming me. You want something to scare the living shit out of you, you get up at five-thirty in the morning like I do and see that old hag floating by in that bonnet. Have mercy!"

They laugh.

Frieda and I are washing Mason jars. We do not hear their words, but with grown-ups we listen to and watch out for their voices.

"Well, I hope don't nobody let me roam around like that when I get senile. It's a shame."

"What they going to do about Della? Don't she have no people?"

"A sister's coming up from North Carolina to look after her. I expect she wants to get aholt of Della's house."

"Oh, come on. That's a evil thought, if ever I heard one."

"What you want to bet? Henry Washington said that sister ain't seen Della in fifteen years."

"I kind of thought Henry would marry her one of these days."

"That old woman?"

"Well, Henry ain't no chicken."

"No, but he ain't no buzzard, either."

"He ever been married to anybody?"

"No."

"How come? Somebody cut it off?"

"He's just picky."

"He ain't picky. You see anything around here you'd marry?"

"Well . . . no."

"He's just sensible. A steady worker with quiet ways. I hope it works out all right."

"It will. How much you charging?"

"Five dollars every two weeks."

"That'll be a big help to you."

"I'll say."

Their conversation is like a gently wicked dance: sound meets sound, curtsies, shimmies, and retires. Another sound enters but is upstaged by still another: the two circle each other and stop. Sometimes their words move in lofty spirals; other times they take strident leaps, and all of it is punctuated with warm-pulsed laughter—like the throb of a heart made of jelly. The edge, the curl, the thrust of their emotions is always clear to Frieda and me. We do not, cannot, know the meanings of all their words, for we are nine and ten years old. So we watch their faces, their hands, their feet, and listen for truth in timbre.

So when Mr. Henry arrived on a Saturday night, we smelled him. He smelled wonderful. Like trees and lemon vanishing cream, and Nu Nile Hair Oil and flecks of Sen-Sen.

He smiled a lot, showing small even teeth with a friendly gap in the middle. Frieda and I were not introduced to him—merely pointed out. Like, here is the bathroom; the clothes closet is here; and these are my kids, Frieda and Claudia; watch out for this window; it don't open all the way.

We looked sideways at him, saying nothing and expecting him to say nothing. Just to nod, as he had done at the clothes closet, acknowledging our existence. To our surprise, he spoke to us.

"Hello there. You must be Greta Garbo, and you must be Ginger Rogers."

We giggled. Even my father was startled into a smile.

"Want a penny?" He held out a shiny coin to us. Frieda lowered her head, too pleased to answer. I reached for it. He snapped his thumb and forefinger, and the penny disappeared. Our shock was laced with delight. We searched all over him, poking our fingers into his socks, looking up the inside back of his coat. If happiness is anticipation with certainty, we were happy. And while we waited for the coin to reappear, we knew we were amusing Mama and Daddy. Daddy was smiling, and Mama's eyes went soft as they followed our hands wandering over Mr. Henry's body.

We loved him. Even after what came later, there was no bitterness in our memory of him.

She slept in the bed with us. Frieda on the outside because she is brave—it never occurs to her that if in her sleep her hand hangs over the edge of the bed "something" will crawl out from under it and bite her fingers off. I sleep near the wall because that thought *has* occurred to me. Pecola, therefore, had to sleep in the middle.

Mama had told us two days earlier that a "case" was coming—a girl who had no place to go. The county had placed her in our house for a few days until they could decide what to do, or, more precisely, until the family was reunited. We were to be nice to her and not fight. Mama didn't know "what got into people," but that old Dog Breedlove had burned up his house, gone upside his wife's head, and everybody, as a result, was outdoors.

Outdoors, we knew, was the real terror of life. The threat of being outdoors surfaced frequently in those days. Every possibility of excess was curtailed with it. If somebody ate too much, he could end up outdoors. If somebody used too much coal, he could end up outdoors. People could gamble themselves outdoors, drink themselves outdoors. Sometimes mothers put their sons outdoors, and when that happened, regardless of what the son had done, all sympathy was with him. He was outdoors, and his own flesh had done it. To be put outdoors by a landlord was one thing—unfortunate, but an aspect of life over which you had no control, since you could not control your income. But to be slack enough to put oneself outdoors, or heartless enough to put one's own kin outdoors—that was criminal.

There is a difference between being put *out* and being put out*doors.* If you are put out, you go somewhere else; if you are outdoors, there is no place to go. The distinction was subtle but final. Outdoors was the end of something, an irrevocable, physical fact, defining and complementing our metaphysical condition. Being a minority in both caste and class, we moved about anyway on the hem of life, struggling to consolidate our weaknesses and hang on, or to creep singly up into the major folds of the garment. Our peripheral existence, however, was something we had learned to deal with—probably because it was abstract. But the concreteness of being outdoors was another matter—like the difference between the concept of death and being, in fact, dead. Dead doesn't change, and outdoors is here to stay.

Knowing that there was such a thing as outdoors bred in us a hunger for property, for ownership. The firm possession of a yard, a porch, a grape arbor. Propertied black people spent all their energies, all their love, on their nests. Like frenzied, desperate birds, they overdecorated everything; fussed and fidgeted over their hard-won homes; canned, jellied, and preserved all summer to fill the cupboards and shelves; they painted, picked, and poked at every corner of their houses. And these houses loomed like hothouse sunflowers among the rows of weeds that were the rented houses. Renting blacks cast furtive glances at these owned yards and porches, and made firmer commitments to buy themselves "some nice little old place." In the meantime, they saved, and scratched, and piled away what they could in the rented hovels, looking forward to the day of property.

Cholly Breedlove, then, a renting black, having put his family outdoors, had catapulted himself beyond the reaches of human consideration. He had joined the animals; was, indeed, an old dog, a snake, a ratty nigger. Mrs. Breedlove was staying with the woman she worked for; the boy, Sammy, was with some other family; and Pecola was to stay with us. Cholly was in jail.

She came with nothing. No little paper bag with the other dress, or a nightgown, or two pair of whitish cotton bloomers. She just appeared with a white woman and sat down.

We had fun in those few days Pecola was with us. Frieda and I stopped fighting each other and concentrated on our guest, trying hard to keep her from feeling outdoors.

When we discovered that she clearly did not want to dominate us, we liked her. She laughed when I clowned for her, and smiled and accepted gracefully the food gifts my sister gave her.

"Would you like some graham crackers?"

"I don't care."

Frieda brought her four graham crackers on a saucer and some milk in a blue-and-white Shirley Temple cup. She was a long time with the milk, and gazed fondly at the silhouette of Shirley Temple's dimpled face. Frieda and she had a loving conversation about how cu-ute Shirley Temple was. I couldn't join them in their adoration because I hated Shirley. Not because she was cute, but because she danced with Bojangles, who was *my* friend, *my* uncle, *my* daddy, and who ought to have been soft-shoeing it and chuckling with me. Instead he was enjoying, sharing, giving a lovely dance thing with one of those little white girls whose socks never slid down under their heels. So I said, "I like Jane Withers."

They gave me a puzzled look, decided I was incomprehensible, and continued their reminiscing about old squint-eyed Shirley.

Younger than both Frieda and Pecola, I had not yet arrived at the turning point in the development of my psyche which would allow me to love her. What I felt at that time was unsullied hatred. But before that I had felt a stranger, more frightening thing than hatred for all the Shirley Temples of the world.

It had begun with Christmas and the gift of dolls. The big, the special, the loving gift was always a big, blue-eyed Baby Doll. From the clucking sounds of adults I knew that the doll represented what they thought was my fondest wish. I was bemused with the thing itself, and the way it looked. What was I supposed to do with it? Pretend I was its mother? I had no interest in babies or the concept of motherhood. I was interested only in humans my own age and size, and could not generate any enthusiasm at the prospect of being a mother. Motherhood was old age, and other remote possibilities. I learned quickly, however, what I was expected to do with the doll: rock it, fabricate storied situations around it, even sleep with it. Picture books were full of little girls sleeping with their dolls. Raggedy Ann dolls usually, but they were out of the question. I was physically revolted by and secretly frightened of those round moronic eyes, the pancake face, and orangeworms hair.

The other dolls, which were supposed to bring me great pleasure, succeeded in doing quite the opposite. When I took it to bed, its hard unyielding limbs resisted my flesh—the tapered fingertips on those dimpled hands scratched. If, in sleep, I turned, the bone-cold head collided with my own. It was a most uncomfortable, patently aggressive sleeping companion. To hold it was no more rewarding. The starched gauze or lace on the cotton dress irritated any embrace. I had only one desire: to dismember it. To see of what it was made, to discover the dearness, to find the beauty, the desirability that had escaped me, but apparently only me. Adults, older girls, shops, magazines, newspapers, window signs—all the world had agreed that a blue-eyed, yellow-haired, pink-skinned doll was what every girl child treasured. "Here," they said, "this is beautiful, and if you are on this day 'worthy' you may have it." I fingered the face, wondering at the single-stroke eyebrows; picked at the pearly teeth stuck like two piano keys between red bowline lips. Traced the turned-up nose, poked the glassy blue eyeballs, twisted the yellow hair. I could not love it. But I could examine it to see what it was that all the world said was lovable. Break off the tiny fingers, bend the flat feet, loosen the hair, twist the head around, and the thing made one sound—a sound they said was the sweet and plaintive cry "Mama," but which sounded to me like the bleat of a dying lamb, or, more precisely, our icebox door opening on rusty hinges in July. Remove the cold and stupid eyeball, it would bleat still, "Ahhhhhh," take off the head, shake out the sawdust, crack the back against the brass bed rail, it would bleat still. The gauze back would split, and I could see the disk with six holes, the secret of the sound. A mere metal roundness.

Grown people frowned and fussed: "You-don't-know-how-to-take-care-of-nothing. I-never-had-a-baby-doll-in-my-whole-life-and-used-to-cry-my-eyes-out-for-them. Now-you-got-one-a-beautiful-one-and-you-tear-it-up-what's-the-matter-with-you?"

How strong was their outrage. Tears threatened to erase the aloofness of their authority. The emotion of years of unfulfilled longing preened in their voices. I did not know why I destroyed those dolls. But I did know that nobody ever asked me what I wanted for Christmas. Had any adult with the power to fulfill my desires taken me seriously and asked me what I wanted, they would have known that I did not want to have anything to own, or to possess any object. I wanted rather to feel something on Christmas day. The real question would have been, "Dear Claudia, what experience would you like on Christmas?" I could have spoken up, "I want to sit on the low stool in Big Mama's kitchen with my lap full of lilacs and listen to Big Papa play his violin for me alone." The lowness of the stool made for my body, the security and warmth of Big Mama's kitchen, the smell of the lilacs, the sound of the music, and, since it would be good to have all of my senses engaged, the taste of a peach, perhaps, afterward.

Instead I tasted and smelled the acridness of tin plates and cups designed for tea parties that bored me. Instead I looked with loathing on new dresses that required a hateful bath in a galvanized zinc tub before wearing. Slipping around on the zinc, no time to play or soak, for the water chilled too fast, no time to enjoy one's nakedness, only time to make curtains of soapy water careen down between the legs. Then the scratchy towels and the dreadful and humiliating absence of dirt. The irritable, unimaginative cleanliness. Gone the ink marks from legs and face, all my creations and accumulations of the day gone, and replaced by goose pimples.

I destroyed white baby dolls.

But the dismembering of dolls was not the true horror. The truly horrifying thing was the transference of the same impulses to little white girls. The indifference with which I could have axed them was shaken only by my desire to do so. To discover what eluded me: the secret of the magic they weaved on others. What made people look at them and say "Awwwww," but not for me? The eye slide of black women as they approached them on the street, and the possessive gentleness of their touch as they handled them.

If I pinched them, their eyes—unlike the crazed glint of the baby doll's eyes—would fold in pain, and their cry would not be the sound of an icebox door, but a fascinating cry of pain. When I learned how repulsive this disinterested violence was, that it was repulsive because it was disinterested, my shame floundered about for refuge. The best hiding place was love. Thus the conversion from pristine sadism to fabricated hatred, to fraudulent love. It was a small step to Shirley Temple. I learned much later to worship her, just as I learned to delight in cleanliness, knowing, even as I learned, that the change was adjustment without improvement.

"Three quarts of milk. That's what was *in* that icebox yesterday. Three whole quarts. Now they ain't none. Not a drop. I don't mind folks coming in and getting what they want, but three quarts of milk! What the devil does *any*body need with *three* quarts of milk?"

The "folks" my mother was referring to was Pecola. The three of us, Pecola, Frieda, and I, listened to her downstairs in the kitchen fussing about the amount of milk Pecola had drunk. We knew she was fond of the Shirley Temple cup and took every opportunity to drink milk out of it just to handle and see sweet Shirley's face. My mother knew that Frieda and I hated milk and assumed Pecola drank it out of greediness. It was certainly not for us to "dispute" her. We didn't initiate talk with grown-ups; we answered their questions.

Ashamed of the insults that were being heaped on our friend, we just sat there: I picked toe jam, Frieda cleaned her fingernails with her teeth, and Pecola finger-traced some scars on her knee—her head cocked to one side. My mother's fussing soliloquies always irritated and depressed us. They were interminable, insulting, and although indirect (Mama never named anybody—just talked about folks and *some* people), extremely painful in their thrust. She would go on like that for hours, connecting one offense to another until all of the things that chagrined her were spewed out. Then, having told everybody and everything off, she would burst into song and sing the rest of the day. But it was such a long time before the singing part came. In the meantime, our stomachs jellying and our necks burning, we listened, avoided each other's eyes, and picked toe jam or whatever.

". . . I don't know what I'm supposed to be running here, a charity ward, I guess. Time for me to get out of the *giving* line and get in the *getting* line. I guess I ain't sup*posed* to have nothing. I'm sup*posed* to end up in the poorhouse. Look like nothing I do is going to keep me out of there. Folks just spend all their time trying to figure out ways to send *me* to the poorhouse. I got about as much business with another mouth to feed as a cat has with side pockets. As if I don't have trouble enough trying to feed my own and keep out the poorhouse, now I got something else in here that's just going to *drink* me on in there. Well, naw, she ain't. Not long as I got strength in my body and a tongue in my head. There's a limit to everything. I ain't got nothing to just throw *away.* Don't *no*body need *three* quarts of milk. Henry *Ford* don't need three quarts of milk. That's just downright *sin*ful. I'm willing to do what I can for folks. Can't nobody say I ain't. But this has got to stop, and I'm just the one to stop it. Bible say watch as *well* as pray. Folks just dump they children off on you and go on 'bout they business. Ain't nobody even *peeped* in here to see whether that child has a loaf of bread. Look like they would just *peep* in to see whether I had a loaf of bread to give her. But naw. That thought don't cross they mind. That old trifling Cholly been out of jail *two* whole days and ain't been here *yet* to see if his own child was 'live or dead. She could be *dead* for all he know. And that *mama* neither. What kind of something is that?"

When Mama got around to Henry Ford and all those people who didn't care whether she had a loaf of bread, it was time to go. We wanted to miss the part about Roosevelt and the CCC camps.

Frieda got up and started down the stairs. Pecola and I followed, making a wide arc to avoid the kitchen doorway. We sat on the steps of the porch, where my mother's words could reach us only in spurts.

It was a lonesome Saturday. The house smelled of Fels Naphtha and the sharp odor of mustard greens cooking. Saturdays were lonesome, fussy, soapy days. Second in misery only to those tight, starchy, cough-drop Sundays, so full of "don'ts" and "set'cha self downs."

If my mother was in a singing mood, it wasn't so bad. She would sing about hard times, bad times, and somebody-done-gone-and-left-me times. But her voice was so sweet and her singing-eyes so melty I found myself longing for those hard times, yearning to be grown without "a thin di-i-ime to my name." I looked forward to the delicious time when "my man" would leave me, when I would "hate to see that evening sun go down . . ." 'cause then I would know "my man has left this town." Misery colored by the greens and blues in my mother's voice took all of the grief out of the words and left me with a conviction that pain was not only endurable, it was sweet.

But without song, those Saturdays sat on my head like a coal scuttle, and if Mama was fussing, as she was now, it was like somebody throwing stones at it.

". . . and here I am poor as a bowl of yak-me. What do they think I am? Some kind of Sandy Claus? Well, they can just take they stocking down 'cause it *ain't* Christmas. . . ."

We fidgeted.

"Let's do something," Frieda said.

"What do you want to do?" I asked.

"I don't know. Nothing." Frieda stared at the tops of the trees. Pecola looked at her feet.

"You want to go up to Mr. Henry's room and look at his girlie magazines?"

Frieda made an ugly face. She didn't like to look at dirty pictures. "Well," I continued, "we could look at his Bible. *That's* pretty." Frieda sucked her teeth and made a *phttt* sound with her lips. "O.K., then. We could go thread needles for the half-blind lady. She'll give us a penny."

Frieda snorted. "Her eyes look like snot. I don't feel like looking at them. What *you* want to do Pecola?"

"I don't care," she said. "Anything you want."

I had another idea. "We could go up the alley and see what's in the trash cans."

"Too cold," said Frieda. She was bored and irritable.

"I know. We could make some fudge."

"You kidding? With Mama in there fussing? When she starts fussing at the walls, you know she's gonna be at it all day. She wouldn't even let us."

"Well, let's go over to the Greek hotel and listen to them cuss."

"Oh, who wants to do *that?* Besides, they say the same old words all the time."

My supply of ideas exhausted, I began to concentrate on the white spots on my fingernails. The total signified the number of boyfriends I would have. Seven.

Mama's soliloquy slid into the silence ". . . Bible say feed the hungry. That's fine. That's all right. But I ain't feeding no elephants. . . . Anybody need three quarts of milk to *live* need to get out of here. They in the wrong place. What is this? Some kind of *dai*ry farm?"

Suddenly Pecola bolted straight up, her eyes wide with terror. A whinnying sound came from her mouth.

"What's the matter with *you?*" Frieda stood up too.

Then we both looked where Pecola was staring. Blood was running down her legs. Some drops were on the steps. I leaped up. "Hey. You cut yourself? Look. It's all over your dress."

A brownish-red stain discolored the back of her dress. She kept whinnying, standing with her legs far apart.

Frieda said, "Oh. Lordy! I know. I know what that is!"

"What?" Pecola's fingers went to her mouth.

"That's ministratin'."

"What's that?"

"You know."

"Am I going to die?" she asked.

"Noooo. You won't die. It just means you can have a baby!"

"What?"

"How do *you* know?" I was sick and tired of Frieda knowing everything.

"Mildred told me, and Mama too."

"I don't believe it."

"You don't have to, dummy. Look. Wait here. Sit down, Pecola. Right here." Frieda was all authority and zest. "And you," she said to me, "you go get some water."

"Water?"

"Yes, stupid. Water. And be quiet, or Mama will hear you."

Pecola sat down again, a little less fear in her eyes. I went into the kitchen.

"What you want, girl?" Mama was rinsing curtains in the sink.

"Some water, ma'am."

"Right where I'm working, naturally. Well, get a glass. Not no one clean one neither. Use that jar."

I got a Mason jar and filled it with water from the faucet. It seemed a long time filling.

"Don't nobody never want nothing till they see me at the sink. Then everybody got to drink water. . . ."

When the jar was full, I moved to leave the room.

"Where you going?"

"Outside."

"Drink that water right here!"

"I ain't gonna break nothing."

"You don't know what you gonna do."

"Yes, ma'am. I do. Lemme take it out. I won't spill none."

"You bed' not."

I got to the porch and stood there with the Mason jar of water. Pecola was crying.

"What you crying for? Does it hurt?"

She shook her head.

"Then stop slinging snot."

Frieda opened the back door. She had something tucked in her blouse. She looked at me in amazement and pointed to the jar. "What's that supposed to do?"

"You told me. You *said* get some water."

"Not a little old jar full. Lots of water. To scrub the steps with, dumbbell!"

"How was I supposed to know?"

"Yeah. How was you. Come on." She pulled Pecola up by the arm. "Let's go back here." They headed for the side of the house where the bushes were thick.

"Hey. What about me? I want to go."

"Shut uuuup," Frieda stage-whispered. "Mama will hear you. You wash the steps."

They disappeared around the corner of the house.

I was going to miss something. Again. Here was something important, and I had to stay behind and not see any of it. I poured the water on the steps, sloshed it with my shoe, and ran to join them.

Frieda was on her knees; a white rectangle of cotton was near her on the ground. She was pulling Pecola's pants off. "Come on. Step out of them." She managed to get the soiled pants down and flung them at me. "Here."

"What am I supposed to do with these?"

"Bury them, moron."

Frieda told Pecola to hold the cotton thing between her legs.

"How she gonna walk like that?" I asked.

Frieda didn't answer. Instead she took two safety pins from the hem of her skirt and began to pin the ends of the napkin to Pecola's dress.

I picked up the pants with two fingers and looked about for something to dig a hole with. A rustling noise in the bushes startled me, and turning toward it, I saw a pair of fascinated eyes in a dough-white face. Rosemary was watching us. I grabbed for her face and succeeded in scratching her nose. She screamed and jumped back.

"Mrs. MacTeer! Mrs. MacTeer!" Rosemary hollered. "Frieda and Claudia are out here playing nasty! Mrs. MacTeer!"

Mama opened the window and looked down at us.

"What?"

"They're playing nasty, Mrs. MacTeer. Look. And Claudia hit me 'cause I seen them!"

Mama slammed the window shut and came running out the back door.

"What you all doing? Oh. Uh-huh. Uh-huh. Playing nasty, huh?"

She reached into the bushes and pulled off a switch. "I'd rather raise pigs than some nasty girls. Least I can slaughter *them!*"

We began to shriek. "No, Mama. No, ma'am. We wasn't! She's a liar! No, ma'am, Mama! No, ma'am, Mama!"

Mama grabbed Frieda by the shoulder, turned her around, and gave her three or four stinging cuts on her legs. "Gonna be nasty, huh? Naw you ain't!"

Frieda was destroyed. Whippings wounded and insulted her.

Mama looked at Pecola. "You too!" she said. "Child of mine or not!" She grabbed Pecola and spun her around. The safety pin snapped open on one end of the napkin, and Mama saw it fall from under her dress. The switch hovered in the air while Mama blinked. "What the devil is going on here?"

Frieda was sobbing. I, next in line, began to explain. "She was bleeding. We was just trying to stop the blood!"

Mama looked at Frieda for verification. Frieda nodded. "She's ministratin'. We was just helping."

Mama released Pecola and stood looking at her. Then she pulled both of them toward her, their heads against her stomach. Her eyes were sorry. "All right, all right. Now, stop crying. I didn't know. Come on, now. Get on in the house. Go on home, Rosemary. The show is over."

We trooped in, Frieda sobbing quietly, Pecola carrying a white tail, me carrying the little-girl-gone-to-woman pants.

Mama led us to the bathroom. She prodded Pecola inside, and taking the underwear from me, told us to stay out.

We could hear water running into the bathtub.

"You think she's going to drown her?"

"Oh, Claudia. You so dumb. She's just going to wash her clothes and all."

"Should we beat up Rosemary?"

"No. Leave her alone."

The water gushed, and over its gushing we could hear the music of my mother's laughter.

That night, in bed, the three of us lay still. We were full of awe and respect for Pecola. Lying next to a real person who was really ministratin' was somehow sacred. She was different from us now—grown-up-like. She, herself, felt the distance, but refused to lord it over us.

After a long while she spoke very softly. "Is it true that I can have a baby now?"

"Sure," said Frieda drowsily. "Sure you can."

"But . . . how?" Her voice was hollow with wonder.

"Oh," said Frieda, "somebody has to love you."

"Oh."

There was a long pause in which Pecola and I thought this over. It would involve, I supposed, "my man," who, before leaving me, would love me. But there weren't any babies in the songs my mother sang. Maybe that's why the women were sad: the men left before they could make a baby.

Then Pecola asked a question that had never entered my mind. "How do you do that? I mean, how do you get somebody to love you?" But Frieda was asleep. And I didn't know.

HEREISTHEHOUSEITISGREENANDWHITEITHASAREDDOOR ITISVERYPRETTYITISVERYPRETTYPRETTYPRETTYPRETT

There is an abandoned store on the southeast corner of Broadway and Thirty-fifth Street in Lorain, Ohio. It does not recede into its background of leaden sky, nor harmonize with the gray frame houses and black telephone poles around it. Rather, it foists itself on the eye of the passerby in a manner that is both irritating and melancholy. Visitors who drive to this tiny town wonder why it has not been torn down, while pedestrians, who are residents of the neighborhood, simply look away when they pass it.

At one time, when the building housed a pizza parlor, people saw only slow-footed teen-aged boys huddled about the corner. These young boys met there to feel their groins, smoke cigarettes, and plan mild outrages. The smoke from their cigarettes they inhaled deeply, forcing it to fill their lungs, their hearts, their thighs, and keep at bay the shiveriness, the energy of their youth. They moved slowly, laughed slowly, but flicked the ashes from their cigarettes too quickly, too often, and exposed themselves, to those who were interested, as novices to the habit. But long before the sound of their lowing and the sight of their preening, the building was leased to a Hungarian baker, modestly famous for his brioche and poppy-seed rolls. Earlier than that, there was a real-estate office there, and even before that, some gypsies used it as a base of operations. The gypsy family gave the large plate-glass window as much distinction and character as it ever had. The girls of the family took turns sitting between yards of velvet draperies and Oriental rugs hanging at the windows. They looked out and occasionally smiled, or winked, or beckoned—only occasionally. Mostly they looked, their elaborate dresses, long-sleeved and long-skirted, hiding the nakedness that stood in their eyes.

So fluid has the population in that area been, that probably no one remembers longer, longer ago, before the time of the gypsies and the time of the teen-agers when the Breedloves lived there, nestled together in the storefront. Festering together in the debris of a realtor's whim. They slipped in and out of the box of peeling gray, making no stir in the neighborhood, no sound in the labor force, and no wave in the mayor's office. Each member of the family in his own cell of consciousness, each making his own patchwork quilt of reality—collecting fragments of experience here, pieces of information there. From the tiny impressions gleaned from one another, they created a sense of belonging and tried to make do with the way they found each other.

The plan of the living quarters was as unimaginative as a first-generation Greek landlord could contrive it to be. The large "store" area was partitioned into two rooms by beaverboard planks that did not reach to the ceiling. There was a living room, which the family called the front room, and the bedroom, where all the living was done. In the front room were two sofas, an upright piano, and a tiny artificial Christmas tree which had been there, decorated and dust-laden, for two years. The bedroom had three beds: a narrow iron bed for Sammy, fourteen years old, another for Pecola, eleven years old, and a double bed for Cholly and Mrs. Breedlove. In the center of the bedroom, for the even distribution of heat, stood a coal stove. Trunks, chairs, a small end table, and a cardboard "wardrobe" closet were placed around the walls. The kitchen was in the back of this apartment, a separate room. There were no bath facilities. Only a toilet bowl, inaccessible to the eye, if not the ear, of the tenants.

There is nothing more to say about the furnishings. They were anything but describable, having been conceived, manufactured, shipped, and sold in various states of thoughtlessness, greed, and indifference. The furniture had aged without ever having become familiar. People had owned it, but never known it. No one had lost a penny or a brooch under the cushions of either sofa and remembered the place and time of the loss or the finding. No one had clucked and said, "But I *had* it just a minute ago. I was sitting right there talking to . . ." or "Here it is. It must have slipped down while I was feeding the baby!" No one had given birth in one of the beds—or remembered with fondness the peeled paint places, because that's what the baby, when he learned to pull himself up, used to pick loose. No thrifty child had tucked a wad of gum under the table. No happy drunk—a friend of the family, with a fat neck, unmarried, you know, but God how he eats!—had sat at the piano and played "You Are My Sunshine." No young girl had stared at the tiny Christmas tree and remembered when she had decorated it, or wondered if that blue ball was going to hold, or if HE would ever come back to see it.

There were no memories among those pieces. Certainly no memories to be cherished. Occasionally an item provoked a physical reaction: an increase of acid irritation in the upper intestinal tract, a light flush of perspiration at the back of the neck as circumstances surrounding the piece of furniture were recalled. The sofa, for example. It had been purchased new, but the fabric had split straight across the back by the time it was delivered. The store would not take the responsibility. . . .

"Looka here, buddy. It was O.K. when I put it on the truck. The store can't do anything about it once it's on the truck. . . ." Listerine and Lucky Strike breath.

"But I don't want no tore couch if'n it's bought new." Pleading eyes and tightened testicles.

"Tough shit, buddy. *Your* tough shit. . . ."

You could hate a sofa, of course—that is, if you could hate a sofa. But it didn't matter. You still had to get together $4.80 a month. If you had to pay $4.80 a month for a sofa that started off split, no good, and humiliating—you couldn't take any joy in owning it. And the joylessness stank, pervading everything. The stink of it kept you from painting the beaverboard walls; from getting a matching piece of material for the chair; even from sewing up the split, which became a gash, which became a gaping chasm that exposed the cheap frame and cheaper upholstery. It withheld the refreshment in a sleep slept on it. It imposed a furtiveness on the loving done on it. Like a sore tooth that is not content to throb in isolation, but must diffuse its own pain to other parts of the body—making breathing difficult, vision limited, nerves unsettled, so a hated piece of furniture produces a fretful malaise that asserts itself throughout the house and limits the delight of things not related to it.

The only living thing in the Breedloves' house was the coal stove, which lived independently of everything and everyone, its fire being "out," "banked," or "up" at its own discretion, in spite of the fact that the family fed it and knew all the details of its regimen: sprinkle, do not dump, not too much. . . . The fire seemed to live, go down, or die according to its own schemata. In the morning, however, it always saw fit to die.

HEREISTHEFAMILYMOTHERFATHERDICKANDJANETHEYL IVEINTHEGREENANDWHITEHOUSETHEYAREVERYHAPPYH

The Breedloves did not live in a storefront because they were having temporary difficulty adjusting to the cutbacks at the plant. They lived there because they were poor and black, and they stayed there because they believed they were ugly. Although their poverty was traditional and stultifying, it was not unique. But their ugliness was unique. No one could have convinced them that they were not relentlessly and aggressively ugly. Except for the father, Cholly, whose ugliness (the result of despair, dissipation, and violence directed toward petty things and weak people) was behavior, the rest of the family—Mrs. Breedlove, Sammy Breedlove, and Pecola Breedlove—wore their ugliness, put it on, so to speak, although it did not belong to them. The eyes, the small eyes set closely together under narrow foreheads. The low, irregular hairlines, which seemed even more irregular in contrast to the straight, heavy eyebrows which nearly met. Keen but crooked noses, with insolent nostrils. They had high cheekbones, and their ears turned forward. Shapely lips which called attention not to themselves but to the rest of the face. You looked at them and wondered why they were so ugly; you looked closely and could not find the source. Then you realized that it came from conviction, their conviction. It was as though some mysterious all-knowing master had given each one a cloak of ugliness to wear, and they had each accepted it without question. The master had said, "You are ugly people." They had looked about themselves and saw nothing to contradict the statement; saw, in fact, support for it leaning at them from every billboard, every movie, every glance. "Yes," they had said. "You are right." And they took the ugliness in their hands, threw it as a mantle over them, and went about the world with it. Dealing with it each according to his way. Mrs. Breedlove handled hers as an actor does a prop: for the articulation of character, for support of a role she frequently imagined was hers —martyrdom. Sammy used his as a weapon to cause others pain. He adjusted his behavior to it, chose his companions on the basis of it: people who could be fascinated, even intimidated by it. And Pecola. She hid behind hers. Concealed, veiled, eclipsed—peeping out from behind the shroud very seldom, and then only to yearn for the return of her mask.

This family, on a Saturday morning in October, began, one by one, to stir out of their dreams of affluence and vengeance into the anonymous misery of their storefront.

Mrs. Breedlove slipped noiselessly out of bed, put a sweater on over her nightgown (which was an old day dress), and walked toward the kitchen. Her one good foot made hard, bony sounds; the twisted one whispered on the linoleum. In the kitchen she made noises with doors, faucets, and pans. The noises were hollow, but the threats they implied were not. Pecola opened her eyes and lay staring at the dead coal stove. Cholly mumbled, thrashed about in the bed for a minute, and then was quiet.

Even from where Pecola lay, she could smell Cholly's whiskey. The noises in the kitchen became louder and less hollow. There was direction and purpose in Mrs. Breedlove's movements that had nothing to do with the preparation of breakfast. This awareness, supported by ample evidence from the past, made Pecola tighten her stomach muscles and ration her breath.

Cholly had come home drunk. Unfortunately he had been too drunk to quarrel, so the whole business would have to erupt this morning. Because it had not taken place immediately, the oncoming fight would lack spontaneity; it would be calculated, uninspired, and deadly.

Mrs. Breedlove came swiftly into the room and stood at the foot of the bed where Cholly lay.

"I need some coal in this house."

Cholly did not move.

"Hear me?" Mrs. Breedlove jabbed Cholly's foot.

Cholly opened his eyes slowly. They were red and menacing. With no exception, Cholly had the meanest eyes in town.

"Awwwwww, woman!"

"I said I need some coal. It's as cold as a witch's tit in this house. Your whiskey ass wouldn't feel hellfire, but I'm cold. I got to do a lot of things, but I ain't got to freeze."

"Leave me lone."

"Not until you get me some coal. If working like a mule don't give me the right to be warm, what am I doing it for? You sure ain't bringing in nothing. If it was left up to you, we'd all be dead. . . ." Her voice was like an earache in the brain. ". . . If you think I'm going to wade out in the cold and get it myself, you'd better think again."

"I don't give a shit how you get it." A bubble of violence burst in his throat.

"You going to get your drunk self out of that bed and get me some coal or not?"

Silence.

"Cholly!"

Silence.

"Don't try me this morning, man. You say one more word, and I'll split you open!"

Silence.

"All right. All right. But if I sneeze once, just once, God help your butt!"

Sammy was awake now too, but pretending to be asleep. Pecola still held her stomach muscles taut and conserved her breath. They all knew that Mrs. Breedlove could have, would have, and had, gotten coal from the shed, or that Sammy or Pecola could be directed to get it. But the unquarreled evening hung like the first note of a dirge in sullenly expectant air. An escapade of drunkenness, no matter how routine, had its own ceremonial close. The tiny, undistinguished days that Mrs. Breedlove lived were identified, grouped, and classed by these quarrels. They gave substance to the minutes and hours otherwise dim and unrecalled. They relieved the tiresomeness of poverty, gave grandeur to the dead rooms. In these violent breaks in routine that were themselves routine, she could display the style and imagination of what she believed to be her own true self. To deprive her of these fights was to deprive her of all the zest and reasonableness of life. Cholly, by his habitual drunkenness and orneriness, provided them both with the material they needed to make their lives tolerable. Mrs. Breedlove considered herself an upright and Christian woman, burdened with a no-count man, whom God wanted her to punish. (Cholly was beyond redemption, of course, and redemption was hardly the point—Mrs. Breedlove was not interested in Christ the Redeemer, but rather Christ the Judge.) Often she could be heard discoursing with Jesus about Cholly, pleading with Him to help her "strike the bastard down from his pea-knuckle of pride." And once when a drunken gesture catapulted Cholly into the red-hot stove, she screamed, "Get him, Jesus! Get him!" If Cholly had stopped drinking, she would never have forgiven Jesus. She needed Cholly's sins desperately. The lower he sank, the wilder and more irresponsible he became, the more splendid she and her task became. In the name of Jesus.

No less did Cholly need her. She was one of the few things abhorrent to him that he could touch and therefore hurt. He poured out on her the sum of all his inarticulate fury and aborted desires. Hating her, he could leave himself intact. When he was still very young, Cholly had been surprised in some bushes by two white men while he was newly but earnestly engaged in eliciting sexual pleasure from a little country girl. The men had shone a flashlight right on his behind. He had stopped, terrified. They chuckled. The beam of the flashlight did not move. "Go on," they said. "Go on and finish. And, nigger, make it good." The flashlight did not move. For some reason Cholly had not hated the white men; he hated, despised, the girl. Even a half-remembrance of this episode, along with myriad other humiliations, defeats, and emasculations, could stir him into flights of depravity that surprised himself—but only himself. Somehow he could not astound. He could only be astounded. So he gave that up, too.

Cholly and Mrs. Breedlove fought each other with a darkly brutal formalism that was paralleled only by their lovemaking. Tacitly they had agreed not to kill each other. He fought her the way a coward fights a man—with feet, the palms of his hands, and teeth. She, in turn, fought back in a purely feminine way—with frying pans and pokers, and occasionally a flat iron would sail toward his head. They did not talk, groan, or curse during these beatings. There was only the muted sound of falling things, and flesh on unsurprised flesh.

There was a difference in the reaction of the children to these battles. Sammy cursed for a while, or left the house, or threw himself into the fray. He was known, by the time he was fourteen, to have run away from home no less than twenty-seven times. Once he got to Buffalo and stayed three months. His returns, whether by force or circumstance, were sullen. Pecola, on the other hand, restricted by youth and sex, experimented with methods of endurance. Though the methods varied, the pain was as consistent as it was deep. She struggled between an overwhelming desire that one would kill the other, and a profound wish that she herself could die. Now she was whispering, "Don't, Mrs. Breedlove. Don't." Pecola, like Sammy and Cholly, always called her mother Mrs. Breedlove.

"Don't, Mrs. Breedlove. Don't."

But Mrs. Breedlove did.

By the grace, no doubt, of God, Mrs. Breedlove sneezed. Just once.

She ran into the bedroom with a dishpan full of cold water and threw it in Cholly's face. He sat up, choking and spitting. Naked and ashen, he leaped from the bed, and with a flying tackle, grabbed his wife around the waist, and they hit the floor. Cholly picked her up and knocked her down with the back of his hand. She fell in a sitting position, her back supported by Sammy's bed frame. She had not let go of the dishpan, and began to hit at Cholly's thighs and groin with it. He put his foot in her chest, and she dropped the pan. Dropping to his knee, he struck her several times in the face, and she might have succumbed early had he not hit his hand against the metal bed frame when his wife ducked. Mrs. Breedlove took advantage of this momentary suspension of blows and slipped out of his reach. Sammy, who had watched in silence their struggling at his bedside, suddenly began to hit his father about the head with both fists, shouting "You naked fuck!" over and over and over. Mrs. Breedlove, having snatched up the round, flat stove lid, ran tippy-toe to Cholly as he was pulling himself up from his knees, and struck him two blows, knocking him right back into the senselessness out of which she had provoked him. Panting, she threw a quilt over him and let him lie.

Sammy screamed, "Kill him! Kill him!"

Mrs. Breedlove looked at Sammy with surprise. "Cut out that noise, boy." She put the stove lid back in place, and walked toward the kitchen. At the doorway she paused long enough to say to her son, "Get up from there anyhow. I need some coal."

Letting herself breathe easy now, Pecola covered her head with the quilt. The sick feeling, which she had tried to prevent by holding in her stomach, came quickly in spite of her precaution. There surged in her the desire to heave, but as always, she knew she would not.

"Please, God," she whispered into the palm of her hand. "Please make me disappear." She squeezed her eyes shut. Little parts of her body faded away. Now slowly, now with a rush. Slowly again. Her fingers went, one by one; then her arms disappeared all the way to the elbow. Her feet now. Yes, that was good. The legs all at once. It was hardest above the thighs. She had to be real still and pull. Her stomach would not go. But finally it, too, went away. Then her chest, her neck. The face was hard, too. Almost done, almost. Only her tight, tight eyes were left. They were always left.

Try as she might, she could never get her eyes to disappear. So what was the point? They were everything. Everything was there, in them. All of those pictures, all of those faces. She had long ago given up the idea of running away to see new pictures, new faces, as Sammy had so often done. He never took her, and he never thought about his going ahead of time, so it was never planned. It wouldn't have worked anyway. As long as she looked the way she did, as long as she was ugly, she would have to stay with these people. Somehow she belonged to them. Long hours she sat looking in the mirror, trying to discover the secret of the ugliness, the ugliness that made her ignored or despised at school, by teachers and classmates alike. She was the only member of her class who sat alone at a double desk. The first letter of her last name forced her to sit in the front of the room always. But what about Marie Appolonaire? Marie was in front of her, but she shared a desk with Luke Angelino. Her teachers had always treated her this way. They tried never to glance at her, and called on her only when everyone was required to respond. She also knew that when one of the girls at school wanted to be particularly insulting to a boy, or wanted to get an immediate response from him, she could say, "Bobby loves Pecola Breedlove! Bobby loves Pecola Breedlove!" and never fail to get peals of laughter from those in earshot, and mock anger from the accused.

It had occurred to Pecola some time ago that if her eyes, those eyes that held the pictures, and knew the sights—if those eyes of hers were different, that is to say, beautiful, she herself would be different. Her teeth were good, and at least her nose was not big and flat like some of those who were thought so cute. If she looked different, beautiful, maybe Cholly would be different, and Mrs. Breedlove too. Maybe they'd say, "Why, look at pretty-eyed Pecola. We mustn't do bad things in front of those pretty eyes."

Pretty eyes. Pretty blue eyes. Big blue pretty eyes. Run, Jip, run. Jip runs, Alice runs. Alice has blue eyes. Jerry has blue eyes. Jerry runs. Alice runs. They run with their blue eyes. Four blue eyes. Four pretty blue eyes. Blue-sky eyes. Blue-like Mrs. Forrest's blue blouse eyes. Morning-glory-blue-eyes. Alice-and-Jerry-blue-storybook-eyes.

Each night, without fail she prayed for blue eyes. Fervently, for a year she had prayed. Although somewhat discouraged, she was not without hope. To have something as wonderful as that happen would take a long, long time.

Thrown, in this way, into the binding conviction that only a miracle could relieve her, she would never know her beauty. She would see only what there was to see: the eyes of other people.

She walks down Garden Avenue to a small grocery store which sells penny candy. Three pennies are in her shoe—slipping back and forth between the sock and the inner sole. With each step she feels the painful press of the coins against her foot. A sweet, endurable, even cherished irritation, full of promise and delicate security. There is plenty of time to consider what to buy. Now, however, she moves down an avenue gently buffeted by the familiar and therefore loved images. The dandelions at the base of the telephone pole. Why, she wonders, do people call them weeds? She thought they were pretty. But grown-ups say, "Miss Dunion keeps her yard so nice. Not a dandelion anywhere." Hunkie women in black babushkas go into the fields with baskets to pull them up. But they do not want the yellow heads—only the jagged leaves. They make dandelion soup. Dandelion wine. Nobody loves the head of a dandelion. Maybe because they are so many, strong, and soon.

There was the sidewalk crack shaped like a Y, and the other one that lifted the concrete up from the dirt floor. Frequently her sloughing step had made her trip over that one. Skates would go well over this sidewalk—old it was, and smooth; it made the wheels glide evenly, with a mild whirr. The newly paved walks were bumpy and uncomfortable, and the sound of skate wheels on new walks was grating.

These and other inanimate things she saw and experienced. They were real to her. She knew them. They were the codes and touchstones of the world, capable of translation and possession. She owned the crack that made her stumble; she owned the clumps of dandelions whose white heads, last fall, she had blown away; whose yellow heads, this fall, she peered into. And owning them made her part of the world, and the world a part of her.

She climbs four wooden steps to the door of Yacobowski's Fresh Veg. Meat and Sundries Store. A bell tinkles as she opens it. Standing before the counter, she looks at the array of candies. All Mary Janes, she decides. Three for a penny. The resistant sweetness that breaks open at last to deliver peanut butter—the oil and salt which complement the sweet pull of caramel. A peal of anticipation unsettles her stomach.

She pulls off her shoe and takes out the three pennies. The gray head of Mr. Yacobowski looms up over the counter. He urges his eyes out of his thoughts to encounter her. Blue eyes. Blear-dropped. Slowly, like Indian summer moving imperceptibly toward fall, he looks toward her. Somewhere between retina and object, between vision and view, his eyes draw back, hesitate, and hover. At some fixed point in time and space he senses that he need not waste the effort of a glance. He does not see her, because for him there is nothing to see. How can a fifty-two-year-old white immigrant storekeeper with the taste of potatoes and beer in his mouth, his mind honed on the doe-eyed Virgin Mary, his sensibilities blunted by a permanent awareness of loss, *see* a little black girl? Nothing in his life even suggested that the feat was possible, not to say desirable or necessary.

"Yeah?"

She looks up at him and sees the vacuum where curiosity ought to lodge. And something more. The total absence of human recognition—the glazed separateness. She does not know what keeps his glance suspended. Perhaps because he is grown, or a man, and she a little girl. But she has seen interest, disgust, even anger in grown male eyes. Yet this vacuum is not new to her. It has an edge; somewhere in the bottom lid is the distaste. She has seen it lurking in the eyes of all white people. So. The distaste must be for her, her blackness. All things in her are flux and anticipation. But her blackness is static and dread. And it is the blackness that accounts for, that creates, the vacuum edged with distaste in white eyes.

She points her finger at the Mary Janes—a little black shaft of finger, its tip pressed on the display window. The quietly inoffensive assertion of a black child's attempt to communicate with a white adult.

"Them." The word is more sigh than sense.

"What? These? These?" Phlegm and impatience mingle in his voice.

She shakes her head, her fingertip fixed on the spot which, in her view, at any rate, identifies the Mary Janes. He cannot see her view—the angle of his vision, the slant of her finger, makes it incomprehensible to him. His lumpy red hand plops around in the glass casing like the agitated head of a chicken outraged by the loss of its body.

"Christ. Kantcha talk?"

His fingers brush the Mary Janes.

She nods.

"Well, why'nt you say so? One? How many?"

Pecola unfolds her fist, showing the three pennies. He scoots three Mary Janes toward her—three yellow rectangles in each packet. She holds the money toward him. He hesitates, not wanting to touch her hand. She does not know how to move the finger of her right hand from the display counter or how to get the coins out of her left hand. Finally he reaches over and takes the pennies from her hand. His nails graze her damp palm.

Outside, Pecola feels the inexplicable shame ebb.

Dandelions. A dart of affection leaps out from her to them. But they do not look at her and do not send love back. She thinks, "They *are* ugly. They *are* weeds." Preoccupied with that revelation, she trips on the sidewalk crack. Anger stirs and wakes in her; it opens its mouth, and like a hot-mouthed puppy, laps up the dredges of her shame.

Anger is better. There is a sense of being in anger. A reality and presence. An awareness of worth. It is a lovely surging. Her thoughts fall back to Mr. Yacobowski's eyes, his phlegmy voice. The anger will not hold; the puppy is too easily surfeited. Its thirst too quickly quenched, it sleeps. The shame wells up again, its muddy rivulets seeping into her eyes. What to do before the tears come. She remembers the Mary Janes.

Each pale yellow wrapper has a picture on it. A picture of little Mary Jane, for whom the candy is named. Smiling white face. Blond hair in gentle disarray, blue eyes looking at her out of a world of clean comfort. The eyes are petulant, mischievous. To Pecola they are simply pretty. She eats the candy, and its sweetness is good. To eat the candy is somehow to eat the eyes, eat Mary Jane. Love Mary Jane. Be Mary Jane.

Three pennies had bought her nine lovely orgasms with Mary Jane. Lovely Mary Jane, for whom a candy is named.

Three whores lived in the apartment above the Breedloves' storefront. China, Poland, and Miss Marie. Pecola loved them, visited them, and ran their errands. They, in turn, did not despise her.

On an October morning, the morning of the stove-lid triumph, Pecola climbed the stairs to their apartment.

Even before the door was opened to her tapping, she could hear Poland singing—her voice sweet and hard, like new strawberries:

I got blues in my mealbarrel
Blues up on the shelf
I got blues in my mealbarrel
Blues up on the shelf
Blues in my bedroom
Cause I'm sleepin' by myself

"Hi, dumplin'. Where your socks?" Marie seldom called Pecola the same thing twice, but invariably her epithets were fond ones chosen from menus and dishes that were forever uppermost in her mind.

"Hello, Miss Marie. Hello, Miss China. Hello, Miss Poland."

"You heard me. Where your socks? You as bare-legged as a yard dog."

"I couldn't find any."

"Couldn't find any? Must be somethin' in your house that loves socks."

China chuckled. Whenever something was missing, Marie attributed its disappearance to "something in the house that loved it." "There is somethin' in this house that loves brassieres," she would say with alarm.

Poland and China were getting ready for the evening. Poland, forever ironing, forever singing. China, sitting on a pale-green kitchen chair, forever and forever curling her hair. Marie never got ready.

The women were friendly, but slow to begin talk. Pecola always took the initiative with Marie, who, once inspired, was difficult to stop.

"How come you got so many boyfriends, Miss Marie?"

"*Boy*friends? *Boy*friends? Chittlin', I ain't seen a *boy* since nineteen and twenty-seven."

"You didn't see none then." China stuck the hot curlers into a tin of Nu Nile hair dressing. The oil hissed at the touch of the hot metal.

"How come, Miss Marie?" Pecola insisted.

"How come what? How come I ain't seen a boy since nineteen and twenty-seven? Because they ain't *been* no boys since then. That's when they stopped. Folks started gettin' born old."

"You mean that's when *you* got old," China said.

"I ain't never got old. Just fat."

"Same thing."

"You think 'cause you skinny, folks think you young? You'd make a haint buy a girdle."

"And you look like the north side of a southbound mule."

"All I know is, them bandy little legs of yours is every bit as old as mine."

"Don't worry 'bout my bandy legs. That's the first thing they push aside."

All three of the women laughed. Marie threw back her head. From deep inside, her laughter came like the sound of many rivers, freely, deeply, muddily, heading for the room of an open sea. China giggled spastically. Each gasp seemed to be yanked out of her by an unseen hand jerking an unseen string. Poland, who seldom spoke unless she was drunk, laughed without sound. When she was sober she hummed mostly or chanted blues songs, of which she knew many.

Pecola fingered the fringe of a scarf that lay on the back of a sofa. "I never seen nobody with as many boyfriends as you got, Miss Marie. How come they all love you?"

Marie opened a bottle of root beer. "What else they gone do? They know I'm rich and good-lookin'. They wants to put their toes in my curly hair, and get at my money."

"You rich, Miss Marie?"

"Puddin', I got money's mammy."

"Where you get it from? You don't do no work."

"Yeah," said China, "where you get it from?"

"Hoover give it me. I did him a favor once, for the F. B. and I."

"What'd you do?"

"I did him a favor. They wanted to catch this crook, you see. Name of Johnny. He was as low-down as they come. . . ."

"We *know* that," China arranged a curl.

". . . the F. B. and I. wanted him bad. He killed more people than TB. And if you *crossed* him? Whoa, Jesus! He'd run you as long as there was ground. Well, I was little and cute then. No more than ninety pounds, soaking wet."

"You ain't never been soaking wet," China said.

"Well, you ain't never been dry. Shut up. Let me tell you, sweetnin'. To tell it true, I was the only one could handle him. He'd go out and rob a bank or kill some people, and I'd say to him, soft-like, 'Johnny, you shouldn't do that.' And he'd say he just had to bring me pretty things. Lacy drawers and all. And every Saturday we'd get a case of beer and fry up some fish. We'd fry it in meal and egg batter, you know, and when it was all brown and crisp—not hard, though—we'd break open that cold beer. . . ." Marie's eyes went soft as the memory of just such a meal sometime, somewhere transfixed her. All her stories were subject to breaking down at descriptions of food. Pecola saw Marie's teeth settling down into the back of crisp sea bass; saw the fat fingers putting back into her mouth tiny flakes of white, hot meat that had escaped from her lips; she heard the "pop" of the beer-bottle cap; smelled the acridness of the first stream of vapor; felt the cold beeriness hit the tongue. She ended the daydream long before Marie.

"But what about the money?" she asked.

China hooted. "She's makin' like she's the Lady in Red that told on Dillinger. Dillinger wouldn't have come near you lessen he was going hunting in Africa and shoot you for a hippo."

"Well, this hippo had a ball back in Chicago. Whoa Jesus, ninety-nine!"

"How come you always say 'Whoa Jesus' and a number?" Pecola had long wanted to know.

"Because my mama taught me never to cuss."

"Did she teach you not to drop your drawers?" China asked.

"Didn't have none," said Marie. "Never saw a pair of drawers till I was fifteen, when I left Jackson and was doing day work in Cincinnati. My white lady gave me some old ones of hers. I thought they was some kind of stocking cap. I put it on my head when I dusted. When she saw me, she liked to fell out."

"You must have been one dumb somebody." China lit a cigarette and cooled her irons.

"How'd I know?" Marie paused. "And what's the use of putting on something you got to keep taking off all the time? Dewey never let me keep them on long enough to get used to them."

"Dewey who?" This was a somebody new to Pecola.

"Dewey who? Chicken! You never heard me tell of *Dewey?"* Marie was shocked by her negligence.

"No, ma'am."

"Oh, honey, you've missed half your life. Whoa Jesus, one-nine-five. You talkin' 'bout smooth! I met him when I was fourteen. We ran away and lived together like married for three years. You know all those klinker-tops you see runnin' up here? Fifty of 'em in a bowl wouldn't make a Dewey Prince ankle bone. Oh, Lord. How that man loved me!"

China arranged a fingerful of hair into a bang effect. "Then why he left you to sell tail?"

"Girl, when I found out I could sell it—that somebody would pay cold cash for it, you could have knocked me over with a feather."

Poland began to laugh. Soundlessly. "Me too. My auntie whipped me good that first time when I told her I didn't get no money. I said 'Money? For what? He didn't owe me nothin'.' She said, 'The hell he didn't!' "

They all dissolved in laughter.

Three merry gargoyles. Three merry harridans. Amused by a long-ago time of ignorance. They did not belong to those generations of prostitutes created in novels, with great and generous hearts, dedicated, because of the horror of circumstance, to ameliorating, the luckless, barren life of men, taking money incidentally and humbly for their "understanding." Nor were they from that sensitive breed of young girl, gone wrong at the hands of fate, forced to cultivate an outward brittleness in order to protect her springtime from further shock, but knowing full well she was cut out for better things, and could make the right man happy. Neither were they the sloppy, inadequate whores who, unable to make a living at it alone, turn to drug consumption and traffic or pimps to help complete their scheme of self-destruction, avoiding suicide only to punish the memory of some absent father or to sustain the misery of some silent mother. Except for Marie's fabled love for Dewey Prince, these women hated men, all men, without shame, apology, or discrimination. They abused their visitors with a scorn grown mechanical from use. Black men, white men, Puerto Ricans, Mexicans, Jews, Poles, whatever—all were inadequate and weak, all came under their jaundiced eyes and were the recipients of their disinterested wrath. They took delight in cheating them. On one occasion the town well knew, they lured a Jew up the stairs, pounced on him, all three, held him up by the heels, shook everything out of his pants pockets, and threw him out of the window.

Neither did they have respect for women, who, although not their colleagues, so to speak, nevertheless deceived their husbands —regularly or irregularly, it made no difference. "Sugar-coated whores," they called them, and did not yearn to be in their shoes. Their only respect was for what they would have described as "good Christian colored women." The woman whose reputation was spotless, and who tended to her family, who didn't drink or smoke or run around. These women had their undying, if covert, affection. They would sleep with their husbands, and take their money, but always with a vengeance.

Nor were they protective and solicitous of youthful innocence. They looked back on their own youth as a period of ignorance, and regretted that they had not made more of it. They were not young girls in whores' clothing, or whores regretting their loss of innocence. They were whores in whores' clothing, whores who had never been young and had no word for innocence. With Pecola they were as free as they were with each other. Marie concocted stories for her because she was a child, but the stories were breezy and rough. If Pecola had announced her intention to live the life they did, they would not have tried to dissuade her or voiced any alarm.

"You and Dewey Prince have any children, Miss Marie?"

"Yeah. Yeah. We had some." Marie fidgeted. She pulled a bobby pin from her hair and began to pick her teeth. That meant she didn't want to talk anymore.

Pecola went to the window and looked down at the empty street. A tuft of grass had forced its way up through a crack in the sidewalk, only to meet a raw October wind. She thought of Dewey Prince and how he loved Miss Marie. What did love feel like? she wondered.

How do grown-ups act when they love each other? Eat fish together? Into her eyes came the picture of Cholly and Mrs. Breedlove in bed. He making sounds as though he were in pain, as though something had him by the throat and wouldn't let go. Terrible as his noises were, they were not nearly as bad as the no noise at all from her mother. It was as though she was not even there. Maybe that was love. Choking sounds and silence.

Turning her eyes from the window, Pecola looked at the women.

China had changed her mind about the bangs and was arranging a small but sturdy pompadour. She was adept in creating any number of hair styles, but each one left her with a pinched and harassed look. Then she applied makeup heavily. Now she gave herself surprised eyebrows and a cupid-bow mouth. Later she would make Oriental eyebrows and an evilly slashed mouth.

Poland, in her sweet strawberry voice, began another song:

I know a boy who is sky-soft brown
I know a boy who is sky-soft brown
The dirt leaps for joy when his feet touch the ground.
  His strut is a peacock
  His eye is burning brass
  His smile is sorghum syrup drippin' slow-sweet to the last
I know a boy who is sky-soft brown

Marie sat shelling peanuts and popping them into her mouth. Pecola looked and looked at the women. Were they real? Marie belched, softly, purringly, lovingly.

Winter

My daddy's face is a study. Winter moves into it and presides there. His eyes become a cliff of snow threatening to avalanche;

his eyebrows bend like black limbs of leafless trees. His skin takes on the pale, cheerless yellow of winter sun; for a jaw he has the edges of a snowbound field dotted with stubble; his high forehead is the frozen sweep of the Erie, hiding currents of gelid thoughts that eddy in darkness. Wolf killer turned hawk fighter, he worked night and day to keep one from the door and the other from under the windowsills. A Vulcan guarding the flames, he gives us instructions about which doors to keep closed or opened for proper distribution of heat, lays kindling by, discusses qualities of coal, and teaches us how to rake, feed, and bank the fire. And he will not unrazor his lips until spring.

Winter tightened our heads with a band of cold and melted our eyes. We put pepper in the feet of our stockings, Vaseline on our faces, and stared through dark icebox mornings at four stewed prunes, slippery lumps of oatmeal, and cocoa with a roof of skin.

But mostly we waited for spring, when there could be gardens.

By the time this winter had stiffened itself into a hateful knot that nothing could loosen, something did loosen it, or rather someone. A someone who splintered the knot into silver threads that tangled us, netted us, made us long for the dull chafe of the previous boredom.

This disrupter of seasons was a new girl in school named Maureen Peal. A high-yellow dream child with long brown hair braided into two lynch ropes that hung down her back. She was rich, at least by our standards, as rich as the richest of the white girls, swaddled in comfort and care. The quality of her clothes threatened to derange Frieda and me. Patent-leather shoes with buckles, a cheaper version of which we got only at Easter and which had disintegrated by the end of May. Fluffy sweaters the color of lemon drops tucked into skirts with pleats so orderly they astounded us. Brightly colored knee socks with white borders, a brown velvet coat trimmed in white rabbit fur, and a matching muff. There was a hint of spring in her sloe green eyes, something summery in her complexion, and a rich autumn ripeness in her walk.

She enchanted the entire school. When teachers called on her, they smiled encouragingly. Black boys didn't trip her in the halls; white boys didn't stone her, white girls didn't suck their teeth when she was assigned to be their work partners; black girls stepped aside when she wanted to use the sink in the girls' toilet, and their eyes genuflected under sliding lids. She never had to search for anybody to eat with in the cafeteria—they flocked to the table of her choice, where she opened fastidious lunches, shaming our jelly-stained bread with egg-salad sandwiches cut into four dainty squares, pink-frosted cupcakes, sticks of celery and carrots, proud, dark apples. She even bought and liked white milk.

Frieda and I were bemused, irritated, and fascinated by her. We looked hard for flaws to restore our equilibrium, but had to be content at first with uglying up her name, changing Maureen Peal to Meringue Pie. Later a minor epiphany was ours when we discovered that she had a dog tooth—a charming one to be sure—but a dog tooth nonetheless. And when we found out that she had been born with six fingers on each hand and that there was a little bump where each extra one had been removed, we smiled. They were small triumphs, but we took what we could get—snickering behind her back and calling her Six-finger-dog-tooth-meringue-pie. But we had to do it alone, for none of the other girls would cooperate with our hostility. They adored her.

When she was assigned a locker next to mine, I could indulge my jealousy four times a day. My sister and I both suspected that we were secretly prepared to be her friend, if she would let us, but I knew it would be a dangerous friendship, for when my eye traced the white border patterns of those Kelly-green knee socks, and felt the pull and slack of my brown stockings, I wanted to kick her. And when I thought of the unearned haughtiness in her eyes, I plotted accidental slammings of locker doors on her hand.

As locker friends, however, we got to know each other a little, and I was even able to hold a sensible conversation with her without visualizing her fall off a cliff, or giggling my way into what I thought was a clever insult.

One day, while I waited at the locker for Frieda, she joined me.

"Hi."

"Hi."

"Waiting for your sister?"

"Uh-huh."

"Which way do you go home?"

"Down Twenty-first Street to Broadway."

"Why don't you go down Twenty-second Street?"

"'Cause I live on Twenty-first Street."

"Oh. I can walk that way, I guess. Partly, anyway."

"Free country."

Frieda came toward us, her brown stockings straining at the knees because she had tucked the toe under to hide a hole in the foot.

"Maureen's gonna walk part way with us."

Frieda and I exchanged glances, her eyes begging my restraint, mine promising nothing.

It was a false spring day, which, like Maureen, had pierced the shell of a deadening winter. There were puddles, mud, and an inviting warmth that deluded us. The kind of day on which we draped our coats over our heads, left our galoshes in school, and came down with croup the following day. We always responded to the slightest change in weather, the most minute shifts in time of day. Long before seeds were stirring, Frieda and I were scruffing and poking at the earth, swallowing air, drinking rain. . . .

As we emerged from the school with Maureen, we began to moult immediately. We put our head scarves in our coat pockets, and our coats on our heads. I was wondering how to maneuver Maureen's fur muff into a gutter when a commotion in the playground distracted us. A group of boys was circling and holding at bay a victim, Pecola Breedlove.

Bay Boy, Woodrow Cain, Buddy Wilson, Junie Bug—like a necklace of semiprecious stones they surrounded her. Heady with the smell of their own musk, thrilled by the easy power of a majority, they gaily harassed her.

"Black e mo. Black e mo. Yadaddsleepsnekked. Black e mo black e mo ya dadd sleeps nekked. Black e mo . . ."

They had extemporized a verse made up of two insults about matters over which the victim had no control; the color of her skin and speculations on the sleeping habits of an adult, wildly fitting in its incoherence. That they themselves were black, or that their own father had similarly relaxed habits was irrelevant. It was their contempt for their own blackness that gave the first insult its teeth. They seemed to have taken all of their smoothly cultivated ignorance, their exquisitely learned self-hatred, their elaborately designed hopelessness and sucked it all up into a fiery cone of scorn that had burned for ages in the hollows of their minds—cooled—and spilled over lips of outrage, consuming whatever was in its path. They danced a macabre ballet around the victim, whom, for their own sake, they were prepared to sacrifice to the flaming pit.

Black e mo Black e mo Ya daddy sleeps nekked.
Stch ta ta stch ta ta
stach ta ta ta ta ta

Pecola edged around the circle crying. She had dropped her notebook, and covered her eyes with her hands.

We watched, afraid they might notice us and turn their energies our way. Then Frieda, with set lips and Mama's eyes, snatched her coat from her head and threw it on the ground. She ran toward them and brought her books down on Woodrow Cain's head. The circle broke. Woodrow Cain grabbed his head.

"Hey, girl!"

"You cut that out, you hear?" I had never heard Frieda's voice so loud and clear.

Maybe because Frieda was taller than he was, maybe because he saw her eyes, maybe because he had lost interest in the game, or maybe because he had a crush on Frieda, in any case Woodrow looked frightened just long enough to give her more courage.

"Leave her 'lone, or I'm gone tell everybody what you did!"

Woodrow did not answer; he just walled his eyes.

Bay Boy piped up, "Go on, gal. Ain't nobody bothering you."

"You shut up, Bullet Head." I had found my tongue.

"Who you calling Bullet Head?"

"I'm calling you Bullet Head, Bullet Head."

Frieda took Pecola's hand. "Come on."

"You want a fat lip?" Bay Boy drew back his fist at me.

"Yeah. Gimme one of yours."

"You gone get one."

Maureen appeared at my elbow, and the boys seemed reluctant to continue under her springtime eyes so wide with interest. They buckled in confusion, not willing to beat up three girls under her watchful gaze. So they listened to a budding male instinct that told them to pretend we were unworthy of their attention.

"Come on, man."

"Yeah. Come on. We ain't got time to fool with them."

Grumbling a few disinterested epithets, they moved away.

I picked up Pecola's notebook and Frieda's coat, and the four of us left the playground.

"Old Bullet Head, he's always picking on girls."

Frieda agreed with me. "Miss Forrester said he was incorrigival."

"Really?" I didn't know what that meant, but it had enough of a doom sound in it to be true of Bay Boy.

While Frieda and I clucked on about the near fight, Maureen, suddenly animated, put her velvet-sleeved arm through Pecola's and began to behave as though they were the closest of friends.

"I just moved here. My name is Maureen Peal. What's yours?"

"Pecola."

"Pecola? Wasn't that the name of the girl in *Imitation of Life?"*

"I don't know. What is that?"

"The picture show, you know. Where this mulatto girl hates her mother 'cause she is black and ugly but then cries at the funeral. It was real sad. Everybody cries in it. Claudette Colbert too."

"Oh." Pecola's voice was no more than a sigh.

"Anyway, her name was Pecola too. She was so pretty. When it comes back, I'm going to see it again. My mother has seen it four times."

Frieda and I walked behind them, surprised at Maureen's friendliness to Pecola, but pleased. Maybe she wasn't so bad, after all. Frieda had put her coat back on her head, and the two of us, so draped, trotted along enjoying the warm breeze and Frieda's heroics.

"You're in my gym class, aren't you?" Maureen asked Pecola.

"Yes."

"Miss Erkmeister's legs sure are bow. I bet she thinks they're cute. How come she gets to wear real shorts, and we have to wear those old bloomers? I want to die every time I put them on."

Pecola smiled but did not look at Maureen.

"Hey." Maureen stopped short. "There's an Isaley's. Want some ice cream? I have money."

She unzipped a hidden pocket in her muff and pulled out a multifolded dollar bill. I forgave her those knee socks.

"My uncle sued Isaley's." Maureen said to the three of us. "He sued the Isaley's in Akron. They said he was disorderly and that that was why they wouldn't serve him, but a friend of his, a policemen, came in and beared the witness, so the suit went through."

"What's a suit?"

"It's when you can beat them up if you want to and won't

anybody do nothing. Our family does it all the time. We believe in suits."

At the entrance to Isaley's Maureen turned to Frieda and me, asking, "You all going to buy some ice cream?"

We looked at each other. "No," Frieda said.

Maureen disappeared into the store with Pecola.

Frieda looked placidly down the street; I opened my mouth, but quickly closed it. It was extremely important that the world not know that I fully expected Maureen to buy us some ice cream, that for the past 120 seconds I had been selecting the flavor, that I had begun to like Maureen, and that neither of us had a penny.

We supposed Maureen was being nice to Pecola because of the boys, and were embarrassed to be caught—even by each other—thinking that she would treat us, or that we deserved it as much as Pecola did.

The girls came out. Pecola with two dips of orange-pineapple, Maureen with black raspberry.

"You should have got some," she said. "They had all kinds. Don't eat down to the tip of the cone," she advised Pecola.

"Why?"

"Because there's a fly in there."

"How you know?"

"Oh, not really. A girl told me she found one in the bottom of hers once, and ever since then she throws that part away."

"Oh."

We passed the Dreamland Theater, and Betty Grable smiled down at us.

"Don't you just love her?" Maureen asked.

"Uh-huh," said Pecola.

I differed. "Hedy Lamarr is better."

Maureen agreed. "Ooooo yes. My mother told me that a girl named Audrey, she went to the beauty parlor where we lived before, and asked the lady to fix her hair like Hedy Lamarr's, and the lady said, 'Yeah, when you grow some hair like Hedy Lamarr's.'" She laughed long and sweet.

"Sounds crazy," said Frieda.

"She sure is. Do you know she doesn't even menstrate yet, and she's sixteen. Do you, yet?"

"Yes." Pecola glanced at us.

"So do I." Maureen made no attempt to disguise her pride. "Two months ago I started. My girl friend in Toledo, where we lived before, said when she started she was scared to death. Thought she had killed herself."

"Do you know what it's for?" Pecola asked the question as though hoping to provide the answer herself.

"For babies." Maureen raised two pencil-stroke eyebrows at the obviousness of the question. "Babies need blood when they are inside you, and if you are having a baby, then you don't menstrate. But when you're not having a baby, then you don't have to save the blood, so it comes out."

"How do babies get the blood?" asked Pecola.

"Through the like-line. You know. Where your belly button is. That is where the like-line grows from and pumps the blood to the baby."

"Well, if the belly buttons are to grow like-lines to give the baby blood, and only girls have babies, how come boys have belly buttons?"

Maureen hesitated. "I don't know," she admitted. "But boys have all sorts of things they don't need." Her tinkling laughter was somehow stronger than our nervous ones. She curled her tongue around the edge of the cone, scooping up a dollop of purple that made my eyes water. We were waiting for a stop light to change. Maureen kept scooping the ice cream from around the cone's edge with her tongue; she didn't bite the edge as I would have done. Her tongue circled the cone. Pecola had finished hers; Maureen evidently liked her things to last. While I was thinking about her ice cream, she must have been thinking about her last remark, for she said to Pecola, "Did you ever see a naked man?"

Pecola blinked, then looked away. "No. Where would I see a naked man?"

"I don't know. I just asked."

"I wouldn't even look at him, even if I did see him. That's dirty. Who wants to see a naked man?" Pecola was agitated. "Nobody's father would be naked in front of his own daughter. Not unless he was dirty too."

"I didn't say 'father.' I just said 'a naked man.'"

"Well . . ."

"How come you said 'father'?" Maureen wanted to know.

"Who else would she see, dog tooth?" I was glad to have a chance to show anger. Not only because of the ice cream, but because we had seen our own father naked and didn't care to be reminded of it and feel the shame brought on by the absence of shame. He had been walking down the hall from the bathroom into his bedroom and passed the open door of our room. We had lain there wide-eyed. He stopped and looked in, trying to see in the dark room whether we were really asleep—or was it his imagination that opened eyes were looking at him? Apparently he convinced himself that we were sleeping. He moved away, confident that his little girls would not lie open-eyed like that, staring, staring. When he had moved on, the dark took, only him away, not his nakedness. That stayed in the room with us. Friendly-like.

"I'm not talking to you," said Maureen. "Besides, I don't care if she sees her father naked. She can look at him all day if she wants to. Who cares?"

"You do," said Frieda. "That's all you talk about."

"It is not."

"It is so. Boys, babies, and somebody's naked daddy. You must be boy-crazy."

"You better be quiet."

"Who's gonna make me?" Frieda put her hand on her hip and jutted her face toward Maureen.

"You all ready made. Mammy made."

"You stop talking about my mama."

"Well, you stop talking about my daddy."

"Who said anything about your old daddy?"

"You did."

"Well, you started it."

"I wasn't even talking to you. I was talking to Pecola."

"Yeah. About seeing her naked daddy."

"So what if she did see him?"

Pecola shouted, "I never saw my daddy naked. Never."

"You did too," Maureen snapped. "Bay Boy said so."

"I did not."

"You did."

"I did not."

"Did. Your own daddy, too!"

Pecola tucked her head in—a funny, sad, helpless movement. A kind of hunching of the shoulders, pulling in of the neck, as though she wanted to cover her ears.

"You stop talking about her daddy," I said.

"What do I care about her old black daddy?" asked Maureen.

"Black? Who you calling black?"

"You!"

"You think you so cute!" I swung at her and missed, hitting Pecola in the face. Furious at my clumsiness, I threw my notebook at her, but it caught her in the small of her velvet back, for she had turned and was flying across the street against traffic.

Safe on the other side, she screamed at us, "I *am* cute! And you ugly! Black and ugly black e mos. I *am* cute!"

She ran down the street, the green knee socks making her legs look like wild dandelion stems that had somehow lost their heads. The weight of her remark stunned us, and it was a second or two before Frieda and I collected ourselves enough to shout, "Six-finger-dog-tooth-meringue-pie!" We chanted this most powerful of our arsenal of insults as long as we could see the green stems and rabbit fur.

Grown people frowned at the three girls on the curbside, two with their coats draped over their heads, the collars framing the eyebrows like nuns' habits, black garters showing where they bit the tops of brown stockings that barely covered the knees, angry faces knotted like dark cauliflowers.

Pecola stood a little apart from us, her eyes hinged in the direction in which Maureen had fled. She seemed to fold into herself, like a pleated wing. Her pain antagonized me. I wanted to open her up, crisp her edges, ram a stick down that hunched and curving spine, force her to stand erect and spit the misery out on the streets. But she held it in where it could lap up into her eyes.

Frieda snatched her coat from her head. "Come on, Claudia. 'Bye, Pecola."

We walked quickly at first, and then slower, pausing every now and then to fasten garters, tie shoelaces, scratch, or examine old scars. We were sinking under the wisdom, accuracy, and relevance of Maureen's last words. If she was cute—and if anything could be believed, she *was*—then we were not. And what did that mean? We were lesser. Nicer, brighter, but still lesser. Dolls we could destroy, but we could not destroy the honey voices of parents and aunts, the obedience in the eyes of our peers, the slippery light in the eyes of our teachers when they encountered the Maureen Peals of the world. What was the secret? What did we lack? Why was it important? And so what? Guileless and without vanity, we were still in love with ourselves then. We felt comfortable in our skins, enjoyed the news that our senses released to us, admired our dirt, cultivated our scars, and could not comprehend this unworthiness.

Jealousy we understood and thought natural—a desire to have what somebody else had; but envy was a strange, new feeling for us. And all the time we knew that Maureen Peal was not the Enemy and not worthy of such intense hatred. The *Thing* to fear was the *Thing* that made *her* beautiful, and not us.

The house was quiet when we opened the door. The acrid smell of simmering turnips filled our cheeks with sour saliva.

"Mama!"

There was no answer, but a sound of feet. Mr. Henry shuffled part of the way down the stairs. One thick, hairless leg leaned out of his bathrobe.

"Hello there, Greta Garbo; hello, Ginger Rogers."

We gave him the giggle he was accustomed to. "Hello, Mr. Henry. Where's Mama?"

"She went to your grandmaw's. Left word for you to cut off the turnips and eat some graham crackers till she got back. They in the kitchen."

We sat in silence at the kitchen table, crumbling the crackers into anthills. In a little while Mr. Henry came back down the stairs. Now he had his trousers on under his robe.

"Say. Wouldn't you all like some cream?"

"Oh, yes, sir."

"Here. Here's a quarter. Gone over to Isaley's and get yourself some cream. You been good girls, ain't you?"

His light-green words restored color to the day. "Yes, sir. Thank you, Mr. Henry. Will you tell Mama for us if she comes?"

"Sure. But she ain't due back for a spell."

Coatless, we left the house and had gotten all the way to the corner when Frieda said, "I don't want to go to Isaley's."

"What?"

"I don't want ice cream. I want potato chips."

"They got potato chips at Isaley's."

"I know, but why go all that long way? Miss Bertha got potato chips."

"But I want ice cream."

"No you don't, Claudia."

"I do too."

"Well, you go on to Isaley's. I'm going to Miss Bertha's."

"But you got the quarter, and I don't want to go all the way up there by myself."

"Then let's go to Miss Bertha's. You like her candy, don't you?"

"It's always stale, and she always runs out of stuff."

"Today is Friday. She orders fresh on Friday."

"And then that crazy old Soaphead Church lives there."

"So what? We're together. We'll run if he does anything at us."

"He scares me."

"Well, I don't want to go up by Isaley's. Suppose Meringue Pie is hanging around. You want to run into her, Claudia?"

"Come on, Frieda. I'll get candy."

Miss Bertha had a small candy, snuff, and tobacco store. One brick room sitting in her front yard. You had to peep in the door, and if she wasn't there, you knocked on the door of her house in back. This day she was sitting behind the counter reading a Bible in a tube of sunlight.

Frieda bought potato chips, and we got three Powerhouse bars for ten cents, and had a dime left. We hurried back home to sit under the lilac bushes on the side of the house. We always did our Candy Dance there so Rosemary could see us and get jealous. The Candy Dance was a humming, skipping, foot-tapping, eating, smacking combination that overtook us when we had sweets. Creeping between the bushes and the side of the house, we heard voices and laughter. We looked into the living-room window, expecting to see Mama. Instead we saw Mr. Henry and two women. In a playful manner, the way grandmothers do with babies, he was sucking the fingers of one of the women, whose laughter filled a tiny place over his head. The other woman was buttoning her coat. We knew immediately who they were, and our flesh crawled. One was China, and the other was called the Maginot Line. The back of my neck itched. These were the fancy women of the maroon nail polish that Mama and Big Mama hated. And in our house.

China was not too terrible, at least not in our imaginations. She was thin, aging, absentminded, and unaggressive. But the Maginot Line. That was the one my mother said she "wouldn't let eat out of one of her plates." That was the one church women never allowed their eyes to rest on. That was the one who had killed people, set them on fire, poisoned them, cooked them in lye. Although I thought the Maginot Line's face, hidden under all that fat, was really sweet, I had heard too many black and red words about her, seen too many mouths go triangle at the mention of her name, to dwell on any redeeming features she might have.

Showing brown teeth, China seemed to be genuinely enjoying Mr. Henry. The sight of him licking her fingers brought to mind the girlie magazines in his room. A cold wind blew somewhere in me, lifting little leaves of terror and obscure longing. I thought I saw a mild lonesomeness cross the face of the Maginot Line. But it may have been my own image that I saw in the slow flaring of her nostrils, in her eyes that reminded me of waterfalls in movies about Hawaii.

The Maginot Line yawned and said, "Come on, China. We can't hang in here all day. Them people be home soon." She moved toward the door.

Frieda and I dropped down to the ground, looking wildly into each other's eyes. When the women were some distance away, we went inside. Mr. Henry was in the kitchen opening a bottle of pop.

"Back already?"

"Yes, sir."

"Cream all gone?" His little teeth looked so kindly and helpless. Was that really our Mr. Henry with China's fingers?

"We got candy instead."

"You did huh? Ole sugar-tooth Greta Garbo."

He wiped the bottle sweat and turned it up to his lips—a gesture that made me uncomfortable.

"Who were those women, Mr. Henry?"

He choked on the pop and looked at Frieda. "What you say?"

"Those women," she repeated, "who just left. Who were they?"

"Oh." He laughed the grown-up getting-ready-to-lie laugh. A heh-heh we knew well.

"Those were some members of my Bible class. We read the scriptures together, and so they came today to read with me."

"Oh," said Frieda. I was looking at his house slippers to keep from seeing those kindly teeth frame a lie. He walked toward the stairs and then turned back to us.

"Bed' not mention it to your mother. She don't take to so much Bible study and don't like me having visitors, even if they good Christians."

"No, sir, Mr. Henry. We won't."

He rapidly mounted the stairs.

"Should we?" I asked. "Tell Mama?"

Frieda sighed. She had not even opened her Powerhouse bar or her potato chips, and now she traced the letters on the candy wrappers with her fingers. Suddenly she lifted her head and began to look all around the kitchen.

"No. I guess not. No plates are out."

"Plates? What you talking about now?"

"No plates are out. The Maginot Line didn't eat out of one of Mama's plates. Besides, Mama would just fuss all day if we told her."

We sat down and looked at the graham-cracker anthills we had made.

"We better cut off the turnips. They'll burn, and Mama will whip us," she said.

"I know."

"But if we let them burn, we won't have to eat them."

"Heyyy, what a lovely idea," I thought.

"Which you want? A whipping and no turnips, or turnips and no whippings?"

"I don't know. Maybe we could burn them just a little so Mama and Daddy can eat them, but we can say we can't."

"O.K."

I made a volcano out of my anthill.

"Frieda?"

"What?"

"What did Woodward do that you was gonna tell?"

"Wet the bed. Mrs. Cain told Mama he won't quit."

"Old nasty."

The sky was getting dark; I looked out of the window and saw snow falling. I poked my finger down into the mouth of my volcano, and it toppled, dispersing the golden grains into little swirls. The turnip pot crackled.

SEETHECATITGOESMEOWMEOWCOMEANDPLAYCOMEPL AYWITHJANETHEKITTENWILLNOTPLAYPLAYPLAYPLAY

They come from Mobile. Aiken. From Newport News. From Marietta. From Meridian. And the sounds of these places in their mouths make you think of love. When you ask them where they are from, they tilt their heads and say "Mobile" and you think you've been kissed. They say "Aiken" and you see a white butterfly glance off a fence with a torn wing. They say "Nagadoches" and you want to say "Yes, I will." You don't know what these towns are like, but you love what happens to the air when they open their lips and let the names ease out.

Meridian. The sound of it opens the windows of a room like the first four notes of a hymn. Few people can say the names of their home towns with such sly affection. Perhaps because they don't have home towns, just places where they were born. But these girls soak up the juice of their home towns, and it never leaves them. They are thin brown girls who have looked long at hollyhocks in the backyards of Meridian, Mobile, Aiken, and Baton Rouge. And like hollyhocks they are narrow, tall, and still. Their roots are deep, their stalks are firm, and only the top blossom nods in the wind. They have the eyes of people who can tell what time it is by the color of the sky. Such girls live in quiet black neighborhoods where everybody is gainfully employed. Where there are porch swings hanging from chains. Where the grass is cut with a scythe, where rooster combs and sunflowers grow in the yards, and pots of bleeding heart, ivy, and mother-in-law tongue line the steps and windowsills. Such girls have bought watermelon and snapbeans from the fruit man's wagon. They have put in the window the cardboard sign that has a pound measure printed on each of three edges—10 lbs., 25 lbs., 50 lbs.—and NO ICE on the fourth. These particular brown girls from Mobile and Aiken are not like some of their sisters. They are not fretful, nervous, or shrill; they do not have lovely black necks that stretch as though against an invisible collar; their eyes do not bite. These sugar-brown Mobile girls move through the streets without a stir. They are as sweet and plain as buttercake. Slim ankles; long, narrow feet. They wash themselves with orange-colored Lifebuoy soap, dust themselves with Cashmere Bouquet talc, clean their teeth with salt on a piece of rag, soften their skin with Jergens Lotion. They smell like wood, newspapers, and vanilla. They straighten their hair with Dixie Peach, and part it on the side. At night they curl it in paper from brown bags, tie a print scarf around their heads, and sleep with hands folded across their stomachs. They do not drink, smoke, or swear, and they still call sex "nookey." They sing second soprano in the choir, and although their voices are clear and steady, they are never picked to solo. They are in the second row, white blouses starched, blue skirts almost purple from ironing.

They go to land-grant colleges, normal schools, and learn how to do the white man's work with refinement: home economics to prepare his food; teacher education to instruct black children in obedience; music to soothe the weary master and entertain his blunted soul. Here they learn the rest of the lesson begun in those soft houses with porch swings and pots of bleeding heart: how to behave. The careful development of thrift, patience, high morals, and good manners. In short, how to get rid of the funkiness. The dreadful funkiness of passion, the funkiness of nature, the funkiness of the wide range of human emotions.

Wherever it erupts, this Funk, they wipe it away; where it crusts, they dissolve it; wherever it drips, flowers, or clings, they find it and fight it until it dies. They fight this battle all the way to the grave. The laugh that is a little too loud; the enunciation a little too round; the gesture a little too generous. They hold their behind in for fear of a sway too free; when they wear lipstick, they never cover the entire mouth for fear of lips too thick, and they worry, worry, worry about the edges of their hair.

They never seem to have boyfriends, but they always marry. Certain men watch them, without seeming to, and know that if such a girl is in his house, he will sleep on sheets boiled white, hung out to dry on juniper bushes, and pressed flat with a heavy iron. There will be pretty paper flowers decorating the picture of his mother, a large Bible in the front room. They feel secure. They know their work clothes will be mended, washed, and ironed on Monday, that their Sunday shirts will billow on hangers from the door jamb, stiffly starched and white. They look at her hands and know what she will do with biscuit dough; they smell the coffee and the fried ham; see the white, smoky grits with a dollop of butter on top. Her hips assure them that she will bear children easily and painlessly. And they are right.

What they do not know is that this plain brown girl will build her nest stick by stick, make it her own inviolable world, and stand guard over its every plant, weed, and doily, even against him. In silence will she return the lamp to where she put it in the first place; remove the dishes from the table as soon as the last bite is taken; wipe the doorknob after a greasy hand has touched it. A sidelong look will be enough to tell him to smoke on the back porch. Children will sense instantly that they cannot come into her yard to retrieve a ball. But the men do not know these things. Nor do they know that she will give him her body sparingly and partially. He must enter her surreptitiously, lifting the hem of her nightgown only to her navel. He must rest his weight on his elbows when they make love, ostensibly to avoid hurting her breasts but actually to keep her from having to touch or feel too much of him.

While he moves inside her, she will wonder why they didn't put the necessary but private parts of the body in some more convenient place—like the armpit, for example, or the palm of the hand. Someplace one could get to easily, and quickly, without undressing. She stiffens when she feels one of her paper curlers coming undone from the activity of love; imprints in her mind which one it is that is coming loose so she can quickly secure it once he is through. She hopes he will not sweat—the damp may get into her hair; and that she will remain dry between her legs—she hates the glucking sound they make when she is moist. When she senses some spasm about to grip him, she will make rapid movements with her hips, press her fingernails into his back, suck in her breath, and pretend she is having an orgasm. She might wonder again, for the six hundredth time, what it would be like to have *that* feeling while her husband's penis is inside her. The closest thing to it was the time she was walking down the street and her napkin slipped free of her sanitary belt. It moved gently between her legs as she walked. Gently, ever so gently. And then a slight and distinctly delicious sensation collected in her crotch. As the delight grew, she had to stop in the street, hold her thighs together to contain it. That must be what it is like, she thinks, but it never happens while he is inside her. When he withdraws, she pulls her nightgown down, slips out of the bed and into the bathroom with relief.

Occasionally some living thing will engage her affections. A cat, perhaps, who will love her order, precision, and constancy; who will be as clean and quiet as she is. The cat will settle quietly on the windowsill and caress her with his eyes. She can hold him in her arms, letting his back paws struggle for footing on her breast and his forepaws cling to her shoulder. She can rub the smooth fur and feel the unresisting flesh underneath. At her gentlest touch he will preen, stretch, and open his mouth. And she will accept the strangely pleasant sensation that comes when he writhes beneath her hand and flattens his eyes with a surfeit of sensual delight. When she stands cooking at the table, he will circle about her shanks, and the trill of his fur spirals up her legs to her thighs, to make her fingers tremble a little in the pie dough.

Or, as she sits reading the "Uplifting Thoughts" in *The Liberty Magazine,* the cat will jump into her lap. She will fondle that soft hill of hair and let the warmth of the animal's body seep over and into the deeply private areas of her lap. Sometimes the magazine drops, and she opens her legs just a little, and the two of them will be still together, perhaps shifting a little together, sleeping a little together, until four o'clock, when the intruder comes home from work vaguely anxious about what's for dinner.

The cat will always know that he is first in her affections. Even after she bears a child. For she does bear a child—easily, and painlessly. But only one. A son. Named Junior.

One such girl from Mobile, or Meridian, or Aiken who did not sweat in her armpits nor between her thighs, who smelled of wood and vanilla, who had made soufflés in the Home Economics Department, moved with her husband, Louis, to Lorain, Ohio. Her name was Geraldine. There she built her nest, ironed shirts, potted bleeding hearts, played with her cat, and birthed Louis Junior.

Geraldine did not allow her baby, Junior, to cry. As long as his needs were physical, she could meet them—comfort and satiety. He was always brushed, bathed, oiled, and shod. Geraldine did not talk to him, coo to him, or indulge him in kissing bouts, but she saw that every other desire was fulfilled. It was not long before the child discovered the difference in his mother's behavior to himself and the cat. As he grew older, he learned how to direct his hatred of his mother to the cat, and spent some happy moments watching it suffer. The cat survived, because Geraldine was seldom away from home, and could effectively soothe the animal when Junior abused him.

Geraldine, Louis, Junior, and the cat lived next to the playground of Washington Irving School. Junior considered the playground his own, and the schoolchildren coveted his freedom to sleep late, go home for lunch, and dominate the playground after school. He hated to see the swings, slides, monkey bars, and seesaws empty and tried to get kids to stick around as long as possible. White kids; his mother did not like him to play with niggers. She had explained to him the difference between colored people and niggers. They were easily identifiable. Colored people were neat and quiet; niggers were dirty and loud. He belonged to the former group: he wore white shirts and blue trousers; his hair was cut as close to his scalp as possible to avoid any suggestion of wool, the part was etched into his hair by the barber. In winter his mother put Jergens Lotion on his face to keep the skin from becoming ashen. Even though he was light-skinned, it was possible to ash. The line between colored and nigger was not always clear; subtle and telltale signs threatened to erode it, and the watch had to be constant.

Junior used to long to play with the black boys. More than anything in the world he wanted to play King of the Mountain and have them push him down the mound of dirt and roll over him. He wanted to feel their hardness pressing on him, smell their wild blackness, and say "Fuck you" with that lovely casualness. He wanted to sit with them on curbstones and compare the sharpness of jackknives, the distance and arcs of spitting. In the toilet he wanted to share with them the laurels of being able to pee far and long. Bay Boy and P. L. had at one time been his idols. Gradually he came to agree with his mother that neither Bay Boy nor P. L. was good enough for him. He played only with Ralph Nisensky, who was two years younger, wore glasses, and didn't want to *do* anything. More and more Junior enjoyed bullying girls. It was easy making them scream and run. How he laughed when they fell down and their bloomers showed. When they got up, their faces red and crinkled, it made him feel good. The nigger girls he did not pick on very much. They usually traveled in packs, and once when he threw a stone at some of them, they chased, caught, and beat him witless. He lied to his mother, saying Bay Boy did it. His mother was very upset. His father just kept on reading the Lorain *Journal.*

When the mood struck him, he would call a child passing by to come play on the swings or the seesaw. If the child wouldn't, or did and left too soon, Junior threw gravel at him. He became a very good shot.

Alternately bored and frightened at home, the playground was his joy. On a day when he had been especially idle, he saw a very black girl taking a shortcut through the playground. She kept her head down as she walked. He had seen her many times before, standing alone, always alone, at recess. Nobody ever played with her. Probably, he thought, because she was ugly.

Now Junior called to her. "Hey! What are you doing walking through my yard?"

The girl stopped.

"Nobody can come through this yard 'less I say so."

"This ain't your yard. It's the school's."

"But I'm in charge of it."

The girl started to walk away.

"Wait." Junior walked toward her. "You can play in it if you want to. What's your name?"

"Pecola. I don't want to play."

"Come on. I'm not going to bother you."

"I got to go home."

"Say, you want to see something? I got something to show you."

"No. What is it?"

"Come on in my house. See, I live right there. Come on. I'll show you."

"Show me what?"

"Some kittens. We got some kittens. You can have one if you want."

"Real kittens?"

"Yeah. Come on."

He pulled gently at her dress. Pecola began to move toward his house. When he knew she had agreed, Junior ran ahead excitedly, stopping only to yell back at her to come on. He held the door open for her, smiling his encouragement. Pecola climbed the porch stairs and hesitated there, afraid to follow him. The house looked dark. Junior said, "There's nobody here. My ma's gone out, and my father's at work. Don't you want to see the kittens?"

Junior turned on the lights. Pecola stepped inside the door.

How beautiful, she thought. What a beautiful house. There was a big red-and-gold Bible on the dining-room table. Little lace doilies were everywhere—on arms and backs of chairs, in the center of a large dining table, on little tables. Potted plants were on all the windowsills. A color picture of Jesus Christ hung on a wall with the prettiest paper flowers fastened on the frame. She wanted to see everything slowly, slowly. But Junior kept saying, "Hey, you. Come on. Come on." He pulled her into another room, even more beautiful than the first. More doilies, a big lamp with green-and-gold base and white shade. There was even a rug on the floor, with enormous dark-red flowers. She was deep in admiration of the flowers when Junior said, "Here!" Pecola turned. "Here is your kitten!" he screeched. And he threw a big black cat right in her face. She sucked in her breath in fear and surprise and felt fur in her mouth. The cat clawed her face and chest in an effort to right itself, then leaped nimbly to the floor.

Junior was laughing and running around the room clutching his stomach delightedly. Pecola touched the scratched place on her face and felt tears coming. When she started toward the doorway, Junior leaped in front of her.

"You can't get out. You're my prisoner," he said. His eyes were merry but hard.

"You let me go."

"No!" He pushed her down, ran out the door that separated the rooms, and held it shut with his hands. Pecola's banging on the door increased his gasping, high-pitched laughter.

The tears came fast, and she held her face in her hands. When something soft and furry moved around her ankles, she jumped, and saw it was the cat. He wound himself in and about her legs. Momentarily distracted from her fear, she squatted down to touch him, her hands wet from the tears. The cat rubbed up against her knee. He was black all over, deep silky black, and his eyes, pointing down toward his nose, were bluish green. The light made them shine like blue ice. Pecola rubbed the cat's head; he whined, his tongue flicking with pleasure. The blue eyes in the black face held her.

Junior, curious at not hearing her sobs, opened the door, and saw her squatting down rubbing the cat's back. He saw the cat stretching its head and flattening its eyes. He had seen that expression many times as the animal responded to his mother's touch.

"Gimme my cat!" His voice broke. With a movement both awkward and sure he snatched the cat by one of its hind legs and began to swing it around his head in a circle.

"Stop that!" Pecola was screaming. The cat's free paws were stiffened, ready to grab anything to restore balance, its mouth wide, its eyes blue streaks of horror.

Still screaming, Pecola reached for Junior's hand. She heard her dress rip under her arm. Junior tried to push her away, but she grabbed the arm which was swinging the cat. They both fell, and in falling, Junior let go the cat, which, having been released in mid-motion, was thrown full force against the window. It slithered down and fell on the radiator behind the sofa. Except for a few shudders, it was still. There was only the slightest smell of singed fur.

Geraldine opened the door.

"What is this?" Her voice was mild, as though asking a perfectly reasonable question. "Who is this girl?"

"She killed our cat," said Junior. "Look." He pointed to the radiator, where the cat lay, its blue eyes closed, leaving only an empty, black, and helpless face.

Geraldine went to the radiator and picked up the cat. He was limp in her arms, but she rubbed her face in his fur. She looked at Pecola. Saw the dirty torn dress, the plaits sticking out on her head, hair matted where the plaits had come undone, the muddy shoes with the wad of gum peeping out from between the cheap soles, the soiled socks, one of which had been walked down into the heel of the shoe. She saw the safety pin holding the hem of the dress up. Up over the hump of the cat's back she looked at her. She had seen this little girl all of her life. Hanging out of windows over saloons in Mobile, crawling over the porches of shotgun houses on the edge of town, sitting in bus stations holding paper bags and crying to mothers who kept saying "Shet up!" Hair uncombed, dresses falling apart, shoes untied and caked with dirt. They had stared at her with great uncomprehending eyes. Eyes that questioned nothing and asked everything. Unblinking and unabashed, they stared up at her. The end of the world lay in their eyes, and the beginning, and all the waste in between.

They were everywhere. They slept six in a bed, all their pee mixing together in the night as they wet their beds each in his own candy-and-potato-chip dream. In the long, hot days, they idled away, picking plaster from the walls and digging into the earth with sticks. They sat in little rows on street curbs, crowded into pews at church, taking space from the nice, neat, colored children; they clowned on the playgrounds, broke things in dime stores, ran in front of you on the street, made ice slides on the sloped sidewalks in winter. The girls grew up knowing nothing of girdles, and the boys announced their manhood by turning the bills of their caps backward. Grass wouldn't grow where they lived. Flowers died. Shades fell down. Tin cans and tires blossomed where they lived. They lived on cold black-eyed peas and orange pop. Like flies they hovered; like flies they settled. And this one had settled in her house. Up over the hump of the cat's back she looked.

"Get out," she said, her voice quiet. "You nasty little black bitch. Get out of my house."

The cat shuddered and flicked his tail.

Pecola backed out of the room, staring at the pretty milk-brown lady in the pretty gold-and-green house who was talking to her through the cat's fur. The pretty lady's words made the cat fur move; the breath of each word parted the fur. Pecola turned to find the front door and saw Jesus looking down at her with sad and unsurprised eyes, his long brown hair parted in the middle, the gay paper flowers twisted around his face.

Outside, the March wind blew into the rip in her dress. She held her head down against the cold. But she could not hold it low enough to avoid seeing the snowflakes falling and dying on the pavement.

Spring

The first twigs are thin, green, and supple. They bend into a complete circle, but will not break. Their delicate, showy hopefulness shooting from forsythia and lilac bushes meant only a change in whipping style. They beat us differently in the spring. Instead of the dull pain of a winter strap, there were these new green switches that lost their sting long after the whipping was over. There was a nervous meanness in these long twigs that made us long for the steady stroke of a strap or the firm but honest slap of a hairbrush. Even now spring for me is shot through with the remembered ache of switchings, and forsythia holds no cheer.

Sunk in the grass of an empty lot on a spring Saturday, I split the stems of milkweed and thought about ants and peach pits and death and where the world went when I closed my eyes. I must have lain long in the grass, for the shadow that was in front of me when I left the house had disappeared when I went back. I entered the house, as the house was bursting with an uneasy quiet. Then I heard my mother singing something about trains and Arkansas. She came in the back door with some folded yellow curtains which she piled on the kitchen table. I sat down on the floor to listen to the song's story, and noticed how strangely she was behaving. She still had her hat on, and her shoes were dusty, as though she had been walking in deep dirt. She put on some water to boil and then swept the porch; then she hauled out the curtain stretcher, but instead of putting the damp curtains on it, she swept the porch again. All the time singing about trains and Arkansas.

When she finished, I went to look for Frieda. I found her upstairs lying on our bed, crying the tired, whimpering cry that follows the first wailings—mostly gasps and shudderings. I lay on the bed and looked at the tiny bunches of wild roses sprinkled over her dress. Many washings had faded their color and dimmed their outlines.

"What happened, Frieda?"

She lifted a swollen face from the crook of her arm. Shuddering still, she sat up, letting her thin legs dangle over the bedside. I knelt on the bed and picked up the hem of my dress to wipe her running nose. She never liked wiping noses on clothes, but this time she let me. It was the way Mama did with her apron.

"Did you get a whipping?"

She shook her head no.

"Then why you crying?"

"Because."

"Because what?"

"Mr. Henry."

"What'd he do?"

"Daddy beat him up."

"What for? The Maginot Line? Did he find out about the Maginot Line?"

"No."

"Well, what, then? Come on, Frieda. How come I can't know?"

"He . . . *picked* at me."

"Picked at you? You mean like Soaphead Church?"

"Sort of."

"He showed his privates at you?"

"Noooo. He touched me."

"Where?"

"Here and here." She pointed to the tiny breasts that, like two fallen acorns, scattered a few faded rose leaves on her dress.

"Really? How did it feel?"

"Oh, Claudia." She sounded put-out. I wasn't asking the right questions.

"It didn't feel like anything."

"But wasn't it supposed to? Feel good, I mean?" Frieda sucked her teeth. "What'd he do? Just walk up and pinch them?"

She sighed. "First he said how pretty I was. Then he grabbed my arm and touched me."

"Where was Mama and Daddy?"

"Over at the garden weeding."

"What'd you say when he did it?"

"Nothing. I just ran out the kitchen and went to the garden."

"Mama said we was never to cross the tracks by ourselves."

"Well, what would you do? Set there and let him pinch you?"

I looked at my chest. "I don't have nothing to pinch. I'm never going to have nothing."

"Oh, Claudia, you're jealous of everything. You *want* him to?"

"No, I just get tired of having everything last."

"You do not. What about scarlet fever? You had that first."

"Yes, but it didn't last. Anyway, what happened at the garden?"

"I told Mama, and she told Daddy, and we all come home, and he was gone, so we waited for him, and when Daddy saw him come up on the porch, he threw our old tricycle at his head and knocked him off the porch."

"Did he die?"

"Naw. He got up and started singing 'Nearer My God to Thee.' Then Mama hit him with a broom and told him to keep the Lord's name out of his mouth, but he wouldn't stop, and Daddy was cussing, and everybody was screaming."

"Oh, shoot, I always miss stuff."

"And Mr. Buford came running out with his gun, and Mama told him to go somewhere and sit down, and Daddy said no, give him the gun, and Mr. Buford did, and Mama screamed, and Mr. Henry shut up and started running, and Daddy shot at him and Mr. Henry jumped out of his shoes and kept on running in his socks. Then Rosemary came out and said that Daddy was going to jail, and I hit her."

"Real hard?"

"Real hard."

"Is that when Mama whipped you?"

"She didn't whip me, I told you."

"Then why you crying?"

"Miss Dunion came in after everybody was quiet, and Mama and Daddy was fussing about who let Mr. Henry in anyway, and she said that Mama should take me to the doctor, because I might be ruined, and Mama started screaming all over again."

"At you?"

"No. At Miss Dunion."

"But why were you crying?"

"I don't want to be *ruined!*"

"What's ruined?"

"You know. Like the Maginot Line. She's ruined. Mama said so." The tears came back.

An image of Frieda, big and fat, came to mind. Her thin legs swollen, her face surrounded by layers of rouged skin. I too begin to feel tears.

"But, Frieda, you could exercise and not eat."

She shrugged.

"Besides, what about China and Poland? They're ruined too, aren't they? And they ain't fat."

"That's because they drink whiskey. Mama says whiskey ate them up."

"You could drink whiskey."

"Where would I get whiskey?"

We thought about this. Nobody would sell it to us; we had no money, anyway. There was never any in our house. Who would have some?

"Pecola," I said. "Her father's always drunk. She can get us some."

"You think so?"

"Sure. Cholly's always drunk. Let's go ask her. We don't have to tell her what for."

"Now?"

"Sure, now."

"What'll we tell Mama?"

"Nothing. Let's just go out the back. One at a time. So she won't notice."

"O.K. You go first, Claudia."

We opened the fence gate at the bottom of the backyard and ran down the alley.

Pecola lived on the other side of Broadway. We had never been in her house, but we knew where it was. A two-story gray building that had been a store downstairs and had an apartment upstairs.

Nobody answered our knock on the front door, so we walked around to the side door. As we approached, we heard radio music and looked to see where it came from. Above us was the second-story porch, lined with slanting, rotting rails, and sitting on the porch was the Maginot Line herself. We stared up and automatically reached for the other's hand. A mountain of flesh, she lay rather than sat in a rocking chair. She had no shoes on, and each foot was poked between a railing: tiny baby toes at the tip of puffy feet; swollen ankles smoothed and tightened the skin; massive legs like tree stumps parted wide at the knees, over which spread two roads of soft flabby inner thigh that kissed each other deep in the shade of her dress and closed. A dark-brown root-beer bottle, like a burned limb, grew out of her dimpled hand. She looked at us down through the porch railings and emitted a low, long belch. Her eyes were as clean as rain, and again I remembered the waterfall. Neither of us could speak. Both of us imagined we were seeing what was to become of Frieda. The Maginot Line smiled at us.

"You all looking for somebody?"

I had to pull my tongue from the roof of my mouth to say, "Pecola—she live here?"

"Uh-huh, but she ain't here now. She gone to her mama's work place to git the wash."

"Yes, ma'am. She coming back?"

"Uh-huh. She got to hang up the clothes before the sun goes down."

"Oh."

"You can wait for her. Wanna come up here and wait?"

We exchanged glances. I looked back up at the broad cinnamon roads that met in the shadow of her dress.

Frieda said, "No, ma'am."

"Well," the Maginot Line seemed interested in our problem. "You can go to her mama's work place, but it's way over by the lake."

"Where by the lake?"

"That big white house with the wheelbarrow full of flowers."

It was a house that we knew, having admired the large white wheelbarrow tilted down on spoked wheels and planted with seasonal flowers.

"Ain't that too far for you all to go walking?"

Frieda scratched her knee.

"Why don't you wait for her? You can come up here. Want some pop?" Those rain-soaked eyes lit up, and her smile was full, not like the pinched and holding-back smile of other grown-ups.

I moved to go up the stairs, but Frieda said, "No, ma'am, we ain't allowed."

I was amazed at her courage, and frightened of her sassiness. The smile of the Maginot Line slipped. "Ain't 'llowed?"

"No'm."

"Ain't 'llowed to what?"

"Go in your house."

"Is that right?" The waterfalls were still. "How come?"

"My mama said so. My mama said you ruined."

The waterfalls began to run again. She put the root-beer bottle to her lips and drank it empty. With a graceful movement of the wrist, a gesture so quick and small we never really saw it, only remembered it afterward, she tossed the bottle over the rail at us. It split at our feet, and shards of brown glass dappled our legs before we could jump back. The Maginot Line put a fat hand on one of the folds of her stomach and laughed. At first just a deep humming with her mouth closed, then a larger, warmer sound. Laughter at once beautiful and frightening. She let her head tilt sideways, closed her eyes, and shook her massive trunk, letting the laughter fall like a wash of red leaves all around us. Scraps and curls of the laughter followed us as we ran. Our breath gave out at the same time our legs did. After we rested against a tree, our heads on crossed forearms, I said, "Let's go home."

Frieda was still angry—fighting, she believed, for her life. "No, we got to get it now."

"We can't go all the way to the lake."

"Yes we can. Come on."

"Mama gone get us."

"No she ain't. Besides, she can't do nothing but whip us."

That was true. She wouldn't kill us, or laugh a terrible laugh at us, or throw a bottle at us.

We walked down tree-lined streets of soft gray houses leaning like tired ladies. . . . The streets changed; houses looked more sturdy, their paint was newer, porch posts straighter, yards deeper. Then came brick houses set well back from the street, fronted by yards edged in shrubbery clipped into smooth cones and balls of velvet green.

The lakefront houses were the loveliest. Garden furniture, ornaments, windows like shiny eyeglasses, and no sign of life. The backyards of these houses fell away in green slopes down to a strip of sand, and then the blue Lake Erie, lapping all the way to Canada. The orange-patched sky of the steel-mill section never reached this part of town. This sky was always blue.

We reached Lake Shore Park, a city park laid out with rosebuds, fountains, bowling greens, picnic tables. It was empty now, but sweetly expectant of clean, white, well-behaved children and parents who would play there above the lake in summer before half-running, half-stumbling down the slope to the welcoming water. Black people were not allowed in the park, and so it filled our dreams.

Right before the entrance to the park was the large white house with the wheelbarrow full of flowers. Short crocus blades sheathed the purple-and-white hearts that so wished to be first they endured the chill and rain of early spring. The walkway was flagged in calculated disorder, hiding the cunning symmetry. Only fear of discovery and the knowledge that we did not belong kept us from loitering. We circled the proud house and went to the back.

There on the tiny railed stoop sat Pecola in a light red sweater and blue cotton dress. A little wagon was parked near her. She seemed glad to see us.

"Hi."

"Hi."

"What you all doing here?" She was smiling, and since it was a rare thing to see on her, I was surprised at the pleasure it gave me.

"We're looking for you."

"Who told you I was here?"

"The Maginot Line."

"Who is that?"

"That big fat lady. She lives over you."

"Oh, you mean Miss Marie. Her name is Miss Marie."

"Well, everybody calls her Miss Maginot Line. Ain't you scared?"

"Scared of what?"

"The Maginot Line."

Pecola looked genuinely puzzled. "What for?"

"Your mama let you go in her house? And eat out of her plates?"

"She don't know I go. Miss Marie is nice. They all nice."

"Oh, yeah," I said, "she tried to kill us."

"Who? Miss Marie? She don't bother nobody."

"Then how come your mama don't let you go in her house if she so nice?"

"I don't know. She say she's bad, but they ain't bad. They give me stuff all the time."

"What stuff?"

"Oh, lots of stuff, pretty dresses, and shoes. I got more shoes than I ever wear. And jewelry and candy and money. They take me to the movies, and once we went to the carnival. China gone take me to Cleveland to see the square, and Poland gone take me to Chicago to see the Loop. We going everywhere together."

"You lying. You don't have no pretty dresses."

"I do, too."

"Oh, come on, Pecola, what you telling us all that junk for?" Frieda asked.

"It ain't junk." Pecola stood up ready to defend her words, when the door opened.

Mrs. Breedlove stuck her head out the door and said, "What's going on out here? Pecola, who are these children?"

"That's Frieda and Claudia, Mrs. Breedlove."

"Whose girls are you?" She came all the way out on the stoop. She looked nicer than I had ever seen her, in her white uniform and her hair in a small pompadour.

"Mrs. MacTeer's girls, ma'am."

"Oh, yes. Live over on Twenty-first Street?"

"Yes, ma'am."

"What are you doing 'way over here?"

"Just walking. We came to see Pecola."

"Well, you better get on back. You can walk with Pecola. Come on in while I get the wash."

We stepped into the kitchen, a large spacious room. Mrs. Breedlove's skin glowed like taffeta in the reflection of white porcelain, white woodwork, polished cabinets, and brilliant copperware. Odors of meat, vegetables, and something freshly baked mixed with a scent of Fels Naphtha.

"I'm gone get the wash. You all stand stock still right there and don't mess up nothing." She disappeared behind a white swinging door, and we could hear the uneven flap of her footsteps as she descended into the basement.

Another door opened, and in walked a little girl, smaller and younger than all of us. She wore a pink sunback dress and pink fluffy bedroom slippers with two bunny ears pointed up from the tips. Her hair was corn yellow and bound in a thick ribbon. When she saw us, fear danced across her face for a second. She looked anxiously around the kitchen.

"Where's Polly?" she asked.

The familiar violence rose in me. Her calling Mrs. Breedlove Polly, when even Pecola called her mother Mrs. Breedlove seemed reason enough to scratch her.

"She's downstairs," I said.

"Polly!" she called.

"Look," Frieda whispered, "look at that." On the counter near the stove in a silvery pan was a deep-dish berry cobbler. The purple juice bursting here and there through crust. We moved closer.

"It's still hot," Frieda said.

Pecola stretched her hand to touch the pan, lightly, to see if it was hot.

"Polly, come here," the little girl called again.

It may have been nervousness, awkwardness, but the pan tilted under Pecola's fingers and fell to the floor, splattering blackish blueberries everywhere. Most of the juice splashed on Pecola's legs, and the burn must have been painful, for she cried out and began hopping about just as Mrs. Breedlove entered with a tightly packed laundry bag. In one gallop she was on Pecola, and with the back of her hand knocked her to the floor. Pecola slid in the pie juice, one leg folding under her. Mrs. Breedlove yanked her up by the arm, slapped her again, and in a voice thin with anger, abused Pecola directly and Frieda and me by implication.

"Crazy fool . . . my floor, mess . . . look what you . . . work . . . get on out . . . now that . . . crazy . . . my floor, my floor . . . my floor." Her words were hotter and darker than the smoking berries, and we backed away in dread.

The little girl in pink started to cry. Mrs. Breedlove turned to her. "Hush, baby, hush. Come here. Oh, Lord, look at your dress. Don't cry no more. Polly will change it." She went to the sink and turned tap water on a fresh towel. Over her shoulder she spit out words to us like rotten pieces of apple. "Pick up that wash and get on out of here, so I can get this mess cleaned up."

Pecola picked up the laundry bag, heavy with wet clothes, and we stepped hurriedly out the door. As Pecola put the laundry bag in the wagon, we could hear Mrs. Breedlove hushing and soothing the tears of the little pink-and-yellow girl.

"Who were they, Polly?"

"Don't worry none, baby."

"You gonna make another pie?"

"'Course I will."

"Who were they, Polly?"

"Hush. Don't worry none," she whispered, and the honey in her words complemented the sundown spilling on the lake.

SEEMOTHERMOTHERISVERYNICEMOTHERWILLYOUPLAY WITHJANEMOTHERLAUGHSLAUGHMOTHERLAUGHLAUGH

The easiest thing to do would be to build a case out of her foot. That is what she herself did. But to find out the truth about how dreams die, one should never take the word of the dreamer. The end of her lovely beginning was probably the cavity in one of her front teeth. She preferred, however, to think always of her foot. Although she was the ninth of eleven children and lived on a ridge of red Alabama clay seven miles from the nearest road, the complete indifference with which a rusty nail was met when it punched clear through her foot during her second year of life saved Pauline Williams from total anonymity. The wound left her with a crooked, archless foot that flopped when she walked—not a limp that would have eventually twisted her spine, but a way of lifting the bad foot as though she were extracting it from little whirlpools that threatened to pull it under. Slight as it was, this deformity explained for her many things that would have been otherwise incomprehensible: why she alone of all the children had no nickname; why there were no funny jokes and anecdotes about funny things she had done; why no one ever remarked on her food preferences—no saving of the wing or neck for her—no cooking of the peas in a separate pot without rice because she did not like rice; why nobody teased her; why she never felt at home anywhere, or that she belonged anyplace. Her general feeling of separateness and unworthiness she blamed on her foot. Restricted, as a child, to this cocoon of her family's spinning, she cultivated quiet and private pleasures. She liked, most of all, to arrange things. To line things up in rows—jars on shelves at canning, peach pits on the step, sticks, stones, leaves—and the members of her family let these arrangements be. When by some accident somebody scattered her rows, they always stopped to retrieve them for her, and she was never angry, for it gave her a chance to rearrange them again. Whatever portable plurality she found, she organized into neat lines, according to their size, shape, or gradations of color. Just as she would never align a pine needle with the leaf of a cottonwood tree, she would never put the jars of tomatoes next to the green beans. During all of her four years of going to school, she was enchanted by numbers and depressed by words. She missed—without knowing what she missed—paints and crayons.

Near the beginning of World War I, the Williamses discovered, from returning neighbors and kin, the possibility of living better in another place. In shifts, lots, batches, mixed in with other families, they migrated, in six months and four journeys, to Kentucky, where there were mines and millwork.

"When all us left from down home and was waiting down by the depot for the truck, it was nighttime. June bugs was shooting everywhere. They lighted up a tree leaf, and I seen a streak of green every now and again. That was the last time I seen real june bugs. These things up here ain't june bugs. They's something else. Folks here call them fireflies. Down home they was different. But I recollect that streak of green. I recollect it well."

In Kentucky they lived in a real town, ten to fifteen houses on a single street, with water piped right into the kitchen. Ada and Fowler Williams found a five-room frame house for their family. The yard was bounded by a once-white fence against which Pauline's mother planted flowers and within which they kept a few chickens. Some of her brothers joined the Army, one sister died, and two got married, increasing the living space and giving the entire Kentucky venture a feel of luxury. The relocation was especially comfortable to Pauline, who was old enough to leave school. Mrs. Williams got a job cleaning and cooking for a white minister on the other side of town, and Pauline, now the oldest girl at home, took over the care of the house. She kept the fence in repair, pulling the pointed stakes erect, securing them with bits of wire, collected eggs, swept, cooked, washed, and minded the two younger children—a pair of twins called Chicken and Pie, who were still in school. She was not only good at housekeeping, she enjoyed it. After her parents left for work and the other children were at school or in mines, the house was quiet. The stillness and isolation both calmed and energized her. She could arrange and clean without interruption until two o'clock, when Chicken and Pie came home.

When the war ended and the twins were ten years old, they too left school to work. Pauline was fifteen, still keeping house, but with less enthusiasm. Fantasies about men and love and touching were drawing her mind and hands away from her work. Changes in weather began to affect her, as did certain sights and sounds. These feelings translated themselves to her in extreme melancholy. She thought of the death of newborn things, lonely roads, and strangers who appear out of nowhere simply to hold one's hand, woods in which the sun was always setting. In church especially did these dreams grow. The songs caressed her, and while she tried to hold her mind on the wages of sin, her body trembled for redemption, salvation, a mysterious rebirth that would simply happen, with no effort on her part. In none of her fantasies was she ever aggressive; she was usually idling by the river bank, or gathering berries in a field when a someone appeared, with gentle and penetrating eyes, who—with no exchange of words—understood; and before whose glance her foot straightened and her eyes dropped. The someone had no face, no form, no voice, no odor. He was a simple Presence, an all-embracing tenderness with strength and a promise of rest. It did not matter that she had no idea of what to do or say to the Presence—after the wordless knowing and the soundless touching, her dreams disintegrated. But the Presence would know what to do. She had only to lay her head on his chest and he would lead her away to the sea, to the city, to the woods . . . forever.

There was a woman named Ivy who seemed to hold in her mouth all of the sounds of Pauline's soul. Standing a little apart from the choir, Ivy sang the dark sweetness that Pauline could not name; she sang the death-defying death that Pauline yearned for; she sang of the Stranger who *knew* . . .

Precious Lord take my hand
Lead me on, let me stand
I am tired, I am weak, I am worn.

Through the storms, through the night
Lead me on to the light
Take my hand, precious Lord, lead me on.

When my way grows drear
Precious Lord linger near,
When my life is almost gone
Hear my cry hear my call
Hold my hand lest I fall
Take my hand, precious Lord, lead me on.

Thus it was that when the Stranger, the someone, did appear out of nowhere, Pauline was grateful but not surprised.

He came, strutting right out of a Kentucky sun on the hottest day of the year. He came big, he came strong, he came with yellow eyes, flaring nostrils, and he came with his own music.

Pauline was leaning idly on the fence, her arms resting on the cross-rail between the pickets. She had just put down some biscuit dough and was cleaning the flour from under her nails. Behind her at some distance she heard whistling. One of these rapid, high-note riffs that black boys make up as they go while sweeping, shoveling, or just walking along. A kind of city-street music where laughter belies anxiety, and joy is as short and straight as the blade of a pocketknife. She listened carefully to the music and let it pull her lips into a smile. The whistling got louder, and still she did not turn around, for she wanted it to last. While smiling to herself and holding fast to the break in somber thoughts, she felt something tickling her foot. She laughed aloud and turned to see. The whistler was bending down tickling her broken foot and kissing her leg. She could not stop her laughter—not until he looked up at her and she saw the Kentucky sun drenching the yellow, heavy-lidded eyes of Cholly Breedlove.

"When I first seed Cholly, I want you to know it was like all the bits of color from that time down home when all us chil'ren went berry picking after a funeral and I put some in the pocket of my Sunday dress, and they mashed up and stained my hips. My whole dress was messed with purple, and it never did wash out. Not the dress nor me. I could feel that purple deep inside me. And that lemonade Mama used to make when Pap came in out the fields. It be cool and yellowish, with seeds floating near the bottom. And that

streak of green them june bugs made on the trees the night we left from down home. All of them colors was in me. Just sitting there. So when Cholly come up and tickled my foot, it was like them berries, that lemonade, them streaks of green the june bugs made, all come together. Cholly was thin then, with real light eyes. He used to whistle, and when I heerd him, shivers come on my skin."

Pauline and Cholly loved each other. He seemed to relish her company and even to enjoy her country ways and lack of knowledge about city things. He talked with her about her foot and asked, when they walked through the town or in the fields, if she were tired. Instead of ignoring her infirmity, pretending it was not there, he made it seem like something special and endearing. For the first time Pauline felt that her bad foot was an asset.

And he did touch her, firmly but gently, just as she had dreamed. But minus the gloom of setting suns and lonely river banks. She was secure and grateful; he was kind and lively. She had not known there was so much laughter in the world.

They agreed to marry and go 'way up north, where Cholly said steel mills were begging for workers. Young, loving, and full of energy, they came to Lorain, Ohio. Cholly found work in the steel mills right away, and Pauline started keeping house.

And then she lost her front tooth. But there must have been a speck, a brown speck easily mistaken for food but which did not leave, which sat on the enamel for months, and grew, until it cut into the surface and then to the brown putty underneath, finally eating away to the root, but avoiding the nerves, so its presence was not noticeable or uncomfortable. Then the weakened roots, having grown accustomed to the poison, responded one day to severe pressure, and the tooth fell free, leaving a ragged stump behind. But even before the little brown speck, there must have been the conditions, the setting that would allow it to exist in the first place.

In that young and growing Ohio town whose side streets, even, were paved with concrete, which sat on the edge of a calm blue lake, which boasted an affinity with Oberlin, the underground railroad station, just thirteen miles away, this melting pot on the lip of America facing the cold but receptive Canada—What could go wrong?

"Me and Cholly was getting along good then. We come up north; supposed to be more jobs and all. We moved into two rooms up over a furniture store, and I set about housekeeping. Cholly was working at the steel plant, and everything was looking good. I don't know what all happened. Everything changed. It was hard to get to know folks up here, and I missed my people. I weren't used to so much white folks. The ones I seed before was something hateful, but they didn't come around too much. I mean, we didn't have too much truck with them. Just now and then in the fields, or at the commissary. But they want all over us. Up north they was everywhere—next door, downstairs, all over the streets—and colored folks few and far between. Northern colored folk was different too. Dicty-like. No better than whites for meanness. They could make you feel just as no-count, 'cept I didn't expect it from them. That was the lonesomest time of my life. I 'member looking out them front windows just waiting for Cholly to come home at three o'clock. I didn't even have a cat to talk to."

In her loneliness, she turned to her husband for reassurance, entertainment, for things to fill the vacant places. Housework was not enough; there were only two rooms, and no yard to keep or move about in. The women in the town wore high-heeled shoes, and when Pauline tried to wear them, they aggravated her shuffle into a pronounced limp. Cholly was kindness still, but began to resist her total dependence on him. They were beginning to have less and less to say to each other. He had no problem finding other people and other things to occupy him—men were always climbing the stairs asking for him, and he was happy to accompany them, leaving her alone.

Pauline felt uncomfortable with the few black women she met. They were amused by her because she did not straighten her hair. When she tried to make up her face as they did, it came off rather badly. Their goading glances and private snickers at her way of talking (saying "chil'ren") and dressing developed in her a desire for new clothes. When Cholly began to quarrel about the money she wanted, she decided to go to work. Taking jobs as a day worker helped with the clothes, and even a few things for the apartment, but it did not help with Cholly. He was not pleased with her purchases and began to tell her so. Their marriage was shredded with quarrels. She was still no more than a girl, and still waiting for that plateau of happiness, that hand of a precious Lord who, when her way grew drear, would always linger near. Only now she had a clearer idea of what drear meant. Money became the focus of all their discussions, hers for clothes, his for drink. The sad thing was that Pauline did not really care for clothes and makeup. She merely wanted other women to cast favorable glances her way.

After several months of doing day work, she took a steady job in the home of a family of slender means and nervous, pretentious ways.

"Cholly commenced to getting meaner and meaner and wanted to fight me all of the time. I give him as good as I got. Had to. Look like working for that woman and fighting Cholly was all I did. Tiresome. But I holt on to my jobs, even though working for that woman was more than a notion. It wasn't so much her meanness as just simpleminded. Her whole family was. Couldn't get along with one another worth nothing. You'd think with a pretty house like that and all the money they could holt on to, they would enjoy one another. She haul off and cry over the leastest thing. If one of her friends cut her short on the telephone, she'd go to crying. She should of been glad she had a telephone. I ain't got one yet. I recollect oncet how her baby brother who she put through dentistry school didn't invite them to some big party he throwed. They was a big to-do about that. Everybody stayed on the telephone for days. Fussing and carrying on. She asked me, 'Pauline, what would you do if your own brother had a party and didn't invite you?' I said ifn I really wanted to go to that party, I reckoned I'd go anyhow. Never mind what he want. She just sucked her teeth a little and made out like what I said was dumb. All the while I was thinking how dumb she was. Whoever told her that her brother was her friend? Folks can't like folks just 'cause they has the same mama. I tried to like that woman myself. She was good about giving me stuff, but I just couldn't like her. Soon as I worked up a good feeling on her account, she'd do something ignorant and start in to telling me how to clean and do. If I left her on her own, she'd drown in dirt. I didn't have to pick up after Chicken and Pie the way I had to pick up after them. None of them knew so much as how to wipe their behinds. I know, 'cause I did the washing. And couldn't pee proper to save their lives. Her husband ain't hit the bowl yet. Nasty white folks is about the nastiest things they is. But I

would have stayed on 'cepting for Cholly come over by where I was working and cut up so. He come there drunk wanting some money. When that white woman see him, she turned red. She tried to act strong-like, but she was scared bad. Anyway, she told Cholly to get out or she would call the police. He cussed her and started pulling on me. I would of gone upside his head, but I don't want no dealings with the police. So I taken my things and left. I tried to get back, but she didn't want me no more if I was going to stay with Cholly. She said she would let me stay if I left him. I thought about that. But later on it didn't seem none too bright for a black woman to leave a black man for a white woman. She didn't never give me the eleven dollars she owed me, neither. That hurt bad. The gas man had cut the gas off, and I couldn't cook none. I really begged that woman for my money. I went to see her. She was mad as a wet hen. Kept on telling me I owed her for uniforms and some old broken-down bed she give me. I didn't know if I owed her or not, but I needed my money. She wouldn't let up none, neither, even when I give her my word that Cholly wouldn't come back there no more. Then I got so desperate I asked her if she would loan it to me. She was quiet for a spell, and then she told me I shouldn't let a man take advantage over me. That I should have more respect, and it was my husband's duty to pay the bills, and if he couldn't, I should leave and get alimony. All such simple stuff. What was he gone give me alimony on? I seen she didn't understand that all I needed from her was my eleven dollars to pay the gas man so I could cook. She couldn't get that one thing through her thick head. 'Are you going to leave him, Pauline?' she kept on saying. I thought she'd give me my money if I said I would, so I said 'Yes, ma'am.' 'All right,' she said. 'You leave him, and then come back to work, and we'll let bygones be bygones.' 'Can I have my money today?' I said. 'No' she said. 'Only when you leave him. I'm only thinking of you and your future. What good is he, Pauline, what good is he to you?' How you going to answer a woman like that, who don't know what good a man is, and say out of one side of her mouth she's thinking of your future but won't give you your own money so you can buy you something besides baloney to eat? So I said, 'No good, ma'am. He ain't no good to me. But just the same, I think I'd best stay on.' She got up, and I left. When I go outside, I felt pains in my crotch, I had held my legs together so tight trying to make that woman understand. But I reckon now she couldn't understand. She married a man with a slash in his face instead of a mouth. So how could she understand?"

One winter Pauline discovered she was pregnant. When she told Cholly, he surprised her by being pleased. He began to drink less and come home more often. They eased back into a relationship more like the early days of their marriage, when he asked if she were tired or wanted him to bring her something from the store. In this state of ease, Pauline stopped doing day work and returned to her own housekeeping. But the loneliness in those two rooms had not gone away. When the winter sun hit the peeling green paint of the kitchen chairs, when the smoked hocks were boiling in the pot, when all she could hear was the truck delivering furniture downstairs, she thought about back home, about how she had been all alone most of the time then too, but that this lonesomeness was different. Then she stopped staring at the green chairs, at the delivery truck; she went to the movies instead. There in the dark her memory was refreshed, and she succumbed to her earlier dreams. Along with the idea of romantic love, she was introduced to another—physical beauty. Probably the most destructive ideas in the history of human thought. Both originated in envy, thrived in insecurity, and ended in disillusion. In equating physical beauty with virtue, she stripped her mind, bound it, and collected self-contempt by the heap. She forgot lust and simple caring for. She regarded love as possessive mating, and romance as the goal of the spirit. It would be for her a well-spring from which she would draw the most destructive emotions, deceiving the lover and seeking to imprison the beloved, curtailing freedom in every way.

She was never able, after her education in the movies, to look at a face and not assign it some category in the scale of absolute beauty, and the scale was one she absorbed in full from the silver screen. There at last were the darkened woods, the lonely roads, the river banks, the gentle knowing eyes. There the flawed became whole, the blind sighted, and the lame and halt threw away their crutches. There death was dead, and people made every gesture in a cloud of music. There the black-and-white images came together, making a magnificent whole—all projected through the ray of light from above and behind.

It was really a simple pleasure, but she learned all there was to love and all there was to hate.

"The onliest time I be happy seem like was when I was in the picture show. Every time I got, I went. I'd go early, before the show started. They'd cut off the lights, and everything be black. Then the screen would light up, and I'd move right on in them pictures. White men taking such good care of they women, and they all dressed up in big clean houses with the bathtubs right in the same room with the toilet. Them pictures gave me a lot of pleasure, but it made coming home hard, and looking at Cholly hard. I don't know. I 'member one time I went to see Clark Gable and Jean Harlow. I fixed my hair up like I'd seen hers on a magazine. A part on the side, with one little curl on my forehead. It looked just like her. Well, almost just like. Anyway, I sat in that show with my hair done up that way and had a good time. I thought I'd see it through to the end again, and I got up to get me some candy. I was sitting back in my seat, and I taken a big bite of that candy, and it pulled a tooth right out of my mouth. I could of cried. I had good teeth, not a rotten one in my head. I don't believe I ever did get over that. There I was, five months pregnant, trying to look like Jean Harlow, and a front tooth gone. Everything went then. Look like I just didn't care no more after that. I let my hair go back, plaited it up, and settled down to just being ugly. I still went to the pictures, though, but the meanness got worse. I wanted my tooth back. Cholly poked fun at me, and we started fighting again. I tried to kill him. He didn't hit me too hard, 'cause I were pregnant I guess, but the fights, once they got started up again, kept up. He begin to make me madder than anything I knowed, and I couldn't keep my hands off him. Well, I had that baby—a boy—and after that got pregnant again with another one. But it weren't like I thought it was gone be. I loved them and all, I guess, but maybe it was having no money, or maybe it was Cholly, but they sure worried the life out of me. Sometimes I'd catch myself hollering at them and beating them, and I'd feel sorry for them, but I couldn't seem to stop. When I had the second one, a girl, I 'member I said I'd love it no matter what it looked like. She looked like a black ball of hair. I don't recollect trying to get pregnant that first time. But that second time, I actually tried to get pregnant. Maybe 'cause I'd had one already and wasn't scairt to do it. Anyway, I felt good, and wasn't thinking on the carrying, just the baby itself. I used to talk to it whilst it be still in the womb. Like good friends we was. You know. I be hanging wash and I knowed lifting weren't good for it. I'd say to it holt on now I

gone hang up these few rags, don't get froggy; it be over soon. It wouldn't leap or nothing. Or I be mixing something in a bowl for the other chile and I'd talk to it then too. You know, just friendly talk. On up til the end I felted good about that baby. I went to the hospital when my time come. So I could be easeful. I didn't want to have it at home like I done with the boy. They put me in a big room with a whole mess of women. The pains was coming, but not too bad. A little old doctor come to examine me. He had all sorts of stuff. He gloved his hand and put some kind of jelly on it and rammed it up between my legs. When he left off, some more doctors come. One old one and some young ones. The old one was learning the young ones about babies. Showing them how to do. When he got to me he said now these here women you don't have any trouble with. They deliver right away and with no pain. Just like horses. The young ones smiled a little. They looked at my stomach and between my legs. They never said nothing to me. Only one looked at me. Looked at my face, I mean. I looked right back at him. He dropped his eyes and turned red. He knowed, I reckon, that maybe I weren't no horse foaling. But them others. They didn't know. They went on. I seed them talking to them white women: 'How you feel? Gonna have twins?' Just shucking them, of course, but nice talk. Nice friendly talk. I got edgy, and when them pains got harder, I was glad. Glad to have something else to think about. I moaned something awful. The pains wasn't as bad as I let on, but I had to let them people know having a baby was more than a bowel movement. I hurt just like them white women. Just 'cause I wasn't hooping and hollering before didn't mean I wasn't feeling pain. What'd they think? That just 'cause I knowed how to have a baby with no fuss that my behind wasn't pulling and aching like theirs? Besides, that doctor don't know what he talking about. He must never seed no mare foal. Who say they don't have no pain? Just 'cause she don't cry? 'Cause she can't say it, they think it ain't there? If they looks in her eyes and see them eyeballs lolling back, see the sorrowful look, they'd know. Anyways, the baby come. Big old healthy thing. She looked different from what I thought. Reckon I talked to it so much before I conjured up a mind's eye view of it. So when I seed it, it was like looking at a picture of your mama when she was a girl. You knows who she is, but she don't look the same. They give her to me for a nursing, and she liked to pull my nipple off right away. She caught on fast. Not like Sammy, he was the hardest child to feed. But Pecola look like she knowed right off what to do. A right smart baby she was. I used to like to watch her. You know they makes them greedy sounds. Eyes all soft and wet. A cross between a puppy and a dying man. But I knowed she was ugly. Head full of pretty hair, but Lord she was ugly."

When Sammy and Pecola were still young Pauline had to go back to work. She was older now, with no time for dreams and movies. It was time to put all of the pieces together, make coherence where before there had been none. The children gave her this need; she herself was no longer a child. So she became, and her process of becoming was like most of ours: she developed a hatred for things that mystified or obstructed her; acquired virtues that were easy to maintain; assigned herself a role in the scheme of things; and harked back to simpler times for gratification.

She took on the full responsibility and recognition of breadwinner and returned to church. First, however, she moved out of the two rooms into a spacious first floor of a building that had been built as a store. She came into her own with the women who had despised her, by being more moral than they; she avenged herself on Cholly by forcing him to indulge in the weaknesses she despised. She joined a church where shouting was frowned upon, served on Stewardess Board No. 3, and became a member of Ladies Circle No. 1. At prayer meeting she moaned and sighed over Cholly's ways, and hoped God would help her keep the children from the sins of the father. She stopped saying "chil'ren" and said "childring" instead. She let another tooth fall, and was outraged by painted ladies who thought only of clothes and men. Holding Cholly as a model of sin and failure, she bore him like a crown of thorns, and her children like a cross.

It was her good fortune to find a permanent job in the home of a well-to-do family whose members were affectionate, appreciative, and generous. She looked at their houses, smelled their linen, touched their silk draperies, and loved all of it. The child's pink nightie, the stacks of white pillow slips edged with embroidery, the sheets with top hems picked out with blue cornflowers. She became what is known as an ideal servant, for such a role filled practically all of her needs. When she bathed the little Fisher girl, it was in a porcelain tub with silvery taps running infinite quantities of hot, clear water. She dried her in fluffy white towels and put her in cuddly night clothes. Then she brushed the yellow hair, enjoying the roll and slip of it between her fingers. No zinc tub, no buckets of stove-heated water, no flaky, stiff, grayish towels washed in a kitchen sink, dried in a dusty backyard, no tangled black puffs of rough wool to comb. Soon she stopped trying to keep her own house. The things she could afford to buy did not last, had no beauty or style, and were absorbed by the dingy storefront. More and more she neglected her house, her children, her man—they were like the afterthoughts one has just before sleep, the early-morning and late-evening edges of her day, the dark edges that made the daily life with the Fishers lighter, more delicate, more lovely. Here she could arrange things, clean things, line things up in neat rows. Here her foot flopped around on deep pile carpets, and there was no uneven sound. Here she found beauty, order, cleanliness, and praise. Mr. Fisher said, "I would rather sell her blueberry cobblers than real estate." She reigned over cupboards stacked high with food that would not be eaten for weeks, even months; she was queen of canned vegetables bought by the case, special fondants and ribbon candy curled up in tiny silver dishes. The creditors and service people who humiliated her when she went to them on her own behalf respected her, were even intimidated by her, when she spoke for the Fishers. She refused beef slighty dark or with edges not properly trimmed. The slightly reeking fish that she accepted for her own family she would all but throw in the fish man's face if he sent it to the Fisher house. Power, praise, and luxury were hers in this household. They even gave her what she had never had—a nickname—Polly. It was her pleasure to stand in her kitchen at the end of a day and survey her handiwork. Knowing there were soap bars by the dozen, bacon by the rasher, and reveling in her shiny pots and pans and polished floors. Hearing, "We'll never let her go. We could never find anybody like Polly. She will *not* leave the kitchen until everything is in order. Really, she is the ideal servant."

Pauline kept this order, this beauty, for herself, a private world, and never introduced it into her storefront, or to her children. Them she bent toward respectability, and in so doing taught them fear: fear of being clumsy, fear of being like their father, fear of not being loved by God, fear of madness like Cholly's mother's. Into her son she beat a loud desire to run away, and into her daughter she beat a fear of growing up, fear of other people, fear of life.

All the meaningfulness of her life was in her work. For her virtues were intact. She was an active church woman, did not drink, smoke, or carouse, defended herself mightily against Cholly, rose above him in every way, and felt she was fulfilling a mother's role conscientiously when she pointed out their father's faults to keep them from having them, or punished them when they showed any slovenliness, no matter how slight, when she worked twelve to sixteen hours a day to support them. And the world itself agreed with her.

It was only sometimes, sometimes, and then rarely, that she thought about the old days, or what her life had turned to. They were musings, idle thoughts, full sometimes of the old dreaminess, but not the kind of thing she cared to dwell on.

"I started to leave him once, but something came up. Once, after he tried to set the house on fire, I was all set in my mind to go. I can't even 'member now what held me. He sure ain't give me much of a life. But it wasn't all bad. Sometimes things wasn't all bad. He used to come easing into bed sometimes, not too drunk. I make out like I'm asleep, 'cause it's late, and he taken three dollars out of my pocketbook that morning or something. I hear him breathing, but I don't look around. I can see in my mind's eye his black arms thrown back behind his head, the muscles like great big peach stones sanded down, with veins running like little swollen rivers down his arms. Without touching him I be feeling those ridges on the tips of my fingers. I sees the palms of his hands calloused to granite, and the long fingers curled up and still. I think about the thick, knotty hair on his chest, and the two big swells his breast muscles make. I want to rub my face hard in his chest and feel the hair cut my skin. I know just where the hair growth slacks out—just above his navel—and how it picks up again and spreads out. Maybe he'll shift a little, and his leg will touch me, or I feel his flank just graze my behind. I don't move even yet. Then he lift his head, turn over, and put his hand on my waist. If I don't move, he'll move his hand over to pull and knead my stomach. Soft and slow-like. I still don't move, because I don't want him to stop. I want to pretend sleep and have him keep on rubbing my stomach. Then he will lean his head down and bite my tit. Then I don't want him to rub my stomach anymore. I want him to put his hand between my legs. I pretend to wake up, and turn to him, but not opening my legs. I want him to open them for me. He does, and I be soft and wet where his fingers are strong and hard. I be softer than I ever been

before. All my strength in his hand. My brain curls up like wilted leaves. A funny, empty feeling is in my hands. I want to grab holt of something, so I hold his head. His mouth is under my chin. Then I don't want his hand between my legs no more, because I think I am softening away. I stretch my legs open, and he is on top of me. Too heavy to hold, and too light not to. He puts his thing in me. In me. In me. I wrap my feet around his back so he can't get away. His face is next to mine. The bed springs sounds like them crickets used to back home. He puts his fingers in mine, and we stretches our arms outwise like Jesus on the cross. I hold on tight. My fingers and my feet hold on tight, because everything else is going, going. I know he wants me to come first. But I can't. Not until he does. Not until I feel him loving me. Just me. Sinking into me. Not until I know that my flesh is all that be on his mind. That he couldn't stop if he had to. That he would die rather than take his thing out of me. Of me. Not until he has let go of all he has, and give it to me. To me. To me. When he does, I feel a power. I be strong, I be pretty, I be young. And then I wait. He shivers and tosses his head. Now I be strong enough, pretty enough, and young enough to let him make me come. I take my fingers out of his and put my hands on his behind. My legs drop back onto the bed. I don't make no noise, because the chil'ren might hear. I begin to feel those little bits of color floating up into me—deep in me. That streak of green from the june-bug light, the purple from the berries trickling along my thighs, Mama's lemonade yellow runs sweet in me. Then I feel like I'm laughing between my legs, and the laughing gets all mixed up with the colors, and I'm afraid I'll come, and afraid I won't. But I know I will. And I do. And it be rainbow all inside. And it lasts and lasts and lasts. I want to thank him, but don't know how, so I pat him like you do a baby. He asks me if I'm all right. I say yes. He gets off me and lies down to sleep. I want to say something, but I don't. I don't want to take my mind offen the rainbow. I should get up and go to the toilet, but I don't. Besides, Cholly is asleep with his leg throwed over me. I can't move and don't want to.

"But it ain't like that anymore. Most times he's thrashing away inside me before I'm woke, and through when I am. The rest of the time I can't even be next to his stinking drunk self. But I don't care 'bout it no more. My Maker will take care of me. I know He will. I know He will. Besides, it don't make no difference about this old

earth. There is sure to be a glory. Only thing I miss sometimes is that rainbow. But like I say, I don't recollect it much anymore."

SEEFATHERHEISBIGANDSTRONGFATHERWILLYOUPLAY WITHJANEFATHERISSMILINGSMILEFATHERSMILESMILES

When Cholly was four days old, his mother wrapped him in two blankets and one newspaper and placed him on a junk heap by the railroad. His Great Aunt Jimmy, who had seen her niece carrying a bundle out of the back door, rescued him. She beat his mother with a razor strap and wouldn't let her near the baby after that. Aunt Jimmy raised Cholly herself, but took delight sometimes in telling him of how she had saved him. He gathered from her that his mother wasn't right in the head. But he never had a chance to find out, because she ran away shortly after the razor strap, and no one had heard of her since.

Cholly was grateful for having been saved. Except sometimes. Sometimes when he watched Aunt Jimmy eating collards with her fingers, sucking her four gold teeth, or smelled her when she wore the asafetida bag around her neck, or when she made him sleep with her for warmth in winter and he could see her old, wrinkled breasts sagging in her nightgown—then he wondered whether it would have been just as well to have died there. Down in the rim of a tire under a soft black Georgia sky.

He had four years of school before he got courage enough to ask his aunt who and where his father was.

"That Fuller boy, I believe it was," his aunt said. "He was hanging around then, but he taken off pretty quick before you was born. I think he gone to Macon. Him or his brother. Maybe both. I hear old man Fuller say something 'bout it once."

"What name he have?" asked Cholly.

"Fuller, Foolish."

"I mean what his given name?"

"Oh." She closed her eyes to think, and sighed. "Can't recollect nothing no more. Sam, was it? Yeh. Samuel. No. No, it wasn't. It was Samson. Samson Fuller."

"How come you all didn't name me Samson?" Cholly's voice was low.

"What for? He wasn't nowhere around when you was born. Your mama didn't name you nothing. The nine days wasn't up before she throwed you on the junk heap. When I got you I named you myself on the ninth day. You named after my dead brother. Charles Breedlove. A good man. Ain't no Samson never come to no good end."

Cholly didn't ask anything else.

Two years later he quit school to take a job at Tyson's Feed and Grain Store. He swept up, ran errands, weighed bags, and lifted them onto the drays. Sometimes they let him ride with the drayman. A nice old man called Blue Jack. Blue used to tell him old-timey stories about how it was when the Emancipation Proclamation came. How the black people hollered, cried, and sang. And ghost stories about how a white man cut off his wife's head and buried her in the swamp, and the headless body came out at night and went stumbling around the yard, knocking over stuff because it couldn't see, and crying all the time for a comb. They talked about the women Blue had had, and the fights he'd been in when he was younger, about how he talked his way out of getting lynched once, and how others hadn't.

Cholly loved Blue. Long after he was a man, he remembered the good times they had had. How on a July 4 at a church picnic a family was about to break open a watermelon. Several children were standing around watching. Blue was hovering about on the periphery of the circle—a faint smile of anticipation softening his face. The father of the family lifted the melon high over his head—his big arms looked taller than the trees to Cholly, and the melon blotted out the sun. Tall, head forward, eyes fastened on a rock, his arms higher than the pines, his hands holding a melon bigger than the sun, he paused an instant to get his bearing and secure his aim. Watching the figure etched against the bright blue sky, Cholly felt goose pimples popping along his arms and neck. He wondered if God looked like that. No. God was a nice old white man, with long white hair, flowing white beard, and little blue eyes that looked sad when people died and mean when they were bad. It must be the devil who looks like that—holding the world in his hands, ready to dash it to the ground and spill the red guts so niggers could eat the sweet, warm insides. If the devil did look like that, Cholly preferred him. He never felt anything thinking about God, but just the idea of the devil excited him. And now the strong, black devil was blotting out the sun and getting ready to split open the world.

Far away somebody was playing a mouth organ; the music slithered over the cane fields and into the pine grove; it spiraled around the tree trunks and mixed itself with the pine scent, so Cholly couldn't tell the difference between the sound and the odor that hung about the heads of the people.

The man swung the melon down to the edge of a rock. A soft cry of disappointment accompanied the sound of smashed rind. The break was a bad one. The melon was jagged, and hunks of rind and red meat scattered on the grass.

Blue jumped. "Aw—awww," he moaned, "dere go da heart." His voice was both sad and pleased. Everybody looked to see the big red chunk from the very center of the melon, free of rind and sparse of seed which had rolled a little distance from Blue's feet. He stooped to pick it up. Blood red, its planes dull and blunted with sweetness, its edges rigid with juice. Too obvious, almost obscene, in the joy it promised.

"Go 'head, Blue," the father laughed. "You can have it."

Blue smiled and walked away. Little children scrambled for the pieces on the ground. Women picked out the seeds for the smallest ones and broke off little bits of the meat for themselves. Blue's eye caught Cholly's. He motioned to him. "Come on, boy. Les' you and me eat the heart."

Together the old man and the boy sat on the grass and shared the heart of the watermelon. The nasty-sweet guts of the earth.

It was in the spring, a very chilly spring, that Aunt Jimmy died of peach cobbler. She went to a camp meeting that took place after a rainstorm, and the damp wood of the benches was bad for her. For four or five days afterward, she felt poorly. Friends came to see about her. Some made camomile tea; others rubbed her with liniment. Miss Alice, her closest friend, read the Bible to her. Still she was declining. Advice was prolific, if contradictory.

"Don't eat no whites of eggs."

"Drink new milk."

"Chew on this root."

Aunt Jimmy ignored all but Miss Alice's Bible reading. She nodded in drowsy appreciation as the words from First Corinthians droned over her. Sweet amens fell from her lips as she was chastised for all her sins. But her body would not respond.

Finally it was decided to fetch M'Dear. M'Dear was a quiet woman who lived in a shack near the woods. She was a competent midwife and decisive diagnostician. Few could remember when M'Dear was not around. In any illness that could not be handled by ordinary means—known cures, intuition, or endurance—the word was always, "Fetch M'Dear."

When she arrived at Aunt Jimmy's house, Cholly was amazed at the sight of her. He had always pictured her as shriveled and hunched over, for he knew she was very, very old. But M'Dear loomed taller than the preacher who accompanied her. She must have been over six feet tall. Four big white knots of hair gave power and authority to her soft black face. Standing straight as a poker, she seemed to need her hickory stick not for support but for communication. She tapped it lightly on the floor as she looked down at Aunt Jimmy's wrinkled face. She stroked the knob with the thumb of her right hand while she ran her left one over Aunt Jimmy's body. The backs of her long fingers she placed on the patient's cheek, then placed her palm on the forehead. She ran her fingers through the sick woman's hair, lightly scratching the scalp, and then looking at what the fingernails revealed. She lifted Aunt Jimmy's hand and looked closely at it—fingernails, back skin, the flesh of the palm she pressed with three fingertips. Later she put her ear on Aunt Jimmy's chest and stomach to listen. At M'Dear's request, the women pulled the slop jar from under the bed to show the stools. M'Dear tapped her stick while looking at them.

"Bury the slop jar and everything in it," she said to the women. To Aunt Jimmy she said, "You done caught cold in your womb. Drink pot liquor and nothing else."

"Will it pass?" asked Aunt Jimmy. "Is I'm gone be all right?"

"I reckon."

M'Dear turned and left the room. The preacher put her in his buggy to take her home.

That evening the women brought bowls of pot liquor from black-eyed peas, from mustards, from cabbage, from kale, from collards, from turnips, from beets, from green beans. Even the juice from a boiling hog jowl.

Two evenings later Aunt Jimmy had gained much strength. When Miss Alice and Mrs. Gaines stopped in to check on her, they remarked on her improvement. The three women sat talking about various miseries they had had, their cure or abatement, what had helped. Over and over again they returned to Aunt Jimmy's condition. Repeating its cause, what could have been done to prevent the misery from taking hold, and M'Dear's infallibility. Their voices blended into a threnody of nostalgia about pain. Rising and falling, complex in harmony, uncertain in pitch, but constant in the recitative of pain. They hugged the memories of illnesses to their bosoms. They licked their lips and clucked their tongues in fond remembrance of pains they had endured—childbirth, rheumatism, croup, sprains, backaches, piles. All of the bruises they had collected from moving about the earth—harvesting, cleaning, hoisting, pitching, stooping, kneeling, picking—always with young ones underfoot.

But they had been young once. The odor of their armpits and haunches had mingled into a lovely musk; their eyes had been furtive, their lips relaxed, and the delicate turn of their heads on those slim black necks had been like nothing other than a doe's. Their laughter had been more touch than sound.

Then they had grown. Edging into life from the back door. Becoming. Everybody in the world was in a position to give them orders. White women said, "Do this." White children said, "Give me that." White men said, "Come here." Black men said, "Lay down." The only people they need not take orders from were black children and each other. But they took all of that and re-created it in their own image. They ran the houses of white people, and knew it. When white men beat their men, they cleaned up the blood and went home to receive abuse from the victim. They beat their children with one hand and stole for them with the other. The hands that felled trees also cut umbilical cords; the hands that wrung the necks of chickens and butchered hogs also nudged African violets into bloom; the arms that loaded sheaves, bales, and sacks rocked babies into sleep. They patted biscuits into flaky ovals of innocence—and shrouded the dead. They plowed all day and came home to nestle like plums under the limbs of their men. The legs that straddled a mule's back were the same ones that straddled their men's hips. And the difference was all the difference there was.

Then they were old. Their bodies honed, their odor sour. Squatting in a cane field, stooping in a cotton field, kneeling by a river bank, they had carried a world on their heads. They had given over the lives of their own children and tendered their grandchildren. With relief they wrapped their heads in rags, and their breasts in flannel; eased their feet into felt. They were through with lust and lactation, beyond tears and terror. They alone could walk the roads of Mississippi, the lanes of Georgia, the fields of Alabama unmolested. They were old enough to be irritable when and where they chose, tired enough to look forward to death, disinterested enough to accept the idea of pain while ignoring the presence of pain. They were, in fact and at last, free. And the lives of these old black women were synthesized in their eyes—a purée of tragedy and humor, wickedness and serenity, truth and fantasy.

They chattered far into the night. Cholly listened and grew sleepy. The lullaby of grief enveloped him, rocked him, and at last numbed him. In his sleep the foul odor of an old woman's stools turned into the healthy smell of horse shit, and the voices of the three women were muted into the pleasant notes of a mouth organ. He was aware, in his sleep, of being curled up in a chair, his hands tucked between his thighs. In a dream his penis changed into a long hickory stick, and the hands caressing it were the hands of M'Dear.

On a wet Saturday night, before Aunt Jimmy felt strong enough to get out of the bed, Essie Foster brought her a peach cobbler. The old lady ate a piece, and the next morning when Cholly went to empty the slop jar, she was dead. Her mouth was a slackened O, and her hands, those long fingers with a man's hard nails, having done their laying by, could now be dainty on the sheet. One open eye looked at him as if to say, "Mind how you take holt of that jar, boy." Cholly stared back, unable to move, until a fly settled at the corner of her mouth. He fanned it away angrily, looked back at the eye, and did its bidding.

Aunt Jimmy's funeral was the first Cholly had ever attended. As a member of the family, one of the bereaved, he was the object of a great deal of attention. The ladies had cleaned the house, aired everything out, notified everybody, and stitched together what looked like a white wedding dress for Aunt Jimmy, a maiden lady, to wear when she met Jesus. They even produced a dark suit, white shirt, and tie for Cholly. The husband of one of them cut his hair. He was enclosed in fastidious tenderness. Nobody talked to him; that is, they treated him like the child he was, never engaging him in serious conversation; but they anticipated wishes he never had: meals appeared, hot water for the wooden tub, clothes laid out. At the wake he was allowed to fall asleep, and arms carried him to bed. Only on the third day after the death—the day of the funeral—did he have to share the spotlight. Aunt Jimmy's people came from nearby towns and farms. Her brother O. V., his children and wife, and lots of cousins. But Cholly was still the major figure, because he was "Jimmy's boy, the last thing she loved," and "the one who found her." The solicitude of the women, the head pats of the men, pleased Cholly, and the creamy conversations fascinated him.

"What'd she die from?"

"Essie's pie."

"Don't say?"

"Uh-huh. She was doing fine, I saw her the very day before. Said she wanted me to bring her some black thread to patch some things for the boy. I should of known just from her wanting black thread that was a sign."

"Sure was."

"Just like Emma. 'Member? She kept asking for thread. Dropped dead that very evening."

"Yeah. Well, she was determined to have it. Kept on reminding me. I told her I had some to home, but naw, she wanted it new. So I sent Li'l June to get some that very morning when she was laying dead. I was just fixing to bring it over, 'long with a piece of sweet bread. You know how she craved my sweet bread."

"Sure did. Always bragged on it. She was a good friend to you."

"I believe it. Well, I had no more got my clothes on when Sally bust in the door hollering about how Cholly here had been over to Miss Alice saying she was dead. You could have knocked me over, I tell you."

"Guess Essie feels mighty bad."

"Oh, Lord, yes. But I told her the Lord giveth and the Lord taketh away. Wasn't her fault none. She makes good peach pies. But she bound to believe it was the pie did it, and I 'spect she right."

"Well, she shouldn't worry herself none 'bout that. She was just doing what we all would of done."

"Yeah. 'Cause I was sure wrapping up that sweet bread, and that could of done it too."

"I doubts that. Sweet bread is pure. But a pie is the worse thing to give anybody ailing. I'm surprised Jimmy didn't know better."

"If she did, she wouldn't let on. She would have tried to please. You know how she was. So good."

"I'll say. Did she leave anything?"

"Not even a pocket handkerchief. The house belongs to some white folks in Clarksville."

"Oh, yeah? I thought she owned it."

"May have at one time. But not no more. I hear the insurance folks been down talking to her brother."

"How much do it come to?"

"Eighty-five dollars, I hear."

"That all?"

"Can she get in the ground on that?"

"Don't see how. When my daddy died last year this April it costed one hundred and fifty dollars. 'Course, we had to have everything just so. Now Jimmy's people may all have to chip in. That undertaker that lays out black folks ain't none too cheap."

"Seems a shame. She been paying on that insurance all her life."

"Don't I know?"

"Well, what about the boy? What he gone do?"

"Well, caint nobody find that mama, so Jimmy's brother gone take him back to his place. They say he got a nice place. Inside toilet and everything."

"That's nice. He seems like a good Christian man. And the boy need a man's hand."

"What time's the funeral?"

"Two clock. She ought to be in the ground by four."

"Where's the banquet? I heard Essie wanted it at her house."

"Naw, it's at Jimmy's. Her brother wanted it so."

"Well, it will be a big one. Everybody liked old Jimmy. Sure will miss her in the pew."

The funeral banquet was a peal of joy after the thunderous beauty of the funeral. It was like a street tragedy with spontaneity tucked softly into the corners of a highly formal structure. The deceased was the tragic hero, the survivors the innocent victims; there was the omnipresence of the deity, strophe and antistrophe of the chorus of mourners led by the preacher. There was grief over the waste of life, the stunned wonder at the ways of God, and the restoration of order in nature at the graveyard.

Thus the banquet was the exultation, the harmony, the acceptance of physical frailty, joy in the termination of misery. Laughter, relief, a steep hunger for food.

Cholly had not yet fully realized his aunt was dead. Everything was so interesting. Even at the graveyard he felt nothing but curiosity, and when his turn had come to view the body at the church, he had put his hand out to touch the corpse to see if it were really ice cold like everybody said. But he drew his hand back quickly. Aunt Jimmy looked so private, and it seemed wrong somehow to disturb that privacy. He had trudged back to his pew dry-eyed amid tearful shrieks and shouts of others, wondering if he should try to cry.

Back in his house, he was free to join in the gaiety and enjoy what he really felt—a kind of carnival spirit. He ate greedily and felt good enough to try to get to know his cousins. There was some question, according to the adults, as to whether they were his real cousins or not, since Jimmy's brother O. V. was only a half-brother, and Cholly's mother had been the daughter of Jimmy's sister, but that sister was from the second marriage of Jimmy's father, and O. V. was from the first marriage.

One of these cousins interested Cholly in particular. He was about fifteen or sixteen years old. Cholly went outside and found the boy standing with some others near the tub where Aunt Jimmy used to boil her clothes.

He ventured a tentative "Hey." They responded with another. The fifteen-year-old named Jake offered Cholly a rolled-up cigarette. Cholly took it, but when he held the cigarette at arm's length and stuck the tip of it into the match flame, instead of putting it in his mouth and drawing on it, they laughed at him. Shamefaced, he threw the cigarette down. He felt it important to do something to reinstate himself with Jake. So when he asked Cholly if he knew any girls, Cholly said, "Sure."

All the girls Cholly knew were at the banquet, and he pointed to a cluster of them standing, hanging, draping on the back porch. Darlene too. Cholly hoped Jake wouldn't pick her.

"Let's get some and walk around," said Jake.

The two boys sauntered over to the porch. Cholly didn't know how to begin. Jake wrapped his legs around the rickety porch rail and just sat there staring off into space as though he had no interest in them at all. He was letting them look him over, and guardedly evaluating them in return.

The girls pretended they didn't see the boys and kept on chattering. Soon their talk got sharp; the gentle teasing they had been engaged in with each other changed to bitchiness, a serious kind of making fun. That was Jake's clue; the girls were reacting to him. They had gotten a whiff of his manhood and were shivering for a place in his attention.

Jake left the porch rail and walked right up to a girl named Suky, the one who had been most bitter in her making fun.

"Want to show me 'round?" He didn't even smile.

Cholly held his breath, waiting for Suky to shut Jake up. She was good at that, and well known for her sharp tongue. To his enormous surprise, she readily agreed, and even lowered her lashes. Taking courage, Cholly turned to Darlene and said, "Come on 'long. We just going down to the gully." He waited for her to screw up her face and say no, or what for, or some such thing. His feelings about her were mostly fear—fear that she would not like him, and fear that she would.

His second fear materialized. She smiled and jumped down the three leaning steps to join him. Her eyes were full of compassion, and Cholly remembered that he was the bereaved.

"If you want to," she said, "but not too far. Mama said we got to leave early, and its getting dark."

The four of them moved away. Some of the other boys had come to the porch and were about to begin that partly hostile, partly indifferent, party desperate mating dance. Suky, Jake, Darlene, and Cholly walked through several backyards until they came to an open field. They ran across it and came to a dry riverbed lined with green. The object of the walk was a wild vineyard where the muscadine grew. Too new, too tight to have much sugar, they were eaten anyway. None of them wanted—not then—the grape's easy relinquishing of all its dark juice. The restraint, the holding off, the promise of sweetness that had yet to unfold, excited them more than full ripeness would have done. At last their teeth were on edge, and the boys diverted themselves by pelting the girls with the grapes. Their slim black boy wrists made G clefs in the air as they executed the tosses. The chase took Cholly and Darlene away from the lip of the gully, and when they paused for breath, Jake and Suky were nowhere in sight. Darlene's white cotton dress was stained with juice. Her big blue hair bow had come undone, and the sundown breeze was picking it up and fluttering it about her head. They were out of breath and sank down in the green-and-purple grass on the edge of the pine woods.

Cholly lay on his back panting. His mouth full of the taste of muscadine, listening to the pine needles rustling loudly in their anticipation of rain. The smell of promised rain, pine, and muscadine made him giddy. The sun had gone and pulled away its shreds of light. Turning his head to see where the moon was, Cholly caught sight of Darlene in moonlight behind him. She was huddled into a D—arms encircling drawn-up knees, on which she rested her head. Cholly could see her bloomers and the muscles of her young thighs.

"We bed' get on back," he said.

"Yeah." She stretched her legs flat on the ground and began to retie her hair ribbon. "Mama gone whup me."

"Naw she ain't."

"Uh-huh. She told me she would if I get dirty."

"You ain't dirty."

"I am too. Looka that." She dropped her hands from the ribbon and smoothed out a place on her dress where the grape stains were heaviest.

Cholly felt sorry for her; it was just as much his fault. Suddenly he realized that Aunt Jimmy was dead, for he missed the fear of being whipped. There was nobody to do it except Uncle O. V., and he was the bereaved too.

"Let me," he said. He rose to his knees facing her and tried to tie her ribbon. Darlene put her hands under his open shirt and rubbed the damp tight skin. When he looked at her in surprise, she stopped and laughed. He smiled and continued knotting the bow. She put her hands back under his shirt.

"Hold still," he said. "How I gone get this?"

She tickled his ribs with her fingertips. He giggled and grabbed his rib cage. They were on top of each other in a moment. She corkscrewing her hands into his clothes. He returning the play, digging into the neck of her dress, and then under her dress. When he got his hand in her bloomers, she suddenly stopped laughing and looked serious. Cholly, frightened, was about to take his hand away, but she held his wrist so he couldn't move it. He examined her then with his fingers, and she kissed his face and mouth. Cholly found her muscadine-lipped mouth distracting. Darlene released his head, shifted her body, and pulled down her pants. After some trouble with the buttons, Cholly dropped his pants down to his knees. Their bodies began to make sense to him, and it was not as difficult as he had thought it would be. She moaned a little, but the excitement collecting inside him made him close his eyes and regard her moans as no more than pine sighs over his head. Just as he felt an explosion threaten, Darlene froze and cried out. He thought he had hurt her, but when he looked at her face, she was staring wildly at something over his shoulder. He jerked around.

There stood two white men. One with a spirit lamp, the other with a flashlight. There was no mistake about their being white; he could smell it. Cholly jumped, trying to kneel, stand, and get his pants up all in one motion. The men had long guns.

"Hee hee hee heeeee." The snicker was a long asthmatic cough.

The other raced the flashlight all over Cholly and Darlene.

"Get on wid it, nigger," said the flashlight one.

"Sir?" said Cholly, trying to find a buttonhole.

"I said, get on wid it. An' make it good, nigger, make it good."

There was no place for Cholly's eyes to go. They slid about furtively searching for shelter, while his body remained paralyzed. The flashlight man lifted his gun down from his shoulder, and Cholly heard the clop of metal. He dropped back to his knees. Darlene had her head averted, her eyes staring out of the lamplight into the surrounding darkness and looking almost unconcerned, as though they had no part in the drama taking place around them. With a violence born of total helplessness, he pulled her dress up, lowered his trousers and underwear.

"Hee hee hee hee heeeeee."

Darlene put her hands over her face as Cholly began to simulate what had gone on before. He could do no more than make-believe. The flashlight made a moon on his behind.

"Hee hee hee hee heeee."

"Come on, coon. Faster. You ain't doing nothing for her."

"Hee hee hee hee heeee."

Cholly, moving faster, looked at Darlene. He hated her. He almost wished he could do it—hard, long, and painfully, he hated her so much. The flashight wormed its way into his guts and turned the sweet taste of muscadine into rotten fetid bile. He stared at Darlene's hands covering her face in the moon and lamplight. They looked like baby claws.

"Hee hee hee hee heee."

Some dogs howled. "Thas them. Thas them. I know thas Old Honey."

"Yep," said the spirit lamp.

"Come on." The flashlight turned away, and one of them whistled to Honey.

"Wait," said the spirit lamp, "the coon ain't comed yet."

"Well, he have to come on his own time. Good luck, coon baby."

They crushed the pine needles underfoot. Cholly could hear them whistling for a long time, and then the dogs' answer no longer a howl, but warm excited yelps of recognition.

Cholly raised himself and in silence buttoned his trousers. Darlene did not move. Cholly wanted to strangle her, but instead he touched her leg with his foot. "We got to get, girl. Come on!"

She reached for her underwear with her eyes closed, and could not find them. The two of them patted about in the moonlight for the panties. When she found them, she put them on with the movements of an old woman. They walked away from the pine woods toward the road. He in front, she plopping along behind. It started to rain. "That's good," Cholly thought. "It will explain away our clothes."

When they got back to the house, some ten or twelve guests were still there. Jake was gone, Suky too. Some people had gone back for more helpings of food—potato pie, ribs. All were engrossed in early-night reminiscences about dreams, figures, premonitions. Their stuffed comfort was narcotic and had produced recollections and fabrications of hallucinations.

Cholly and Darlene's entrance produced only a mild stir.

"Ya'll soaked, ain't you?"

Darlene's mother was only vaguely fussy. She had eaten and drunk too much. Her shoes were under her chair, and the side snaps of her dress were opened. "Girl. Come on in here. Thought I told you . . ."

Some of the guests thought they would wait for the rain to slacken. Others, who had come in wagons, thought they'd best leave now. Cholly went into the little storeroom which had been made into a bedroom for him. Three infants were sleeping on his cot. He took off his rain- and pine-soaked clothes and put on his coveralls. He didn't know where to go. Aunt Jimmy's room was out of the question, and Uncle O. V. and his wife would be using it later anyway. He took a quilt from a trunk, spread it on the floor, and lay down. Somebody was brewing coffee, and he had a sharp craving for it, just before falling asleep.

The next day was cleaning-out day, settling accounts, distributing Aunt Jimmy's goods. Mouths were set in downward crescents, eyes veiled, feet tentative.

Cholly floated about aimlessly, doing chores as he was told. All the glamour and warmth the adults had given him on the previous day were replaced by a sharpness that agreed with his mood. He could think only of the flashlight, the muscadines, and Darlene's hands. And when he was not thinking of them, the vacancy in his head was like the space left by a newly pulled tooth still conscious of the rottenness that had once filled it. Afraid of running into Darlene, he would not go far from the house, but neither could he endure the atmosphere of his dead Aunt's house. The picking through her things, the comments on the "condition" of her goods. Sullen, irritable, he cultivated his hatred of Darlene. Never did he once consider directing his hatred toward the hunters. Such an emotion would have destroyed him. They were big, white, armed men. He was small, black, helpless. His subconscious knew what his conscious mind did not guess—that hating them would have consumed him, burned him up like a piece of soft coal, leaving only flakes of ash and a question mark of smoke. He was, in time, to discover that hatred of white men—but not now. Not in impotence but later, when the hatred could find sweet expression. For now, he hated the one who had created the situation, the one who bore witness to his failure, his impotence. The one whom he had not been able to protect, to spare, to cover from the round moon glow of the flashlight. The hee-hee-hee's. He recalled Darlene's dripping hair ribbon, flapping against her face as they walked back in silence in the rain. The loathing that galloped through him made him tremble. There was no one to talk to. Old Blue was too drunk too often these days to make sense. Besides, Cholly doubted if he could reveal his shame to Blue. He would have to lie a little to tell Blue, Blue the woman-killer. It seemed to him that lonely was much better than alone.

The day Cholly's uncle was ready to leave, when everything was packed, when the quarrels about who gets what had seethed down to a sticking gravy on everybody's tongue, Cholly sat on the back porch waiting. It had occurred to him that Darlene might be pregnant. It was a wildly irrational, completely uninformed idea, but the fear it produced was complete enough.

He had to get away. Never mind the fact that he was leaving that very day. A town or two away was not far enough, especially since he did not like or trust his uncle, and Darlene's mother could surely find him, and Uncle O. V. would turn him over to her. Cholly knew it was wrong to run out on a pregnant girl, and recalled, with sympathy, that his father had done just that. Now he understood. He knew then what he must do—find his father. His father would understand. Aunt Jimmy said he had gone to Macon.

With no more thought than a chick leaving its shell, he stepped off the porch. He had gotten a little way when he remembered the treasure; Aunt Jimmy had left something, and he had forgotten all about it. In a stove flue no longer used, she had hidden a little meal bag which she called her treasure. He slipped into the house and found the room empty. Digging into the flue, he encountered webs and soot, and then the soft bag. He sorted the money; fourteen one-dollar bills, two two-dollar bills, and lots of silver change

. . . twenty-three dollars in all. Surely that would be enough to get to Macon. What a good, strong-sounding word, *Macon.*

Running away from home for a Georgia black boy was not a great problem. You just sneaked away and started walking. When night came you slept in a barn, if there were no dogs, a cane field, or an empty sawmill. You ate from the ground and bought root beer and licorice in little country stores. There was always an easy tale of woe to tell inquiring black adults, and whites didn't care, unless they were looking for sport.

When he was several days away, he could go to the back door of nice houses and tell the black cook or white mistress that he wanted a job weeding, plowing, picking, cleaning, and that he lived nearby. A week or more there, and he could take off. He lived this way through the turn of summer, and only the following October did he reach a town big enough to have a regular bus station. Dry-mouthed with excitement and apprehension, he went to the colored side of the counter to buy his ticket.

"How much to Macon, sir?"

"Eleven dollars. Five-fifty for children under twelve."

Cholly had twelve dollars and four cents.

"How old you be?"

"Just on twelve, sir, but my mama only give me ten dollars."

"You jest about the biggest twelve I ever seed."

"Please, sir, I got to get to Macon. My mama's sick."

"Thought you said you mama give you ten dollars."

"That's my play mama. My real mama is in Macon, sir."

"I reckon I knows a lying nigger when I sees one, but jest in case you ain't, jest in case one of them mammies is really dyin' and wants to see her little old smoke before she meets her maker, I gone do it."

Cholly heard nothing. The insults were part of the nuisances of life, like lice. He was happier than he had ever remembered being, except that time with Blue and the watermelon. The bus wasn't leaving for four hours, and the minutes of those hours struggled like gnats on fly paper—dying slow, exhausted with the fight to stay alive. Cholly was afraid to stir, even to relieve himself. The bus might leave while he was gone. Finally, rigid with constipation, he boarded the bus to Macon.

He found a window seat in the back all to himself, and all of Georgia slid before his eyes, until the sun shrugged out of sight. Even in the dark, he hungered to see, and only after the fiercest fight to keep his eyes open did he fall asleep. When he awoke it was very well into day, and a fat black lady was nudging him with a biscuit gashed with cold bacon. With the taste of bacon still in his teeth, they sidled into Macon.

At the end of the alley he could see men clustered like grapes. One large whooping voice spiraled over the heads of the bended forms. The kneeling forms, the leaning forms, all intent on one ground spot. As he came closer, he inhaled a rife and stimulating man smell. The men were gathered, just as the man in the pool hall had said, for and about dice and money. Each figure was decorated some way with the slight pieces of green. Some of them had separated their money, folded the bills around their fingers, clenched the fingers into fists, so the neat ends of the money stuck out in a blend of daintiness and violence. Others had stacked their bills, creased them down the middle, and held the wad as though they were about to deal cards. Still others had left their money in loosely crumpled balls. One man had money sticking out from under his cap. Another stroked his bills with a thumb and forefinger. There was more money in those black hands than Cholly had ever seen before. He shared their excitement, and the dry-mouthed apprehension on meeting his father gave way to the saliva flow of excitement. He glanced at the faces, looking for the one who might be his father. How would he know him? Would he look like a larger version of himself? At that moment Cholly could not remember what his own self looked like. He only knew he was fourteen years old, black, and already six feet tall. He searched the faces and saw only eyes, pleading eyes, cold eyes, eyes gone flat with malice, others laced with fear—all focused on the movement of a pair of dice that one man was throwing, snatching up, and throwing again. Chanting a kind of litany to which the others responded, rubbing the dice as though they were two hot coals, he whispered to them. Then with a whoop the cubes flew from his hand to a chorus of amazements and disappointments. Then the thrower scooped up money, and someone shouted, "Take it and crawl, you water dog, you, the best I know." There was some laughter, and a noticeable release of tension, during which some men exchanged money.

Cholly tapped an old white-haired man on the back.

"Can you tell me is Samson Fuller 'round here somewhere?"

"Fuller?" The name was familiar to the man's tongue. "I don't know, he here somewhere. They he is. In the brown jacket." The man pointed.

A man in a light-brown jacket stood at the far end of the group. He was gesturing in a quarrelsome, agitated manner with another man. Both of them had folded their faces in anger. Cholly edged around to where they stood, hardly believing he was at the end of his journey. There was his father, a man like any other man, but there indeed were his eyes, his mouth, his whole head. His shoulders lurked beneath that jacket, his voice, his hands—all real. They existed, really existed, somewhere. Right here. Cholly had always thought of his father as a giant of a man, so when he was very close it was with a shock that he discovered that he was taller than his father. In fact, he was staring at a balding spot on his father's head, which he suddenly wanted to stroke. While thus fascinated by the pitiable clean space hedged around by neglected tufts of wool, the man turned a hard, belligerent face to him.

"What you want, boy?"

"Uh. I mean . . . is you Samson Fuller?"

"Who sent you?"

"Huh?"

"You Melba's boy?"

"No, sir, I'm . . ." Cholly blinked. He could not remember his mother's name. Had he ever known it? What could he say? Whose boy was he? He couldn't say, "I'm your boy." That sounded disrespectful.

The man was impatient. "Something wrong with your head? Who told you to come after me?"

"Nobody." Cholly's hands were sweating. The man's eyes frightened him. "I just thought . . . I mean, I was just wandering around, and, uh, my name is Cholly. . . ."

But Fuller had turned back to the game that was about to begin anew. He bent down to toss a bill on the ground, and waited for a throw. When it was gone, he stood up and in a vexed and whiny voice shouted at Cholly, "Tell that bitch she get her money. Now, get the fuck outta my face!"

Cholly was a long time picking his foot up from the ground. He was trying to back up and walk away. Only with extreme effort could he get the first muscle to cooperate. When it did, he walked back up the alley, out of its shade, toward the blazing light of the street. As he emerged into the sun, he felt something in his legs give way. An orange crate with a picture of clasping hands pasted on its side was upended on the sidewalk. Cholly sat down on it. The sunshine dropped like honey on his head. A horse-drawn fruit wagon went by, its driver singing: "Fresh from the vine, sweet as sugar, red as wine."

Noises seemed to increase in volume. The clic-cloc of the women's heels, the laughter of idling men in doorways. There was a streetcar somewhere. Cholly sat. He knew if he was very still he would be all right. But then the trace of pain edged his eyes, and he had to use everything to send it away. If he was very still, he thought, and kept his eyes on one thing, the tears would not come. So he sat in the dripping honey sun, pulling every nerve and muscle into service to stop the fall of water from his eyes. While straining in this way, focusing every erg of energy on his eyes, his bowels suddenly opened up, and before he could realize what he knew, liquid stools were running down his legs. At the mouth of the alley where his father was, on an orange crate in the sun, on a street full of grown men and women, he had soiled himself like a baby.

In panic he wondered should he wait there, not moving until nighttime? No. His father would surely emerge and see him and laugh. Oh, Lord. He would laugh. Everybody would laugh. There was only one thing to do.

Cholly ran down the street, aware only of silence. People's mouths moved, their feet moved, a car jugged by—but with no sound. A door slammed in perfect soundlessness. His own feet made no sound. The air seemed to strangle him, hold him back. He was pushing through a world of invisible pine sap that threatened to smother him. Still he ran, seeing only silent moving things, until he came to the end of buildings, the beginning of open space, and saw the Ocmulgee River winding ahead. He scooted down a gravelly slope to a pier jutting out over the shallow water. Finding the deepest shadow under the pier, he crouched in it, behind one of the posts. He remained knotted there in fetal position, paralyzed, his fists covering his eyes, for a long time. No sound, no sight, only darkness and heat and the press of his knuckles on his eyelids. He even forgot his messed-up trousers.

Evening came. The dark, the warmth, the quiet, enclosed Cholly like the skin and flesh of an elderberry protecting its own seed.

Cholly stirred. The ache in his head was all he felt. Soon, like bright bits of glass, the events of that afternoon cut into him. At first he saw only money in black fingers, then he thought he was sitting on an uncomfortable chair, but when he looked, it turned out to be the head of a man, a head with a bald spot the size of an orange. When finally these bits merged into full memory, Cholly began to smell himself. He stood up and found himself weak, trembling, and dizzy. He leaned for a moment on the pier post, then took off his pants, underwear, socks, and shoes. He rubbed handfuls of dirt on his shoes; then he crawled to the river edge. He had to find the water's beginning with his hands, for he could not see it clearly. Slowly he swirled his clothes in the water and rubbed them until he thought they were clean. Back near his post, he took off his shirt and wrapped it around his waist, then spread his trousers and underwear on the ground. He squatted down and picked at the rotted wood of the pier. Suddenly he thought of his Aunt Jimmy, her asafetida bag, her four gold teeth, and the purple rag she wore around her head. With a longing that almost split him open, he thought of her handing him a bit of smoked hock out of her dish. He remembered just how she held it—clumsy-like, in three fingers, but with so much affection. No words, just picking up a bit of meat and holding it out to him. And then the tears rushed down his cheeks, to make a bouquet under his chin.

Three women are leaning out of two windows. They see the long clean neck of a new young boy and call to him. He goes to where they are. Inside, it is dark and warm. They give him lemonade in a Mason jar. As he drinks, their eyes float up to him through the bottom of the jar, through the slick sweet water. They give him back his manhood, which he takes aimlessly.

The pieces of Cholly's life could become coherent only in the head of a musician. Only those who talk their talk through the gold of curved metal, or in the touch of black-and-white rectangles and taut skins and strings echoing from wooden corridors, could give true form to his life. Only they would know how to connect the heart of a red watermelon to the asafetida bag to the muscadine to the flashlight on his behind to the fists of money to the lemonade in a Mason jar to a man called Blue and come up with what all of that meant in joy, in pain, in anger, in love, and give it its final and pervading ache of freedom. Only a musician would sense, know, without even knowing that he knew, that Cholly was free. Dangerously free. Free to feel whatever he felt—fear, guilt, shame, love, grief, pity. Free to be tender or violent, to whistle or weep. Free to sleep in doorways or between the white sheets of a singing woman. Free to take a job, free to leave it. He could go to jail and not feel imprisoned, for he had already seen the furtiveness in the eyes of his jailer, free to say, "No, suh," and smile, for he had already killed three white men. Free to take a woman's insults, for his body had already conquered hers. Free even to knock her in the head, for he had already cradled that head in his arms. Free to be gentle when she was sick, or mop her floor, for she knew what and where his maleness was. He was free to drink himself into a silly helplessness, for he had already been a gandy dancer, done thirty days on a chain gang, and picked a woman's bullet out of the calf of his leg. He was free to live his fantasies, and free even to die, the how and the when of which held no interest for him. In those days, Cholly was truly free. Abandoned in a junk heap by his mother, rejected for a crap game by his father, there was nothing more to lose. He was alone with his own perceptions and appetites, and they alone interested him.

It was in this godlike state that he met Pauline Williams. And it was Pauline, or rather marrying her, that did for him what the flashlight did not do. The constantness, varietylessness, the sheer weight of sameness drove him to despair and froze his imagination. To be required to sleep with the same woman forever was a curious and unnatural idea to him; to be expected to dredge up enthusiasms for old acts, and routine ploys; he wondered at the arrogance of the female. When he had met Pauline in Kentucky, she was hanging over a fence scratching herself with a broken foot. The neatness, the charm, the joy he awakened in her made him want to nest with her. He had yet to discover what destroyed that desire. But he did not dwell on it. He thought rather of whatever had happened to the curiosity he used to feel. Nothing, nothing, interested him now. Not himself, not other people. Only in drink was there some break, some floodlight, and when that closed, there was oblivion.

But the aspect of married life that dumbfounded him and rendered him totally disfunctional was the appearance of children. Having no idea of how to raise children, and having never watched any parent raise himself, he could not even comprehend what such a relationship should be. Had he been interested in the accumulation of things, he could have thought of them as his material heirs; had he needed to prove himself to some nameless "others," he could have wanted them to excel in his own image and for his own sake. He had been alone in the world since he was thirteen, knowing only a dying old woman who felt responsible for him, but whose age, sex, and interests were so remote from his own, he might have felt a stable connection between himself and the children. As it was, he reacted to them, and his reactions were based on what he felt at the moment.

So it was on a Saturday afternoon, in the thin light of spring, he staggered home reeling drunk and saw his daughter in the kitchen.

She was washing dishes. Her small back hunched over the sink. Cholly saw her dimly and could not tell what he saw or what he felt. Then he became aware that he was uncomfortable; next he felt the discomfort dissolve into pleasure. The sequence of his emotions was revulsion, guilt, pity, then love. His revulsion was a reaction to her young, helpless, hopeless presence. Her back hunched that way; her head to one side as though crouching from a permanent and unrelieved blow. Why did she have to look so whipped? She was a child—unburdened—why wasn't she happy? The clear statement of her misery was an accusation. He wanted to break her neck—but tenderly. Guilt and impotence rose in a bilious duet. What could he do for her—ever? What give her? What say to her? What could a burned-out black man say to the hunched back of his eleven-year-old daughter? If he looked into her face, he would see those haunted, loving eyes. The hauntedness would irritate him—the love would move him to fury. How dare she love him? Hadn't she any sense at all? What was he supposed to do about that? Return it? How? What could his calloused hands produce to make her smile? What of his knowledge of the world and of life could be useful to her? What could his heavy arms and befuddled brain accomplish that would earn him his own respect, that would in turn allow him to accept her love? His hatred of her slimed in his stomach and threatened to become vomit. But just before the puke moved from anticipation to sensation, she shifted her weight and stood on one foot scratching the back of her calf with her toe. It was a quiet and pitiful gesture. Her hands were going around and around a frying pan, scraping flecks of black into cold, greasy dishwater. The timid, tucked-in look of the scratching toe—that was what Pauline was doing the first time he saw her in Kentucky. Leaning over a fence staring at nothing in particular. The creamy toe of her bare foot scratching a velvet leg. It was such a small and simple gesture, but it filled him then with a wondering softness. Not the usual lust to part tight legs with his own, but a tenderness, a protectiveness. A desire to cover her foot with his hand and gently nibble away the itch from the calf with his teeth. He did it then, and startled Pauline into laughter. He did it now.

The tenderness welled up in him, and he sank to his knees, his eyes on the foot of his daughter. Crawling on all fours toward her, he raised his hand and caught the foot in an upward stroke. Pecola lost her balance and was about to careen to the floor. Cholly raised his other hand to her hips to save her from falling. He put his head down and nibbled at the back of her leg. His mouth trembled at the firm sweetness of the flesh. He closed his eyes, letting his fingers dig into her waist. The rigidness of her shocked body, the silence of her stunned throat, was better than Pauline's easy laughter had been. The confused mixture of his memories of Pauline and the doing of a wild and forbidden thing excited him, and a bolt of desire ran down his genitals, giving it length, and softening the lips of his anus. Surrounding all of this lust was a border of politeness. He wanted to fuck her—tenderly. But the tenderness would not hold. The tightness of her vagina was more than he could bear. His soul seemed to slip down to his guts and fly out into her, and the gigantic thrust he made into her then provoked the only sound she made—a hollow suck of air in the back of her throat. Like the rapid loss of air from a circus balloon.

Following the disintegration—the falling away—of sexual desire, he was conscious of her wet, soapy hands on his wrists, the fingers clenching, but whether her grip was from a hopeless but stubborn struggle to be free, or from some other emotion, he could not tell.

Removing himself from her was so painful to him he cut it short and snatched his genitals out of the dry harbor of her vagina. She appeared to have fainted. Cholly stood up and could see only her grayish panties, so sad and limp around her ankles. Again the hatred mixed with tenderness. The hatred would not let him pick her up; the tenderness forced him to cover her.

So when the child regained consciousness, she was lying on the kitchen floor under a heavy quilt, trying to connect the pain between her legs with the face of her mother looming over her.

SEETHEDOGBOWBOWGOESTHEDOGDOYOUWANTTOPLAY DOYOUWANTTOPLAYWITHJANESEETHEDOGRUNRUNRUNR

Once there was an old man who loved things, for the slightest contact with people produced in him a faint but persistent nausea. He could not remember when this distaste began, nor could he remember ever being free of it. As a young boy he had been greatly disturbed by this revulsion which others did not seem to share, but having got a fine education, he learned, among other things, the word "misanthrope." Knowing his label provided him with both comfort and courage, he believed that to name an evil was to neutralize if not annihilate it. Then, too, he had read several books and made the acquaintance of several great misanthropes of the ages, whose spiritual company soothed him and provided him with yardsticks for measuring his whims, his yearnings, and his antipathies. Moreover, he found misanthropy an excellent means of developing character: when he subdued his revulsion and occasionally touched, helped, counseled, or befriended somebody, he was able to think of his behavior as generous and his intentions as noble. When he was enraged by some human effort or flaw, he was able to regard himself as discriminating, fastidious, and full of nice scruples.

As in the case of many misanthropes, his disdain for people led him into a profession designed to serve them. He was engaged in a line of work that was dependent solely on his ability to win the trust of others, and one in which the most intimate relationships were necessary. Having dallied with the priesthood in the Anglican Church, he abandoned it to become a caseworker. Time and misfortune, however, conspired against him, and he settled finally on a profession that brought him both freedom and satisfaction. He became a "Reader, Adviser, and Interpreter of Dreams." It was a profession that suited him well. His hours were his own, the competition was slight, the clientele was already persuaded and therefore manageable, and he had numerous opportunities to witness human stupidity without sharing it or being compromised by it, and to nurture his fastidiousness by viewing physical decay. Although his income was small, he had no taste for luxury—his experience in the monastery had solidified his natural asceticism while it developed his preference for solitude. Celibacy was a haven, silence a shield.

All his life he had had a fondness for things—not the acquisition of wealth or beautiful objects, but a genuine love of worn objects: a coffee pot that had been his mother's, a welcome mat from the door of a rooming house he once lived in, a quilt from a Salvation Army store counter. It was as though his disdain of human contact had converted itself into a craving for things humans had touched. The residue of the human spirit smeared on inanimate objects was all he could withstand of humanity. To contemplate, for example, evidence of human footsteps on the mat—absorb the smell of the quilt and wallow in the sweet certainty that many bodies had sweated, slept, dreamed, made love, been ill, and even died under it. Wherever he went, he took along his things, and was always searching for others. This thirst for worn things led him to casual but habitual examinations of trash barrels in alleys and wastebaskets in public places. . . .

All in all, his personality was an arabesque: intricate, symmetrical, balanced, and tightly constructed—except for one flaw. The careful design was marred occasionally by rare but keen sexual cravings.

He could have been an active homosexual but lacked the courage. Bestiality did not occur to him, and sodomy was quite out of the question, for he did not experience sustained erections and could not endure the thought of somebody else's. And besides, the one thing that disgusted him more than entering and caressing a woman was caressing and being caressed by a man. In any case his cravings, although intense, never relished physical contact. He abhorred flesh on flesh. Body odor, breath odor, overwhelmed him. The sight of dried matter in the corner of the eye, decayed or missing teeth, ear wax, blackheads, moles, blisters, skin crusts—all the natural excretions and protections the body was capable of—disquieted him. His attentions therefore gradually settled on those humans whose bodies were least offensive—children. And since he was too diffident to confront homosexuality, and since little boys were insulting, scary, and stubborn, he further limited his interest to little girls. They were usually manageable and frequently seductive. His sexuality was anything but lewd; his patronage of little girls smacked of innocence and was associated in his mind with cleanliness. He was what one might call a very clean old man.

A cinnamon-eyed West Indian with lightly browned skin.

Although his given name was printed on the sign in his kitchen window, and on the business cards he circulated, he was called by the townspeople Soaphead Church. No one knew where the "Church" part came from—perhaps somebody's recollection of his days as a guest preacher—those reverends who had been called but who had no flock or coop, and were constantly visiting other churches, sitting on the altar with the host preacher. But everybody knew what "Soaphead" meant—the tight, curly hair that took on and held a sheen and wave when pomaded with soap lather. A sort of primitive process.

He had been reared in a family proud of its academic accomplishments and its mixed blood—in fact, they believed the former was based on the latter. A Sir Whitcomb, some decaying British nobleman, who chose to disintegrate under a sun more easeful than England's, had introduced the white strain into the family in the early 1800's. Being a gentleman by order of the King, he had done the civilized thing for his mulatto bastard—provided it with three hundred pounds sterling, to the great satisfaction of the bastard's mother, who felt that fortune had smiled on her. The bastard too was grateful, and regarded as his life's goal the hoarding of this white strain. He bestowed his favors on a fifteen-year-old girl of similar parentage. She, like a good Victorian parody, learned from her husband all that was worth learning—to separate herself in body, mind, and spirit from all that suggested Africa; to cultivate the habits, tastes, preferences that her absent father-in-law and foolish mother-in-law would have approved.

They transferred this Anglophilia to their six children and sixteen grandchildren. Except for an occasional and unaccountable insurgent who chose a restive black, they married "up," lightening the family complexion and thinning out the family features.

With the confidence born of a conviction of superiority, they performed well at schools. They were industrious, orderly, and energetic, hoping to prove beyond a doubt De Gobineau's hypothesis that "all civilizations derive from the white race, that none can exist without its help, and that a society is great and brilliant only so far as it preserves the blood of the noble group that created it." Thus, they were seldom overlooked by schoolmasters who recommended promising students for study abroad. The men studied medicine, law, theology, and emerged repeatedly in the powerless government offices available to the native population. That they were corrupt in public and private practice, both lecherous and lascivious, was considered their noble right, and thoroughly enjoyed by most of the less gifted population.

As the years passed, due to the carelessness of some of the Whitcomb brothers, it became difficult to maintain their whiteness, and some distant and some not so distant relatives married each other. No obviously bad effects were noticed from these ill-advised unions, but one or two old maids or gardener boys marked a weakening of faculties and a disposition toward eccentricity in some of the children. Some flaw outside the usual alcoholism and lechery. They blamed the flaw on intermarriage with the family, however, not on the original genes of the decaying lord. In any case, there were flukes. No more than in any other family, to be sure, but more dangerous because more powerful. One of them was a religious fanatic who founded his own secret sect and fathered four sons, one of whom became a schoolmaster known for the precision of his justice and the control in his violence. This schoolmaster married a sweet, indolent half-Chinese girl for whom the fatigue of bearing a son was too much. She died soon after childbirth. Her son, named Elihue Micah Whitcomb, provided the schoolmaster with ample opportunity to work out his theories of education, discipline, and the good life. Little Elihue learned everything he needed to know well, particularly the fine art of self-deception. He read greedily but understood selectively, choosing the bits and pieces of other men's ideas that supported whatever predilection he had at the moment. Thus he chose to remember Hamlet's abuse of Ophelia, but not Christ's love of Mary Magdalene; Hamlet's frivolous politics, but not Christ's serious anarchy. He noticed Gibbon's acidity, but not his tolerance, Othello's love for the fair Desdemona, but not Iago's perverted love of Othello. The works he admired most were Dante's; those he despised most were Dostoyevsky's. For all his exposure to the best minds of the western world, he allowed only the narrowest interpretation to touch him. He responded to his father's controlled violence by developing hard habits and a soft imagination. A hatred of, and fascination with, any hint of disorder or decay.

At seventeen, however, he met his Beatrice, who was three years his senior. A lovely, laughing big-legged girl who worked as a clerk in a Chinese department store. Velma. So strong was her affection and zest for life, she did not eliminate the frail, sickly Elihue from it. She found his fastidiousness and complete lack of humor touching, and longed to introduce him to the idea of delight. He resisted the introduction, but she married him anyway, only to discover that he was suffering from and enjoying an invincible melancholy. When she learned two months into the marriage how important his melancholy was to him, that he was very interested in altering her joy to a more academic gloom, that he equated lovemaking with communion and the Holy Grail, she simply left. She had not lived by the sea all those years, listened to the wharfman's songs all that time, to spend her life in the soundless cave of Elihue's mind.

He never got over her desertion. She was to have been the answer to his unstated, unacknowledged question—where was the life to counter the encroaching nonlife? Velma was to rescue him from the nonlife he had learned on the flat side of his father's belt. But he resisted her with such skill that she was finally driven out to escape the inevitable boredom produced by such a dainty life.

Young Elihue was saved from visible shattering by the steady hand of his father, who reminded him of the family's reputation and Velma's questionable one. He then pursued his studies with more vigor than before and decided at last to enter the ministry. When he was advised that he had no avocation, he left the island, came to America to study the then budding field of psychiatry. But the subject required too much truth, too many confrontations, and offered too little support to a failing ego. He drifted into sociology, then physical therapy. This diverse education continued for six years, when his father refused to support him any longer, until he "found" himself. Elihue, not knowing where to look, was thrown back on his own devices, and "found" himself quite unable to earn money. He began to sink into a rapidly fraying gentility, punctuated with a few of the white-collar occupations available to black people, regardless of their noble bloodlines, in America: desk clerk at a colored hotel in Chicago, insurance agent, traveling salesman for a cosmetics firm catering to blacks. He finally settled in Lorain, Ohio, in 1936, palming himself off as a minister, and inspiring awe with the way he spoke English. The women of the town early discovered his celibacy, and not being able to comprehend his rejection of them, decided that he was supernatural rather than unnatural.

Once he understood their decision, he quickly followed through, accepting the name (Soaphead Church) and the role they had given him. He rented a kind of back-room apartment from a deeply religious old lady named Bertha Reese. She was clean, quiet, and very close to total deafness. The lodgings were ideal in every way but one. Bertha Reese had an old dog, Bob, who, although as deaf and quiet as she, was not as clean. He slept most of his days away on the back porch, which was Elihue's entrance. The dog was too old to be of any use, and Bertha Reese had not the strength or presence of mind to care for him properly. She fed him, and watered him, left him alone. The dog was mangy; his exhausted eyes ran with a sea-green matter around which gnats and flies clustered. Soaphead was revolted by Bob and wished he would hurry up and die. He regarded this wish for the dog's death as humane, for he could not bear, he told himself, to see anything suffer. It did not occur to him that he was really concerned about his own suffering, since the dog had adjusted himself to frailty and old age. Soaphead finally determined to put an end to the animal's misery, and bought some poison with which to do it. Only the horror of having to go near him had prevented Soaphead from completing his mission. He waited for rage or blinding revulsion to spur him.

Living there among his worn things, rising early every morning from dreamless sleeps, he counseled those who sought his advice.

His business was dread. People came to him in dread, whispered in dread, wept and pleaded in dread. And dread was what he counseled.

Singly they found their way to his door, wrapped each in a shroud stitched with anger, yearning, pride, vengeance, loneliness, misery, defeat, and hunger. They asked for the simplest of things: love, health, and money. Make him love me. Tell me what this dream means. Help me get rid of this woman. Make my mother give me back my clothes. Stop my left hand from shaking. Keep my baby's ghost off the stove. Break so-and-so's fix. To all of these requests he addressed himself. His practice was to do what he was bid—not to suggest to a party that perhaps the request was unfair, mean, or hopeless.

With only occasional, and increasingly rare, encounters with the little girls he could persuade to be entertained by him, he lived rather peaceably among his things, admitting to no regrets. He was aware, of course, that something was awry in his life, and all lives, but put the problem where it belonged, at the foot of the Originator of Life. He believed that since decay, vice, filth, and disorder were pervasive, they must be in the Nature of Things. Evil existed because God had created it. He, God, had made a sloven and unforgivable error in judgment: designing an imperfect universe. Theologians justified the presence of corruption as a means by which men strove, were tested, and triumphed. A triumph of cosmic neatness. But this neatness, the neatness of Dante, was in the orderly sectioning and segregating of all levels of evil and decay. In the world it was not so. The most exquisite-looking ladies sat on toilets, and the most dreadful-looking had pure and holy yearnings. God had done a poor job, and Soaphead suspected that he himself could have done better. It was in fact a pity that the Maker had not sought his counsel.

Soaphead was reflecting once again on these thoughts one late hot afternoon when he heard a tap on his door. Opening it, he saw a little girl, quite unknown to him. She was about twelve or so, he thought, and seemed to him pitifully unattractive. When he asked her what she wanted, she did not answer, but held out to him one of his cards advertising his gifts and services: "If you are overcome with trouble and conditions that are not natural, I can remove them; Overcome Spells, Bad Luck, and Evil Influences. Remember, I am a true Spiritualist and Psychic Reader, born with power, and I will help you. Satisfaction in one visit. During many years of practice I have brought together many in marriage and reunited many who were separated. If you are unhappy, discouraged, or in distress, I can help you. Does bad luck seem to follow you? Has the one you love changed? I can tell you why. I will tell you who your enemies and friends are, and if the one you love is true or false. If you are sick, I can show you the way to health. I locate lost and stolen articles. Satisfaction guaranteed."

Soaphead Church told her to come in.

"What can I do for you, my child?"

She stood there, her hands folded across her stomach, a little protruding pot of tummy. "Maybe. Maybe you can do it for me."

"Do what for you?"

"I can't go to school no more. And I thought maybe you could help me."

"Help you how? Tell me. Don't be frightened."

"My eyes."

"What about your eyes?"

"I want them blue."

Soaphead pursed his lips, and let his tongue stroke a gold inlay. He thought it was at once the most fantastic and the most logical petition he had ever received. Here was an ugly little girl asking for beauty. A surge of love and understanding swept through him, but was quickly replaced by anger. Anger that he was powerless to help her. Of all the wishes people had brought him—money, love, revenge—this seemed to him the most poignant and the one most deserving of fulfillment. A little black girl who wanted to rise up out of the pit of her blackness and see the world with blue eyes. His outrage grew and felt like power. For the first time he honestly wished he could work miracles. Never before had he really wanted the true and holy power—only the power to make others believe he had it. It seemed so sad, so frivolous, that mere mortality, not judgment, kept him from it. Or did it?

With a trembling hand he made the sign of the cross over her. His flesh crawled; in that hot, dim little room of worn things, he was chilled.

"I can do nothing for you, my child. I am not a magician. I work only through the Lord. He sometimes uses me to help people. All I can do is offer myself to Him as the instrument through which He works. If He wants your wish granted, He will do it."

Soaphead walked to the window, his back to the girl. His mind raced, stumbled, and raced again. How to frame the next sentence? How to hang on to the feeling of power. His eye fell on old Bob sleeping on the porch.

"We must make, ah, some offering, that is, some contact with nature. Perhaps some simple creature might be the vehicle through which He will speak. Let us see."

He knelt down at the window, and moved his lips. After what seemed a suitable length of time, he rose and went to the icebox that stood near the other window. From it he removed a small packet wrapped in pinkish butcher paper. From a shelf he took a small brown bottle and sprinkled some of its contents on the substance inside the paper. He put the packet, partly opened, on the table.

"Take this food and give it to the creature sleeping on the porch. Make sure he eats it. And mark well how he behaves. If nothing happens, you will know that God has refused you. If the animal behaves strangely, your wish will be granted on the day following this one."

The girl picked up the packet; the odor of the dark, sticky meat made her want to vomit. She put a hand on her stomach.

"Courage. Courage, my child. These things are not granted to faint hearts."

She nodded and swallowed visibly, holding down the vomit. Soaphead opened the door, and she stepped over the threshold.

"Good-bye, God bless," he said and quickly shut the door. At the window he stood watching her, his eyebrows pulled together into waves of compassion, his tongue fondling the worn gold in his upper jaw. He saw the girl bending down to the sleeping dog, who, at her touch, opened one liquid eye, matted in the corners with what looked like green glue. She reached out and touched the dog's head, stroking him gently. She placed the meat on the floor of the porch, near his nose. The odor roused him; he lifted his head, and got up to smell it better. He ate it in three or four gulps. The girl stroked his head again, and the dog looked up at her with soft triangle eyes. Suddenly he coughed, the cough of a phlegmy old man—and got to his feet. The girl jumped. The dog gagged, his mouth chomping the air, and promptly fell down. He tried to raise himself, could not, tried again, and half-fell down the steps. Choking, stumbling, he moved like a broken toy around the yard. The girl's mouth was open, a little petal of tongue showing. She made a wild, pointless gesture with one hand and then covered her mouth with both hands. She was trying not to vomit. The dog fell again, a spasm jerking his body. Then he was quiet. The girl's hands covering her mouth, she backed away a few feet, then turned, ran out of the yard and down the walk.

Soaphead Church went to the table. He sat down, with folded hands balancing his forehead on the balls of his thumbs. Then he rose and went to a tiny night table with a drawer, from which he took paper and a fountain pen. A bottle of ink was on the same shelf that held the poison. With these things he sat again at the table. Slowly, carefully, relishing his penmanship, he wrote the following letter:

Att: TO HE WHO GREATLY ENNOBLED HUMAN NATURE BY CREATING IT

Dear God:

The Purpose of this letter is to familiarize you with facts which either have escaped your notice, or which you have chosen to ignore.

Once upon a time I lived greenly and youngish on one of your islands. An island of the archipelago in the South Atlantic between North and South America, enclosing the Caribbean Sea and the Gulf of Mexico: divided into the Greater Antilles, the Lesser Antilles, and the Bahama Islands. Not the Windward or Leeward Island colonies, mark you, but within, of course, the Greater of the two Antilles (while the precision of my prose may be, at times, laborious, it is necessary that I identify myself to you clearly).

Now.

We in this colony took as our own the most dramatic, and the most obvious, of our white master's characteristics, which were, of course, their worst. In retaining the identity of our race, we held fast to those characteristics most gratifying to sustain and least troublesome to maintain. Consequently we were not royal but snobbish, not aristocratic but class-conscious; we believed authority was cruelty to our inferiors, and education was being at school. We mistook violence for passion, indolence for leisure, and thought recklessness was freedom. We raised our children and reared our crops; we let infants grow, and property develop. Our manhood was defined by acquisitions. Our womanhood by acquiescence. And the smell of your fruit and the labor of your days we abhorred.

This morning, before the little black girl came, I cried—for Velma. Oh, not aloud. There is no wind to carry, bear, or even refuse to bear, a sound so heavy with regret. But in my silent own lone way, I cried—for Velma. You need to know about Velma to understand what I did today.

She (Velma) left me the way people leave a hotel room. A hotel room is a place to be when you are doing something else. Of itself it is of no consequence to one's major scheme. A hotel room is convenient. But its convenience is limited to the time you need it while you are in that particular town on that particular business; you hope it is comfortable, but prefer, rather, that it be anonymous. It is not, after all, where you *live.*

When you no longer need it, you pay a little something for its use; say, "Thank you, sir," and when your business in that town is over, you go away from that room. Does anybody regret leaving a hotel room? Does anybody, who has a home, a real home somewhere, want to stay there? Does anybody look back with affection, or even disgust, at a hotel room when they leave it? You can only love or despise whatever *living* was done in that room. But the room itself? But you take a souvenir. Not, oh, not, to remember the room. To remember, rather, the time and the place of your business, your adventure. What can anyone feel for a hotel room? One doesn't any more feel for a hotel room than one expects a hotel room to feel for its occupant.

That, heavenly, heavenly Father, was how she left me; or rather, she never left me, because she was never ever there.

You remember, do you, how and of what we are made? Let me tell you now about the breasts of little girls. I apologize for the inappropriateness (is that it?), the imbalance of loving them at awkward times of day, and in awkward places, and the tastelessness of loving those which belonged to members of my family. Do I have to apologize for loving strangers?

But you too are amiss here, Lord. How, why, did you allow it to happen? How is it I could lift my eyes from the contemplation of Your Body and fall deeply into the contemplation of theirs? The buds. The buds on some of these saplings. They were mean, you know, mean and tender. Mean little buds resisting the touch, springing like rubber. But aggressive. Daring me to touch. Commanding me to touch. Not a bit shy, as you'd suppose. They stuck out at me, oh yes, at me. Slender-chested, finger-chested lassies. Have you ever seen them, Lord? I mean, really seen them? One could not see them and not love them. You who made them must have considered them lovely even as an idea—how much more lovely is the manifestation of that idea. I couldn't, as you must recall, keep my hands, my mouth, off them. Salt-sweet. Like not quite ripe strawberries covered with the light salt sweat of running days and hopping, skipping, jumping hours.

The love of them—the touch, taste, and feel of them—was not just an easy luxurious human vice; they were, for me, A Thing To Do Instead. Instead of papa, instead of the Cloth, instead of Velma, and I *chose* not to do without them. But I didn't go into the church. At least I didn't do that. As to what I did do? I told people I knew all about You. That I had received Your Powers. It was not a complete *lie;* but it was a *complete* lie. I should never have, I admit, I should never have taken their money in exchange for well-phrased, well-placed, well-faced lies. But, mark you, I hated it. Not for a moment did I love the lies or the money.

But consider: The woman who left the hotel room.

Consider: The greentime, the noontime of the archipelago.

Consider: Their hopeful eyes that were outdone only by their hoping breasts.

Consider: How I needed a comfortable evil to prevent my knowing what I could not bear to know.

Consider: How I hated and despised the money.

And now, consider: Not according to my just deserts, but according to *my* mercy, the little black girl that came a-looning at me today. Tell me, Lord, how could you leave a lass so long so lone that she could find her way to me? How could you? I weep for you, Lord. And it is because I weep for You that I had to do your work for You.

Do you know what she came for? Blue eyes. New, blue eyes, she said. Like she was buying shoes. "I'd like a pair of new blue eyes." She must have asked you for them for a very long time, and you hadn't replied. (A habit, I could have told her, a long-ago habit broken for Job—but no more.) She came to *me* for them. She had one of my cards. (Card enclosed.) By the way, I added the Micah —Micah Elihue Whitcomb. But I am called Soaphead Church. I cannot remember how or why I got the name. What makes one name more a person than another? Is the name the real thing, then? And the person only what his name says? Is that why to the simplest and friendliest of questions: "What is your name?" put to you by Moses, You would not say, and said instead "I am who I am." Like Popeye? I Yam What I Yam? Afraid you were, weren't you, to give out your name? Afraid they would know the name and then know you? Then they wouldn't fear you? It's quite all right. Don't be vexed. I mean no offense. I understand. I have been a bad man too, and an unhappy man too. But someday *I* will die. I was always so kind. Why do I have to die? The little girls. The little girls are the only things I'll miss. Do you know that when I touched their sturdy little tits and bit them—just a little—I felt I was being friendly? I didn't want to kiss their mouths or sleep in the bed with them or take a child bride for my own. Playful, I felt, and friendly. Not like the newspapers said. Not like the people whispered. And they didn't mind at all. Not at all. Remember how so many of them came back? No one would even try to understand that. If I'd been hurting them, would they have come back? Two of them, Doreen and Sugar Babe, they'd come together. I gave them mints, money, and they'd eat ice cream with their legs open while I played with them. It was like a party. And there wasn't nastiness, and there wasn't any filth, and there wasn't any odor, and there wasn't any groaning—just the light white laughter of little girls and me. And there wasn't any look—any long funny look—any long funny Velma look afterward. No look that makes you feel dirty afterward. That makes you want to die. With little girls it is all clean and good and friendly.

You have to understand that, Lord. You said, "Suffer little children to come unto me, and harm them not." Did you forget? Did you forget about the children? Yes. You forgot. You let them go wanting, sit on road shoulders, crying next to their dead mothers. I've seen them charred, lame, halt. You forgot, Lord. You forgot how and when to be God.

That's why I changed the little black girl's eyes for her, and I didn't touch her; not a finger did I lay on her. But I gave her those blue eyes she wanted. Not for pleasure, and not for money. I did what You did not, could not, would not do: I looked at that ugly little black girl, and I loved her. I played You. And it was a very good show!

I, I have caused a miracle. I gave her the eyes. I gave her the blue, blue, two blue eyes. Cobalt blue. A streak of it right out of your own blue heaven. No one else will see her blue eyes. But *she* will. And she will live happily ever after. I, I have found it meet and right so to do.

Now you are jealous. You are jealous of me.

You see? I, too, have created. Not aboriginally, like you, but creation is a heady wine, more for the taster than the brewer.

Having therefore imbibed, as it were, of the nectar, I am not afraid of You, of Death, not even of Life, and it's all right about Velma; and it's all right about Papa; and it's all right about the Greater and the Lesser Antilles. Quite all right. Quite.

With kindest regards, I remain,

Your,

Micah Elihue Whitcomb

Soaphead Church folded the sheets of paper into three equal parts and slipped them into an envelope. Although he had no seal, he longed for sealing wax. He removed a cigar box from under the bed and rummaged about in it. There were some of his most precious things: a sliver of jade that had dislodged from a cuff link at the Chicago hotel; a gold pendant shaped like a Y with a piece of coral attached to it that had belonged to the mother he never knew; four large hairpins that Velma had left on the rim of the bathroom sink; a powder blue grosgrain ribbon from the head of a little girl named Precious Jewel; a blackened faucet head from the sink in a jail cell in Cincinnati; two marbles he had found under a bench in Morningside Park on a very fine spring day; an old Lucky Hart catalog that smelled still of nut-brown and mocha face powder, and lemon vanishing cream. Distracted by his things, he forgot what he had been looking for. The effort to recall was too great; there was a buzzing in his head, and a wash of fatigue overcame him. He closed his box, eased himself out on the bed, and slipped into an ivory sleep from which he could not hear the tiny yelps of an old lady who had come out of her candy store and found the still carcass of an old dog named Bob.

Summer

I have only to break into the tightness of a strawberry, and I see summer—its dust and lowering skies. It remains for me a season of storms. The parched days and sticky nights are undistinguished in my mind, but the storms, the violent sudden storms, both frightened and quenched me. But my memory is uncertain; I recall a summer storm in the town where we lived and imagine a summer my mother knew in 1929. There was a tornado that year, she said, that blew away half of south Lorain. I mix up her summer with my own. Biting the strawberry, thinking of storms, I see her. A slim young girl in a pink crepe dress. One hand is on her hip; the other lolls about her thigh—waiting. The wind swoops her up, high above the houses, but she is still standing, hand on hip. Smiling. The anticipation and promise in her lolling hand are not altered by the holocaust. In the summer tornado of 1929, my mother's hand is unextinguished. She is strong, smiling, and relaxed while the world falls down about her. So much for memory. Public fact becomes private reality, and the seasons of a Midwestern town become the *Moirai* of our small lives.

The summer was already thick when Frieda and I received our seeds. We had waited since April for the magic package containing the packets and packets of seeds we were to sell for five cents each, which would entitle us to a new bicycle. We believed it, and spent a major part of every day trooping about the town selling them. Although Mama had restricted us to the homes of people she knew or the neighborhoods familiar to us, we knocked on all doors, and floated in and out of every house that opened to us: twelve-room houses that sheltered half as many families, smelling of grease and urine; tiny wooden four-room houses tucked into bushes near the railroad tracks; the up-over places—apartments up over fish markets, butcher shops, furniture stores, saloons, restaurants; tidy brick houses with flowered carpets and glass bowls with fluted edges.

During that summer of the seed selling we thought about the money, thought about the seeds, and listened with only half an ear to what people were saying. In the houses of people who knew us we were asked to come in and sit, given cold water or lemonade; and while we sat there being refreshed, the people continued their conversations or went about their chores. Little by little we began to piece a story together, a secret, terrible, awful story. And it was only after two or three such vaguely overheard conversations that we realized that the story was about Pecola. Properly placed, the fragments of talk ran like this:

"Did you hear about that girl?"

"What? Pregnant?"

"Yas. But guess who?"

"Who? I don't know all these little old boys."

"That's just it. Ain't no little old boy. They say it's Cholly."

"Cholly? Her daddy?"

"Uh-huh."

"Lord. Have mercy. That dirty nigger."

"'Member that time he tried to burn them up? I knew he was crazy for sure then."

"What's she gone do? The mama?"

"Keep on like she been, I reckon. He taken off."

"County ain't gone let her keep that baby, is they?"

"Don't know."

"None of them Breedloves seem right anyhow. That boy is off somewhere every minute, and the girl was always foolish."

"Don't nobody know nothing about them anyway. Where they come from or nothing. Don't seem to have no people."

"What you reckon make him do a thing like that?"

"Beats me. Just nasty."

"Well, they ought to take her out of school."

"Ought to. She carry some of the blame."

"Oh, come on. She ain't but twelve or so."

"Yeah. But you never know. How come she didn't fight him?"

"Maybe she did."

"Yeah? You never know."

"Well, it probably won't live. They say the way her mama beat her she lucky to be alive herself."

"She be lucky if it don't live. Bound to be the ugliest thing walking."

"Can't help but be. Ought to be a law: two ugly people doubling up like that to make more ugly. Be better off in the ground."

"Well, I wouldn't worry none. It be a miracle if it live."

Our astonishment was short-lived, for it gave way to a curious kind of defensive shame; we were embarrassed for Pecola, hurt for her, and finally we just felt sorry for her. Our sorrow drove out all thoughts of the new bicycle. And I believe our sorrow was the more intense because nobody else seemed to share it. They were disgusted, amused, shocked, outraged, or even excited by the story. But we listened for the one who would say, "Poor little girl," or, "Poor baby," but there was only head-wagging where those words should have been. We looked for eyes creased with concern, but saw only veils.

I thought about the baby that everybody wanted dead, and saw it very clearly. It was in a dark, wet place, its head covered with great O's of wool, the black face holding, like nickels, two clean black eyes, the flared nose, kissing-thick lips, and the living, breathing silk of black skin. No synthetic yellow bangs suspended over marble-blue eyes, no pinched nose and bowline mouth. More strongly than my fondness for Pecola, I felt a need for someone to want the black baby to live—just to counteract the universal love of white baby dolls, Shirley Temples, and Maureen Peals. And Frieda must have felt the same thing. We did not think of the fact that Pecola was not married; lots of girls had babies who were not married. And we did not dwell on the fact that the baby's father was Pecola's father too; the process of having a baby by any male was incomprehensible to us—at least she knew her father. We thought only of this overwhelming hatred for the unborn baby. We remembered Mrs. Breedlove knocking Pecola down and soothing the pink tears of the frozen doll baby that sounded like the door of our icebox. We remembered the knuckled eyes of schoolchildren under the gaze of Meringue Pie and the eyes of these same children when they looked at Pecola. Or maybe we didn't remember; we just knew. We had defended ourselves since memory against everything and everybody, considered all speech a code to be broken by us, and all gestures subject to careful analysis; we had become headstrong, devious, and arrogant. Nobody paid us any attention, so we paid very good attention to ourselves. Our limitations were not known to us—not then. Our only handicap was our size; people gave us orders because they were bigger and stronger. So it was with confidence, strengthened by pity and pride, that we decided to change the course of events and alter a human life.

"What we gone do, Frieda?"

"What can we do? Miss Johnson said it would be a miracle if it lived."

"So let's make it a miracle."

"Yeah, but how?"

"We could pray."

"That's not enough. Remember last time with the bird?"

"That was different; it was half-dead when we found it."

"I don't care, I still think we have to do something really strong this time."

"Let's ask Him to let Pecola's baby live and promise to be good for a whole month."

"O.K. But we better give up something so He'll know we really mean it this time."

"Give up what? We ain't got nothing. Nothing but the seed money, two dollars."

"We could give that. Or, you know what? We could give up the bicycle. Bury the money and . . . plant the seeds."

"All of the money?"

"Claudia, do you want to do it or not?"

"O.K. I just thought . . . O.K."

"We have to do it *right,* now. We'll bury the money over by her house so we can't go back and dig it up, and we'll plant the seeds out back of our house so we can watch over them. And when they come up, we'll know everything is all right. All right?"

"All right. Only let me sing this time. You say the magic words."

LOOKLOOKHERECOMESAFRIENDTHEFRIENDWILLPLAYW ITHJANETHEYWILLPLAYAGOODGAMEPLAYJANEPLAYPLAY

How many times a minute are you going to look inside that old thing?

I didn't look in a long time.

You did too—

So what? I can look if I want to.

I didn't say you couldn't. I just don't know why you have to look every minute. They aren't going anywhere.

I know it. I just like to look.

You scared they might go away?

Of course not. How can they go away?

The others went away.

They didn't go away. They changed.

Go away. Change. What's the difference?

A lot. Mr. Soaphead said they would last forever.

Forever and ever Amen?

Yes, if you want to know.

You don't have to be so smarty when you talk to me.

I'm not being smarty. You started it.

I'd just like to do something else besides watch you stare in that mirror.

You're just jealous.

I am not.

You are. You wish you had them.

Ha. What would I look like with blue eyes?

Nothing much.

If you're going to keep this up, I may as well go on off by myself.

No. Don't go. What you want to do?

We could go outside and play, I guess.

But it's too hot.

You can take your old mirror. Put it in your coat pocket, and you can look at yourself up and down the street.

Boy! I never would have thought you'd be so jealous.

Oh, come on!

You are.

Are what?

Jealous.

O.K. So I'm jealous.

See. I told you.

No. I told you.

Are they really nice?

Yes. Very nice.

Just "very nice"?

Really, truly, very nice.

Really, truly, bluely nice?

Oh, God. You are crazy.

I am not!

I didn't meant it that way.

Well, what did you mean?

Come on. It's too hot in here.

Wait a minute. I can't find my shoes.

Here they are.

Oh. Thank you.

Got your mirror?

Yes dearie. . . .

Well, let's go then. . . . Ow!

What's the matter?

The sun is too bright. It hurts my eyes.

Not mine. I don't even blink. Look. I can look right at the sun.

Don't do that.

Why not? It doesn't hurt. I don't even have to blink.

Well, blink anyway. You make me feel funny, staring at the sun like that.

Feel funny how?

I don't know.

Yes, you do. Feel funny how?

I told you, I don't know.

Why don't you look at me when you say that? You're looking drop-eyed like Mrs. Breedlove.

Mrs. Breedlove looked drop-eyed at you?

Yes. Now she does. Ever since I got my blue eyes, she look away from me all of the time. Do you suppose she's jealous too?

Could be. They are pretty, you know.

I know. He really did a good job. Everybody's jealous. Every time I look at somebody, they look off.

Is that why nobody has told you how pretty they are?

Sure it is. Can you imagine? Something like that happening to a person, and nobody but nobody saying anything about it? They all try to pretend they don't see them. Isn't that funny? . . . I said, isn't that funny?

Yes.

You are the only one who tells me how pretty they are.

Yes.

You are a real friend. I'm sorry about picking on you before. I mean, saying you were jealous and all.

That's all right.

No. Really. You are my very best friend. Why didn't I know you before?

You didn't need me before.

Didn't need you?

I mean . . . you were so unhappy before. I guess you didn't notice me before.

I guess you're right. And I was so lonely for friends. And you were right here. Right before my eyes.

No, honey. Right after your eyes.

What?

What does Maureen think about your eyes?

She doesn't say anything about them. Has she said anything to you about them?

No. Nothing.

Do you like Maureen?

Oh. She's all right. For a half-white girl, that is.

I know what you mean. But would you like to be her friend? I mean, would you like to go around with her or anything?

No.

Me neither. But she sure is popular.

Who wants to be popular.

Not me.

Me neither.

But you couldn't be popular anyway. You don't even go to school.

You don't either.

I know. But I used to.

What did you stop for?

They made me.

Who made you?

I don't know. After that first day at school when I had my blue eyes. Well, the next day they had Mrs. Breedlove come out. Now I don't go anymore. But I don't care.

You don't?

No, I don't. They're just prejudiced, that's all.

Yes, they sure are prejudiced.

Just because I got blue eyes, bluer than theirs, they're prejudiced.

That's right.

They are bluer, aren't they?

Oh, yes. Much bluer.

Bluer than Joanna's?

Much bluer than Joanna's.

And bluer than Michelena's?

Much bluer than Michelena's.

I thought so. Did Michelena say anything to you about my eyes?

No. Nothing.

Did you say anything to her?

No.

How come?

How come what?

How come you don't talk to anybody?

I talk to you.

Besides me.

I don't like anybody besides you.

Where do you live?

I told you once.

What is your mother's name?

Why are you so busy meddling me?

I just wondered. You don't talk to anybody. You don't go to school. And nobody talks to you.

How do you know nobody talks to me?

They don't. When you're in the house with me, even Mrs. Breedlove doesn't say anything to you. Ever. Sometimes I wonder if she even sees you.

Why wouldn't she see me?

I don't know. She almost walks right over you.

Maybe she doesn't feel too good since Cholly's gone.

Oh, yes. You must be right.

She probably misses him.

I don't know why she would. All he did was get drunk and beat her up.

Well, you know how grown-ups are.

Yes. No. How are they?

Well, she probably loved him anyway.

HIM?

Sure. Why not? Anyway, if she didn't love him, she sure let him do it to her a lot.

That's nothing.

How do you know?

I saw them all the time. She didn't like it.

Then why'd she let him do it to her?

Because he made her.

How could somebody make you do something like that?

Easy.

Oh, yeah? How easy?

They just make you, that's all.

I guess you're right. And Cholly could make anybody do anything.

He could not.

He made you, didn't he?

Shut up!

I was only teasing.

Shut up!

O.K. O.K.

He just tried, see? He didn't do anything. You hear me?

I'm shutting up.

You'd better. I don't like that kind of talk.

I said I'm shutting up.

You always talk so dirty. Who told you about that, anyway?

I forget.

Sammy?

No. You did.

I did not.

You did. You said he tried to do it to you when you were sleeping on the couch.

See there! You don't even know what you're talking about. It was when I was washing dishes.

Oh, yes. Dishes.

By myself. In the kitchen.

Well, I'm glad you didn't let him.

Yes.

Did you?

Did I what?

Let him.

Now who's crazy?

I am, I guess.

You sure are.

Still . . .

Well. Go ahead. Still what?

I wonder what it would be like.

Horrible.

Really?

Yes. Horrible.

Then why didn't you tell Mrs. Breedlove?

I did tell her!

I don't mean about the first time. I mean about the second time, when you were sleeping on the couch.

I wasn't sleeping! I was reading!

You don't have to shout.

You don't understand anything, do you? She didn't even believe me when I told her.

So that's why you didn't tell her about the second time?

She wouldn't have believed me then either.

You're right. No use telling her when she wouldn't believe you.

That's what I'm trying to get through your thick head.

O.K. I understand now. Just about.

What do you mean, just about?

You sure are mean today.

You keep on saying mean and sneaky things. I thought you were my friend.

I am. I am.

Then leave me alone about Cholly.

OK.

There's nothing more to say about him, anyway. He's gone, anyway.

Yes. Good riddance.

Yes. Good riddance.

And Sammy's gone too.

And Sammy's gone too.

So there's no use talking about it. I mean them.

No. No use at all.

It's all over now.

Yes.

And you don't have to be afraid of Cholly coming at you anymore.

No.

That was horrible, wasn't it?

Yes.

The second time too?

Yes.

Really? The second time too?

Leave me alone! You better leave me alone.

Can't you take a joke? I was only funning.

I don't like to talk about dirty things.

Me neither. Let's talk about something else.

What? What will we talk about?

Why, your eyes.

Oh, yes. My eyes. My blue eyes. Let me look again.

See how pretty they are.

Yes. They get prettier each time I look at them.

They are the prettiest I've ever seen.

Really?

Oh, yes.

Prettier than the sky?

Oh, yes. Much prettier than the sky.

Prettier than Alice-and-Jerry Storybook eyes?

Oh, yes. Much prettier than Alice-and-Jerry Storybook eyes.

And prettier than Joanna's?

Oh, yes. And bluer too.

Bluer than Michelena's?

Yes.

Are you sure?

Of course I'm sure.

You don't sound sure. . . .

Well, I am sure. Unless. . . .

Unless what?

Oh, nothing. I was just thinking about a lady I saw yesterday. Her eyes sure were blue. But no. Not bluer than yours.

Are you sure?

Yes. I remember them now. Yours are bluer.

I'm glad.

Me too. I'd hate to think that there was anybody around with bluer eyes than yours. I'm sure there isn't. Not around here, anyway.

But you don't know, do you? You haven't seen everybody, have you?

No. I haven't.

So there could be, couldn't there?

Not hardly.

But maybe. Maybe. You said "around here." Nobody "around here" probably has bluer eyes. What about someplace else? Even if my eyes are bluer than Joanna's and bluer than Michelena's and bluer than that lady's you saw, suppose there is somebody way off somewhere with bluer eyes than mine?

Don't be silly.

There could be. Couldn't there?

Not hardly.

But suppose. Suppose a long way off. In Cincinnati, say, there is somebody whose eyes are bluer than mine? Suppose there are *two* people with bluer eyes?

So what? You asked for blue eyes. You got blue eyes.

He should have made them bluer.

Who?

Mr. Soaphead.

Did you say what color blue you wanted them?

No. I forgot.

Oh. Well.

Look. Look over there. At that girl. Look at her eyes. Are they bluer than mine?

No, I don't think so.

Did you look real good?

Yes.

Here comes someone. Look at his. See if they're bluer.

You're being silly. I'm not going to look at everybody's eyes.

You have to.

No I don't.

Please. If there is somebody with bluer eyes than mine, then maybe there is somebody with the bluest eyes. The bluest eyes in the whole world.

That's just too bad, isn't it?

Please help me look.

No.

But suppose my eyes aren't blue enough?

Blue enough for what?

Blue enough for . . . I don't know. Blue enough for something. Blue enough . . . for you!

I'm not going to play with you anymore.

Oh. Don't leave me.

Yes. I am.

Why? Are you mad at me?

Yes.

Because my eyes aren't blue enough? Because I don't have the bluest eyes?

No. Because you're acting silly.

Don't go. Don't leave me. Will you come back if I get them?

Get what?

The bluest eyes. Will you come back then?

Of course I will. I'm just going away for a little while.

You promise?

Sure. I'll be back. Right before your very eyes.

So it was.

A little black girl yearns for the blue eyes of a little white girl, and the horror at the heart of her yearning is exceeded only by the evil of fulfillment.

We saw her sometimes, Frieda and I—after the baby came too soon and died. After the gossip and the slow wagging of heads. She was so sad to see. Grown people looked away; children, those who were not frightened by her, laughed outright.

The damage done was total. She spent her days, her tendril,

sap-green days, walking up and down, up and down, her head jerking to the beat of a drummer so distant only she could hear. Elbows bent, hands on shoulders, she flailed her arms like a bird in an eternal, grotesquely futile effort to fly. Beating the air, a winged but grounded bird, intent on the blue void it could not reach—could not even see—but which filled the valleys of the mind.

We tried to see her without looking at her, and never, never went near. Not because she was absurd, or repulsive, or because we were frightened, but because we had failed her. Our flowers never grew. I was convinced that Frieda was right, that I had planted them too deeply. How could I have been so sloven? So we avoided Pecola Breedlove—forever.

And the years folded up like pocket handkerchiefs. Sammy left town long ago; Cholly died in the workhouse; Mrs. Breedlove still does housework. And Pecola is somewhere in that little brown house she and her mother moved to on the edge of town, where you can see her even now, once in a while. The birdlike gestures are worn away to a mere picking and plucking her way between the tire rims and the sunflowers, between Coke bottles and milkweed, among all the waste and beauty of the world—which is what she herself was. All of our waste which we dumped on her and which she absorbed. And all of our beauty, which was hers first and which she gave to us. All of us—all who knew her—felt so wholesome after we cleaned ourselves on her. We were so beautiful when we stood astride her ugliness. Her simplicity decorated us, her guilt sanctified us, her pain made us glow with health, her awkwardness made us think we had a sense of humor. Her inarticulateness made us believe we were eloquent. Her poverty kept us generous. Even her waking dreams we used—to silence our own nightmares. And she let us, and thereby deserved our contempt. We honed our egos on her, padded our characters with her frailty, and yawned in the fantasy of our strength.

And fantasy it was, for we were not strong, only aggressive; we were not free, merely licensed; we were not compassionate, we were polite; not good, but well behaved. We courted death in order to call ourselves brave, and hid like thieves from life. We substituted good grammar for intellect; we switched habits to simulate maturity; we rearranged lies and called it truth, seeing in the new pattern of an old idea the Revelation and the Word.

She, however, stepped over into madness, a madness which protected her from us simply because it bored us in the end.

Oh, some of us "loved" her. The Maginot Line. And Cholly loved her. I'm sure he did. He, at any rate, was the one who loved her enough to touch her, envelop her, give something of himself to her. But his touch was fatal, and the something he gave her filled the matrix of her agony with death. Love is never any better than the lover. Wicked people love wickedly, violent people love violently, weak people love weakly, stupid people love stupidly, but the love of a free man is never safe. There is no gift for the beloved. The lover alone possesses his gift of love. The loved one is shorn, neutralized, frozen in the glare of the lover's inward eye.

And now when I see her searching the garbage—for what? The thing we assassinated? I talk about how I did *not* plant the seeds too deeply, how it was the fault of the earth, the land, of our town. I even think now that the land of the entire country was hostile to marigolds that year. This soil is bad for certain kinds of flowers. Certain seeds it will not nurture, certain fruit it will not bear, and when the land kills of its own volition, we acquiesce and say the victim had no right to live. We are wrong, of course, but it doesn't matter. It's too late. At least on the edge of my town, among the garbage and the sunflowers of my town, it's much, much, much too late.

TOPICS FOR PAPERS AND DISCUSSION

1. *Rape and incest.* "Rape and incest are quite literal in *The Bluest Eye,* yet a close examination of the novel shows they become a condition of existence—people of similar and different sex ravish each other; families grow incestuous spiritually." Verify the validity of this statement. Start with Cholly's physical rape of Pecola. How does it grow logically out of his history? Consider Pecola's various experiences. Look closely at the fights between Pauline and Cholly, including the reactions of the children, Sammy and Pecola. What have Soaphead Church and the boy Junior to do with rape and incest? Include black-white relationships. What connotations do "rape" and "incest" assume, and what do they symbolize?

2. *Pecola as victim.* Morrison sees the little girl "as a total and complete victim of whatever was around her." The author also said of her: "I wrote about a child who was ugly—Pecola was a perfect, defeated victim—only she was also beautiful." Show how Pecola was abused by her father, ignored by her mother, taunted by schoolmates, and eventually driven to madness. Also, is it possible to accept a reverse idea that Morrison shows "wide-spirited sympathy for the villains as well as the

victims"? For example, it has been said that "Cholly becomes truly tragic, trapped by social circumstances"; the rape is his only way "to express love." Keeping in mind the destruction of a child-victim, do you agree? disagree? Explain.

3. *The pecking order.* Much resonance is gained by the author's inclusion and treatment of a wide range of castes and classes: whores, "niggers," poor blacks, middle-class "coloreds," rich "high-yellows," black-white families, as well as a few whites. Analyze the change undergone by Pauline to Polly in the white household. Ruminate about the novel's broad social spectrum, and then try to answer these questions: What is Morrison attempting to say by her inclusiveness? How does she dramatize the nature of each group? What are the characteristics of each and their relationships to those below and above them? In what ways do history, social conditions, industry, business, etc., strengthen the class and caste system?

4. *People and settings.* Many black writers of the past were obsessed with black-white conflicts; Morrison is more concerned with interrelationships among blacks. Thus her work is mostly about black characters. Account for its accomplishments on the basis of its absence of white characters. Also, the town in *The Bluest Eye* is Lorain, Ohio, where the author was born and raised. Does the locale seem presented strictly as autobiographical information? Morrison's fiction is noted for its extraordinary sense of place, especially of settings she creates imaginatively. What details, feelings, moods are conveyed in her treatment of interiors like rooms and houses, or exteriors like neighborhoods, communities, and geographical landscapes?

5. *"Blue eyes."* Explain the preoccupation with blue eyes. Look first toward the end of the third section, "Spring," beginning with Pecola's request of Soaphead Church that he give her blue eyes. Examine Soaphead's letter to God and the paragraph that starts "Do you know what she came for? Blue Eyes. New, blue eyes, she said." What do you make of the "dialogue" (regular print and italics) almost at the end? Does anyone see Pecola's "blue eyes" except herself? Consider a countervailing idea: hatred of blue eyes rather than a desire to have them. An illustrative paragraph on the destruction of white baby dolls is located in the first part, "Autumn," beginning "It had begun with Christmas and the gift of dolls."

6. *Form and meaning.* Repeatedly Morrison creates scenes of a peaceful, happy, friendly, domestic, or romantic nature, often touched with humor, only to have the same scenes erupt into their opposites. Consider these scenes: Claudia, Frieda, Maureen, and Pecola walking home; Cholly's first erotic experience; Junior, Pecola, and the cat, then Geraldine's return home; Pecola's "ministratin'"; friendly Henry Washington and Frieda; "the Maginot Line," Claudia, and Frieda together;

Pauline's spotless kitchen in the white home and the spilled blueberry cobbler. Based upon these episodes, how does the author's view of life define the existence of her characters? What philosophical interpretation is she dramatizing?

7. *Music is the soul of humanity.* Morrison's novels include musical passages, references to musical instruments, chants, rhymes, patter songs, snatches of popular tunes, folk songs, etc. Her own prose style is musical, whether or not music is the principal subject. The paragraph located three-fourths through the "Spring" section beginning "The pieces of Cholly's life could become coherent only in the head of a musician" reads as though it is set to a plucked or strummed instrument, perhaps a guitar. Why would such sound and rhythm be appropriate to the content of this Cholly passage? Study closely other uses of music in *The Bluest Eye.* Point out the multiple functions of music in the overall design.

8. *A key paradigm?* The story of Cholly Breedlove forms this pattern: birth, abandonment, rescue; death [Aunt Jimmy's], funeral, banquet; the mating dance, mating, violence, violence turned against a partner [Darlene], indifference to the partner; hunting and finding "the treasure," flight, seeking lost parent [Samson Fuller], rejection, and humiliation. Show how valid this pattern, or some variation on it, is (or is not) for defining the life and fate of other characters and the black race as presented in the novel. If the paradigm is not entirely valid—certain elements might need rearrangement—modify it and test out the modifications. What meanings emerge from the patterns of these events?

9. *The garden of the post-lapsarian world.* The garden is life itself, our existence. But too often flowers, fruit, and trees become bitter, rank, rotten. Seeds refuse to sprout—fruitfulness is denied. With this observation in mind, examine botanical imagery and its function in the novel. Consider its positive and negative aspects. What conditions cause blight, infertility, and deformity? Conduct research in the basic symbolic meanings of *seasons.* Ponder the use of the seasons in this novel and discuss their arrangement. The novel begins with autumn, a time of fulfillment and harvest—what happens in it? How does each of the four parts of the novel reflect or invert our expectations of each designated season?

10. *Novel as critique of violence.* Violence is ubiquitous in *The Bluest Eye.* It may grow out of *humiliation* (Cholly's savage hate of Darlene) or *frustration* (Claudia's destructive reaction to her white dolls) or *love* (Cholly's attack on Pecola) or *hostility* (Junior turns hatred of his mother into bullying other children and the family pet). Violence may serve a number of purposes such as the "ritualized" beatings in the Breedlove quarrels, the "sacrifice" of the dog, or the escape into insanity when the world's brutality becomes intolerable. Discuss these and the many other

instances of violence, asking why it erupts and what purposes it serves. Link your answers to the topic about form and meaning in the novel.

11. *Innovative form.* The look of the novel is striking in many ways. Examine the following physical and narrative features and comment on their functions: (1) At the beginning, the children's primer story which loses its punctuation and spacing and visibly shrinks. (2) As altered excerpts of the same story, the headings in run-on boldface type, and their relation to what follows. (3) The liberal use of italicized sections, like Pauline's monologue. (4) Soaphead's letter to God. (5) Pecola's "conversation" in alternately italicized and regular type. (6) Bracketing the novel at beginning and end with Claudia's melancholy commentary on seeds and soil. What other contrasts of normalized and unnormalized features do you find?

12. *The faces of love.* Much is said about love, and in the penultimate paragraph, the narrative voice of Claudia enters to proclaim: "Oh, some of us 'loved' her [Pecola]. . . . Love is never any better than the lover." Claudia next differentiates lovers who are wicked, violent, weak, stupid, or free. Look for various kinds of love, for what happens to love under the pressure of living, for distortions and perversions of love and their causes. Examine the relationship of love and sexuality. From what sources do the various characters derive their ideas and expectations of love? If love is denied or withdrawn, what happens to them? At what levels would you place the varied consequences of love gone wrong: tragedy? pathos? bathos?

13. *Beauty and ugliness.* Among varied dualities, beauty-ugliness is significant. What is considered beautiful in Claudia's world? What ugly? As the novel progresses, both concepts lose their dictionary meanings and assume ironic overtones. What are they? In the "Spring" section on Pauline Breedlove, the narrator speaks of romantic love and physical beauty as "probably the most destructive ideas in the history of human thought." What is meant? Pecola in particular and the blacks in general may indeed be victims of these "destructive ideas." How does the author wish us to judge beauty and ugliness? Morrison loves her country and its black people, and yet her characters are brutalized by life in an ugly America. Why? Explain.

14. *Minor characters.* The novel is filled with minor characters who give it life, density, richness even though some make only brief appearances. What are their functions? How are eccentrics like Soaphead and the boarder, Mr. Henry, alike and different? Consider the three whores, China, Poland, and Miss Marie, "the Maginot Line." Based on the uncomplimentary generalities made about women moving from "Mobile or Meridian or Aiken or Baton Rouge," analyze a mother like Geraldine. Comment on children like Maureen Peal and Junior. Why was the old man Blue Jack important in Cholly's youth? Whites appear rarely—is

the storekeeper Mr. Yacobowski typical of them? Incidentally, how and why is little Shirley Temple important in this novel?

15. *Narrative methods.* Unusual narrative techniques distinguish this novel. The first-person narrator is at times the child Claudia. Yet often the author shifts to an older, wisely reflective Claudia or an omniscient point of view well beyond the means of Claudia's perception. How does the author handle these shifting viewpoints? Do they violate credibility and consistency? Defend or refute their use. Account, too, for the mixture of past and present verb tenses. Which family do you take to be central, the MacTeers or the Breedloves? Or are the families meant as counter balances? In view of the differing viewpoints, does the tone of the work tend to alternate back and forth between positive and negative positions?

Being There

Jerzy Kosinski

For Katherina v. F.
who taught me that love
is more than the longing
to be together

ONE

It was Sunday. Chance was in the garden. He moved slowly, dragging the green hose from one path to the next, carefully watching the flow of the water. Very gently he let the stream touch every plant, every flower, every branch of the garden. Plants were like people; they needed care to live, to survive their diseases, and to die peacefully.

Yet plants were different from people. No plant is able to think about itself or able to know itself; there is no mirror in which the plant can recognize its face; no plant can do anything intentionally: it cannot help growing, and its growth has no meaning, since a plant cannot reason or dream.

It was safe and secure in the garden, which was separated from the street by a high, red brick wall covered with ivy, and not even the sounds of the passing cars disturbed the peace. Chance ignored the streets. Though he had never stepped outside the house and its garden, he was not curious about life on the other side of the wall.

The front part of the house where the Old Man lived might just as well have been another part of the wall or the street. He could not tell if anything in it was alive or not. In the rear of the ground floor facing the garden, the maid lived. Across the hall Chance had his room and his bathroom and his corridor leading to the garden.

What was particularly nice about the garden was that, at any moment, standing in the narrow paths or amidst the bushes and trees, Chance could start to wander, never knowing whether he was going forward or backward, unsure whether he was ahead of or behind his previous steps. All that mattered was moving in his own time, like the growing plants.

Once in a while Chance would turn off the water and sit on the grass and think. The wind, mindless of direction, intermittently swayed the bushes and trees. The city's dust settled evenly, darkening the flowers, which waited patiently to be rinsed by the rain and dried by the sunshine. And yet, with all its life, even at the peak of its bloom, the garden was its own graveyard. Under every tree and bush lay rotten trunks and disintegrated and decomposing roots. It was hard to know which was more important: the garden's surface or the graveyard from which it grew and into which it was constantly lapsing. For example, there were some hedges at the wall which grew in complete disregard of the other plants; they grew faster, dwarfing the smaller flowers, and spreading onto the territory of weaker bushes.

Chance went inside and turned on the TV. The set created its own light, its own color, its own time. It did not follow the law of gravity that forever bent all plants downward. Everything on TV was tangled and mixed and yet smoothed out: night and day, big and small, tough and brittle, soft and rough, hot and cold, far and near. In this colored world of television, gardening was the white cane of a blind man.

By changing the channel he could change himself. He could go through phases, as garden plants went through phases, but he could change as rapidly as he wished by twisting the dial backward and forward. In some cases he could spread out into the screen without stopping, just as on TV people spread out into the screen. By turning the dial, Chance could bring others inside his eyelids. Thus he came to believe that it was he, Chance, and no one else, who made himself be.

The figure on the TV screen looked like his own reflection in a mirror. Though Chance could not read or write, he resembled the man on TV more than he differed from him. For example, their voices were alike.

He sank into the screen. Like sunlight and fresh air and mild rain, the world from outside the garden entered Chance, and Chance, like a TV image, floated into the world, buoyed up by a force he did not see and could not name.

He suddenly heard the creak of a window opening above his head and the voice of the fat maid calling. Reluctantly he got up, carefully turned off the TV, and stepped outside. The fat maid was leaning out of the upstairs window flapping her arms. He did not like her. She had come some time after black Louise had gotten sick and returned to Jamaica. She was fat. She was from abroad, and spoke with a strange accent. She admitted that she did not understand the talk on the TV, which she watched in her room. As a rule he listened to her rapid speech only when she was bringing him food and telling him what the Old Man had eaten and what she thought he had said. Now she wanted him to come up quickly.

Chance began walking the three flights upstairs. He did not trust the elevator since the time black Louise had been trapped in it for hours. He walked down the long corridor until he reached the front of the house.

The last time he had seen this part of the house, some of the trees in the garden, now tall and lofty, had been quite small and insignificant. There was no TV then. Catching sight of his reflection in the large hall mirror, Chance saw the image of himself as a small boy and then the image of the Old Man sitting in a huge chair. His hair was gray, his hands wrinkled and shriveled. The Old Man breathed heavily and had to pause frequently between words.

Chance walked through the rooms, which seemed empty; the heavily curtained windows barely admitted the daylight. Slowly he looked at the large pieces of furniture shrouded in old linen covers, and at the veiled mirrors. The words that the Old Man had spoken to him the first time had wormed their way into his memory like firm roots. Chance was an orphan, and it was the Old Man himself who had sheltered him in the house ever since Chance was a child. Chance's mother had died when he was born. No one, not even the Old Man, would tell him who his father was. While some could learn to read and write, Chance would never be able to manage this. Nor would he ever be able to understand much of what others were saying to him or around him. Chance was to work in the garden, where he would care for plants and grasses and trees which grew there peacefully. He would be as one of them: quiet, openhearted in the sunshine and heavy when it rained. His name was Chance because he had been born by chance. He had no family. Although his mother had been very pretty, her mind had been as damaged as his: the soft soil of his brain, the ground from which all his thoughts shot up, had been ruined forever. Therefore, he could not look for a place in the life led by people outside the house or the garden gate. Chance must limit his life to his quarters and to the garden; he must not enter other parts of the household or walk out into the street. His food would always be brought to his room by Louise, who would be the only person to see Chance and talk to him. No one else was allowed to enter Chance's room. Only the Old Man himself might walk and sit in the garden. Chance would do exactly what he was told or else he would be sent to a special home for the insane where, the Old Man said, he would be locked in a cell and forgotten.

Chance did what he was told. So did black Louise.

*

As Chance gripped the handle of the heavy door, he heard the screeching voice of the maid. He entered and saw a room twice the height of all the others. Its walls were lined with built-in shelves, filled with books. On the large table flat leather folders were spread around.

The maid was shouting into the phone. She turned and, seeing him, pointed to the bed. Chance approached. The Old Man was propped against the stiff pillows and seemed poised intently, as if he were listening to a trickling whisper in the gutter. His shoulders sloped down at sharp angles, and his head, like a heavy fruit on a twig, hung down to one side. Chance stared into the Old Man's face. It was white, the upper jaw overlapped the lower lip of his mouth, and only one eye remained open, like the eye of a dead bird that sometimes lay in the garden. The maid put down the receiver, saying that she had just called the doctor, and he would come right away.

Chance gazed once more at the Old Man, mumbled good-bye, and walked out. He entered his room and turned on the TV.

TWO

Later in the day, watching TV, Chance heard the sounds of a struggle coming from the upper floors of the house. He left his room and, hidden behind the large sculpture in the front hall, watched the men carry out the Old Man's body. With the Old Man gone, someone would have to decide what was going to happen to the house, to the new maid, and to himself. On TV, after people died, all kinds of changes took place—changes brought about by relatives, bank officials, lawyers, and businessmen.

But the day passed and no one came. Chance ate a simple dinner, watched a TV show and went to sleep.

* * *

He rose early as always, found the breakfast that had been left at his door by the maid, ate it, and went into the garden.

He checked the soil under the plants, inspected the flowers, snipped away dead leaves, and pruned the bushes. Everything was in order. It had rained during the night, and many fresh buds had emerged. He sat down and dozed in the sun.

As long as one didn't look at people, they did not exist. They began to exist, as on TV, when one turned one's eyes on them. Only then could they stay in one's mind before being erased by new images. The same was true of him. By looking at him, others could make him be clear, could open him up and unfold him; not to be seen was to blur and to fade out. Perhaps he was missing a lot by simply watching others on TV and not being watched by them. He was glad that now, after the Old Man had died, he was going to be seen by people he had never been seen by before.

*

When he heard the phone ring in his room, he rushed inside. A man's voice asked him to come to the study.

Chance quickly changed from working clothes into one of his best suits, carefully trimmed and combed his hair, put on a pair of large sunglasses, which he wore when working in the garden, and went upstairs. In the narrow, dim book-lined room, a man and a woman were looking at him. Both sat behind the large desk, where various papers were spread out before them. Chance remained in the center of the room, not knowing what to do. The man got up and took a few steps toward him, his hand outstretched.

"I am Thomas Franklin, of Hancock, Adams and Colby. We are the lawyers handling this estate. And this," he said, turning to the woman, "is my assistant, Miss Hayes." Chance shook the man's hand and looked at the woman. She smiled.

"The maid told me that a man has been living in the house, and works as the gardener." Franklin inclined his head toward Chance.

"However, we have no record of a man—any man—either being employed by the deceased or residing in his house during any of the last forty years. May I ask you how many days you have been here?"

Chance was surprised that in so many papers spread on the desk his name was nowhere mentioned; it occurred to him that perhaps the garden was not mentioned there either. He hesitated. "I have lived in this house for as long as I can remember, ever since I was little, a long time before the Old Man broke his hip and began staying in bed most of the time. I was here before there were big bushes and before there were automatic sprinklers in the garden. Before television."

"You what?" Franklin asked. "You lived here—in this house—since you were a child? May I ask you what your name is?"

Chance was uneasy. He knew that a man's name had an important connection with his life. That was why people on TV always had two names—their own, outside of TV, and the one they adopted each time they performed. "My name is Chance," he said.

"Mr. Chance?" the lawyer asked.

Chance nodded.

"Let's look through our records," Mr. Franklin said. He picked up some of the papers heaped in front of him. "I have a complete record here of all those who were at any time employed by the deceased and by his estate. Although he was supposed to have a will, we were unable to find it. Indeed, the deceased left very few personal documents behind. However, we do have a list of all his employees," he emphasized, looking down at a document he held in his hand.

Chance waited.

"Please sit down, Mr. Chance," said the woman. Chance pulled a chair toward the desk and sat down.

Mr. Franklin rested his head in his hand. "I am very puzzled, Mr. Chance," he said, without lifting his eyes from the paper he was studying, "but your name does not appear anywhere in our records. No one by the name of Chance has ever been connected with the deceased. Are you certain, Mr. Chance—truly certain—that you have indeed been employed in this house?"

Chance answered very deliberately: "I have always been the gardener here. I have worked in the garden in back of the house all my life. As long as I can remember. I was a little boy when I began. The trees were small, and there were practically no hedges. Look at the garden now."

Mr. Franklin quickly interrupted. "But there is not a single indication that a gardener has been living in this house and working here. We, that is—Miss Hayes and I—have been put in charge of the deceased's estate by our firm. We are in possession of all the inventories. I can assure you," he said, "that there is no account of your being employed. It is clear that at no time during the last forty years was a man employed in this house. Are you a professional gardener?"

"I am a gardener," said Chance. "No one knows the garden better than I. From the time I was a child, I am the only one who has ever worked here. There was someone else before me—a tall black man; he stayed only long enough to tell me what to do and show me how to do it; from that time, I have been on my own. I planted some of the trees," he said, his whole body pointing in the direction of the garden, "and the flowers, and I cleaned the paths and watered the plants. The Old Man himself used to come down to sit in the garden and read and rest there. But then he stopped."

Mr. Franklin walked from the window to the desk. "I would like to believe you, Mr. Chance," he said, "but, you see, if what you say is true, as you claim it to be, then—for some reason difficult to fathom—your presence in this house, your employment, hasn't been recorded in any of the existing documents. True," he murmured to his assistant, "there were very few people employed here; he retired from our firm at the age of seventy-two, more than twenty-five years ago, when his broken hip immobilized him. And yet," he said, "in spite of his advanced age, the deceased was always in control of his affairs, and those who were employed by him have always been properly listed with our firm—paid, insured, et cetera. We have a record, after Miss Louise left, of the employment of one 'imported' maid, and that's all."

"I know old Louise; she can tell you that I have lived and worked here. She was here ever since I can remember, ever since I was little. She brought my food to my room every day, and once in a while she would sit with me in the garden."

"Louise died, Mr. Chance," interrupted Franklin.

"She left for Jamaica," said Chance.

"Yes, but she fell ill and died recently," Miss Hayes explained.

"I did not know that she had died," said Chance quietly.

"Nevertheless," Mr. Franklin persisted, "anyone ever employed by the deceased has always been properly paid, and our firm has been in charge of all such matters; hence our complete record of the estate's affairs."

"I did not know any of the other people working in the house. I always stayed in my room and worked in the garden."

"I'd like to believe you. However, as far as your former existence in this house is concerned, there just isn't any trace of you. The new maid has no idea of how long you have been here. Our firm has been in possession of all the pertinent deeds, checks, insurance claims, for the last fifty years." He smiled. "At the time the deceased was a partner in the firm, some of us were not even born, or were very, very young." Miss Hayes laughed. Chance did not understand why she laughed.

Mr. Franklin returned to the documents. "During your employment and your residence here, Mr. Chance, can you recall signing any papers?"

"No, sir."

"Then in what manner were you paid?"

"I have never been given any money. I was given my meals, very good meals, and as much to eat as I wanted; I have my room with a bathroom and a window that looks out on the garden, and a new door was put in leading out into the garden. I was given a radio and then a television, a big color television set with remote control changer. It also has an alarm in it to wake me up in the morning."

"I know the kind you're referring to," said Mr. Franklin.

"I can go to the attic and choose any of the Old Man's suits. They all fit me very well. Look." Chance pointed to his suit. "I can also have his coats, and his shoes, even though they are a bit tight, and his shirts, though the collars are a bit small, and his ties and . . ."

"I understand," Mr. Franklin said.

"It's quite amazing how fashionable your clothes look," interjected Miss Hayes suddenly.

Chance smiled at her.

"It's astonishing how men's fashions of today have reverted to the styles of the twenties," she added.

"Well, well," Mr. Franklin said, attempting lightheartedness, "are you implying that my wardrobe is out of style?" He turned to Chance: "And so you haven't in any way been contracted for your work."

"I don't think I have."

"The deceased never promised you a salary or any other form of payment?" Mr. Franklin persisted.

"No. No one promised me anything. I hardly ever saw the Old

Man. He did not come into the garden since the bushes on the left side were planted, and they're shoulder-high now. As a matter of fact, they were planted when there was no television yet, only radio. I remember listening to the radio while I was working in the garden and Louise coming downstairs and asking me to turn it down because the Old Man was asleep. He was already very old and sick."

Mr. Franklin almost jumped out of his chair. "Mr. Chance, I think it would simplify matters if you could produce some personal identification indicating your address. That would be a start. You know, a checkbook or driver's license or medical insurance card . . . you know."

"I don't have any of those things," said Chance.

"Just any card that states your name and address and your age."

Chance was silent.

"Perhaps your birth certificate?" Miss Hayes asked kindly.

"I don't have any papers."

"We shall need some proof of your having lived here," Mr. Franklin said firmly.

"But," said Chance, "you have me. I am here. What more proof do you need?"

"Have you ever been ill—that is, have you ever had to go to the hospital or to a doctor? Please understand," Mr. Franklin said tonelessly, "all we want is some evidence that you actually have been employed and resided here."

"I have never been ill," said Chance. "Never."

Mr. Franklin noticed the admiring look Miss Hayes gave the gardener. "I know," he said. "Tell me the name of your dentist."

"I have never gone to a dentist or to a doctor. I have never been outside of this house, and no one has ever been allowed to visit me. Louise went out sometimes, but I did not."

"I must be frank with you," Mr. Franklin said wearily. "There is no record of your having been here, of any wages paid to you, of any medical insurance." He stopped. "Have you paid any taxes?"

"No," said Chance.

"Have you served in the army?"

"No. I have seen the army on TV."

"Are you, by chance, related to the deceased?"

"No, I am not."

"Assuming that what you say is true," said Franklin flatly, "do you plan to make any claim against the estate of the deceased?"

Chance did not understand. "I am perfectly all right, sir," he said cautiously. "I'm fine. The garden is a good one. The sprinklers are only a few years old."

"Tell me," Miss Hayes interrupted, straightening up and throwing her head back, "what are your plans now? Are you going to work for someone else?"

Chance adjusted his sunglasses. He did not know what to say. Why would he have to leave the garden? "I would like to stay here and work in this garden," he said quietly.

Mr. Franklin shuffled the papers on the desk and drew out a page filled with fine print. "It's a simple formality," he said, handing the paper to Chance. "Would you be kind enough to read it now and—if you agree to it—to sign it where indicated?"

Chance picked up the paper. He held it in both hands and stared at it. He tried to calculate the time needed to read a page. On TV the time it took people to read legal papers varied. Chance knew that he should not reveal that he could not read or write. On TV programs people who did not know how to read or write were often mocked and ridiculed. He assumed a look of concentration, wrinkling his brow, scowling, now holding his chin between the thumb and the forefinger of his hand. "I can't sign it," he said returning the sheet to the lawyer. "I just can't."

"I see," Mr. Franklin said. "You mean therefore that you refuse to withdraw your claim?"

"I can't sign it, that's all," said Chance.

"As you wish," said Mr. Franklin. He gathered his documents together. "I must inform you, Mr. Chance," he said, "that this house will be closed tomorrow at noon. At that time, both doors and the gate to the garden will be locked. If, indeed, you do reside here, you will have to move out and take with you all your personal effects." He reached into his pocket and drew out a small calling card. "My name and the address and phone number of our firm are on this card."

Chance took the card and slipped it into the pocket of his vest. He knew that he had to leave the study now and go to his room. There was an afternoon TV program he always watched and did not want to miss. He got up, said good-bye, and left. On the stairs he threw the card away.

THREE

Early Tuesday morning Chance carried a large heavy leather suitcase down from the attic, noting for the last time the portraits lining the walls. He packed, left his room, and then, his hand on the garden gate, thought suddenly of postponing his departure and returning to the garden, where he would be able to hide unseen for some time. He set the suitcase down and went back into the garden. All was peaceful there. The flowers stood slender and erect. The electric water sprinkler spurted out a formless cloud of mist onto the shrubs. Chance felt with his fingers the prickly pine needles and the sprawling twigs of the hedge. They seemed to reach toward him.

For some time he stood in the garden looking around lazily in the morning sun. Then he disconnected the sprinkler and walked back to his room. He turned on the TV, sat down on the bed, and flicked the channel changer several times. Country houses, skyscrapers, newly built apartment houses, churches shot across the screen. He turned the set off. The image died; only a small blue dot hung in the center of the screen, as if forgotten by the rest of the world to which it belonged; then it too disappeared. The screen filled with grayness; it might have been a slab of stone.

Chance got up and now, on the way to the gate, he remembered to pick up the old key that for years had hung untouched on a board in the corridor next to his room. He walked to the gate and inserted the key; then, pulling the gate open, he crossed the threshold, abandoned the key in the lock, and closed the gate behind him. Now he could never return to the garden.

He was outside the gate. The sunlight dazzled his eyes. The sidewalks carried the passers-by away, the tops of the parked cars shimmered in the heat.

He was surprised: the street, the cars, the buildings, the people, the faint sounds were images already burned into his memory. So far, everything outside the gate resembled what he had seen on TV; if anything, objects and people were bigger, yet slower, simpler and more cumbersome. He had the feeling that he had seen it all.

He began to walk. In the middle of the block, he became conscious of the weight of his suitcase and of the heat: he was walking in the sun. He had found a narrow space between the cars parked against the curb and turned to leave the sidewalk, when suddenly he saw a car rapidly backing toward him. He attempted to leap out past the car's rear bumper, but the suitcase slowed him. He jumped, but too late. He was struck and jammed against the headlights of the stationary car behind him. Chance barely managed to raise one knee; he could not raise his other leg. He felt a piercing pain, and cried out, hammering against the trunk of the moving vehicle with his fist. The limousine stopped abruptly. Chance, his right leg raised above the bumper, his left one still trapped, could not move. The sweat drenched his body.

The chauffeur leaped from the limousine. He was black, in uniform, and carried his hat in his hand. He began to mumble words, then realized that Chance's leg was still pinned. Frightened, he ran back into the car and drove a few inches forward. Chance's calf was freed. He tried to stand on both feet, but collapsed onto the edge of the sidewalk. Instantly, the rear door of the car opened and a slender woman emerged. She bent over him. "I hope you're not badly hurt?"

Chance looked up at her. He had seen many women who looked like her on TV. "It's only my leg," he said, but his voice was trembling. "I think it was crushed a bit."

"Oh, dear God!" the woman said hoarsely. "Can you—would you please raise your trouser-leg so I can take a look?"

Chance pulled up his left trouser-leg. The middle of the calf was an already swelling red-bluish blotch.

"I hope nothing is broken," the woman said. "I can't tell you how sorry I am. My chauffeur has never had an accident before."

"It's all right," Chance said. "I feel somewhat better now."

"My husband has been very ill. We have his doctor and several nurses staying with us. The best thing, I think, would be to take you right home, unless, of course, you'd prefer to consult your own physician."

"I don't know what to do," said Chance.

"Do you mind seeing our doctor, then?"

"I don't mind at all," said Chance.

"Let's go," said the woman. "If the doctor advises it, we'll drive you straight to the hospital."

Chance leaned on the arm that the woman proffered him. Inside the limousine she sat next to him. The chauffeur installed Chance's suitcase, and the limousine smoothly joined the morning traffic.

The woman introduced herself. "I am Mrs. Benjamin Rand. I am called EE by my friends, from my Christian names, Elizabeth Eve."

"EE," Chance repeated gravely.

"EE," said the lady, amused.

Chance recalled that in similar situations men on TV introduced themselves. "I am Chance," he stuttered and, when this didn't seem to be enough, added, "the gardener."

"Chauncey Gardiner," she repeated. Chance noticed that she had changed his name. He assumed that, as on TV, he must use his new name from now on. "My husband and I are very old friends of Basil and Perdita Gardiner," the woman continued. "Are you by any chance a relative of theirs, Mr. Gardiner?"

"No, I am not," Chance replied.

"Would you care for a little whisky or perhaps a little cognac?"

Chance was puzzled. The Old Man did not drink and had not permitted his servants to drink. But once in a while, black Louise had secretly drunk in the kitchen and, on her insistence a very few times, Chance had tasted alcohol.

"Thank you. Perhaps some cognac," he replied, suddenly feeling the pain in his leg.

"I see that you are suffering," said the woman. She hastened to open a built-in bar in front of them, and from a silverish flask poured dark liquid into a monogrammed glass. "Please drink it all," she said. "It will do you good." Chance tasted the drink and sputtered. The woman smiled. "That's better. We'll be home soon and you'll be cared for. Just a little patience."

Chance sipped the drink. It was strong. He noticed a small TV set cleverly concealed above the bar. He was tempted to turn it on. He sipped his drink again as the car maneuvered slowly through the congested streets. "Does the TV work?" Chance asked.

"Yes. Of course it does."

"Can you—would you turn it on, please?"

"Certainly. It will take your mind off your pain." She leaned forward and pressed a button: images filled the screen. "Is there any particular channel, any program, that you want to watch?"

"No. This one is fine."

The small screen and the sounds of the TV separated them from the noise of the street. A car suddenly pulled in front of them, and the chauffeur braked sharply. As Chance braced himself for the sudden lurch, a pain pierced his leg. Everything spun around him; then his mind blanked, like a TV suddenly switched off.

*

He awoke in a room flooded with sunshine. EE was there. He lay on a very large bed.

"Mr. Gardiner," she was saying slowly. "You lost consciousness. But meanwhile we're home."

There was a knock at the door; it opened and a man appeared wearing a white smock and thick black-rimmed glasses and carrying a fat leather case. "I am your doctor," he said, "and you must be Mr. Gardiner, crushed and kidnaped by our charming hostess." Chance nodded. The doctor joked, "Your victim is very handsome. But now I'll have to examine him, and I'm sure you will prefer to leave us alone."

Before EE left, the doctor told her that Mr. Rand was asleep and should not be disturbed until late in the afternoon.

Chance's leg was tender; a purple bruise covered almost the entire calf.

"I'm afraid," said the doctor, "that I'll have to give you an injection so I can examine your leg without making you faint when I press it."

The doctor removed a syringe from his case. While he was filling it, Chance visualized all the TV incidents in which he had seen injections being given. He expected the injection to be painful, but he did not know how to show that he was afraid.

The doctor evidently noticed it. "Now, now," he said. "It's just a mild state of shock you're in, sir, and, though I doubt it, there may have been some damage to the bone." The injection was surprisingly quick, and Chance felt no pain.

After a few minutes the doctor reported that there had been no injury to the bone. "All you must do," he said, "is rest until this evening. Then if you feel like it, you can get up for dinner. Just make sure you don't put any weight on the injured leg. Meanwhile I'll instruct the nurse about your injections; you'll have one every three hours and a pill at mealtimes. If necessary, we'll arrange for X rays tomorrow. Now, have a good rest, sir." He left the room.

Chance was tired and sleepy. But when EE returned, he opened his eyes.

When one was addressed and viewed by others, one was safe. Whatever one did would then be interpreted by the others in the same way that one interpreted what they did. They could never know more about one than one knew about them.

"Mrs. Rand," he said. "I almost fell asleep."

"I am sorry if I disturbed you," she said. "But I've just been speaking to the doctor and he tells me that all you need is rest. Now, Mr. Gardiner—" She sat on a chair next to his bed. "I must tell you how very guilty I am and how responsible I feel for your accident. I do hope it will not inconvenience you too much."

"Please don't worry," Chance said. "I am very grateful for your help. I don't . . . I wouldn't . . ."

"It was the least we could do. Now is there anyone you would like to notify? Your wife? Your family?"

"I have no wife, no family."

"Perhaps your business associates? Please do feel free to use the telephone or send a cable or use our Telex. Would you like a secretary? My husband has been ill for so long that at present his staff has very little to do."

"No, thank you. There isn't anything I need."

"Surely there must be someone you would like to contact . . . I hope you don't feel . . ."

"There is no one."

"Mr. Gardiner, if this is so—and please don't think that what I say is mere politeness—if you have no particular business to attend to right away, I would like you to stay here with us until your injury has completely healed. It would be dreadful for you to have to look after yourself in such a state. We've lots of room, and the best medical attention will be available to you. I hope you will not refuse."

Chance accepted the invitation. EE thanked him, and he then heard her order the servants to unpack his suitcase.

* * *

Chance woke up as a strip of light moved across his face from the opening in the heavy curtains. It was late in the afternoon. He felt dizzy; he was aware of the pain in his leg and uncertain of where he was. Then he recalled the accident, the car, the woman, and the doctor. Standing close to the bed, within reach of his hand, was a TV. He turned it on and gazed at the reassuring images. Then, just as he decided to get up and open the curtains, the phone rang. EE was calling him. She asked about his leg and wanted to know whether he was ready to have tea and sandwiches brought to him and whether she could come up and visit him now. He said yes.

A maid entered with a tray, which she set down on the bed. Slowly and carefully, Chance ate the delicate food, remembering such meals from TV.

He was resting against the pillows, watching television, when EE entered the room. As she pulled a chair closer to his bed, he reluctantly turned the set off. She wanted to know about his leg. He admitted to some pain. In his presence she telephoned the doctor, assuring him that the patient appeared to be feeling better.

She told Chance that Mr. Rand was much older than she; he was well into his seventies. Until his recent illness, her husband had been a vigorous man, and even now, in spite of his age and illness, he remained interested and active in his business. She regretted, she said, that they had no children of their own, particularly since Rand had broken off all relations with his former wife and with his grown son of that marriage. EE confessed that she felt responsible for the rupture between father and son, since Benjamin Rand had divorced the boy's mother to marry her.

Thinking that he ought to show a keen interest in what EE was saying, Chance resorted to repeating to her parts of her own sentences, a practice he had observed on TV. In this fashion he encouraged her to continue and elaborate. Each time Chance repeated EE's words, she brightened and looked more confident. In fact, she became so at ease that she began to punctuate her speech by touching, now his shoulder, now his arm. Her words seemed to float inside his head; he observed her as if she were on television. EE rested her weight back in the chair. A knock at the door interrupted her in mid-sentence.

It was the nurse with the injection. Before leaving, EE invited Chance to have dinner with her and Mr. Rand, who was beginning to feel better.

Chance wondered whether Mr. Rand would ask him to leave the house. The thought that he might have to leave did not upset him; he knew that eventually he would have to go but that, as on TV, what would follow next was hidden; he knew the actors on the new program were unknown. He did not have to be afraid, for everything that happened had its sequel, and the best that he could do was to wait patiently for his own forthcoming appearance.

Just as he was turning on the TV, a valet—a black man—came, carrying his clothes, which had been cleaned and pressed. The man's smile brought back the easy smile of old Louise.

* * *

EE called again, asking him to come down and join her and her husband for a drink before dinner. At the bottom of the stairs a servant escorted him to the drawing room, where EE and an elderly man were waiting. Chance noticed that EE's husband was old, almost as old as the Old Man. Chance took his hand, which was dry and hot; his handshake was weak. The man was looking at Chance's leg. "Don't put any strain on it," he said in a slow, clear voice. "How are you feeling? EE told me about your accident. A damned shame! No excuse for it!"

Chance hesitated a moment. "It's really nothing, sir. I feel quite well already. This is the first time in my life that I have had an accident."

A servant poured champagne. Chance had barely begun to sip his when dinner was announced. The men followed EE to the dining room, where a a table was laid for three. Chance noted the gleaming silver and the frosty sculptures in the corners of the room.

In deciding how to behave, Chance chose the TV program of a young businessman who often dined with his boss and the boss's daughter.

"You look like a healthy man, Mr. Gardiner," said Rand. "That's your good luck. But doesn't this accident prevent you from attending to your business?"

"As I have already told Mrs. Rand," Chance began slowly, "my house has been closed up, and I do not have any urgent business." He cut and ate his food carefully. "I was just expecting something to happen when I had the accident."

Mr. Rand removed his glasses, breathed onto the lenses, and polished them with his handkerchief. Then he settled the glasses back on and stared at Chance with expectation. Chance realized that his answer was not satisfactory. He looked up and saw EE's gaze.

"It is not easy, sir," he said, "to obtain a suitable place, a garden, in which one can work without interference and grow with the seasons. There can't be too many opportunities left any more. On TV . . ." he faltered. It dawned on him. "I've never seen a garden. I've seen forests and jungles and sometimes a tree or two. But a garden in which I can work and watch the things I've planted in it grow . . ." He felt sad.

Mr. Rand leaned across the table to him. "Very well put, Mr. Gardiner—I hope you don't mind if I call you Chauncey? A gardener! Isn't that the perfect description of what a real businessman is? A person who makes a flinty soil productive with the labor of his own hands, who waters it with the sweat of his own brow, and who creates a place of value for his family and for the community. Yes, Chauncey, what an excellent metaphor! A productive businessman is indeed a laborer in his own vineyard!"

The alacrity with which Mr. Rand responded relieved Chance; all was well. "Thank you sir," he murmured.

"Please . . . do call me Ben."

"Ben." Chance nodded. "The garden I left was such a place, and I know I won't ever find anything as wonderful. Everything which grew there was of my own doing: I planted seeds, I watered them, I watched them grow. But now it's all gone, and all that's left is the room upstairs." He pointed toward the ceiling.

Rand regarded him gently. "You're young, Chauncey, why do you have to talk about 'the room upstairs'? That's where I'm going soon, not you. You could almost be my son, you're so young. You and EE: both of you, so young."

"Ben, dear—" began EE.

"I know, I know," he interrupted, "you don't like my bringing up our ages. But for me all that's left is a room upstairs."

Chance wondered what Rand meant by saying that he'd soon be in the room upstairs. How could he move in up there while he, Chance, was still in the house?

They ate in silence, Chance chewing slowly and ignoring the wine. On TV, wine put people in a state they could not control.

"Well," said Rand, "if you can't find a good opportunity soon, how will you take care of your family?"

"I have no family."

Rand's face clouded. "I don't understand it—a handsome, young man like you without a family? How can that be?"

"I've not had the time," said Chance.

Rand shook his head, impressed. "Your work was that demanding?"

"Ben, please—" EE broke in.

"I'm sure Chauncey doesn't mind answering my questions? Do you, Chauncey?"

Chance shook his head.

"Well . . . didn't you ever want a family?"

"I don't know what it is to have a family."

Rand murmured: "Then, indeed, you are alone, aren't you?"

After a silence, the servants brought in another course. Rand looked over at Chance.

"You know," he said, "there's something about you that I like. I'm an old man, and I can speak to you frankly. You're direct: you grasp things quickly and you state them plainly. As you may be aware," Rand continued, "I am chairman of the board of the First American Financial Corporation. We have just begun a program to assist American businesses that have been harassed by inflation, excessive taxation, riots, and other indecencies. We want to offer the decent 'gardeners' of the business community a helping hand, so to speak. After all, they are our strongest defense against the conglomerates and the pollutants who so threaten our basic freedoms and the well-being of our middle class. We must discuss this at greater length; perhaps, when you are up and around, you can meet some of the other members of the board, who will acquaint you further with our projects and our goals."

Chance was glad that Rand immediately added: "I know, I know, you are not a man to act on the spur of the moment. But do think about what I've said, and remember that I'm very ill and don't know how much longer I'm going to be around. . . ."

EE began to protest, but Rand continued: "I am sick and weary with age. I feel like a tree whose roots have come to the surface. . . ."

Chance stopped listening. He missed his garden; in the Old Man's garden none of the trees ever had their roots surface or wither. There, all the trees were young and well cared for. In the silence he now felt widening around him, he said quickly: "I will consider what you've said. My leg still hurts, and it is difficult to decide."

"Good. Don't rush, Chauncey." Rand leaned over and patted Chance's shoulder. They rose and went into the library.

FOUR

On Wednesday, as Chance was dressing, the phone rang. He heard the voice of Rand: "Good morning, Chauncey. Mrs. Rand wanted me to wish you good morning for her too, since she won't be at home today. She had to fly to Denver. But there's another reason I called. The President will address the annual meeting of the Financial Institute today; he is flying to New York and has just telephoned me from his plane. He knows I am ill and that, as the chairman, I won't be able to preside over the meeting as scheduled. But as I am feeling somewhat better today, the President has graciously decided to visit me before the luncheon. It's nice of him, don't you think? Well, he's going to land at Kennedy and then come over to Manhattan by helicopter. We can expect him here in about an hour." He stopped; Chance could hear his labored breathing. "I want you to meet him, Chauncey. You'll enjoy it. The President is quite a man, quite a man, and I know that he'll like and appreciate you. Now listen: the Secret Service people will be here before long to look over the place. It's strictly routine, something they have to do, no matter what, no matter where. If you don't mind, my secretary will notify you when they arrive."

"All right, Benjamin, thank you."

"Oh, yes, one more thing, Chauncey. I hope you won't mind . . . but they will have to search you personally as well. Nowadays, no one in close proximity to the President is allowed to have any sharp objects on his person—so don't show them your mind, Chauncey, they may take it away from you! See you soon, my friend!" He hung up.

There must be no sharp objects. Chance quickly removed his tie clip and put his comb on the table. But what had Rand meant when he said "your mind"? Chance looked at himself in the mirror. He liked what he saw: his hair glistened, his skin was ruddy, his freshly pressed dark suit fitted his body as bark covers a tree. Pleased, he turned on the TV.

After a while, Rand's secretary called to say that the President's men were ready to come up. Four men entered the room, talking and smiling easily, and began to go through it with an assortment of complicated instruments.

Chance sat at the desk, watching TV. Changing channels, he suddenly saw a huge helicopter descending in a field in Central Park. The announcer explained that at that very moment the President of the United States was landing in the heart of New York City.

The Secret Service men stopped working to watch too. "Well, the Boss has arrived," one of them said. "We better hurry with the other rooms." Chance was alone when Rand's secretary called to announce the President's imminent arrival.

"Thank you," he said. "I guess I'd better go down right now, don't you think?" He stammered a bit.

"I think it is time, sir."

Chance walked downstairs. The Secret Service men were quietly moving around the corridors, the front hall and the elevator entrance. Some stood near the windows of the study; others were in the dining room, the living room, and in front of the library. Chance was searched by an agent, who quickly apologized and then opened the door to the library for him.

Rand approached and patted Chance's shoulder. "I'm so glad that you'll have the opportunity to meet the Chief Executive. He's a fine man, with a sense of justice nicely contained by the law and an excellent judgment of both the pulse and purse of the electorate. I must say, it's very thoughtful of him to come to visit me now. Don't you agree?"

Chance agreed.

"What a pity EE isn't here," Rand declared. "She's a great fan of the President and finds him very attractive. She telephoned from Denver, you know."

Chance said that he knew about EE's call.

"And you didn't talk to her? Well, she'll call again; she'll want to know your impressions of the President and of how things went. . . . If I should be asleep, Chauncey, you will speak to her, won't you, and tell her all about the meeting?"

"I'll be glad to. I hope you're feeling well, sir. You do look better."

Rand moved uneasily in his chair. "It's all make-up, Chauncey—all make-up. The nurse was here all night and through the morning, and I asked her to fix me up so the President won't feel I'm going to die during our talk. No one likes a dying man, Chauncey, because few know what death is. All we know is the terror of it. You're an exception, Chauncey, I can tell. I know that you're not afraid. That's what EE and I admire in you: your marvelous balance. You don't stagger back and forth between fear and hope; you're a truly peaceful man! Don't disagree; I'm old enough to be your father. I've lived a lot, trembled a lot, was surrounded by little men who forgot that we enter naked and exit naked and that no accountant can audit life in our favor."

Rand looked pallid. He reached for a pill, swallowed it, and sipped some water from a glass. A phone rang. He picked up the receiver and said briskly: "Mr. Gardiner and I are ready. Show the President into the library." He replaced the receiver and then removed the glass of water from the desk top, placing it behind him on a bookshelf. "The President is here, Chauncey. He's on the way."

Chance remembered seeing the President on a recent television program. In the sunshine of a cloudless day, a military parade had been in progress. The President stood on a raised platform, surrounded by military men in uniforms covered with glittering medals, and by civilians in dark glasses. Below, in the open field, never-ending columns of soldiers marched, their faces riveted upon their leader, who waved his hand. The President's eyes were veiled with distant thought. He watched the thousands in their ranks, who were reduced by the TV screen to mere mounds of lifeless leaves swept forward by a driving wind. Suddenly, down from the skies, jets swooped in tight, faultless formations. The military observers and the civilians on the reviewing stand barely had time to raise their heads when, like bolts of lightning, the planes streaked past the President, hurling down thunderous booms. The President's head once more pervaded the screen. He gazed up at the disappearing planes; a fleeting smile softened his face.

* * *

"It's good to see you, Mr. President," Rand said, rising from his chair to greet a man of medium height who entered the room smiling. "How thoughtful of you to come all this way to look in on a dying man."

The President embraced him and led him to a chair. "Nonsense, Benjamin. Do sit down, now, and let me see you." The President seated himself on a sofa and turned to Chance.

"Mr. President," Rand said, "I want to introduce my dear friend,

Mr. Chauncey Gardiner. Mr. Gardiner—the President of the United States of America." Rand sank into a chair, while the President extended his hand, a wide smile on his face. Remembering that during his TV press conferences, the President always looked straight at the viewers, Chance stared directly into the President's eyes.

"I'm delighted to meet you, Mr. Gardiner," the President said, leaning back on a sofa. "I've heard so much about you."

Chance wondered how the President could have heard anything about him. "Please do sit down, Mr. Gardiner," the President said. "Together, let's reprimand our friend Benjamin for the way he shuts himself up at home. Ben . . ." he leaned toward the old man—"this country needs you, and I, as your Chief Executive, haven't authorized you to retire."

"I am ready for oblivion, Mr. President," said Rand mildly, "and, what's more, I'm not complaining; the world parts with Rand, and Rand parts with the world: a fair trade, don't you agree? Security, tranquility, a well-deserved rest: all the aims I have pursued will soon be realized."

"Now be serious, Ben!" The President waved his hand. "I have known you to be a philosopher, but above all you're a strong, active businessman! Let's talk about life!" He paused to light a cigarette. "What's this I hear about your not addressing the meeting of the Financial Institute today?"

"I can't, Mr. President," said Rand. "Doctor's orders. And what's more," he added, "I obey pain."

"Well . . . yes . . . after all, it's just another meeting. And even if you're not there in person, you'll be there in spirit. The Institute remains your creation; your life's stamp is on all its proceedings."

The men began a long conversation. Chance understood almost nothing of what they were saying, even though they often looked in his direction, as if to invite his participation. Chance thought that they purposely spoke in another language for reasons of secrecy, when suddenly the President addressed him: "And you, Mr. Gardiner? What do you think about the bad season on The Street?"

Chance shrank. He felt that the roots of his thoughts had been suddenly yanked out of their wet earth and thrust, tangled, into the unfriendly air. He stared at the carpet. Finally, he spoke: "In a garden," he said, "growth has its season. There are spring and summer, but there are also fall and winter. And then spring and summer again. As long as the roots are not severed, all is well and all will be well." He raised his eyes. Rand was looking at him, nodding. The President seemed quite pleased.

"I must admit, Mr. Gardiner," the President said, "that what you've just said is one of the most refreshing and optimistic statements I've heard in a very, very long time." He rose and stood erect, with his back to the fireplace. "Many of us forget that nature and society are one! Yes, though we have tried to cut ourselves off from nature, we are still part of it. Like nature, our economic system remains, in the long run, stable and rational, and that's why we must not fear to be at its mercy." The President hesitated for a moment, then turned to Rand. "We welcome the inevitable seasons of nature, yet we are upset by the seasons of our economy! How foolish of us!" He smiled at Chance. "I envy Mr. Gardiner his good solid sense. This is just what we lack on Capitol Hill." The President glanced at his watch, then lifted a hand to prevent Rand from rising. "No, no, Ben—you rest. I do hope to see you again soon. When you're feeling better, you and EE must come to visit us in Washington. And you, Mr. Gardiner . . . You will also honor me and my family with a visit, won't you? We'll all look forward to that!" He embraced Rand, shook hands swiftly with Chance, and strode out the door.

Rand hastily retrieved his glass of water, gulped down another pill, and slumped in his chair. "He is a decent fellow, the President, isn't he?" he asked Chance.

"Yes," said Chance, "though he looks taller on television."

"Oh, he certainly does!" Rand exclaimed. "But remember that he is a political being, who diplomatically waters with kindness every plant on his way, no matter what he really thinks. I do like him! By the way, Chauncey, did you agree with my position on credit and tight money as I presented it to the President?"

"I'm not sure I understood it. That's why I kept quiet."

"You said a lot, my dear Chauncey, quite a lot, and it is what you said and how you said it that pleased the President so much. He hears my sort of analysis from everyone, but, yours, unfortunately . . . seldom if ever at all."

The phone rang. Rand answered it and then informed Chance that the President and the Secret Service men had departed and that the nurse was waiting with an injection. He embraced Chance and excused himself. Chance went upstairs. When he turned the TV on, he saw the presidential motorcade moving along Fifth Avenue. Small crowds gathered on sidewalks; the President's hand waved from the limousine's window. Chance did not know if he had actually shaken that hand only moments before.

* * *

The annual meeting of the Financial Institute opened in an atmosphere of expectation and high tension, following the disclosure that morning of the rise in national unemployment to an unprecedented level. Administration officials were reluctant to divulge what measures the President would propose to combat further stagnation of the economy. All of the public news media were on the alert.

In his speech the President reassured the public that no drastic governmental measures were forthcoming, even though there had been another sudden decline in productivity. "There was a time for spring," he said, "and a time for summer; but, unfortunately, as in a garden of the earth, there is also a time for the inevitable chill and storm of autumn and winter." The President stressed that as long as the seeds of industry remained firmly embedded in the life of the country, the economy was certain to flourish again.

In the short, informal question-and-answer period, the President revealed that he had "conducted multiple-level consultations" with members of the "Cabinet, House, and Senate, and also with prominent leaders of the business community." Here he paid tribute to Benjamin Turnbull Rand, chairman of the Institute, absent because of illness; he added that at Mr. Rand's home he had engaged in a most fruitful discussion with Rand and with Mr. Chauncey Gardiner on the beneficial effects of inflation. "Inflation would prune the dead limbs of savings, thus enlivening the vigorous trunk of industry." It was in the context of the President's speech that Chance's name first came to the attention of the news media.

* * *

In the afternoon Rand's secretary said to Chance: "I have Mr. Tom Courtney of the New York *Times* on the line. Could you talk to him, sir, just for a few minutes? I think he wants to get some facts about you."

"I'll talk to him," said Chance.

The secretary put Courtney on. "I'm sorry to disturb you, Mr. Gardiner; I wouldn't have if I hadn't first talked to Mr. Rand." He paused for effect.

"Mr. Rand is a very sick man," said Chance.

"Well, yes . . . Anyway, he mentioned that because of your character and your vision there is a possibility of your joining the board of the First American Financial Corporation. Do you wish to comment on this?"

"No," said Chance. "Not now."

Another pause. "Since the New York *Times* is covering the President's speech and his visit to New York, we would like to be as exact as possible. Would you care to comment on the nature of the discussion that took place between you, Mr. Rand, and the President?"

"I enjoyed it very much."

"Good, sir. And so, it seems, did the President. But Mr. Gardiner," Courtney went on, with feigned casualness, "we at the *Times* would like very much to update our information on you, if you see what I mean. . . ." He laughed nervously. "To start with, what, for example, is the relationship between your business and that of the First American Financial Corporation?"

"I think you ought to ask Mr. Rand that," said Chance.

"Yes, of course. But since he is ill, I am taking the liberty of asking you."

Chance was silent. Courtney waited for an answer.

"I have nothing more to say," said Chance and hung up.

Courtney leaned back in his chair, frowning. It was getting late. He called his staff, and when they had come in he assumed his old casual manner. "All right, gentlemen. Let's start with the President's visit and speech. I talked to Rand. Chauncey Gardiner, the man mentioned by the President, is a businessman, it seems, a financier, and, according to Rand, a strong candidate for one of the vacant seats on the board of the First American Financial Corporation." He looked at his staffers, who expected to hear more.

"I also talked to Gardiner. Well . . ." Courtney paused. "He's very laconic and matter-of-fact. Anyway, we won't have enough time to round up all the information on Gardiner, so let's play up his prospective affiliation with Rand, his joining the board of the First American Financial, his advice to the President, and so forth."

* * *

Chance watched TV in his room. The President's speech at the luncheon of the Financial Institute was telecast on several channels; the few remaining programs showed only family games and children's adventures. Chance ate lunch in his room, continued to watch TV, and was just about to fall asleep when Rand's secretary called.

"The executives of the THIS EVENING television program have just phoned," she said excitedly, "and they want you to appear on the show tonight. They apologized for giving you such short notice, but they've only just now heard that the Vice President will be unable to appear on the show to discuss the President's speech. Because Mr. Rand is so ill, he will, of course, also be unable to appear; but he has suggested that you—a financier who has made so favorable an impression on the President—might be willing to come instead."

Chance could not imagine what being on TV involved. He wanted to see himself reduced to the size of the screen; he wanted to become an image, to dwell inside the set.

The secretary waited on the phone.

"It's all right with me," said Chance. "What do I have to do?"

"You don't have to do anything, sir," she said cheerfully. "The producer himself will pick you up in time for the show. It's a live program, so you have to be there half an hour before it goes on. You'll be THIS EVENING's main attraction tonight. I'll call them right back; they'll be delighted with your acceptance."

Chance turned on the TV. He wondered whether a person changed before or after appearing on the screen. Would he be changed forever or only during the time of his appearance? What part of himself would he leave behind when he finished the program? Would there be two Chances after the show: one Chance who watched TV and another who appeared on it?

Early that evening, Chance was visited by the producer of THIS EVENING—a short man in a dark suit. The producer explained that the President's speech had heightened interest in the nation's economic situation. ". . . and since the Vice President won't be able to appear on our show tonight," he continued, "we would be very grateful to have you tell our viewers exactly what is going on in the country's economy. Occupying, as you do, a position of such intimacy with the

President, you are a man ideally suited to provide the country with an explanation. On the show you can be as direct as you'd like to be. The host won't interrupt you at all while you're talking, but if he wants to break in he'll let you know by raising his left forefinger to his left eyebrow. This will mean that he wants either to ask you a new question or to emphasize what you've already said."

"I understand," said Chance.

"Well, if you're ready, sir, we can go; our make-up man will have to do only a minor touch-up." He smiled. "Our host, by the way, would be honored to meet you before the show goes on."

In the large limousine sent by the network, there were two small TV sets. As they drove along Park Avenue, Chance asked if a set could be turned on. He and the producer watched the program in silence.

The interior of the studio looked like all the TV studios Chance had ever seen on TV. He was escorted quickly to a large adjoining office and offered a drink, which he refused; instead, he had a cup of coffee. The host of the show appeared. Chance recognized him instantly; he had seen him many times on THIS EVENING, although he did not like talk shows very much.

While the host talked on and on to him, Chance wondered what was going to happen next and when he would actually be televised. The host grew quiet at last, and the producer returned promptly with the make-up man. Chance sat in front of a mirror as the man covered his face with a thin layer of brownish powder. "Have you appeared on television a lot?" asked the make-up man.

"No," said Chance, "but I watch it all the time."

The make-up man and the producer chuckled politely. "Ready," said the make-up man, nodding and closing his case. "Good luck, sir." He turned and left.

Chance waited in an adjacent room. In one corner stood a large, bulky TV set. He saw the host appear and introduce the show. The audience applauded; the host laughed. The big, sharp-nosed cameras rolled smoothly around the stage. There was music, and the band leader flashed on screen, grinning.

Chance was astonished that television could portray itself; cameras watched themselves and, as they watched, they televised a program. This self-portrait was telecast on TV screens facing the stage and watched by the studio audience. Of all the manifold things there were in all the world—trees, grass, flowers, telephones, radios, elevators

—only TV constantly held up a mirror to its own neither solid nor fluid face.

Suddenly the producer appeared and signaled Chance to follow him. They walked through the door and on past a heavy curtain. Chance heard the host pronounce his name. Then, as the producer stepped away, he found himself in the glare of the lights. He saw the audience in front of him; unlike the audiences he had seen on his own TV set, he could not distinguish individual faces in the crowd. Three large cameras stood on the small, square stage; on the right, the host sat at a leather-padded table. He beamed at Chance, rose with dignity, and introduced him; the audience applauded loudly. Imitating what he had so often seen on TV, Chance moved toward the vacant chair at the table. He sat down, and so did the host. The cameramen wheeled the cameras silently around them. The host leaned across the table toward Chance.

Facing the cameras and the audience, now barely visible in the background of the studio, Chance abandoned himself to what would happen. He was drained of thought, engaged, yet removed. The cameras were licking up the image of his body, were recording his every movement and noiselessly hurling them into millions of TV screens scattered throughout the world—into rooms, cars, boats, planes, living rooms, and bedrooms. He would be seen by more people than he could ever meet in his entire life—people who would never meet him. The people who watched him on their sets did not know who actually faced them; how could they, if they had never met him? Television reflected only people's surfaces; it also kept peeling their images from their bodies until they were sucked into the caverns of their viewers' eyes, forever beyond retrieval, to disappear. Facing the cameras with their unsensing triple lenses pointed at him like snouts, Chance became only an image for millions of real people. They would never know how real he was, since his thinking could not be televised. And to him, the viewers existed only as projections of his own thought, as images. He would never know how real they were, since he had never met them and did not know what they thought.

Chance heard the host say: "We here in the studio are very honored to have you with us tonight, Mr. Chauncey Gardiner, and so, I'm sure, are the more than forty million Americans who watch THIS EVENING nightly. We are especially grateful to you for filling in on such short notice for the Vice President, who was unfortunately prevented by pressing business from being with us tonight." The host paused for a second; there was complete silence in the studio. "I will be frank, Mr. Gardiner. Do you agree with the President's view of our economy?"

"Which view?" asked Chance.

The host smiled knowingly. "The view which the President set forth this afternoon in his major address to the Financial Institute of America. Before his speech, the President consulted with you, among his other financial advisers. . . ."

"Yes . . . ?" said Chance.

"What I mean is . . ." The host hesitated and glanced at his notes. "Well . . . let me give you an example: the President compared the economy of this country to a garden, and indicated that after a period of decline a time of growth would naturally follow. . . ."

"I know the garden very well," said Chance firmly. "I have worked in it all of my life. It's a good garden and a healthy one; its trees are healthy and so are its shrubs and flowers, as long as they are trimmed and watered in the right seasons. The garden needs a lot of care. I do agree with the President: everything in it will grow strong in due course. And there is still plenty of room in it for new trees and new flowers of all kinds."

Part of the audience interrupted to applaud and part booed. Looking at the TV set that stood to his right, Chance saw first his own face fill the screen. Then some faces in the audience were shown—they evidently approved his words; others appeared angry. The host's face returned to the screen, and Chance turned away from the set and faced him.

"Well, Mr. Gardiner," the host said, "that was very well put indeed, and I think it was a booster for all of us who do not like to wallow in complaints or take delight in gloomy predictions! Let us be clear, Mr. Gardiner. It is your view, then, that the slowing of the economy, the downtrend in the stock market, the increase in unemployment . . . you believe that all of this is just another phase, another season, so to speak, in the growth of a garden. . . ."

"In a garden, things grow . . . but first, they must wither; trees have to lose their leaves in order to put forth new leaves, and to grow thicker and stronger and taller. Some trees die, but fresh saplings replace them. Gardens need a lot of care. But if you love your garden, you don't mind working in it, and waiting. Then in the proper season you will surely see it flourish."

Chance's last words were partly lost in the excited murmuring of the audience. Behind him, members of the band tapped their instruments; a few cried out loud bravos. Chance turned to the set beside him and saw his own face with the eyes turned to one side. The host lifted his hand to silence the audience, but the applause continued, punctuated by isolated boos. He rose slowly and motioned Chance to join him at center stage, where he embraced him ceremoniously. The applause mounted to uproar. Chance stood uncertainly. As the noise subsided, the host took Chance's hand and said: "Thank you, thank you, Mr. Gardiner. Yours is the spirit which this country so greatly needs. Let's hope it will help usher spring into our economy. Thank you again, Mr. Chauncey Gardiner—financier, presidential adviser, and true statesman!"

He escorted Chance back to the curtain, where the producer gently took him in hand. "You were great, sir, just great!" the producer exclaimed. "I've been producing this show for almost three years and I can't remember anything like it! I can tell you that the boss really loved it. It was great, really great!" He led Chance to the rear of the studio. Several employees waved to him warmly, while others turned away.

* * *

After dining with his wife and children, Thomas Franklin went into the den to work. There was simply not enough time for him to finish his work in the office, especially as Miss Hayes, his assistant, was on vacation.

He worked until he could no longer concentrate, then went to the bedroom. His wife was already in bed, watching a TV program of commentary on the President's speech. Franklin glanced at the set as he undressed. In the last two years, Franklin's stock market holdings had fallen to one third of their value, his savings were gone, and his share in the profits of his firm had recently diminished. He was not encouraged by the President's speech and hoped that the Vice President or, in his absence, this fellow Gardiner, might brighten his gloomy predicament. He threw off his trousers clumsily, neglecting to hang them in the automatic trouser-press which his wife had given him on his birthday, and sat down on the bed to watch THIS EVENING, which was just starting.

The host introduced Chauncey Gardiner. The guest moved forward. The image was sharp and the color faithful. But even before that full face materialized clearly on the screen, Franklin felt he had seen this man before somewhere. Had it been on TV, during one of the in-depth interviews through which the restless cameras showed every angle of a man's head and body? Perhaps he had even met Gardiner in person? There was something familiar about him, especially the way he was dressed.

He was so absorbed in trying to remember if and when he had actually met the man that he did not hear at all what Gardiner said and what it was exactly that had prompted the loudly applauding audience.

"What was that he said, dear?" he asked his wife.

"Wow!" she said, "how did you miss it? He just said that the economy is doing fine! The economy is supposed to be something like a garden: you know, things grow and things wilt. Gardiner thinks things will be okay!" She sat in bed looking at Franklin ruefully. "I told you that there was no need to give up our option on that place in Vermont or to put off the cruise. It's just like you—you're always the first one to panic! Ha! I told you so! It's only a mild frost—in the garden!"

Franklin once again stared distractedly at the screen. When and where the devil had he seen this fellow before?

"This Gardiner has quite a personality," his wife mused. "Manly; well-groomed; beautiful voice; sort of a cross between Ted Kennedy and Cary Grant. He's not one of those phony idealists, or IBM-ized technocrats."

Franklin reached for a sleeping pill. It was late and he was tired. Perhaps becoming a lawyer had been a mistake. Business . . . finance . . . Wall Street; they were probably better. But at forty he was too old to start taking chances. He envied Gardiner his looks, his success, his self-assurance. "Like a garden." He sighed audibly. Sure. If one could only believe that.

* * *

On his way home from the studio, alone in the limousine, watching TV, Chance saw the host with his next guest, a voluptuous actress clad in an almost transparent gown. He heard his name mentioned by both the host and his guest; the actress smiled often and said that she found Chance good-looking and very masculine.

At Rand's house, one of the servants rushed out to open the door for him.

"That was a very fine speech you made, Mr. Gardiner." He trailed Chance to the elevator.

Another servant opened the elevator door. "Thank you, Mr. Gardiner," he said. "Just 'thank you' from a simple man who has seen a lot."

In the elevator Chance gazed at the small portable TV set built into a side panel. THIS EVENING was still going strong. The host was now talking to another guest, a heavily bearded singer, and Chance once again heard his name mentioned.

Upstairs, Chance was met by Rand's secretary: "That was a truly remarkable performance, sir," the woman said. "I have never seen anyone more at ease, or truer to himself. Thank goodness, we still have people like you in this country. Oh, and by the way, Mr. Rand saw you on television and though he's not feeling too well he insisted that when you got back you pay him a visit."

Chance entered Rand's bedroom. "Chauncey," said Rand, struggling to prop himself up in his enormous bed. "Let me congratulate you most warmly! Your speech was so good, so good. I hope the whole country watched you." He smoothed his blanket. "You have the great gift . . . of being natural, and that, my dear man, is a rare talent, and the true mark of a leader. You were strong and brave, yet you did not moralize. Everything you said was directly to the point."

The two men regarded each other silently.

"Chauncey, my dear friend," Rand went on, in a serious and almost reverential manner. "You will be interested in the fact that EE is chairman of the Hospitality Committee of the United Nations. It is only right that she should be present at the U.N. reception tomorrow. Since I won't be able to escort her, I would like you to do so for me. Your speech will be uppermost in many people's minds; and many, I know, would like very much to meet you. You will escort her, won't you?"

"Yes. Of course I'll be glad to accompany EE."

For a moment, Rand's face seemed blurred, as if it were frozen inwardly. He moistened his lips; his eyes aimlessly scanned the room. Then he focused them on Chance. "Thank you, Chauncey. And . . . by the way," he said quietly, "if anything should happen to me, please do take care of her. She needs someone like you . . . very much."

They shook hands and said good-bye. Chance went to his room.

* * *

On the plane back to New York from Denver, EE thought more and more about Gardiner. She tried to discover a unifying thread in the events of the last two days. She remembered that when she first saw him after the accident, he did not seem surprised; his face was without expression, his manner calm and detached. He behaved as if he had expected the accident, the pain, and even her appearance.

Two days had passed, but she did not know who he was and where he had come from. He steadily avoided any talk about himself. The day before, while the servants were eating in the kitchen and Chance was asleep, she had carefully gone through all of his belongings, but there were no documents among them, no checks, no money, no credit cards; she was not able to find even the stray stub of a theater ticket. It puzzled her that he traveled this way. Presumably, his personal affairs were attended to by a business or a bank which remained at his instant disposal. For he was obviously well-to-do. His suits were hand-tailored from an exquisite cloth, his shirts handmade from the most delicate silks and his shoes handmade from the softest leather. His suitcase was almost new, though its shape and lock were of an old-fashioned design.

On several occasions she had attempted to question him about his past. He had resorted to one or another of his favorite comparisons drawn on television or taken from nature; she guessed that he was troubled by a business loss, or even a bankruptcy—so common nowadays—or perhaps by the loss of a woman's love. Perhaps he had decided to leave the woman on the spur of the moment and was still wondering if he should return. Somewhere in this country there was the community where he had lived, a place which contained his home, his business, and his past.

He had not dropped names; nor had he referred to places or events. Indeed, she could not remember encountering anyone who relied more on his own self. Gardiner's manner alone indicated social confidence and financial security.

She could not define the feelings that he kindled in her. She was aware that her pulse raced when she was near him, aware of his image in her thoughts and of the difficulty she had in speaking to him in cool, even tones. She wanted to know him, and she wanted to yield to that knowledge. There were innumerable selves that he evoked in her. Yet she was not able to discover a single motive in any of his actions and for a brief instant she feared him. From the beginning, she noticed the meticulous care he took to insure that nothing he said to her or to anyone else was definite enough to reveal what he thought of her or of anyone or, indeed, of anything.

But unlike the other men with whom she was intimate, Gardiner neither restrained nor repulsed her. The thought of seducing him, of making him lose his composure, excited her. The more withdrawn he was, the more she wanted him to look at her and to acknowledge her desire, to recognize her as a willing mistress. She saw herself making love to him—abandoned, wanton, without reticence or reserve.

She arrived home late that evening and called Chance, asking him whether she could come to his room. He agreed.

She looked tired. "I am so sorry I had to be away. I missed your television appearance—and I missed you," she murmured in a timid voice.

She sat down on the edge of the bed; Chance moved back to give her more room.

She brushed her hair from her forehead, and, looking at him quietly, put her hand on his arm. "Please don't . . . run away from me! Don't!" She sat motionless, her head resting against Chance's shoulder.

Chance was bewildered: there was clearly no place to which he could run away. He searched his memory and recalled situations on TV in which a woman advanced toward a man on a couch or a bed or inside a car. Usually, after a while, they would come very close to each other, and, often they would be partly undressed. They would then kiss and embrace. But on TV what happened next was always obscured: a brand-new image would appear on the screen: the embrace of man and woman was utterly forgotten. And yet, Chance knew, there could be other gestures and other kinds of closeness following such intimacies. Chance had just a fleeting memory of a maintenance man who, years ago, used to come to the Old Man's house to take care of the incinerator. On several occasions after he was through with the work, he would come out into the garden and drink beer. Once he showed Chance a number of small photographs of a man and woman who were completely naked. In one of these photographs, a woman held the man's unnaturally long and thickened organ in her hand. In another, the organ was lost between her legs.

As the maintenance man talked about the photographs and what they portrayed, Chance scrutinized them closely. The images on paper were vaguely disturbing; on television he had never seen the unnaturally enlarged hidden parts of men and women, or these freakish embraces. When the maintenance man left, Chance stooped down to look over his own body. His organ was small and limp; it did not protrude in the slightest. The maintenance man insisted that in this organ hidden seeds grew, and that they came forth in a spurt whenever a man took his pleasure. Though Chance prodded and massaged his organ, he felt nothing; even in the early morning, when he woke up and often found it somewhat enlarged, his organ refused to stiffen out: it gave him no pleasure at all.

Later, Chance tried hard to figure out what connection there was—if any—between a woman's private parts and the birth of a child. In some of the TV series about doctors and hospitals and operations, Chance had often seen the mystery of birth depicted: the pain and agony of the mother, the joy of the father, the pink, wet body of the newborn infant. But he had never watched any show which explained why some women had babies and others did not. Once or twice Chance was tempted to ask Louise about it, but he decided against it. Instead, he watched TV, for a while, with closer attention. Eventually, he forgot about it.

EE had begun to smooth his shirt. Her hand was warm; now it touched his chin. Chance did not move. "I am sure . . ." EE whispered, "you must . . . you do know that I want us, want you and me to become very close. . . ." Suddenly, she began to cry quietly, like a child. Sobbing and blowing her nose, she took out her handkerchief and patted her eyes; but still she kept on crying.

Chance assumed that he was in some way responsible for her sorrow, but he did not know how. He put his arms around EE. She, as if expecting his touch, leaned heavily against him, and they tumbled over together on the bed. EE bent over his chest, her hair brushing his face. She kissed his neck and forehead; she kissed his eyes and his ears. Her tears wet his skin, and Chance smelled her perfume, all the while thinking of what he should do next. Now EE's hand touched his waist, and Chance felt the hand exploring his thighs. After a while, the hand withdrew. EE was not crying any longer; she lay quietly next to him, still and peaceful.

"I am grateful to you, Chauncey," she said. "You are a man of restraint. You know that with one touch of your hand, just one touch, I would open to you. But you do not wish to exploit another," she reflected. "In some ways you are not really American. You are more of a European man, do you know that?" She smiled. "What I mean is that, unlike men I have known, you do not practice all of those American lovers'-lane tricks, all of that fingering, kissing, tickling, stroking, hugging: that coy meandering toward the target, which is both feared and desired." She paused. "Do you know that you're very brainy, very cerebral, really, Chauncey, that you want to conquer the woman from within her very own self, that you want to infuse in her the need and the desire and the longing for your love?"

Chance was confused when she said that he wasn't really American. Why should she say that? On TV, he had often seen the dirty, hairy, noisy men and women who openly declared themselves anti-American, or were declared so by police, well-dressed officials of the government and businessmen, neat people who called themselves American. On TV, these confrontations often ended in violence, bloodshed, and death.

EE stood up and rearranged her clothes. She looked at him; there was no enmity in her look. "I might just as well tell you this, Chauncey," she said. "I am in love with you. I love you, and I want you. And I know that you know it, and I am grateful that you have decided to wait until . . . until . . ." She searched, but could not find the words. She left the room. Chance got up and patted down his hair. He sat by his desk and turned on the TV. The image appeared instantly.

FIVE

It was Thursday. As soon as he opened his eyes, Chance turned on the TV, then called the kitchen for his breakfast.

The maid brought in the neatly arranged breakfast tray. She told him that Mr. Rand had had a relapse, that two additional doctors had been summoned, and that they had been at his bedside since midnight. She handed Chance a pile of newspapers and a typed note. Chance did not know whom the note was from.

He had just finished eating when EE called. "Chauncey—darling—did you get my note? And did you see this morning's papers?" she asked. "It seems you've been described as one of the chief architects of the President's policy speech. And your own comments on THIS EVENING are quoted side by side with the President's. Oh, Chauncey, you were marvelous! Even the President was impressed by you!"

"I like the President," said Chance.

"I hear you looked absolutely smashing on TV! All my friends want to meet you. Chauncey, you are still going to the U.N. reception with me this afternoon?"

"Yes, I'd be happy to go."

"You are a dear. I hope you won't find all the fuss too boring. We don't have to stay late. After the reception we can go and see some friends of mine if you like; they're giving a large dinner party."

"I'll be glad to go with you."

"Oh, I'm so happy," EE exclaimed. Her voice dropped: "Can I see you? I've missed you so very much. . . ."

"Yes, of course."

She entered the room, her face flushed. "I have to tell you something that's very important to me, and I must say it as I look at you," she said, catching her breath and stopping to grope for words. "I wonder if you would consider remaining here with us, Chauncey, at least for a while. This invitation is Ben's as well as mine." She did not wait for an answer. "Think of it! You can live here in this house with us! Chauncey, please, don't say no! Benjamin is so ill; he said he feels so much more secure with you under the same roof." She threw her arms around him and pressed her body hard against his. "Chauncey, my dearest, you must, you must," she whispered. There was an unguarded quaver in her voice.

Chance agreed.

EE hugged him and kissed his cheek; then she broke away from him and began circling the room. "I know! We must get you a secretary. Now that you are in the public eye, you'll want someone experienced to help you with your affairs and screen your callers, to protect you from the people you don't want to talk to or meet. But perhaps there's someone you already had in mind? Someone who's worked for you in the past?"

"No," Chance answered. "There's no one."

"Then I'll start looking for someone right away," she said huskily.

Before lunch, while Chance was watching TV, EE rang his room. "Chauncey, I hope I'm not disturbing you," she said in a measured voice. "But I would like you to meet Mrs. Aubrey, who is here in the library with me. She would like to be considered for the post of temporary secretary until we can find a permanent one. Can you see her now?"

"Yes, I can," said Chance.

When Chance entered the library, he saw a gray-haired woman sitting beside EE on the sofa.

EE introduced them.

Chance shook hands and sat down. Under the inquisitive stare of Mrs. Aubrey, he drummed his fingers on the desk top. "Mrs. Aubrey has been Mr. Rand's trusted secretary at the First American Financial Corporation for years," EE exclaimed.

"I see," Chance said.

"Mrs. Aubrey does not want to retire—she's certainly not the type for that." Chance had nothing to say. He rubbed his thumb over his cheek. EE pulled up her wristwatch, which had slipped down on her hand.

"If you'd like, Chauncey," EE continued, "Mrs. Aubrey can make herself available immediately. . . ."

"Good," he said, finally. "I hope Mrs. Aubrey will enjoy working here. This is a fine household."

EE sought his glance across the desk. "In that case," she said, "it's settled. I've got to run now. I have to get dressed for the reception. I'll speak to you later, Chauncey."

Chance watched Mrs. Aubrey. She had turned her head to one side and seemed almost wistful. She resembled a solitary dandelion.

He liked her. He did not know what to say. He waited for Mrs. Aubrey to speak. At length, she caught his stare and said softly: "Perhaps we can start. If you would care to give me an outline of the general nature of your business and social activities . . ."

"Please speak to Mrs. Rand about it," said Chance, rising.

Mrs. Aubrey hastily got to her feet. "I quite understand," she said.

"In any case, sir, I am at your disposal. My office is just next to that of Mr. Rand's private secretary."

Chance said, "Thank you again," and walked out of the room.

* * *

At the United Nations fete, Chance and EE were greeted by members of the U.N. Hospitality Committee and escorted to one of the most prominent tables. The Secretary-General approached; he greeted EE by kissing her hand and asking about Rand's health. Chance could not recall ever having seen the man on TV.

"This," said EE to the Secretary-General, "is Mr. Chauncey Gardiner, a very dear friend of Benjamin's."

The men shook hands. "I know this gentleman," the Secretary said, still smiling. "I admired Mr. Gardiner so much on television last night. I am honored by your presence here, sir."

They all sat down; waiters arrived with canapés of caviar, salmon, and egg, and trays crowded with glasses of champagne; photographers hovered about and snapped pictures. A tall florid man approached the table, and the Secretary-General rose like a shot. "Mr. Ambassador," he said, "how good of you to come over." He turned to EE. "May I have the honor of introducing His Excellency Vladimir Skrapinov, Ambassador of the Union of Soviet Socialist Republics?"

"Mr. Ambassador and I have already had the pleasure of meeting, haven't we?" EE smiled. "I recall a warm exchange between Mr. Rand and Ambassador Skrapinov two years ago in Washington." She paused. "Unfortunately, Mr. Rand is ill and must forgo the pleasure of your company here today." The Ambassador bowed cordially, seated himself, and talked loudly with EE and the Secretary-General. Chance fell silent and looked over the crowd. After a time the Secretary-General rose, reaffirmed his pleasure at meeting Chance, said good-bye, and departed. EE caught sight of her old friend, the Ambassador of Venezuela, who was just passing by, excused herself and went over to him.

The Soviet Ambassador moved his chair closer to Chance's. The flashbulbs of the photographers flashed away. "I'm sorry we didn't meet sooner," he said. "I saw you on THIS EVENING and must say that I listened with great interest to your down-to-earth philosophy. I'm not surprised that it was so quickly endorsed by your President." He drew his chair still closer. "Tell me, Mr. Gardiner, how is our mutual friend, Benjamin Rand? I hear that his illness is actually very serious. I did not want to upset Mrs. Rand by discussing it in detail."

"He's ill," Chance said. "He's not well at all."

"So I understand, so I've heard." The Ambassador nodded, looking intently at Chance. "Mr. Gardiner," he said, "I want to be candid. Considering the gravity of your country's economic situation, it is clear that you will be called upon to play an important role in the administration. I have detected in you a certain . . . reticence regarding political issues. But, Mr. Gardiner, after all . . . shouldn't we, the diplomats, and you, the businessmen, get together more often? We are not so far from each other, not so far!"

Chance touched his forehead with his hand. "We are not," he said. "Our chairs are almost touching."

The Ambassador laughed aloud. The photographers clicked. "Bravo, very good!" the Ambassador exclaimed. "Our chairs are indeed almost touching! And—how shall I put it—we both want to remain seated on them, don't we? Neither of us wants his chair snatched from under him, am I right? Am I correct? Good! Excellent! Because if one goes, the other goes and then—boom!—we are both down, and no one wants to be down before his time, eh?" Chance smiled, and the Ambassador laughed loudly once again.

Skrapinov suddenly bent toward him. "Tell me, Mr. Gardiner, do you by any chance like Krylov's fables? I ask this because you have that certain Krylovian touch."

Chance looked around and saw that he and Skrapinov were being filmed by cameramen. "Krylovian touch? Do I really?" he asked and smiled.

"I knew it, I knew it!" Skrapinov almost shouted. "So you know Krylov!" The Ambassador paused and then spoke rapidly in another language. The words sounded soft, and the Ambassador's features took on the look of an animal. Chance, who had never been addressed in a foreign language, raised his eyebrows and then laughed. The Ambassador looked astonished. "So . . . so! I was correct, wasn't I? You do know your Krylov in Russian, don't you? Mr. Gardiner, I must confess that I suspected as much all along. I know an educated man when I meet one." Chance was about to deny it when the Ambassador winked. "I appreciate your discretion, my friend." Again he spoke to Chance in a foreign tongue; this time Chance did not react.

Just then, EE returned to the table, accompanied by two diplomats, whom she introduced as Gaufridi, a *député* from Paris, and His

Excellency Count von Brockburg-Schulendorff, of West Germany. "Benjamin and I," she reminisced, "had the pleasure of visiting the Count's ancient castle near Munich. . . ."

The men were seated, and the photographers kept shooting. Von Brockburg-Schulendorff smiled, waiting for the Russian to speak. Skrapinov responded by smiling. Gaufridi looked from EE to Chance.

"Mr. Gardiner and I," began Skrapinov, "have just been sharing our enthusiasm for Russian fables. It appears that Mr. Gardiner is an avid reader and admirer of our poetry, which, incidentally, he reads in the original."

The German pulled his chair closer to Chance's. "Allow me to say, Mr. Gardiner, how much I admired your naturalistic approach to politics and economics on television. Of course, now that I know you have a literary background, I feel that I can understand your remarks much better." He looked at the Ambassador, then lifted his eyes to the ceiling. "Russian literature," he announced, "has inspired some of the greatest minds of our age."

"—Not to speak of German literature!" Skrapinov exclaimed. "My dear Count, may I remind you of Pushkin's lifelong admiration for the literature of your country. Why, after Pushkin translated *Faust* into Russian, Goethe sent him his own pen! Not to mention Turgenev, who settled in Germany, and the love of Tolstoy and Dostoevsky for Schiller."

Von Brockburg-Schulendorff nodded. "Yes, but can you calculate the effect of reading the Russian masters on Hauptmann, Nietzsche, and Thomas Mann? And how about Rilke: how often did Rilke declare that whatever was English was foreign to him, while whatever was Russian was his ancestral homeland . . . ?"

Gaufridi abruptly finished a glass of champagne. His face was flushed. He leaned across the table toward Skrapinov. "When we first met during World War II," he said, "you and I were dressed in soldiers' uniforms, fighting the common enemy, the cruelest enemy in the annals of our nations' histories. Sharing literary influences is one thing, sharing blood another."

Skrapinov attempted a smile. "But, Mr. Gaufridi," he said, "you speak of the time of war, many years ago—another era altogether. Today, our uniforms and decorations are on display in museums. Today, we . . . we are soldiers of peace." He had scarcely finished when Von Brockburg-Schulendorff excused himself; he rose abruptly, shoved his chair aside, kissed EE's hand, shook hands with

Skrapinov and Chance, and, bowing in the direction of the Frenchman, strode off. The photographers popped away.

EE exchanged seats with the Frenchman so that he and Chance could sit next to each other. "Mr. Gardiner," the *député* began mildly, as if nothing had occurred, "I heard the President's speech, in which he referred to his consultations with you. I have read a lot about you, and I've also had the pleasure of watching you on television." He lit a long cigarette which he had carefully inserted into a holder. "I understand from the remarks of Ambassador Skrapinov that, among your many other accomplishments, you are also a man of letters." He looked sharply at Chance. "My dear Mr. Gardiner, it is only by . . . accepting fables as reality sometimes that we can advance a little way along the path of power and peace. . . ." Chance lifted his glass. "It will come as no surprise to you," he went on, "that many of our own industrialists, financiers, and members of government have the keenest interest in developments of the First American Financial Corporation. Ever since the illness of our mutual friend, Benjamin, their view of the course which the Corporation will pursue has been somewhat . . . shall we say, obstructed." He halted, but Chance said nothing. "We are pleased to hear that you may fill Rand's place, should Benjamin fail to get well. . . ."

"Benjamin will get well," said Chance. "The President said so."

"Let us hope so," declared the Frenchman. "Let us hope. And yet none of us, not even the President, can be sure. Death hovers nearby, always ready to swoop down. . . ."

Gaufridi was interrupted by the departure of the Soviet Ambassador. Everyone stood up. Skrapinov edged toward Chance. "A most interesting meeting, Mr. Gardiner," he said quietly. "Most instructive. If you should ever visit our country, my government would be most honored to offer you its hospitality." He pressed Chance's hand while film cameras rolled and photographers took photographs.

Gaufridi sat with Chance and EE at the table.

"Chauncey," said EE, "you must have really impressed our stiff Russian friend! A pity Benjamin couldn't have been here—he so enjoys talking politics!" She put her head closer to Chance. "It's no secret that you were talking Russian to Skrapinov—I didn't know you knew the language! That's incredible!"

Gaufridi sputtered: "It's extremely useful to speak Russian these days. Are you proficient in other languages, Mr. Gardiner?"

"Mr. Gardiner's a modest man," EE blurted out. "He doesn't advertise his accomplishments! His knowledge is for himself!"

A tall man approached to pay his respects to EE: Lord Beauclerk, chairman of the board of the British Broadcasting Company. He turned toward Chance.

"I enormously enjoyed the bluntness of your statement on television. Very cunning of you, very cunning indeed! One doesn't want to work things out too finely, does one? I mean—not for the videots. It's what they want, after all: *'a god to punish, not a man of their infirmity.'* Eh?"

As they were about to leave, they found themselves surrounded by men carrying open tape recorders and motion picture and portable TV cameras. One after the other, EE introduced them to Chance. One of the younger reporters stepped forward. "Would you be so kind as to answer a few questions, Mr. Gardiner?"

EE stepped in front of Chance. "Let's get this straight right now," she said. "You will not keep Mr. Gardiner too long; he must leave soon. Agreed?"

A reporter called out: "What do you think of the editorial on the President's speech in the New York *Times?*"

Chance looked at EE, but she returned his inquiring glance. He had to say something. "I didn't read it," he declared.

"You didn't read the *Times* editorial on the President's address?"

"I did not," said Chance.

Several journalists exchanged leers. EE gazed at Chance with mild astonishment, and then with growing admiration.

"But, sir," one of the reporters persisted coldly, "you must at least have glanced at it."

"I did not read the *Times,*" Chance repeated.

"The *Post* spoke of your 'peculiar brand of optimism,'" said another man. "Did you read that?"

"No. I didn't read that either."

"Well," the reporter persisted, "what about the phrase, 'peculiar brand of optimism'?"

"I don't know what it means," Chance replied.

EE stepped forward proudly. "Mr. Gardiner has many responsibilities," she said, "especially since Mr. Rand has been ill. He finds out what is in the newspapers from the staff briefings."

An older reporter stepped forward. "I am sorry to persist, Mr. Gardiner, but it would nonetheless be of great interest to me to know which newspapers you 'read,' so to speak, via your staff briefings."

"I do not read any newspapers," said Chance. "I watch TV."

The journalists stood, silent and embarrassed. "Do you mean," one finally asked, "that you find TV's coverage more objective than that of the newspapers?"

"As I've said," explained Chance, "I watch TV."

The older reporter half-turned away. "Thank you, Mr. Gardiner," he said, "for what is probably the most honest admission to come from a public figure in recent years. Few men in public life have had the courage not to read newspapers. None have had the guts to admit it!"

As EE and Chance were about to leave the building, they were overtaken by a young woman photographer. "I am sorry for pursuing you, Mr. Gardiner," she said breathlessly, "but can I have just one more picture of you—you're a very photogenic man, you know!"

Chance smiled at her politely; EE recoiled slightly. Chance was surprised by her anger. He did not know what had upset her.

* * *

The President casually glanced at the press digest of the day before. All the major papers reported the text of his speech at the Financial Institute of America and included his remarks about Benjamin Rand and Chauncey Gardiner. It occurred to the President that he ought to know more about Gardiner.

He called his personal secretary and asked her to gather all available information about Gardiner. Later, between appointments, he summoned her to his office.

The President took the file she handed him. He opened it, found a complete dossier on Rand, which he immediately laid aside, a brief interview with Rand's chauffeur sketchily describing Gardiner's accident and a transcript of Gardiner's remarks on THIS EVENING.

"There seems to be no other information, Mr. President," his secretary said hesitantly.

"All I want is the usual material we always get before inviting guests to the White House; that's all."

The secretary fidgeted uneasily. "I did consult our standard sources, Mr. President, but they don't seem to contain anything on Mr. Chauncey Gardiner."

The President's brows knitted and he said icily: "I assume that Mr. Chauncey Gardiner, like all the rest of us, was born of certain parents, grew up in certain places, made certain connections, and like the rest of us contributed, through his taxes, to the wealth of this nation. And so, I'm sure, did his family. Just give me the basics, please."

The secretary looked uncomfortable. "I'm sorry, Mr. President, but I wasn't able to find out anything more than what I've just given you. As I said, I did try all of our usual sources."

"You mean to say," the President muttered gravely, pointing tensely at the file, "that this is absolutely all they have on him?"

"That is correct, sir."

"Am I to assume that none of our agencies knows a single thing about a man with whom I spent half an hour, face-to-face, and whose name and words I quoted in my speech? Have you by any chance tried *Who's Who?* And, for God's sake, if that fails, try the Manhattan telephone book!"

The secretary laughed nervously. "I'll keep trying, sir."

"I certainly would appreciate it if you would."

The secretary left the room, and the President reached for his calendar and scribbled in its margin: *Gardiner?*

* * *

Immediately after leaving the United Nations reception, Ambassador Skrapinov prepared a secret report about Gardiner. Chauncey Gardiner, he maintained, was shrewd, and highly educated. He emphasized Gardiner's knowledge of Russian and of Russian literature, and saw in Gardiner "the spokesman of those American business circles which, in view of deepening depression and widening civil unrest, were bent on maintaining their threatened *status quo,* even at the price of political and economic concessions to the Soviet bloc."

At home, in the Soviet Mission to the United Nations, the Ambassador telephoned his embassy in Washington and spoke to the chief of the Special Section. He requested, on a top-priority basis, all information concerning Gardiner: he wanted details on his family, education, his friends and associates, and his relationship with Rand, and he wanted to find out the real reason why, of all his economic advisers, the President had singled him out. The chief of the Special Section promised to deliver a complete dossier by the following morning.

Next, the Ambassador personally supervised the preparation of small gift packages to be delivered to Gardiner and Rand. Each package contained several pounds of Beluga caviar and bottles of specially distilled Russian vodka. In addition, he had a rare first edition of Krylov's *Fables,* with Krylov's own notes handwritten on many of the pages, inserted into Gardiner's package. The volume had been requisitioned from the private collection of a recently arrested Jewish member of the Academy of Sciences in Leningrad.

Later, as he was shaving, the Ambassador decided to take a chance: he decided to include Gardiner's name in the speech that he was to deliver that evening to the International Congress of the Mercantile Association, convening in Philadelphia. The paragraph, introduced into the speech after it had already been approved by his superiors in Moscow, welcomed the emergence in the United States of "Those enlightened statesmen—personified by, among others, Mr. Chauncey Gardiner—who are clearly aware that, unless the leaders of the opposing political systems move the chairs on which they sit closer to each other, all of their seats will be pulled out from under them by rapid social and political changes."

Skrapinov's speech was a hit. The allusion to Gardiner was picked up by the major news media. At midnight, watching TV, Skrapinov heard his speech quoted and saw a close-up of Gardiner—a man who, according to the announcer, had been "within the space of two days cited by both the President of the United States and the Soviet Ambassador to the United Nations."

On the frontispiece of Krylov's works, the Ambassador had inscribed: *"'One could make this fable clearer still: but let us not provoke the geese' (Krylov).—To Mr. Chauncey Gardiner, with admiration and in the hope of future meetings, warmly, Skrapinov."*

* * *

After arriving at the home of EE's friends from the United Nations, EE and Chance found themselves in a room that was at least three stories high; at half its height along the wall ran the ornately carved balustrade of a gallery. The room was full of sculptures and glass cases containing shiny objects; the chandelier, hanging on a golden rope, resembled a tree whose leaves had been replaced by flickering candles.

Groups of guests were scattered around the room, and the waiters circulated with trays of drinks. The hostess, a fat woman in a green gown, with thick strings of jewels on her exposed chest, walked toward them, arms outstretched. She and EE embraced and kissed each other on the cheek; then EE introduced Chance. The woman put out her hand and held Chance's for a moment. "At last, at last," she exclaimed cheerfully, "the famous Chauncey Gardiner! EE has told me that you cherish your privacy more than anything else." She stopped, as if a more profound second thought had come to her, then threw back her head a bit and measured him up and down. "But now, when I see how good-looking you are, I suspect it has been EE who cherishes her privacy—with you!"

"Sophie, dear," EE pleaded coyly.

"I know, I know. Suddenly, you are embarrassed! There is nothing wrong with being fond of one's privacy, EE, dear!" She laughed and, with her hand on Chance's arm, continued gaily: "Please do forgive me, Mr. Gardiner. EE and I always joke like this when we're together. You look even handsomer than your photographs, and I must say I agree with *Women's Wear Daily*—you're obviously one of the best-dressed businessmen today. Of course, with your height and broad shoulders and narrow hips and long legs and . . ."

"Sophie, please—" EE broke in, blushing.

"I'll be quiet now, I will. Do follow me, both of you; let's meet some interesting people. Everybody is so anxious to talk to Mr. Gardiner."

Chance was introduced to a number of guests. He shook their hands, met the stares of women and men, and, barely catching their names, gave his own. A short, bald man succeeded in cornering him next to an imposing piece of furniture, full of sharp edges.

"I'm Ronald Stiegler, of Eidolon Books. Delighted to meet you, sir." The man extended his hand. "We watched your TV performance with great interest," said Stiegler. "And just now, coming over here in my car, I heard on the radio that the Soviet Ambassador mentioned your name in Philadelphia . . ."

"On your radio? Don't you have television in your car?" Chance asked. Stiegler pretended to be amused. "I hardly even listen to my radio. With traffic so hectic, one has to pay attention to everything." He stopped a waiter and asked for a vodka martini on the rocks with a twist of orange.

"I've been thinking," he said, leaning against the wall, "and so have some of my editors: Would you consider writing a book for us? Something on your special subject. Clearly, the view from the White

House is different from the view of the egghead or the hardhat. What do you say?" He drained off his drink in several gulps and when a servant passed by carrying a tray of glasses, grabbed another. "One for you?" He grinned at Chance.

"No, thank you. I don't drink."

"Sir, I'm thinking: it would be only fair and it would certainly be to the country's advantage to promote your philosophy more widely. Eidolon Books would be very happy to perform this service for you. Right here and now I think I could promise you a six-figure advance against royalties and a very agreeable royalty and reprint clause. The contract could be drawn up and signed in a day or two, and you could have the book for us, let's say, in about a year or two."

"I can't write," said Chance.

Stiegler smiled deprecatingly. "Of course—but who can, nowadays? It's no problem. We can provide you with our best editors and research assistants. I can't even write a simple postcard to my children. So what?"

"I can't even read," said Chance.

"Of course not!" Stiegler exclaimed. "Who has time? One glances at things, talks, listens, watches. Mr. Gardiner, I admit that as a publisher I should be the last one to tell you this . . . but publishing isn't exactly a flowering garden these days."

"What kind of garden is it?" asked Chance with interest.

"Well, whatever it was once, it isn't any more. Of course, we're still growing, still expanding. But too many books are being published. And what with recession, stagnation, unemployment . . . Well, as you must know, books aren't selling any more. But, as I say, for a tree of your height, there is still a sizable plot reserved. Yes, I can see a Chauncey Gardiner blooming under the Eidolon imprint! Let me drop you a little note, outlining our thoughts and—our figures. Are you still at the Rands'?"

"Yes, I am."

Dinner was announced. The guests were seated around several small tables arranged symmetrically throughout the dining room. There were ten at Chance's table; he was flanked on each side by a woman. The conversation quickly turned to politics. An older man sitting across from Chance addressed him, and Chance stiffened uneasily.

"Mr. Gardiner, when is the government going to stop calling industrial by-products poisons? I went along with the banning of

DDT because DDT is a poison and there's no problem finding some new chemicals. But it's a damn sight different when we stop the manufacture of heating oils, let's say, because we don't like the decomposition products of kerosene!" Chance stared silently at the old man. "I say, by God, that there's a helluva difference between petroleum ash and bug powder! Any idiot could see that!"

"I have seen ashes and I have seen powders," said Chance. "I know that both are bad for growth in a garden."

"Hear, hear!" the woman sitting on Chance's right cried out. "He's marvelous!" she whispered to the companion on her right in a voice loud enough for everyone to hear. To the others, she said: "Mr. Gardiner has the uncanny ability of reducing complex matters to the simplest of human terms. But by bringing this down to earth, to our own home," the woman continued, "I can see the priority and urgency which Mr. Gardiner and the influential men like him, including our President, who quotes him so often, give to this matter." Several of the others smiled.

A distinguished-looking man in pince-nez addressed Chance: "All right, Mr. Gardiner," he said, "the President's speech was reassuring. Still and all, these are the facts: unemployment is approaching catastrophic proportions, unprecedented in this country; the market continues to fall toward 1929 levels; some of the largest and finest companies in our country have collapsed. Tell me, sir, do you honestly believe that the President will be able to halt this downward trend?"

"Mr. Rand said that the President knows what he is doing," said Chance slowly. "They spoke; I was there; that is what Mr. Rand said after they were finished."

"What about the war?" the young woman sitting on Chance's left said, leaning close to him.

"The war? Which war?" said Chance. "I've seen many wars on TV."

"Alas," the woman said, "in this country, when we dream of reality, television wakes us. To millions, the war, I suppose, is just another TV program. But out there, at the front, real men are giving their lives."

While Chance sipped coffee in one of the adjoining sitting rooms, he was discreetly approached by one of the guests. The man introduced himself and sat down next to Chance, regarding him intently. He was older than Chance. He looked like some of the men Chance often saw on TV. His long silky gray hair was combed straight from his forehead to the nape of his neck. His eyes were large and expressive and shaded with unusually long eyelashes. He talked softly and from time to time uttered a short dry laugh. Chance did not understand what he said or why he laughed. Every time he felt that the man expected an answer from him, Chance said yes. More often, he simply smiled and nodded. Suddenly, the man bent over and whispered a question to which he wanted a definite answer. Yet Chance was not certain what he had asked and so gave no reply. The man repeated himself. Again Chance remained silent. The man leaned still closer and looked at him hard; apparently, he caught something in Chance's expression which made him ask, in a cold toneless voice: "Do you want to do it now? We can go upstairs and do it."

Chance did not know what the man wanted him to do. What if it were something he couldn't do? Finally he said, "I would like to watch."

"Watch? You mean, watch me? Just doing it alone?" The man made no effort to hide his amazement.

"Yes," said Chance, "I like to watch very much." The man averted his eyes and then turned to Chance once more. "If that's what you want, then I want it too," he declared boldly.

After liqueurs were served, the man gazed into Chance's eyes and impatiently slid his hand under Chance's arm. With his surprisingly strong forearm he pressed Chance to him. "It's time for us," he whispered. "Let's go upstairs."

Chance did not know if he should leave without letting EE know where he was going.

"I want to tell EE," Chance said.

The man stared wildly at him. "Tell EE?" He paused. "I see. Well, it's all the same: tell her later."

"Not now?"

"Please," said the man. "Let's go. She'll never miss you in this crowd. We'll walk casually down to the rear elevator and go straight upstairs. Do come with me."

They moved through the crowded room. Chance looked around, but EE was not in sight.

The elevator was narrow, its walls covered with soft purple fabric. The man stood next to Chance and suddenly thrust his hand into

Chance's groin. Chance did not know what to do. The man's face was friendly; there was an eager look on it. His hand continued to probe Chance's trousers. Chance decided that the best thing was to do nothing.

The elevator stopped. The man got out first and led Chance by the arm. All was quiet. They entered a bedroom. The man asked Chance to sit down. He opened a small concealed bar and offered Chance a drink. Chance was afraid that he might pass out as he had done that time in the car with EE; therefore he refused. He also refused to smoke a strange-smelling pipe which the man offered him. The man poured himself a large drink, which he drank almost at once. Then he approached Chance and embraced him, pressing his thighs against Chance's. Chance remained still. The man now kissed his neck and cheeks, then sniffed and mussed his hair. Chance wondered what he had said or done to prompt such affection. He tried very hard to recall seeing something like this on TV but could remember only a single scene in a film in which a man kissed another man. Even then it had not been clear what was actually happening. He remained still.

The man clearly did not mind this; his eyes were closed, his lips parted. He slipped his hands under Chance's jacket, searching insistently; then he stepped away, looked at Chance, and, hurrying, began to undress. He kicked off his shoes and lay naked on the bed. He gestured to Chance: Chance stood beside the bed and looked down at the prostrate form. To Chance's surprise, the man cupped his own flesh in a hand, groaning and jerking and trembling as he did so.

The man was certainly ill. Chance often saw people having fits on TV. He leaned over and the man suddenly grabbed him. Chance lost his balance and almost fell upon the naked body. The man reached for Chance's leg, and without a word raised and pressed the sole of Chance's shoe against his hardened organ.

Seeing how the erect extended part grew stiffer under the edge of his shoe and how it protruded from the man's underbelly, Chance recalled the photographs of the man and woman shown to him by the maintenance man in the Old Man's house. He felt uneasy. But he lent his foot to the man's flesh, watched the man's body tremble and saw how his naked legs stretched out, straining tautly, and heard how he screamed out of some inner agony. And then the man again pressed Chance's shoe into his flesh. From under the shoe a white substance coursed forth in short spurts. The man's face went pale: his head jerked from side to side. The man twitched for the last time; the trembling and shivering of his body subsided and his muscles tensed under Chance's shoe, calmed and softened as if they had been suddenly unplugged from a source of energy. He closed his eyes. Chance reclaimed his foot and quietly left.

He found his way back to the elevator and on the ground floor walked down a long corridor, guided by the sound of voices. Soon he was back among the guests. He was searching for EE when someone tapped him on the shoulder. It was she.

"I was afraid you got bored and left," she said. "Or that you were kidnaped. There are loads of women here who wouldn't mind making off with you, you know."

Chance did not know why anyone would want to kidnap him. He was silent and finally said, "I wasn't with a woman. I was with a man. We went upstairs but he got sick and so I came down."

"Upstairs? Chauncey, you're always engaged in some kind of discussion; I do wish you'd just relax and enjoy the party."

"He got sick," said Chance. "I stayed with him for a while."

"Very few men are as healthy as you are; they can't take all this drink and chattering," said EE. "You're an angel, my dear. Thank God there are still men like you around to give aid and comfort."

* * *

When they returned from the dinner party, Chance got into bed and watched TV. The room was dark; the screen cast an uneasy light on the walls. Chance heard the door open. EE entered in her dressing gown and approached his bed.

"I couldn't sleep, Chauncey," she said. She touched his shoulder.

Chance wanted to turn off the TV and turn on the lights.

"Please, don't," said EE. "Let's stay like this."

She sat on the bed, next to him, and put her arms around her knees. "I had to see you," she said, "and I know—I know," she whispered in short bursts, "that you don't mind my coming here—to your room. You don't mind, do you?"

"I don't," Chance said.

Slowly, she moved closer; her hair brushed his face. In an instant she threw off her robe and slipped under his blanket.

She moved her body next to his, and he felt her hand run over the length of his bare chest and hip, stroking, squeezing, reaching down; he felt her fingers pressing feverishly into his skin. He extended his hand and let it slide over her neck and breasts and belly. He felt her trembling; he felt her limbs unfolding. He did not know what else to do and so he withdrew his hand. She continued to tremble and shiver, pressing his head and his face to her damp flesh, as if she wanted him to devour her. She cried out brokenly, uttered ruptured sounds, spoke in phrases which barely began, making noises that resembled animal gasps. Kissing his body over and over again, she wailed softly and began to half-moan and half-laugh, her tongue lunging down toward his flaccid flesh, her head bobbing, her legs beating together. She quivered, and he felt her wet thighs.

He wanted to tell her how much he preferred to look at her, that only by watching could he memorize her and take her and possess her. He did not know how to explain to her that he could not touch better or more fully with his hands than he could with his eyes. Seeing encompassed all at once; a touch was limited to one spot at a time. EE should no more have wanted to be touched by him than should the TV screen have wanted it.

Chance neither moved nor resisted. Suddenly EE went limp and let her head fall on his chest. "You don't want me," she said. "You don't feel anything for me. Nothing at all."

Chance gently pushed her aside and sat up heavily at the edge of the bed.

"I know, I know," she cried. "I don't excite you!" Chance did not know what she meant. "I'm right, aren't I, Chauncey?"

He turned and looked at her. "I like to watch you," he said.

She stared at him. "To watch me?"

"Yes. I like to watch."

She sat up breathless, gasping for air. "Is that why . . . is that all you want, to watch me?"

"Yes. I like to watch you."

"But aren't you excited?" She reached down and took his flesh and held it in her hand. In turn, Chance touched her; his fingers moved inside her. She jerked again, turned her head to him, and in a fiery attempt pulled and sucked his flesh into her mouth, licking it with her tongue, nibbling at it with her teeth, trying desperately to breathe life into it. Chance waited patiently until she stopped.

She wept bitterly. "You don't love me," she cried. "You can't stand it when I touch you!"

"I like to watch you," said Chance.

"I don't understand what you mean," she moaned. "No matter

what I do, I can't arouse you. And you keep saying that you like to watch me. . . . Watch me! You mean . . . when . . . when I'm alone . . . ?"

"Yes. I like to watch you."

In the bluish light emanating from the TV, EE looked at him, her eyes veiled. "You want me to come while you watch."

Chance said nothing.

"If I touched myself, you'd get excited and then you'd make love to me?"

Chance did not understand. "I would like to watch you," he repeated.

"I think I understand now." She got up, paced swiftly up and down the room, crossing in front of the TV screen; every now and then a word escaped her lips, a word scarcely louder than her breath.

She returned to the bed. She stretched out on her back and let her hand run over her body; languidly, she spread her legs wide apart and then her hands crept froglike toward her belly. She swayed back and forth and shoved her body from side to side as if it were pricked by rough grass. Her fingers caressed her breasts, buttocks, thighs. In a quick motion, her legs and arms wrapped around Chance like a web of sprawling branches. She shook violently: a delicate tremor ran through her. She no longer stirred; she was half-asleep.

Chance covered her with the blanket. Then he changed the channels several times, keeping the sound low. They rested together in bed and he watched TV, afraid to move.

Sometime later, EE said to him: "I am so free with you. Up until the time I met you, every man I knew barely acknowledged me. I was a vessel that he could take hold of, pierce, and pollute. I was merely an aspect of somebody's love-making. Do you know what I mean?"

Chance looked at her but said nothing.

"Dearest . . . You uncoil my wants: desire flows within me, and when you watch me my passion dissolves it. You make me free. I reveal myself to myself and I am drenched and purged."

He remained silent.

EE stretched and smiled. "Chauncey, dear, I've been meaning to bring this up: Ben wants you to fly to Washington with me tomorrow and take me to the Capitol Hill Ball. I must go; I'm chairman of the Fund-Raising Committee. You will come with me, won't you?"

"I would like to go with you," said Chance.

She cuddled up next to him and dozed off again. Chance watched TV until he too fell asleep.

SIX

Mrs. Aubrey rang Chance in the morning. "Sir, I've just seen this morning's papers. You're in every one of them, and the photographs are stunning! There's one of you with Ambassador Skrapinov . . . and one with the Secretary-General . . . and another with . . . a German Count Somebody. The *Daily News* has a full page picture of you with Mrs. Rand. Even the *Village Voice* . . ."

"I don't read newspapers," said Chance.

"Well, anyway, a number of the major networks have invited you for exclusive TV appearances. Also, *Fortune, Newsweek, Life, Look, Vogue, House & Garden* want to do stories on you. The *Irish Times* called and so did *Spectator, Sunday Telegraph,* and *The Guardian;* they want a press conference. A Lord Beauclerk wanted me to inform you that the BBC is ready to fly you to London for a TV special; he hopes that you will be his house guest. The New York bureaus of *Jours de France, Der Spiegel, L'Osservatore Romano, Pravda, Neue Zürcher Zeitung* have called for appointments. Count von Brockburg-Schulendorff just called to tell you that *Stern,* of Germany, will have you on its cover; *Stern* would like to acquire world rights to your remarks on television, and they're waiting for your terms. French *L'Express* wants you to discuss the challenge of the American depression in their round-table interview: they'll pay your travel expenses. Mr. Gaufridi called twice to offer you his hospitality when you are in France. The directors of the Tokyo Stock Exchange would like you to inspect a new Japanese-made data retrieving computer . . ."

Chance interrupted: "I don't want to meet these people."

"I understand, sir. Just two final points: The *Wall Street Journal* has predicted your imminent appointment to the board of the First American Financial Corporation, and they would like to have a statement from you. In my view, sir, if you could give them a prognosis at this time, you could help their stock enormously. . . ."

"I cannot give them anything."

"Very well, sir. The other thing is that the trustees of the Eastshore University would like to confer an honorary doctor of laws degree on you at this year's commencement exercises, but they want to make sure beforehand that you'll accept."

"I do not need a doctor," said Chance.

"Do you want to talk to the trustees?"

"No."

"I see. And what about the newspapers?"

"I don't like newspapers."

"Will you see the foreign correspondents?"

"I see them often enough on TV."

"Very good, sir. Oh, yes, Mrs. Rand wanted me to remind you that the Rand plane will be leaving for Washington at four o'clock. And she wanted me to inform you that you'll be staying at your hostess's home."

* * *

Karpatov, the chief of the Special Section, arrived on Friday to see Ambassador Skrapinov. He was immediately ushered into the Ambassador's office.

"There is no additional information in Gardiner's file," he said, placing a thin folder on the Ambassador's desk.

Skrapinov tossed the file to one side. "Where is the rest?" he asked crisply.

"There is no record of him anywhere, Comrade Skrapinov."

"Karpatov, I want the facts!"

Karpatov spoke haltingly: "Comrade Ambassador, I have been able to determine that the White House is eager to find out what we know about Gardiner. This should indicate that Gardiner has political importance of the first magnitude."

Skrapinov glared at Karpatov, then got up and began pacing back and forth behind his desk. "I want," he said, "from your Section one thing only: the facts about Gardiner."

Karpatov stood there sullenly. "Comrade Ambassador," he answered, "it is my duty to report that we have been unable to discover even the most elementary information about him. It is almost as if he had never existed before." The Ambassador's hand came down on his desk, and a small statuette toppled to the floor. Trembling, Karpatov stooped, picked it up and carefully put it back on the desk.

"Don't imagine," the Ambassador hissed, "that you can palm such rot off on me! I won't accept it! 'As if he had never existed'! Do you realize that Gardiner happens to be one of the most important men in this country and that this country happens to be not Soviet Georgia but the United States of America, the biggest imperialist state in the world! People like Gardiner decide the fate of millions every day! 'As if he had never existed'! Are you mad? Do you realize that I mentioned the man in my speech?" He paused, then bent forward toward Karpatov. "Unlike the people of your Section, I do not believe in twentieth-century 'dead souls'—nor do I believe in people from other planets coming down to haunt us, as they do on American television programs. I hereby demand all data on Chauncey Gardiner to be delivered to me personally within four hours!"

Hunching his shoulders, Karpatov left the room.

* * *

When four hours had passed and Skrapinov had still not heard from Karpatov, he decided to teach him a lesson. He summoned to his office Sulkin, ostensibly a minor official at the Mission, but actually one of the most powerful men in the Foreign Department.

Skrapinov complained bitterly to Sulkin about Karpatov's ineptitude, stressed the extraordinary importance of obtaining information on Gardiner, and asked that Sulkin help him get a clear picture of Gardiner's past.

After lunch, Sulkin arranged a private conference with Skrapinov. They proceeded to a room at the Mission known as "The Cellar," which was specially protected against listening devices. Sulkin opened his attaché case and with ceremony drew from a black folder a single blank piece of paper. Skrapinov waited expectantly.

"This, my dear Comrade, is your picture of Gardiner's past!" Sulkin growled.

Skrapinov glanced at the page, saw that it was blank, dropped it, glared at Sulkin, and said: "I don't understand, Comrade Sulkin. This page is empty. Does this mean that I am not to be entrusted with the facts about Gardiner?"

Sulkin sat down and lit a cigarette, slowly shaking the match out. "Investigating the background of Mr. Gardiner, my dear Comrade Ambassador, has apparently proven so difficult a task for the agents of the Special Section that it has already resulted in the loss of one of them, without his being able to uncover the tiniest detail of Gardiner's background!" Sulkin paused to puff on his cigarette. "It was fortunate, however, that on Wednesday night I took the precaution of photowiring to Moscow a tape of Gardiner's television appearance on THIS EVENING. This tape, you might be interested in knowing, was submitted to prompt psychiatric, neurological, and linguistic examination. With the aid of our latest-model computers, our teams have analyzed Gardiner's vocabulary, syntax, accent, gestures, facial and other characteristics. The results, my dear Skrapinov, may surprise you. It proved impossible to determine in any way whatsoever his ethnic background or to ascribe his accent to any single community in the entire United States!"

Skrapinov looked at Sulkin in bewilderment.

Smiling wanly, Sulkin continued: "Moreover, it may interest you to know that Gardiner appears to be emotionally one of the most well-adjusted American public figures to have emerged in recent years. However," Sulkin went on, "your Mr. Chauncey Gardiner remains, to all intents and purposes," and here he held up the sheet of paper by its corner, "a blank page."

"Blank page?"

"Blank page," echoed Sulkin. "Exactly. Gardiner's code name!"

Skrapinov quickly reached for a glass of water and gulped it down. "Excuse me, Comrade," he said. "But on Thursday evening when I took it upon myself to allude to Gardiner in my speech in Philadelphia, I naturally assumed that he was an established member of the Wall Street elite. After all, he was mentioned by the American President. But if, as it seems . . ."

Sulkin held up his hand. "Seems? What reason do you have to suggest that Chauncey Gardiner is not in actual fact the man whom you described?"

Skrapinov could barely mutter: "Blank page . . . the lack of any facts . . ."

Again Sulkin interrupted. "Comrade Ambassador," he said, "I am here actually to congratulate you on your perceptiveness. It is, I must tell you, our firm conviction that Gardiner is, in fact, a leading member of an American elitist faction that has for some years been planning a *coup d'état.* He must be of such great importance to this group that they have succeeded in masking every detail of his identity until his emergence Tuesday afternoon."

"Did you say *coup d'état?*" asked Skrapinov.

"I did," replied Sulkin. "Do you doubt the possibility?"

"Well, no. Certainly not. Lenin himself seems to have foreseen it."

"Good, very good," said Sulkin, snapping the lock of his attaché case. "It appears that your intuition has proven itself well-founded. Your initial decision to latch onto Gardiner has been justified. You have a good instinct, Comrade Skrapinov—a true Marxist instinct!" He got up to leave. "You will shortly receive special instructions about the attitude to adopt toward Gardiner."

When Sulkin had gone, Skrapinov thought: It's incredible! Billions of rubles are spent each year on clever Japanese gadgetry, on superspies trained and camouflaged for years, on reconnaissance satellites, overstaffed embassies, trade missions, cultural exchanges, bribes, and gifts—but all that matters in the end is a good Marxist instinct! He thought of Gardiner and envied him his youth, his composure, his future as a leader. *Blank Page, Blank Page*—The code name brought back to him memories of World War II, of the Partisans he had led to so many victories. Maybe diplomacy had been the wrong career for him; maybe the army would have been better. . . . But he was old.

* * *

On Friday afternoon, the President's secretary reported to him. "I'm sorry, Mr. President, but since yesterday, I have been able to collect only a few additional press clippings about Gardiner. They are the speech of the Soviet Ambassador, who mentioned him, and the transcript of Gardiner's interview with the press at the United Nations."

The President was annoyed. "Let's stop this! Have you asked Benjamin Rand about Gardiner?"

"I have telephoned the Rands, sir. Unfortunately, Mr. Rand has had a serious relapse and is on powerful sedatives. He can't talk."

"Did you speak to Mrs. Rand, then?"

"I did, sir. She was at her husband's bedside. She said only that Mr. Gardiner cherishes his privacy and that she respects this aspect of

Mr. Gardiner's personality very much. She said that she feels—but only feels, you understand—that Mr. Gardiner intends to become much more active now that Mr. Rand is bedridden. But she did not connect Mr. Gardiner with any specific business or with any family situation."

"That's even less than what I read in the *Times!* What about our investigative sources? Have you talked to Steven?"

"I did, Mr. President. He hasn't been able to find a single thing. He's checked twice, and not one agency could help him. Gardiner's photograph and fingerprints were checked out, of course, just before your visit to Rand's and, having no record of any kind—as Rand's guest—he was cleared. And I guess that's really all I have to tell you."

"All right, all right. Call Grunmann. Tell him what you know, or, rather, don't know, and have him call me as soon as he gets something on Gardiner."

Grunmann called in a short time. "Mr. President, all of us here have been trying desperately. There just isn't a thing on him. The man doesn't seem to have existed until he moved into Rand's house three days ago!"

"I am very disturbed by this, very disturbed," said the President. "I want you to try again. I want you to keep on it, do you understand? And by the way, Walter: there's a TV program, isn't there, in which some ordinary Americans turn out to be really invaders from another planet? Well, Walter, I refuse to believe that I talked to one of these intruders in New York! I expect you to come up with a large file on Gardiner. If not, I warn you that I shall personally authorize an immediate investigation of those who are responsible for such a flagrant breach in our security!"

Grunmann called back. "Mr. President," he said in a low voice, "I am afraid that our initial fears are now confirmed. We have no record of this man's birth, of his parents, or of his family. We do know, however, beyond any doubt, and I can vouch for it, that he has never been in any legal trouble with any individual or any private, state, or federal organization, corporation, or agency. He was never the cause of any accident or of any damage and—aside from the Rand accident—he was never involved as a third party in any such situation. He has never been hospitalized; he carries no insurance;

nor, for that matter, can he possibly have any other documents or personal identification. He doesn't drive a car or fly a plane, and no license of any kind has ever been issued to him. He has no credit cards, no checks, no calling cards. He does not own a property in this country. . . . Mr. President, we snooped on him a bit in New York: he doesn't talk business or politics on the phone or at home. All he does is watch TV; the set is always on in his room: there's a constant racket—"

"He what?" interrupted the President. "What did you say, Walter?"

"I said he watches television—all the channels—practically all the time. Even when Mrs. Rand . . . is with him in his bedroom, sir . . ."

The President cut in sharply: "Walter, there's no excuse for such investigations, and, damn it, I don't want to know anything of that sort! Who the hell cares what Gardiner does in his bedroom?"

"I'm sorry, Mr. President, but we've had to try everything." He cleared his throat. "Sir, we have been getting quite apprehensive about this man Gardiner. We recorded his conversations at the United Nations reception, but he hardly said a thing. Frankly, sir, it has occurred to us that he might be the agent of a foreign power. But the fact of the matter is that those people almost invariably have too much documentation provided, too much American identity. There's absolutely nothing un-American about them; it's a miracle, as the Director always says, that none of them gets elected to the highest office of this land—" Grunmann caught himself, but it was too late for him to brush off his remark.

"That's a very poor joke, Walter," the President said sternly.

"I'm sorry, sir, I didn't mean . . . I do apologize—"

"Go ahead with your report."

"Well, sir, first, we feel that Mr. Gardiner is not one of these transplants. Definitely not, and then, the Soviets have put out an alert for information on his background. I'm happy to tell you, Mr. President, that even this unprecedented display of Soviet curiosity has failed; not only were they unable to come up with anything beyond—I am not joking, Mr. President—newspaper clippings from our press, but as a result of their eagerness they broke their cover and lost one of their most able agents to us! What's more, eight other foreign powers have put Gardiner on their spying priorities lists. All I can say is that we shall keep on it, Mr. President . . . we shall continue investigating on a round-the-clock basis, sir, and I'll let you know just as soon as we come up with anything."

The President went upstairs to his apartment to rest. It's simply incredible, he thought, incredible. Millions of dollars are allocated each year to each of these agencies, and they can't supply me with even the most rudimentary facts about a man now living in one of the best town houses of New York City as a guest of one of our most prominent businessmen. Is the Federal Government being undermined? By whom? He sighed, turned on TV, and dropped off to sleep.

SEVEN

The man sitting on the sofa faced the small group assembled in his suite. "Gentlemen," he began slowly, "some of you already know that Duncan has decided not to run with me. That leaves us, at present, without a candidate. My friends, we've got to announce someone soon, someone as good as Duncan, and I say this despite the distressing discoveries about Duncan's past that have unfortunately surfaced."

Schneider spoke out. "It wasn't easy to come up even with Duncan," he said, "and let's not kid ourselves . . . whom can we possibly get at this late date? Shellman is going to stay with his firm. I don't think Frank can even be considered given his miserable record as president of the university."

"What about George?" a voice asked.

"George has just had another operation—the second in three months. He's an obvious health risk."

There was silence in the room. It was then that O'Flaherty spoke. "I think I have someone," he said quietly. "What about Chauncey Gardiner?" All eyes turned to the man on the sofa who was drinking his coffee.

"Gardiner?" the man on the sofa said. "Chauncey Gardiner? We don't really know anything about him, do we? Our people haven't been able to find out one single blessed thing. And he certainly hasn't been of any help: he hasn't said a thing about himself ever since he moved in with the Rands four days ago. . . ."

"Then I would like to state," said O'Flaherty, "that this makes me think of Gardiner as an even better bet."

"Why?" several men chorused.

O'Flaherty spoke easily: "What was the trouble with Duncan? With Frank and with Shellman, for that matter, and with so many of the others we've considered and have had to reject? The damn trouble was that they all had background, too much background! A man's past cripples him: his background turns into a swamp and invites scrutiny!"

He waved his arms excitedly. "But just consider Gardiner. May I stress what you have just heard from a most authoritative voice: Gardiner has no background! And so he's not and cannot be objectionable to anyone! He's personable, well-spoken, and he comes across well on TV! And, as far as his thinking goes, he appears to be one of us. That's all. It's clear what he isn't. Gardiner is our one chance."

Schneider crushed out his cigar. "O'Flaherty just tapped something," he said. "Something big. Hmmmm . . . Gardiner, Gardiner . . ."

A waiter entered with steaming pots of fresh coffee and the discussion continued.

* * *

Chance pushed his way through the throng of dancing couples toward the exit. In his eyes there lingered yet a faint, blurred image of the grand ballroom, of the trays of refreshments at the buffet, the multicolored flowers, brilliant bottles, rows upon rows of shining glasses on the table. He caught sight of EE as she was embraced by a tall, heavily decorated general. He passed through a blaze of photographers' flash-guns as through a cloud. The image of all he had seen outside the garden faded.

Chance was bewildered. He reflected and saw the withered image of Chauncey Gardiner: it was cut by the stroke of a stick through a stagnant pool of rain water. His own image was gone as well.

He crossed the hall. Chilled air streamed in through an open window. Chance pushed the heavy glass door open and stepped out into the garden. Taut branches laden with fresh shoots, slender stems with tiny sprouting buds shot upward. The garden lay calm, still sunk in repose. Wisps of clouds floated by and left the moon polished. Now and then, boughs rustled and gently shook off their drops of water. A breeze fell upon the foliage and nestled under the cover of its moist leaves. Not a thought lifted itself from Chance's brain. Peace filled his chest.

TOPICS FOR PAPERS AND DISCUSSION

1. *Characters.* The characters in this novel are "flat" (see E. M. Forster's *Aspects of the Novel),* with the possible exception of Chance, and he is a nonentity. Elizabeth Eve, for instance, in spite of being young, beautiful, and energetic, is principally characterized by the stultifying clichés of her speeches and actions. Apparently Kosinski wishes to create a picture of particularly "videotized" types, if we grasp the pun tucked away in that word. Write an analysis of the "typing of humanity in the world of *Being There.*" Examine Kosinski's presentation of all the characters. What is gained (and lost) when a writer rigorously pursues this technique?

2. *Satire and the media.* How does the novel satirize TV? What does it say about the influence of television on the behavior of viewers and the formation of ideas? Does the phrase "the boob tube" have relevance? How are newspapers, magazines, and journalists in general depicted? What does the novel suggest about the phenomenon of "instant fame," which can be bestowed by the media? Review Mrs. Aubrey's summary in Chapter Six of the worldwide fame achieved by Chance virtually overnight. What are the novel's other satiric targets? Beyond ridiculing man's foolishness, abuses, and vices, the aim of satire is to reform. What does *Being There* try to correct?

3. *Power.* In a world which seems to have lost its moral, ethical, religious, and philosophical basis, "power" appears to be the new *modus vivendi.* In this sense, *Being There* is a sly analysis and exposure, if not an outright condemnation, of how some people and institutions cultivate, garner, and exploit power. What specifically does the novel show about those aspects of the "power play" that motivate persons, institutions, and countries? Gather examples of the power theme and discuss their ramifications. Who, paradoxically, is the most powerful character of all, and what aspects of personality engender that power?

4. *Revitalized myth—"a new man, a new woman."* Using as the basis of his novel the myth of Eden, Kosinski works modern variations on it. For instance, this time Adam (Chance) is forced from the garden before he

meets his Eve. The accident in which she figures is a "damned shame," as Rand says. Ponder these clues further, asking questions about mythic purpose. How does the myth organize and focus the materials? What does it hint about the future—the new parents of the human race? Are there loose ends? Ponder implications about the nature of the new man and new woman in a new kind of garden-world. What is the garden-world they cultivate to be like?

5. *Extrapolation.* For all its brevity, the novel covers a wide variety of topics: politics, business, news, law, economics, diplomacy, communications, sex, illness, publishing, celebrity status, and many more. With all these subjects, the novel points up human tendencies to hear only what we want to hear, and then leap to exaggerative inferences to suit our own needs and desires. In the novel, ambiguity occurs in the double ways people and Chance view each other and phenomena. He looks at, understands, and treats people and things one way, they quite another. What does our bent for extrapolation imply about absolutes? About existence in general?

6. *A new pantheon.* In announcing that "God is dead," Nietzsche meant that Judeo-Christian worship of God as practiced in the late nineteenth century was no longer viable. When *Being There* opens we learn that "the Old Man had died." In Chapter Five, Lord Beauclerk says that what TV and its viewers want is *"a god to punish, not a man of their infirmity."* Discuss the plausibility that TV may be the new god. Gather evidence to support your discussion. Recall Beauclerk's punning remark about *"videots."* In Chapter One, "Chance . . . turned on the TV. The set *created its own light, its own color, its own time."* (editors' italics) What kind of god is evident, and what is the nature of the world this god creates?

7. *Social psychology.* Kosinski was educated as a social psychologist. This profession studies various relationships such as those between individuals, between the individual and the group, and between groups. It examines the influence of social institutions on individual development, communication, leadership, cooperation, competition, problem solving within groups, the nature and measurement of attitudes within groups, and the study of imitation and suggestion and their effect on fashion and fads. Analyze the novel from several of these vantages. Then determine if any or all of these categories satisfactorily account for the artistry of *Being There.*

8. *Narrative techniques.* Kosinski writes most of the novel in the third person, staying close to the severely limited central intelligence of Chance. However, on occasion he uses other points of view (the President, EE, Thomas Franklin, Ambassador Skrapinov, etc.). Why is it necessary to shift points of view in this particular work? What is accomplished? Furthermore, Kosinski depends heavily upon chance, coincidence, ironic reversals, and other obvious forms of plot manipula-

tion to keep the story going. Yet he seems to get away with every stretching of credibility. Explain why.

9. *Comedy.* What is comic about this novel? View from the uncorrupted, innocent Chance's point of view: his personal life before expulsion from the garden, his budding political career, his erotic adventures. Comedy grew from boisterous dialogue in fertility rites for the feasts of the Greek god Dionysus. Farce, fantasy, satire, parody, political propaganda, ending in a lyrical celebration of unity, were its elements. What vestiges of the origins do you find in *Being There,* and in what way are these elements transformed in the twentieth century? How do they clarify certain scenes? What is the aim of the humor? Discuss the novel as "black comedy."

10. *Nuances of meaning.* Study the following for thematic implications, enriching symbolism, or ironic overtones: the title, numbers *(seven* chapters), computers and other machines, titles of newspapers and journals, Chance's "fashionable clothes," the lawyer's proof of being, the magic effect on Eve of Chance's repeating her words (a TV practice), the erotic photographs, the Soviets, Krylov's tales, the power of silence, reticence, and stupidity, O'Flaherty's declaration to the politicos (Chapter Seven): "[Gardiner] appears to be one us. . . . Gardiner is our one chance," and the progressive fading of everything from Chance's brain on the last page.

11. *Personal psychology.* M.-L. von Franz explains that when an instinctual reaction to an unfamiliar experience is blocked by the unconscious, the reaction is often displaced to an erotic one. What does this idea tell the reader about the differing erotic situations in which Chance finds himself? What does it say about individuals, classes, and institutions? The ironic, comic, and satirical modes convey what overtones about eros in the world of *Being There?* Explain the refreshing light that is thrown on pornography, emotional eunuchry, autoeroticism, fetishism, and romantic love. What devastating revelations are made about Chance's innocent remark, "I like to watch"?

12. *Projection.* Ponder this statement: "Psychologically projection means that an individual's or an institution's needs, instincts, appetites, wishes, and fears are unconsciously cast on others, particularly those who are 'blank pages,' where they may find a sympathetic 'hook' upon which to depend." The brain-damaged Chance is an egregious twentieth-century example of this kind of *tabula rasa;* he is a living, ambulatory TV screen for others; in turn, he absorbs his entire life from TV itself. In the TV studio, "the viewers existed only as projections" of Chance's thought. Analyze "projection" as a psychological condition and as a writing technique in the novel.

13. *Setting: gardens and graveyards.* "And yet, with all its life, even at the peak of its bloom, the garden was its own graveyard" (Chapter One).

Read the entire paragraph for a key to the novel's underlying metaphorical structure and its way of viewing life. What possibilities and examples of metaphorical graveyards appear and what metaphorical gardens grow from them? Ponder Chance's progress between gardens: Manhattan townhouse, TV studio, United Nations fête, wealthy New York home, Capitol Hill ballroom. Weigh and judge this "snowballing" effect in manipulation of setting. What is revealed about settings individually and then collectively?

14. *The "blank page": to be seen is to exist.* The imagistic texture of this novel is relatively slight compared with others here. Kosinski, however, finely controls these related words, on which he plays multiple variations: *screen, mirror, image, reflection,* and *sight.* What themes are carried by these images? Chance's code name is "blank page," which, in turn, may be a code for one or more prominent American political figures of the Sixties and Seventies. Attempt to "crack the code." How might EE, Benjamin, and others be encoded? What social (and media-related) phenomena of recent politics, on which a number of books have been published, are caustically satirized?

15. *Important messages.* One observer of Kosinski writes that "deep below his stories there is an important meaning and a sincere message about the frightful world we are living in. His questions are the old, but never satisfactorily answered questions: What is man? What is our life really about? What to do in this world where one must be indifferent to avoid one shock after another?" Evaluate this statement, with reference to *Being There.* Is there any hope for mankind at all? For instance, would a return to an Edenic state make any difference? How does Kosinski's manipulation of tone breed a remnant of hope for humanity?

Surfacing

Margaret Atwood

I

CHAPTER ONE

I can't believe I'm on this road again, twisting along past the lake where the white birches are dying, the disease is spreading up from the south, and I notice they now have seaplanes for hire. But this is still near the city limits; we didn't go through, it's swelled enough to have a bypass, that's success.

I never thought of it as a city but as the last or first outpost depending on which way we were going, an accumulation of sheds and boxes and one main street with a movie theater, the itz, the oyal, red *R* burned out, and two restaurants which served identical gray hamburger steaks plastered with mud gravy and canned peas, watery and pallid as fisheyes, and french fries bleary with lard. Order a poached egg, my mother said, you can tell if it's fresh by the edges.

In one of those restaurants before I was born my brother got under the table and slid his hands up and down the waitress's legs while she was bringing the food; it was during the war and she had on shiny orange rayon stockings, he'd never seen them before, my mother didn't wear them. A different year there we ran through the snow across the sidewalk in our bare feet because we had no shoes, they'd worn out during the summer. In the car that time we sat with our feet wrapped in blankets, pretending we were wounded. My brother said the Germans shot our feet off.

Now though I'm in another car, David's and Anna's; it's sharp-finned and striped with chrome, a lumbering monster left over from ten years ago, he has to reach under the instrument panel to turn on the lights. David says they can't afford a newer one, which probably isn't true. He's a good driver, I realize that, I keep my outside hand on the door in spite of it. To brace myself and so I can get out quickly if I have to. I've driven in the same car with them before but on this road it doesn't seem right, either the three of them are in the wrong place or I am.

I'm in the back seat with the packsacks; this one, Joe, is sitting beside me chewing gum and holding my hand, they both pass the time. I examine the hand: the palm is broad, the short fingers tighten and relax, fiddling with my gold ring, turning it, it's a reflex of his. He has peasant hands, I have peasant feet, Anna told us that. Everyone now can do a little magic, she reads hands at parties, she says it's a substitute for conversation. When she did mine she said "Do you have a twin?" I said No. "Are you positive," she said, "because some of your lines are double." Her index finger traced me: "You had a good childhood but then there's this funny break." She puckered her forehead and I said I just wanted to know how long I was going to live, she could skip the rest. After that she told us Joe's hands were dependable but not sensitive and I laughed, which was a mistake.

From the side he's like the buffalo on the U.S. nickel, shaggy and blunt-snouted, with small clenched eyes and the defiant but insane look of a species once dominant, now threatened with extinction. That's how he thinks of himself, too: deposed, unjustly. Secretly he would like them to set up a kind of park for him, like a bird sanctuary. Beautiful Joe.

He feels me watching him and lets go of my hand. Then he takes his gum out, bundling it in the silver wrapper, and sticks it in the ashtray and crosses his arms. That means I'm not supposed to observe him; I face front.

In the first few hours of driving we moved through flattened cow-sprinkled hills and leaf trees and dead elm skeletons, then into the needle trees and the cuttings dynamited in pink and gray granite and the flimsy tourist cabins, and the signs saying GATEWAY TO THE NORTH, at least four towns claim to be that. The future is in the North, that was a political slogan once; when my father heard it he said there was nothing in the North but the past and not much of that either. Wherever he is now, dead or alive and nobody knows which, he's no longer making epigrams. They have no right to get old. I envy people whose parents died when they were young, that's easier to remember, they stay unchanged. I was sure mine would anyway, I could leave and return much later and everything would be the same. I thought of them as living in some other time, going about their own concerns closed safe behind a wall as translucent as Jell-O, mammoths frozen in a glacier. All I would have to do was come back when I was ready but I kept putting it off, there would be too many explanations.

Now we're passing the turnoff to the pit the Americans hollowed out. From here it looks like an innocent hill, spruce-covered, but the thick power lines running into the forest give it away. I heard they'd left, maybe that was a ruse, they could easily still be living in there, the generals in concrete bunkers and the ordinary soldiers in underground apartment buildings where the lights burn all the time. There's no way of checking because we aren't allowed in. The city invited them to stay, they were good for business, they drank a lot.

"That's where the rockets are," I say. *Were.* I don't correct it.

David says "Bloody fascist pig Yanks," as though he's commenting on the weather.

Anna says nothing. Her head rests on the back of the seat, the ends of her light hair whipping in the draft from the side window that won't close properly. Earlier she was singing, House of the Rising Sun and Lili Marlene, both of them several times, trying to make her voice go throaty and deep; but it came out like a hoarse child's. David turned on the radio, he couldn't get anything, we were between stations. When she was in the middle of St. Louis Blues he began to whistle and she stopped. She's my best friend, my best woman friend; I've known her two months.

I lean forward and say to David, "The bottle house is around this next curve and to the left," and he nods and slows the car. I told them about it earlier, I guessed it was the kind of object that would interest them. They're making a movie, Joe is doing the camera work, he's never done it before but David says they're the new Renaissance Men, you teach yourself what you need to learn. It was mostly David's idea, he calls himself the director: they already have the credits worked out. He wants to get shots of things they come across, random samples he calls them, and that will be the name of the movie too: *Random Samples.* When they've used up their supply of film (which was all they could afford; and the camera is rented) they're going to look at what they've collected and rearrange it.

"How can you tell what to put in if you don't already know what it's about?" I asked David when he was describing it. He gave me one of his initiate-to-novice stares. "If you close your mind in advance like that you wreck it. What you need is flow." Anna, over by the stove measuring out the coffee, said everyone she knew was making a movie, and David said that was no fucking reason why he shouldn't. She said "You're right, sorry"; but she laughs about it behind his back, she calls it Random Pimples.

The bottle house is built of pop bottles cemented together with the bottoms facing out, green ones and brown ones in zigzag patterns like the ones they taught us in school to draw on tepees; there's a wall around it made of bottles, too, arranged in letters so the brown ones spell BOTTLE VILLA.

"Neat," David says, and they get out of the car with the camera. Anna and I climb out after them; we stretch our arms, and Anna has a cigarette. She's wearing a purple tunic and white bellbottoms, they have a smear on them already, grease from the car. I told her she should wear jeans or something but she said she looks fat in them.

"Who made it, Christ, think of the work," she says, but I don't know anything about it except that it's been there forever, the tangled black spruce swamp around it making it even more unlikely, a preposterous monument to some quirkish person exiled or perhaps a voluntary recluse like my father, choosing this swamp because it was the only place where he could fulfill his lifelong dream of living in a house of bottles. Inside the wall is an attempted lawn and a border with orange mattress-tuft marigolds.

"Great," says David, "really neat," and he puts his arm around Anna and hugs her briefly to show he's pleased, as though she is somehow responsible for the Bottle Villa herself. We get back in the car.

I watch the side window as though it's a TV screen. There's nothing I can remember till we reach the border, marked by the sign that says BIENVENUE on one side and WELCOME on the other. The sign has bullet holes in it, rusting red around the edges. It always did, in the fall the hunters use it for target practice; no matter how many times they replace it or paint it the bullet holes reappear, as though they aren't put there but grow by a kind of inner logic or infection, like mold or boils. Joe wants to film the sign but David says, "Naaa, what for?"

Now we're on my home ground, foreign territory. My throat constricts, as it learned to do when I discovered people could say words that would go into my ears meaning nothing. To be deaf and dumb would be easier. The cards they poke at you when they want a quarter, with the hand alphabet on them. Even so, you would need to learn spelling.

The first smell is the mill, sawdust, there are mounds of it in the yard with the stacked timber slabs. The pulpwood goes elsewhere to the paper mill, but the bigger logs are corralled in a boom on the river, a ring of logs chained together with the free ones nudging each other inside it; they travel to the saws in a clanking overhead chute, that hasn't been changed. The car goes under it and we're curving up into the tiny company town, neatly planned with public flowerbeds and an eighteenth-century fountain in the middle, stone dolphins and a cherub with part of the face missing. It looks like an imitation but it may be real.

Anna says "Oh wow, what a great fountain."

"The company built the whole thing," I say, and David says "Rotten capitalist bastards" and begins to whistle again.

I tell him to turn right and he does. The road ought to be here, but instead there's a battered checkerboard, the way is blocked.

"Now what," says David.

We didn't bring a map, because I knew we wouldn't need one. "I'll have to ask," I say, so he backs the car out and we drive along the main street till we come to a corner store, magazines and candy.

"You must mean the old road," the woman says with only a trace of an accent. "It's been closed for years, what you need is the new one." I buy four vanilla cones because you aren't supposed to ask without buying anything. She gouges down into the cardboard barrel with a metal scoop. Before, the ice cream came rolled in pieces of paper which they would peel off like bark, pressing the short logs of ice cream into the cones with their thumbs. Those must be obsolete.

I go back to the car and tell David the directions. Joe says he likes chocolate better.

Nothing is the same, I don't know the way any more. I slide my tongue around the ice cream, trying to concentrate on it, they put seaweed in it now, but I'm starting to shake, why is the road different, he shouldn't have allowed them to do it, I want to turn around and go back to the city and never find out what happened to him. I'll start crying, that would be horrible, none of them would know what to do and neither would I. I bite down into the cone and I can't feel anything for a minute but the knife-hard pain up the side of my face. Anesthesia, that's one technique: if it hurts invent a different pain. I'm all right.

David finishes his cone, tossing the carton-flavored tip out the window, and starts the car. We go through a part that's spread out from the town since I was here, freshly built square bungalows like city ones except for the pink and baby-blue trim, and a few oblong shacks farther along, tar paper and bare boards. A clutch of children playing in the wet mud that substitutes for lawns; most of them are dressed in clothes too big for them, which makes them seem stunted.

"They must fuck a lot here," Anna says, "I guess it's the Church." Then she says "Aren't I awful."

David says "The true north strong and free."

Beyond the houses, two older children, dark faced, hold out tin cans toward the car. Raspberries perhaps.

We come to the gas station where the woman said to turn left and David groans with joy, "Oh god look at that," and they pile out as though it will escape if they aren't quick enough. What they're after is the three stuffed moose on a platform near the pumps: they're dressed in human clothes and wired standing up on their hind legs, a father moose with a trench coat and a pipe in his mouth, a mother moose in a print dress and flowered hat and a little boy moose in short pants, a striped jersey and a baseball cap, waving an American flag.

Anna and I follow. I go up behind David and say "Don't you need some gas," he shouldn't use the moose without paying, like the washrooms they're here to attract customers.

"Oh look," Anna says, hand going to her mouth, "there's another one on the roof," and there is, a little girl moose in a frilly skirt and a pigtailed blond wig, holding a red parasol in one hoof. They get her too. The owner of the gas station is standing behind his plate glass show window in his undershirt, scowling at us through the film of dust.

When we're back in the car I say as though defending myself, "Those weren't here before." Anna's head swivels around, my voice must sound odd.

"Before what?" she says.

The new road is paved and straight, two lanes with a line down the middle. Already it's beginning to gather landmarks, a few advertisement signs, a roadside crucifix with a wooden Christ, ribs sticking out, the alien god, mysterious to me as ever. Underneath it are a couple of jam jars with flowers, daisies and red devil's paintbrush and the white ones you can dry, Indian Posies, Everlasting, there must have been a car accident.

At intervals the old road crosses us; it was dirt, full of bumps and potholes, it followed the way the land went, up and down the hills and around the cliffs and boulders. They used to go over it as fast as possible, their father knew every inch of it and could take it (he said) blindfolded, which was what they often seemed to be doing, grinding up past the signs that said PETITE VITESSE and plunging down over the elevator edges and scraping around the rockfaces, GARDEZ LE DROIT, horn hooting; the rest of them clamped onto the inside of the car, getting sicker and sicker despite the Lifesavers their mother would hand out, and finally throwing up groggily by the side of the road, blue asters and pink fireweed, if he could stop in time or out the car window if he couldn't or into paper bags, he anticipated emergencies, if he was in a hurry and didn't want to stop at all.

That won't work, I can't call them "they" as if they were somebody else's family: I have to keep myself from telling that story. Still though, seeing the old road billowing along at a distance through the trees (ruts and traces already blurring with grass and saplings, soon it will be gone) makes me reach into my bag for the Lifesavers I brought. But they aren't needed anymore, even though the new road turns from pavement into gravel ("Must've elected the wrong guy last time around," David says jokingly) and the familiar smell of road dust fuming behind and around us mixes with the gas-and-upholstery smell of the car.

"Thought you said this would be bad," David says over his shoulder, "it's not bad at all." We're nearly to the village already, the two roads joining here but widened—rock blasted, trees bulldozed over, roots in the air, needles reddening—past the flat cliff where the election slogans are painted and painted over, some faded and defaced, others fresh yellow and white, VOTEZ GODET, VOTEZ OBRIEN, along with hearts and initials and words and advertisements, THÉ SALADA, BLUE MOON COTTAGES ½ MILE, QUÉBEC LIBRE, FUCK YOU, BUVEZ COCA-COLA GLACÉ, JESUS SAVES, mélange of demands and languages, an X ray of it would be the district's entire history.

But they've cheated, we're here too soon and I feel deprived of something, as though I can't really get here unless I've suffered; as though the first view of the lake, which we can see now, blue and cool as redemption, should be through tears and a haze of vomit.

CHAPTER TWO

We slur down the last hill, gravel pinging off the underside of the car, and suddenly there's a thing that isn't supposed to be here. MOTEL, BAR BIÈRE BEER the sign reads, neon even, someone is trying; but to no avail, there aren't any cars parked outside and the VACANCY notice is up. The building is like any other cheap motel, long gray stucco with aluminum doors; the earth around it is still chunky and raw, not yet overgrown with the road weeds.

"Let's pick up a few," David says, to Joe; he's already swerved the car.

We head towards the door but then I stop, it's the best place to leave them, and say "You go in and have a beer or something, I'll be back in about half an hour."

"Right," David says. He knows what to avoid.

"Want me to come?" Joe offers, but when I say No, relief gleams through his beard. The three of them disappear through the screen door of the bar and I walk the rest of the way down the hill.

I like them, I trust them, I can't think of anyone else I like better, but right now I wish they weren't here. Though they're necessary: David's and Anna's car was the only way I could make it, there's no bus and no train and I never hitch. They're doing me a favor, which they disguised by saying it would be fun, they like to travel. But my reason for being here embarrasses them, they don't understand it. They all disowned their parents long ago, the way you are supposed to: Joe never mentions his mother and father, Anna says hers were nothing people and David calls his The Pigs.

There was a covered bridge here once, but it was too far north to be quaint. They tore it down three years before I left, to improve the dam, and replaced it with the concrete bridge which is here now, enormous, monumental, dwarfing the village. It's the dam that controls the lake: sixty years ago they raised the lake level so that whenever they wanted to flush the logs down the narrow outflow river to the mill they would have enough water power. But they don't do much logging here any more. A few men work on railway maintenance, one freight train a day; a couple of families run the stores, the small one where they used to speak English, the other where they wouldn't. The rest process the tourists, businessmen in plaid shirts still creased from the cellophane packages, and wives, if they come, who sit in twos on the screened blackfly-proof porches of the single-room cabins and complain to each other while the men play at fishing.

I pause to lean over the railing on the river side. The floodgates are open, the froth-colored and brown rapids topple over the rocks, the sound rushes. The sound is one of the first things I remember, that was what warned them. It was night, I was lying in the bottom of the canoe; they had started out from the village but a heavy fog had risen, so thick they could hardly see the water. They found the shoreline and followed it along; it was dead silent, they could hear what they thought was the howling of wolves, muffled by forest and mist, it meant they had taken the right direction. Then there was the pouring noise of the rapids and they saw where they were, just as the current caught them. They were going backwards, the howling was the village dogs. If the canoe had tipped over we would have been killed, but they were calm, they didn't act like danger; what stayed in my head was only the mist whiteness, the hush of moving water and the rocking motion, total safety.

Anna was right, I had a good childhood; it was in the middle of the war, flecked gray newsreels I never saw, bombs and concentration camps, the leaders roaring at the crowds from inside their uniforms, pain and useless death, flags rippling in time to the anthems. But I didn't know about that till later, when my brother found out and told me. At the time it felt like peace.

Now I'm in the village, walking through it, waiting for the nostalgia to hit, for the cluster of nondescript buildings to be irradiated with inner light like a plug-in crêche, as it has been so often in memory; but nothing happens. It hasn't gotten any bigger, these days the children probably move to the city. The same two-story frame houses with nasturtiums on the windowsills and squared roof-corners, motley lines of washing trailing from them like the tails of kites; though some of the houses are slicker and have changed color. The white dollhouse-sized church above on the rock hillside is neglected, peeling paint and a broken window, the old priest must be gone. What I mean is dead.

Down by the shore, a lot of boats are tied up at the government dock but not many cars parked: more boats than cars, a bad season. I try to decide which of the cars is my father's but as I scan them I realize I no longer know what kind of car he would be driving.

I reach the turnoff to Paul's, a rough dirt path rutted by tires, crossing the railroad tracks and continuing through a swamp field, logs laid side by side over the soggy parts. A few blackflies catch up with me, it's July, past the breeding time, but as usual there are some left.

The road goes up and I climb it, along the backs of the houses Paul built for his son and his son-in-law and his other son, his clan. Paul's is the original, yellow with maroon trim, squat farmhouse pattern; though this isn't farming country, it's mostly rock and where there's any soil it's thin and sandy. The closest Paul ever got to farming was to have a cow, killed by the milk bottle. The shed where it and the horses used to live is now a garage.

In the clearing behind the house two 1950s cars are resting, a pink one and a red one, raised on wooden blocks, no wheels; scattered around them are the rusting remains of older cars: like my father, Paul saves everything useful. The house has added a pointed structure like a church spire, made of former car parts welded together; on top of it is a TV antenna and on top of that a lightning rod.

Paul is at home, he's in the vegetable garden at the side of the house. He straightens up to watch me, his face leathery and retained as ever, like a closed suitcase; I don't think he knows who I am.

"Bonjour monsieur," I say when I'm at the fence. He takes a step toward me, still guarding, and I say "Don't you remember me," and smile. Again the strangling feeling, paralysis of the throat; but Paul speaks English, he's been outside. "It was very kind of you to write."

"Ah," he says, not recognizing me but deducing who I must be, *"bonjour,"* and then he smiles, too. He clasps his hands in front of him like a priest or a porcelain mandarin; he doesn't say anything else. We stand there on either side of the fence, our faces petrified in well-intentioned curves, mouths wreathed in parentheses, until I say "Has he come back yet?"

At this his chin plummets, his head teeters on his neck. "Ah. No." He gazes sideways, accusingly, down at a potato plant near his left foot. Then his head jerks up again and he says gaily, "Not yet, ay? But maybe soon. Your fadder, he knows the bush."

Madame has appeared in the kitchen doorway and Paul speaks with her in the nasal slanted French I can't interpret because I learned all but a few early words of mine in school. Folk songs and Christmas carols and, from the later grades, memorized passages of Racine and Baudelaire are no help to me here.

"You must come in," he says to me, "and take a tea," and he bends and undoes the hook of the wooden gate. I go forward to the door where Madame is waiting for me, hands outstretched in welcome, smiling and shaking her head mournfully as though through no fault of my own I'm doomed.

Madame makes the tea on a new electric stove, a blue ceramic Madonna with pink child hanging above it; when I glimpsed the stove on my way through the kitchen I felt betrayed, she should have remained loyal to her wood range. We sit on the screened porch overlooking the lake, balancing our teacups and rocking side by side in three rocking chairs; I've been given the store cushion, which has an embroidered view of Niagara Falls. The black-and-white collie, either the identical one I used to be afraid of or its offshoot, lies on the braided rug by our feet.

Madame, who is the same thickness all the way down, is in a long-skirted dress and black stockings and a print apron with a bib, Paul in high-waisted trousers with braces, flannel shirtsleeves rolled. I'm annoyed with them for looking so much like carvings, the habitant kind they sell in tourist handicraft shops, but of course it's the other way around, it's the carvings that look like them. I wonder what they think I look like, they may find my jeans and sweatshirt and fringed over-the-shoulder bag strange, perhaps immoral, though such things may be more common in the village since the tourists and the TV; besides, I can be forgiven because my family was, by reputation, peculiar as well as *anglais*.

I lift my cup, they are watching me anxiously: it's imperative that I mention the tea. *"Très bon,"* I manage to get out in the direction of Madame. *"Délicieux."* Doubt seizes me, *thé* may be feminine.

What I'm remembering are the visits our mother was obliged to pay Madame while our father was visiting Paul. My father and Paul would be outside, talking about boats or motors or forest fires or one of their expeditions, and my mother and Madame would be inside in the rocking chairs (my mother with the Niagara Falls cushion), trying with great goodwill to make conversation. Neither knew more than five words of the other's language and after the opening *Bonjour* both would unconsciously raise their voices as though talking to a deaf person.

"Il fait beau," my mother would shout, no matter what the weather was like, and Madame would grin with strain and say *"Pardon? Ah, il fait* beau, *oui, il fait beau, ban oui."* When she had ground to a stop both would think desperately, chairs rocking.

"'Ow are *you?"* Madame would scream, and my mother, after deciphering this, would say *"Fine,* I am fine." Then she would repeat the question: "How are *you,* madame?" But Madame would not have the answer and both, still smiling, would glance furtively out through the screen to see if the men were yet coming to rescue them.

Meanwhile my father would be giving Paul the cabbages or the string beans he had brought from his garden and Paul would be replying with tomatoes or lettuces from his. Since their gardens had the same things in them this exchange of vegetables was purely ritual: after it had taken place we would know the visit would be officially over.

Madame is stirring her tea now and sighing. She says something to Paul and Paul says, "Your mother, she was a good woman, Madame says it is very sad; so young too."

"Yes," I say. Mother and Madame were about the same age and no one would call Madame young; but then my mother never got fat like Madame.

I went to see her in the hospital, where she allowed herself to be taken only when she could no longer walk; one of the doctors told me that. She must have concealed the pain for weeks, tricked my father into believing it was only one of her usual headaches, that would be her kind of lie. She hated hospitals and doctors; she must have been afraid they would experiment on her, keep her alive as long as they could with tubes and needles even though it was what they call terminal, in the head it always is; and in fact that's what they did.

They had her on morphine, she said there were webs floating in the air in front of her. She was very thin, much older than I'd ever thought possible, skin tight over her curved beak nose, hands on the sheet curled like bird claws clinging to a perch. She peered at me with bright blank eyes. She may not have known who I was: she didn't ask me why I left or where I'd been, though she might not have asked anyway, feeling as she always had that personal questions were rude.

"I'm not going to your funeral," I said. I had to lean close to her, the hearing in one of her ears was gone. I wanted her to understand in advance, and approve.

"I never enjoyed them," she said to me, one word at a time. "You have to wear a hat. I don't like liquor." She must have been talking about church or cocktail parties. She lifted her hand, slowly as if through water, and felt the top of her head; there was a tuft of white hair standing straight up. "I didn't get the bulbs in. Is there snow outside?"

On the bedside table with the flowers, chrysanthemums, I saw her diary; she kept one every year. All she put in it was a record of the weather and the work done on that day: no reflections, no emotions. She would refer to it when she wanted to compare the years, decide whether the spring had been late or early, whether it had been a wet summer. It made me angry to see it in that windowless room where it was no use; I waited till her eyes were closed and slipped it into my shoulder bag. When I got outside I leafed through it, I thought there might be something about me, but except for the dates the pages were blank, she had given up months ago.

"Do what you think best," she said from behind her closed eyes. "Is there snow?"

We rock some more. I want to ask Paul about my father but he ought to begin, he must have news to tell me. Maybe he's avoiding it; or maybe he's being tactful, waiting until I'm ready. Finally I say "What happened to him?"

Paul shrugs. "He is just gone," he says. "I go there one day to see him, the door is open, the boats is there, I think maybe he is off somewheres near and I wait awhile. Next day I go back, everything the same, I begin to worry, where he is, I don't know. So I write to you, he has leaved your *caisse postale* and the keys, I lock up the place. His car she is here, with me." He gestures towards the back, the garage. My father trusted Paul, he said Paul could build anything and fix anything. They were once caught in a three-week rainstorm, my father said if you could spend three weeks in a wet tent with a man without killing him or having him kill you then he was a good man. Paul justified for him his own ideal of the simple life; but for Paul the anachronism was imposed, he'd never chosen it.

"Did you look on the island?" I say. "If the boats are there he can't have gone off the island."

"I look, sure," Paul says, "I tell the police from down-the-road, they look around, nobody find nothing. Your husband here too?" he asks irrelevantly.

"Yes, he's here," I say, skipping over the lie even in my own mind. What he means is that a man should be handling this; Joe will do as a stand-in. My status is a problem, they obviously think I'm married. But I'm safe, I'm wearing my ring, I never threw it out, it's useful for landladies. I sent my parents a postcard after the wedding, they must have mentioned it to Paul; that, but not the divorce. It isn't part of the vocabulary here, there's no reason to upset them.

I'm waiting for Madame to ask about the baby, I'm prepared, alerted, I'll tell her I left him in the city; that would be perfectly true, only it was a different city, he's better off with my husband, former husband.

But Madame doesn't mention it, she lifts another cube of sugar from the tray by her side and he intrudes, across from me, a coffee shop, not city but roadside, on the way to or from somewhere, some goal or encounter. He peels the advertisement paper from the sugar and lets one square fall into the cup, I'm talking and his mouth turns indulgent, it must have been before the child. He smiles and I smile too, thinking of the slice of cucumber pickle that was stuck to the top of his club sandwich. A round historical plaque, on a supermarket wall or in a parking lot, marking the site where a building once stood in which an event of little importance once took place, ridiculous. He puts his hand on mine, he tries that a lot but he's easy to get rid of, easier and easier. I don't have time for him, I switch problems.

I sip at my tea and rock, by my feet the dog stirs, the lake below flutters in the wind which is beginning. My father has simply disappeared then, vanished into nothing. When I got Paul's letter —"Your father is gone, nobody can't find him"—it seemed incredible, but it appears to be true.

There used to be a barometer on the porch wall, a wooden house with two doors and a man and a woman who lived inside. When it was going to be fair the woman in her long skirt and apron would emerge from her door, when it was going to rain she would go in and the man would come out, carrying an axe. When it was first explained to me I thought they controlled the weather instead of merely responding to it. My eyes seek the house now, I need a prediction, but it's not there.

"I think I'll go down the lake," I say.

Paul raises his hands, palms outward. "We look two, three times already."

But they must have missed something, I feel it will be different if I look myself. Probably when we get there my father will have returned from wherever he has been, he will be sitting in the cabin waiting for us.

CHAPTER THREE

On my way back to the motel I detour to the store, the one where they're supposed to speak English: we will need some food. I go up the wooden steps, past a drowsing mop-furred mongrel roped to the porch with a length of clothesline. The screen door has a BLACK CAT CIGARETTES handle; I open it and step into the store smell, the elusive sweetish odor given off by the packaged cookies and the soft-drink cooler. For a brief time the post office was here, a DÉFENSE DE CRACHER SUR LE PLANCHER sign stamped with a government coat of arms.

Behind the counter there's a woman about my age, but with brassiere-shaped breasts and a light auburn moustache; her hair is in rollers covered by a pink net and she has on slacks and a sleeveless jersey top. The old priest is definitely gone, he disapproved of slacks, the women had to wear long concealing skirts and dark stockings and keep their arms covered in church. Shorts were against the law, and many of them lived all their lives beside the lake without learning to swim because they were ashamed to put on bathing suits.

The woman looks at me, inquisitive but not smiling, and the two men still in Elvis Presley haircuts, duck's ass at the back and greased pompadours curving out over their foreheads, stop talking and look at me, too; they keep their elbows on the counter. I hesitate: maybe the tradition has changed, maybe they no longer speak English.

"Avez-vous du viande hâché?" I ask her, blushing because of my accent.

She grins then and the two men grin also, not at me but at each other. I see I've made a mistake, I should have pretended to be an American.

"Amburger, oh yes, we have lots. *H*ow much?" she asks, adding the *H* carelessly to show she can if she feels like it. This is border country.

"A pound, no, two pounds," I say, blushing even more because I've been so easily discovered, they're making fun of me and I have no way of letting them know I share the joke. Also I agree with them, if you live in a place you should speak the language. But this isn't where I lived.

She hacks with a cleaver at a cube of frozen meat, weighs it. "Doo leevers," she says, mimicking my school accent. The two men snigger. I solace myself by replaying the man from the government, he was at a gallery opening, a handicraft exhibit, string wall hangings, woven place mats, stoneware breakfast sets; Joe wanted to go so he could resent not being in it. The man seemed to be a cultural attaché of some sort, an ambassador; I asked him if he knew this part of the country, my part, and he shook his head and said "*Des barbares,* they are not civilized." At the time that annoyed me.

I pick up some fly dope in a spray can for the others, also some eggs and bacon, bread and butter, miscellaneous tins. Everything is more expensive here than in the city; no one keeps hens or cows or pigs any more, it's all imported from more fertile districts. The bread is in wax-paper wrappers, *tranché.*

I would like to back out the door, I don't want them staring at me from behind; but I force myself to walk slowly, frontwards.

There used to be only one store. It was in the front part of a house, run by an old woman who was also called Madame: none of the women had names then. Madame sold khaki-colored penny candies which we were forbidden to eat, but her main source of power was that she had only one hand. Her other arm ended in a soft pink snout like an elephant's trunk and she broke the parcel string by wrapping it around her stump and pulling. This arm devoid of a hand was for me a great mystery, almost as puzzling as Jesus. I wanted to know how the hand had come off (perhaps she had taken it off herself) and where it was now, and especially whether my own hand could ever come off like that; but I never asked, I must have been afraid of the answers. Going down the steps, I try to remember what the rest of her was like, her face, but I can see only the potent candies, inaccessible in their glass reliquary, and the arm, miraculous in an unspecified way like the toes of saints or the cut-off pieces of early martyrs, the eyes on the plate, the severed breasts, the heart with letters on it shining like a light bulb through the trim hole painted in the chest, art history.

I find the others in the small chilly room labelled BAR; they're the only customers. They have six beer bottles and four glasses on their orange formica-topped table. A mottled boy with a haircut like the ones of the men in the store, only blond, is sitting with them.

David waves at me as I come in: he's happy about something. "Have a beer," he says. "This is Claude, his father owns this joint."

Claude shambles off morosely to get me a beer. Underneath the bar itself is a crudely carved wooden fish with red and blue dots on it, intended possibly for a speckled trout; on its leaping back it supports the fake marble surface. Above the bar is a TV, turned off or broken, and the regulation picture, scrolled gilt frame, blown-up photograph of a stream with trees and rapids and a man fishing. It's an imitation of other places, more southern ones, which are themselves imitations, the original someone's distorted memory of a nineteenth-century English gentleman's shooting lodge, the kind with trophy heads and furniture made from deer antlers, Queen Victoria had a set like that. But if this is what succeeds why shouldn't they do it?

"Claude told us business is bad this year," David says, "on accounta word is around the lake's fished out. They're going to other lakes, Claude's dad flies them in his seaplane, neat eh? But he says some of the men went out in the spring with a dragnet and there's all kinds of them down there, real big ones, they're just gettin' too smart." David is slipping into his yokel dialect; he does it for fun, it's a parody of himself, the way he says he talked back in the fifties when he wanted to be a minister and was selling Bibles door to door to put himself through theological seminary: "Hey, lady, wanna buy a dirty book?" Now though it seems to be unconscious, maybe he's doing it for Claude, to make it clear he too is a man of the people. Or maybe it's an experiment in Communications, that's what he teaches, at night, the same place Joe works; it's an Adult Education program. David calls it Adult Vegetation; he got the job because he was once a radio announcer.

"Any news?" Joe asks, in a neutral mumble that signals he'd prefer it if I kept from showing any reaction, no matter what has happened.

"No," I say, "nothing different." Voice level, calm. Perhaps that was what he liked about me, there must have been something, though I can't reconstruct our first meeting, now I can: it was in a store, I was buying some new brushes and a spray tin of fixative. He said Do you live around here and we went to the corner for a coffee, except I had a 7-up instead. What impressed him that time, he even mentioned it later, cool he called it, was the way I took off my clothes and put them on again later very smoothly as if I were feeling no emotion. But I really wasn't.

Claude comes back with the beer and I say "Thank you" and glance up at him and his face dissolves and re-forms, he was about eight the last time I was here; he used to peddle worms in rusted tin cans to the fishermen down by the government dock. He's uneasy now, he can tell I recognize him.

"I'd like to go down the lake for a couple of days," I say, to David because it's his car. "I'd like to look around, if that's okay."

"Great," says David, "I'm gonna get me one of them smart fish." He brought along a borrowed fishing rod, though I warned him he might not have a chance to use it: if my father had turned up after all we would have gone away without letting him find out we were here. If he's safe I don't want to see him. There's no point, they never forgave me, they didn't understand the divorce; I don't think they even understood the marriage, which wasn't surprising since I didn't understand it myself. What upset them was the way I did it, so suddenly, and then running off and leaving my husband and child, my attractive full-color magazine illustrations, suitable for framing. Leaving my child, that was the unpardonable sin; it was no use trying to explain to them why it wasn't really mine. But I admit I was stupid, stupidity is the same as evil if you judge by the results, and I didn't have any excuses, I was never good at them. My brother was, he used to make them up in advance of the transgressions; that's the logical way.

"Oh god," Anna says, "David thinks he's a great white hunter." She's teasing him, she does that a lot; but he doesn't hear, he's getting up, Claude is hustling him off to make him out a license, it seems Claude is in charge of the licenses. When David comes back I want to ask how much he paid, but he's too pleased, I don't want to spoil it. Claude is pleased also.

We find out from Claude we can hire Evans, who owns the Blue Moon Cabins, to run us down the lake. Paul would take us for nothing, he offered, but I wouldn't feel right about it; also I'm sure he would misinterpret Joe's amorphous beard and David's moustache and Three Musketeers hair. They're just a style now, like crew cuts, but Paul might feel they are dangerous, they mean riots.

David eases the car down the turnoff, two ruts and a rock hump in the center that scrapes the car's belly. We brake in front of the cabin marked OFFICE; Evans is there, a bulky laconic American in checked shirt and peaked cap and a thick knitted jacket with an eagle on the back. He knows where my father's place is, all the older guides know every house on the lake. He moves his cigarette butt to the corner of his mouth and says he'll take us there, ten miles, for five dollars; for another five he'll pick us up two days from now, in the morning. That will give us the rest of the day to drive back to the city. He's heard of the disappearance, of course, but he doesn't mention it.

"A groovy old guy, eh?" David says when we're outside. He's enjoying himself, he thinks this is reality: a marginal economy and grizzled elderly men, it's straight out of Depression photo essays. He spent four years in New York and became political, he was studying something; it was during the sixties, I'm not sure when. My friends' pasts are vague to me and to each other also, any one of us could have amnesia for years and the others wouldn't notice.

When David has backed the car down to the Blue Moon dock we unload our stuff, the packsacks of clothes, the camera equipment, the Samsonite case with my career in it, the half-dozen Red Caps they got at the motel and the paper bag of food. We scramble into the boat, a battered wood-hulled launch; Evans starts the motor and we churn out slowly. Summer cottages beginning to sprout here, they spread like measles, it must be the paved road.

David sits in front beside Evans. "Gettin' many fish?" he asks, folksy, chummy, crafty. "Here and there, here and there," Evans says, giving no free handouts; then he switches the motor into high gear and I can't hear any more.

I wait until we're into the middle of the lake. At the right moment I look over my shoulder as I always did and there is the village, suddenly distanced and clear, the houses receding and grouping, the white church startling against the dark of the trees. The feeling I expected before but failed to have comes now, homesickness, for a place where I never lived, I'm far enough away; then the village shrinks, optical illusion, and we're around a point of land, it's behind us.

The three of us are together on the back seat, Anna beside me. "This is good," she says to me, voice shrilling over the engine roar, "it's good for us to get away from the city"; but when I turn to answer there are tears on her cheek and I wonder why, she's always so cheerful. Then I realize they aren't tears, it's started to drizzle. The raincoats are in our packsacks; I didn't notice it had clouded over. We won't be very wet though, with this boat it will only take half an hour; before, with the heavier boats and primitive motors, it took two to three hours depending on the wind. In the city people would say to my mother, "Aren't you afraid? What if something happened?" They were thinking of the time it would take to get to a doctor.

I'm cold, I huddle my shoulders up; drops ping onto my skin. The shoreline unrolls and folds together again as we go past; forty miles from here there's another village, in between there's nothing but a tangled maze, low hills curving out of the water, bays branching in, peninsulas which turn into islands, islands, necks of land leading to other lakes. On a map or in an aerial photograph the water pattern radiates like a spider, but in a boat you can see only a small part of it, the part you're in.

The lake is tricky, the weather shifts, the wind swells up quickly; people drown every year, boats loaded topheavy or drunken fishermen running at high speed into deadheads, old pieces of tree waterlogged and partly decayed, floating under the surface, there are a lot of them left over from the logging and the time they raised the lake level. Because of the convolutions it's easy to lose the way if you haven't memorized the landmarks and I watch for them now, dome-shaped hill, point with dead pine, stubble of cut trunks poking up from a shallows, I don't trust Evans.

But he's taken the right turns so far, we're coming into my territory, two short bends and through a passage between granite shores and out into a wider bay. The peninsula is where I left it, pushing out from the island shore with the house not even showing through the trees, though I know where it is; camouflage was one of my father's policies.

Evans arches the boat around the point and slows for the dock. The dock slants, the ice takes something away from it every winter and the water warps and rots it; it's been repaired so much all the materials are different, but it's the same dock my brother fell off the time he drowned.

He used to be kept in a chicken-wire enclosure my father built for him, large cage or small playground, with trees, a swing, rocks, a sandpile. The fence was too high for him to climb over but there was a gate and one day he learned how to open it. My mother was alone in the house; she glanced out the window, checking, and he was no longer in the cage. It was a still day, no wind noise, and she heard something down by the water. She ran to the dock, he wasn't there, she went out to the end of it and looked down. My brother was under the water, face upturned, eyes open and unconscious, sinking gently; air was coming out of his mouth.

It was before I was born but I can remember it as clearly as if I saw it, and perhaps I did see it: I believe that an unborn baby has its eyes open and can look out through the walls of the mother's stomach, like a frog in a jar.

CHAPTER FOUR

We unload our baggage while Evans idles the motor. When David has paid him he gives us an uninterested nod and backs the boat out, then turns it and swings around the point, the sound dwindling to a whine and fading as land and distance move between us. The lake jiggles against the shore, the waves subside, nothing remains but a faint irridescent film of gasoline, purple and pink and green. The space is quiet, the wind has gone down and the lake is flat, silver-white, it's the first time all day (and for a long time, for years) we have been out of the reach of motors. My ears and body tingle, aftermath of the vibration, like feet taken out of roller skates.

The others are standing aimlessly; they seem to be waiting for me to tell them what comes next. "We'll take the things up," I say. I warn them about the dock: it's slippery with the drizzle, which is lighter now, almost a mist; also some of the boards may be soft and treacherous.

What I want to do is shout "Hello!" or "We're here!" but I don't, I don't want to hear the absence.

I hoist a packsack and walk along the dock and onto the land and towards the cabin, following the path and climbing the steps set into the hillside, lengths of split cedar held in place by a stake pounded at each end. The house is built on a sand hill, part of a ridge left by the retreating glaciers; only a few inches of soil and a thin coating of trees hold it down. On the lake side the sand is exposed, raw, it's been crumbling away: the stones and charcoal from the fireplace they used when they first lived here in tents have long since vanished, and the edge trees fall gradually, several I remember upright are leaning now. Red pines, bark scaling, needles bunched on the top branches. A kingfisher is perched on one of them, making its staccato alarm-clock cry; they nest in the cliff, burrowing into the sand, it speeds up the erosion.

In front of the house the chicken-wire fence is still here, though one end is almost over the brink. They never dismantled it; even the dwarf swing is there, ropes frayed, sagging and blotched with weather. It wasn't like them to keep something when it was no longer needed; perhaps they expected grandchildren, visiting here. He would have wanted a dynasty, like Paul's, houses and descendants proliferating around him. The fence is a reproach, it points to my failure.

But I couldn't have brought the child here, I never identified it as mine; I didn't name it before it was born even, the way you're supposed to. It was my husband's, he imposed it on me, all the time it was growing in me I felt like an incubator. He measured everything he would let me eat, he was feeding it on me, he wanted a replica of himself; after it was born I was no more use. I couldn't prove it though he was clever: he kept saying he loved me.

The house is smaller, because (I realize) the trees around it have grown. It's turned grayer in nine years too, like hair. The cedar logs are upright instead of horizontal, upright logs are shorter and easier for one man to handle. Cedar isn't the best wood, it decays quickly. Once my father said "I didn't build it to last forever" and I thought then, Why not? Why didn't you?

I hope the door will be open but it's padlocked, as Paul said he left it. I dig the keys he gave me out of my bag and approach warily: whatever I find inside will be a clue. What if he returned after Paul locked it and couldn't get in? But there are other ways of getting in, he could have broken a window.

Joe and David are here now with the other packsacks and the beer. Anna is behind them with my case and the paper bag; she's singing again, Mockingbird Hill.

I open the wooden door and the screen door inside it and scan the room cautiously, then step inside. Table covered with blue oilcloth, bench, another bench which is a wooden box built against the wall, sofa with metal frame and thin mattress, it folds out into a bed. That was where our mother used to be: all day she would lie unmoving, covered with a brown plaid blanket, her face bloodless and shrunken. We would talk in whispers, she looked so different and she didn't hear if we spoke to her; but the next day she would be the same as she had always been. We came to have faith in her ability to recover, from anything; we ceased to take her illnesses seriously, they were only natural phases, like cocoons. When she died I was disappointed in her.

Nothing is out of place. Water drops fall on the roof, down from the trees.

They follow me inside. "Is this where you lived?" Joe asks. It's unusual for him to ask me anything about myself: I can't tell whether he's pleased or discouraged. He goes over to the snowshoes on the wall and lifts one down, taking refuge in his hands.

Anna puts the groceries on the counter and wraps her arms around herself. "It must have been weird," she says. "Cut off from everything like that."

"No," I say. To me it felt normal.

"Depends what you're used to," David says. "I think it's neat." But he's not certain.

There are two other rooms and I open the doors quickly. A bed in each, shelves, clothes hanging on nails: jackets, raincoats, they were always left here. A gray hat, he had several of those. In the right-hand room is a map of the district, tacked to the wall. In the other are some pictures, watercolors, I recall now having painted them when I was twelve or thirteen; the fact that I'd forgotten about them is the only thing that makes me uneasy.

I go back to the living room. David has dropped his packsack on the floor and unfolded himself along the sofa. "Christ, am I wiped," he says. "Somebody break me out a beer." Anna brings him one and he pats her on the rear and says "That's what I like, service." She takes out cans for herself and us and we sit on the benches and drink it. Now that we're no longer moving the cabin is chilly.

The right smell, cedar and wood stove and tar from the oakum stuffed between the logs to keep out the mice. I look up at the ceiling, the shelves: there's a stack of papers beside the lamp, perhaps he was working on them just before whatever it was happened, before he left. There might be something for me, a note, a message, a will. I kept expecting that after my mother died, word of some kind, not money but an object, a token. For a while I went twice a day to the post-office box which was the only one of my addresses I'd given them; but nothing arrived, maybe she didn't have time.

No dirty dishes, no clothing strewn around, no evidence. It doesn't feel like a house that's been lived in all winter.

"What time is it?" I ask David. He holds up his watch: it's almost five. It will be up to me to organize dinner, since in a way this is my place, they are my guests.

There's kindling in the box behind the stove and a few pieces of white birch; the disease hasn't yet hit this part of the country. I find the matches and kneel in front of the stove, I've almost forgotten how to do this but after three or four matches I get it lit.

I take the round enameled bowl down from its hook, and the big knife. They watch me: none of them asks me where I'm going, though Joe seems worried. Perhaps he's been expecting me to have hysterics and he's anxious because I'm not having any. "I'm going to the garden," I say to reassure them. They know where that is, they could see it from the lake coming in.

Grass is growing up in the path and in front of the gate; the weeds are a month tall. Ordinarily I would spend a few hours pulling them out, but it isn't worth it, we'll be here only two days.

Frogs hop everywhere out of my way, they like it here; it's close to the lake, damp, my canvas shoes are soaked through. I pick some of the leaf lettuce that hasn't flowered and turned bitter, then I pull up an onion, sliding the loose brown outer skin off from the bulb, white and eyelike.

The garden's been rearranged: before there were scarlet runners up one side of the fence. The blossoms were redder than anything else in the garden, the hummingbirds went into them, hovering, their wings a blur. The beans that were left too long would yellow after the first frost and split open. Inside were pebbles, purple-black and frightening. I knew that if I could get some of them and keep them for myself I would be all-powerful; but later when I was tall enough and could finally reach to pick them it didn't work. Just as well, I think, as I had no idea what I would do with the power once I got it; if I'd turned out like the others with power I would have been evil.

I go to the carrot row and pull up a carrot but they haven't been thinned properly, it's forked and stubby. I cut off the onion leaves and the carrot top and throw them on the compost heap, then put the things in the bowl and start back towards the gate, adding up the time, growing time, in my head. In the middle of June he was here surely, it can't be longer than that.

Anna is outside the fence, she's come to look for me. "Where's the can?" she says. "I'm about to burst."

I take her to the beginning of the trail and point her along it.

"Are you okay?" she says.

"Sure," I say; the question surprises me.

"I'm sorry he wasn't here," she says mournfully, gazing at me out of her round green eyes as though it's her grief, her catastrophe.

"It's all right," I tell her, comforting her, "just keep going along the path and you'll find it, though it's quite a distance," I laugh, "don't get lost."

I carry the bowl down to the dock and wash the vegetables in the lake. Below me in the water there's a leech, the good kind with red dots on the back, undulating along like a streamer held at one end and shaken. The bad kind is mottled gray and yellow. It was my brother who made up these moral distinctions, at some point he became obsessed with them, he must have picked them up from the war. There had to be a good kind and a bad kind of everything.

I cook the hamburgers and we eat and I wash the dishes in the chipped dishpan, Anna drying; then it's almost dark. I lift the bedding out from the wall bench and make up our bed, Anna can do theirs. He must have been sleeping in the main room, on the sofa.

They aren't used to going to bed as soon as it's dark, though, and neither am I any more. I'm afraid they'll be bored because there's no TV or anything, I search for entertainments. A box of dominoes, a deck of cards, those were under the folded blankets. There are a lot of paperbacks on the shelves in the bedrooms, detective novels mostly, recreational reading. Beside them are the technical books on trees and the other reference books, *Edible Plants and Shoots, Tying the Dry Fly, The Common Mushrooms, Log Cabin Construction, A Field Guide to the Birds, Exploring Your Camera,* he believed that with the proper guidebooks you could do everything yourself; and his cache of serious books: the King James Bible which he said he enjoyed for its literary qualities, a complete Robert Burns, Boswell's *Life,* Thompson's *Seasons,* selections from Goldsmith and Cowper. He admired what he called the eighteenth-century rationalists: he thought of them as men who had avoided the corruptions of the Industrial Revolution and learned the secret of the golden mean, the balanced life, he was sure they all practiced organic farming. It astounded me to discover much later, in fact my husband told me, that Burns was an alcoholic, Cowper a madman, Dr. Johnson a manic-depressive and Goldsmith a pauper. There was something wrong with Thompson also; "escapist" was the term he used. After that I liked them better, they weren't paragons any more.

"I'll light the lamp," I say, "and we can read."

But David says "Naaa, why read when you can do that in the city?" He's twiddling the dial on his transistor radio; he can't pick up anything but static and a wail that might be music, wavering in and out, and a tiny insect voice whispering in French. "Shit," he says, "I wish I could get the scores." He means baseball, he's a fan.

"We could play bridge," I say, but no one wants to.

After a while David says "Well, children, time to break out the grass." He opens his packsack and gropes around inside, and Anna says "What a dumb place to put them, it's the first place they'd look."

"Up your ass," David says, smiling at her, "that's where they'd look first, they grab a good thing when they see one. Don't worry, baby, I know what I'm doing."

"Sometimes I wonder," Anna says.

We go outside and down to the dock and sit on the damp wood, watching the sunset, smoking a little. The clouds to the west are yellow and gray, fading, and in the clear sky southeast of us the moon is rising.

"This is great," David says, "it's better than in the city. If we could only kick out the fascist pig Yanks and the capitalists this would be a neat country. But then who would be left?"

"Oh Christ," Anna says, "don't get going on that."

"How?" I say. "How would you kick them out?"

"Organize the beavers," David says, "chew them to pieces, it's the only way. This Yank stockbroker is going along Bay Street and the beavers ambush him, drop on him from a telephone pole, chomp chomp and it's all over. You heard about the latest national flag? Nine beavers pissing on a frog."

It's old and shoddy but I laugh anyway. A little beer, a little pot, some jokes, a little political chitchat, the golden mean; we're the new bourgeoisie, this might as well be a Rec Room. Still I'm glad they're with me, I wouldn't want to be here alone; at any moment the loss, vacancy, will overtake me, they ward it off.

"Do you realize," David says, "that this country is founded on the bodies of dead animals? Dead fish, dead seals, and historically dead beavers, the beaver is to this country what the black man is to the United States. Not only that, in New York it's now a dirty word, beaver. I think that's very significant." He sits up and glares at me through the semidarkness.

"We aren't your students," Anna says, "lie down." His head rests in her lap, she's stroking his forehead, I can see her hand moving back and forth. They've been married nine years, Anna told me, they must have got married about the same time I did; but she's older than I am. They must have some special method, formula, some knowledge I missed out on; or maybe he was the wrong person. I thought it would happen without my doing anything about it, I'd turn into part of a couple, two people linked together and balancing each other, like the wooden man and woman in the barometer house at Paul's. It was good at first but he changed after I married him, he married me, we committed that paper act. I still don't see why signing a name should make any difference but he began to expect things, he wanted to be pleased. We should have kept sleeping together and left it at that.

Joe puts his arm around me, I take hold of his fingers. What I'm seeing is the black-and-white tugboat that used to be on the lake, or was it flat like a barge, it towed the log booms slowly down towards the dam, I waved at it whenever we went past in our boat and the men would wave back. It had a little house on it for them to live in, with windows and a stovepipe coming out through the roof. I felt that would be the best way to live, in a floating house carrying everything you needed with you and some other people you liked; when you wanted to move somewhere else it would be easy.

Joe is swaying back and forth, rocking, which may mean he's happy. The wind starts again, brushing over us, the air warm-cool and fluid, the trees behind us moving their leaves, the sound ripples; the water gives off icy light, zinc moon breaking on small waves. Loon voice, each hair on my body lifting with the shiver; the echoes deflect from all sides, surrounding us, here everything echoes.

CHAPTER FIVE

Birdsong wakes me. It's pre-dawn, earlier than the traffic starts in the city, but I've learned to sleep through that. I used to know the species; I listen, my ears are rusty, there's nothing but a jumble of sound. They sing for the same reason trucks honk, to proclaim their territories: a rudimentary language. Linguistics, I should have studied that instead of art.

Joe is half awake too and groaning to himself, the sheet pulled around his head like a cowl. He's torn the blankets up from the bottom of the bed and his lean feet stick out, toes with the deprived look of potatoes sprouted in the bag. I wonder if he'll remember he woke me when it was still dark, sitting up and saying "Where is this?" Every time we're in a new place he does that. "It's all right," I said, "I'm here," and though he said "Who? Who?," repeating it like an owl, he allowed me to ease him back down into the bed. I'm afraid to touch him at these times, he might mistake me for one of the enemies in his nightmare; but he's beginning to trust my voice.

I examine the part of his face that shows, an eyelid and the side of his nose, the skin pallid as though he's been living in a cellar, which we have been; his beard is dark brown, almost black, it continues around his neck and merges under the sheet with the hair on his back. His back is hairier than most men's, a warm texture, it's like teddy-bear fur, though when I told him that he seemed to take it as an insult to his dignity.

I'm trying to decide whether or not I love him. It shouldn't matter, but there's always a moment when curiosity becomes more important to them than peace and they need to ask; though he hasn't yet. It's best to have the answer worked out in advance: whether you evade or do it the hard way and tell the truth, at least you aren't caught off guard. I sum him up, dividing him into categories: he's good in bed, better than the one before; he's moody but he's not much bother, we split the rent and he doesn't talk much, that's an advantage. When he suggested we should live together I didn't hesitate. It wasn't even a real decision, it was more like buying a goldfish or a potted cactus plant, not because you want one in advance but because you happen to be in the store and you see them lined up on the counter. I'm fond of him, I'd rather have him around than not; though it would be nice if he meant something more to me. The fact that he doesn't makes me sad: no one has since my husband. A divorce is like an amputation, you survive but there's less of you.

I lie for a while with my eyes open. This used to be my room; Anna and David are in the one with the map, this one has the pictures. Ladies in exotic costumes, sausage rolls of hair across their foreheads, with puffed red mouths and eyelashes like toothbrush bristles: when I was ten I believed in glamour, it was a kind of religion and these were my icons. Their arms and legs are constrained in fashion-model poses, one gloved hand on the hip, one foot stuck out in front. They're wearing shoes with Petunia Pig toes and perpendicular heels, and their dresses have cantaloupe strapless tops like Rita Hayworth's and ballerina skirts with blotches meant for spangles. I didn't draw very well then, there's something wrong with the proportions, the necks are too short and the shoulders are enormous. I must have been imitating the paper dolls they had in the city, cardboard movie stars, Jane Powell, Esther Williams, with two-piece bathing suits printed on their bodies and cutout wardrobes of formal gowns and lacy negligées. Little girls in gray jumpers and white blouses, braids clipped to their heads with pink plastic barrettes, owned and directed them; they would bring them to school and parade them at recess, propping them up against the worn brick wall, feet in the snow, paper dresses no protection against the icy wind, inventing for them dances and parties, celebrations, interminable changing of costumes, a slavery of pleasure.

Below the pictures at the foot of the bed there's a gray leather jacket hanging on a nail. It's dirty and the leather is cracked and peeling. I see it for a while before I recognize it: it belonged to my mother a long time ago, she kept sunflower seeds in the pockets. I thought she'd thrown it out; it shouldn't still be here, he should have got rid of it after the funeral. Dead people's clothes ought to be buried with them.

I turn over and shove Joe further against the wall so I can curl up.

I surface again later; Joe is wide awake now, he's come out from under the sheet. "You talked in your sleep again," I tell him. Sometimes I think he says more when he's asleep than he does when he's awake.

He gives a noncommittal growl. "I'm hungry." Then, after a pause, "What did I say?"

"The usual. You wanted to know where you were and who I was." I'd like to hear about the dream itself; I used to have dreams but I don't any longer.

"That's pretty boring," he says. "Was that all?"

I throw back the covers and lower my feet to the floor, a minor ordeal: even in midsummer here the nights are cold. I get dressed as fast as possible and go out to start the fire. Anna is there, still in her sleeveless nylon nightgown and bare feet, standing in front of the wavery yellowish mirror. There's a zippered case on the counter in front of her, she's putting on makeup. I realize I've never seen her without it before; shorn of the pink cheeks and heightened eyes her face is curiously battered, a worn doll's, her artificial face is the natural one. The backs of her arms have goose pimples.

"You don't need that here," I say, "there's no one to look at you." My mother's phrase, used to me once when I was fourteen; she was watching, dismayed, as I covered my mouth with Tango Tangerine. I told her I was just practicing.

Anna says in a low voice, "He doesn't like to see me without it," and then, contradicting herself, "He doesn't know I wear it." I glimpse the subterfuge this must involve, or is it devotion: does she have to sneak out of the bed before he's awake every morning and into it at night with the lights out? Maybe David is telling generous lies; but she blends and mutes herself so well he may not notice.

While the stove is heating I go outside, first up to the outhouse and down again to the lake to dip my hands and face, then to the refrigerator, a metal garbage can sunk in the ground with a tight-fitting raccoon-proof lid and over that a heavy wooden cover. When the game wardens arrived in their police launch, as they did once a year, they could never believe we didn't have an icebox, they used to search everywhere for hidden, illegal fish.

I reach down for the eggs; the bacon is in a screened box under the cabin, ventilated but protected from flies and mice. In a settler's house these would have been root cellar and smokehouse; my father is an improvisor on standard themes.

I carry the food inside and start the breakfast. Joe and David are up, Joe sitting on the wall bench, face still fuzzy with sleep, David examining his chin in the mirror.

"I can make you hot water if you want to shave," I suggest, but his reflection grins and he shakes his head.

"Naaa," he says, "I'm gonna grow me a little old beard."

"Don't you dare," Anna says. "I don't like him kissing me when he has a beard, it reminds me of a cunt." Her hand goes over her mouth as though she is shocked. "Isn't that awful?"

"Filthy talk, woman," David says, "she's uncultured and vulgar."

"Oh I know. I've always been like that."

It's a quick skit, Joe and I are the audience, but Joe is still off in the place inside himself where he spends most of his time and I'm at the stove turning the bacon, I can't watch them, so they stop.

I crouch down in front of the stove and open the firebox door to make the toast over the coals. There are no dirty words any more, they've been neutered, now they're only parts of speech; but I recall the feeling, puzzled, baffled, when I found out some words were dirty and the rest were clean. The bad ones in French were the religious ones, the worst ones in any language were what they were most afraid of and in English it was the body, that was even scarier than God. You could also say Jeesus Christ, but it meant you were angry or disgusted. I learned about religion the way most children then learned about sex, not in the gutter but in the gravel-and-cement schoolyard, during the winter months of real school. They would cluster in groups, holding each other's mittened hands and whispering. They terrified me by telling me there was a dead man in the sky watching everything I did and I retaliated by explaining where babies came from. Some of their mothers phoned mine to complain, though I think I was more upset than they were: they didn't believe me but I believed them.

I finish the toast; the bacon is done too, I dish it out, pouring the fat afterwards into the fire, keeping my hand back from the spurt of flame.

After breakfast David says "What's on the agenda?" I tell them I would like to search the trail that runs for half a mile close to the shore; my father may have gone along it to get wood. There was another trail that went back almost as far as the swamp but it was my brother's and secret, by now it must be illegible.

He can't have left the island, both canoes are in the toolshed and the aluminum motorboat is padlocked to a tree near the dock; the gas tanks for the motor are empty.

"Anyway," I say, "there's only two places he can be, on the island or in the lake." My head contradicts me: someone could have picked him up here and taken him to the village at the other end of the lake, it would be the perfect way to vanish; maybe he wasn't here during the winter at all.

But that's avoiding, it's not unusual for a man to disappear in the bush, it happens dozens of times each year. All it takes is a small mistake, going too far from the house in winter, blizzards are sudden, or twisting your leg so you can't walk out, in spring the blackflies would finish you, they crawl inside your clothes, you'd be covered with blood and delirious in a day. I can't accept it though, he knew too much, he was too careful.

I give David the machete, I don't know what shape the trail will be in, we may have to brush it out; Joe carries the hatchet. Before we start I coat their wrists and ankles with bug spray, and my own also. I used to be immune to mosquitoes, I'd been bitten so much, but I've lost it: on my legs and body are several itchy pink bumps from last night. The sound of love in the north, a kiss, a slap.

It's overcast, low-hanging cloud; there's a slight wind from the southeast, it may rain later or it may miss us, the weather here comes in pockets, like oil. We go in through the neck-high grass mixed with wild raspberry canes between the garden and the lake, past the burn heap and the compost heap. I should have unearthed the garbage, to see how recent it is; there's a pit also, where the burned tin cans are smashed flat and buried, that could be excavated. My father viewed as an archeological problem.

We're on the trail inside the forest; the first part is fairly open, though now and then we pass gigantic stumps, level and saw-cut, remnants of the trees that were here before the district was logged out. The trees will never be allowed to grow that tall again, they're killed as soon as they're valuable, big trees are scarce as whales.

The forest thickens and I watch for the blazes, still visible after fourteen years; the trees they're cut on have grown swollen edges around the wounds, scar tissue.

We begin to climb and my husband catches up with me again, making one of the brief appearances, framed memories he specializes in: crystal-clear image enclosed by a blank wall. He's writing his own initials on a fence, graceful scrolls to show me how, lettering was one of the things he taught. There are other initials on the fence but he's making his bigger, leaving his mark. I can't identify the date or place, it was a city, before we were married; I lean beside him, admiring the fall of winter sunlight over his cheekbone and the engraved nose, noble and sloped like a Roman coin profile; that was when everything he did was perfect. On his hand is a leather glove. He said he loved me, the magic word, it was supposed to make everything light up, I'll never trust that word again.

My bitterness about him surprises me: I was what's known as the offending party, the one who left, he didn't do anything to me. He wanted a child, that's normal, he wanted us to be married.

In the morning while we were doing the dishes I decided to ask Anna. She was wiping a plate, humming snatches of The Big Rock Candy Mountain under her breath. "How do you manage it?" I said.

She stopped humming. "Manage what?"

"Being married. How do you keep it together?"

She glanced at me quickly as though she was suspicious. "We tell a lot of jokes."

"No, but really," I said. If there was a secret trick I wanted to learn it.

She talked to me then, or not to me exactly but to an invisible microphone suspended above her head: people's voices go radio when they give advice. She said you just had to make an emotional commitment, it was like skiing, you couldn't see in advance what would happen but you had to let go. Let go of what, I wanted to ask her; I was measuring myself against what she was saying. Maybe that was why I failed, because I didn't know what I had to let go of. For me it hadn't been like skiing, it was more like jumping off a cliff. That was the feeling I had all the time I was married; in the air, going down, waiting for the smash at the bottom.

"How come it didn't work out, with you?" Anna said.

"I don't know," I said, "I guess I was too young."

She nodded sympathetically. "You're lucky you didn't have kids, though."

"Yes," I said. She doesn't have any herself; if she did she couldn't have said that to me. I've never told her about the baby; I haven't told Joe either, there's no reason to. He won't find out the usual way, there aren't any pictures of it peering out from a crib or a window or through the bars of a playpen in my bureau drawer or my billfold where he could stumble across them and act astonished or outraged or sad. I have to behave as though it doesn't exist, because for me it can't, it was taken away from me, exported, deported. A section of my own life, sliced off from me like a Siamese twin, my own flesh canceled. Lapse, relapse, I have to forget.

The trail's winding now through high ground where there are boulders coming up out of the earth, carried and dropped by glaciers, moss on them and ferns, it's a damp climate. I keep my eyes on the ground, names reappearing, wintergreen, wild mint, Indian cucumber; at one time I could list every plant here that could be used or eaten. I memorized survival manuals, *How to Stay Alive in the Bush, Animal Tracks and Signs, The Woods in Winter,* at the age when the ones in the city were reading True Romance magazines: it wasn't till then I realized it was in fact possible to lose your way. Maxims float up: always carry matches and you will not starve, in a snowstorm dig a hole, avoid unclassified mushrooms, your hands and feet are the most important, if they freeze you're finished. Worthless knowledge; the pulp magazines with their cautionary tales, maidens who give in and get punished with Mongoloid infants, fractured spines, dead mothers or men stolen by their best friends would have been more practical.

The trail dips down and across a swamp inlet at the tip of a bay, cedars here and bullrushes, blueflags, ooze. I go slowly, looking for footprints. There's nothing but a deer track, no sign of anyone: apparently Paul and the searchers didn't make it this far. The mosquitoes have scented us and swarm around our heads; Joe swears gently, David loudly, at the end of the line I hear Anna slapping.

We swing away from the shore and here it's a jungle, branches growing in across the path, hazel and moose maple, pithy junk trees. Sight is blocked two feet in, trunks and leaves a solid interlocking fence, green, green-gray, gray-brown. None of the branches is chopped or broken back, if he's been here he's gone miraculously around and between them rather than through. I stand aside and David hacks at the wall with his machete, not very well: he tatters and bends rather than slicing.

We come up against a tree fallen aross the trail. It's brought several young balsams down with it: they lie tangled together, logjam. "I don't think anyone's been through here," I say, and Joe says "Right on," he's annoyed: it's obvious. I peer into the forest to see if another trail has been cut around the windfall but there's no sign; or there are too many signs, since I'm anxious every opening between two trees looks like a path.

David prods at the dead trunk with the machete, poking holes in the bark. Joe sits down on the ground: he's breathing hard, too much city, and the flies are getting to him, he scratches his neck and the backs of his hands. "I guess that's it," I say because I have to be the one to confess defeat, and Anna says "Thank God, they're eating me alive."

We start back. He could still be in there somewhere but I see now the impossibility of searching the island for him, it's two miles long. It would take twenty or thirty men at least, strung out at intervals and walking straight through the forest, and even then they could miss him, dead or alive, accident or suicide or murder. Or if for some unfathomable reason he's chosen this absence and is hiding, they'd never find him: there would be nothing easier in this country than to let the searchers get ahead of you and then follow at a distance, stopping when they stop, keeping them in sight so that no matter which way they turned you would always be behind them. That's what I would do.

We walk through the green light, feet muffled on wet decaying leaves. The trail is altered going back: I'm at the end now. Every few steps I glance to each side, eyes straining, scanning the ground for evidence, for anything human: a button, a cartridge, a discarded bit of paper.

It's like the times he used to play hide and seek with us in the semi-dark after supper, it was different from playing in a house, the space to hide in was endless; even when we knew which tree he had gone behind there was the fear that what would come out when you called would be someone else.

CHAPTER SIX

No one can expect anything else from me. I checked everything, I tried; now I'm absolved from knowing. I should be telling someone official, filling in forms, getting help as you're supposed to in an emergency. But it's like searching for a ring lost on a beach or in the snow: futile. There's no act I can perform except waiting; tomorrow Evans will ship us to the village, and after that we'll travel to the city and the present tense. I've finished what I came for and I don't want to stay here, I want to go back to where there is electricity and distraction. I'm used to it now, filling the time without it is an effort.

The others are trying to amuse themselves. Joe and David are out in one of the canoes; I should have made them take life jackets, neither of them can steer, they're shifting their paddles from side to side. I can see them from the front window and from the side window I can see Anna, partly hidden by trees. She's lying on her belly in bikini and sunglasses, reading a murder mystery, though she must be cold: the sky has cleared a little, but when the clouds move in front of the sun the heat shuts off.

Except for the bikini and the color of her hair she could be me at sixteen, sulking on the dock, resentful at being away from the city and the boy friend I'd proved my normality by obtaining; I wore his ring, too big for any of my fingers, around my neck on a chain, like a crucifix or a military decoration. Joe and David, when distance has disguised their faces and their awkwardness, might be my brother and my father. The only place left for me is that of my mother; a problem, what she did in the afternoons between the routines of lunch and supper. Sometimes she would take breadcrumbs or seeds out to the bird-feeder tray and wait for the jays, standing quiet as a tree, or she would pull weeds in the garden; but on some days she would simply vanish, walk off by herself into the forest. Impossible to be like my mother, it would need a time warp; she was either ten thousand years behind the rest or fifty years ahead of them.

I brush my hair in front of the mirror, delaying; then I turn back to my work, my deadline, the career I suddenly found myself having, I didn't intend to but I had to find something I could sell. I'm still awkward with it, I don't know what clothes to wear to interviews: it feels strapped to me, like an aqualung or an extra, artificial limb. I have a title though, a classification, and that helps: I'm what they call a commercial artist, or, when the job is more pretentious, an illustrator. I do posters, covers, a little advertising and magazine work and the occasional commissioned book like this one. For a while I was going to be a real artist; he thought that was cute but misguided, he said I should study something I'd be able to use because there have never been any important women artists. That was before we were married and I still listened to what he said, so I went into Design and did fabric patterns. But he was right, there never have been any.

This is the fifth book I've done; the first was a Department of Manpower employment manual, young people with lobotomized grins, rapturous in their padded slots: Computer Programmer, Welder, Executive Secretary, Lab Technician. Line drawings and a few graphs. The others were children's books and so is this one, *Quebec Folk Tales,* it's a translation. It isn't my territory but I need the money. I've had the typescript three weeks, I haven't come up with any final illustrations yet. As a rule I work faster than that.

The stories aren't what I expected; they're like German fairy tales, except for the absence of red-hot iron slippers and nail-studded casks. I wonder if this mercy descends from the original tellers, from the translator or from the publisher; probably it's Mr. Percival the publisher, he's a cautious man, he shies away from anything he calls "disturbing." We had an argument about that: he said one of my drawings was too frightening and I said children like being frightened. "It isn't the children who buy the books," he said, "it's their parents." So I compromised; now I compromise before I take the work in, it saves time. I've learned the sort of thing he wants: elegant and stylized, decoratively colored, like patisserie cakes. I can do that, I can imitate anything: fake Walt Disney, Victorian etchings in sepia, Bavarian cookies, ersatz Eskimo for the home market. Though what they like best is something they hope will interest the English and American publishers too.

Clean water in a glass, brushes in another glass, watercolors and acrylics in their metal toothpaste tubes. Bluebottle fly near my elbow, metallic abdomen gleaming, sucker tongue walking on the oilcloth like a seventh foot. When it was raining we would sit at this table and draw in our scrapbooks with crayons or colored pencils, anything we liked. In school you had to do what the rest were doing.

On the crest of the hill for all to see
God planted a Scarlet Maple Tree

printed thirty-five times, strung out along the top of the blackboard, each page with a preserved maple leaf glued to it, ironed between sheets of wax paper.

I outline a princess, an ordinary one, emaciated fashion-model torso and infantile face, like those I did for *Favourite Fairy Tales.* Earlier they annoyed me, the stories never revealed the essential things about them, such as what they ate or whether their towers and dungeons had bathrooms, it was as though their bodies were pure air. It wasn't Peter Pan's ability to fly that made him incredible for me, it was the lack of an outhouse near his underground burrow.

My princess tilts her head: she's gazing up at a bird rising from a nest of flames, wings outspread like a heraldic emblem or a fire-insurance trademark: The Tale of the Golden Phoenix. The bird has to be yellow and the fire can only be yellow too, they have to keep the cost down, so I can't use red; that way I lose orange and purple also. I asked for red instead of yellow but Mr. Percival wanted "a cool tone."

I pause to judge: the princess looks stupefied rather than filled with wonder. I discard her and try again, but this time she's crosseyed and has one breast bigger than the other. My fingers are stiff, maybe I'm getting arthritis.

I skim the story again for a different episode, but no pictures form. It's hard to believe that anyone here, even the grandmothers, ever knew these stories: this isn't a country of princesses, The Fountain of Youth and The Castle of the Seven Splendours don't belong here. They must have told stories about something as they sat around the kitchen range at night: bewitched dogs and malevolent trees perhaps, and the magic powers of rival political candidates, whose effigies in straw they burned during elections.

But the truth is that I don't know what the villagers thought or talked about, I was so shut off from them. The older ones occasionally crossed themselves when we passed, possibly because my mother was wearing slacks, but even that was never explained. Although we played during visits with the solemn, slightly hostile children of Paul and Madame, the games were brief and wordless. We never could find out what went on inside the tiny hillside church they filed into on Sundays: our parents wouldn't let us sneak up and peer through the windows, which made it illicit and attractive. After my brother began going to school in the winters he told me it was called the Mass and what they did inside was eat; I imagined it as a sort of birthday party, with ice cream—birthday parties were my only experience then of people eating in groups—but according to my brother all they had was soda crackers.

When I started school myself I begged to be allowed to go to Sunday School, like everyone else; I wanted to find out, also I wanted to be less conspicuous. My father didn't approve, he reacted as though I'd asked to go to a pool hall: Christianity was something he'd escaped from, he wished to protect us from its distortions. But after a couple of years he decided I was old enough, I could see for myself, reason would defend me.

I knew what you wore, itchy white stockings and a hat and gloves; I went with one of the girls from school whose family took a pursed-mouth missionary interest in me. It was a United Church, it stood on a long gray street of block-shaped buildings. On the steeple instead of a cross there was a thing like an onion going around which they said was a ventilator, and inside it smelled of face powder and damp wool trousers. The Sunday-School part was in the cellar; it had blackboards like a regular school, with KICKAPOO JOY JUICE printed on one of them in orange chalk and underneath, in green chalk, the mysterious initials C.G.I.T. This was a possible clue, until they translated it for me, Canadian Girls In Training. The teacher wore maroon nail polish and a blue pancake-sized hat clipped to her head by two prongs; she told us a lot about her admirers and their cars. At the end she handed out pictures of Jesus, who didn't have thorns and ribs but was alive and draped in a bedsheet, tired-looking, surely incapable of miracles.

After church every time, the family I went with drove to a hill above the railway terminal to watch the trains shunting back and forth; it was their Sunday treat. Then they would have me to lunch, which was always the same thing, pork and beans, and canned pineapple for dessert. At the beginning the father would say grace, "For what we are about to receive may the Lord make us truly thankful, Amen," while the four children pinched and kicked each other under the table; and at the end he would say:

Pork and beans and musical fruit
The more you eat the more you toot.

The mother, who had a bun of graying hair and prickles around her mouth like a schmoo, would frown and ask me what I'd learned about Jesus that morning, and the father would grin feebly, ignored by all; he was a clerk in a bank, the Sunday trains his only diversion, the little rhyme his only impropriety. For some time I had a confused notion that canned pineapple really was musical and would make you sing better, until my brother set me straight.

"Maybe I'll be a Catholic," I said to my brother; I was afraid to say it to my parents.

"Catholics are crazy," he said. The Catholics went to a school down the street from ours and the boys threw snowballs at them in winter and rocks in spring and fall. "They believe in the B.V.M."

I didn't know what that was and neither did he, so he said "They believe if you don't go to Mass you'll turn into a wolf."

"Will you?" I said.

"We don't go," he said, "and we haven't."

Maybe that's why they didn't waste any sweat searching for my father, they were afraid to, they thought he'd turned into a wolf; he'd be a prime candidate since he never went to Mass at all. *Les maudits anglais,* the damned English, they mean it; they're sure we're all damned literally. There should be a *loup-garou* story in *Quebec Folk Tales,* perhaps there was and Mr. Percival took it out, it was too rough for him. But in some of the stories they do it the other way around, the animals are human inside and they take their fur skins off as easily as getting undressed.

I remember the hair on Joe's back, vestigial, like appendices and little toes: soon we'll evolve into total baldness. I like the hair, though, and the heavy teeth, thick shoulders, unexpectedly slight hips, hands whose texture I can still feel on my skin, roughened and leathery from the clay. Everything I value about him seems to be physical: the rest is either unknown, disagreeable or ridiculous. I don't care much for his temperament, which alternates between surliness and gloom, or for the overgrown pots he throws so skillfully on the wheel and then mutilates, cutting holes in them, strangling them, slashing them open. That's unfair, he never uses a knife, only his fingers, and a lot of the time he only bends them, doubles them over; even so they have a disagreeable mutant quality. Nobody else admires them either: the aspiring housewives he teaches two evenings a week, Pottery and Ceramics 432-A, want to make ashtrays and plates with cheerful daisies on them instead, and the things don't sell at all in the few handicraft shops that will even stock them. So they accumulate in our already cluttered basement apartment like fragmentary memories or murder victims. I can't even put flowers in them, the water would run out through the rips. Their only function is to uphold Joe's unvoiced claim to superior artistic seriousness: every time I sell a poster design or get a new commission he mangles another pot.

I wanted my third princess to be running lightly through a meadow but the paper's too wet, she gets out of control, sprouting an enormous rear; I try to salvage it by turning it into a bustle, but it's not convincing. I give up and doodle, adding fangs and a moustache, surrounding her with moons and fish and a wolf with bristling hackles and a snarl; but that doesn't work either, it's more like an overweight collie. What's the alternative to princesses, what else will parents buy for their children? Humanoid bears and talking pigs, Protestant choo-choo trains who make the grade and become successful.

Perhaps it's not only his body I like, perhaps it's his failure; that also has a kind of purity.

I crumple up my third princess, dump the paint water into the slop pail and clean the brushes. I survey from the windows: David and Joe are still out on the lake but they seem to be heading back now. Anna is halfway up the hillside stairs, towel over her arm. I see her for a moment faceted by the screen door and then she's inside.

"Hi," she says, "get anything done?"

"Not much," I say.

She comes over to the table and smooths out my botched princesses. "That's good," she says without conviction.

"Those are mistakes," I say.

"Oh." She turns the sheets over, face down. "Did you believe that stuff when you were little?" she says. "I did, I thought I was really a princess and I'd end up living in a castle. They shouldn't let kids have stuff like that." She goes to the mirror, blots and smooths her face, then stands on tiptoe, checking her back to see if it's pink. "What was he *doing* up here?" she asks suddenly.

It takes me a moment to understand what she means. My father, his work. "I don't know," I say. "Just, you know."

She gives me an odd glance, as though I've violated a propriety, and I'm puzzled, she told me once you shouldn't define yourself by your job but by who you are. When they ask her what she does she talks about fluidity and Being rather than Doing; though if she doesn't like the person she just says "I'm David's wife."

"He was living," I say. This is almost right, it satisfies her, she goes into the bedroom to change her clothes.

All at once I'm furious with him for vanishing like this, unresolved, leaving me with no answers to give them when they ask. If he was going to die he should have done it visibly, out in the open, so they could mark him with a stone and get it over with.

They must find it strange, a man his age staying alone the whole winter in a cabin ten miles from nowhere; I never questioned it, to me it was logical. They always intended to move here permanently as soon as they could, when he retired: isolation was to him desirable. He didn't dislike people, he merely found them irrational; animals, he said, were more consistent, their behavior at least was predictable. To him that's what Hitler exemplified: not the triumph of evil but the failure of reason. He found war irrational too, both of my parents were pacifists, but he would have fought anyway, in defense of science perhaps, if he'd been permitted; this must be the only country where a botanist can be classified as crucial to the national defense.

As it was he withdrew; we could have lived all year in the company town but he split us between two anonymities, the city and the bush. In the city we lived in a succession of apartments and in the bush he picked the most remote lake he could find, when my brother was born there wasn't yet a road to it. Even the village had too many people for him, he needed an island, a place where he could recreate not the settled farm life of his own father but that of the earliest ones who arrived when there was nothing but forest and no ideologies but the ones they brought with them. When they say Freedom they never quite mean it, what they mean is freedom from interference.

The stack of papers is still up on the shelf by the lamp. I've been avoiding it, looking through it would be an intrusion if he were still alive. But now I've admitted he's dead I might as well find out what he left for me. Executor.

I was expecting a report of some kind, tree growth or diseases, unfinished business; but on the top page there's only a crude drawing of a hand, done with a felt pen or a brush, and some notations: numbers, a name. I flip through the next few pages. More hands, then a stiff childish figure, faceless and minus the hands and feet, and on the next page a similar creature with two things like tree branches or antlers protruding from its head. On each of the pages are the numbers, and on some a few scrawled words: LICHENS RED CLOTHING LEFT. I can't make sense out of them. The handwriting is my father's, but changed, more hasty or careless.

Outside I hear the crunch of wood on wood as the canoe hits the dock, they've brought it in too fast; then their laughter. I reach the stack of papers back to the shelf, I don't want them to see.

That's what he was doing here all winter, he was shut up in this cabin making these unintelligible drawings. I sit at the table, my heart speeded up as if I've opened what I thought was an empty closet and found myself face to face with a thing that isn't supposed to be there, like a claw or a bone. This is the forgotten possibility: he might have gone insane. Crazy, loony. Bushed, the trappers call it when you stay in the forest by yourself too long. And if insane, perhaps not dead: none of the rules would be the same.

Anna walks out of the bedroom, dressed in jeans and shirt again. She combs her hair in front of the mirror, light ends, dark roots, humming to herself, You Are My Sunshine; smoke twines up from her cigarette. *Help,* I think at her silently, *talk.* And she does.

"What's for dinner?" she says; then, waving, "Here they come."

CHAPTER SEVEN

At supper we finish off the beer. David wants to go fishing, it's the last night, so I leave the dishes for Anna and go down to the garden with the shovel and the tin can saved from the peas.

I dig in the weediest part near the compost heap, lifting the earth and letting it crumble, sieving the worms out with my fingers. The soil is rich, the worms scramble, red ones and pink ones.

Nobody loves me
Everybody hates me
I'm going to the garden to eat worms.

They sang that back and forth at recess: it was an insult, but perhaps they are edible. They're sold like apples in season, VERS 5c on the roadside signs, sometimes VERƧ 5c, later VERS 10c, inflation. French class, *vers libre,* I translated it the first time as Free Worms and she thought I was being smart.

I put the worms in the can and some dirt for them. As I walk back to the cabin I hold my palm over the top; already they're nudging with their head ends, trying to get out. I make them a cover from a piece of paper torn off the grocery bag, keeping it on with a rubber band. My mother was a saver: rubber bands, string, safety pins, jam jars, for her the Depression never ended.

David is fitting the sections of his borrowed fishing rod together; it's fiberglass, I have no faith in it. I take the steel trolling rod from its hooks on the wall. "Come on," I tell David, "you can use that one for still-fishing."

"Show me how to light the lamp," Anna says, "I'll stay here and read."

I don't want to leave her alone. What I'm afraid of is my father, hidden on the island somewhere and attracted by the light perhaps, looming up at the window like a huge ragged moth; or, if he's still at all lucid, asking her who she is and ordering her out of his house. As long as there are four of us he'll keep away, he never liked groups.

"Poor sport," David says.

I tell her I need her in the canoe for extra weight, which is a lie as we'll be too heavy already, but she takes my expert word.

While they're getting into the canoe I return to the garden and catch a small leopard frog as an emergency weapon. I put it in a jam jar and punch a few airholes in the lid.

Tackle box, smelling of stale fish, old captures; worm can and frog bottle, knife and heap of bracken fronds for the fish to bleed on. Joe in the bow, Anna behind him on a life jacket facing me, David on another life jacket with his back to me and his legs tangled in amongst Anna's. Before I push off I clip a silver and gold spinner with glass ruby eyes to David's line and hook a worm on, looping its body seductively. Both ends twirl.

"Ech," says Anna, who can see what I'm doing.

"It doesn't hurt them," my brother said, "they don't feel it." "Then why do they squirm?" I said. He said it was nervous tension.

"Whatever happens," I tell them, "stay in the middle." We move ponderously out of the bay. I've taken on too much: I haven't been in a canoe for years, my muscles are shot, Joe paddles as though he's stirring the lake with a ladle and we're down by the bow. But none of them will know the difference. I think, it's a good thing our lives don't depend on catching a fish. Starvation, bite your arm and suck the blood, that's what they do on lifeboats; or the Indian way, if there's no bait try a chunk of your flesh.

The island shoreline recedes behind us, he can't follow us here. Above the trees streaky mackerel clouds are spreading in over the sky, paint on a wet page; no wind at lake level, soft feel of the air before rain. The fish like this, the mosquitoes too, but I can't use any bug spray because it would get on the bait and the fish would smell it.

I steer us along the mainland shore. A blue heron lifts from a bay where it's been fishing and flaps overhead, neck and beak craning forward and long legs stretched back, winged snake. It notes us with a rasping pterodactyl croak and rises higher, heading southeast, there was a colony of them, it must still be there. But now I have to pay more attention to David. The copper line slants down, cutting the water, vibrating slightly.

"Any action?" I ask.

"It's just sort of jigging."

"That's the spoon turning," I say. "Keep the tip down; if you feel a nibble wait a second and then give it a sharp tug, okay?"

"Right," he says.

My arms are tired. Behind me I can hear the tick tock of the frog hopping up and hitting its muzzle against the jar lid.

When we're getting near the sheer cliff I tell him to reel in, we'll still-fish and he can use his own rod.

"Lie down, Anna," he says, "I'm gonna use my own rod."

Anna says "Oh Christ, you have to do that about everything, don't you?"

He chuckles at her and reels and the line comes in, the water slipping off it; the pale gleam of the spoon wavers up out of the lake. When it skips over the surface toward us I can see the worm is gone.

On one hook is a shred of worm skin; I used to wonder how the lures with their crude African-idol eyes could deceive the fish, but perhaps they've learned.

We're opposite the cliff, gray slab of rock straight as a monument, overhanging slightly, ledge like a step halfway up, brown rock-lichen growing in the fissures. I put a lead sinker and a different spoon and a fresh worm on David's line and toss it over; the worm drops, pink, pink-brown, till it disappears in the shadow of the cliff. The dark torpedo shapes of the fish are seeing it, sniffing at it, prodding it with their noses. I believe in them the way other people believe in God: I can't see them but I know they are there.

"Keep right still," I say to Anna, who's beginning to shift uncomfortably. They can hear.

Light fading, silence; back in the forest, liquid spiral thrush voice, they call at sunset. David's arm moves up and down.

When nothing happens I tell him to reel in; the worm is gone again. I take out the little frog, the ultimate solution, and hook it on securely while it squeaks. Other people always did that for me.

"God you're coldblooded," Anna says. The frog goes down through the water, kicking like a man swimming.

Everyone concentrates, even Anna: they sense this is my last trick. I stare into the water, it was always a kind of meditation. My brother fished by technique, he outguessed them, but I fished by prayer, listening.

Our father who art in heaven
Please let the fish be caught.

Later when I knew that wouldn't work, just *Please be caught,* invocation or hypnosis. He got more fish but I could pretend mine were willing, they had chosen to die and forgiven me in advance.

I begin to think the frog has failed. But it's still magic, the rod bends like a diviner's and Anna shrieks with surprise.

I say "Keep the line tight," but David is oblivious, he's reeling like a mixmaster and saying "Wow, wow" to himself and it's up to the surface, it jumps clear and hangs in the air like a framed photo over a bar, only moving. It dives and pulls, the line slackens, it's doubling back trying to shake loose; but when it jumps again David jerks the rod with his whole body and it sails across and flops into the canoe, a dumb move, he could've lost it, on top of Anna and she lurches, screaming "Get it off me! Get it off me!" and we almost tip. Joe says

"Holy shit" and grabs at the side, I bend the other way, counterbalancing, David is snatching at it. It slithers over the canoe ribs, flippering and snapping.

"Here," I say, "hit it back of the eyes." I reach him the sheathed knife, I'd rather not kill it myself.

David swipes at it, misses; Anna covers her eyes and says "Ugh. Ugh." It flops towards me and I step down on it with my foot and grab the knife and whack it quickly with the knife handle, crushing the skull, and it trembles stiffly all over, that's done it.

"What is it?" David asks, amazed by what he's caught but proud too. They are laughing, joyful with victory and relief, like the newsreels of parades at the end of the war, and that makes me glad. Their voices bounce off the cliff.

"Walleye," I say. "Pickerel. We'll have it for breakfast."

It's a good size. I pick it up, fingers hooked under the gills and holding firmly, they can bite and jerk loose even when they're dead. I put it on the bracken fronds and rinse my hand and the knife. One of its eyes is bulging out and I feel a little sick, it's because I've killed something, made it dead; but I know that's irrational, killing certain things is all right, food and enemies, fish and mosquitoes; and wasps, when there are too many of them you pour boiling water down their tunnels. "Don't bother them and they won't bother you," our mother would say when they lit on our plates. That was before the house was built, we were living outside in tents. Our father said they went in cycles.

"Neat, eh?" David says to the others; he's excited, he wants praise. "Ugh," says Anna, "it's slimy, I'm not going to eat any of it." Joe grunts, I wonder if he's jealous.

David wants to try for another; it's like gambling, you only stop if you lose. I don't remind him I have no more magic frogs; I get out a worm for him and let him hook it on himself.

He fishes for a while but he's having no luck. Just as Anna's beginning to fidget again I hear a whine, motorboat. I listen, it may be going somewhere else, but it rounds a point and becomes a roar, homing in on us, big powerboat, the white water veeing from the bow. The engine cuts and it skids in beside us, its wash rocking us sharply. American flag on the front and another at the back, two irritated-looking businessmen with pug-dog faces and nifty outfits and a thin shabby man from the village, guiding. I see it's Claude from the motel, he scowls at us, he feels we're poaching on his preserve.

"Getting any?" one of the Americans yells, teeth bared, friendly as a shark.

I say "No" and nudge David with my foot. He'd want to tell, if only to spite them.

The other American throws his cigar butt over the side. "This don't look like much of a place," he says to Claude.

"Used to be," Claude says.

"Next year I'm goin' to Florida," the first American says.

"Reel in," I say to David. There's no sense in staying here now. If they catch one they'll be here all night, if they don't get anything in fifteen minutes they'll blast off and scream around the lake in their souped-up boat, deafening the fish. They're the kind who catch more than they can eat and they'd do it with dynamite if they could get away with it.

We used to think they were harmless and funny and inept and faintly lovable, like President Eisenhower. We met two of them once on the way to the bass lake, they were carrying their tin motorboat and the motor over the portage so they wouldn't have to paddle once they were on the inner lake; when we first heard them thrashing along through the underbrush we thought they were bears. Another one turned up with a spinning reel and stepped in our campfire, scorching his new boots; when he tried to cast he sent his plug, a real minnow sealed in transparent plastic, into the bushes on the other side of the bay. We laughed at him behind his back and asked if he was catching squirrels but he didn't mind, he showed us his automatic firelighter and his cook set with detachable handles and his collapsible armchair. They liked everything collapsible.

On the way back we hug the shore, avoiding the open lake in case the Americans take it into their heads to zoom past us as close as possible, they sometimes do that for fun, their wake could tip us. But before we're half the distance they whoosh away into nowhere like Martians in a late movie, and I relax.

When we get back I'll hang up the fish and wash the scales and the salty armpit odor off my hands with soap. After that I'll light the lamp and the fire and make some cocoa. Being here feels right to me for the first time, and I know it's because we're leaving tomorrow. My father will have the island to himself; madness is private, I respect that, however he may be living it's better than an institution. Before we go I'll burn his drawings, they're evidence of the wrong sort.

The sun has set, we slide back through the gradual dusk. Loon voices in the distance; bats flitter past us, dipping over the water surface, flat calm now, the shore things, white-gray rocks and dead trees, doubling themselves in the dark mirror. Around us the illusion of infinite space or of no space, ourselves and the obscure shore which it seems we could touch, the water between an absence. The canoe's reflection floats with us, the paddles twin in the lake. It's like moving on air, nothing beneath us holding us up; suspended, we drift home.

CHAPTER EIGHT

In the early morning Joe wakes me; his hands at any rate are intelligent, they move over me delicately as a blind man's reading braille, skilled, molding me like a vase, they're learning me; they repeat patterns he's tried before, they've found out what works, and my body responds that way too, anticipates him, educated, crisp as a typewriter. It's best when you don't know them. A phrase comes to me, a joke then but mournful now, someone in a parked car after a high-school dance who said *With a paper bag over their head they're all the same.* At the time I didn't understand what he meant, but since then I've pondered it. It's almost like a coat of arms: two people making love with paper bags over their heads, not even any eyeholes. Would that be good or bad?

When we're finished and after we rest I get up and dress and go out to prepare the fish. It's been hanging all night, the string through its gills looped to a tree branch out of the reach of scavengers, racoons, otters, mink, skunks. A squeezing of fish shit, like a bird's only browner, drools from the anus. I untie the string and carry the fish down to the lake to clean and fillet it.

I kneel on the flat rock beside the lake, the knife and the plate for the fillets beside me. This was never my job; someone else did it, my brother or my father. I cut off the head and tail and slit the belly and open the fish into its two halves. Inside the stomach is a partly digested leech and some shreds of crayfish. I divide along the backbone, then along the two lateral lines: four pieces, bluish white, translucent. The entrails will be buried in the garden, they're fertilizer.

As I'm washing the fillets David saunters down to the dock with his toothbrush. "Hey," he says, "is that my fish?" He regards the guts on the plate with interest. "Hold it," he says, "that's a Random Sample." He goes for Joe and the camera and the two of them solemnly film the fish innards, collapsed bladders and tubes and soft ropes, rearranging them between takes for better angles. It would never occur to David to have someone snap him with a Brownie camera holding his fish up by the tail and grinning, nor would he ever have it stuffed and mounted; still, he wants to immortalize it, in his own way. Photo album, I'm in it somewhere, successive incarnations of me preserved and flattened like flowers pressed in dictionaries; that was the other book she kept, the leather album, a logbook like the diaries. I used to hate standing still, waiting for the click.

I dip the fillets in flour and fry them and we eat them with strips of bacon. "Good food, good meat, Good God, let's eat," David says; and later, smacking his lips, "Couldn't get this in the city."

Anna says "Sure you could, frozen. You can get anything there now."

After breakfast I go into my room and begin to pack. Through the plywood wall I hear Anna walking, pouring more coffee, the creak as David stretches out on the couch.

Perhaps I should fold up all the bedding and towels and the abandoned clothes, tie them into bundles and take them back with me. No one will be living here now and the moths and the mice will get in eventually. If he doesn't ever decide to return I suppose it belongs to me, or half to me and half to my brother; but my brother won't do anything about it, after he left he's evaded them as much as I have. He set it up better though, he simply went as far away as he could: if I stuck a knitting needle straight through the earth the point would emerge where he is now, camped in the outback, inaccessible; he probably hasn't even got my letter yet. Mineral rights, that's what he explores, for one of the big international companies, a prospector; but I can't believe in that, nothing he's done since we grew up is real to me.

"I like it here," David says. No sound from the others. "Let's stay on for a while, a week, it'd be great."

"Don't you have that seminar?" Anna says dubiously. "Man and his Electricity Environment, or something?"

"Electrifying. That's not till August."

"I don't think we should," Anna says.

"How come you never want us to do anything I want to do?" David says, and there's a pause. Then he says "What d'you think?" and Joe says "Okay by me."

"Great," says David, "we'll do some more fishing."

I sit down on the bed. They might have asked me first, it's my house. Though maybe they're waiting till I come out, they'll ask then. If I say I don't want to they can't very well stay; but what reason can I give? I can't tell them about my father, betray him; anyway they might think I was making it up. There's my work, but they know I have it with me. I could leave by myself with Evans but I'd only get as far as the village: it's David's car, I'd have to steal the keys, and also, I remind myself, I never learned to drive.

Anna makes a last feeble attempt. "I'll run out of cigarettes."

"Do you good," David says cheerfully, "filthy habit. Get you back into shape." He's older than we are, he's over thirty, he's beginning to worry about that; every now and then he hits himself in the stomach and says "Flab."

"I'll get crabby," Anna says, but David only laughs and says "Try it."

I could tell them there isn't enough food. But they'd spot that as a lie, there's the garden and the rows of cans on the shelves, corned beef, Spam, baked beans, chicken, powdered milk, everything.

I go to the room door, open it. "You'll have to pay Evans the five anyway," I say.

For a moment they're startled, they realize I've overheard. Then David says "No sweat." He gives me a quick look, triumphant and appraising, as though he's just won something: not a war but a lottery.

When Evans turns up at the appointed time David and Joe go down to the dock to arrange things with him. I warned them not to say anything about the fish: if they do, this part of the lake will be swarming with Americans, they have an uncanny way of passing the word, like ants about sugar, or lobsters. After a few minutes I hear the boat starting again and accelerating and diminishing, he's gone.

I've avoided Evans and the explanation and negotiations by going up to the outhouse and latching myself in. That was where I went when there was something I didn't want to do, like weeding the garden. It's the new outhouse, the old one got used up. This one is built of logs, my brother and I made the hole for it, he dug with the shovel and I hauled the sand up in a pail. Once a porcupine fell in, they like to chew axe handles and toilet seats.

In the city I never hid in bathrooms; I didn't like them, they were too hard and white. The only city place I can remember hiding is behind opened doors at birthday parties. I despised them, the pew-purple velvet dresses with antimacassar lace collars and the presents, voices going Oooo with envy when they were opened, and the pointless games, finding a thimble or memorizing clutter on a tray. There were only two things you could be, a winner or a loser; the mothers tried to rig it so everyone got a prize, but they couldn't figure out what to do about me since I wouldn't play. At first I ran away, but after that my mother said I had to go, I had to learn to be polite; "civilized," she called it. So I watched from behind the door. When I finally joined in a game of Musical Chairs I was welcomed with triumph, like a religious convert or a political defector.

Some were disappointed, they found my hermit-crab habits amusing, they found me amusing in general. Each year it was a different school, in October or November when the first snow hit the lake, and I was the one who didn't know the local customs, like a person from another culture: on me they could try out the tricks and minor tortures they'd already used up on each other. When the boys chased and captured the girls after school and tied them up with their own skipping ropes, I was the one they would forget on purpose to untie. I spent many afternoons looped to fences and gates and convenient trees, waiting for a benevolent adult to pass and free me; later I became an escape artist of sorts, expert at undoing knots. On better days they would gather around, competing for me.

"Adam and Eve and Pinch Me," they shouted,

"Went to the river to bathe;
Adam and Eve fell in,
So who do you think was saved?"

"I don't know," I said.

"You have to answer," they said, "that's the rules."

"Adam and Eve," I said craftily. "*They* were saved."

"If you don't do it right we won't play with you," they said. Being socially retarded is like being mentally retarded, it arouses in others disgust and pity and the desire to torment and reform.

It was harder for my brother; our mother had taught him that fighting was wrong so he came home every day beaten to a pulp. Finally she had to back down: he could fight, but only if they hit first.

I didn't last long at Sunday School. One girl told me she had prayed for a Barbara Ann Scott doll with figure skates and swansdown trim on the costume and she got it for her birthday; so I decided to pray too, not like the Lord's Prayer or the fish prayer but for something real. I prayed to be made invisible, and when in the morning everyone could still see me I knew they had the wrong God.

A mosquito lights on my arm and I let it bite me, waiting till its abdomen globes with blood before I pop it with my thumb like a grape. They need the blood before they can lay their eggs. There's a breeze, filtering through the screened window; it's better here than in the city, with the exhaust-pipe fumes and the damp heat, the burnt-rubber smell of the subway, the brown grease that congeals on your skin if you walk around outside. How have I been able to live so long in the city, it isn't safe. I always felt safe here, even at night.

That's a lie, my own voice says out loud. I think hard about it, considering it, and it is a lie: sometimes I was terrified, I would shine the flashlight ahead of me on the path, I would hear a rustling in the forest and know it was hunting me, a bear, a wolf or some indefinite thing with no name, that was worse.

I look around at the walls, the window; it's the same, it hasn't changed, but the shapes are inaccurate as though everything has warped slightly. I have to be more careful about my memories, I have to be sure they're my own and not the memories of other people telling me what I felt, how I acted, what I said: if the events are wrong the feelings I remember about them will be wrong too, I'll start inventing them and there will be no way of correcting it, the ones who could help are gone. I run quickly over my version of it, my life, checking it like an alibi; it fits, it's all there till the time I left. Then static, like a jumped track, for a moment I've lost it, wiped clean; my exact age even, I shut my eyes, what is it? To have the past but not the present, that means you're going senile.

I refuse to panic, I force my eyes open, my hand, life etched on it, reference: I flatten the palm and the lines fragment, spread like ripples. I concentrate on the spiderweb near the window, flyhusks caught in it catching in turn the sun, in my mouth tongue forming my name, repeating it like a chant. . . .

Then someone knocks on the door. "Ready or not, you must be caught," says a voice, it's David, I can identify him, relief, I slip back into place.

"Just a minute," I say, and he knocks again and says "Snappy with the crap in there," giving a Woody Woodpecker laugh.

Before lunch I tell them I'm going for a swim. The others don't want to, they say it will be too cold, and it is cold, like ice water. I shouldn't be going by myself, we were taught that, I might get cramps.

What I used to do was run to the end of the dock and jump, it was like a heart attack or lightning, but as I walk towards the lake I find I no longer have the nerve for that.

This was where he drowned, he got saved only by accident; if there had been a wind she wouldn't have heard him. She leaned over and reached down and grabbed him by the hair, hauled him up and poured the water out of him. His drowning never seemed to have affected him as much as I thought it should, he couldn't even remember it. If it had happened to me I would have felt there was something special about me, to be raised from the dead like that; I would have returned with secrets, I would have known things most people didn't.

After she'd told the story I asked our mother where he would have gone if she hadn't saved him. She said she didn't know. My father explained everything but my mother never did, which only convinced me that she had the answers but wouldn't tell. "Would he be in the graveyard?" I said. They had a verse about the graveyard at school too:

Stick him in the bread pan,
Sock him in the jaw;
Now he's in the graveyard,
Haw, haw haw.

"Nobody knows," she said. She was making a pie crust and she gave me a piece of the dough to distract me. My father would have said Yes; he said you died when your brain died. I wonder if he still believes that.

I go off the dock and wade in from the shore, slowly, splashing water over my shoulders and neck, the cold climbing my thighs; my footsoles feel the sand and the twigs and sunk leaves. At that time I would dive and coast along the lake floor with my eyes open, distance and my own body blurred and eroding; or out further, diving from the canoe or the raft and turning on my back under the water to look up, the bubbles fleeing from my mouth. We would stay in until our skins became numbed and turned a strange color, bluish purple. I must have been superhuman, I couldn't do it now. Perhaps I'm growing old, at last, can that be possible?

I stand there shivering, seeing my reflection and my feet down through it, white as fish flesh on the sand, till finally being in the air is more painful than being in the water and I bend and push myself reluctantly into the lake.

II

CHAPTER NINE

The trouble is all in the knob at the top of our bodies. I'm not against the body or the head either: only the neck, which creates the illusion that they are separate. The language is wrong, it shouldn't have different words for them. If the head extended directly into the shoulders like a worm's or a frog's without that constriction, that lie, they wouldn't be able to look down at their bodies and move them around as if they were robots or puppets; they would have to realize that if the head is detached from the body both of them will die.

I'm not sure when I began to suspect the truth, about myself and about them, what I was and what they were turning into. Part of it arrived swift as flags, as mushrooms, unfurling and sudden growth, but it was there in me, the evidence, only needing to be deciphered. From where I am now it seems as if I've always known, everything, time is compressed like the fist I close on my knee in the darkening bedroom, I hold inside it the clues and solutions and the power for what I must do now.

I was seeing poorly, translating badly, a dialect problem, I should have used my own. In the experiments they did with children, shutting them up with deaf-and-dumb nurses, locking them in closets, depriving them of words, they found that after a certain age the mind is incapable of absorbing any language; but how could they tell the child hadn't invented one, unrecognizable to everyone but itself? That was in the green book at high school, *Your Health,* along with the photographs of cretins and people with thyroid deficiencies, the crippled and deformed, the examples, with black oblongs across their eyes like condemned criminals: the only pictures of naked bodies it was judged proper for us to see. The rest were diagrams, transparencies with labels and arrows, the ovaries purple sea creatures, the womb a pear.

The voices of the others and the riffle and slap of cards reach me through the closed door. Canned laughter, they carry it with them, the midget reels of tape and the On switch concealed somewhere in their chests, instant playback.

After Evans left that day I was uneasy: the island wasn't safe, we were trapped on it. They didn't realize it but I did, I was responsible for them. The sense of watching eyes, his presence lurking just behind the green leafscreen, ready to pounce or take flight, he wasn't predictable, I was trying to think of ways to keep them out of danger; they would be all right as long as they didn't go anywhere alone. He might be harmless but I couldn't be sure.

We finished lunch and I took the breadcrumbs out to the tray for the birds. The jays had discovered there were people living in the cabin; they're intelligent, they knew a figure near the tray signaled food; or perhaps a few of them were old enough to remember the image of my mother, hand outstretched. Two or three of them stood sentinel now, out of reach, wary.

Joe followed me out and watched as I spread the crumbs. He put his fingers on my arm, frowning at me, which may have meant he wanted to talk to me: speech to him was a task, a battle, words mustered behind his beard and issued one at a time, heavy and square like tanks. His hand gripped me in a preliminary spasm, but David was there with the axe.

"Hey, lady," he said, "I see your woodpile's gettin' low. You could use a handyman."

He wanted to do something useful; and he was right, if we were staying a week we would need a fresh supply. I asked him to find standing trees, dead but not too old or rotten, "Yes'm," he said, giving me a burlesque salute.

Joe took the small hatchet and went with him. They were from the city, I was afraid they might chop their feet; though that would be a way out, I thought, we'd have to go back. But I didn't need to warn them about him, they had weapons. He would see that and run away.

When they'd disappeared along the trail into the forest I said I was going down to weed the garden, another job that had to be done. I wanted to keep busy, preserve at least the signs of order, conceal my fear, both from others and from him. Fear has a smell, as love does.

Anna could tell she was expected to help; she abandoned her murder mystery and stubbed out her cigarette, only half smoked, she was rationing them. We tied scarves around our heads and I went to the toolshed for the rake.

The garden was full in sunlight and steaming hot, moist as a greenhouse. We knelt down and began to pull at the weeds; they resisted, holding on or taking clumps of soil out with them or breaking their stems, leaving their roots in the earth to regenerate; I dug for the feet in the warm dirt, my hands green with weed blood. Gradually the vegetables emerged, pallid and stunted most of them, all but strangled. We raked the weeds into piles between the rows, where they wilted, dying slowly; later they would be burned, like witches, to keep them from reappearing. There were a few mosquitoes and the deer flies with their iridescent rainbow eyes and stings like heated needles.

From time to time I paused, checking the fence, the border, but no one was there. Perhaps he would be unrecognizable, his former shape transfigured by age and madness and the forest, rag bundle of decaying clothes, the skin of his face woolly with dead leaves. History, I thought, quick.

It took them years to make the garden, the real soil was too sandy and anemic. This oblong was artificial, the product of skill and of compost spaded in, black muck dredged from swamps, horse dung ferried by boat from the winter logging camps when they still kept horses to drag the logs to the frozen lake. My father and mother would carry it in bushel baskets on the handbarrow, two poles with boards nailed across, each of them lifting an end.

I could remember before that, when we lived in tents. It was about here we found the lard pail, ripped open like a paper bag, claw scratches and toothmarks scarring the paint. Our father had gone on a long trip as he often did to investigate trees for the paper company or the government, I was never certain which he worked for. Our mother was given a three-week supply of food. The bear walked through the back of the food tent, we heard it in the night. It stepped on the eggs and tomatoes and pried open all the storage tins and scattered the wax-paper bread and smashed the jam jars, we salvaged what we could in the morning. The only thing it didn't bother with was the potatoes, and we were eating them for breakfast around the campfire when it materialized on the path, snuffling along bulky and flatfooted, an enormous fanged rug, returning for more. My mother stood up and walked toward it; it hesitated and grunted. She yelled a word at it that sounded like "Scat!" and waved her arms, and it turned around and thudded off into the forest.

That was the picture I kept, my mother seen from the back, arms upraised as though she was flying, and the bear terrified. When she told the story later she said she'd been scared to death but I couldn't believe that, she had been so positive, assured, as if she knew a foolproof magic formula: gesture and word. She was wearing her leather jacket.

"You on the pill?" Anna asked suddenly.

I looked at her, startled. It took me a minute, why did she want to know? That was what they used to call a personal question.

"Not any more," I said.

"Me neither," she said glumly. "I don't know anyone who still is any more. I got a blood clot in my leg, what did you get?" She had a smear of mud across her cheek, her pink face layer was softening in the heat, like tar.

"I couldn't see," I said. "Things were blurry. They said it would clear up after a couple of months but it didn't." It was like having vaseline on my eyes but I didn't say that.

Anna nodded; she was tugging at the weeds as though she was

pulling hair. "Bastards," she said, "they're so smart, you think they'd be able to come up with something that'd work without killing you. David wants me to go back on, he says it's no worse for you than aspirin, but next time it could be the heart or something. I mean, I'm not taking those kinds of chances."

Love without fear, sex without risk, that's what they wanted to be true; and they almost did it, I thought, they almost pulled it off, but as in magicians' tricks or burglaries half-success is failure and we're back to the other things. Love is taking precautions. Did you take any precautions, they say, not before but after. Sex used to smell like rubber gloves and now it does again, no more handy green plastic packages, moon-shaped so that the woman can pretend she's still natural, cyclical, instead of a chemical slot machine. But soon they'll have the artificial womb, I wonder how I feel about that. After the first I didn't ever want to have another child, it was too much to go through for nothing, they shut you into a hospital, they shave the hair off you and tie your hands down and they don't let you see, they don't want you to understand, they want you to believe it's their power, not yours. They stick needles into you so you won't hear anything, you might as well be a dead pig, your legs are up in a metal frame, they bend over you, technicians, mechanics, butchers, students clumsy or snickering practicing on your body, they take the baby out with a fork like a pickle out of a pickle jar. After that they fill your veins up with red plastic, I saw it running down through the tube. I won't let them do that to me ever again.

He wasn't there with me, I couldn't remember why; he should have been, since it was his idea, his fault. But he brought his car to collect me afterward, I didn't have to take a taxi.

From the forest behind us came the sound of sporadic chopping: a few blows, the echoes, a pause, a few more blows, one of them laughing, echo of the laughter. It was my brother who cut the trail, the year before he left, the axe hacking and the machete slashing through the undergrowth marking his progress as he worked his way around the shore.

"Haven't we done enough?" Anna asked. "I bet I'm getting sunstroke." She sat back on her heels and took out the unsmoked half of her cigarette. I think she wanted us to exchange more confidences, she wanted to talk about her other diseases, but I kept on weeding. Potatoes, onions; the strawberry patch was a hopeless jungle, we wouldn't do that; in any case the season was over.

David and Joe appeared in the long grass outside the fence, one at either end of a thinnish log. They were proud, they'd caught something. The log was notched in many places as though they'd attacked it.

"Hi," David called. "How are the ol' plantation workers coming?"

Anna stood up. "Fuck off," she said, squinting at them against the sun.

"You've hardly done anything," David said, unquenchable, "you call that a garden?"

I measured their axework with my father's summarizing eye. In the city he would shake hands with them, estimating them shrewdly: could they handle an axe, what did they know about manure? They would stand there embarrassed in their washed suburban skins and high-school clothes, uncertain what was expected of them.

"That's great," I said.

David wanted us to get the movie camera and take some footage of both of them carrying the log, for *Random Samples;* he said it would be his cameo appearance. Joe said we couldn't work the camera. David said all you did was press a button, an idiot could do it, anyway it might be even better if it was out of focus or overexposed, it would introduce the element of chance, like a painter throwing paint at a canvas, it would be organic. But Joe said what if we wrecked the camera, who would pay for it. In the end they stuck the axe in the log, after several tries, and took turns shooting each other standing beside it, arms folded and one foot on it as if it was a lion or a rhinoceros.

In the evening we played bridge, with the set of slightly greasy cards that had always been there, blue seahorses on one deck, red seahorses on the other. David and Anna played against us. They won easily: Joe didn't know how, exactly, and I hadn't played for years. I was never any good; the only part I liked was picking up the cards and arranging them.

Afterward I waited for Anna to walk up to the outhouse with me; usually I went first, alone. We took both flashlights; they made protective circles of weak yellow light, moving with our feet as they walked. Rustlings, toads in the dry leaves; once the quick warning thump of a rabbit. The sounds would be safe as long as I knew what they were.

"I wish I had a warmer sweater," Anna said, "I didn't know it got so cold."

"There's some raincoats," I said, "you could try those."

When we got back to the cabin the other two were in bed; they didn't bother going as far as the outhouse after dark, they peed on the ground. I brushed my teeth; Anna started taking off her makeup by the light of a candle and her flashlight propped on end, they'd blown out the lamp.

I went into my room and got undressed. Joe mumbled, he was half asleep; I curled my arm over him.

Outside was the wind, trees moving in it, nothing else. The yellow target from Anna's flashlight was on the ceiling; it shifted, she was going into their room and I could hear them, Anna breathing, a fast panic sound as though she was running; then her voice began, not like her real voice but twisted as her face must have been, a desperate beggar's whine, *please please.* I put the pillow over my head, I didn't want to listen, I wanted it to be through but it kept on, *Shut up* I whispered but she wouldn't. She was praying to herself, it was as if David wasn't there at all. *Jesus jesus oh yes please jesus.* Then something different, not a word but pure pain, clear as water, an animal's at the moment the trap closes.

It's like death, I thought, the bad part isn't the thing itself but being a witness. I suppose they could hear us too; the times before. But I never say anything.

CHAPTER TEN

The sunset had been red, reddish purple, and the next day the sun held as I guessed it would; without a radio or a barometer you have to make your own prophecies. It was the second day of the week, I was ticking them off in my head, prisoner's scratches on the wall; I felt stretched, pulled tight like a drying rope, the fact that he had not yet appeared only increased the possibility that he would. The seventh day seemed a great distance away.

I wanted to get them off the island, to protect them from him, to protect him from them, save all of them from knowledge. They might start to explore, cut other trails; already they were beginning to be restless: fire and food, the only two necessities, were taken care of and there was nothing left to be done. Sun rising, drifting across the sky, shadows changing without help, uninterrupted air, absence of defining borders, the only break an occasional distant plane, vapor streak, for them it must have been like living in a hammock.

In the morning David fished from the dock, catching nothing; Anna read, she was on her fourth or fifth paperback. I swept the floor, the broom webbing itself with long threads, dark and light, from where Anna and I brushed our hair in front of the mirror; then I tried to work. Joe stayed on the wall bench, arms wrapped around his knees in lawn-dwarf position, watching me. Every time I glanced up his eyes would be there, blue as ballpoint pens or Superman; even with my head turned away I could feel his X-ray vision prying under my skin, a slight prickling sensation as though he was tracing me. It was hard to concentrate; I reread two of the folk tales, about the king who learned to speak with animals and the fountain of life, but I got no further than a rough sketch of a thing that looked like a football player. It was supposed to be a giant.

"What's wrong?" I said to him finally, putting down my brush, giving up.

"Nothing," he said. He took the cover off the butter dish and started carving holes in the butter with his forefinger.

I should have realized much earlier what was happening, I should have got out of it when we were still in the city. It was unfair of me to stay with him, he'd become used to it, hooked on it, but I didn't realize that and neither did he. When you can't tell the difference between your own pleasure and your pain then you're an addict. I did that, I fed him unlimited supplies of nothing, he wasn't ready for it, it was too strong for him, he had to fill it up, like people isolated in a blank room who see patterns.

After lunch they all sat around expectantly, as though waiting for me to dole out the crayons and plasticine or regiment the sing-song, tell them what to play. I searched through the past: what did we do when it was sunny and there was no work?

"How would you like," I said, "to pick some blueberries?" Offering it as a surprise; work disguised in some other form, it had to be a game.

They seized on it, glad of the novelty. "A groove," David said. Anna and I made peanut-butter sandwiches for a midafternoon snack; then we basted our noses and the lobes of our ears with Anna's suntan lotion and started out.

David and Anna went in the green canoe, we took the heavier one.

They still couldn't paddle very well but there wasn't much wind. I had to use a lot of energy just to keep us pointed straight, because Joe didn't know how to steer; also he wouldn't admit it, which made it harder.

We wavered around the stone point where the trail goes; then we were in the archipelago of islands, tips of sunken hills, once possibly a single ridge before the lake was flooded. None of them is big enough to have a name; some are no more than rocks, with a few trees clutched and knotted to them by the roots. On one of them, further along, was the heron colony. I had to strain my eyes to spot it: the young in the nests were keeping their serpent necks and blade heads immobile, imitating dead branches. The nests were all in a single tree, white pine, grouped for mutual protection like bungalows on the outskirts. If the herons get within pecking range they fight.

"See them?" I said to Joe, pointing.

"See what?" he said. He was sweating, overworked, the wind was against us. He scowled up at the sky but he couldn't make them out until one of them lifted and settled, wings balancing.

Beyond the herons' island was a larger one, flattish, with several red pines rising straight as masts from a ground harsh with blueberry bushes. We landed and tied the canoes and I gave each of them a tin cup. The blueberries were only beginning to ripen, the dots of them showing against the green like first rain pocking the lake. I took my own cup and started to work along the shore, they ripen earlier there.

During the war or was it after they would pay us a cent a cup; there was nowhere to spend it, I didn't understand at first what the metal disks were for: leaves on one side and a man's head chopped off at the neck on the reverse.

I was remembering the others who used to come. There weren't many of them on the lake even then, the government had put them somewhere else, corralled them, but there was one family left. Every year they would appear on the lake in blueberry season and visit the good places the same way we did, condensing as though from the air, five or six of them in a weatherbeaten canoe: father in the stern, head wizened and corded like a dried root, mother with her gourd body and hair pared back to her nape, the rest children or grandchildren. They would check to see how many blueberries there were, faces neutral and distanced, but when they saw that we were picking they would move on, gliding unhurried along near the shore and then disappearing around a point or into a bay as though they had never been there. No one knew where they lived during the winter; once, though, we passed two of the children standing by the side of the road with tin cans of blueberries for sale. It never occurred to me till now that they must have hated us.

The shore bushes rustled: it was Joe, coming down behind me. He squatted on the stone beside me; his cup was only a third full, sprinkled with leaves and green-white berries.

"Take a rest," he said.

"In a minute." I was almost finished. It was hot, light glared from the lake; in the sun the berries were so blue they seemed lit up from within. Falling into the cup they made a plink like water.

"We should get married," Joe said.

I set the cup down carefully on the rock and turned to look at him, shielding my eyes. I wanted to laugh, it was incongruous, it wasn't what he would call his trip, the legal phrases and the paperwork and the vows, especially the finality; and he'd got the order wrong, he'd never asked whether I loved him, that was supposed to come first, I would have been prepared for that. "Why?" I said. "We're living together anyway. We don't need a certificate for that."

"I think we should," he said, "we might as well."

"But it wouldn't make any difference," I said. "Everything would be the same."

"Then why not do it?" He had moved closer, he was being logical, he was threatening me with something. I swiveled, scouting for help, but they were at the far end of the island, Anna's pink shirt tiny and blazing like a gas station banner.

"No," I said, the only answer to logic. It was because I didn't want to, that's why it would gratify him, it would be a sacrifice, of my reluctance, my distaste.

"Sometimes," he said, placing the words evenly and deliberately, pegs in a pegboard, "I get the feeling you don't give a shit about me."

"I do," I said. "I do give a shit about you," repeating it like a skipping rhyme. I wondered if that was the equivalent of saying I loved him. I was calculating how much getaway money I had in the bank, how long it would take me to pack and move out, away from the clay dust and the cellar mold smell and the monstrous humanoid pots, how soon I could find a new place. Prove your love, they say. You really want to marry me, let me fuck you instead. You really want to fuck, let me marry you instead. As long as there's a victory, some flag I can wave, parade I can have in my head.

"No, you don't, I can tell," he said, unhappy rather than angry; that was worse, I could cope with his anger. He was growing larger, becoming alien, three-dimensional; panic began.

"Look," I said, "I've been married before and it didn't work out. I had a baby too." My ace, voice patient. "I don't want to go through that again." It was true, but the words were coming out of me like the mechanical words from a talking doll, the kind with the pull tape at the back; the whole speech was unwinding, everything in order, a spool. I would always be able to say what I'd just finished saying: I've tried and failed, I'm inoculated, exempt, classified as wounded. It wasn't that I didn't suffer, I was conscientious about that, that's what qualified me. But marriage was like playing Monopoly or doing crossword puzzles, either your mind worked that way, like Anna's, or it didn't; and I'd proved mine didn't. A small neutral country.

"It would be different with us," he said, disregarding what I said about the baby.

At my wedding we filled out forms, name, age, birthplace, blood type. We had it in a post office, a J.P. did it, oil portraits of former postmasters presided from the beige walls. I could recall the exact smells, glue and humid socks and the odor of second-day blouse and crystallized deodorant from the irritated secretary, and, from another doorway, the chill of antiseptic. It was a hot day, when we stepped out into the sun we couldn't see for an instant; then there was a flock of draggled pigeons pecking at the scuffed post-office lawn beside the fountain. The fountain had dolphins and a cherub with part of the face missing.

"It's over," he said, "feel better?"

He coiled his arms around me, protecting me from something, the future, and kissed me on the forehead. "You're cold," he said. My legs were shaking so much I could hardly stand up and there was an ache, slow like a groan. "Come on," he said, "we'd better get you home." He lifted my face, scrutinizing it in the light. "Maybe I should carry you to the car."

He was talking to me as though I was an invalid, not a bride. In one hand I carried a purse or a suitcase; the other was closed. We walked through the pigeons and they blew up around us, confetti. In the car I didn't cry, I didn't want to look at him. "I know it's tough," he said, "but it's better this way." Quote, unquote. His flexible hands on the wheel. It turned, perfect circle, and the gears interlocked and spun, the engine ticked like a clock, the voice of reason.

"Why are you doing this to me?" I said, losing control. "You'll ruin it." Then I was sorry, as though I'd stepped on a small animal by accident, he was so miserable: he'd abdicated, betrayed what I'd assumed were his principles, in order to be saved, by me, from me, and he'd got nothing by it.

I took his hand; he let me hold it, frowning at me, sullen as a doormat. "I'm not good enough for you," I said, motto, the words printed on a scroll like a fortune cookie. I kissed him on the side of the face. I was stalling for time, also I was afraid of him: the look he gave me as I drew away was one of baffled rage.

We were sitting outside in the chicken-wire enclosure; Joe was in the sandbox with his back half turned to us, scraping together a large mound of sand. He'd finished his pie, the rest of us were still eating. It was too hot to eat in the house, we had to keep the stove going for two hours. They had purple mouths and blue teeth which showed when they talked or laughed.

"That's the best pie I ever ate," David said. "Just like mother used to make." He smacked his lips and posed, pretending to be a TV ad.

"Stuff it," Anna said, "you can't afford just one measly compliment, can you?"

David's purple mouth grinned. "Aw," he said, "that *was* a compliment."

"The hell," Anna said. "I've met your mother."

David sighed and leaned back against his tree, rolling his eyes to Joe for sympathy. But he got none and so he gazed up at the sky instead. "This is the life," he said after a while. "We ought to start a colony, I mean a community up here, get it together with some other people, break away from the urban nuclear family. It wouldn't be a bad country if only we could kick out the fucking pig Americans, eh? Then we could have some peace."

Nobody answered him; he took off one of his shoes and began scratching the sole of his foot thoughtfully.

"I think it would be a copout," Anna said abruptly.

"What would?" David said, overly tolerant, as though she'd interrupted him in mid-sentence. "Kicking out the pigs?"

"Oh shit," Anna said, "you just won't."

"What the hell are you talking about?" he said, feigning hurt. But she sat hugging her knees, smoke breathing through her nostrils. I got up and started to collect the plates.

"It turns me on when she bends over," David said. "She's got a neat ass. I'm really into the whole ass thing. Joe, don't you think she's got a neat ass?"

"You can have it," Joe said. He was leveling the sand mound he had built, he was still angry.

I scraped the ends of crust into the stove and washed the plates, the water turning reddish blue, vein color. The others ambled in; they didn't feel like playing bridge, they sat around the table reading detective novels and back issues of magazines, *Maclean's* and *The National Geographic,* some of them were ten years old. I'd read them all, so I went into David's and Anna's room with a candle to look for more.

I had to climb up on the bed to reach the shelf. There was a high pile of books; I lifted it down to where the candle was. On top was a layer of paperbacks, the average kind, but underneath them were some things that were out of place: the brown leather photo album that ought to have been in a trunk in the city, along with my mother's unused wedding presents, tarnished silver bowls and lace tablecloths, and the scrapbooks we used to draw in when it rained. I thought she'd thrown them out; I wondered who had brought them here, which one of them.

There were several scrapbooks; I sat down on the bed and opened one at random, feeling as though I was opening someone else's private diary. It was my brother's: explosions in red and orange, soldiers dismembering in the air, planes and tanks; he must have been going to school by then, he knew enough to draw little swastikas on the sides. Further on there were flying men with comic-book capes and explorers on another planet, he spent hours explaining these pictures to me. The purple jungles I'd forgotten, the green sun with seven red moons, the animals with scales and spines and tentacles; and a man-eating plant, engulfing a careless victim, a balloon with HELP in it squeezing out of his mouth like bubble gum. The other explorers were rescuing him with their weapons: flamethrowers, trumpet-shaped pistols, ray guns. In the background was their spaceship, bristling with gadgets.

The next scrapbook was mine. I searched through it carefully, looking for something I could recognize as myself, where I had come from or gone wrong; but there were no drawings at all, just illustrations cut from magazines and pasted in. They were ladies, all kinds: holding up cans of cleanser, knitting, smiling, modeling toeless high heels and nylons with dark seams and pillbox hats and veils. A lady was what you dressed up as on Halloween when you couldn't think of anything else and didn't want to be a ghost; or it was what you said at school when they asked you what you were going to be when you grew up, you said "A lady" or "A mother," either one was safe; and it wasn't a lie, I did want to be those things. On some of the pages were women's dresses clipped from mail-order catalogues, no bodies in them.

I tried another one: mine also, earlier. The drawings were of ornately decorated Easter eggs, singly and in groups. Some of them had people-shaped rabbits climbing up them on rope ladders; apparently the rabbits lived inside the eggs, there were doors at the tops, they could pull the ladders up after them. Beside the larger eggs were smaller ones connected to them by bridges, the outhouses. Page after page of eggs and rabbits, grass and trees, normal and green, surrounding them, flowers blooming, sun in the upper right-hand corner of each picture, moon symmetrically in the left. All the rabbits were smiling and some were laughing hilariously; several were shown eating ice-cream cones from the safety of their egg-tops. No monsters, no wars, no explosions, no heroism. I couldn't remember ever having drawn these pictures. I was disappointed in myself: I must have been a hedonistic child, I thought, and quite stodgy also, interested in nothing but social welfare. Or perhaps it was a vision of Heaven.

Behind me someone came into the room, it was David. "Hey lady," he said, "what're you doing in my bed? You a customer or something?"

"Sorry," I said. I put the album back on the shelf but I took the scrapbooks into my room and hid them under the mattress; I didn't want them spying.

CHAPTER ELEVEN

At night Joe kept turned away from me, he wasn't going to compromise. I ran my fingers over his furry back to show I wanted a truce, the borders restored to where they'd been, but after he twitched me off and grunted irritably I withdrew. I curled up, concentrating on excluding him: he was merely an object in the bed, like a sack or a large turnip. There's more than one way to skin a cat, my father used to say; it bothered me, I didn't see why they would want to skin a cat even one way. I stared at the wall and thought of maxims: two can play that game, marry in haste, repent at leisure, least said soonest mended, traditional wisdom which was never any help.

At breakfast he ignored me and the others too, hunching over his plate, mumbling replies.

"What's with him?" David said. His new beard was sprouting, a brown smudge on his chin.

"Shut up," Anna said; but she glanced at me, inquisitive, holding me responsible for it whatever it was.

Joe wiped his sweatshirt sleeve across his mouth and went out of the house, letting the screen door slam behind him.

"Maybe he's constipated," David said, "it makes them grouchy. You sure he's been getting enough exercise?" Then he went "Arf, arf" like Popeye, wiggling his ears.

"Stupid," Anna said fondly; she rumpled his hair.

"Hey, don't do that," he said, "it'll all fall out." He jumped up and went to the mirror and rearranged the hair down over his forehead; I hadn't noticed before that he combed it that way to cover the patches where it had once grown.

I gathered up the bacon rinds and the crusts from the toast and took them out to the bird tray. The jays were there, they saw I had food and told each other about it with hoarse cries. I stood quietly with my hand outstretched but they wouldn't fly down; they winged overhead, reconnoitering. Perhaps I was moving without knowing it, you had to convince them you were a thing, not an enemy. Our mother made us watch from inside the house, she said we frightened them. Once people believed the flight of birds was a portent: augury.

I heard the mosquito whine of a motor approaching; I left my handful of crumbs on the tray and went out on the point to watch. It was Paul's boat, white-painted and squarish, handmade; he waved to me from the stern. There was another man with him, sitting in the bow, backwards.

They pulled in to the dock and I ran down the steps to greet them; I caught the rope and tied it. "Careful," I said as they stepped out, "it's rotten in places."

Paul had brought me a huge wad of vegetables from his garden: he handed me a bouquet of swiss chard, a quart basket of green beans, a bundle of carrots, a brain-sized cauliflower, bashfully, as though the gift might not be acceptable. The proper reply would have been an equally large or perhaps larger assortment. I thought with dismay of the spindly broccoli and the radishes already gone to seed.

"Here is a man," he said. "They send him to me because I know your father." He stepped backwards, effacing himself, and almost slipped off the dock.

"Malmstrom," the man said as though it was a secret code; his hand shot toward me. I transferred the swiss chard to the crook of my arm and took the hand, which squeezed mine confidentially. "Bill Malmstrom, please call me Bill." He had trimmed gray hair and an executive moustache like the shirt ads, the vodka ads; his clothes were woodsy, semiworn, verging on the authentic. Slung around his neck was a pair of binoculars in a suede case.

We walked to the land; he had taken out a pipe and was lighting it. I wondered if he was from the government. "Paul, here, was telling me," he said, looking around for Paul, "what a nice place you have."

"It's my father's," I said.

His face drooped into the appropriate downward curve; if he'd been wearing a hat he would have taken it off. "Ah yes," he said, "a tragedy." I distrusted him: I couldn't place the accent, the name sounded German.

"Where are you from?" I asked, trying to be polite.

"Michigan," he said as though it was something to be proud of. "I'm a member of the Detroit branch of the Wildlife Protection Association of America; we have a branch in this country, quite a flourishing little branch." He beamed at me, condescending. "As a matter of fact that's what I wanted to discuss with you. Our place on Lake Erie is, ah, giving out, so to say. I believe I can speak for the rest of the Michigan members in saying we'd be prepared to make you an offer."

"What for?" I said. He sounded as though he wanted me to buy something, a magazine or a membership.

He swept his pipe in a semicircle. "This lovely piece of property," he said. "What we'd use it for would be a kind of retreat lodge, where the members could meditate and observe," he puffed, "the beauties of nature. And maybe do a little hunting and fishing."

"Don't you want to see it?" I asked. "I mean, the house and all."

"I must admit that I've already seen it; we've had our eye on this piece for quite some time. I've been coming up here to fish for years, and I've taken the liberty, when no one seemed to be here, of having a stroll around." He gave a small harumph, a voyeur of good social standing caught in the act; then he named a price that meant I could forget about *Quebec Folk Tales* and children's books and everything else, at least for a while.

"Would you change it?" I asked. I foresaw motels, highrises.

"Well, we'd have to install a power generator, of course, and a septic tank; but apart from that, no, I expect we'd like to leave it the way it is, it has a definite," he stroked his moustache, "rural charm."

"I'm sorry but it's not for sale," I said, "not right now; maybe later." If my father had been dead he might have liked the proposal but as it was he would be furious if he returned and found I'd sold his house. I wasn't sure I'd be the owner in any case. There must be deeds hidden, property titles, legal papers, I'd never had any dealings with lawyers; I would have to sign forms or charters, I might have to pay death duties.

"Well," he said with the heartiness of a loser. "I'm sure the offer will still be open. Indefinitely, you might say." He drew out his wallet and gave me a card: *Bill Malmstrom, Teenie Town,* it said, *Togs for Toddlers 'n Tots.*

"Thank you," I said, "I'll keep it in mind."

I took Paul by the arm and led him to the garden, as though to reciprocate for the vegetables: I felt I had to explain, at least to him, he had gone to a lot of trouble for me.

"Your garden, she is not doing so good, ay?" he said, inspecting.

"No," I said, "we just got it weeded; but I want you to have . . ." I gazed desperately around, seized on a withered lettuce and presented it to him, roots and all, as gracefully as I could.

He held it, blinking, discouraged. "Madame will like that," he said.

"Paul," I said, lowering my voice, "the reason I can't sell is that my father's still alive."

"Yes?" he said, perking up. "He came back, he is here?"

"Not exactly," I said. "He's away right now, on a sort of trip; but perhaps he will be here soon." For all I could tell he might have been listening to us at that moment, from behind the raspberry canes or the burn heap.

"He went for the trees?" Paul said, hurt that he hadn't been consulted: he used to go, too. "You saw him first, before?"

"No," I said, "he was gone when I got here; but he left me a note, more or less."

"Ah," he said, glancing nervously over my shoulder into the forest. It was clear he didn't believe me.

For lunch we had Paul's cauliflower and some tins, corn and fried ham. During the canned pears David said "Who were those two old guys?" He must have seen them from the window.

"It was a man who wanted to buy the place," I said.

"I bet he was a Yank," David said, "I can spot them in a crowded room."

"Yes," I said, "but he was from a wildlife association, that's who he was buying it for."

"Bullshit," David said, "he was a front man for the C.I.A."

I laughed. "No," I said; I showed him the *Teenie Town* card.

But David was serious. "You haven't seen them in operation the way I have," he said darkly, invoking his New York past.

"What would they want up here?" I said.

"A snooping base," he said. "Bird watchers, binoculars, it all fits. They know this is the kind of place that will be strategically important during the war."

"What war?" I asked, and Anna said "Here we go."

"It's obvious. They're running out of water, clean water, they're dirtying up all of theirs, right? Which is what we have a lot of, this country is almost all water if you look at a map. So in a while, I give it ten years, they'll be up against the wall. They'll try to swing a deal with the government, get us to give them the water cheap or for nothing in exchange for more soapflakes or something, and the government will give in, they'll be a bunch of puppets as usual. But by that time the Nationalist Movement will be strong enough so they'll force the government to back down; riots or kidnappings or something. Then the Yank pigs will send in the Marines, they'll have to; people in New York and Chicago will be dropping like flies, industry will be stalled, there'll be a black market in water, they'll be shipping it in tankers from Alaska. They'll come in through Quebec, it will have separated by then; the Pepsis will even help them, they'll be having a good old laugh. They'll hit the big cities and knock out communications and take over, maybe shoot a few kids, and the Movement guerrillas will go into the bush and start blowing up the water pipelines the

Yanks will be building in places like this, to get the water down there."

He seemed very positive about it, as if it had happened already. I thought about the survival manuals: if the Movement guerrillas were anything like David and Joe they would never make it through the winters. They couldn't get help from the cities, they would be too far, and the people there would be apathetic, they wouldn't mind another change of flag. If they tried at the outlying farms the farmers would take after them with shotguns. The Americans wouldn't even have to defoliate the trees, the guerrillas would die of starvation and exposure anyway.

"Where will you get food?" I said.

"What do you mean 'you'?" he said. "I'm just speculating."

I thought of how it would appear in the history books when it was over: a paragraph with dates and a short summary of what happened. That's how it was in high school, they taught it neutrally, a long list of wars and treaties and alliances, people taking and losing power over other people; but nobody would ever go into the motives, why they wanted it, whether it was good or bad. They used long words like "demarcation" and "sovereignty," they wouldn't say what they meant and you couldn't ask: in high school the right thing was to stare fixedly at the teacher as though at a movie screen, and it was worse for a girl to ask questions than for a boy. If a boy asked a question the other boys would make derisive sucking noises with their mouths, but if a girl asked one the other girls would say "Think you're so great" in the washroom afterward. In the margins around the Treaty of Versailles I drew ornaments, plants with scrolled branches, hearts and stars instead of flowers. I got so I could draw invisibly, my fingers scarcely moving.

The generals and the historic moments looked better framed. If you put your eye down close to the photograph they disintegrated into gray dots.

Anna was squeezed in beside David on the bench, playing with one of his hands while he talked. "Did I ever tell you that you have Murderer's Thumb?" she said.

"Don't interrupt," he said, but when she made a whimpering face he said "Yep, you did, almost every day," and patted her arm.

"It's spread flat at the end," she said, explaining to us.

"I hope you didn't sell out," David said to me. I shook my head. "Good girl," he said, "your heart's in the right place. And the rest of her too," he said to Joe, "I like it round and firm and fully packed. Anna, you're eating too much."

I washed and Anna dried, as usual. Suddenly Anna said "David is a schmuck. He's one of the schmuckiest people I know."

I looked around at her: her voice was like fingernails, I'd never heard her talk that way about David.

"Why?" I said. "What's wrong?" He hadn't said anything at lunch that could have upset her.

"I guess you think he's hot for you." Her mouth stretched down tight with the lips inside, a toad's.

"No," I said, bewildered, "why would I think that?"

"Those things he says, you know, like about your ass and being fully packed," she said impatiently.

"I thought he was teasing." I had thought that too, it was just a habit like picking your nose, only verbal.

"Teasing, shit. He was doing it to me. He always does stuff like that to other women in front of me, he'd screw them with me in the room if he could. Instead he screws them somewhere else and tells me about it afterwards."

"Oh," I said. I hadn't deduced that. "Why? I mean, why does he tell you?"

Anna brooded, her dish towel slack. "He says it's being honest. What a turd. When I get mad he says I'm jealous and possessive and I shouldn't get uptight, he says jealousy is bourgeois, it's a leftover from the property ethic, he thinks we should all be swingers and share it around. But I say there are these basic emotions, if you feel something you should let it out, right?" It was an article of faith, she glared at me, challenging me to affirm or deny; I wasn't certain, so I didn't say anything. "He pretends he doesn't feel those things, he's so cool," she said, "but really it's just to show me he can do it and get away with it, I can't stop him; all that theorizing about it is cover-up bullshit garbage." She raised her head, smiling, friendly again. "I thought I should warn you so you'd know if he grabs you or anything it won't have much to do with you, it's all about me really."

"Thank you," I said. I was sorry she'd told me; I still wanted to believe that what they called a good marriage had remained possible, for someone. But it was kind of her, thoughtful; I knew in her place I wouldn't have done it, I would have let her take care of herself, My Brother's Keeper always reminded me of zoos and insane asylums.

CHAPTER TWELVE

The slop pail was full; I carried it to the garden to pour the dirty water into the trench. Joe was lying by himself on the dock, face down; when I came to rinse the pail he didn't move. Anna passed me on the steps, wearing her orange bikini, oiled for her sun ritual.

In the cabin I set the pail under the counter. David was pondering his chin bristles in the mirror; he slid his arm half around me and said in a guttural voice, "Come wiz me to zee outhouse."

"Not right now," I said, "I have to do some work."

He mimed regret. "Ah well," he said, "some other time."

I took out my Samsonite case and sat down at the table. He leaned over my shoulder. "Where's old Joe?"

"Down on the dock," I said.

"He seems out of sorts," David said, "maybe he has worms; when you get back to the city you should take him to the vet." And a moment later, "How come you never laugh at my jokes?"

He hung around while I set out the brushes and paper. Finally he said, "Well, Nature calls," and soft-shoed out the door like the end of a vaudeville act.

I swiveled the caps back onto the paint tubes, I had no intention of working: now they were all out of the way I would search for the will, the deed, the property title. Paul had been certain he was dead, that made me doubt my theory. Perhaps the C.I.A. had done away with him to get the land, Mr. Malmstrom was not quite plausible; but that was preposterous, I couldn't start suspecting people for no reason.

I rummaged in the cavity under the wall bench, went through the shelves, groped under the beds where the tents were stored. He might have filed the papers in a safe-deposit box, earlier, in a city bank, I'd never find them. Or he might have burned them. At any rate they weren't here.

Unless they were in among the pages of a book: I checked Goldsmith and Burns, holding them by the spines and shaking, then I thought of his lunatic drawings, the only clue I had that he might not be dead. I'd never gone through all of them. In a way that would be the logical hiding place; he'd always been logical, and madness is only an amplification of what you already are.

I lifted down the stack of drawings and began to look. The paper was thin and soft, like rice paper. First the hands and antlered figures, always with numbers scrawled in the corner, then a larger sheet, a half moon with four sticks coming out of it, bulbed at the ends. I righted the page, judging by the numbers, and it became a boat with people, the knobs were their heads. It was reassuring to find I could interpret it, it made sense.

But the next one was nothing I could recognize. The body was long, a snake or a fish; it had four limbs or arms and a tail and on the head were two branched horns. Lengthwise it was like an animal, an alligator; upright it was more human, but only in the positions of the arms and the front-facing eyes.

Total derangement. I wondered when it had started; it must have been the snow and the loneliness, he'd pushed himself too far, it gets in through your eyes, the thin black cold of midwinter night, the white days dense with sunlight, outer space melting and freezing again into different shapes, your mind starts doing the same thing. The drawing was something he saw, a hallucination; or it might have been himself, what he thought he was turning into.

I uncovered the next page. But it wasn't a drawing, it was a typed letter, I skimmed it quickly. Addressed to my father.

DEAR SIR:

Many thanks for forwarding the photographs and tracings and the corresponding map. The material is most valuable and I shall include some of it in my forthcoming work on the subject, with your permission and giving due credit. Details of any subsequent discoveries you may make would be most welcome.

I include a copy of one of my recent studies which you may find of interest.

Yours sincerely,

The letter had an illegible signature and a university crest. Paper-clipped to it were half a dozen Xeroxed sheets: "Rock Paintings of the Central Shield," by Dr. Robin M. Grove. The first few pages were maps and graphs and statistics; I skimmed them quickly. At the end of the article there were three short paragraphs, subtitled "Aesthetic Qualities and Possible Significance":

> The subject matter falls into the following categories: Hands, Abstract Symbols, Humans, Animals and Mythological Creatures. In treatment they are reminiscent, with their elongated limbs and extreme distortion, of the drawings of children. The static rigidity is in marked contrast to the rock paintings of other cultures, most notably the European cave paintings.
>
> From the above features we may deduce that the creators of the paintings were interested exclusively in symbolic content, at the expense of expressiveness and form. However, we can only indulge in conjecture as to the nature of this content, since no historical records exist. Informants questioned have supplied conflicting traditions. Some state that the sites of the paintings are the abodes of powerful or protective spirits, which may explain the custom, persisting in remote areas, of leaving offerings of clothing and small bundles of "prayer" sticks. One gives more credence to the theory that the paintings are associated with the practice of fasting to produce significant or predictive dreams.
>
> Doubtful also is the technique employed. The paintings seem to have been executed either with the fingers or with a crude brush of some sort. The predominant colour is red, with minor occurrences of white and yellow; this may be due either to the fact that red among the Indians is a sacred colour or to the relative availability of iron oxides. The bonding agent is being investigated; it may prove to be bear's fat or birds' eggs, or perhaps blood or spittle.

The academic prose breathed reason; my hypotheses crumbled like sand. This was the solution, the explanation: he never failed to explain.

His drawings were not originals then, only copies. He must have been doing them as a sort of retirement hobby, he was an incurable amateur and enthusiast: if he'd become hooked on these rock paintings he would have combed the area for them, collecting them with his camera, pestering the experts by letter whenever he found one; an old man's delusion of usefulness.

I pressed my fingers into my eyes, hard, to make the pool of blackness ringed with violent color. Release, red spreading back in, abrupt as pain. The secret had come clear, it had never been a secret, I'd made it one, that was easier. My eyes came open, I began to arrange.

I thought, I suppose I knew it from the beginning, I shouldn't have tried to find out, it's killed him. I had the proof now, indisputable, of sanity and therefore of death. Relief, grief, I must have felt one or the other. A blank, a disappointment: crazy people can come back, from wherever they go to take refuge, but dead people can't, they are prohibited. I tried to recall him, picture his face, the way he'd been when he was alive, I found I couldn't; all I could see was the cards he used to hold up, testing us: $3 \times 9 = ?$ He was as absent now as a number, a zero, the question mark in place of the missing answer. Unknown quantity. His way. Everything had to be measured.

I was staring down at the drawings, they were framed by my two arms lain parallel on the table. I began to notice them again. There was a gap, something not accounted for, something left over.

I spread the first six pages out on the table and studied them, using what they called my intelligence, it short-circuits those other things. The notes and numbers were apparently a location code, it was like a puzzle he'd left for me to solve, an arithmetic problem; he taught us arithmetic, our mother taught us to read and write. Geometry, the first thing I learned was how to draw flowers with compasses, they were like acid patterns. Once they thought you could see God that way but all I saw was landscapes and geometrical shapes; which would be the same thing if you believed God was a mountain or a circle. He said Jesus was a historical figure and God was a superstition, and a superstition was a thing that didn't exist. If you tell your children God doesn't exist they will be forced to believe you are the god, but what happens when they find out you are human after all, you have to grow old and die? Resurrection is like plants, Jesus Christ is risen today they sang at Sunday school, celebrating the daffodils; but people are not onions, as he so reasonably pointed out, they stay under.

The numbers were a system, a game; I would play it with him, it would make him seem less dead. I lined up the pages and compared the notes, carefully as a jeweler.

On one of the drawings, another antlered figure, I finally spotted the key: a name I recognized, White Birch Lake where we went bass fishing, it was connected to the main lake by a portage. I went into David's and Anna's room, where the map of the district was tacked to the wall. Marked on a point of land was a tiny red X and a number, identical with the number on the drawing. The printed name was different, Lac des Verges Blanches, the government had been translating all the English names into French ones, though the Indian names remained the same. Scattered here and there were other X's, like a treasure map.

I wanted to go there and verify, match the drawing with reality; that way I'd be sure I'd followed the rules and done it right. I could disguise it as a fishing trip, David hadn't caught anything since his first attempt, though he'd been trying. We'd have time to go there and get back with two days to spare.

I heard Anna's voice approaching, singing, the words trailing off as her breath gave out climbing the steps. I went back to the main room.

"Hi," she said, "do I look burnt?"

She was pink now, parboiled, white showing around the orange edges of her suit, neck dividing body color from applied face color. "A little," I said.

"Listen," she said, her voice shifting into concern, "what's wrong with Joe? I was down on the dock with him and he didn't say one word."

"He doesn't talk much," I said.

"I know, but this was different. He was just lying there." She was pushing, demanding answers.

"He thinks we should get married," I said.

Her eyebrows lifted like antennae. "Really? Joe? That's not—"

"I don't want to."

"Oh," she said, "then that's awful. You must feel awful." She'd found out; now she was rubbing after-sun lotion on her shoulders. "Mind?" she said, handing me the plastic tube.

I didn't feel awful; I realized I didn't feel much of anything, I hadn't for a long time. Perhaps I'd been like that all my life, just as some babies are born deaf or without a sense of touch; but if that was true I wouldn't have noticed the absence. At some point my neck must have closed over, pond freezing or a wound, shutting me into my head; since then everything had been glancing off me, it was like being in a vase, or the village where I could see them but not hear them because I couldn't understand what was being said. Bottles distort for the observer too: frogs in the jam jar stretched wide, to them watching I must have appeared grotesque.

"Thanks," Anna said, "I hope I won't peel. I think you should go talk to him, or something."

"I have," I said; but her eyes were accusing, I hadn't done enough, conciliation, expiation. I went obediently toward the door.

"Maybe you can work it out," she called after me.

Joe was still on the dock but he was sitting on the edge now with his feet in the water, I crouched down beside him. His toes had dark hairs on the tops, spaced like the needles on a balsam twig.

"What is it?" I said. "Are you sick?"

"You know fucking well," he said after a minute.

"Let's go back to the city," I said, "the way it was before." I took hold of his hand so I could feel the calloused palm, thickened by the wheel, concrete.

"You're screwing around with me," he said, still not looking at me. "All I want is a straight answer."

"About what?" I said. Near the dock there were some water skippers, surface tension holding them up; the fragile shadows of the dents where their feet touched fell on the sand underwater, moving when they moved. His vulnerability embarrassed me, he could still feel, I should have been more careful with him.

"Do you love me, that's all," he said. "That's the only thing that matters."

It was the language again, I couldn't use it because it wasn't mine. He must have known what he meant but it was an imprecise word; the Eskimos had fifty-two names for snow because it was important to them, there ought to be as many for love.

"I want to," I said. "I do in a way." I hunted through my brain for any emotion that would coincide with what I'd said. I did want to, but it was like thinking God should exist and not being able to believe.

"Fucking jesus," he said, pulling his hand away, "just yes or no, don't mess around."

"I'm trying to tell the truth," I said. The voice wasn't mine, it came from someone dressed as me, imitating me.

"The truth is," he said bitterly, "you think my work is crap, you think I'm a loser and I'm not worth it." His face contorted, it was pain: I envied him.

"No," I said, but I couldn't say it right and he needed more than that.

"Come up to the cabin," I said; Anna was there, she would help. "I'll make some tea." I got up but he wouldn't follow.

While the stove was heating I took the leather album from the shelf in their room and opened it on the table, where Anna was reading. It was no longer his death but my own that concerned me; perhaps I would be able to tell when the change occurred by the differences in my former faces, alive up to a year, a day, then frozen. The duchess at the French court before the Revolution, who stopped laughing or crying so her skin would never change or wrinkle, it worked, she died immortal.

Grandmothers and grandfathers first, distant ancestors, strangers, in face-front firing-squad poses: cameras weren't ordinary then, maybe they thought their souls were being stolen, as the Indians did. Underneath them were labels in white, my mother's cautious printing. My mother before she was married, another stranger, with bobbed hair and a knitted hat. Wedding pictures, corseted smiles. My brother before I was born, then pictures of me beginning to appear. Paul taking us down the lake with his sleigh and horses before the ice went out. My mother, in her leather jacket and odd long 1940s hair, standing beside the tray for the birds, her hand stretched out; the jays were there too, she's training them, one is on her shoulder, peering at her with clever thumbtack eyes, another is landing on her wrist, wings caught as a blur. Sun sifting around her through the pines, her eyes looking straight at the camera, frightened, receding into the shadows of her head like a skull's, a trick of the light.

I watched myself grow larger. Mother and father in alternate shots, building the house, walls and then the roof, planting the garden. Around them were borders of blank paper, at each corner a hinge, they were like small gray-and-white windows opening into a place I could no longer reach. I was in most of the pictures, shut in behind the paper; or not me but the missing part of me.

School pictures, my face lined up with forty others, colossal teachers towering above us. I could find myself always, I was the one smudged with movement or turning the other way. Further on, glossy color prints, forgotten boys with pimples and carnations, myself in the stiff dresses, crinolines and tulle, layered like store birthday cakes; I was civilized at last, the finished product. She would say "You look very nice, dear," as though she believed it; but I wasn't convinced, I knew by then she was no judge of the normal.

"Is that you?" Anna said, putting down *The Mystery at Sturbridge*. "Christ, how could we ever wear that stuff?"

The last pages of the album were blank, with some loose prints stuck in between the black leaves as though my mother hadn't wanted to finish. After the formal dresses I disappeared; no wedding pictures, but of course we hadn't taken any. I closed the cover, straightening the edges.

No hints or facts, I didn't know when it had happened. I must have been all right then; but after that I'd allowed myself to be cut in two.

Woman sawn apart in a wooden crate, wearing a bathing suit, smiling, a trick done with mirrors, I read it in a comic book; only with me there had been an accident and I came apart. The other half, the one locked away, was the only one that could live; I was the wrong half, detached, terminal. I was nothing but a head, or, no, something minor like a severed thumb; numb. At school they used to play a joke, they would bring little boxes with cotton wool in them and a hole cut in the bottom; they would poke their finger through the hole and pretend it was a dead finger.

CHAPTER THIRTEEN

We pushed off from the dock at ten by David's watch. The sky was watercolor blue, the cloud bunches white on the backs and gray on the bellies. Wind from the stern, waves overtaking, my arms lifting and swinging, light and automatic as though they knew what to do. I was at the front, figurehead; behind me Joe shoved at the water, the canoe surged forward.

The landmarks passed, unscrolling, one-dimensional map thickening into stone and wood around us: point, cliff, leaning dead tree, heron island with the intricate bird silhouettes, blueberry island sailed by its mast pines, foregrounds. On the next island there was once a trapper's cabin, logs chinked with grass and a straw mound where the bed had been; I could see nothing left but a muddle of rotting timber.

In the morning we talked, uselessly but in calm rational voices as though discussing the phone bill; which meant it was final. We were still in bed, his feet stuck out at the bottom. I could hardly wait till I was old so I wouldn't have to do this any more.

"When we get back to the city," I said, "I'll move out."

"I will if you like," he said generously.

"No, you've got all your pots and things there."

"Have it your way," he said, "you always do."

He thought of it as a contest, like the children at school who would twist your arm and say Give in? Give in? until you did; then they would let go. He didn't love me, it was an idea of himself he loved and he wanted someone to join him, anyone would do, I didn't matter so I didn't have to care.

The sun was at twelve. We had lunch on a jagged island almost out in the wide part of the lake. After we landed we found that someone had built a fireplace already, on the shore ledge of bare granite; trash was strewn around it, orange peelings and tin cans and a rancid bulge of greasy paper, the tracks of humans. It was like dogs pissing on a fence, as if the endlessness, anonymous water and unclaimed land, compelled them to leave their signature, stake their territory, and garbage was the only thing they had to do it with. I picked up the pieces of clutter and piled them to one side, I would burn them afterward.

"That's disgusting," Anna said. "How can you touch it?"

"It's the sign of a free country," David said. "Germany under Hitler was very tidy."

We didn't need to use the axe, the island was covered with dry sticks, branches discarded from trees. I boiled the water and made tea and we had chicken noodle soup, out of a package, and sardines and tinned applesauce.

We sat in the shade, white smoke and the smell of scorching orange peels wrapping over us when the wind swerved. I hooked the billy tin off the fire and poured the tea; ashes and bits of twig were floating in it.

"Gentlemen," David said, raising his tin cup, "Up the Queen. Did that once in a bar in New York and these three Limeys came over and wanted to start a fight, they thought we were Yanks insulting their Queen. But I said she was our Queen too so we had the right, and they ended up buying us a drink."

"I think it would be more fair," Anna said, "if you did it, 'Ladies and Gentlemen, Up the Queen and the Duke.'"

"None of that Women's Lib," David said, his eyes lidding, "or you'll be out on the street. I won't have one in the house, they're preaching random castration, they get off on that, they're roving the streets in savage bands armed with garden shears."

"I'll join if you will," Anna said to me, joking.

I said "I think men ought to be superior." But neither of them heard the actual words; Anna looked at me as though I'd betrayed her and said "Wow, are you ever brain-washed," and David said "Want a job?" and to Joe, "Hear that, you're superior." But when

Joe only grunted he said "You should wire him for sound. Or fix him up with a plug and a shade, he'd make a great end-table lamp. I'm having him give a guest lecture in Adult Vegetation next year, 'How Pots Communicate,' he'll walk in and say nothing for two hours, that'll freak them." Joe smiled at last, wanly.

In the night I had wanted rescue, if my body could be made to sense, respond, move strongly enough, some of the red light-bulb synapses, blue neurons, incandescent molecules might seep into my head through the closed throat, neck membrane. Pleasure and pain are side by side they said but most of the brain is neutral; nerveless, like fat. I rehearsed emotions, naming them: joy, peace, guilt, release, love and hate, react, relate; what to feel was like what to wear, you watched the others and memorized it. But the only thing there was the fear that I wasn't alive: a negative, the difference between the shadow of a pin and what it's like when you stick it in your arm, in school caged in the desk I used to do that, with pen nibs and compass points too, instruments of knowledge, English and geometry; they've discovered rats prefer any sensation to none. The insides of my arms were stippled with tiny wounds, like an addict's. They slipped the needle into the vein and I was falling down, it was like diving, sinking from one layer of darkness to a deeper, deepest; when I rose up through the anaesthetic, pale green and then daylight, I could remember nothing.

"Don't bother him," Anna said.

"Or maybe I'll make it a short course this time," David said. "For the businessmen how to open the *Playboy* centerfold with the left hand only, keeping the right free for action, for the housewives how to switch on the TV and switch off their heads, that's all they need to know, then we can go home."

But he wouldn't, he needed to be rescued himself and neither of us would put on the cape and boots and the thunderbolt sweatshirt, we were both afraid of failure; we lay with our backs to each other, pretending to sleep, while Anna prayed to nobody through the plywood wall. Romance comic books, on the cover always a pink face oozing tears like a melting popsicle; men's magazines were about pleasure, cars and women, the skins bald as inner tubes. In a way it was a relief, to be exempt from feeling.

"The trouble with you is you hate women," Anna said savagely; she threw the rest of her tea and the tea leaves out of her tin cup into the lake, they hit with a splat.

David grinned. "That's what they call a delayed reaction," he said. "Goose Anna in the bum and three days later she squeals. Cheer up, you're so cute when you're mad." He crawled over to her on all fours and rubbed his bristly burdock chin against her face and asked her how she would like to be raped by a porcupine. "You know that one?" he said. "How do porcupines do it? Carefully!" Anna smiled at him as though he was a brain-damaged child.

The next minute he had scrambled up and was capering on the point, shaking his clenched fist and yelling "Pigs! Pigs!" as loud as he could. It was some Americans, going past on their way to the village, their boat sloshing up and down in the waves, spray pluming, flags cocked fore and aft. They couldn't hear him because of the wind and the motor, they thought he was greeting, they waved and smiled.

I washed the dishes and soaked the fireplace, the hot stones sizzling, and we packed and started again. It was rougher, there were whitecaps on the open lake, the canoe rolled under us, we had to fight to keep it from turning broadside on; foam trailed on the dark water, spent waves. Paddle digging the lake, ears filled with moving air; breath and sweat, muscle hurt, my body at any rate was alive.

The wind was too strong, we had to change course; we headed across to the lee shore and followed it, as close to the land as possible, threading the maze of rocks and shallows. It was the long way around but the trees sheltered us.

Finally we reached the narrow bay where the portage was; the sun was at four, we'd been delayed by the wind. I hoped I would be able to find the place, the beginning of the path; I knew it was on the opposite side. As we rounded the point I heard a sound, human sound. At first it was like an outboard starting; then it was a snarl. Chain saw, I could see them now, two men in yellow helmets. They'd left a trail, trees felled at intervals into the bay, trunks cut cleanly as though by a knife.

Surveyors, the paper company or the government, the power company. If it was the power company I knew what it meant: they were going to raise the lake level as they had sixty years ago, they were plotting the new shoreline. Twenty feet up again and this time they wouldn't cut off the trees as they had before, it would cost too much, they would be left to rot. The garden would go but the cabin would survive; the hill would become an eroding sand island surrounded by dead trees.

As we went by they glanced up at us, then turned back to their work, indifferent. Advance men, agents. Swish and crackle as the tree tottered, whump and splash as it hit. Near them was a post driven into the ground, numbers on it in fresh red paint. The lake didn't matter to them, only the system: it would be a reservoir. During the war. I would be able to do nothing, I didn't live there.

The landing place at the portage was clogged with driftwood, sodden and moss-grown. We pushed in among the slippery logs as far as we could, then clambered out and waded, dragging the canoes up over, soaking our shoes. It was bad for the canoes, it scraped the keels. There were other paint marks, recent.

We unloaded the canoes and I knotted the paddles into position across the thwarts. They said they would take the tents and the canoes and Anna and I could take the packs and the leftovers, the fishing rods and the tackle box with the jar of frogs I'd caught that morning, the movie equipment. David had insisted on it, though I warned him we might tip.

"We have to use up the film," he said, "we've only got it rented for another week."

Anna said "But there won't be anything you want," and David said "How do you know what I want?"

"There's an Indian rock painting," I said, "prehistoric. You might take that." A point of interest, it would go with the Bottle Villa and the stuffed moose family, a new anomaly for their collection.

"Wow," David said, "Is there? Neat," and Anna said "For God's sake don't encourage him."

Neither of them had portaged before; we had to help them lift and balance the canoes. I said maybe they should double up, both of them under one canoe, but David insisted they could do it the real way. I said they should be careful; if the canoe slipped sideways and you didn't get out in time it would break your neck. "What's the matter," he said, "don't you trust us?"

The trail hadn't been brushed out recently but there were deep footprints, bootprints, in the muddy places. Two sets, they pointed in but not out: whoever they were, Americans maybe, spies, they were still in there.

The packs were heavy, food for three days in case the weather turned bad and marooned us; the straps cut into my shoulders, I leaned forward against the weight, feet squishing in the wet shoes as I walked.

The portage was up over a steep ridge of rock, watershed, then down through ferns and saplings to an oblong pond, a shallow mudhole we'd have to paddle across to reach the second portage. Anna and I got there first and set down the packs; Anna had time to smoke half a cigarette before David and Joe came staggering down the trail, bumping into the sides like blinkered horses. We held the canoes and they crouched out from under, they were pink and breathless.

"Better be fish in there," David said, sleeving off his forehead.

"The next one's shorter," I told them.

The water was covered with lily pads, the globular yellow lilies with their thick center snouts pushing up from among them. It swarmed with leeches, I could see them undulating sluggishly under the brown surface. When the paddles hit bottom on the way across, gas bubbles from decomposing vegetation rose and burst with a stench of rotten eggs or farts. The air fogged with mosquitoes.

We reached the second portage, marked by a trapper's blaze weathered to the color of the tree. I got out and stood holding the canoe steady while Joe climbed forward.

It was behind me, I smelled it before I saw it; then I heard the flies. The smell was like decaying fish. I turned around and it was hanging upside down by a thin blue nylon rope tied round its feet and looped over a tree branch, its wings fallen open. It looked at me with its mashed eye.

CHAPTER FOURTEEN

"Heavy," David said. "What is it?"

"A dead bird," Anna said. She held her nose with two fingers.

I said "It's a heron. You can't eat them." I couldn't tell how it had been done, bullet, smashed with a stone, hit with a stick. This would be a good place for herons, they would come to fish in the shallow water, standing on one leg and striking with the long spear bill. They must have got it before it had time to rise.

"We need that," David said, "we can put it next to the fish guts."

"Shit," Joe said, "it really stinks."

"That won't show in the movie," David said, "you can stand it for five minutes, it looks so great, you have to admit." They began to set up the camera; Anna and I waited, sitting on the packs.

I saw a beetle on it, blueblack and oval; when the camera whirred it burrowed in under the feathers. Carrion beetle, death beetle. Why had they strung it up like a lynch victim, why didn't they just throw it away like the trash? To prove they could do it, they had the power to kill. Otherwise it was valueless; beautiful from a distance but it couldn't be tamed or cooked or trained to talk, the only relation they could have to a thing like that was to destroy it. Food, slave or corpse, limited choices; horned and fanged heads sawed off and mounted on the billiard room wall, stuffed fish, trophies. It must have been the Americans; they were in there now, we would meet them.

The second portage was shorter but more thickly overgrown: leaves brushed, branches pushed into the corridor of air over the trail as though preventing. Newly broken stubs, wood and pith exposed like splintered bones, ferns trampled, they'd been here, their tractor-tread footsteps dinting the mud path in front of me like excavations, craters. The slope descended, slits of the lake gleamed through the trees. I wondered what I would say to them, what could be said; if I asked them why, it would mean nothing. But when we reached the end of the portage they were nowhere in sight.

The lake was a narrow crescent, the far end was hidden. Lac des Verges Blanches, the white birch grew in clumps by the shore edge, doomed eventually by the disease, tree cancer, but not yet. The wind swayed the tops of them; it was blowing crossways over the lake. The surface corrugated, water flapping against the shore.

We got into the canoes again and paddled towards the bend; I remembered there was an open space where we could camp. On the way there were several abandoned beaver lodges shaped like dilapidated beehives or wooden haystacks; I memorized them, the bass liked underwater tangle.

We were later than I had planned, the sun was red and weakening. David wanted to fish right away but I said we had to pitch the tents and collect wood first. There was garbage at this site too but it was ancient garbage, the labels on the beer bottles illegible, the cans corroded. I gathered it up and took it with me when I went back among the trees to dig the toilet hole.

Layer of leaves and needles, layer of roots, damp sand. That was what used to bother me most about the cities, the white zero-mouthed toilets in their clean tiled cubicles. Flush toilets and vacuum cleaners, they roared and made things vanish, at that time I was afraid there was a machine that could make people vanish like that too, go nowhere, like a camera that could steal not only your soul but your body also. Levers and buttons, triggers, the machines sent them up as roots sent up flowers; tiny circles and oblongs, logic become visible, you couldn't tell in advance what would happen if you pressed them.

I showed the three of them where I had dug the hole. "Where do you sit?" Anna asked, squeamish.

"On the ground," David said, "good for you, toughen you up. You could use an ass job." Anna poked him on the belt buckle and said "Flab," imitating him.

I opened more tins and heated them, baked beans and peas, and we ate them with smoky tea. From the rock where I washed the dishes I could see part of a tent, in among the cedars at the distant end of the lake: their bunker. Binoculars trained on me, I could feel the eye rays, cross of the rifle sight on my forehead, in case I made a false move.

David was impatient, he wanted his money's worth, what he'd come for. Anna said she'd stay at the campsite: fishing didn't interest her. We left her the insect spray and the three of us got into the green canoe with the fishing rods. I put the frog jar in the stern where I could reach it. David was facing me this time; Joe sat in the bow, he was going to fish, too, though he didn't have a license.

The wind had dwindled, the lake was pink and orange. We went along the shore, birches cool, overhanging us, ice pillars. I was dizzy, too much water and sun glare, the skin of my face was shimmering as though burned, afterglow. In my head when I closed my eyes the shape of the heron dangled, upside down. I should have buried it.

The canoe steered over to the nearest beaver lodge and they tied up to it. I opened the tackle box and clipped a lure onto David's line. He was happy, whistling under his breath.

"Hey, maybe I'll hook a beaver," he said. "The national emblem. That's what they should've put on the flag instead of a maple leaf, a split beaver; I'd salute that."

"Why should it be split?" I said. It was like skinning the cat, I didn't get it.

He looked exasperated. "It's a joke," he said; and when I still didn't laugh, "Where've you been living? It's slang for cunt. The Maple Beaver Forever, that would be neat." He lowered his line into the water and began to sing, off key:

"In days of yore, from Britain's shore
Wolfe, the gallant hero, came:
It spread all o'er the hooerhouse floor
On Canada's fair domain . . .

They sing that at your school?"

"The fish will hear you," I said, and he stopped.

A part of the body, a dead animal. I wondered what part of them the heron was, that they needed so much to kill it.

Into my head the tugboat floated, the one that was on the lake before, log boom trailing it, men waving from the cabin, sunlight and blue sky, the perfect way. But it didn't last. One spring when we got to the village it was beached near the government dock, abandoned. I wanted to see what the little house was like, how they had lived; I was sure there would be a miniature table and chairs, beds that folded down out of the walls, flowered window curtains. We climbed up; the door was open but inside it was bare wood, not even painted; there was no furniture at all and the stove was gone. The only things we could find were two rusted razor blades on the windowsill and some pictures drawn on the walls in pencil.

I thought they were plants or fish, some of them were shaped like clams, but my brother laughed, which meant he knew something I didn't; I nagged at him until he explained. I was shocked, not by those parts of the body, we'd been told about those, but that they should be cut off like that from the bodies that ought to have gone with them, as though they could detach themselves and crawl around on their own like snails.

I'd forgotten about that; but of course they were magic drawings like the ones in caves. You draw on the wall what's important to you, what you're hunting. They had enough food, no need to draw tinned peas and Argentine corned beef, and that's what they wanted instead during those monotonous and not at all idyllic trips up and down the lake, nothing to do but play cards, they must have detested it, back and forth chained to the logs. All of them dead now or old, they probably hated each other.

The bass struck on both lines at once. They fought hard, the rods doubled over. David landed one but Joe let his escape into the labyrinth of sticks, where it wound the line around a branch and snapped it.

"Hey," David was saying, "kill it for me." The bass was fierce, it was flipping around the inside of the canoe. It spat water from its undershot jaw with a hissing sound; it was either terrified or enraged, I couldn't tell which.

"You do it," I said, handing him the knife. "I showed you how, remember?"

Thud of metal on fishbone, skull, neckless headbody, the fish is whole, I couldn't anymore, I had no right to. We didn't need it, our proper food was tin cans. We were committing this act, violation, for sport or amusement or pleasure, recreation they call it, these were no longer the right reasons. That's an explanation but no excuse my father used to say, a favorite maxim.

While they admired David's murder, cadaver, I took the bottle with the frogs in it out of the tackle box and unscrewed the top; they slipped into the water, green with black leopard spots and gold eyes, rescued. High school, each desk with a tray on it and a frog, exhaling ether, spread and pinned flat as a doily and slit open, the organs explored and clipped out, the detached heart still gulping slowly like an adam's apple, no martyr's letters on it, the intestines messy string. Pickled cat pumped full of plastic, red for the arteries, blue for the veins, at the hospital, the undertaker's. Find the brain of the worm, donate your body to science. Anything we could do to the animals we could do to each other: we practiced on them first.

Joe flipped his broken line back to me and I rummaged among the lures and found another leader, a lead sinker, another hook: accessory, accomplice.

The Americans had rounded the point, two of them in a silver canoe; they were barging towards us. I assessed them, their disguises: they weren't the bloated middle-aged kind, those would stick to powerboats and guides; they were younger, trimmer, with the candid, tanned astronaut finish valued by the magazines. When they were even with us their mouths curved open, showing duplicate sets of teeth, white and even as false ones.

"Gettin' any?" the front man said with a Midwestern accent; traditional greeting.

"Lots," David said, smiling back. I was expecting him to say something to them, insult them, but he didn't. They were quite large.

"Us too," the front one said. "We been in here three-four days, they been biting the whole time, caught our limit every day." They had a starry flag like all of them, a miniature decal sticker on the canoe bow. To show us we were in occupied territory.

"Well, see ya," the back one said. Their canoe moved past us towards the next beaver house.

Raygun fishing rods, faces impermeable as space-suit helmets, sniper eyes, they did it; guilt glittered on them like tinfoil. My brain recited the stories I'd been told about them: the ones who stuffed the pontoons of their seaplane with illegal fish, the ones who had a false bottom to their car, two hundred lake trout on dry ice, the game warden caught them by accident. "This is a lousy country," they said when he wouldn't take the bribe, "we ain't never coming back here." They got drunk and chased loons in their powerboats for fun, backtracking on the loon as it dived, not giving it a chance to fly, until it drowned or got chopped up in the propeller blades. Senseless killing, it was a game; after the war they'd been bored.

The sunset was fading, at the other side of the sky the black was coming up. We took the fish back, four of them by now, and I cut a Y-shaped sapling stringer to go through the gills.

"Poo," Anna said to us, "you smell like a fish market."

David said "Wish we had some beer. Maybe we could get some off the Yanks, they're the type."

I went down to the lake with the bar of soap to wash the fish blood off my hands. Anna followed me.

"God," she said, "what'm I going to do? I forgot my makeup, he'll kill me."

I studied her: in the twilight her face was gray. "Maybe he won't notice," I said.

"He'll notice, don't you worry. Not now maybe, it hasn't all rubbed off, but in the morning. He wants me to look like a young chick all the time, if I don't he gets mad."

"You could let your face get really dirty," I said.

She didn't answer that. She sat down on the rock and rested her forehead on her knees. "He'll get me for it," she said fatalistically. "He's got this little set of rules. If I break one of them I get punished, except he keeps changing them so I'm never sure. He's crazy, there's something missing in him, you know what I mean? He likes to make me cry because he can't do it himself."

"But that can't be serious," I said, "the makeup thing."

A sound came out of her throat, a cough or a laugh. "It's not just that; it's something for him to use. He watches me all the time, he waits for excuses. Then either he won't screw at all or he slams it in so hard it hurts. I guess it's awful of me to say that." Her eggwhite eyes turned toward me in the half-darkness. "But if you said any of this to him he'd just make funny cracks about it, he says I have a mind like a soap opera, he says I invent it. But I really don't, you know." She was appealing to me for judgment but she didn't trust me, she was afraid I would talk to him about it behind her back.

"Maybe you should leave," I said, offering my solution, "or get a divorce."

"Sometimes I think he wants me to, I can't tell anymore. It used to be good, then I started to really love him and he can't stand that, he can't stand having me love him. Isn't that funny?" She had my mother's leather jacket over her shoulders, she'd brought it because she didn't have a heavy sweater. With Anna's head attached to it it was incongruous, diminished. I tried to think about my mother but she was blanked out; the only thing that remained was a story she once told about how, when she was little, she and her sister had made wings for themselves out of an old umbrella; they'd jumped off the barn roof, attempting to fly, and she broke both her ankles. She would laugh about it but the story seemed to me then chilly and sad, the failure unbearable.

"Sometimes I think he'd like me to die," Anna said, "I have dreams about it."

We walked back and I built up the fire and mixed some cocoa, using powdered milk. Everything was dark now except for the flames, sparks going up in spirals, coals underneath pulsing red when the night breeze hit them. We sat on the groundsheets, David with his arm around Anna, Joe and I a foot apart.

"This reminds me of Girl Guides," Anna said in the cheerful voice I once thought was hers. She began to sing, the notes hesitant, quavering:

"There'll be bluebirds over
The white cliffs of Dover
Tomorrow, when the world is free. . . ."

The words went out towards the shadows, smoke-thin, evaporating. Across the lake a barred owl was calling, quick and soft like a wing beating against the eardrum, cutting across the pattern of her voice, negating her. She glanced behind her: she felt it.

"Now everybody sing," she said, clapping her hands.

David said "Well, goodnight, children," and he and Anna went into their tent. The tent lit up from inside for a moment, flashlight, then went out.

"Coming?" Joe said.

"In a minute." I wanted to give him time to go to sleep.

I sat in the dark, the stroking sound of the night lake surrounding me. In the distance the Americans' campfire glowed, a dull red cyclops eye: the enemy lines. I wished evil toward them: Let them suffer, I prayed, tip their canoe, burn them, rip them open. Owl: answer, no answer.

I crawled into the tent through the mosquito netting; I groped for the flashlight but didn't switch it on, I didn't want to disturb him. I undressed by touch; he was obscure beside me, inert, comforting as a log. Perhaps that was the only time there could be anything like love, when he was asleep, demanding nothing. I passed my hand lightly over his shoulder as I would touch a tree or a stone.

But he wasn't sleeping; he moved, reached over for me.

"I'm sorry," I said, "I thought you were asleep."

"Okay," he said, "I give up, you win. We'll forget everything I said and do it like you want, back to the way it was before, right?"

It was too late, I couldn't. "No," I said. I had already moved out.

His hand tightened in anger on my arm; then he let go. "Sweet flaming balls of Christ," he said. His outline lifted in the darkness, I crouched down, he was going to hit me; but he turned over away from me, muffling himself in the sleeping bag.

My heart bumped, I held still, translating the noises on the other side of the canvas wall. Squeaks, shuffling in the dry leaves, grunting, nocturnal animals; no danger.

CHAPTER FIFTEEN

The tent roof was translucent, wet parchment, spotted on the outside with early dew. Bird voices twirled over my ears, intricate as skaters or running water, the air filling with liquid syllables.

In the middle of the night there was a roar, Joe having a nightmare. I touched him, it was safe, he was trapped in the straitjacket sleeping bag. He sat up, not yet awake.

"This is the wrong room," he said.

"What was it?" I asked. "What were you dreaming?" I wanted to know, perhaps I could remember how. But he folded over and went back.

My hand was beside me; it had the cured-hide smell of wood smoke mingled with sweat and earth, fish lingering, smell of the past. At the cabin we could soak the clothes we'd been wearing, scrub the forest out of them, renew our coating of soap and lotion.

I dressed and went down to the lake and dipped my face into it. This water was not clear like the water in the main lake: it was brownish, complicated by more kinds of life crowded more closely together, and it was colder. The rock ledge dropped straight down, lake of the edge. I woke the others.

After I'd cleaned the fish I dipped them in flour and fried them and boiled coffee. The fish flesh was white, blue-veined; it tasted like underwater and reeds. They ate, not talking much; they hadn't slept well.

Anna's face in the daylight was dried and slightly shriveled without its cream underfilm and pink highlights; her nose was sunburned and she had prune crinkles under her eyes. She kept turned away from David, but he didn't seem to notice, he didn't say anything, except when she knocked her foot against his cup and tipped some of his coffee out onto the ground. Then all he said was "Watch it Anna, you're getting sloppy."

"Do you want to fish anymore this morning?" I said to David, but he shook his head: "Let's go take that rock painting."

I burned the fishbones, the spines fragile as petals; the innards I planted in the forest. They were not seeds, in the spring no minnows would sprout up. Deer skeleton we found on the island, shreds of flesh on it still, he said the wolves had killed it in the winter because it was old, that was natural. If we dived for them and used our teeth to catch them, fighting on their own grounds, that would be fair, but hooks were substitutes and air wasn't their place.

The two of them fiddled with the movie camera, adjusting and discussing it; then we could start.

According to the map the rock painting was in a bay near the Americans' camp. They didn't seem to be up yet, there was no smoke coming from their fireplace. I thought, maybe it worked and they're dead.

I looked for a dip in the shore, a line that would fit the mapline. It was there, site of the X, unmistakable: cliff with sheer face, the kind they would have chosen to paint on, no other flat rock in sight. He had been here and long before him the original ones, the first explorers, leaving behind them their sign, word, but not its meaning. I leaned forward, scanning the cliff surface; we let the canoes drift in sideways till they scraped the stone.

"Where is it?" David said; and to Joe, "You'll have to steady the canoe, there's no way we can shoot from land."

"It might be hard to see at first," I said. "Faded. It ought to be right here somewhere." But it wasn't: no man with antlers, nothing like red paint or even a stain, the rock surface extended under my hand, coarse-grained, lunar, broken only by a pink-white vein of quartz that ran across it, a diagonal marking the slow tilt of the land; nothing human.

Either I hadn't remembered the map properly or what he'd written on the map was wrong. I'd reasoned it out, unraveled the clues in his puzzle the way he taught us and they'd led nowhere. I felt as though he'd lied to me.

"Who told you about it?" David said, cross-examining.

"I just thought it was here," I said. "Someone mentioned it. Maybe it was another lake." For a moment I knew: of course, the lake had been flooded, it would be twenty feet under water. But that was the other lake, this one was part of a separate system, the watershed divided them. The map said he'd found them on the main lake too; according to the letter he'd been taking pictures of them. But when I'd searched the cabin there had been no camera. No drawings, no camera, I'd done it wrong, I would have to look again.

They were disappointed, they'd expected something picturesque or bizarre, something they could utilize. He hadn't followed the rules, he'd cheated, I wanted to confront him, demand an explanation: You said it would be here.

We turned back. The Americans were up, they were still alive; they were setting out in their canoe, the front one had his fishing rod trailing over the bow. Joe and I were ahead, we approached them at right angles.

"Hi," the front one said, to me, bleached grin. "Any luck?" That was their armor, bland ignorance, heads empty as weather balloons: with that they could defend themselves against anything. Straight power, they mainlined it; I imagined the surge of electricity, nerve juice, as they hit it, brought it down, flapping like a crippled plane. The innocents get slaughtered because they exist, I thought, there is nothing inside the happy killers to restrain them, no conscience or piety; for them the only things worthy of life were human, their own kind of human, framed in the proper clothes and gimmicks, laminated. It would have been different in those countries where an animal is the soul of an ancestor or the child of a god, at least they would have felt guilt.

"We aren't fishing," I said, my lips clipping the words. My arm wanted to swing the paddle sideways, blade into his head: his eyes would blossom outward, his skull shatter like an egg.

The corners of his mouth wilted. "Oh," he said. "Say, what part of the States are you all from? It's hard to tell, from your accent. Fred and me guessed Ohio."

"We're not from the States," I said, annoyed that he'd mistaken me for one of them.

"No kidding?" His face lit up, he'd seen a real native. "You from here?"

"Yes," I said. "We all are."

"So are we," said the back one unexpectedly.

The front one held out his hand, though five feet of water separated us. "I'm from Sarnia and Fred here, my brother-in-law, is from Toronto. We thought you were Yanks, with the hair and all."

I was furious with them, they'd disguised themselves. "What're you doing with that flag on your boat then?" I said, my voice loud, it surprised them. The front one withdrew his hand.

"Oh that," he said with a shrug. "I'm a Mets fan, have been for years, I always root for the underdog. Bought that when I was down there for the game, the year they won the pennant." I looked more closely at the sticker: it wasn't a flag at all, it was a blue-and-white oblong with red printing, GO METS.

David and Anna had caught up with us. "You a Mets fan?" David said. "Out of sight." He slid his canoe in beside theirs and they shook hands.

But they'd killed the heron anyway. It doesn't matter what country they're from, my head said, they're still Americans, they're what's in store for us, what we are turning into. They spread themselves like a virus, they get into the brain and take over the cells and the cells change from inside and the ones that have the disease can't tell the difference. Like the Late Show sci-fi movies, creatures from outer space, body snatchers injecting themselves into you, dispossessing your brain, their eyes blank eggshells behind the dark glasses. If you look like them and talk like them and think like them then you are them, I was saying, you speak their language, a language is everything you do.

But how did they evolve, where did the first one come from, they weren't an invasion from another planet, they were terrestrial. How did we get bad. For us when we were small the origin was Hitler, he was the great evil, many-tentacled, ancient and indestructible as the Devil. It didn't matter that he had shrunk to a few cinders and teeth by the time I heard about him; I was certain he was alive, he was in the comic books my brother brought home in the winters and he was in my brother's scrapbook too, he was the swastikas on the tanks, if only he could be destroyed everyone would be saved, safe. When our father made bonfires to burn the weeds we would throw sticks into the flames and chant "Hitler's house is burning down, My Fair Lady-O"; we knew it helped. All possible horrors were measured against him. But Hitler was gone and the thing remained; whatever it was, even then, moving away from them as they smirked and waved goodbye, I was asking Are the Americans worse than Hitler. It was like cutting up a tapeworm, the pieces grew.

We landed at the campsite and rolled up the sleeping bags and struck the tents and packed them. I covered the toilet hole and smoothed it, camouflaging it with sticks and needles. Leave no traces.

David wanted to stay and have lunch with the Americans and talk about baseball scores, but I said the wind was against us, we would need the time. I hurried them, I wanted to get away, from my own anger as well as from the friendly metal killers.

We reached the first portage at eleven. My feet moved over the rocks and mud, stepping in my own day-old footprints, back-tracking; in my brain the filaments, trails reconnected and branched, we killed other people besides Hitler, before my brother went to school and learned about him and the games became war games. Earlier we would play we were animals; our parents were the humans, the enemies who might shoot us or catch us, we would hide from them. But sometimes the animals had power too: one time we were a swarm of bees, we gnawed the fingers, feet and nose off our least favorite doll, ripped her cloth body open and pulled out the stuffing, it was gray and fluffy like the insides of mattresses; then we threw her into the lake. She floated and they found the body and asked us how she got lost, and we lied and said we didn't know. Killing was wrong, we had been told that: only enemies and food could be killed. Of course the doll wasn't hurt, it wasn't alive; though children think everything is alive.

At the midway pond the heron was still there, hanging in the hot sunlight like something in a butcher's window, desecrated, unredeemed. It smelled worse. Around its head the flies vibrated, laying their eggs. The king who learned to speak with animals, in the story he ate a magic leaf and they revealed a treasure, a conspiracy, they saved his life; what would they really say? Accusation, lament, an outcry of rage; but they had no spokesman.

I felt a sickening complicity, sticky as glue, blood on my hands, as though I had been there and watched without saying No or doing anything to stop it: one of the silent guarded faces in the crowd. The trouble some people have being German, I thought, I have being human. In a way it was stupid to be more disturbed by a dead bird than by those other things, the wars and riots and the massacres in the newspapers. But for the wars and riots there was always an explanation, people wrote books about them saying why they happened: the death of the heron was causeless, undiluted.

The laboratory, he was older then. He never caught birds, they were too quick for him, what he caught was the slower things. He kept them in jars and tin cans on a board shelf back in the forest, near the swamp; to reach them he made a secret path, marked only by small notches on the trees, a code. Sometimes he forgot to feed them or perhaps it was too cold at night, because when I went there by myself that day one of the snakes was dead and several of the frogs, their skin dry and their yellow stomachs puffed up, and the crayfish was floating in the clouded water with its legs uppermost like a spider's. I emptied those bottles into the swamp. The other things, the ones still alive, I let out. I rinsed the jars and tins and left them in a row on the board.

After lunch I hid but I had to come out finally for dinner. He couldn't say anything in front of them but he knew it was me, there was no one else. He was so angry he was pale, his eyes twisted as though they couldn't see me. "They were mine," he said. Afterward he trapped other things and changed the place; this time he wouldn't tell me. I found it anyway but I was afraid to let them out again. Because of my fear they were killed.

I didn't want there to be wars and death, I wanted them not to exist; only rabbits with their colored egg houses, sun and moon orderly above the flat earth, summer always, I wanted everyone to be happy. But his pictures were more accurate, the weapons, the disintegrating soldiers: he was a realist, that protected him. He almost drowned once but he would never allow that to happen again, by the time he left he was ready.

The leeches were there again in the tepid pond water, clumps of young ones hanging from the lily-pad stems like fingers, larger ones swimming, flat and soft as noodles. I didn't like them but distaste excused nothing. In the other lake they never bothered us when we were swimming but we would catch the mottled kind, the bad kind he called them, and throw them on the campfire when our mother wasn't watching, she prohibited cruelty. I didn't mind that so much, if only they would die; but they would writhe out and crawl painfully, coated with ashes and pine needles, back towards the lake, seeming to be able to smell where the water was. Then he would pick them up with two sticks and put them back in the flames again.

It wasn't the city that was wrong, the inquisitors in the schoolyard, we weren't better than they were; we just had different victims. To become like a little child again, a barbarian, a vandal: it was in us too, it was innate. A thing closed in my head, hand, synapse, cutting off my escape: that was the wrong way, the entrance, redemption was elsewhere, I must have overlooked it.

We reached the main lake and reloaded the canoes and shoved them out over the snarl of logs. In the bay the felled trees and numbered posts showed where the surveyors had been, power company. My country, sold or drowned, a reservoir; the people were sold along with the land and the animals, a bargain, sale, *solde. Les soldes* they called them, sellouts, the flood would depend on who got elected, not here but somewhere else.

CHAPTER SIXTEEN

It was the sixth day, I had to find out; it would be my last chance, tomorrow Evans was coming to take us back. My brain was rushing, covering over the bad things and filling the empty spaces with an embroidery of calculations and numbers, I needed to finish, I had never finished anything. To be exact, to condense myself to a pinpoint, impaling a fact, a certainty.

As soon as I could I rechecked the map. The X was where it should have been, I hadn't made a mistake. There was only one theory I could retreat to: some of the crosses might be places he thought suitable for paintings but hadn't examined yet. I ran my finger around the shore, looking for the nearest marked site; it was the cliff where we had been fishing the first evening, it would be underwater, I would have to dive. If I found something it would vindicate him, I would know he'd been right; if not I could try the next X, near the heron island, and then the next one.

I had my bathing suit on already; we'd been washing the clothes down on the dock, rubbing them on the ribbed washboard with the worn-down bar of yellow soap, standing in the lake to rinse them. They were pegged out to dry now on the line behind the cabin, shirts, jeans, socks, Anna's colored lingerie, our cast skins. Anna had seemed more relaxed, she hummed from behind her fresh façade of makeup. She had stayed down by the lake to shampoo the smoke out of her hair. I pulled on a sweatshirt in case there were Americans. Before leaving I searched once more for his camera, the one he must have used to take the photographs, but it wasn't there; he must have had it with him. At the time, the last time.

I had started down the steps before I saw them. The three of them were on the dock, split into parts by the tree-trunk bars. Anna was kneeling in her orange bikini, with a towel draped over her head like a nun; David was standing over her, hands on hips. Joe was further back with the movie camera, sitting on the dock with his legs dangling, head averted as if waiting politely for them to be through. When I heard what they were saying I stood still. The canoes were there and I needed one of them but it was too dangerous. It was a calm day, the sound carried.

"Come on, take it off," David said; his light-humor voice.

"I wasn't bothering you." Anna was muted, avoiding.

"It won't hurt you, we need a naked lady."

"What the hell for?" Anna was peevish now, her veiled head upturned; her eyes would be squinting.

"Random Samples," David said patiently, and I thought, They've used up everything, there's nothing left here now for them to take pictures of except each other, next it will be me. "You'll go in beside the dead bird, it's your chance for stardom, you've always wanted fame. You'll get to be on Educational TV," he added as though it was a special bribe.

"Oh for Christ's sake," Anna said. She picked up her murder mystery again and pretended to read.

"Come on, we need a naked lady with big tits and a big ass," David said in the same tender voice; I recognized that menacing gentleness, at school it always went before the trick, the punchline.

"Look, will you leave me alone?" Anna said. "I'm minding my own business, mind yours why don't you." She stood up, her towel sliding off, and tried to get past him to the land, but he sidestepped in front of her.

"I won't take her if she doesn't want to," Joe said.

"It's token resistance," David said, "she wants to, she's an exhibitionist at heart. She likes her lush body, don't you? Even if she is getting too fat."

"Don't think I don't know what you're trying to do," Anna said, as though she guessed a riddle. "You're trying to humiliate me."

"What's humiliating about your body, darling?" David said caressingly. "We all love it, you ashamed of it? That's pretty stingy of you, you should share the wealth; not that you don't."

Anna was furious now, goaded, her voice rose. "Fuck off, you want bloody everything, don't you, you can't use that stuff on me."

"Why not," David said evenly, "it works. Now just take it off like a good girl or I'll have to take it off for you."

"Leave her alone," Joe said, swinging his legs, bored or excited, it was impossible to tell.

I wanted to run down to the dock and stop them, fighting was wrong, we weren't allowed to, if we did both sides got punished as in a real war. So we battled in secret, undeclared, and after a while I no longer fought back because I never won. The only defense was flight, invisibility. I sat down on the top step.

"Shut up, she's my wife," David said. His hand clamped down above her elbow. She jerked away, then I saw his arms go around her as if to kiss her and she was in the air, upside down over his shoulder, hair hanging in damp ropes. "Okay, twatface," he said, "is it off or into the lake?"

Anna's fists grabbed bunches of his shirt. "If I go in, you go in too." The words spurted from behind her fallen hair, she was kicking, I couldn't see whether she was laughing or crying.

"Shoot," David said to Joe, and to Anna, "I'll count to ten."

Joe swiveled the camera and trained it on them like a bazooka or a strange instrument of torture and pressed the button, lever, sinister whirr.

"All right," Anna said under its coercion, "you shmuck bastard, God damn you." He set her down and stepped aside. Her arms, elbows out, struggled with the fastener like a beetle's on its back and the top dropped away: I saw her cut in half, one breast on either side of a thin tree.

"Bottoms too," David said as though to a recalcitrant child. Anna glanced at him, contemptuous, and bent. "Look sexy now, move it; give us a little dance."

Anna stood for a moment, brown-red with yellow fur and white markings like underwear, glaring at them. Then she stuck her middle finger in the air at them and ran to the end of the dock and jumped into the lake. It was a bellyflop, the water splattered out like a dropped egg. She came up with her hair in streaks over her forehead and started to swim around toward the sand point, clumsy, arms flailing.

"Get that?" David said mildly over his shoulder.

"Some of it," Joe said. "Maybe you could order her to do it again." I thought he was being sarcastic but I wasn't sure. He began to unscrew the camera from the tripod.

I could hear Anna splashing and then stumbling below on the sand point; she was really crying now, her indrawn breaths rasping. The bushes rustled, she swore; then she appeared over the top of the hill, she must have climbed up by holding on to the leaning trees. Her pink face was dissolving, her skin was covered with sand and pine needles like a burned leech. She went into the cabin without looking at me or saying anything.

I stood up. Joe was gone but David was still on the dock, sitting now crosslegged. One at a time they were safer; I went down for the canoe.

"Hi," he said, "how goes it?" He didn't know I'd been watching. He had his shoes off and was picking at a toenail as though nothing had happened.

David is like me, I thought, we are the ones that don't know how to love, there is something essential missing in us, we were born that way, Madame at the store with one hand, atrophy of the heart. Joe and Anna are lucky, they do it badly and suffer because of it: but it's better to see than to be blind, even though that way you had to let in the crimes and atrocities too. Or perhaps we are normal and the ones who can love are freaks, they have an extra organ, like the vestigial eye in the foreheads of amphibians they've never found the use for.

Anna's bikini lay on the dock, crumpled, a shed chrysalis. He picked up the top and began pleating and unpleating the strap. I hadn't meant to say anything about it, it wasn't my concern, but I found myself asking him anyway. "Why did you do that?" My voice was neutral and I realized it wasn't for Anna I was asking, I wasn't defending her; it was for myself, I needed to understand.

For a moment he acted. "What?" he said, grinning and innocent.

"What you just did to her."

He looked hard at me to see if I was accusing him but I was untying the canoe, I was impersonal as a wall, a confessional, and that reassured him. "You don't know what she does to me," he said with a slight whine. "She asks for it, she makes me do it." His voice turned crafty. "She goes with other men, she thinks she can get away with it, but she's too dumb, every time I find out; I can smell it on her. Not that I'd mind if she'd do it openly and be honest about it, God knows, it's not that I'm jealous." He smiled broadmindedly. "But she's devious, I can't stand that."

Anna hadn't told me, she had left something out; or else he was lying. "But she loves you," I said.

"Bullshit," he said, "she's trying to cut my balls off." His eyes were sad rather than hostile, as though he had once believed better of her.

"She loves you," I repeated, petals off a daisy; it was the magic word but it couldn't work because I had no faith. My husband, saying it over and over like a Dial the Weather recording, trying to engrave it on me; and with the same bewilderment, as though I was the one who'd been hurting him and not the other way round. An accident, that's what he called it.

"She never tells *me* that," he said. "I get the impression she wants out, she's waiting for the chance to leave. But I haven't asked, we don't talk much any more except with other people around."

"Maybe you should," I said; unconvinced, unconvincing.

He shrugged. "What would we talk about? She's too dumb, she can't figure out what I'm saying to her, Jesus, she moves her lips when she watches the TV even. She doesn't know anything, every time she opens her mouth she makes an ass of herself. I know what you're thinking," he said, almost pleading, "but I'm all for the equality of women; she just doesn't happen to be equal and that's not my fault, is it? What I married was a pair of boobs, she manipulated me into it, it was when I was studying for the ministry, nobody knew any better then. But that's life." He wiggled his moustache and gave a Woody Woodpecker laugh, his eyes baffled.

"I think you could work it out," I said. I braced the paddle across the gunwales and clambered into the canoe. I remembered what Anna had said about emotional commitments: they've made one, I thought, they hate each other; that must be almost as absorbing as love. The barometer couple in their wooden house, enshrined in their niche on Paul's front porch, my ideal; except they were glued there, condemned to oscillate back and forth, sun and rain, without escape. When he saw her next there would be no recantations, no elaborate reconciliation or forgiveness, they were beyond that. Neither of them would mention it, they had reached a balance almost like peace. Our mother and father at the sawhorse behind the cabin, mother holding the tree, white birch, father sawing, sun through the branches lighting their hair, grace.

The canoe pivoted. "Hey," he said, "where you off to?"

"Oh . . ." I gestured towards the lake.

"Want a stern paddler?" he said. "I'm great, I've had lots of practice by now."

He sounded wistful, as though he needed company, but I didn't want him with me, I'd have to explain what I was doing and he wouldn't be able to help. "No," I said, "thanks just the same." I knelt, slanting the canoe to one side.

"Okay," he said, "see you later, alligator." He unwound his legs and stood up and strolled off the dock toward the cabin, his striped T-shirt flashing between the slats of the trees, receding behind me as I glided from the bay into the open water.

CHAPTER SEVENTEEN

I moved toward the cliff. The sun sloped, it was morning still, the light not yellow but clear white. Overhead a plane, so far up I could hardly hear it, threading the cities together with its trail of smoke; an X in the sky, unsacred crucifix. The shape of the heron flying above us the first evening we fished, legs and neck stretched, wings outspread, a blue-gray cross, and the other heron or was it the same one, hanging wrecked from the tree. Whether it died willingly, consented, whether Christ died willingly, anything that suffers and dies instead of us is Christ; if they didn't kill birds and fish they would have killed us. The animals die that we may live, they are substitute people, hunters in the fall killing the deer, that is Christ also. And we eat them, out of cans or otherwise; we are eaters of death, dead Christ-flesh resurrecting inside us, granting us life. Canned Spam, canned Jesus, even the plants must be Christ. But we refuse to worship; the body worships with blood and muscle but the thing in the knob head will not, wills not to, the head is greedy, it consumes but does not give thanks.

I reached the cliff, there were no Americans. I edged along it, estimating the best place to dive: it faced east, the sun was on it, it was the right time of day; I would start at the left-hand side. Diving by myself was hazardous, there ought to be another person. But I thought I remembered how: we took the canoes or we built rafts from strayed logs and board ends, they would often snap their ropes and escape in the spring when the ice went out; sometimes we would come across them again later, drifting loose like pieces broken from a glacier.

I shipped the paddle and took off my sweatshirt. I would dive several feet out from the rockface and then swim down and in: otherwise I'd risk hitting my head, the drop looked sheer but there might be a ledge underwater. I knelt, facing backwards with both knees on the stern seat, then put a foot on each gunwale and stood up slowly. I bent my knees and straightened, the canoe teetered like a springboard. My other shape was in the water, not my reflection but my shadow, foreshortened, outline blurred, rays streaming out from around the head.

My spine whipped, I hit the water and kicked myself down, sliding through the lake strata, gray to darker gray, cool to cold. I arched sideways and the rockface loomed up, gray pink brown; I worked along it, touching it with my fingers, snail touch on slimesurface, the water unfocusing my eyes. Then my lungs began to clutch and I curled and rose, letting out air like a frog, my hair swirling over my face, toward the canoe, where it hung split between water and air, mediator and life raft. I canted it with my weight and rolled into it over the side and rested; I hadn't seen anything. My arms ached from the day before and the new effort, my body stumbled, it remembered the motions only imperfectly, like learning to walk after illness.

I waited a few minutes, then moved the canoe farther along and dived again, my eyes straining, not knowing what shape to expect, handprint or animal, the lizard body with horns and tail and front-facing head, bird or canoe with stick paddlers; or a small thing, an abstraction, a circle, a moon; or a long distorted figure, stiff and childish, a human. Air gave out, I broke surface. Not here, it must be further along or deeper down; I was convinced it was there, he would not have marked and numbered the map so methodically for nothing, that would not be consistent, he always observed his own rules, axioms.

On the next try I thought I saw it, a blotch, a shadow, just as I turned to go up. I was dizzy, my vision was beginning to cloud, while I rested my ribs panted, I ought to pause, half an hour at least; but I was elated, it was down there, I would find it. Reckless, I balanced and plunged.

Pale green, then darkness, layer after layer, deeper than before, seabottom; the water seemed to have thickened, in it pinprick lights flicked and darted, red and blue, yellow and white, and I saw they were fish, the chasm-dwellers, fins lined with phosphorescent sparks, teeth neon. It was wonderful that I was down so far, I watched the fish, they swam like patterns on closed eyes, my legs and arms were weightless, free-floating; I almost forgot to look for the cliff and the shape.

It was there but it wasn't a painting, it wasn't on the rock. It was below me, drifting towards me from the furthest level where there was no life, a dark oval trailing limbs. It was blurred but it had eyes, they were open, it was something I knew about, a dead thing, it was dead.

I turned, fear gushing out of my mouth in silver, panic closing my throat, the scream kept in and choking me. The green canoe was far above me, sunlight radiating around it, a beacon, safety.

But there was not one canoe, there were two, the canoe had twinned or I was seeing double. My hand came out of the water and gripped the gunwale, then my head; water ran from my nose, I gulped breath, stomach and lungs contracting, my hair sticky like weeds, the lake was horrible, it was filled with death, it was touching me.

Joe was in the other canoe. "He told me you went over this way," he said. He must have been almost there before I dived but I hadn't seen him. I couldn't say anything, my lungs were urgent, my arms would hardly pull me into the canoe.

"What the hell are you doing?" he said.

I lay on the bottom of the canoe and closed my eyes; I wanted him not to be there. It formed again in my head: at first I thought it was my drowned brother, hair floating around the face, image I'd kept from before I was born; but it couldn't be him, he had not drowned after all, he was elsewhere. Then I recognized it: it wasn't ever my brother I'd been remembering, that had been a disguise.

I knew when it was, it was in a bottle curled up, staring out at me like a cat pickled; it had huge jelly eyes and fins instead of hands, fish gills, I couldn't let it out, it was dead already, it had drowned in air. It was there when I woke up, suspended in the air above me like a chalice, an evil grail and I thought, Whatever it is, part of myself or a separate creature, I killed it. It wasn't a child but it could have been one, I didn't allow it.

Water was dripping from me into the canoe, I lay in a puddle. I had been furious with them, I knocked it off the table, my life on the floor, glass egg and shattered blood, nothing could be done.

That was wrong, I never saw it. They scraped it into a bucket and threw it wherever they throw them, it was traveling through the sewers by the time I woke, back to the sea, I stretched my hand up to it and it vanished. The bottle had been logical, pure logic, remnant of the trapped and decaying animals, secreted by my head, enclosure, something to keep the death away from me. Not even a hospital, not even that sanction of legality, official procedures. A house it was, shabby front room with magazines, purple runner on the hall floor, vines and blossoms, the smell of lemon polish, furtive doors and whispers, they wanted you out fast. Pretense of the non-nurse, her armpits acid, face powdered with solicitude. Stumble along the hall, from flower to flower, her criminal hand on my elbow, other arm against the wall. Ring on my finger. It was all real enough, it was enough reality for ever, I couldn't accept it, that mutilation, ruin I'd made, I needed a different version. I pieced it together the best way I could, flattening it, scrapbook, collage, pasting over the wrong parts. A faked album, the memories fraudulent as passports; but a paper house was better than none and I could almost live in it, I'd lived in it until now.

He hadn't gone with me to the place where they did it; his own children, the real ones, were having a birthday party. But he came afterward to collect me. It was a hot day, when we stepped out into the sun we couldn't see for an instant. It wasn't a wedding, there were no pigeons, the post office and the lawn were in another part of the city where I went for stamps; the fountain with the dolphins and the cherub with half a face was from the company town, I'd put it in so there would be something of mine.

"It's over," he said, "feel better?"

I was emptied, amputated; I stank of salt and antiseptic, they had planted death in me like a seed.

"You're cold," he said, "come on, we'd better get you home." Scrutinizing my face in the light, hands on the wheel, tough, better this way. In my deflated lap there was a purse, suitcase. I couldn't go there, home, I never went there again, I sent them a postcard.

They never knew, about that or why I left. Their own innocence, the reason I couldn't tell them; perilous innocence, closing them in glass, their artificial garden, greenhouse. They didn't teach us about evil, they didn't understand about it, how could I describe it to them? They were from another age, prehistoric, when everyone got married and had a family, children growing in the yard like sunflowers; remote as Eskimos or mastodons.

I opened my eyes and sat up. Joe was still there beside me; he was holding on to the edge of my canoe.

"You all right?" he said. His voice came to me faintly, as though muffled.

He said I should do it, he made me do it; he talked about it as though it was legal, simple, like getting a wart removed. He said it wasn't a person, only an animal; I should have seen that was no different, it was hiding in me as if in a burrow and instead of granting it sanctuary I let them catch it. I could have said No but I didn't; that made me one of them too, a killer. After the slaughter, the murder, he couldn't believe I didn't want to see him any more; it bewildered him, he resented me for it, he expected gratitude because he arranged it for me, fixed me so I was as good as new; others, he said, wouldn't have bothered. Since then I'd carried that death around inside me, layering it over, a cyst, a tumor, black pearl; the gratitude I felt now was not for him.

I had to go onto the shore and leave something: that was what you were supposed to do, leave a piece of your clothing as an offering. I regretted the nickels I'd taken dutifully for the collection plate, I got so little in return: no power remained in their bland oleo-tinted Jesus prints or in the statues of the other ones, rigid and stylized, holy triple name shrunken to swearwords. These gods, here on the shore or in the water, unacknowledged or forgotten, were the only ones who had ever given me anything I needed; and freely.

The map crosses and the drawings made sense now: at the beginning he must have been only locating the rock paintings, deducing them, tracing and photographing them, a retirement hobby; but then he found out about them. The Indians did not own salvation but they had once known where it lived and their signs marked the sacred places, the places where you could learn the truth. There was no painting at White Birch Lake and none here, because his later drawings weren't copied from things on the rocks. He had discovered new places, new oracles, they were things he was seeing the way I had seen, true vision; at the end, after the failure of logic. When it happened the first time he must have been terrified, it would be like stepping through a usual door and finding yourself in a different galaxy, purple trees and red moons and a green sun.

I swung the paddle and Joe's hand came unstuck and the canoe went towards the shore. I slipped on my canvas shoes and bundled up the sweatshirt and stepped out, looping the rope to a tree, then I climbed the slope towards the cliff, trees on one side, rockface on the other, balsam smell, underbrush scratching my bare legs. There was a ledge, I'd noticed it from the lake, I could throw my sweatshirt onto it. I didn't know the names of the ones I was making the offering to; but they were there, they had power. Candles in front of statues, crutches on the steps, flowers in jam jars by the roadside crosses, gratitude for cures, however wished-for and partial. Clothing was better, it was closer and more essential; and the gift had been greater, more than a hand or an eye, feeling was beginning to seep back into me, I tingled like a foot that's been asleep.

I was opposite the ledge; reindeer moss feathered it, clumps intricate with branches, the tips red, glowing in the sun. It was only an arm's length away on the sheer cliff; I folded my sweatshirt neatly and reached it across.

Behind me something lumbered, crashing. It was Joe, I'd forgotten about him. When he caught up with me he took me by the shoulders.

"You all right?" he said again.

I didn't love him, I was far away from him, it was as though I was seeing him through a smeared window or glossy paper; he didn't belong here. But he existed, he deserved to be alive. I was wishing I could tell him how to change so he could get there, the place where I was.

"Yes," I said. I touched him on the arm with my hand. My hand touched his arm. Hand touched arm. Language divides us into fragments, I wanted to be whole.

He kissed me; I stood on my side of the window. When his head drew away I said "I don't love you," I was going to explain but he didn't seem to hear me, mouth on my shoulder, fingers at the clasp behind my back, then sliding down my flanks, he was pushing on me as though trying to fold up a lawn chair, he wanted me to lie down on the ground.

I stretched out inside my body, twigs and pine needles under me. At that moment I thought, Perhaps for him I am the entrance, as the lake was the entrance for me. The forest condensed in him, it was noon, the sun was behind his head; his face was invisible, the sun's rays coming out from a center of darkness, my shadow.

His hands descended, zipper sound, metal teeth on metal teeth, he was rising out of the fur husk, solid and heavy; but the cloth separated from him and I saw he was human, I didn't want him in me, sacrilege, he was one of the killers, the clay victims damaged and strewn behind him, and he hadn't seen, he didn't know about himself, his own capacity for death.

"Don't," I said, he was lowering himself down on me, "I don't want you to."

"What's wrong with you?" he said, angry; then he was pinning me, hands manacles, teeth against my lips, censoring me, he was shoving against me, his body insistent as one side of an argument.

I slid my arm between us, against his throat, windpipe, and pried his head away. "I'll get pregnant," I said, "it's the right time." It was the truth, it stopped him: flesh making more flesh, miracle, that frightens all of them.

He reached the dock first, outdistancing me, his fury propelling the canoe like a motor. By the time I got there he had vanished.

CHAPTER EIGHTEEN

There was no one in the cabin. It was different, larger, as though I hadn't been there for a long time: the half of me that had begun to return was not yet used to it. I went back outside and unhooked the gate of the fenced oblong and sat down on the swing, carefully, the ropes still held my weight; I swayed myself gently back and forth, keeping my feet on the ground. Rocks, trees, sandbox where I made houses with stones for windows. The birds were there, chicadees and jays; but they were wary of me, they weren't trained.

I turned the ring on my left-hand finger, souvenir: he gave it to me, plain gold, he said he didn't like ostentation, it got us into the motels easier, opener of doors; in the intervening time I wore it on a chain around my neck. The cold bathrooms, interchangeable, feel of tile on footsoles, walking into them wrapped in someone else's towel in the days of rubber sex, precautions. He would prop his watch on the night tables to be sure he wasn't late.

For him I could have been anyone but for me he was unique, the first, that's where I learned. I worshiped him, non-child-bride, idolater, I kept the scraps of his handwriting like saints' relics, he never wrote letters, all I had was the criticisms in red pencil he paperclipped to my drawings. C's and D's, he was an idealist, he said he didn't want our relationship as he called it to influence his aesthetic judgment. He didn't want our relationship to influence anything; it was to be kept separate from life. A certificate framed on the wall, his proof that he was still young.

He did say he loved me though, that part was true; I didn't make it up. It was the night I locked myself in and turned on the water in the bathtub and he cried on the other side of the door. When I gave up and came out he showed me snapshots of his wife and children, his reasons, his stuffed and mounted family, they had names, he said I should be mature.

I heard the thin dentist's-drill sound of a powerboat approaching, more Americans; I got off the swing and went halfway down the steps where I would be shielded by the trees. They slowed their motor and curved into the bay. I crouched and watched, at first I thought they were going to land: but they were only gazing, surveying, planning the attack and the takeover. They pointed up at the cabin and talked, flash of binoculars. Then they accelerated and headed off towards the cliff where the gods lived. But they wouldn't catch anything, they wouldn't be allowed. It was dangerous for them to go there without knowing about the power; they might hurt themselves, a false move, metal hooks lowered into the sacred water, that could touch it off like electricity or a grenade. I had endured it only because I had a talisman, my father had left me the guides, the man-animals and the maze of numbers.

It would be right for my mother to have left something for me also, a legacy. His was complicated, tangled, but hers would be simple as a hand, it would be final. I was not completed yet; there had to be a gift from each of them.

I wanted to search for it but David was jogging down the path from the outhouse. "Hi," he called, "you seen Anna?"

"No," I said. If I went back to the house or into the garden he would follow me and talk. I stood up and walked down the rest of the steps and ducked into the trail entrance through the long grass.

In the cool green among the trees, new trees and stumps, the stumps with charcoal crusts on them, scabby and crippled, survivors of an old disaster. Sight flowing ahead of me over the ground, eyes filtering the shapes, the names of things fading but their forms and uses remaining, the animals learned what to eat without nouns. Six leaves, three leaves, the root of this is crisp. White stems curved like question marks, fish-colored in the dim light, corpse plants, inedible. Finger-shaped yellow fungi, unclassified, I never memorized all of them; and further along a mushroom with cup and ring and chalk gills and a name: Death Angel, deadly poison. Beneath it the invisible part, threadlike underground network of which this was the solid flower, temporary as an icicle, growth frozen; tomorrow it would be melted but the roots would stay. If our bodies lived in the earth with only the hair sprouting up through the leaf mold it would seem as if that was all we were, filament plants.

The reason they invented coffins, to lock the dead in, preserve them, they put makeup on them; they didn't want them spreading or changing into anything else. The stone with the name and the date was on them to weight them down. She would have hated it, that box, she would have tried to get out; I ought to have stolen her out of that room and brought her here and let her go away by herself into the forest, she would have died anyway but quicker, lucidly, not in that glass case.

It sprang up from the earth, pure joy, pure death, burning white like snow.

The dry leaves shuffled behind me: he had shadowed me along the trail. "Hi, whatcha doin'?" he said.

I didn't turn or speak but he didn't wait for an answer, he sat down beside me and said "What's that?"

I had to concentrate in order to talk to him, the English words seemed imported, foreign; it was like trying to listen to two separate conversations, each interrupting the other. "A mushroom," I said. That wouldn't be enough, he would want a specific term. My mouth jumped like a stutterer's and the Latin appeared. "Amanita."

"Neat," he said, but he wasn't interested. I willed him to go away but he didn't; after a while he put his hand on my knee.

"Well?" he said.

I looked at him. His smile was like a benevolent uncle's; under his forehead there was a plan, it corrugated the skin. I pushed his hand off and he put it back again.

"How about it?" he said. "You wanted me to follow you."

His fingers were squeezing, he was drawing away some of the power, I would lose it and come apart again, the lies would recapture. "Please don't," I said.

"Come on now, don't give me a hassle," he said. "You're a groovy chick, you know the score, you aren't married." He reached his arm around me, invading, and pulled me over toward him; his neck was creased and freckled, soon he would have jowls, he smelled like scalp. His moustache whisked my face.

I twisted away and stood up. "Why are you doing this?" I said. "You're interfering." I wiped at my arm where he had touched it.

He didn't understand what I meant, he smiled even harder. "Don't get uptight," he said, "I won't tell Joe. It'll be great, it's good for you, keeps you healthy." Then he went "Yuk, yuk" like Goofy.

He was speaking about it as though it was an exercising program, athletic demonstration, ornamental swimming in a chlorine swimming pool noplace in California. "It wouldn't keep me healthy," I said, "I'd get pregnant."

He lifted his eyebrows, incredulous. "You're putting me on," he said, "this is the twentieth century."

"No it isn't," I said. "Not here."

He stood up also and took a step toward me. I backed away. He was turning mottled pink, turkey neck, but his voice was still rational. "Listen," he said, "I realize you walk around in never-never land but don't tell me you don't know where Joe is; he's not so noble, he's off in the bushes somewhere with that cunt on four legs, right about now he's shoving it into her." He glanced quickly at his wristwatch as though timing them; he seemed elated by what he'd said, his eyes gleamed like test tubes.

"Oh," I said; I thought about it for a minute. "Maybe they love each other." It would be logical, they were the ones who could. "Do you love me," I asked in case I hadn't understood him, "is that why you want me to?"

He thought I was being either smart or stupid and said "Christ." Then he paused, aiming. "You aren't going to let him get away with it, are you?" he said. "Tit for tat, as they say." He folded his arms, resting his case, retaliation was his ultimate argument: he must have felt it was a duty, an obligation on my part, it would be justice. Geometrical sex, he needed me for an abstract principle; it would be enough for him if our genitals could be detached like two kitchen appliances and copulate in mid-air, that would complete his equation.

His wristwatch glittered, glass and silver: perhaps it was his dial, the key that wound him, the switch. There must be a phrase, a vocabulary that would work. "I'm sorry," I said, "but you don't turn me on."

"You," he said, searching for words, not controlled any more, "tight-ass bitch."

The power flowed into my eyes, I could see into him, he was an impostor, a pastiche, layers of political handbills, pages from magazines, *affiches,* verbs and nouns glued on to him and shredding away, the original surface littered with fragments and tatters. In a black suit knocking on doors, young once, even that had been a costume, a uniform; now his hair was falling off and he didn't know what language to use, he'd forgotten his own, he had to copy. Secondhand American was spreading over him in patches, like mange or lichen. He was infested, garbled, and I couldn't help him: it would take such time to heal, unearth him, scrape down to where he was true.

"Keep it to yourself then," he said, "I'm not going to sit up and beg for a little third-rate cold tail."

I detoured around past him, back towards the cabin. More than ever I needed to find it, the thing she had hidden; the power from my father's intercession wasn't enough to protect me, it gave only knowledge and there were more gods than his, his were the gods of the head, antlers rooted in the brain. Not only how to see but how to act.

I thought he would stay there, at least till I was out of range, but he followed along behind me. "Sorry I blew my cool," he said. His voice had changed again, now it was deferential. "It's between us, okay? No need to mention it to Anna, right?" If he'd succeeded he would have told her as soon as he could. "I respect you for it, I really do."

"That's all right," I said; I knew he was lying.

They sat around the table in the regular places and I served dinner. There hadn't been any lunch but no one mentioned that.

"What time is Evans coming tomorrow?" I said.

"Ten, ten-thirty," David said. "Have a nice afternoon?" he said to Anna. Joe stuck a new potato with his fork and put it into his mouth.

"Fantastic," Anna said. "I got some sun and finished my book, then I had a long talk with Joe and went for a stroll." Joe chewed, his closed mouth moving, silent refutation. "And you?"

"Great," David said, his voice buoyant, inflated. He bent his arm onto the table, his hand brushing mine casually, as though by accident, for her to see. I flinched away, he was lying about me, the animals don't lie.

Anna smiled mournfully at him. I watched him, he wasn't laughing, he was staring at her, the lines in his face deepening and sagging. They know everything about each other, I thought, that's why they're so sad; but Anna was more than sad, she was desperate, her body her only weapon and she was fighting for her life, he was her life, her life was the fight: she was fighting him because if she ever surrendered the balance of power would be broken and he would go elsewhere. To continue the war.

I didn't want to join. "It's not what you think," I said to Anna. "He asked me to but I wouldn't." I wanted to tell her I hadn't acted against her.

Her eyes flicked from him to me. "That was pure of you," she said. I'd made a mistake, she resented me because I hadn't given in, it commented on her.

"She's pure all right," David said, "she's a little purist."

"Joe told me she won't put out for him anymore," Anna said, still looking at me. Joe didn't say anything; he was eating another potato.

"She hates men," David said lightly. "Either that or she wants to be one. Right?"

A ring of eyes, tribunal; in a minute they would join hands and dance around me, and after that the rope and the pyre, cure for heresy.

Maybe it was true, I leafed through all the men I had known to see whether or not I hated them. But then I realized it wasn't the men I hated, it was the Americans, the human beings, men and women both. They'd had their chance but they had turned against the gods, and it was time for me to choose sides. I wanted there to be a machine that could make them vanish, a button I could press that would evaporate them without disturbing anything else, that way there would be more room for the animals, they would be rescued.

"Aren't you going to answer?" Anna said, taunting.

"No," I said.

Anna said, "God, she really is inhuman," and they both laughed a little, sorrowfully.

CHAPTER NINETEEN

I cleared the table and scraped the canned-ham fat scraps from the plates into the fire, food for the dead. If you fed them enough they would come back; or was it the reverse, if you fed them enough they would stay away, it was in one of the books but I'd forgotten.

Anna said she would wash the dishes. It was an apology perhaps, reparation for the fact that she'd found it easier to fight on his side than against him. For once. She rattled the cutlery in the pan, singing to avoid discussion, we were beyond the time for confidences; her voice occupied the room, territorial.

It had to be inside the house. Before supper I searched the toolshed, while I was getting the shovel, and the garden when I dug up the potatoes; but it wasn't there, I would have recognized it. It had to be something out of place, something that wasn't here when I left, apple in the row of oranges like the old arithmetic workbooks. She would have brought it here especially for me and hidden it where I would discover it when I was ready; like my father's puzzle it would mediate, we cannot approach them directly. I dried the dishes as Anna washed, inspecting each one to make sure it was familiar. But nothing had been added since I'd been here, the gift was not a dish.

It wasn't anywhere in the main room. When we'd finished I went into David's and Anna's room: her leather jacket was there, hanging up, it hadn't been put back since the trip. I examined the pockets; there was nothing in them but an empty metal aspirin container and an ancient Kleenex, and the husks from sunflower seeds; and a charred filter from one of Anna's cigarettes, which I dropped on the floor and crushed with my foot.

My room was the only one remaining. As soon as I stepped inside it I sensed the power, in my hands and running along my arms, I was close to it. I scanned the walls and shelves, it wasn't there; my painted ladies watched me with their bristling eyes. Then I was certain: it was in the scrapbooks, I'd shoved them under the mattress without reading through all of them. They were the last possibility and they weren't supposed to be here, they belonged in the city, in the trunk.

I heard a motor droning from down the lake, a different pitch, deeper than a powerboat.

"Hey look," Anna called from the main room, "a big boat!" We went out on the point: it was a police launch like the ones driven by the game wardens, they were checking us the way they used to, to see if we had any dead fish and a license to go with them; it was routine.

The launch slowed and drew in to the dock. David was down there anyway, I would let him meet it, he was the one with the papers. I reentered the house and stood by the window. Anna, inquisitive, sauntered down to join them.

There were two men, police or probably game wardens, they were wearing ordinary clothes; and a third man, blond, Claude from the village probably, and a fourth one, older, the size of Paul. It was odd that Paul was on the launch: if he were coming for a visit he would bring his own boat. David shook hands with them and they clustered on the dock, talking in low voices. David dug into his pocket, for the license; then he scratched his neck as if worried. Joe appeared from the outhouse path and the talking started over again; Anna's head turned up towards me.

Then I saw David hurrying, taking the hill steps two at a time. The screen door banged shut behind him. "They found your father," he said, breathing hard from the climb. He squinted his face, as if to show sympathy.

The door slammed again, it was Anna; he put his arm around her and they both studied me with the intent pouncing look they'd had at supper.

"Oh," I said. "Where?"

"Some American guys found him in the lake. They were fishing, they hooked him by mistake; the body was unrecognizable but an old guy named Paul something-or-other down there, says he knows you, he identified the clothes. They figured he'd fallen off a cliff or something, he had a skull fracture." Seedy department-store magician, producing my father out of nowhere like a stuffed rabbit out of a hat.

"Where?" I said again.

"It's awful," Anna said, "I'm really sorry."

"They don't know where it happened," David said, "he must've drifted; he had a camera around his neck, big one, they think the weight kept him down or he would've been found sooner." His eyes gloating.

It was clever of him to have guessed the missing camera, since I'd told them nothing. He must have thought quickly in order to make it all up in such a short time: I knew it was a lie, he was doing it to get back at me. "Did they ask to see your fishing license?" I said.

"No," he said, faking surprise. "You want to talk to them?"

That was a risk, he should have calculated better, it would expose his whole false construction. Maybe that's what he wanted, maybe it was intended as a practical joke. I decide to act as though I believed him, see how he'd get out of it. "No," I said, "tell them I'm too upset. I'll speak to Paul tomorrow when we get to the village, about the arrangements." That was what they were called, the arrangements. "He'd want to be buried around here." Convincing details, if he could invent I could invent also, I'd read enough murder mysteries. The detectives, eccentric hermits, orchid raisers, sharp blue-haired old ladies, girls with jackknives and flashlights, for them everything fitted. But not in real life, I wanted to tell him, you've outsmarted yourself.

He and Anna glanced at each other: they'd planned on hurting me. "Okay," he said.

Anna said, "Wouldn't you rather . . ." and then stopped. They walked back down the steps, disappointed both of them, their trap had failed.

I went into the other room and took the scrapbooks out from under the mattress. There was still enough light to see by but I closed my eyes, touching the covers with my hands, fingertips. One of them was heavier and warmer; I lifted it, let it fall open. My mother's gift was there for me, I could look.

The rest of the scrapbook had early people, hairs blazing out of their heads like rays or spikes, and suns with faces, but the gift itself was a loose page, the edge torn, the figures drawn in crayon. On the left was a woman with a round moon stomach: the baby was sitting up inside her gazing out. Opposite her was a man with horns on his head like cow horns and a barbed tail.

The picture was mine, I had made it. The baby was myself before I was born, the man was God, I'd drawn him when my brother learned in the winter about the Devil and God: if the Devil was allowed a tail and horns, God needed them also, they were advantages.

That was what the pictures had meant then but their first meaning was lost now like the meanings of the rock paintings. They were my guides, she had saved them for me, pictographs, I had to read their new meaning with the help of the power. The gods, their likenesses: to see them in their true shape is fatal. While you are human; but after the transformation they could be reached. First I had to immerse myself in the other language.

Launch vibration, going away. I slid the page back into the scrapbook and replaced it under the mattress. Trample of the others on the hill, I stayed inside the room.

They lit the lamp. Noise of David fumbling and then the cards, he was laying out a game of solitaire; then Anna's voice, she wanted to set up the other deck. They were playing doubles, slapping the cards down expertly as gamblers, monosyllables as they gained or lost. Joe sat in the corner on the bench, I could hear him scuffling against the wall.

For him truth might still be possible, what will preserve him is the absence of words; but the others are already turning to metal, skins galvanizing, heads congealing to brass knobs, components and intricate wires ripening inside. The cards tick on the table.

I unclose my fist, releasing, it becomes a hand again, palm a network of trails, lifeline, past present and future, the break in it closing together as I purse my fingers. When the heartline and the headline are one, Anna told us, you are either a criminal, an idiot or a saint. How to act.

Their voices murmur, they can't discuss me, they know I'm listening. They're avoiding me, they find me inappropriate; they think I should be filled with death, I should be in mourning. But nothing has died, everything is alive, everything is waiting to become alive.

III

CHAPTER TWENTY

The sunset was red, a clear tulip color paling to flesh webs, membrane. Now there are only streaks of it, mauve and purple, sky visible through the window, divided by the window squares and then by the interlacing branches, leaves overlapping leaves. I'm in the bed, covered up, clothes in a pile on the floor, he will be here soon, they can't postpone it forever.

Mumbles, cards gathered, swish and spit of teeth being brushed. Blown breath and guttering, the lamp goes out, the flashlight beams wash over the ceiling. He opens the door and stands hesitating, darkening the light he holds, after the morning and the afternoon he isn't sure how to approach me. I feign sleep and he feels his way into the room, stealthy as moss, and unzips his human skin.

He thinks I'm in pain, he wants to evade it, he bends himself away from me; but I stroke him, move my hand over his body, he's startled because I'm awake. After a minute he turns to me, stiffening, arms going around me and over me and I smell Anna on him, suntan lotion and pink face grease and smoke, but that doesn't matter; what matters is the other smell, smells, the sheets, wool and soap, chemically treated hides, I can't here. I sit up, swing my legs out of the bed.

"Now what?" he says, whispers.

I tug at his hands. "Not here."

"Christ!" He tries to pull me back down but I brace my legs, hooking them onto the side.

"Don't talk," I say.

He stumbles out of the bed then and follows me, from this room to the other and across the outer floor. When I've unlatched the screen door and the wooden door I take his hand: there is something outside which I have protection against but he doesn't, I have to keep him close to me, inside the radius.

We go over the ground, feet and skin bare; the moon is rising, in the gray-green light his body gleams and the trunks of trees, the white ovals of his eyes. He walks as though blind, blundering into the shadow clumps, toes stubbing, he has not yet learned to see in the dark. My tentacled feet and free hand scent out the way, shoes are a barrier between touch and the earth. Double thump, clutched heartbeat: rabbits, warning us and each other. On the far shore an owl, its voice feathered and clawed, black on black, blood in the heart.

I lie down, keeping the moon on my left hand and the absent sun on my right. He kneels, he is shivering, the leaves under and around us are damp from the dew, or is it the lake, soaking up through the rock and sand, we are near the shore, the small waves riffle. He needs to grow more fur.

"What is it?" he says. "What's wrong?" My hands are on his shoulders, he is thick, undefined, outline but no features, hair and beard a mane, moon behind him. He turns to curve over me; his eyes glint, he is shaking, fear or tensed flesh or the cold. I pull him down, his beard and hair fall over me like ferns, mouth as soft as water. Heavy on me, warm stone, almost alive.

"I love you," he says into the side of my neck, catechism. Teeth grinding, he's holding back, he wants it to be like the city, baroque scrollwork, intricate as a computer, but I'm impatient, pleasure is redundant, the animals don't have pleasure. I guide him into me, it's the right season, I hurry.

He trembles and then I can feel my lost child surfacing within me, forgiving me, rising from the lake where it has been prisoned for so long, its eyes and teeth phosphorescent; the two halves clasp, interlocking like fingers, it buds, it sends out fronds. This time I will do it by myself, squatting, on old newspapers in a corner alone; or on leaves, dry leaves, a heap of them, that's cleaner. The baby will slip out easily as an egg, a kitten, and I'll lick it off and bite the cord, the blood returning to the ground where it belongs; the moon will be full, pulling. In the morning I will be able to see it: it will be covered with shining fur, a god, I will never teach it any words.

I press my arms around him, smoothing his back; I'm grateful to him, he's given me the part of himself I needed. I'll take him back to the cabin, through the force that presses in on us now like deep sea on a diver, then I can let him go.

"Is it all right?" he says. He's lying on top of me, breathing, molten. "Was it all right?"

He means two different things; but "Yes" I say, answer to a third question, unasked. Nobody must find out or they will do that to me again, strap me to the death machine, emptiness machine, legs in the metal framework, secret knives. This time I won't let them.

"Then it's okay," he says; he's leaning on his elbows, with his fingers and lips he soothes me, my cheek, hair. "It wasn't anything this afternoon, it didn't mean anything; it was her that wanted it." He rolls off me, lies beside me, nuzzling against my shoulder for warmth; he's shivering again. "Shit," he says, "it's bloody freezing." Then, cautiously, "Now do you?"

It's love, the ritual word, he wants to know again; but I can't give redemption, even as a lie. We both wait for my answer. The wind moves, rustling of tree lungs, water lapping all around us.

CHAPTER TWENTY-ONE

When I wake up it's morning, we're in the bed again. He is awake already, head hovering above me, he was surveying me while I slept. He smiles, a plump smile, contented, his beard puffed up like a singing toad throat, and lowers his face to kiss me. He still doesn't understand, he thinks he has won, act of his flesh a rope noosed round my neck, leash, he will lead me back to the city and tie me to fences, doorknobs.

"You slept in," he says. He begins to shift himself over onto me but I look at the sun, it's late, eight-thirty almost. In the main room I can hear metal on metal, they're up.

"There's no hurry," he says, but I push him away and get dressed.

Anna is making food, scraping a spoon in the frying pan. She has her purple tunic on and her white bellbottoms, urban costume, and her makeup is slabbed down over her face like a visor.

"I thought I'd do it," she says, "so you two could sleep in." She must have heard the door opening and closing in the night; she produces a smile, warm, conspiratorial, and I know what circuits are closing in her head: by screwing Joe she's brought us back together. Saving the world, everyone wants to; men think they can do it with guns, women with their bodies, love conquers all, conquerors love all, mirages raised by words.

She dishes out breakfast. It's baked beans from a can, the usual morning food is gone.

"Pork and beans and musical fruit, the more you eat the more you toot," David says and quacks like Daffy Duck, jaunty, mimicking satisfaction.

Anna helps him, cooperative community life, she taps him on the knuckles with her fork and says "Oh you." Then she remembers and adjusts to her Tragedy mask: "How long will it take you, in the village I mean?"

"I don't know," I say. "Not very long."

We pack and I help them carry the baggage down, my own also, caseful of alien words and failed pictures, canvas bundle of clothes, nothing I need. They sit on the dock talking; Anna is smoking, she's reduced to the last one.

"Christ," she says, "I'll be glad to hit the city. Stock up again."

I go up the steps once more to make sure they haven't left anything. The jays are there, flowing from tree to tree, voices semaphoring, tribal; they retreat to the upper branches, they still haven't decided whether I can be trusted. The cabin is the way we found it; when Evans arrives I'll snap the lock.

"You should take the canoes up before he comes," I say when I'm back down. "They go in the toolshed."

"Right," David says. He consults his watch, but they don't get up. They have the camera out, they're discussing the movie; the zipper bag of equipment is beside them, the tripod, the reels of film in their canisters.

"I figure we can start cutting it in two or three weeks," David says, his version of a pro. "We'll take it into the lab first thing."

"There's part of a reel left," Anna says. "You should get her, you got me but you never got her." She looks at me, fumes ascending from her nose and mouth.

"Now that's an idea," David says. "The rest of us are in it, she's the only one who isn't." He assesses me. "Where would we fit her in, though? We don't have anyone fucking yet; but I'd have to do it," he says to Joe, "we need you running the camera."

"I could run the camera," Anna says, "you could both do it," and everyone laughs.

They get up after a while and hoist the red canoe, one at each end, and carry it up the hill. I stay with Anna on the dock.

"Is my nose peeling?" she says, rubbing it. From her handbag she takes a round gilt compact with violets on the cover. She opens it, unclosing her other self, and runs her fingertip around the corners of her mouth left one, right one; then she unswivels a pink stick and dots her cheeks and blends them, changing her shape, performing the only magic left to her.

Rump on a packsack, harem cushion, pink on the cheeks and black discreetly around the eyes, as red as blood as black as ebony, a seamed and folded imitation of a magazine picture that is itself an imitation of a woman who is also an imitation, the original nowhere, hairless lobed angel in the same heaven where God is a circle, captive princess in someone's head. She is locked in, she isn't allowed to eat or shit or cry or give birth, nothing goes in, nothing comes out. She takes her clothes off or puts them on, paper-doll wardrobe, she copulates under strobe lights with the man's torso while his brain watches from its glassed-in control cubicle at the other end of the room, her face twists into poses of exultation and total abandonment, that is all. She is not bored, she has no other interests.

Anna sits, darkness in her eye sockets, skull with a candle. She clicks the compact shut and stubs out her cigarette against the dock; I remember the way she was crying, climbing up the sand hill, it was yesterday, since then she has crystallized. The machine is gradual, it takes a little of you at a time, it leaves the shell. It was all right as long as they stuck to dead things, the dead can defend themselves, to be half dead is worse. They did it to each other also, without knowing.

I unzip the bag with the camera equipment and lift out the cannisters of film.

"What're you doing?" Anna says, listlessly, however.

I unwind the film, standing full in the sun, and let it spiral into the lake. "You better not do that," Anna says, "they'll kill you." But she doesn't interfere, she doesn't call them.

When I've unraveled the reels I open the back of the camera. The film coils onto the sand under the water, weighted down by its containers; the invisible captured images are swimming away into the lake like tadpoles, Joe and David beside their defeated log, axemen, arms folded, Anna with no clothes on jumping off the end of the dock, finger up, hundreds of tiny naked Annas no longer bottled and shelved.

I study her to see if her release has made any difference, but the green eyes regard me unaltered from the enamel face. "They'll get you," she says, doleful as a prophet. "You shouldn't have done it."

They're at the top of the hill now, coming back for the other canoe. I run quickly towards it, flip it over right side up, throw a paddle inside and drag it along the dock.

"Hey!" David calls. "What're you doing?" They're almost here, Anna watches me, biting a knuckle, she can't decide whether or not to tell: if she keeps quiet they'll treat her as an accomplice.

I slide the canoe stern first into the water, squat, step in, shove.

"She dumped out your film," Anna says behind me.

I push the blade into the water, I don't turn, I can hear them peering down into the lake.

"Shit," David says, "shit, shit, oh shit, why the shit didn't you stop her?"

When I'm as far as the sand point I look back. Anna stands, arms slack at her sides, uninvolved; David is kneeling, his hands fishing in the water, pulling up the film in spaghetti handfuls though he must know it's futile, everything has escaped.

Joe is not there. He appears then at the top of the sand cliff, running, halting. He yells my name, furiously: if he had a rock he would throw it.

The canoe glides, carrying the two of us, around past the leaning trees and out of range. It's too late for them to get the other canoe and follow; probably they haven't thought of it, surprise attacks work by confusing. The direction is clear, I see I've been planning this, for how long I can't tell.

I go along near the trees, boat and arms one movement, amphibian; the water closes behind me, no track. The land bends and we bend with it, a narrowing and then a space and I'm safe, hidden in the shore maze.

Here there are boulders; they loom under the water, brown

shadows like clouds or threats, barricade. Slope of ground on either side, rock hung with creepers. The lake floor, once land floor, slants upward, so shallow now a motor could not pass. Another turning and I'm in the bay, land-locked swamp, layer of tepid water with reeds and cattails nosing up through the black vegetable ooze, around the sawed stumps of the once tower-high trees. This is where I threw the dead things and rinsed the tins and jars.

I float, no need to paddle. Further in, the trees they didn't cut before the flood are marooned, broken and gray-white, tipped on their sides, their giant contorted roots bleached and skinless; on the sodden trunks are colonies of plants, feeding on disintegration, laurel, sundew the insect-eater, its toenail-sized leaves sticky with red hairs. Out of the leaf nests the flowers rise, pure white, flesh of gnats and midges, petals now, metamorphosis.

I lie down on the bottom of the canoe and wait. The still water gathers the heat; birds, off in the forest a woodpecker, somewhere a thrush. Through the trees the sun glances; the swamp around me smolders, energy of decay turning to growth, greenfire. I remember the heron; by now it will be insects, frogs, fish, other herons. My body also changes, the creature in me, plant-animal, sends out filaments in me; I ferry it secure between death and life, I multiply.

The motor approaching wakes me: it's out on the lake, it will be Evans. I beach the canoe, knot the rope to a tree. They won't be expecting me, not from this direction; I have to make sure they leave with him as they should, it would be their way to pretend but stay behind to catch me when I come back.

It's less than a quarter of a mile through the trees, swerving to avoid branches, careful where I step, along the vestiges of the coded trail to where the laboratory shelves were, if I didn't know the trail was there I could never find it. As Evans' boat pulls into the dock I am behind them, near the piled wood, head down and lying flat, I can see them through the screen of plant stems.

They stoop, they're loading the things into the boat. I wonder if they're taking mine as well, my clothes, fragments of pictures.

They stand talking with Evans, their voices low, inaudible; but they'll be explaining, they'll have to invent some reason, accident, say why I'm not with them. They will be plotting a strategy for recapture; or will they really go off and discard me, vanish into the catacombs of the city, giving me up for lost, stashing me away in their heads with all the obsolete costumes and phrases? For them I'll soon be ancient as crew cuts and World War songs, a half-remembered face in a high-school year book, a captured enemy medal: memorabilia, or possibly not even that.

Joe comes up the steps, shouting; Anna shouts, too, shrill, like a train whistle before departure, my name. It's too late, I no longer have a name. I tried for all those years to be civilized but I'm not and I'm through pretending.

Joe goes around to the front of the cabin, concealed from me. After a minute he reappears, stumping back down the hill to them, shoulders sloped in defeat. Perhaps by now he understands.

They clamber into the boat. Anna pauses for a moment, turned directly toward me, face in the sunlight puzzled, oddly forlorn: does she see me, is she going to wave goodbye? Then the others reach out hands to her and lift her in, a gesture that looks from a distance almost like love.

The boat chugs backwards into the bay, then swings into forward and roars. Bullhead Evans at the wheel, check-shirted and stolid, American, they are all Americans now. But they are really going, really gone, a ringing in my ears and then a silence. I get to my feet slowly, my body is cramped from not moving; on the bare flesh of my legs are the imprints of leaves and twigs.

I walk to the hill and scan the shoreline, finding the place, opening, where they disappeared: checking, reassuring. It's true, I am by myself; this is what I wanted, to stay here alone. From any rational point of view I am absurd; but there are no longer any rational points of view.

CHAPTER TWENTY-TWO

They've locked the doors, on the toolshed, on the cabin; it was Joe, he may have assumed I'd take the canoe to the village. No, it was ill will. I shouldn't have left the keys hanging on the nail, I should have put them in my pocket. But it was stupid of them to think they could keep me out. Soon they will reach the village, the car, the city; what are they saying about me now? That I was running away; but to go with them would have been running away, the truth is here.

I stand on the front step and lean sideways, clutching the window ledge, looking in. The canvas packsack with my clothes has been moved, it's back inside now, on the table with my case; beside it is Anna's detective novel, her last one, cold comfort but comfort, death is logical, there's always a motive. Perhaps that's why she read them, for the theology.

Sun gone, sky darkening, it may rain later. Clouds building over the hills, anvils, ominous hammerheads, it will be a storm; it might miss, though, sometimes they eddy for days, approaching but never striking. I'll have to get inside. Breaking into my own house, go in and out the window, they used to sing, holding their arms up like bridges; as we have done before.

The handbarrow is underneath the cabin, beside the stacked wood where it was always kept, two poles with boards nailed across like rungs. I haul it out and prop it against the wall under the window, the one with no screen. The window is hooked on the inside at the corners, I'll have to break four of the little squares of glass. I do it with a rock, my head turned away, eyes closed because of the splinters. I reach carefully in through the jagged holes and undo the hooks and lift the window inward onto the couch. If I could open the toolshed I could use the screwdriver to take the padlock hasp off the door, but the toolshed has no windows. Axe and machete inside it, saw, metal utensils.

I step on the couch and then on the floor, I'm in. I sweep up the broken glass; after that I hook the window back in place. It will be a nuisance, climbing in and out, removing the window each time, but the other windows have screens and I've nothing to cut them with. I could try the knife: If I had to leave in a hurry it would be better to use one of the back windows, they're nearer the ground.

I've succeeded; I don't know what to do now. I pause in the middle of the room, listening: no wind, stillness, held breath of the lake, the trees.

To be busy I unpack my clothes again and hang them on the nails in my room. My mother's jacket is back, I last saw it in Anna's room, it's been shifted. My footsteps are the only sounds, reverberation of shoes on wood.

There must be something that comes next but the power has drained away, my fingers are empty as gloves, eyes ordinary, nothing guides me.

I sit down at the table and leaf through an old magazine, shepherds knitting their own socks, weather gnarling their faces, women in laced bodices and red lipstick balancing washing baskets on their heads, smiling to show their teeth and happiness; rubber plantations and deserted temples, jungle crawling over the serene carved gods. Ring from a wet cup on the cover, printed there yesterday or ten years ago.

I open a can of peaches and eat two of the yellow fibrous halves, sugary juice dribbling from the spoon. Then I lie down on the couch and sleep descends over my face, black oblong, dreamless.

When I wake up the diffused light outside is further west, it feels late, it must be almost six, dinner hour; David had the only watch. Hunger is there in me, a contained whimper. I unhook the window and climb out, one foot on the wobbling handbarrow, scraping my knee as I let myself drop to the ground. I should build a ladder; but there are no implements, no boards.

I go down to the garden. I've forgotten the knife and the bowl but they aren't needed, fingers will do. I unlatch the gate, the chicken-wire walls are around me; outside the fence the trees droop as though wilting, the plants inside are pale in the grayish light; the air is heavy, oppressive. I start to pull up the onions and the carrots.

I'm crying finally, it's the first time, I watch myself doing it: I'm crouching down beside the lettuces, flowers finished now, gone to seed, my breath knots, my body tightens against it; the water fills my mouth, fish taste. But I'm not mourning, I'm accusing them, *Why did you?* They chose it, they had control over their death, they decided it was time to leave and they left, they set up this barrier. They didn't consider how I would feel, who would take care of me. I'm furious because they let it happen.

"Here I am," I call. "I'm here!" Voice rising and rising with the frustration and then the terror of hearing no answer, the time we were playing after supper and I hid too well, too far away and they couldn't find me. The tree trunks are so much alike, the same size, the same color, impossible to retrace the path, instead locate the sun, the direction, whichever way you go you're bound to hit water. The dangerous thing is to panic, to walk in circles.

"I'm here!" But nothing happens. I wipe the salt off my face, my fingers earth-smeared.

If I will it, if I pray, I can bring them back. They're here now, I can sense them waiting, beyond sight on the path or in the long grass outside the fence, they are pulling against me but I can make them come out, from wherever it is they are hiding.

I start a fire in the stove and cook the food in the darkening room. There's no reason to set out plates; I eat from the pot and the frying pan with a spoon. I'll save the dirty dishes till there are enough; when the dishwasher pail is full I will have to lower it through the window with a rope.

I climb out again and set the scraps from the tinned meat on the tray for the birds. Deep gray, the clouds descending, closing in; the puffs of wind have begun, they advance across the lake like shudders; to the south there's a column of rain. Flickers of light but no thunder, gust of leaves.

I walk up the hill to the outhouse, forcing myself to go slowly, holding the panic at a distance, looking at it. Inside I hook the door shut, it's doors I'm afraid of because I can't see through them, it's the door opening by itself in the wind I'm afraid of. I run back down the path, telling myself to stop it, I'm old enough, I'm old.

The power would have protected me but it's gone, exhausted, no more use now than silver bullets or the sign of the cross. But the house will defend me, it's the right shape. Back inside I put the window up again, hooking it to the frame, barricading myself in, wood bars. The four broken panes, how can I close them. I try stuffing them with pages torn from the magazines and crumpled, *National Geographic, Maclean's,* but it doesn't work, the holes are too big, the wads of paper fall to the floor. If only I had nails, a hammer.

I light the lamp but the air drafting in through the broken window makes it flutter and turn blue, and with the lamp on I can't see what's happening outside. I blow it out and sit in darkness, listening to the gush of the wind, but it doesn't rain.

After a while I decide to go to bed. I'm not tired, I slept in the afternoon, but there's nothing else to do. In my room I stand for a long time wondering why I'm afraid to take off my clothes: am I worried that they'll come back for me, if they do I'll have to get out quickly; but they wouldn't try it in a storm, Evans knows better than that, the open lake is the worst place because of the electricity, flesh and water both conduct.

I tie back the curtain so there will be more light. My mother's jacket is hanging on a nail beside the window, there's nobody in it; I press my forehead against it. Leather smell, the smell of loss; irrecoverable. But I can't think about that. I lie down on the bed in my clothes and in a moment the first rain hits the roof. It patters, changes to a steady drumming, sound of an avalanche, surrounding. I feel the lake rising, up over the shore and the hill, the trees toppling into it like sand collapsing, roots overturned, the house unmoored and floating like a boat, rocking and rocking.

In the middle of the night silence wakes me, the rain has stopped. Blank dark, I can see nothing, I try to move my hands but I can't. The fear arrives like waves, like footfalls, it has no center; it encloses me like armor, it's my skin that is afraid, rigid. They want to get in, they want me to open the windows, the door, they can't do it by themselves. I'm the only one, they are depending on me but I don't know any longer who they are; however they come back they won't be the same, they will have changed. I willed it, I called to them, that they should arrive is logical; but logic is a wall, I built it, on the other side is terror.

Above on the roof is the finger-tapping of water dripping from the trees. I hear breathing, withheld, observant, not in the house but all around it.

CHAPTER TWENTY-THREE

In the morning I remember the window outline, beginning to emerge; I must have been watching till nearly dawn. Then I think it might have been a dream, the kind that creates the illusion of being awake.

For breakfast I eat canned stew, heating it first in a pot, and instant coffee. There are too many windows, I move so I'm sitting on the wall bench, from there I can see all of them.

I stack the dishes in the pan with the ones from last night and pour the rest of the hot water over them. Then I turn to the mirror to brush my hair.

But when I pick up the brush there is a surge of fear in my hand, the power is there again in a different form, it must have seeped up through the ground during the lightning. I know that the brush is forbidden, I must stop being in the mirror. I look for the last time at my distorted glass face: eyes light blue in dark-red skin, hair standing tangled out from my head, reflection intruding between my eyes and vision. Not to see myself but to see. I reverse the mirror so it's toward the wall, it no longer traps me, Anna's soul closed in the gold compact, that and not the camera is what I should have broken.

I unfasten the window and go out; at once the fear leaves me like a hand lifting from my throat. There must be rules: places I'm permitted to be, other places I'm not. I'll have to listen carefully, if I trust them they will tell me what is allowed. I ought to have let them in, it may have been the only chance they will give me.

The enclosure with the swing and the sand pile is forbidden, I know that without touching it. I walk down to the lake. It is flat calm, the water is pollen-streaked, mist is drifting up off the bays and from behind the islands, the sun burning it away as it rises, the sun itself hot and bright as light through a lens. Something glimmers out on the surface, a swimming animal or a dead log; when there is no wind things venture out from the shore. The air smells of earth, midsummer.

I step on the dock: the fear says No, I can be near the lake but not on the dock. I wash my hands from the flat stone. If I do everything in the right order, if I think of nothing else. What sacrifice, what do they want?

When I'm certain I've guessed what is required I go back to the cabin, enter it. The fire I made for breakfast is still smoldering: I add another stick of wood and open the draft.

I snap the catches on my case and take out the drawings and the typescript, *Quebec Folk Tales,* it's easily replaceable for them in the city, and my bungled princesses, the Golden Phoenix awkward and dead as a mummified parrot. The pages bunch in my hands; I add them one by one so the fire will not be smothered, then the paint tubes and brushes, this is no longer my future. There must be some way of canceling the Samsonite case, it can't be burned. I draw the big knife across it, X-ing it out.

I slip the ring from my left hand, non-husband, he is the next thing I must discard finally, and drop it into the fire, altar, it may not melt but it will at least be purified, the blood will burn off. Everything from history must be eliminated, the circles and the arrogant square pages. I rummage under the mattress and bring out the scrapbooks, ripping them up, the ladies, dress forms with decorated china heads, the suns and the moons, the rabbits and their archaic eggs, my false peace, his wars, airplanes and tanks and the helmeted explorers; perhaps at the other side of the world my brother feels the weight lifting, freedom feathering his arms. Even the guides, the miraculous double woman and the god with horns, they must be translated. The ladies on the wall too with their watermelon breasts and lampshade skirts, all my artifacts.

Theirs too, the map torn from the wall, the rock paintings, left to me by my father's will; and the album, the sequence of my mother's life, the confining photographs. My own faces curl, blacken, the imitation mother and father change to flat ashes. It is time that separates us, I was a coward, I would not let them into my age, my place. Now I must enter theirs.

When the paper things are burned I smash the glasses and plates and the chimney of the lamp. I rip one page from each of the books, Boswell and *The Mystery at Sturbridge,* the Bible and the common mushrooms and *Log Cabin Construction,* to burn through all the words would take too long. Everything I can't break, frying pan, enamel bowl, spoons and forks, I throw on the floor. After that I use the big knife to slash once through the blankets, the sheets and the beds and the tents and at the end my own clothes and my mother's gray leather jacket, my father's gray felt hat, the raincoats: these husks are not needed any longer, I abolish them, I have to clear a space.

When nothing is left intact and the fire is only smoldering I leave, carrying one of the wounded blankets with me, I will need it until the fur grows. The house shuts with a click behind me.

I untie my feet from the shoes and walk down to the shore; the earth is damp, cold, pockmarked with raindrops. I pile the blanket on the rock and step into the water and lie down. When every part of me is wet I take off my clothes, peeling them away from my flesh like wallpaper. They sway beside me, inflated, the sleeves bladders of air.

My back is on the sand, my head rests against the rock, innocent as plankton; my hair spreads out, moving and fluid in the water. The earth rotates, holding my body down to it as it holds the moon; the sun pounds in the sky, red flames and rays pulsing from it, searing away the wrong form that encases me, dry rain soaking through me, warming the blood egg I carry. I dip my head beneath the water, washing my eyes.

Inshore a loon; it lowers its head, then lifts it again and calls. It sees me but it ignores me, accepts me as part of the land.

When I am clean I come up out of the lake, leaving my false body floated on the surface, a cloth decoy; it jiggles in the waves I make, nudges gently against the dock.

They offered clothing as a token, formerly; that was partial but the gods are demanding, absolute, they want all.

The sun is three-quarters, I have become hungry. The food in the cabin is forbidden, I'm not allowed to go back into that cage, wooden rectangle. Also tin cans and jars are forbidden; they are glass and metal. I head for the garden and prowl through it, then squat, wrapped in my blanket. I eat the green peas out of their shells and the raw yellow beans, I scrape the carrots from the earth with my fingers, I will wash them in the lake first. There is one late strawberry, I find it among the matted weeds and suckers. Red foods, heart color, they are the best kind, they are sacred; then yellow, then blue; green foods are mixed from blue and yellow. I pull up one of the beets and scratch the dirt from it and gnaw at it but the rind is tough, I'm not strong enough yet.

At sunset I devour the washed carrots, taking them from the grass where I've concealed them, and part of a cabbage. The outhouse is forbidden so I leave my dung, droppings, on the ground and kick earth over. All animals with dens do that.

I hollow a lair near the woodpile, dry leaves underneath and dead branches leaned over, with fresh needled branches woven to cover. Inside it I curl with the blanket over my head. There are mosquitoes, they bite through; it's best not to slap them, the blood smell brings others. I sleep in relays like a cat, my stomach hurts. Around me the space rustles; owl sound, across the lake or inside me, distance contracts. A light wind, the small waves talking against the shore, multilingual water.

CHAPTER TWENTY-FOUR

The light wakes me, speckled through the roof branches. My bones ache, hunger is loose in me, belly a balloon, floating shark stomach. It's hot, the sun is almost at noon, I've slept most of the morning. I crawl outside and run towards the garden where the food is.

The gate stops me. Yesterday I could go in but not today: they are doing it gradually. I lean against the fence, my feet pawprinting the mud damp from the rain, the dew, the lake oozing up through the ground. Then my belly cramps and I step to one side and lie down in the long grass. A frog is there, leopard frog with green spots and gold-rimmed eyes, ancestor. It includes me, it shines, nothing moves but its throat breathing.

I rest on the ground, head propped on hands, trying to forget the hunger, looking through the wire hexagons at the garden: rows, squares, stakes, markers. The plants are flourishing, they grow almost visibly, sucking moisture up through the roots and succulent stems, their leaves sweating, flushed in the sunrays to a violent green, weeds and legitimate plants alike, there is no difference. Under the ground the worms twine, pink veins.

The fence is impregnable; it can keep out everything but weed seeds, birds, insects and the weather. Beneath it is a two-foot-deep moat, paved with broken glass, smashed jars and bottles, and covered with gravel and earth, the woodchucks and skunks can't burrow under. Frogs and snakes get through but they are permitted.

The garden is a stunt, a trick. It could not exist without the fence.

Now I understand the rule. They can't be anywhere that's marked out, enclosed: even if I opened the doors and fences they could not pass in, to houses and cages, they can move only in the spaces between them, they are against borders. To talk with them I must approach the condition they themselves have entered; in spite of my hunger I must resist the fence, I'm too close now to turn back.

But there must be something else I can eat, something that is not forbidden. I think of what I might catch, crayfish, leeches, no not yet. Along the trail the edible plants, the mushrooms, I know the poisonous kinds and the ones we used to collect, some of them can be eaten raw.

There are raspberries on the canes, shriveled and not many but they are red. I suck those, their sweetness, sourness, piercing in my mouth, teeth crackling on the seeds. Into the trail, tunnel, cool of the trees, as I walk I search the ground for shapes I can eat, anything. Provisions, they will provide, they have always favored survival.

I find the six-leaved plants again, two of them, and dig up the crisp white roots and chew them, not waiting to take them back to the lake to wash them. Earth caked beneath my jagged nails.

The mushrooms are still there, the deadly white one, I'll save that till I'm immune, ready, and the yellow food, yellow fingers. By now many of them are too old, wrinkled, but I break off the softer ones. I hold them in my mouth a long time before swallowing, they taste musty, mildewed canvas, I'm not sure of them.

What else, what else? Enough for a while. I sit down, wrapping myself in the blanket which is damp from the grass, my feet have gone cold. I will need other things, perhaps I can catch a bird or a fish, with my hands, that will be fair. Inside me it is growing, they take what they require, if I don't feed it it will absorb my teeth, bones, my hair will thin, come out in handfuls. But I put it there, I invoked it, the fur god with tail and horns, already forming. The mothers of gods, how do they feel, voices and light glaring from the belly, do they feel sick, dizzy? Pain squeezes my stomach, I bend, head pressed against knees.

Slowly I retrace the trail. Something has happened to my eyes, my feet are released, they alternate, several inches from the ground. I'm ice-clear, transparent, my bones and the child inside me showing through the green webs of my flesh, the ribs are shadows, the muscles jelly, the trees are like this too, they shimmer, their cores glow through the wood and bark.

The forest leaps upward, enormous, the way it was before they cut it, columns of sunlight frozen; the boulders float, melt, everything is made of water, even the rocks. In one of the languages there are no nouns, only verbs held for a longer moment.

The animals have no need for speech, why talk when you are a word

I lean against a tree, I am a tree leaning

I break out again into the bright sun and crumple, head against the ground

I am not an animal or a tree, I am the thing in which the trees and animals move and grow, I am a place

I have to get up, I get up. Through the ground, break surface, I'm standing now; separate again. I pull the blanket over my shoulders, head forward.

I can hear the jays, crying and crying as if they've found an enemy or food. They are near the cabin, I walk toward them up the hill. I see them in the trees and swooping between the trees, the air forming itself into birds, they continue to call.

Then I see her. She is standing in front of the cabin, her hand stretched out, she is wearing her gray leather jacket; her hair is long, down to her shoulders in the style of thirty years ago, before I was born; she is turned half away from me, I can see only the side of her face. She doesn't move, she is feeding them: one perches on her wrist, another on her shoulder.

I've stopped walking. At first I feel nothing except a lack of surprise: that is where she would be, she has been standing there all along. Then as I watch and it doesn't change I'm afraid, I'm cold with fear, I'm afraid it isn't real, paper doll cut by my eyes, burnt picture, if I blink she will vanish.

She must have sensed it, my fear. She turns her head quietly and looks at me, past me, as though she knows something is there but she can't quite see it. The jays cry again, they fly up from her, the shadows of their wings ripple over the ground and she's gone.

I go up to where she was. The jays are there in the trees, cawing at me; there are a few scraps on the feeding tray still, they've knocked some to the ground. I squint up at them, trying to see her, trying to see which one she is; they hop, twitch their feathers, turn their heads, fixing me first with one eye, then the other.

CHAPTER TWENTY-FIVE

It's day again, my body jumps out of sleep. What I heard was a powerboat, attacking. It's almost too late, they were pulling around into the bay and slowing and nearly to the dock when I woke up. I scramble on hands and knees out of my den, blanket over me, brown plaid camouflage, and run stooping further back among the trees and flatten, worming into a thicket, hazel bushes, where I can see.

They may have been sent to hunt for me, perhaps the others asked them to, they may be the police; or they may be sightseers, curious tourists. Evans will have told at the store, the whole village will know. Or the war may have started, the invasion, they are Americans.

They can't be trusted. They'll mistake me for a human being, a naked woman wrapped in a blanket: possibly that's what they've come here for, if it's running around loose, ownerless, why not take it. They won't be able to tell what I really am. But if they guess my true form, identity, they will shoot me or bludgeon in my skull and hang me up by the feet from a tree.

They're hulking out of the boat now, four or five of them. I can't see them clearly, their faces, the stems and leaves are in the way; but

I can smell them and the scent brings nausea, it's stale air, bus stations and nicotine smoke, mouths lined with soiled plush, acid taste of copper wiring or money. Their skins are red, green in squares, blue in lines, and it's a minute before I remember that these are fake skins, flags. Their real skins above the collars are white and plucked, with tufts of hair on top, piebald blend of fur and no fur like moldy sausages or the rumps of baboons. They are evolving, they are halfway to machine, the leftover flesh atrophied and diseased, porous like an appendix.

Two of them climb the hill to the cabin. They are talking, their voices are distinct but they penetrate my ears as sounds only, foreign radio. It must be either English or French but I can't recognize it as any language I've ever heard or known. Scrapes and grunts, they're getting in, through the door or the open window, crunch of their boots inside on the broken glass. One of them laughs, spike scratched on slate.

The other three are still on the dock. Then they shout: they must have found my clothes, one is kneeling down. Is it Joe, I try to picture what Joe looks like. But it makes no difference, he wouldn't help me, he would be on their side; he may have given them the keys.

The two come out of the cabin and thud down to the dock again, their false skins flapping. They cluster, they chitter and sizzle like a speeded-up tape, the forks and spoons on the ends of their arms waving excitedly. Perhaps they think I drowned myself, that would be the kind of blunder they would make.

Keep quiet, I say, I bite into my arm but I can't hold it back, the laughter extrudes. It startles me, I stop at once but it's too late, they've heard me. Rubber feet stomping off the dock and bulletproof heads moving toward me, who could they be, David and Joe, Claude from the village, Evans, Malmstrom the spy, the Americans, the humans, they're here because I wouldn't sell. I don't own it, nobody owns it I tell them, you don't have to kill me. Rabbit's choices: freeze, take the chance they won't see you; then bolt.

I have a good start on them and no shoes. I run silently, dodging branches, heading for the path to the swamp, the canoe is there, I can easily reach it first. On the open lake they could cut me off with the motorboat but if I go into the swamp, among the dead tree roots, I'll be safe, they'd have to wade for me, the mud is soft, they'll sink like bulldozers. Behind me they crash, their boots crash, language ululating, electronic signals thrown back and forth between them, hooo, hooo, they talk in numbers, the voice of reason. They clank, heavy with weapons and iron plating.

But they've half-circled and are closing, five metal fingers converging to a fist. I double back. Other tricks: up a tree, but no time and no tree is big enough. Crouch behind boulders, at night yes but not now and there are no boulders, they've pulled themselves back into the earth just when I need them. Flight, there's no alternative, though I'm praying the power has deserted me, nothing is on my side, not even the sun.

I swerve toward the lake, there's a high bank here, steep slope, sand mostly. I go over the edge and slide down it, on a knee and elbow it seems, gouging furrows, I hope they won't see the tracks. I keep the blanket over me so the white won't show and crouch with my face against the tree roots that dangle over the eroded side. Twisted: cedars. One of my feet is gashed and the arm, I can feel the blood swelling out like sap.

The clangs and shouts thrash past me and continue, further away, then nearer. I stay unmoving, don't give yourself away. Back in the woods they group: talking, laughter. Maybe they've brought food, in hampers and thermos botles, maybe they thought of it as a picnic. My heart clenches, unclenches, I listen to it.

The sound of the starting motor prods me. I pull myself up onto the bank and squat behind the hedge of trunks, if I stay by the shore they might see me. The noise surges out from behind the point and they rocket past, so near I could hit them with a stone. I count them, making sure, five.

That is the way they are, they will not let you have peace, they don't want you to have anything they don't have themselves. I stay on the bank, resting, licking the scratches; no fur yet on my skin, it's too early.

I make my way back towards the cabin, resenting the gods although perhaps they saved me, limping, blood is still coming out of my foot but not as much. I wonder if they have set traps; I will have to avoid my shelter. Caught animals gnaw off their arms and legs to get free, could I do that.

I haven't had time to be hungry and even now the hunger is detached from me, it does not insist; I must be getting used to it, soon I will be able to go without food altogether. Later I will search along the other trail; at the end of it is the stone point, it has blueberry bushes.

As I approach the toolshed the fear, the power is there, in the soles of my feet, coming out of the ground, a soundless humming. I am forbidden to walk on the paths. Anything that metal has touched, scarred; axe and machete cleared the trails, order is made with knives. His job was wrong, he was really a surveyor, he learned the trees, naming and counting them so the others could level and excavate. He must know that by now. I step to one side, skirting the worn places where shoes have been, descending towards the lake.

He is standing near the fence with his back to me, looking in at the garden. The late afternoon sunlight falls obliquely between the tree trunks on the hill, down on him, clouding him in an orange haze, he wavers as if through water.

He has realized he was an intruder; the cabin, the fences, the fires and paths were violations; now his own fence excludes him, as logic excludes love. He wants it ended, the borders abolished, he wants the forest to flow back into the places his mind cleared: reparation.

I say Father.

He turns toward me and it's not my father. It is what my father saw, the thing you meet when you've stayed here too long alone.

I'm not frightened, it's too dangerous for me to be frightened of it; it gazes at me for a time with its yellow eyes, wolf's eyes, depthless but lambent as the eyes of animals seen at night in the car headlights. Reflectors. It does not approve of me or disapprove of me, it tells me it has nothing to tell me, only the fact of itself.

Then its head swings away with an awkward, almost crippled motion: I do not interest it, I am part of the landscape, I could be anything, a tree, a deer skeleton, a rock.

I see now that although it isn't my father it is what my father has become. I knew he wasn't dead.

From the lake a fish jumps

An idea of a fish jumps

A fish jumps, carved wooden fish with dots painted on the sides, no, antlered fish thing drawn in red on cliffstone, protecting spirit. It hangs in the air suspended, flesh turned to icon, he has changed again, returned to the water. How many shapes can he take.

I watch it for an hour or so; then it drops and softens, the circles widen, it becomes an ordinary fish again.

When I go to the fence the footprints are there, side by side in the mud. My breath quickens, it was true, I saw it. But the prints are too small, they have toes; I place my feet in them and find that they are my own.

CHAPTER TWENTY-SIX

In the evening I make a different lair, further back and better hidden. I eat nothing but I lie down on the rocks and drink from the lake. During the night I have a dream about them, the way they were when they were alive and becoming older; they are in a boat, the green canoe, heading out of the bay.

When I wake in the morning I know they have gone finally, back into the earth, the air, the water, wherever they were when I summoned them. The rules are over. I can go anywhere now, into the cabin, into the garden, I can walk on the paths. I am the only one left alive on the island.

They were here though, I trust that. I saw them and they spoke to me, in the other language.

I'm not hungry any more but I trudge back to the cabin and climb through the window again and open a tin of yellow beans. To prefer life, I owe them that. I sit cross-legged on the wall bench and eat the beans out of the can with my fingers, a few at a time, too much at first is bad. Junk on the floor, things broken, did I do that?

David and Anna were here, they slept in the far bedroom; I remember them, but indistinctly and with nostalgia, as I remember people I once knew. They live in the city now, in a different time. I can remember him, fake husband, more clearly though, and now I feel nothing for him but sorrow. He was neither of the things I believed, he was only a normal man, middle-aged, second-rate, selfish and kind in the average proportions; but I was not prepared for the average, its needless cruelties and lies. My brother saw the danger early. To immerse oneself, join in the war, or to be destroyed. Though there ought to be other choices.

Soon it will be autumn, then winter; the leaves will turn by late August, as early as October it will begin to snow and it will keep on until the snow is level with the tops of the windows or the bottom of the roof, the lake will freeze solid. Or before that they'll close the floodgates on the dam and the water will rise, I'll watch it day by day, perhaps that's why they came in the motorboat, not to hunt but to warn me. In any case I can't stay here forever, there isn't enough food. The garden won't last and the tins and bottles will give out; the link between me and the factories is broken, I have no money.

If they were searchers they will go back and say maybe that they saw me, maybe that they only thought they did. If they weren't searchers they'll say nothing.

I could take the canoe that's roped up in the swamp and paddle the ten miles to the village, now, tomorrow, when I've eaten and I'm strong enough. Then back to the city and the pervasive menace, the Americans. They exist, they're advancing, they must be dealt with, but possibly they can be watched and predicted and stopped without being copied.

No gods to help me now, they're questionable once more, theoretical as Jesus. They've receded, back to the past, inside the skull, is it the same place. They'll never appear to me again, I can't afford it; from now on I'll have to live in the usual way, defining them by their absence; and love by its failures, power by its loss, its renunciation. I regret them; but they give only one kind of truth, one hand.

No total salvation, resurrection, Our father, Our mother, I pray, Reach down for me, but it won't work: they dwindle, grow, become what they were, human. Something I never gave them credit for; but their totalitarian innocence was my own.

I try to think for the first time what it was like to be them: our father, islanding his life, protecting both us and himself, in the midst of war and in a poor country, the effort it must have taken to sustain his illusions of reason and benevolent order, and perhaps he didn't. Our mother, collecting the seasons and the weather and her children's faces, the meticulous records that allowed her to omit the other things, the pain and isolation and whatever it was she was fighting against, something in a vanished history, I can never know. They are out of reach now, they belong to themselves, more than ever.

I set the half-empty tin down on the table and walk carefully across the floor, my bare feet avoiding the broken glass. I turn the mirror around: in it there's a creature neither animal nor human, furless, only a dirty blanket, shoulders huddled over into a crouch, eyes staring blue as ice from the deep sockets; the lips move by themselves. This was the stereotype, straws in the hair, talking nonsense or not talking at all. To have someone to speak to and words that can be understood: their definition of sanity.

That is the real danger now, the hospital or the zoo, where we are put, species and individual, when we can no longer cope. They would never believe it's only a natural woman, state of nature, they think of that as a tanned body on a beach with washed hair waving like scarves; not this, face dirt-caked and streaked, skin grimed and scabby, hair like a frayed bathmat stuck with leaves and twigs. A new kind of centerfold.

I laugh, and a noise comes out like something being killed: a mouse, a bird?

CHAPTER TWENTY-SEVEN

This above all, to refuse to be a victim. Unless I can do that I can do nothing. I have to recant, give up the old belief that I am powerless and because of it nothing I can do will ever hurt anyone. A lie which was always more disastrous than the truth would have been. The word games, the winning and losing games are finished; at the moment there are no others but they will have to be invented, withdrawing is no longer possible and the alternative is death.

I drop the blanket on the floor and go into my dismantled room. My spare clothes are here, knife slashes in them but I can still wear them. I dress, clumsily, unfamiliar with buttons; I reenter my own time.

But I bring with me from the distant past five nights ago the time-traveler, the primeval one who will have to learn, shape of a goldfish now in my belly, undergoing its watery changes. Word furrows potential already in its proto-brain, untraveled paths. No god and perhaps not real, even that is uncertain; I can't know yet, it's too early. But I assume it: if I die it dies, if I starve it starves with me. It might be the first one, the first true human; it must be born, allowed.

I'm outside in the garden when the boat comes. It isn't Evans; it's Paul's boat, thick and slow and painted white, he built it himself. Paul is at the back, beside the antique motor; in the front is Joe.

I go out through the gate and retreat behind the trees, white birches clumped beside the path, not hurrying, not running away but cautious.

The motor cuts, the nose of the boat bumps the dock. Paul stands up with an oar, pulling in; Joe gets out and ropes the boat and takes several steps towards the land.

He calls my name, then pauses, "Are you here?" Echo: here, here?

He must have been waiting in the village, the searchers must have told him they'd seen me, perhaps he was with them. He stayed behind when David and Anna went away in their car, or he drove to the city with them and then hitched back, walked back, what's important is that he's here, a mediator, an ambassador, offering me something: captivity in any of its forms, a new freedom?

I watch him, my love for him useless as a third eye or a possibility. If I go with him we will have to talk, wooden houses are obsolete, we can no longer live in spurious peace by avoiding each other, the way it was before, we will have to begin. For us it's necessary, the intercession of words; and we will probably fail, sooner or later, more or less painfully. That's normal, it's the way it happens now and I don't know whether it's worth it or even if I can depend on him, he may have been sent as a trick. But he isn't an American, I can see that now; he isn't anything, he is only half formed, and for that reason I can trust him.

To trust is to let go. I tense forward, toward the demands and questions, though my feet do not move yet.

He calls for me again, balancing on the dock which is neither land nor water, hands on hips, head thrown back and eyes scanning. His voice is annoyed: he won't wait much longer. But right now he waits.

The lake is quiet, the trees surround me, asking and giving nothing.

TOPICS FOR PAPERS AND DISCUSSION

1. *The protagonist.* Write an analysis of the protagonist's character. Examine the quality of her mind and range of ideas, her past experiences, relationships to her "husband," brother, David, Joe, father, mother, Anna, and others. Consider her sex and her physical and psychological trauma. A superficial interpretation might show her as interested principally in herself, a bit ruthless in her dealings with others, and, perhaps, to paraphrase David in Chapter Thirteen, "a women's libber." What contrary evidence appears? For instance, what light is thrown on her character when she feels responsible for others, wishes to save them, desires to protect, rescue, and redeem them?

2. *Minor characters.* Atwood's techniques for developing minor characters include: typical actions, unique ways of speaking, individual interests, various kinds of relationships to the narrator (and each other), different occupations, identification with certain objects, attitudes toward life, and recurrent ideas. Also she uses the techniques of dividing a character in two, each a part of the whole, twinning, doubling (the *doppelgänger),*

or direct identity (when she identifies herself with Anna, David, etc.). With reference to these techniques, analyze both a male and a female minor character and their relationships to the protagonist and the principal themes of *Surfacing*.

3. *Action as meaning*. For psychologists, "the way down is the way up" (the way in is the way out); for the Bible, "Except a corn of wheat fall into the ground and die, it abideth alone: but if it die, it bringeth forth much fruit" (John 12:24). Examine these paradoxes as revelatory of the novel's intentions, by referring to specific actions of the protagonist; trace the general course her actions take. Consider driving through "dead elm skeletons" (Chapter One) and diving for the rock painting. Ponder her actions in section III. Deliberate the two-way consequences of Joe's proposal of marriage. Apply the statements to the actions of her father and mother. What happens to those who refuse the way down?

4. *Victor and victim*. Speaking of her purposes in writing *Power Politics,* a book of poems, Atwood says, "I don't think it's about the plight of women or the villainy of men . . . . I'd say it has to do with the creation, exploration, and eventual destruction of, or by, certain mythologies, especially those involving victor and victim patterns with their endless variations of pose, accusation, complicity, and subversion of the human." Evaluate "intentions" in *Surfacing* from this point of view. Take into account especially the relationships among pairs of characters: the narrator and her "husband," the narrator and Joe, Anna and David, and the narrator's mother and father.

5. *Quest for wholeness*. Writes one critic, "For the protagonist, there occurs a 'failure of logic,' for her journey 'home' is an exploration of a world beyond logic. Her quest . . . is for an identity, a vision of self. She must find that self—not only through the father for whom she searches . . . but also through the mother for whom she must search in the depths of her own psyche." *Surfacing* joins the ranks of quest literature if we remember that the protagonist's endeavor is to achieve "wholeness of self." Discuss the novel from this vantage. (Books that will help: "The Process of Individuation," M.-L. von Franz in C. G. Jung, *Man and His Symbols; The Great Mother,* Erich Neumann; *The Living Symbol,* Gerhard Adler.)

6. *Schizophrenia*. Enumerate the ways the novel may be seen as a schizoid crisis provoked by the narrator's sex, the abortion, the death of her father, and the unsuspected proposal of marriage. (Consult R. D. Laing's short book *The Divided Self.)* Discuss how the idea informs almost every part of the novel, or its restriction to the principal character. Explain how schizophrenia is one way of defining Atwood's "world view" or interpretation of existence. How much of the novel is excluded from such a reading? Cite specific evidence that militates against this interpretation. Discuss the thematic subject of schizophrenia as a variation on others, such as doubling, cutting off, dividing, dwarfing, etc.

7. *Transformation.* The word *metamorphosis* occurs near the end of the novel, but multiple variations on it also appear, especially in the third section: *change, growth, multiplication, fluidity (tears, rain, mist, dew, water, blood),* and, to give a few examples of verbs: *eliminate, sacrifice, purge, translate, destroy, form,* and *reform.* What has this concentration of terms for transformation to do with the development of the protagonist and other characters? Why specifically are the terms concentrated in the third section? On the other hand, consider the opposite, *resistance to change,* as it appears in ideas, objects, images, and characters.

8. *Power.* Show how power is central to an understanding of *Surfacing.* As a child, the narrator thought the beans would make her "all-powerful," but the power didn't work (Chapter Four). Besides, she says, "if I'd turned out like the others with power I would have been evil." Images of power are ubiquitous. "Power" changes toward the end to "the powers" (beneficent but dangerous) whom she has sought out. Explain. Consider other evidence of power and power-plays among the characters. Examine "war" (declared and undeclared), money and purchasing, gratuitous, even wanton exercises of power. If "power" and "the powers" are both negative and positive, how does the novel reconcile the seeming contradictions?

9. *Themes and ideas.* For such a short novel, it is surprising that *Surfacing* contains so many ideas, partially or wholly developed, all coherent with principal themes. Select what you take to be a major, overriding theme from the several themes in the novel. Then explore the possibility that one theme you have chosen controls and unifies these various idea strands: logic, order, language, education, war, Americanism (why is the narrator so anti-American?), disease, death, cosmetics, food, eating, religion, nature and civilization, parents and children, art and making money, making films, games people play, mythology, and so on.

10. *An organizing principle.* Examine *Surfacing* from the point of view of thesis, antithesis, synthesis. This critical method might be organized by ideas *(thesis:* women's slavery, *antithesis:* women's liberation, *synthesis:* equal rights of men and women); or by imagery *(thesis:* mechanical objects, *antithesis:* natural entities, *synthesis:* unification and metamorphosis of both). Do the same for action, character, image, sound. What syntheses might result from such binary thematic contrasts as: nature and civilization? new and old gods? head and heart? construction and destruction? the powerful and the weak? madness and sanity?

11. *Submerging and surfacing.* Many kinds of sinking and surfacing occur in this novel. The word *surfacing* is deliberately ambiguous. It implies (1) living on the surface of life—fashions, social behavior, slogans, rejection of the past, canned or bottled ideas, and so on. It means (2) rising from the depths to the surface (literally or psychologically—from the unconscious to the conscious, from repression to acknowledgment, from mystery to disclosure, division to wholeness, etc.). Examine various aspects of the text for kinds of surfacing and sinking; determine what

they mean for governing ideas. Consider character, action, image, commentary, time, ideas, and narrative method.

12. *Thematic structure.* "It moves through three sections, beginning with the private or personal—in which mythologies are presented mostly as burlesques—through the social to the mythic," says Atwood of her poems in *Power Politics. Surfacing* also moves through three sections. Evaluate thematic structure from clues in Atwood's statement (it might need some modification when applied to the novel). Consider structural triplets such as: (1) paralysis, letting go, change; (2) lies, dissolution of lies, truth; (3) repression and distortion, coming to consciousness and surfacing, consciousness and transformation; (4) powerlessness, growing strength, power; (5) submersion, ascension, surfacing.

13. *The spirit world.* "The operation of the spirit(s) is a balancing of opposites, in the conjunction of female (passive, earthly, cold) and male (active, upper, warm)," writes psychologist C. G. Jung. "Through the warm participation of consciousness (male) the unconscious (female) is changed and imprinted." To what extent does Jung's idea clarify the narrator's situation? Apply his statement to the narrator's sense of balance achieved at the end of *Surfacing.* What opposites are balanced for her, however temporarily and tenuously? Why does she need specific gifts from her spirit father and spirit mother? Why indeed does she apparently need whatever it is that Joe brings when he returns for her at the end?

14. *Key passages.* In Chapter Seventeen, the protagonist dives "deeper than before, [to] sea bottom" and discovers something familiar, "a dark oval trailing limbs . . . . It wasn't ever my brother I'd been remembering, that had been a disguise." Then the repressed memory of her abortion surfaces. Reread the passage, paying close attention to the words. How do the details "color" the rest of the novel, her memories, her attitude toward life, human beings, religion, feeling, love, etc.? In what terms does she report them? Do the same for this sentence: "The *bottle* had been *logical,* pure logic, *remnant* of the *trapped and decaying animals, secreted by my head, enclosure,* something *to keep the death away from me*" (editors' italics).

15. *Image, motif, symbol.* Because Atwood is also a poet, she is sensitive to the use of recurrent verbal patterns. The result in *Surfacing* is a web of images, motifs, and symbols, each identified with some aspect of character, theme, or fragment of theme. Examine some of the following for their thematic significances: scrapbooks (and variations), paintings (and movies), clothing, geometrical forms, colors, cars, roads, mother with hand outstretched, games, birds, reptiles (leeches), Americanism, war, thread, machines, mirrors, powerboats, glass, cameras, moose family, landscape, couples, amnesia (paralysis), hairiness, cosmetics, books, gifts, crossing water, etc.

Seize the Day

SAUL BELLOW

1

When it came to concealing his troubles, Tommy Wilhelm was not less capable than the next fellow. So at least he thought, and there was a certain amount of evidence to back him up. He had once been an actor—no, not quite, an extra—and he knew what acting should be. Also, he was smoking a cigar, and when a man is smoking a cigar, wearing a hat, he has an advantage; it is harder to find out how he feels. He came from the twenty-third floor down to the lobby on the mezzanine to collect his mail before breakfast, and he believed—he hoped—that he looked passably well: doing all right. It was a matter of sheer hope, because there was not much that he could add to his present effort. On the fourteenth floor he looked for his father to enter the elevator; they often met at this hour, on the way to breakfast. If he worried about his appearance it was mainly for his old father's sake. But there was no stop on the fourteenth, and the elevator sank and sank. Then the smooth door opened and the great dark red uneven carpet that covered the lobby billowed toward Wilhelm's feet. In the foreground the lobby was dark, sleepy. French drapes like sails kept out the sun, but three high, narrow windows were open, and in the blue air Wilhelm saw a pigeon about to light on the great chain that supported the marquee of the movie house directly underneath the lobby. For one moment he heard the wings beating strongly.

Most of the guests at the Hotel Gloriana were past the age of retirement. Along Broadway in the Seventies, Eighties, and Nineties, a great part of New York's vast population of old men and women lives. Unless the weather is too cold or wet they fill the benches about the tiny railed parks and along the subway gratings from Verdi Square to Columbia University, they crowd the shops and cafeterias, the dime stores, the tea-rooms, the bakeries, the beauty parlors, the reading rooms and club rooms. Among these old people at the Gloriana, Wilhelm felt out of place. He was comparatively young, in his middle forties, large and blond, with big shoulders; his back was heavy and strong, if already a little stooped or thickened. After breakfast the old guests sat down on the green leather armchairs and sofas in the lobby and began to gossip and look into the papers; they had nothing to do but wait out the day. But Wilhelm was used to an active life and liked to go out energetically in the morning. And for several months, because he had no position, he had kept up his morale by rising early; he was shaved and in the lobby by eight o'clock. He bought the paper and some cigars and drank a Coca-Cola or two before he went in to breakfast with his father. After breakfast—out, out, out to attend to business. The getting out had in itself become the chief business. But he had realized that he could not keep this up much longer, and today he was afraid. He was aware that his routine was about to break up and he sensed that a huge trouble long presaged but till now formless was due. Before evening, he'd know.

Nevertheless he followed his daily course and crossed the lobby.

Rubin, the man at the newsstand, had poor eyes. They may not have been actually weak but they were poor in expression, with lacy lids that furled down at the corners. He dressed well. It didn't seem necessary—he was behind the counter most of the time—but he dressed very well. He had on a rich brown suit; the cuffs embarrassed the hairs on his small hands. He wore a Countess Mara painted necktie. As Wilhelm approached, Rubin did not see him; he was looking out dreamily at the Hotel Ansonia, which was visible from his corner, several blocks away. The Ansonia, the neighborhood's great landmark, was built by Stanford White. It looks like a baroque palace from Prague or Munich enlarged a hundred times, with towers, domes, huge swells and bubbles of metal gone green from exposure, iron fretwork and festoons. Black television antennae are densely planted on its round summits. Under the changes of weather it may look like marble or like sea water, black as slate in the fog, white as tufa in sunlight. This morning it looked like the image of itself reflected in deep water, white and cumulous above, with cavernous distortions underneath. Together, the two men gazed at it.

Then Rubin said, "Your dad is in to breakfast already, the old gentleman."

"Oh, yes? Ahead of me today?"

"That's a real knocked-out shirt you got on," said Rubin. "Where's it from, Saks?"

"No, it's a Jack Fagman—Chicago."

Even when his spirits were low, Wilhelm could still wrinkle his forehead in a pleasing way. Some of the slow, silent movements of his face were very attractive. He went back a step, as if to stand away from himself and get a better look at his shirt. His glance was comic, a comment upon his untidiness. He liked to wear good clothes, but once he had put it on each article appeared to go its own way. Wilhelm, laughing, panted a little; his teeth were small; his cheeks when he laughed and puffed grew round, and he looked much younger than his years. In the old days when he was a college freshman and wore a raccoon coat and a beanie on his large blond head his father used to say that, big as he was, he could charm a bird out of a tree. Wilhelm had great charm still.

"I like this dove-gray color," he said in his sociable, good-natured way. "It isn't washable. You have to send it to the cleaner. It never smells as good as washed. But it's a nice shirt. It cost sixteen, eighteen bucks."

This shirt had not been bought by Wilhelm; it was a present from his boss—his former boss, with whom he had had a falling out. But there was no reason why he should tell Rubin the history of it. Although perhaps Rubin knew—Rubin was the kind of man who knew, and knew and knew. Wilhelm also knew many things about Rubin, for that matter, about Rubin's wife and Rubin's business, Rubin's health. None of these could be mentioned, and the great weight of the unspoken left them little to talk about.

"Well, y'lookin' pretty sharp today," Rubin said.

And Wilhelm said gladly, "Am I? Do you really think so?" He could not believe it. He saw his reflection in the glass cupboard full of cigar boxes, among the grand seals and paper damask and the gold-embossed portraits of famous men, García, Edward the Seventh, Cyrus the Great. You had to allow for the darkness and deformations of the glass, but he thought he didn't look too good. A wide wrinkle like a comprehensive bracket sign was written upon his forehead, the point between his brows, and there were patches of brown on his dark blond skin. He began to be half amused at the shadow of his own marveling, troubled, desirous eyes, and his nostrils and his lips. Fair-haired hippopotamus!—that was how he looked to himself. He saw a big round face, a wide, flourishing red mouth, stump teeth. And the hat, too; and the cigar, too. I should have done hard labor all my life, he reflected. Hard honest labor that tires you out and makes you sleep. I'd have worked off my energy and felt better. Instead, I had to distinguish myself—yet.

He had put forth plenty of effort, but that was not the same as working hard, was it? And if as a young man he had got off to a bad start it was due to this very same face. Early in the nineteen-thirties, because of his striking looks, he had been very briefly considered star material, and he had gone to Hollywood. There for seven years, stubbornly, he had tried to become a screen artist. Long before that time his ambition or delusion had ended, but through pride and perhaps also through laziness he had remained in California. At last he turned to other things, but those seven years of persistence and defeat had unfitted him somehow for trades and businesses, and then it was too late to go into one of the professions. He had been slow to mature, and he had lost ground, and so he hadn't been able to get rid of his energy and he was convinced that this energy itself had done him the greatest harm.

"I didn't see you at the gin game last night," said Rubin.

"I had to miss it. How did it go?"

For the last few weeks Wilhelm had played gin almost nightly, but yesterday he had felt that he couldn't afford to lose any more. He had never won. Not once. And while the losses were small they weren't gains, were they? They were losses. He was tired of losing, and tired also of the company, and so he had gone by himself to the movies.

"Oh," said Rubin, "it went okay. Carl made a chump of himself yelling at the guys. This time Doctor Tamkin didn't let him get away with it. He told him the psychological reason why."

"What was the reason?"

Rubin said, "I can't quote him. Who could? You know the way Tamkin talks. Don't ask me. Do you want the *Trib?* Aren't you going to look at the closing quotations?"

"It won't help much to look. I know what they were yesterday at three," said Wilhelm. "But I suppose I better had get the paper." It seemed necessary for him to lift one shoulder in order to put his hand into his jacket pocket. There, among little packets of pills and crushed cigarette butts and strings of cellophane, the red tapes of packages which he sometimes used as dental floss, he recalled that he had dropped some pennies.

"That doesn't sound so good," said Rubin. He meant to be conversationally playful, but his voice had no tone and his eyes, slack and lid-blinded, turned elsewhere. He didn't want to hear. It was all the same to him. Maybe he already knew, being the sort of man who knew and knew.

No, it wasn't good. Wilhelm held three orders of lard in the commodities market. He and Dr. Tamkin had bought this lard together four days ago at 12.96, and the price at once began to fall and was still falling. In the mail this morning there was sure to be a call for additional margin payment. One came every day.

The psychologist, Dr. Tamkin, had got him into this. Tamkin lived at the Gloriana and attended the card game. He had explained to Wilhelm that you could speculate in commodities at one of the uptown branches of a good Wall Street house without making the full deposit of margin legally required. It was up to the branch manager. If he knew you—and all the branch managers knew Tamkin—he would allow you to make short-term purchases. You needed only to open a small account.

"The whole secret of this type of speculation," Tamkin had told him, "is in the alertness. You have to act fast—buy it and sell it; sell it and buy it again. But quick! Get to the window and have them wire Chicago at just the right second. Strike and strike again! Then get out the same day. In no time at all you turn over fifteen, twenty thousand dollars' worth of soy beans, coffee, corn, hides, wheat, cotton." Obviously the doctor understood the market well. Otherwise he could not make it sound so simple. "People lose because they are greedy and can't get out when it starts to go up. They gamble, but I do it scientifically. This is not guesswork. You must take a few points and get out. Why, ye gods!" said Dr. Tamkin with his bulging eyes, his bald head, and his drooping lip. "Have you stopped to think how much dough people are making in the market?"

Wilhelm with a quick shift from gloomy attention to the panting laugh which entirely changed his face had said, "Ho, have I ever! What do you think? Who doesn't know it's way beyond nineteen-twenty-eight—twenty-nine and still on the rise? Who hasn't read the Fulbright investigation? There's money everywhere. Everyone is shoveling it in. Money is—is—"

"And can you rest—can you sit still while this is going on?" said Dr. Tamkin. "I confess to you I can't. I think about people, just because they have a few bucks to invest, making fortunes. They have no sense, they have no talent, they just have the extra dough and it makes them more dough. I get so worked up and tormented and restless, so restless! I haven't even been able to practice my profession. With all this money around you don't want to be a fool while everyone else is making. I know guys who make five, ten thousand a week just by fooling around. I know a guy at the Hotel Pierre. There's nothing to him, but he has a whole case of Mumm's champagne at lunch. I know another guy on Central Park South—But what's the use of talking. They make millions. They have smart lawyers who get them out of taxes by a thousand schemes."

"Whereas I got taken," said Wilhelm. "My wife refused to sign a joint return. One fairly good year and I got into the thirty-two-percent bracket and was stripped bare. What of all my bad years?"

"It's a businessmen's government," said Dr. Tamkin. "You can be sure that these men making five thousand a week—"

"I don't need that sort of money," Wilhelm had said. "But oh! if I could only work out a little steady income from this. Not much. I don't ask much. But how badly I need—! I'd be so grateful if you'd show me how to work it."

"Sure I will. *I* do it regularly. I'll bring you my receipts if you like. And do you want to know something? I approve of your attitude very much. You want to avoid catching the money fever. This type of activity is filled with hostile feeling and lust. You should see what it does to some of these fellows. They go on the market with murder in their hearts."

"What's that I once heard a guy say?" Wilhelm remarked. "A man is only as good as what he loves."

"That's it—just it," Tamkin said. "You don't have to go about it their way. There's also a calm and rational, a psychological approach."

Wilhelm's father, old Dr. Adler, lived in an entirely different world from his son, but he had warned him once against Dr. Tamkin. Rather casually—he was a very bland old man—he said, "Wilky, perhaps you listen too much to this Tamkin. He's interesting to talk to. I don't doubt it. I think he's pretty common but he's a persuasive man. However, I don't know how reliable he may be."

It made Wilhelm profoundly bitter that his father should speak to him with such detachment about his welfare. Dr. Adler liked to appear affable. Affable! His own son, his one and only son, could not speak his mind or ease his heart to him. I wouldn't turn to Tamkin, he thought, if I could turn to him. At least Tamkin sympathizes with me and tries to give me a hand, whereas Dad doesn't want to be disturbed.

Old Dr. Adler had retired from practice; he had a considerable fortune and could easily have helped his son. Recently Wilhelm had told him, "Father—it so happens that I'm in a bad way now. I hate to have to say it. You realize that I'd rather have good news to bring you. But it's true. And since it's true, Dad— What else am I supposed to say? It's true."

Another father might have appreciated how difficult this confession was—so much bad luck, weariness, weakness, and failure. Wilhelm had tried to copy the old man's tone and made himself sound gentlemanly, low-voiced, tasteful. He didn't allow his voice to tremble; he made no stupid gesture. But the doctor had no answer. He only nodded. You might have told him that Seattle was near Puget Sound, or that the Giants and Dodgers were playing a night game, so little was he moved from his expression of healthy, handsome, good-humored old age. He behaved toward his son as he had formerly done toward his patients, and it was a great grief to Wilhelm; it was almost too much to bear. Couldn't he see—couldn't he feel? Had he lost his family sense?

Greatly hurt, Wilhelm struggled however to be fair. Old people are bound to change, he said. They have hard things to think about. They must prepare for where they are going. They can't live by the old schedule any longer and all their perspectives change, and other people become alike, kin and acquaintances. Dad is no longer the same person, Wilhelm reflected. He was thirty-two when I was born, and now he's going on eighty. Furthermore, it's time I stopped feeling like a kid toward him, a small son.

The handsome old doctor stood well above the other old people in the hotel. He was idolized by everyone. This was what people said: "That's old Professor Adler, who used to teach internal medicine. He was a diagnostician, one of the best in New York, and had a tremendous practice. Isn't he a wonderful-looking old guy? It's a pleasure to see such a fine old scientist, clean and immaculate. He stands straight and understands every single thing you say. He still has all his buttons. You can discuss any subject with him." The clerks, the elevator operators, the telephone girls and waitresses and chambermaids, the management flattered and pampered him. That was what he wanted. He had always been a vain man. To see how his father loved himself sometimes made Wilhelm madly indignant.

He folded over the *Tribune* with its heavy, black, crashing sensational print and read without recognizing any of the words, for his mind was still on his father's vanity. The doctor had created his own praise. People were primed and did not know it. And what did he need praise for? In a hotel where everyone was busy and contacts were so brief and had such small weight, how could it satisfy him? He could be in people's thoughts here and there for a moment; in and then out. He could never matter much to them. Wilhelm let out a long, hard breath and raised the brows of his round and somewhat circular eyes. He stared beyond the thick borders of the paper.

> . . . love that well which thou must leave ere long.

Involuntary memory brought him this line. At first he thought it referred to his father, but then he understood that it was for himself, rather. *He* should love that well. "This thou perceivest, which makes *thy* love more strong." Under Dr. Tamkin's influence Wilhelm had recently begun to remember the poems he used to read. Dr. Tamkin knew, or said he knew, the great English poets and once in a while he mentioned a poem of his own. It was a long time since anyone had spoken to Wilhelm about this sort of thing. He didn't like to think about his college days, but if there was one course that now made sense it was Literature I. The textbook was Lieder and Lovett's *British Poetry and Prose,* a black heavy book with thin pages. Did I read that? he asked himself. Yes, he had read it and there was one accomplishment at least he could recall with pleasure. He had read "Yet once more, O ye laurels." How pure this was to say! It was beautiful.

> Sunk though he be beneath the wat'ry floor . . .

Such things had always swayed him, and now the power of such words was far, far greater.

Wilhelm respected the truth, but he could lie and one of the things he lied often about was his education. He said he was an alumnus of Penn State; in fact he had left school before his sophomore year was finished. His sister Catherine had a B.S. degree. Wilhelm's late mother was a graduate of Bryn Mawr. He was the only member of the family who had no education. This was another sore point. His father was ashamed of him.

But he had heard the old man bragging to another old man, saying, "My son is a sales executive. He didn't have the patience to finish school. But he does all right for himself. His income is up in the five figures somewhere."

"What—thirty, forty thousand?" said his stooped old friend.

"Well, he needs at least that much for his style of life. Yes, he needs that."

Despite his troubles, Wilhelm almost laughed. Why, that boasting old hypocrite. He knew the sales executive was no more. For many weeks there had been no executive, no sales, no income. But how we love looking fine in the eyes of the world—how beautiful are the old when they are doing a snow job! It's Dad, thought Wilhelm, who is the salesman. He's selling me. *He* should have gone on the road.

But what of the truth? Ah, the truth was that there were problems, and of these problems his father wanted no part. His father was ashamed of him. The truth, Wilhelm thought, was very awkward. He pressed his lips together, and his tongue went soft; it pained him far at the back, in the cords and throat, and a knot of ill formed in his chest. Dad never was a pal to me when I was young, he reflected. He was at the office or the hospital, or lecturing. He expected me to look out for myself and never gave me much thought. Now he looks down on me. And maybe in some respects he's right.

No wonder Wilhelm delayed the moment when he would have to go into the dining room. He had moved to the end of Rubin's counter. He had opened the *Tribune;* the fresh pages drooped from his hands; the cigar was smoked out and the hat did not defend him. He was wrong to suppose that he was more capable than the next fellow when it came to concealing his troubles. They were clearly written out upon his face. He wasn't even aware of it.

There was the matter of the different names, which, in the hotel, came up frequently. "Are you Doctor Adler's son?" "Yes, but my name is Tommy Wilhelm." And the doctor would say, "My son and I use different monickers. I uphold tradition. He's for the new." The Tommy was Wilhelm's own invention. He adopted it when he went to Hollywood, and dropped the Adler. Hollywood was his own idea, too. He used to pretend that it had all been the doing of a certain talent scout named Maurice Venice. But the scout had never made him a definite offer of a studio connection. He had approached him, but the results of the screen tests had not been good. After the test Wilhelm took the initiative and pressed Maurice Venice until he got him to say, "Well, I suppose you might make it out there." On the strength of this Wilhelm had left college and had gone to California.

Someone had said, and Wilhelm agreed with the saying, that in Los

Angeles all the loose objects in the country were collected, as if America had been tilted and everything that wasn't tightly screwed down had slid into Southern California. He himself had been one of these loose objects. Sometimes he told people, "I was too mature for college. I was a big boy, you see. Well, I thought, when do you start to become a man?" After he had driven a painted flivver and had worn a yellow slicker with slogans on it, and played illegal poker, and gone out on Coke dates, he had *had* college. He wanted to try something new and quarreled with his parents about his career. And then a letter came from Maurice Venice.

The story of the scout was long and intricate and there were several versions of it. The truth about it was never told. Wilhelm had lied first boastfully and then out of charity to himself. But his memory was good, he could still separate what he had invented from the actual happenings, and this morning he found it necessary as he stood by Rubin's showcase with his *Tribune* to recall the crazy course of the true events.

I didn't seem even to realize that there was a depression. How could I have been such a jerk as not to prepare for anything and just go on luck and inspiration? With round gray eyes expanded and his large shapely lips closed in severity toward himself he forced open all that had been hidden. Dad I couldn't affect one way or another. Mama was the one who tried to stop me, and we carried on and yelled and pleaded. The more I lied the louder I raised my voice, and charged—like a hippopotamus. Poor Mother! How I disappointed her. Rubin heard Wilhelm give a broken sigh as he stood with the forgotten *Tribune* crushed under his arm.

When Wilhelm was aware that Rubin watched him, loitering and idle, apparently not knowing what to do with himself this morning, he turned to the Coca-Cola machine. He swallowed hard at the Coke bottle and coughed over it, but he ignored his coughing, for he was still thinking, his eyes upcast and his lips closed behind his hand. By a peculiar twist of habit he wore his coat collar turned up always, as though there were a wind. It never lay flat. But on his broad back, stooped with its own weight, its strength warped almost into deformity, the collar of his sports coat appeared anyway to be no wider than a ribbon.

He was listening to the sound of his own voice as he explained, twenty-five years ago in the living room on West End Avenue, "But Mother, if I don't pan out as an actor I can still go back to school."

But she was afraid he was going to destroy himself. She said,

"Wilky, Dad could make it easy for you if you wanted to go into medicine." To remember this stifled him.

"I can't bear hospitals. Besides, I might make a mistake and hurt someone or even kill a patient. I couldn't stand that. Besides, I haven't got that sort of brains."

Then his mother had made the mistake of mentioning her nephew Artie, Wilhelm's cousin, who was an honor student at Columbia in math and languages. That dark little gloomy Artie with his disgusting narrow face, and his moles and self-sniffing ways and his unclean table manners, the boring habit he had of conjugating verbs when you went for a walk with him. "Roumanian is an easy language. You just add a *tl* to everything." He was now a professor, this same Artie with whom Wilhelm had played near the soldiers' and sailors' monument on Riverside Drive. Not that to be a professor was in itself so great. How could anyone bear to know so many languages? And Artie also had to remain Artie, which was a bad deal. But perhaps success had changed him. Now that he had a place in the world perhaps he was better. Did Artie love his languages, and live for them, or was he also, in his heart, cynical? So many people nowadays were. No one seemed satisfied, and Wilhelm was especially horrified by the cynicism of successful people. Cynicism was bread and meat to everyone. And irony, too. Maybe it couldn't be helped. It was probably even necessary. Wilhelm, however, feared it intensely. Whenever at the end of the day he was unusually fatigued he attributed it to cynicism. Too much of the world's business done. Too much falsity. He had various words to express the effect this had on him. Chicken! Unclean! Congestion! he exclaimed in his heart. Rat race! Phony! Murder! Play the Game! Buggers!

At first the letter from the talent scout was nothing but a flattering sort of joke. Wilhelm's picture in the college paper when he was running for class treasurer was seen by Maurice Venice, who wrote to him about a screen test. Wilhelm at once took the train to New York. He found the scout to be huge and oxlike, so stout that his arms seemed caught from beneath in a grip of flesh and fat; it looked as though it must be positively painful. He had little hair. Yet he enjoyed a healthy complexion. His breath was noisy and his voice rather difficult and husky because of the fat in his throat. He had on a double-breasted suit of the type then known as the pillbox; it was chalk-striped, pink on blue; the trousers hugged his ankles.

They met and shook hands and sat down. Together these two big men dwarfed the tiny Broadway office and made the furnishings look like toys. Wilhelm had the color of a Golden Grimes apple when he was well, and then his thick blond hair had been vigorous and his wide shoulders unwarped; he was leaner in the jaws, his eyes fresher and wider; his legs were then still awkward but he was impressively handsome. And he was about to make his first great mistake. Like, he sometimes thought, I was going to pick up a weapon and strike myself a blow with it.

Looming over the desk in the small office darkened by overbuilt midtown—sheer walls, gray spaces, dry lagoons of tar and pebbles —Maurice Venice proceeded to establish his credentials. He said, "My letter was on the regular stationery, but maybe you want to check on me?"

"Who, *me?*" said Wilhelm. "Why?"

"There's guys who think I'm in a racket and make a charge for the test. I don't ask a cent. I'm no agent. There ain't no commission."

"I never even thought of it," said Wilhelm. Was there perhaps something fishy about this Maurice Venice? He protested too much.

In his husky, fat-weakened voice he finally challenged Wilhelm, "If you're not sure, you can call the distributor and find out who I am, Maurice Venice."

Wilhelm wondered at him. "Why shouldn't I be sure? Of course I am."

"Because I can see the way you size me up, and because this is a dinky office. Like you don't believe me. Go ahead. Call. I won't care if you're cautious. I mean it. There's quite a few people who doubt me at first. They can't really believe that fame and fortune are going to hit 'em."

"But I tell you I do believe you," Wilhelm had said, and bent inward to accommodate the pressure of his warm, panting laugh. It was purely nervous. His neck was ruddy and neatly shaved about the ears—he was fresh from the barbershop; his face anxiously glowed with his desire to make a pleasing impression. It was all wasted on Venice, who was just as concerned about the impression *he* was making.

"If you're surprised, I'll just show you what I mean," Venice had said. "It was about fifteen months ago right in this identical same office when I saw a beautiful thing in the paper. It wasn't even a photo but a drawing, a brassière ad, but I knew right away that this was star material. I called up the paper to ask who the girl was, they gave me the name of the advertising agency; I phoned the agency and they gave me the name of the artist; I got hold of the artist and he gave me the number of the model agency. Finally, finally I got her number and phoned her and said, 'This is Maurice Venice, scout for Kaskaskia Films.' So right away she says, 'Yah, so's your old lady.' Well, when I saw I wasn't getting nowhere with her I said to her, 'Well, miss. I don't blame you. You're a very beautiful thing and must have a dozen admirers after you all the time, boy friends who like to call and pull your leg and give a tease. But as I happen to be a very busy fellow and don't have the time to horse around or argue, I tell you what to do. Here's my number, and here's the number of the Kaskaskia Distributors, Inc. Ask them who am I, Maurice Venice. The scout.' She did it. A little while later she phoned me back, all apologies and excuses, but I didn't want to embarrass her and get off on the wrong foot with an artist. I know better than to do that. So I told her it was a natural precaution, never mind. I wanted to run a screen test right away. Because I seldom am wrong about talent. If I see it, it's there. Get that, please. And do you know who that little girl is today?"

"No," Wilhelm said eagerly. "Who is she?"

Venice said impressively, "'Nita Christenberry."

Wilhelm sat utterly blank. This was failure. He didn't know the name, and Venice was waiting for his response and would be angry.

And in fact Venice had been offended. He said, "What's the matter with you! Don't you read a magazine? She's a starlet."

"I'm sorry," Wilhelm answered. "I'm at school and don't have time to keep up. If I don't know her, it doesn't mean a thing. She made a big hit, I'll bet."

"You can say that again. Here's a photo of her." He handed Wilhelm some pictures. She was a bathing beauty—short, the usual breasts, hips, and smooth thighs. Yes, quite good, as Wilhelm recalled. She stood on high heels and wore a Spanish comb and mantilla. In her hand was a fan.

He had said, "She looks awfully peppy."

"Isn't she a divine girl? And what personality! Not just another broad in the show business, believe me." He had a surprise for Wilhelm. "I have found happiness with her," he said.

"You have?" said Wilhelm, slow to understand.

"Yes, boy, we're engaged."

Wilhelm saw another photograph, taken on the beach. Venice was dressed in a terry-cloth beach outfit, and he and the girl, cheek to cheek, were looking into the camera. Below, in white ink, was written "Love at Malibu Colony."

"I'm sure you'll be very happy. I wish you—"

"I *know,*" said Venice firmly, "I'm going to be happy. When I saw that drawing, the breath of fate breathed on me. I felt it over my entire body."

"Say, it strikes a bell suddenly," Wilhelm had said. "Aren't you related to Martial Venice the producer?"

Venice was either a nephew of the producer or the son of a first cousin. Decidedly he had not made good. It was easy enough for Wilhelm to see this now. The office was so poor, and Venice bragged so nervously and identified himself so scrupulously—the poor guy. He was the obscure failure of an aggressive and powerful clan. As such he had the greatest sympathy from Wilhelm.

Venice had said, "Now I suppose you want to know where you come in. I seen your school paper, by accident. You take quite a remarkable picture."

"It can't be so much," said Wilhelm, more panting than laughing.

"You don't want to tell me my business," Venice said. "Leave it to me. I studied up on this."

"I never imagined— Well, what kind of roles do you think I'd fit?"

"All this time that we've been talking, I've been watching. Don't think I haven't. You remind me of someone. Let's see who it can be—one of the great old-timers. Is it Milton Sills? No, that's not the one. Conway Tearle, Jack Mulhall? George Bancroft? No, his face was ruggeder. One thing I can tell you, though, a George Raft type you're not—those tough, smooth, black little characters."

"No, I wouldn't seem to be."

"No, you're not that flyweight type, with the fists, from a nightclub, and the glamorous sideburns, doing the tango or the bolero. Not Edward G. Robinson, either—I'm thinking aloud. Or the Cagney fly-in-your-face role, a cabbie, with that mouth and those punches."

"I realize that."

"Not suave like William Powell, or a lyric juvenile like Buddy Rogers. I suppose you don't play the sax? No. But—"

"But what?"

"I have you placed as the type that loses the girl to the George Raft type or the William Powell type. You are steady, faithful, you get stood up. The older women would know better. The mothers are on your side. With what they been through, if it was up to them, they'd take you in a minute. You're very sympathetic, even the young girls feel that. You'd make a good provider. But they go more for the other types. It's as clear as anything."

This was not how Wilhelm saw himself. And as he surveyed the old ground he recognized now that he had been not only confused but hurt. Why, he thought, he cast me even then for a loser.

Wilhelm had said, with half a mind to be defiant, "Is that your opinion?"

It never occurred to Venice that a man might object to stardom in such a role. "Here is your chance," he said. "Now you're just in college. What are you studying?" He snapped his fingers. "Stuff." Wilhelm himself felt this way about it. "You may plug along fifty years before you get anywheres. This way, in one jump, the world knows who you are. You become a name like Roosevelt, Swanson. From east to west, out to China, into South America. This is no bunk. You become a lover to the whole world. The world wants it, needs it. One fellow smiles, a billion people also smile. One fellow cries, the other billion sob with him. Listen, bud—" Venice had pulled himself together to make an effort. On his imagination there was some great weight which he could not discharge. He wanted Wilhelm, too, to feel it. He twisted his large, clean, well-meaning, rather foolish features as though he were their unwilling captive, and said in his choked, fat-obstructed voice, "Listen, everywhere there are people trying hard, miserable, in trouble, downcast, tired, trying and trying. They need a break, right? A break through, a help, luck or sympathy."

"That certainly is the truth," said Wilhelm. He had seized the feeling and he waited for Venice to go on. But Venice had no more to say; he had concluded. He gave Wilhelm several pages of blue hectographed script, stapled together, and told him to prepare for the screen test. "Study your lines in front of a mirror," he said. "Let yourself go. The part should take ahold of you. Don't be afraid to make faces and be emotional. Shoot the works. Because when you start to act you're no more an ordinary person, and those things don't apply to you. You don't behave the same way as the average."

And so Wilhelm had never returned to Penn State. His roommate sent his things to New York for him, and the school authorities had to write to Dr. Adler to find out what had happened.

Still, for three months Wilhelm delayed his trip to California. He wanted to start out with the blessings of his family, but they were never given. He quarreled with his parents and his sister. And then, when he was best aware of the risks and knew a hundred reasons against going and had made himself sick with fear, he left home. This was typical of Wilhelm. After much thought and hesitation and debate he invariably took the course he had rejected innumerable times. Ten such decisions made up the history of his life. He had decided that it would be a bad mistake to go to Hollywood, and then he went. He had made up his mind not to marry his wife, but ran off and got married. He had resolved not to invest money with Tamkin, and then had given him a check.

But Wilhelm had been eager for life to start. College was merely another delay. Venice had approached him and said that the world had named Wilhelm to shine before it. He was to be freed from the anxious and narrow life of the average. Moreover, Venice had claimed that he never made a mistake. His instinct for talent was infallible, he said.

But when Venice saw the results of the screen test he did a quick about-face. In those days Wilhelm had had a speech difficulty. It was not a true stammer, it was a thickness of speech which the sound track exaggerated. The film showed that he had many peculiarities, otherwise unnoticeable. When he shrugged, his hands drew up within his sleeves. The vault of his chest was huge, but he really didn't look strong under the lights. Though he called himself a hippopotamus, he more nearly resembled a bear. His walk was bearlike, quick and rather soft, toes turned inward, as though his shoes were an impediment. About one thing Venice had been right. Wilhelm was photogenic, and his wavy blond hair (now graying) came out well, but after the test Venice refused to encourage him. He tried to get rid of him. He couldn't afford to take a chance on him, he had made too many mistakes already and lived in fear of his powerful relatives.

Wilhelm had told his parents, "Venice says I owe it to myself to go." How ashamed he was now of this lie! He had begged Venice not to give him up. He had said, "Can't you help me out? It would kill me to go back to school now."

Then when he reached the Coast he learned that a recommendation from Maurice Venice was the kiss of death. Venice needed help and charity more than he, Wilhelm, ever had. A few years later when Wilhelm was down on his luck and working as an orderly in a Los

Angeles hospital, he saw Venice's picture in the papers. He was under indictment for pandering. Closely following the trial, Wilhelm found out that Venice had indeed been employed by Kaskaskia Films but that he had evidently made use of the connection to organize a ring of call girls. Then what did he want with me? Wilhelm had cried to himself. He was unwilling to believe anything very bad about Venice. Perhaps he was foolish and unlucky, a fall guy, a dupe, a sucker. You didn't give a man fifteen years in prison for that. Wilhelm often thought that he might write him a letter to say how sorry he was. He remembered the breath of fate and Venice's certainty that he would be happy. 'Nita Christenberry was sentenced to three years. Wilhelm recognized her although she had changed her name.

By that time Wilhelm too had taken his new name. In California he became Tommy Wilhelm. Dr. Adler would not accept the change. Today he still called his son Wilky, as he had done for more than forty years. Well, now, Wilhelm was thinking, the paper crowded in disarray under his arm, there's really very little that a man can change at will. He can't change his lungs, or nerves, or constitution or temperament. They're not under his control. When he's young and strong and impulsive and dissatisfied with the way things are he wants to rearrange them to assert his freedom. He can't overthrow the government or be differently born; he only has a little scope and maybe a foreboding, too, that essentially you can't change. Nevertheless, he makes a gesture and becomes Tommy Wilhelm. Wilhelm had always had a great longing to be Tommy. He had never, however, succeeded in feeling like Tommy, and in his soul had always remained Wilky. When he was drunk he reproached himself horribly as Wilky. "You fool, you clunk, you Wilky!" he called himself. He thought that it was a good thing perhaps that he had not become a success as Tommy since that would not have been a genuine success. Wilhelm would have feared that not he but Tommy had brought it off, cheating Wilky of his birthright. Yes, it had been a stupid thing to do, but it was his imperfect judgment at the age of twenty which should be blamed. He had cast off his father's name, and with it his father's opinion of him. It was, he knew it was, his bid for liberty, Adler being in his mind the title of the species, Tommy the freedom of the person. But Wilky was his inescapable self.

In middle age you no longer thought such thoughts about free choice. Then it came over you that from one grandfather you had inherited such and such a head of hair which looked like honey when it whitens or sugars in the jar; from another, broad thick shoulders; an oddity of speech from one uncle, and small teeth from another, and the gray eyes with darkness diffused even into the whites, and a wide-lipped mouth like a statue from Peru. Wandering races have such looks, the bones of one tribe, the skin of another. From his mother he had gotten sensitive feelings, a soft heart, a brooding nature, a tendency to be confused under pressure.

The changed name was a mistake, and he would admit it as freely as you liked. But this mistake couldn't be undone now, so why must his father continually remind him how he had sinned? It was too late. He would have to go back to the pathetic day when the sin was committed. And where was that day? Past and dead. Whose humiliating memories were these? His and not his father's. What had he to think back on that he could call good? Very, very little. You had to forgive. First, to forgive yourself, and then general forgiveness. Didn't he suffer from his mistakes far more than his father could?

"Oh, God," Wilhelm prayed. "Let me out of my trouble. Let me out of my thoughts, and let me do something better with myself. For all the time I have wasted I am very sorry. Let me out of this clutch and into a different life. For I am all balled up. Have mercy."

2

The mail.

The clerk who gave it to him did not care what sort of appearance he made this morning. He only glanced at him from under his brows, upward, as the letters changed hands. Why should the hotel people waste courtesies on him? They had his number. The clerk knew that he was handing him, along with the letters, a bill for his rent. Wilhelm assumed a look that removed him from all such things. But it was bad. To pay the bill he would have to withdraw money from his brokerage account, and the account was being watched because of the drop in lard. According to the *Tribune's* figures lard was still twenty points below last year's level. There were government price supports. Wilhelm didn't know how these worked but he understood that the farmer was protected and that the SEC kept an eye on the market and therefore he believed that lard would rise again and he wasn't greatly worried as yet. But in the meantime his father might have offered to pick up his hotel tab. Why didn't he? What a selfish old man he was! He saw his son's hardships; he could so easily help him. How little it would mean to him, and how much to Wilhelm! Where was the old man's heart? Maybe, thought Wilhelm, I was sentimental in the past and exaggerated his kindliness—warm family life. It may never have been there.

Not long ago his father had said to him in his usual affable, pleasant way, "Well, Wilky, here we are under the same roof again, after all these years."

Wilhelm was glad for an instant. At last they would talk over old times. But he was also on guard against insinuations. Wasn't his father saying, "Why are you here in a hotel with me and not at home in Brooklyn with your wife and two boys? You're neither a widower nor a bachelor. You have brought me all your confusions. What do you expect me to do with them?"

So Wilhelm studied the remark for a bit, then said, "The roof is twenty-six stories up. But how many years has it been?"

"That's what I was asking you."

"Gosh, Dad, I'm not sure. Wasn't it the year Mother died? What year was that?"

He asked this question with an innocent frown on his Golden Grimes, dark blond face. *What year was it!* As though he didn't know the year, the month, the day, the very hour of his mother's death.

"Wasn't it nineteen-thirty-one?" said Dr. Adler.

"Oh, was it?" said Wilhelm. And in hiding the sadness and the overwhelming irony of the question he gave a nervous shiver and wagged his head and felt the ends of his collar rapidly.

"Do you know?" his father said. "You must realize, an old fellow's memory becomes unreliable. It was in winter, that I'm sure of. Nineteen-thirty-two?"

Yes, it was age. Don't make an issue of it, Wilhelm advised himself. If you were to ask the old doctor in what year he had interned, he'd tell you correctly. All the same, don't make an issue. Don't quarrel with your own father. Have pity on an old man's failings.

"I believe the year was closer to nineteen-thirty-four, Dad," he said.

But Dr. Adler was thinking, Why the devil can't he stand still when we're talking? He's either hoisting his pants up and down by the pockets or jittering with his feet. A regular mountain of tics, he's getting to be. Wilhelm had a habit of moving his feet back and forth as though, hurrying into a house, he had to clean his shoes first on the doormat.

Then Wilhelm had said, "Yes, that was the beginning of the end, wasn't it, Father?"

Wilhelm often astonished Dr. Adler. Beginning of the end? What could he mean—what was he fishing for? Whose end? The end of family life? The old man was puzzled but he would not give Wilhelm an opening to introduce his complaints. He had learned that it was better not to take up Wilhelm's strange challenges. So he merely agreed pleasantly, for he was a master of social behavior, and said, "It was an awful misfortune for us all."

He thought, What business has he to complain to *me* of his mother's death?

Face to face they had stood, each declaring himself silently after his own way. It was: it was not, the beginning of the end—*some* end.

Unaware of anything odd in his doing it, for he did it all the time, Wilhelm had pinched out the coal of his cigarette and dropped the butt in his pocket, where there were many more. And as he gazed at his father the little finger of his right hand began to twitch and tremble; of that he was unconscious, too.

And yet Wilhelm believed that when he put his mind to it he could have perfect and even distinguished manners, outdoing his father. Despite the slight thickness in his speech—it amounted almost to a stammer when he started the same phrase over several times in his effort to eliminate the thick sound—he could be fluent. Otherwise he would never have made a good salesman. He claimed also that he was a good listener. When he listened he made a tight mouth and rolled his eyes thoughtfully. He would soon tire and begin to utter short, loud, impatient breaths, and he would say, "Oh yes . . . yes . . . yes. I couldn't agree more." When he was forced to differ he would declare, "Well, I'm not sure. I don't really see it that way. I'm of two minds about it." He would never willingly hurt any man's feelings.

But in conversation with his father he was apt to lose control of himself. After any talk with Dr. Adler, Wilhelm generally felt dissatisfied, and his dissatisfaction reached its greatest intensity when they discussed family matters. Ostensibly he had been trying to help the old man to remember a date, but in reality he meant to tell him, "You were set free when Ma died. You wanted to forget her. You'd like to get rid of Catherine, too. Me, too. You're not kidding anyone"—Wilhelm striving to put this across, and the old man not having it. In the end he was left struggling, while his father seemed unmoved.

And then once more Wilhelm had said to himself, "But man! you're not a kid. Even then you weren't a kid!" He looked down over the front of his big, indecently big, spoiled body. He was beginning to lose his shape, his gut was fat, and he looked like a hippopotamus. His younger son called him "a hummuspotamus"; that was little Paul. And here he was still struggling with his old dad, filled with ancient grievances. Instead of saying, "Good-by, youth! Oh, good-by those marvelous, foolish wasted days. What a big clunk I was—I *am.*"

Wilhelm was still paying heavily for his mistakes. His wife Margaret would not give him a divorce, and he had to support her and the two children. She would regularly agree to divorce him, and then think things over again and set new and more difficult conditions. No court would have awarded her the amounts he paid. One of today's letters, as he had expected, was from her. For the first time he had sent her a postdated check, and she protested. She also enclosed bills for the boys' educational insurance policies, due next week. Wilhelm's mother-in-law had taken out these policies in Beverly Hills, and since her death two years ago he had to pay the premiums. Why couldn't she have minded her own business! They were his kids, and he took care of them and always would. He had planned to set up a trust fund. But that was on his former expectations. Now he had to rethink the future, because of the money problem. Meanwhile, here were the bills to be paid. When he saw the two sums punched out so neatly on the cards he cursed the company and its IBM equipment. His heart and his head were congested with anger. Everyone was supposed to have money. It was nothing to the company. It published pictures of funerals in the magazines and frightened the suckers, and then punched out little holes, and the customers would lie awake to think out ways to raise the dough. They'd be ashamed not to have it. They couldn't let a great company down, either, and they got the scratch. In the old days a man was put in prison for debt, but there were subtler things now. They made it a shame not to have money and set everybody to work.

Well, and what else had Margaret sent him? He tore the envelope open with his thumb, swearing that he would send any other bills back to her. There was, luckily, nothing more. He put the hole-punched cards in his pocket. Didn't Margaret know that he was nearly at the end of his rope? Of course. Her instinct told her that this was her opportunity, and she was giving him the works.

He went into the dining room, which was under Austro-Hungarian management at the Hotel Gloriana. It was run like a European establishment. The pastries were excellent, especially the strudel. He often had apple strudel and coffee in the afternoon.

As soon as he entered he saw his father's small head in the sunny bay at the farther end, and heard his precise voice. It was with an odd sort of perilous expression that Wilhelm crossed the dining room.

Dr. Adler liked to sit in a corner that looked across Broadway down to the Hudson and New Jersey. On the other side of the street was a supermodern cafeteria with gold and purple mosaic columns. On the second floor a private-eye school, a dental laboratory, a reducing parlor, a veteran's club, and a Hebrew school shared the space. The old man was sprinkling sugar on his strawberries. Small hoops of brilliance were cast by the water glasses on the white tablecloth, despite a faint murkiness in the sunshine. It was early summer, and the long window was turned inward; a moth was on the pane; the putty was broken and the white enamel on the frames was streaming with wrinkles.

"Ha, Wilky," said the old man to his tardy son. "You haven't met our neighbor Mr. Perls, have you? From the fifteenth floor."

"How d'do," Wilhelm said. He did not welcome this stranger; he began at once to find fault with him. Mr. Perls carried a heavy cane with a crutch tip. Dyed hair, a skinny forehead—these were not reasons for bias. Nor was it Mr. Perls's fault that Dr. Adler was using him, not wishing to have breakfast with his son alone. But a gruffer voice within Wilhelm spoke, asking, "Who is this damn frazzle-faced herring with his dyed hair and his fish teeth and this drippy mustache? Another one of Dad's German friends. Where does he collect all these guys? What is the stuff on his teeth? I never saw such pointed crowns. Are they stainless steel, or a kind of silver? How can a human face get into this condition. Uch!" Staring with his widely spaced gray eyes, Wilhelm sat, his broad back stooped under the sports jacket. He clasped his hands on the table with an implication of suppliance. Then he began to relent a little toward Mr. Perls, beginning at the teeth. Each of those crowns represented a tooth ground to the quick, and estimating a man's grief with his teeth as two per cent of the total, and adding to that his flight from Germany and the probable origin of his wincing wrinkles, not to be confused with the wrinkles of his smile, it came to a sizable load.

"Mr. Perls was a hosiery wholesaler," said Dr. Adler.

"Is this the son you told me was in the selling line?" said Mr. Perls.

Dr. Adler replied, "I have only this one son. One daughter. She was a medical technician before she got married—anesthetist. At one time she had an important position in Mount Sinai."

He couldn't mention his children without boasting. In Wilhelm's opinion, there was little to boast of. Catherine, like Wilhelm, was big and fair-haired. She had married a court reporter who had a pretty hard time of it. She had taken a professional name, too—Philippa. At forty she was still ambitious to become a painter. Wilhelm didn't venture to criticize her work. It didn't do much to him, he said, but then he was no critic. Anyway, he and his sister were generally on the outs and he didn't often see her paintings. She worked very hard, but there were fifty thousand people in New York with paints and brushes, each practically a law unto himself. It was the Tower of Babel in paint. *He* didn't want to go far into this. Things were chaotic all over.

Dr. Adler thought that Wilhelm looked particularly untidy this morning—unrested, too, his eyes red-rimmed from excessive smoking. He was breathing through his mouth and he was evidently much distracted and rolled his red-shot eyes barbarously. As usual, his coat collar was turned up as though he had had to go out in the rain. When he went to business he pulled himself together a little; otherwise he let himself go and looked like hell.

"What's the matter, Wilky, didn't you sleep last night?"

"Not very much."

"You take too many pills of every kind—first stimulants and then depressants, anodynes followed by analeptics, until the poor organism doesn't know what's happened. Then the luminal won't put people to sleep, and the Pervitin or Benzedrine won't wake them. God knows! These things get to be as serious as poisons, and yet everyone puts all their faith in them."

"No, Dad, it's not the pills. It's that I'm not used to New York any more. For a native, that's very peculiar, isn't it? It was never so noisy at night as now, and every little thing is a strain. Like the alternate parking. You have to run out at eight to move your car. And where can you put it? If you forget for a minute they tow you away. Then some fool puts advertising leaflets under your windshield wiper and you have heart failure a block away because you think you've got a ticket. When you do get stung with a ticket, you can't argue. You haven't got a chance in court and the city wants the revenue."

"But in your line you have to have a car, eh?" said Mr. Perls.

"Lord knows why any lunatic would want one in the city who didn't need it for his livelihood."

Wilhelm's old Pontiac was parked in the street. Formerly, when on an expense account, he had always put it up in a garage. Now he was afraid to move the car from Riverside Drive lest he lose his space, and he used it only on Saturdays when the Dodgers were playing in Ebbets Field and he took his boys to the game. Last Saturday, when the Dodgers were out of town, he had gone out to visit his mother's grave.

Dr. Adler had refused to go along. He couldn't bear his son's driving. Forgetfully, Wilhelm traveled for miles in second gear; he was seldom in the right lane and he neither gave signals nor watched for lights. The upholstery of his Pontiac was filthy with grease and ashes. One cigarette burned in the ashtray, another in his hand, a third on the floor with maps and other waste paper and Coca-Cola bottles. He dreamed at the wheel or argued and gestured, and therefore the old doctor would not ride with him.

Then Wilhelm had come back from the cemetery angry because the stone bench between his mother's and his grandmother's graves had been overturned and broken by vandals. "Those damn teen-age hoodlums get worse and worse," he said. "Why, they must have used a sledge-hammer to break the seat smack in half like that. If I could catch one of them!" He wanted the doctor to pay for a new seat, but his father was cool to the idea. He said he was going to have himself cremated.

Mr. Perls said, "I don't blame you if you get no sleep up where you are." His voice was tuned somewhat sharp, as though he were slightly deaf. "Don't you have Parigi the singing teacher there? God, they have some queer elements in this hotel. On which floor is that Estonian woman with all her cats and dogs? They should have made her leave long ago."

"They've moved her down to twelve," said Dr. Adler.

Wilhelm ordered a large Coca-Cola with his breakfast. Working in secret at the small envelopes in his pocket, he found two pills by touch. Much fingering had worn and weakened the paper. Under cover of a napkin he swallowed a Phenaphen sedative and a Unicap, but the doctor was sharp-eyed and said, "Wilky, what are you taking now?"

"Just my vitamin pills." He put his cigar butt in an ashtray on the table behind him, for his father did not like the odor. Then he drank his Coca-Cola.

"That's what you drink for breakfast, and not orange juice?" said Mr. Perls. He seemed to sense that he would not lose Dr. Adler's favor by taking an ironic tone with his son.

"The caffeine stimulates brain activity," said the old doctor. "It does all kinds of things to the respiratory center."

"It's just a habit of the road, that's all," Wilhelm said. "If you drive around long enough it turns your brains, your stomach, and everything else."

His father explained, "Wilky used to be with the Rojax Corporation. He was their northeastern sales representative for a good many years but recently ended the connection."

"Yes," said Wilhelm, "I was with them from the end of the war." He sipped the Coca-Cola and chewed the ice, glancing at one and the other with his attitude of large, shaky, patient dignity. The waitress set two boiled eggs before him.

"What kind of line does this Rojax company manufacture?" said Mr. Perls.

"Kiddies' furniture. Little chairs, rockers, tables, Jungle-Gyms, slides, swings, seesaws."

Wilhelm let his father do the explaining. Large and stiff-backed, he tried to sit patiently, but his feet were abnormally restless. All right! His father had to impress Mr. Perls? He would go along once more, and play his part. Fine! He would play along and help his father maintain his style. Style was the main consideration. That was just fine!

"I was with the Rojax Corporation for almost ten years," he said. "We parted ways because they wanted me to share my territory. They took a son-in-law into the business—a new fellow. It was his idea."

To himself, Wilhelm said, Now God alone can tell why I have to lay my whole life bare to this blasted herring here. I'm sure nobody else does it. Other people keep their business to themselves. Not me.

He continued, "But the rationalization was that it was too big a territory for one man. I had a monopoly. That wasn't so. The real reason was that they had gotten to the place where they would have to make me an officer of the corporation. Vice presidency. I was in line for it, but instead this son-in-law got in, and—"

Dr. Adler thought Wilhelm was discussing his grievances much too openly and said, "My son's income was up in the five figures."

As soon as money was mentioned, Mr. Perls's voice grew eagerly sharper. "Yes? What, the thirty-two-per-cent bracket? Higher even, I guess?" He asked for a hint, and he named the figures not idly but with a sort of hugging relish. Uch! How they love money, thought Wilhelm. They adore money! Holy money! Beautiful money! It was getting so that people were feeble-minded about everything except money. While if you didn't have it you were a dummy, a dummy! You had to excuse yourself from the face of the earth. Chicken! that's what it was. The world's business. If only he could find a way out of it.

Such thinking brought on the usual congestion. It would grow into a fit of passion if he allowed it to continue. Therefore he stopped talking and began to eat.

Before he struck the egg with his spoon he dried the moisture with his napkin. Then he battered it (in his father's opinion) more than was necessary. A faint grime was left by his fingers on the white of the egg after he had picked away the shell. Dr. Adler saw it with silent repugnance. What a Wilky he had given to the world! Why, he didn't even wash his hands in the morning. He used an electric razor so that he didn't have to touch water. The doctor couldn't bear Wilky's dirty habits. Only once—and never again, he swore—had he visited his room. Wilhelm, in pajamas and stockings had sat on his bed, drinking gin from a coffee mug and rooting for the Dodgers on television. "That's two and two on you, Duke. Come on—hit it, now." He came down on the mattress—bam! The bed looked kicked to pieces. Then he drank the gin as though it were tea, and urged his team on with his fist. The smell of dirty clothes was outrageous. By the bedside lay a quart bottle and foolish magazines and mystery stories for the hours of insomnia. Wilhelm lived in worse filth than a savage. When the Doctor spoke to him about this he answered, "Well, I have no wife to look after my things." And who—*who!* —had done the leaving? Not Margaret. The Doctor was certain that she wanted him back.

Wilhelm drank his coffee with a trembling hand. In his full face his abused bloodshot gray eyes, moved back and forth. Jerkily he set his cup back and put half the length of a cigarette into his mouth; he seemed to hold it with his teeth, as though it were a cigar.

"I can't let them get away with it," he said. "It's also a question of morale."

His father corrected him. "Don't you mean a moral question, Wilky?"

"I mean that, too. I have to do something to protect myself. I was promised executive standing." Correction before a stranger mortified him, and his dark blond face changed color, more pale, and then more dark. He went on talking to Perls but his eyes spied on his father. "I was the one who opened the territory for them. I could go back for one of their competitors and take away their customers. *My* customers. Morale enters into it because they've tried to take away my confidence."

"Would you offer a different line to the same people?" Mr. Perls wondered.

"Why not? I know what's wrong with the Rojax product."

"Nonsense," said his father. "Just nonsense and kid's talk, Wilky. You're only looking for trouble and embarrassment that way. What would you gain by such a silly feud? You have to think about making a living and meeting your obligations."

Hot and bitter, Wilhelm said with pride, while his feet moved angrily under the table, "I don't have to be told about my obligations. I've been meeting them for years. In more than twenty years I've never had a penny of help from anybody. I preferred to dig a ditch on the WPA but never asked anyone to meet my obligations for me."

"Wilky has had all kinds of experiences," said Dr. Adler.

The old doctor's face had a wholesome reddish and almost translucent color, like a ripe apricot. The wrinkles beside his ears were deep because the skin conformed so tightly to his bones. With all his might, he was a healthy and fine small old man. He wore a white vest of a light check pattern. His hearing-aid doodad was in the pocket. An unusual shirt of red and black stripes covered his chest. He bought his clothes in a college shop farther uptown. Wilhelm thought he had no business to get himself up like a jockey, out of respect for his profession.

"Well," said Mr. Perls. "I can understand how you feel. You want to fight it out. By a certain time of life, to have to start all over again can't be a pleasure, though a good man can always do it. But anyway you want to keep on with a business you know already, and not have to meet a whole lot of new contacts."

Wilhelm again thought, Why does it have to be me and my life that's discussed, and not him and his life? He would never allow it. But I am an idiot. I have no reserve. To me it can be done. I talk. I must ask for it. Everybody wants to have intimate conversations, but the smart fellows don't give out, only the fools. The smart fellows talk intimately about the fools, and examine them all over and give them advice. Why do I allow it? The hint about his age had hurt him. No, you can't admit it's as good as ever, he conceded. Things do give out.

"In the meanwhile," Dr. Adler said, "Wilky is taking it easy and considering various propositions. Isn't that so?"

"More or less," said Wilhelm. He suffered his father to increase Mr. Perls's respect for him. The WPA ditch had brought the family into contempt. He was a little tired. The spirit, the peculiar burden of his existence lay upon him like an accretion, a load, a hump. In any moment of quiet, when sheer fatigue prevented him from struggling, he was apt to feel this mysterious weight, this growth or collection of nameless things which it was the business of his life to carry about. That must be what a man was for. This large, odd, excited, fleshy, blond, abrupt personality named Wilhelm, or Tommy, was here present, in the present—Dr. Tamkin had been putting into his mind many suggestions about the present moment, the here and now—this Wilky, or Tommy Wilhelm, forty-four years old, father of two sons, at present living in the Hotel Gloriana, was assigned to be the carrier of a load which was his own self, his characteristic self. There was no figure or estimate for the value of this load. But it is probably exaggerated by the subject, T. W. Who is a visionary sort of animal. Who has to believe that he can know why he exists. Though he has never seriously tried to find out why.

Mr. Perls said, "If he wants time to think things over and have a rest, why doesn't he run down to Florida for a while? Off season it's cheap and quiet. Fairyland. The mangoes are just coming in. I got two acres down there. You'd think you were in India."

Mr. Perls utterly astonished Wilhelm when he spoke of fairyland with a foreign accent. Mangoes—India? What did he mean, India?

"Once upon a time," said Wilhelm, "I did some public-relations work for a big hotel down in Cuba. If I could get them a notice in Leonard Lyons or one of the other columns it might be good for another holiday there, gratis. I haven't had a vacation for a long time, and I could stand a rest after going so hard. You know that's true, Father." He meant that his father knew how deep the crisis was becoming; how badly he was strapped for money; and that he could not rest but would be crushed if he stumbled; and that his obligations would destroy him. He couldn't falter. He thought, The money! When I had it, I flowed money. They bled it away from me. I hemorrhaged money. But now it's almost all gone, and where am I supposed to turn for more?

He said, "As a matter of fact, Father, I am tired as hell."

But Mr. Perls began to smile and said, "I understand from Doctor Tamkin that you're going into some kind of investment with him, partners."

"You know, he's a very ingenious fellow," said Dr. Adler. "I really enjoy hearing him go on. I wonder if he really is a medical doctor."

"Isn't he?" said Perls. "Everybody thinks he is. He talks about his patients. Doesn't he write prescriptions?"

"I don't really know what he does," said Dr. Adler. "He's a cunning man."

"He's a psychologist, I understand," said Wilhelm.

"I don't know what sort of psychologist or psychiatrist he may be," said his father. "He's a little vague. It's growing into a major industry, and a very expensive one. Fellows have to hold down very big jobs in order to pay those fees. Anyway, this Tamkin is clever. He never said he practiced here, but I believe he was a doctor in California. They don't seem to have much legislation out there to cover these things, and I hear a thousand dollars will get you a degree from a Los Angeles correspondence school. He gives the impression of knowing something about chemistry, and things like hypnotism. I wouldn't trust him, though."

"And why wouldn't you?" Wilhelm demanded.

"Because he's probably a liar. Do you believe he invented all he things he claims?"

Mr. Perls was grinning.

"He was written up in *Fortune,*" said Wilhelm. "Yes, in *Fortune* magazine. He showed me the article. I've seen his clippings."

"That doesn't make him legitimate," said Dr. Adler. "It might have been another Tamkin. Make no mistake, he's an operator. Perhaps even crazy."

"Crazy, you say?"

Mr. Perls put in, "He could be both sane and crazy. In these days nobody can tell for sure which is which."

"An electrical device for truck drivers to wear in their caps," said Dr. Adler, describing one of Tamkin's proposed inventions. "To wake them with a shock when they begin to be drowsy at the wheel. It's triggered by the change in blood-pressure when they start to doze."

"It doesn't sound like such an impossible thing to me," said Wilhelm.

Mr. Perls said, "To me he described an underwater suit so a man could walk on the bed of the Hudson in case of an atomic attack. He said he could walk to Albany in it."

"Ha, ha, ha, ha, ha!" cried Dr. Adler in his old man's voice. "Tamkin's Folly. You could go on a camping trip under Niagara Falls."

"This is just his kind of fantasy," said Wilhelm. "It doesn't mean a thing. Inventors are supposed to be like that. I get funny ideas myself. Everybody wants to make something. Any American does."

But his father ignored this and said to Perls, "What other inventions did he describe?"

While the frazzle-faced Mr. Perls and his father in the unseemly, monkey-striped shirt were laughing, Wilhelm could not restrain himself and joined in with his own panting laugh. But he was in despair. They were laughing at the man to whom he had given a power of attorney over his last seven hundred dollars to speculate for him in the commodities market. They had bought all that lard. It had to rise today. By ten o'clock, or half-past ten, trading would be active, and he would see.

3

Between white tablecloths and glassware and glancing silverware, through overfull light, the long figure of Mr. Perls went away into the darkness of the lobby. He thrust with his cane, and dragged a large built-up shoe which Wilhelm had not included in his estimate of troubles. Dr. Adler wanted to talk about him. "There's a poor man," he said, "with a bone condition which is gradually breaking him up."

"One of those progressive diseases?" said Wilhelm.

"Very bad. I've learned," the doctor told him, "to keep my sympathy for the real ailments. This Perls is more to be pitied than any man I know."

Wilhelm understood he was being put on notice and did not express his opinion. He ate and ate. He did not hurry but kept putting food on his plate until he had gone through the muffins and his father's strawberries, and then some pieces of bacon that were left; he had several cups of coffee, and when he was finished he sat gigantically in a state of arrest and didn't seem to know what he should do next.

For a while father and son were uncommonly still. Wilhelm's

preparations to please Dr. Adler had failed completely, for the old man kept thinking, You'd never guess he had a clean upbringing, and, What a dirty devil this son of mine is. Why can't he try to sweeten his appearance a little? Why does he want to drag himself like this? And he makes himself look so idealistic.

Wilhelm sat, mountainous. He was not really so slovenly as his father found him to be. In some aspects he even had a certain delicacy. His mouth, though broad, had a fine outline, and his brow and his gradually incurved nose, dignity, and in his blond hair there was white but there were also shades of gold and chestnut. When he was with the Rojax Corporation Wilhelm had kept a small apartment in Roxbury, two rooms in a large house with a small porch and garden, and on mornings of leisure, in late spring weather like this, he used to sit expanded in a wicker chair with the sunlight pouring through the weave, and sunlight through the slug-eaten holes of the young hollyhocks and as deeply as the grass allowed into small flowers. This peace (he forgot that that time had had its troubles, too), this peace was gone. It must not have belonged to him, really, for to be here in New York with his old father was more genuinely like his life. He was well aware that he didn't stand a chance of getting sympathy from his father, who said he kept his for real ailments. Moreover, he advised himself repeatedly not to discuss his vexatious problems with him, for his father, with some justice, wanted to be left in peace. Wilhelm also knew that when he began to talk about these things he made himself feel worse, he became congested with them and worked himself into a clutch. Therefore he warned himself, Lay off, pal. It'll only be an aggravation. From a deeper source, however, came other promptings. If he didn't keep his troubles before him he risked losing them altogether, and he knew by experience that this was worse. And furthermore, he could not succeed in excusing his father on the ground of old age. No. No, he could not. I am his son, he thought. He is my father. He is as much father as I am son—old or not. Affirming this, though in complete silence, he sat, and, sitting, he kept his father at the table with him.

"Wilky," said the old man, "have you gone down to the baths here yet?"

"No, Dad, not yet."

"Well, you know the Gloriana has one of the finest pools in New York. Eighty feet, blue tile. It's a beauty."

Wilhelm had seen it. On the way to the gin game you passed the stairway to the pool. He did not care for the odor of the wall-locked and chlorinated water.

"You ought to investigate the Russian and Turkish baths, and the sunlamps and massage. I don't hold with sunlamps. But the massage does a world of good, and there's nothing better than hydrotherapy when you come right down to it. Simple water has a calming effect and would do you more good than all the barbiturates and alcohol in the world."

Wilhelm reflected that this advice was as far as his father's help and sympathy would extend.

"I thought," he said, "that the water cure was for lunatics."

The doctor received this as one of his son's jokes and said with a smile, "Well, it won't turn a sane man into a lunatic. It does a great deal for me. I couldn't live without my massages and steam."

"You're probably right. I ought to try it one of these days. Yesterday, late in the afternoon, my head was about to bust and I just had to have a little air, so I walked around the reservoir, and I sat down for a while in a playground. It rests me to watch the kids play potsy and skiprope."

The doctor said with approval, "Well, now that's more like the idea."

"It's the end of the lilacs," said Wilhelm. "When they burn it's the beginning of summer. At least, in the city. Around the time of year when the candy stores take down the windows and start to sell sodas on the sidewalk. But even though I was raised here, Dad, I can't take city life any more, and I miss the country. There's too much push here for me. It works me up too much. I take things too hard. I wonder why you never retired to a quieter place."

The doctor opened his small hand on the table in a gesture so old and so typical that Wilhelm felt it like an actual touch upon the foundations of his life. "I am a city boy myself, you must remember," Dr. Adler explained. "But if you find the city so hard on you, you ought to get out."

"I'll do that," said Wilhelm, "as soon as I can make the right connection. Meanwhile—"

His father interrupted, "Meanwhile I suggest you cut down on drugs."

"You exaggerate that, Dad. I don't really—I give myself a little boost against—" He almost pronounced the word "misery" but he kept his resolution not to complain.

The doctor, however, fell into the error of pushing his advice too hard. It was all he had to give his son and he gave it once more. "Water and exercise," he said.

He wants a young, smart, successful son, thought Wilhelm, and he said, "Oh, Father, it's nice of you to give me this medical advice, but steam isn't going to cure what ails me."

The doctor measurably drew back, warned by the sudden weak strain of Wilhelm's voice and all that the droop of his face, the swell of his belly against the restraint of his belt intimated.

"Some new business?" he asked unwillingly.

Wilhelm made a great preliminary summary which involved the whole of his body. He drew and held a long breath, and his color changed and his eyes swam. "New?" he said.

"You make too much of your problems," said the doctor. "They ought not to be turned into a career. Concentrate on real troubles—fatal sickness, accidents." The old man's whole manner said, Wilky, don't start this on me. I have a right to be spared.

Wilhelm himself prayed for restraint; he knew this weakness of his and fought it. He knew, also, his father's character. And he began mildly, "As far as the fatal part of it goes, everyone on this side of the grave is the same distance from death. No, I guess my trouble is not exactly new. I've got to pay premiums on two policies for the boys. Margaret sent them to me. She unloads everything on me. Her mother left her an income. She won't even file a joint tax return. I get stuck. Etcetera. But you've heard the whole story before."

"I certainly have," said the old man. "And I've told you to stop giving her so much money."

Wilhelm worked his lips in silence before he could speak. The congestion was growing. "Oh, but my kids, Father. My kids. I love them. I don't want them to lack anything."

The doctor said with a half-deaf benevolence, "Well, naturally. And she, I'll bet, is the beneficiary of that policy."

"Let her be. I'd sooner die myself before I collected a cent of such money."

"Ah, yes." The old man sighed. He did not like the mention of death. "Did I tell you that your sister Catherine—Philippa—is after me again."

"What for?"

"She wants to rent a gallery for an exhibition."

Stiffly fair-minded, Wilhelm said, "Well, of course that's up to you, Father."

The round-headed old man with his fine, feather-white, ferny hair said, "No, Wilky. There's not a thing on those canvases. I don't believe it; it's a case of the emperor's clothes. I may be old enough for my second childhood, but at least the first is well behind me. I was glad enough to buy crayons for her when she was four. But now she's a woman of forty and too old to be encouraged in her delusions. She's no painter."

"I wouldn't go so far as to call her a born artist," said Wilhelm, "but you can't blame her for trying something worth while."

"Let her husband pamper her."

Wilhelm had done his best to be just to his sister, and he had sincerely meant to spare his father, but the old man's tight, benevolent deafness had its usual effect on him. He said, "When it comes to women and money, I'm completely in the dark. What makes Margaret act like this?"

"She's showing you that you can't make it without her," said the doctor. "She aims to bring you back by financial force."

"But if she ruins me, Dad, how can she expect me to come back? No, I have a sense of honor. What you don't see is that she's trying to put an end to me."

His father stared. To him this was absurd. And Wilhelm thought, Once a guy starts to slip, he figures he might as well be a clunk. A real big clunk. He even takes pride in it. But there's nothing to be proud of—hey, boy? Nothing. I don't blame Dad for his attitude. And it's no cause for pride.

"I don't understand that. But if you feel like this why don't you settle with her once and for all?"

"What do you mean, Dad?" said Wilhelm, surprised. "I thought I told you. Do you think I'm not willing to settle? Four years ago when we broke up I gave her everything—goods, furniture, savings. I tried to show good will, but I didn't get anywhere. Why when I wanted Scissors, the dog, because the animal and I were so attached to each other—it was bad enough to leave the kids—she absolutely refused me. Not that she cared a damn about the animal. I don't think you've seen him. He's an Australian sheep dog. They usually have one blank or whitish eye which gives a misleading look, but they're the gentlest dogs and have unusual delicacy about eating or talking. Let me at least have the companionship of this animal. Never." Wilhelm was greatly moved. He wiped his face at all corners with his napkin. Dr. Adler felt that his son was indulging himself too much in his emotions.

"Whenever she can hit me, she hits, and she seems to live for that alone. And she demands more and more, and still more. Two years ago she wanted to go back to college and get another degree. It increased my burden but I thought it would be wiser in the end if she got a better job through it. But still she takes as much from me as before. Next thing she'll want to be a Doctor of Philosophy. She says the women in her family live long, and I'll have to pay and pay for the rest of my life."

The doctor said impatiently, "Well, these are details, not principles. Just details which you can leave out. The dog! You're mixing up all kinds of irrelevant things. Go to a good lawyer."

"But I've already told you, Dad. I got a lawyer, and she got one, too, and both of them talk and send me bills, and I eat my heart out. Oh, Dad, Dad, what a hole I'm in!" said Wilhelm in utter misery. "The lawyers—see?—draw up an agreement, and she says okay on Monday and wants more money on Tuesday. And it begins again."

"I always thought she was a strange kind of woman," said Dr. Adler. He felt that by disliking Margaret from the first and disapproving of the marriage he had done all that he could be expected to do.

"Strange, Father? I'll show you what she's like." Wilhelm took hold of his broad throat with brown-stained fingers and bitten nails and began to choke himself.

"What are you doing?" cried the old man.

"I'm showing you what she does to me."

"Stop that—stop it!" the old man said and tapped the table commandingly.

"Well, Dad, she hates me. I feel that she's strangling me. I can't catch my breath. She just has fixed herself on me to kill me. She can do it at long distance. One of these days I'll be struck down by suffocation or apoplexy because of her. I just can't catch my breath."

"Take your hands off your throat, you foolish man," said his father. "Stop this bunk. Don't expect me to believe in all kinds of voodoo."

"If that's what you want to call it, all right." His face flamed and paled and swelled and his breath was laborious.

"But I'm telling you that from the time I met her I've been a slave. The Emancipation Proclamation was only for colored people. A husband like me is a slave, with an iron collar. The churches go up to Albany and supervise the law. They won't have divorces. The court says, 'You want to be free. Then you have to work twice as hard—twice, at least! Work! you bum.' So then guys kill each other for the buck, and they may be free of a wife who hates them but they are sold to the company. The company knows a guy has got to have his salary, and takes full advantage of him. Don't talk to me about being free. A rich man may be free on an income of a million net. A poor man may be free because nobody cares what he does. But a fellow in my position has to sweat it out until he drops dead."

His father replied to this, "Wilky, it's entirely your own fault. You don't have to allow it."

Stopped in his eloquence, Wilhelm could not speak for a while. Dumb and incompetent, he struggled for breath and frowned with effort into his father's face.

"I don't understand your problems," said the old man. "I never had any like them."

By now Wilhelm had lost his head and he waved his hands and said over and over, "Oh, Dad, don't give me that stuff, don't give me that. Please don't give me that sort of thing."

"It's true," said his father. "I come from a different world. Your mother and I led an entirely different life."

"Oh, how can you compare Mother," Wilhelm said. "Mother was a help to you. Did she harm you ever?"

"There's no need to carry on like an opera, Wilky," said the doctor. "This is only your side of things."

"What? It's the truth," said Wilhelm.

The old man could not be persuaded and shook his round head and drew his vest down over the gilded shirt, and leaned back with a completeness of style that made this look, to anyone out of hearing, like an ordinary conversation between a middle-aged man and his respected father. Wilhelm towered and swayed, big and sloven, with his gray eyes red-shot and his honey-colored hair twisted in flaming shapes upward. Injustice made him angry, made him beg. But he wanted an understanding with his father, and he tried to capitulate to him. He said, "You can't compare Mother and Margaret, and neither can you and I be compared, because you, Dad, were a success. And a success—is a success. I never made a success."

The doctor's old face lost all of its composure and became hard and angry. His small breast rose sharply under the red and black shirt and he said, "Yes. Because of hard work. I was not self-indulgent, not lazy. My old man sold dry goods in Williamsburg. We were nothing, do you understand? I knew I couldn't afford to waste my chances."

"I wouldn't admit for one minute that I was lazy," said Wilhelm. "If anything, I tried too hard. I admit I made many mistakes. Like I thought I shouldn't do things you had done already. Study chemistry. You had done it already. It was in the family."

His father continued, "I didn't run around with fifty women, either. I was not a Hollywood star. I didn't have time to go to Cuba for a vacation. I stayed at home and took care of my children."

Oh, thought Wilhelm, eyes turning upward. Why did I come here in the first place, to live near him? New York is like a gas. The colors are running. My head feels so tight, I don't know what I'm doing. He thinks I want to take away his money or that I envy him. He doesn't see what I want.

"Dad," Wilhelm said aloud, "you're being very unfair. It's true the movies was a false step. But I love my boys. I didn't abandon them. I left Margaret because I had to."

"Why did you have to?"

"Well—" said Wilhelm, struggling to condense his many reasons into a few plain words. "I had to—I had to."

With sudden and surprising bluntness his father said, "Did you have bed-trouble with her? Then you should have stuck it out. Sooner or later everyone has it. Normal people stay with it. It passes. But you wouldn't, so now you pay for your stupid romantic notions. Have I made my view clear?"

It was very clear. Wilhelm seemed to hear it repeated from various sides and inclined his head different ways, and listened and thought. Finally he said, "I guess that's the medical standpoint. You may be right. I just couldn't live with Margaret. I wanted to stick it out, but I was getting very sick. She was one way and I was another. She wouldn't be like me, so I tried to be like her, and I couldn't do it."

"Are you sure she didn't tell *you* to go?" the doctor said.

"I wish she had. I'd be in a better position now. No, it was me. I didn't want to leave, but I couldn't stay. Somebody had to take the initiative. I did. Now I'm the fall guy too."

Pushing aside in advance all the objections that his son would make, the doctor said, "Why did you lose your job with Rojax?"

"I didn't, I've told you."

"You're lying. You wouldn't have ended the connection. You need the money too badly. But you must have got into trouble." The small old man spoke concisely and with great strength. "Since you have to talk and can't let it alone, tell the truth. Was there a scandal—a woman?"

Wilhelm fiercely defended himself. "No, Dad, there wasn't any woman. I told you how it was."

"Maybe it was a man, then," the old man said wickedly.

Shocked, Wilhelm stared at him with burning pallor and dry lips. His skin looked a little yellow. "I don't think you know what you're talking about," he answered after a moment. "You shouldn't let your imagination run so free. Since you're been living here on Broadway you must think you understand life, up to date. You ought to know your own son a little better. Let's drop that, now."

"All right, Wilky, I'll withdraw it. But something must have happened in Roxbury nevertheless. You'll never go back. You're just talking wildly about representing a rival company. You won't. You've done something to spoil your reputation, I think. But you've got girl friends who are expecting you back, isn't that so?"

"I take a lady out now and then while on the road," said Wilhelm. "I'm not a monk."

"No one special? Are you sure you haven't gotten into complications?"

He had tried to unburden himself and instead, Wilhelm thought, he had to undergo an inquisition to prove himself worthy of a sympathetic word. Because his father believed that he did all kinds of gross things.

"There is a woman in Roxbury that I went with. We fell in love and wanted to marry, but she got tired of waiting for my divorce. Margaret figured that. On top of which the girl was a Catholic and I had to go with her to the priest and make an explanation."

Neither did this last confession touch Dr. Adler's sympathies or sway his calm old head or affect the color of his complexion.

"No, no, no, no; all wrong," he said.

Again Wilhelm cautioned himself. Remember his age. He is no longer the same person. He can't bear trouble. I'm so choked up and congested anyway I can't see straight. Will I ever get out of the woods, and recover my balance? You're never the same afterward. Trouble rusts out the system.

"You really *want* a divorce?" said the old man.

"For the price I pay I should be getting something."

"In that case," Dr. Adler said, "it seems to me no normal person would stand for such treatment from a woman."

"Ah, Father, Father!" said Wilhelm. "It's always the same thing with you. Look how you lead me on. You always start out to help me with my problems, and be sympathetic and so forth. It gets my hopes up and I begin to be grateful. But before we're through I'm a hundred times more depressed than before. Why is that? You have no sympathy. You want to shift all the blame on to me. Maybe you're wise to do it." Wilhelm was beginning to lose himself. "All you seem to think about is your death. Well, I'm sorry. But I'm going to die too. And I'm your son. It isn't my fault in the first place. There ought to be a right way to do this, and be fair to each other. But what I want to know is, why do you start up with me if you're not going to help me? What do you want to know about my problems for, Father? So you can lay the whole responsibility on me—so that you won't have to help me? D'you want me to comfort you for having such a son?" Wilhelm had a great knot of wrong tied tight within his chest, and tears approached his eyes but he didn't let them out. He looked shabby enough as it was. His voice was thick and hazy, and he was stammering and could not bring his awful feelings forth.

"You have some purpose of your own," said the doctor, "in acting so unreasonable. What do you want from me? What do you expect?"

"What do I expect?" said Wilhelm. He felt as though he were unable to recover something. Like a ball in the surf, washed beyond reach, his self-control was going out. "I expect *help!*" The words escaped him in a loud, wild, frantic cry and startled the old man, and two or three breakfasters within hearing glanced their way. Wilhelm's hair, the color of whitened honey, rose dense and tall with the expansion of his face, and he said, "When I suffer—you aren't even sorry. That's because you have no affection for me, and you don't want any part of me."

"Why must I like the way you behave? No, I don't like it," said Dr. Adler.

"All right. You want me to change myself. But suppose I could do it—what would I become? What could I? Let's suppose that all my life I have had the wrong ideas about myself and wasn't what I thought I was. And wasn't even careful to take a few precautions, as most people do—like a woodchuck has a few exits to his tunnel. But what shall I do now? More than half my life is over. More than half. And now you tell me I'm not even normal."

The old man too had lost his calm. "You cry about being helped," he said. "When you thought you had to go into the service I sent a check to Margaret every month. As a family man you could have had an exemption. But no! The war couldn't be fought without you and you had to get yourself drafted and be an office-boy in the Pacific theater. Any clerk could have done what you did. You could find nothing better to become than a GI."

Wilhelm was going to reply, and half raised his bearish figure from the chair, his fingers spread and whitened by their grip on the table, but the old man would not let him begin. He said, "I see other elderly people here with children who aren't much good, and they keep backing them and holding them up at a great sacrifice. But I'm not going to make that mistake. It doesn't enter your mind that when I die—a year, two years from now—you'll still be here. I do think of it."

He had intended to say that he had a right to be left in peace. Instead he gave Wilhelm the impression that he meant it was not fair for the better man of the two, and the more useful, the more admired, to leave the world first. Perhaps he meant that, too—a little; but he would not under other circumstances have come out with it so flatly.

"Father," said Wilhelm with an unusual openness of appeal. "Don't you think I know how you feel? I have pity. I want you to live on and on. If you outlive me, that's perfectly okay by me." As his father did not answer this avowal and turned away his glance, Wilhelm suddenly burst out, "No, but you hate me. And if I had money you wouldn't. By God, you have to admit it. The money makes the difference. Then we would be a fine father and son, if I was a credit to you—so you could boast and brag about me all over the hotel. But I'm not the right type of son. I'm too old, I'm too old and too unlucky."

His father said, "I can't give you any money. There would be no end to it if I started. You and your sister would take every last buck from me. I'm still alive, not dead. I am still here. Life isn't over yet. I am as much alive as you or anyone. And I want nobody on my back. Get off! And I give you the same advice, Wilky. Carry nobody on your back."

"Just keep your money," said Wilhelm miserably. "Keep it and enjoy it yourself. That's the ticket!"

4

Ass! Idiot! Wild Boar! Dumb mule! Slave! Lousy, wallowing hippopotamus! Wilhelm called himself as his bending legs carried him from the dining room. His pride! His inflamed feelings! His begging and feebleness! And trading insults with his old father—and spreading confusion over everything. Oh, how poor, contemptible, and ridiculous he was! When he remembered how he had said, with great reproof, "You ought to know your own son"—why, how corny and abominable it was.

He could not get out of the sharply brilliant dining room fast enough. He was horribly worked up; his neck and shoulders, his entire chest ached as though they had been tightly tied with ropes. He smelled the salt odor of tears in his nose.

But at the same time, since there were depths in Wilhelm not unsuspected by himself, he received a suggestion from some remote element in his thoughts that the business of life, the real business—to carry his peculiar burden, to feel shame and impotence, to taste these quelled tears—the only important business, the highest business was being done. Maybe the making of mistakes expressed the very purpose of his life and the essence of his being here. Maybe he was supposed to make them and suffer from them on this earth. And though he had raised himself above Mr. Perls and his father because they adored money, still they were called to act energetically and this was better than to yell and cry, pray and beg, poke and blunder and go by fits and starts and fall upon the thorns of life. And finally sink beneath that watery floor—would that be tough luck, or would it be good riddance?

But he raged once more against his father. Other people with money, while they're still alive, want to see it do some good. Granted, he shouldn't support me. But have I ever asked him to do that? Have I ever asked for dough at all, either for Margaret or for the kids or for myself? It isn't the money, but only the assistance; not even assistance, but just the feeling. But he may be trying to teach me that a grown man should be cured of such feeling. Feeling got me in dutch at Rojax. I had the *feeling* that I belonged to the firm, and my *feelings* were hurt when they put Gerber in over me. Dad thinks I'm too simple. But I'm not so simple as he thinks. What about his feelings? He doesn't forget death for one single second, and that's what makes him like this. And not only is death on his mind but through money he forces me to think about it, too. It gives him power over me. He forces me that way, he himself, and then he's sore. If he was poor, I could care for him and show it. The way I *could* care, too, if I only had a chance. He'd see how much love and respect I had in me. It would make him a different man, too. He'd put his hands on me and give me his blessing.

Someone in a gray straw hat with a wide cocoa-colored band spoke to Wilhelm in the lobby. The light was dusky, splotched with red underfoot; green, the leather furniture; yellow, the indirect lighting.

"Hey, Tommy. Say, there."

"Excuse me," said Wilhelm, trying to reach a house phone. But this was Dr. Tamkin, whom he was just about to call.

"You have a very obsessional look on your face," said Dr. Tamkin.

Wilhelm thought, Here he is, Here he is. If I could only figure this guy out.

"Oh," he said to Tamkin. "Have I got such a look? Well, whatever it is, you name it and I'm sure to have it."

The sight of Dr. Tamkin brought his quarrel with his father to a close. He found himself flowing into another channel.

"What are we doing?" he said. "What's going to happen to lard today?"

"Don't worry yourself about that. All we have to do is hold on to it and it's sure to go up. But what's made you so hot under the collar, Wilhelm?"

"Oh, one of those family situations." This was the moment to take a new look at Tamkin, and he viewed him closely but gained nothing by the new effort. It was conceivable that Tamkin was everything that he claimed to be, and all the gossip false. But was he a scientific man, or not? If he was not, this might be a case for the district attorney's office to investigate. Was he a liar? That was a delicate question. Even a liar might be trustworthy in some ways. Could he trust Tamkin—could he? He feverishly, fruitlessly sought an answer.

But the time for this question was past, and he had to trust him now. After a long struggle to come to a decision, he had given him the money. Practical judgment was in abeyance. He had worn himself out, and the decision was no decision. How had this happened? But how had his Hollywood career begun? It was not because of Maurice Venice, who turned out to be a pimp. It was because Wilhelm himself was ripe for the mistake. His marriage, too, had been like that. Through such decisions somehow his life had taken form. And so, from the moment when he tasted the peculiar flavor of fatality in Dr. Tamkin, he could no longer keep back the money.

Five days ago Tamkin had said, "Meet me tomorrow, and we'll go to the market." Wilhelm, therefore, had had to go. At eleven o'clock they had walked to the brokerage office. On the way, Tamkin broke the news to Wilhelm that though this was an equal partnership he couldn't put up his half of the money just yet; it was tied up for a week or so in one of his patents. Today he would be two hundred dollars short; next week, he'd make it up. But neither of them needed an income from the market, of course. This was only a sporting proposition anyhow, Tamkin said. Wilhelm had to answer, "Of course." It was too late to withdraw. What else could he do? Then came the formal part of the transaction, and it was frightening. The very shade of green of Tamkin's check looked wrong; it was a false, disheartening color. His handwriting was peculiar, even monstrous; the e's were like i's, the t's and l's the same, and the h's like wasps' bellies. He wrote like a fourth-grader. Scientists, however, dealt mostly in symbols; they printed. This was Wilhelm's explanation.

Dr. Tamkin had given him his check for three hundred dollars. Wilhelm, in a blinded and convulsed aberration, pressed and pressed to try to kill the trembling of his hand as he wrote out his check for a thousand. He set his lips tight, crouched with his huge back over the table, and wrote with crumbling, terrified fingers, knowing that if Tamkin's check bounced his own would not be honored either. His sole cleverness was to set the date ahead by one day to give the green check time to clear.

Next he had signed a power of attorney, allowing Tamkin to speculate with his money, and this was an even more frightening document. Tamkin had never said a word about it, but here they were and it had to be done.

After delivering his signatures, the only precaution Wilhelm took was to come back to the manager of the brokerage office and ask him privately, "Uh, about Doctor Tamkin. We were in here a few minutes ago, remember?"

That day had been a weeping, smoky one and Wilhelm had gotten away from Tamkin on the pretext of having to run to the post office. Tamkin had gone to lunch alone, and here was Wilhelm, back again, breathless, his hat dripping, needlessly asking the manager if he remembered.

"Yes, sir, I know," the manager had said. He was a cold, mild, lean German who dressed correctly and around his neck wore a pair of opera glasses with which he read the board. He was an extremely correct person except that he never shaved in the morning, not caring, probably, how he looked to the fumblers and the old people and the operators and the gamblers and the idlers of Broadway uptown. The market closed at three. Maybe, Wilhelm guessed, he had a thick beard and took a lady out to dinner later and wanted to look fresh-shaven.

"Just a question," said Wilhelm. "A few minutes ago I signed a power of attorney so Doctor Tamkin could invest for me. You gave me the blanks."

"Yes, sir, I remember."

"Now this is what I want to know," Wilhelm had said. "I'm no lawyer and I only gave the paper a glance. Does this give Doctor Tamkin power of attorney over any other assets of mine—money, or property?"

The rain had dribbled from Wilhelm's deformed, transparent raincoat; the buttons of his shirt, which always seemed tiny, were partly broken, in pearly quarters of the moon, and some of the dark, thick golden hairs that grew on his belly stood out. It was the manager's business to conceal his opinion of him; he was shrewd, gray, correct (although unshaven) and had little to say except on matters that came to his desk. He must have recognized in Wilhelm a man who reflected long and then made the decision he had rejected twenty separate times. Silvery, cool, level, long-profiled, experienced, indifferent, observant, with unshaven refinement, he scarcely looked at Wilhelm, who trembled with fearful awkwardness. The manager's face, low-colored, long-nostriled, acted as a unit of perception; his eyes merely did their reduced share. Here was a man, like Rubin, who knew and knew and knew. He, a foreigner, knew; Wilhelm, in the city of his birth, was ignorant.

The manager had said, "No, sir, it does not give him."

"Only over the funds I deposited with you?"

"Yes, that is right, sir."

"Thank you, that's what I wanted to find out," Wilhelm had said, grateful.

The answer comforted him. However, the question had no value. None at all. For Wilhelm had no other assets. He had given Tamkin his last money. There wasn't enough of it to cover his obligations anyway, and Wilhelm had reckoned that he might as well go bankrupt now as next month. "Either broke or rich," was how he had figured, and that formula had encouraged him to make the gamble.

Well, not rich; he did not expect that, but perhaps Tamkin might really show him how to earn what he needed in the market. By now, however, he had forgotten his own reckoning and was aware only that he stood to lose his seven hundred dollars to the last cent.

Dr. Tamkin took the attitude that they were a pair of gentlemen experimenting with lard and grain futures. The money, a few hundred dollars, meant nothing much to either of them. He said to Wilhelm, "Watch. You'll get a big kick out of this and wonder why more people don't go into it. You think the Wall Street guys are so smart —geniuses? That's because most of us are psychologically afraid to think about the details. Tell me this. When you're on the road, and you don't understand what goes on under the hood of your car, you'll worry what'll happen if something goes wrong with the engine. Am I wrong?" No, he was right. "Well," said Dr. Tamkin with an expression of quiet triumph about his mouth, almost the suggestion of a jeer. "It's the same psychological principle, Wilhelm. They are rich because you don't understand what goes on. But it's no mystery, and by putting in a little money and applying certain principles of observation, you begin to grasp it. It can't be studied in the abstract. You have to take a specimen risk so that you feel the process, the money-flow, the whole complex. To know how it feels to be a seaweed you have to get in the water. In a very short time we'll take out a hundred-per-cent profit." Thus Wilhelm had had to pretend at the outset that his interest in the market was theoretical.

"Well," said Tamkin when he met him now in the lobby, "what's the problem, what is this family situation? Tell me." He put himself forward as the keen mental scientist. Whenever this happened Wilhelm didn't know what to reply. No matter what he said or did it seemed that Dr. Tamkin saw through him.

"I had some words with my dad."

Dr. Tamkin found nothing extraordinary in this. "It's the eternal same story," he said. "The elemental conflict of parent and child. It won't end, ever. Even with a fine old gentleman like your dad."

"I don't suppose it will. I've never been able to get anywhere with him. He objects to my feelings. He thinks they're sordid. I upset him and he gets mad at me. But maybe all old men are alike."

"Sons, too. Take it from one of them," said Dr. Tamkin. "All the same, you should be proud of such a fine old patriarch of a father. It should give you hope. The longer he lives, the longer your life-expectancy becomes."

Wilhelm answered, brooding, "I guess so. But I think I inherit more from my mother's side, and she died in her fifties."

"A problem arose between a young fellow I'm treating and his dad—I just had a consultation," said Dr. Tamkin as he removed his dark gray hat.

"So early in the morning?" said Wilhelm with suspicion.

"Over the telephone, of course."

What a creature Tamkin was when he took off his hat! The indirect light showed the many complexities of his bald skull, his gull's nose, his rather handsome eyebrows, his vain mustache, his deceiver's brown eyes. His figure was stocky, rigid, short in the neck, so that the large ball of the occiput touched his collar. His bones were peculiarly formed, as though twisted twice where the ordinary human bone was turned only once, and his shoulders rose in two pagoda-like points. At midbody he was thick. He stood pigeon-toed, a sign perhaps that he was devious or had much to hide. The skin of his hands was aging, and his nails were moonless, concave, clawlike, and they appeared loose. His eyes were as brown as beaver fur and full of strange lines. The two large brown naked balls looked thoughtful—but were they? And honest—but was Dr. Tamkin honest? There was a hypnotic power in his eyes, but this was not always of the same strength, nor was Wilhelm convinced that it was completely natural. He felt that Tamkin tried to make his eyes deliberately conspicuous, with studied art, and that he brought forth his hypnotic effect by an exertion. Occasionally it failed or drooped, and when this happened the sense of his face passed downward to his heavy (possibly foolish?) red underlip.

Wilhelm wanted to talk about the lard holdings, but Dr. Tamkin said, "This father-and-son case of mine would be instructive to you. It's a different psychological type completely than your dad. This man's father thinks that he isn't his son."

"Why not?"

"Because he has found out something about the mother carrying on with a friend of the family for twenty-five years."

"Well, what do you know!" said Wilhelm. His silent thought was, Pure bull. Nothing but bull!

"You must note how interesting the woman is, too. She has two husbands. Whose are the kids? The fellow detected her and she gave a signed confession that two of the four children were not the father's."

"It's amazing," said Wilhelm, but he said it in a rather distant way.

He was always hearing such stories from Dr. Tamkin. If you were to believe Tamkin, most of the world was like this. Everybody in the hotel had a mental disorder, a secret history, a concealed disease. The wife of Rubin at the newsstand was supposed to be kept by Carl, the yelling, loud-mouthed gin-rummy player. The wife of Frank in the barbershop had disappeared with a GI while he was waiting for her to disembark at the French Lines pier. Everyone was like the faces on a playing card, upside down either way. Every public figure had a character-neurosis. Maddest of all were the businessmen, the heartless, flaunting, boisterous business class who ruled this country with their hard manners and their bold lies and their absurd words that nobody could believe. They were crazier than anyone. They spread the plague. Wilhelm, thinking of the Rojax Corporation, was inclined to agree that many businessmen were insane. And he supposed that Tamkin, for all his peculiarities, spoke a kind of truth and did some people a sort of good. It confirmed Wilhelm's suspicions to hear that there was a plague, and he said, "I couldn't agree with you more. They trade on anything, they steal everything, they're cynical right to the bones."

"You have to realize," said Tamkin, speaking of his patient, or his client, "that the mother's confession isn't good. It's a confession of duress. I try to tell the young fellow he shouldn't worry about a phony confession. But what does it help him if I am rational with him?"

"No?" said Wilhelm, intensely nervous. "I think we ought to go over to the market. It'll be opening pretty soon."

"Oh, come on," said Tamkin. "It isn't even nine o'clock, and there isn't much trading the first hour anyway. Things don't get hot in Chicago until half-past ten, and they're an hour behind us, don't forget. Anyway, I say lard will go up, and it will. Take my word. I've made a study of the guilt-aggression cycle which is behind it. I ought to know *something* about that. Straighten your collar."

"But meantime," said Wilhelm, "we have taken a licking this week. Are you sure your insight is at its best? Maybe when it isn't we should lay off and wait."

"Don't you realize," Dr. Tamkin told him, "you can't march in a straight line to the victory? You fluctuate toward it. From Euclid to Newton there was straight lines. The modern age analyzes the wavers. On my own accounts, I took a licking in hides and coffee. But I have confidence. I'm sure I'll out-guess them." He gave Wilhelm a narrow smile, friendly, calming, shrewd, and wizard-like, patronizing, secret, potent. He saw his fears and smiled at them. "It's something," he remarked, "to see how the competition-factor will manifest itself in different individuals."

"So? Let's go over."

"But I haven't had my breakfast yet."

"I've had mine."

"Come, have a cup of coffee."

"I wouldn't want to meet my dad." Looking through the glass doors, Wilhelm saw that his father had left by the other exit. Wilhelm thought, He didn't want to run into me, either. He said to Dr. Tamkin, "Okay, I'll sit with you, but let's hurry it up because I'd like to get to the market while there's still a place to sit. Everybody and his uncle gets in ahead of you."

"I want to tell you about this boy and his dad. It's highly absorbing. The father was a nudist. Everybody went naked in the house. Maybe the woman found men *with* clothes attractive. Her husband didn't believe in cutting his hair, either. He practiced dentistry. In his office he wore riding pants and a pair of boots, and he wore a green eyeshade."

"Oh, come off it," said Wilhelm.

"This is a true case history."

Without warning, Wilhelm began to laugh. He himself had had no premonition of his change of humor. His face became warm and pleasant, and he forgot his father, his anxieties; he panted bearlike, happily, through his teeth. "This sounds like a horse-dentist. He wouldn't have to put on pants to treat a horse. Now what else are you going to tell me? Did the wife play the mandolin? Does the boy join the cavalry? Oh, Tamkin, you really are a killer-diller."

"Oh, you think I'm trying to amuse you," said Tamkin. "That's because you aren't familiar with my outlook. I deal in facts. Facts always are sensational. I'll say that a second time. Facts *always!* are sensational."

Wilhelm was reluctant to part with his good mood. The doctor had little sense of humor. He was looking at him earnestly.

"I'd bet you any amount of money," said Tamkin, "that the facts about you are sensational."

"Oh—ha, ha! You want them? You can sell them to a true confession magazine."

"People forget how sensational the things are that they do. They don't see it on themselves. It blends into the background of their daily life."

Wilhelm smiled. "Are you sure this boy tells you the truth?"

"Yes, because I've known the whole family for years."

"And you do psychological work with your own friends? I didn't know that was allowed."

"Well, I'm a radical in the profession. I have to do good wherever I can."

Wilhelm's face became ponderous again and pale. His whitened gold hair lay heavy on his head, and he clasped uneasy fingers on the table. Sensational, but oddly enough, dull, too. Now how do you figure that out? It blends with the background. Funny but unfunny. True but false. Casual but laborious, Tamkin was. Wilhelm was most suspicious of him when he took his driest tone.

"With me," said Dr. Tamkin, "I am at my most efficient when I don't need the fee. When I only love. Without a financial reward. I remove myself from the social influence. Especially money. The spiritual compensation is what I look for. Bringing people into the here-and-now. The real universe. That's the present moment. The past is no good to us. The future is full of anxiety. Only the present is real—the here-and-now. Seize the day."

"Well," said Wilhelm, his earnestness returning. "I know you are a very unusual man. I like what you say about here-and-now. Are all the people who come to see you personal friends and patients too? Like that tall handsome girl, the one who always wears those beautiful broomstick skirts and belts?"

"She was an epileptic, and a most bad and serious pathology, too. I'm curing her successfully. She hasn't had a seizure in six months, and she used to have one every week."

"And that young cameraman, the one who showed us those movies from the jungles of Brazil, isn't he related to her?"

"Her brother. He's under my care, too. He has some terrible tendencies, which are to be expected when you have an epileptic sibling. I came into their lives when they needed help desperately, and took hold of them. A certain man forty years older than she had her in his control and used to give her fits by suggestion whenever she tried to leave him. If you only knew one per cent of what goes on in the city of New York! You see, I understand what it is when the lonely person begins to feel like an animal. When the night comes and he feels like howling from his window like a wolf. I'm taking complete care of that young fellow and his sister. I have to steady him down or he'll go from Brazil to Australia the next day. The way I keep him in the here-and-now is by teaching him Greek."

This was a complete surprise! "What, do you know Greek?"

"A friend of mine taught me when I was in Cairo. I studied Aristotle with him to keep from being idle."

Wilhelm tried to take in these new claims and examine them. Howling from the window like a wolf when night comes sounded genuine to him. That was something really to think about. But the Greek! He realized that Tamkin was watching to see how he took it. More elements were continually being added. A few days ago Tamkin had hinted that he had once been in the underworld, one of the Detroit Purple Gang. He was once head of a mental clinic in Toledo. He had worked with a Polish inventor on an unsinkable ship. He was a technical consultant in the field of television. In the life of a man of genius, all of these things might happen. But had they happened to Tamkin? Was he a genuis? He often said that he had attended some of the Egyptian royal family as a psychiatrist. "But everybody is alike, common or aristocrat," he told Wilhelm. "The aristocrat knows less about life."

An Egyptian princess whom he had treated in California, for horrible disorders he had described to Wilhelm, retained him to come back to the old country with her, and there he had had many of her friends and relatives under his care. They turned over a villa on the Nile to him. "For ethical reasons, I can't tell you many of the details about them," he said—but Wilhelm had already heard all these details, and strange and shocking they were, if true. *If* true—he could not be free from doubt. For instance, the general who had to wear ladies' silk stockings and stand otherwise naked before the mirror—and all the rest. Listening to the doctor when he was so strangely factual, Wilhelm had to translate his words into his own language, and he could not translate fast enough or find terms to fit what he heard.

"Those Egyptian big shots invested in the market, too, for the heck of it. What did they need extra money for? By association, I almost became a millionaire myself, and if I had played it smart there's no telling what might have happened. I could have been the ambassador." The American? The Egyptian ambassador? "A friend of mine tipped me off on the cotton. I made a heavy purchase of it. I didn't have that kind of money, but everybody there knew me. It never entered their minds that a person of their social circle didn't have dough. The sale was made on the phone. Then, while the cotton shipment was at sea, the price tripled. When the stuff suddenly became so valuable all hell broke loose on the world cotton market, they looked to see who was the owner of this big shipment. Me! They investigated my credit and found out I was a mere doctor, and they canceled. This was illegal. I sued them. But as I didn't have the money to fight them I sold the suit to a Wall Street lawyer for twenty thousand dollars. He fought it and was winning. They settled with him out of court for more than a million. But on the way back from Cairo, flying, there was a crash. All on board died. I have this guilt on my conscience, of being the murderer of that lawyer. Although he was a crook."

Wilhelm thought, I must be a real jerk to sit and listen to such impossible stories. I guess I am a sucker for people who talk about the deeper things of life, even the way he does.

"We scientific men speak of irrational guilt, Wilhelm," said Dr. Tamkin, as if Wilhelm were a pupil in his class. "But in such a situation, because of the money, I wished him harm. I realize it. This isn't the time to describe all the details, but the money made me guilty. *M*oney and *M*urder both begin with *M*. *M*achinery. *M*ischief."

Wilhelm, his mind thinking for him at random, said, "What about *M*ercy? *M*ilk-of-human-kindness?"

"One fact should be clear to you by now. Money-making is aggression. That's the whole thing. The functionalistic explanation is the only one. People come to the market to kill. They say, 'I'm going to make a killing.' It's not accidental. Only they haven't got the genuine courage to kill, and they erect a symbol of it. The money. They make a killing by a fantasy. Now, counting and number is always a sadistic activity. Like hitting. In the Bible, the Jews wouldn't allow you to count them. They knew it was sadistic."

"I don't understand what you mean," said Wilhelm. A strange uneasiness tore at him. The day was growing too warm and his head felt dim. "What makes them want to kill?"

"By and by, you'll get the drift," Dr. Tamkin assured him. His amazing eyes had some of the rich dryness of a brown fur. Innumerable crystalline hairs or spicules of light glittered in their bold surfaces. "You can't understand without first spending years on the study of the ultimates of human and animal behavior, the deep chemical, organismic, and spiritual secrets of life. I am a psychological poet."

"If you're this kind of poet," said Wilhelm, whose fingers in his pocket were feeling in the little envelopes for the Phenaphen capsules, "what are you doing on the market?"

"That's a good question. Maybe I am better at speculation because

I don't care. Basically, I don't wish hard enough for money, and therefore I come with a cool head to it."

Wilhelm thought, Oh, sure! That's an answer, is it? I bet that if I took a strong attitude he'd back down on everything. He'd grovel in front of me. The way he looks at me on the sly, to see if I'm being taken in! He swallowed his Phenaphen pill with a long gulp of water. The rims of his eyes grew red as it went down. And then he felt calmer.

"Let me see if I can give you an answer that will satisfy you," said Dr. Tamkin. His flapjacks were set before him. He spread the butter on them, poured on brown maple syrup, quartered them, and began to eat with hard, active, muscular jaws which sometimes gave a creak at the hinges. He pressed the handle of his knife against his chest and said, "In here, the human bosom—mine, yours, everybody's—there isn't just one soul. There's a lot of souls. But there are two main ones, the real soul and a pretender soul. Now! Every man realizes that he has to love something or somebody. He feels that he must go outward. 'If thou canst not love, what art thou?' Are you with me?"

"Yes, Doc, I think so," said Wilhelm listening—a little skeptically but nonetheless hard.

"'What are thou?' Nothing. That's the answer. Nothing. In the heart of hearts—Nothing! So of course you can't stand that and want to be Something, and you try. But instead of being this Something, the man puts it over on everybody instead. You can't be that strict to yourself. You love a *little*. Like you have a dog" *(Scissors!)* "or give some money to a charity drive. Now that isn't love, is it? What is it? Egotism, pure and simple. It's a way to love the pretender soul. Vanity. Only vanity, is what it is. And social control. The interest of the pretender soul is the same as the interest of the social life, the society mechanism. This is the main tragedy of human life. Oh, it is terrible! Terrible! You are not free. Your own betrayer is inside of you and sells you out. You have to obey him like a slave. He makes you work like a horse. And for what? For who?"

"Yes, for what?" The doctor's words caught Wilhelm's heart. "I couldn't agree more," he said. "When do we get free?"

"The purpose is to keep the whole thing going. The true soul is the one that pays the price. It suffers and gets sick, and it realizes that the pretender can't be loved. Because the pretender is a lie. The true soul loves the truth. And when the true soul feels like this, it wants to kill the pretender. The love has turned into hate. Then you become dangerous. A killer. You have to kill the deceiver."

"Does this happen to everybody?"

The doctor answered simply, "Yes, to everybody. Of course, for simplification purposes, I have spoken of the soul; it isn't a scientific term, but it helps you to understand it. Whenever the slayer slays, he wants to slay the soul in him which has gypped and deceived him. Who is his enemy? Him. And his lover? Also. Therefore, all suicide is murder, and all murder is suicide. It's the one and identical phenomenon. Biologically, the pretender soul takes away the energy of the true soul and makes it feeble, like a parasite. It happens unconsciously, unawaringly, in the depths of the organism. Ever take up parasitology?"

"No, it's my dad who's the doctor."

"You should read a book about it."

Wilhelm said, "But this means that the world is full of murderers. So it's not the world. It's a kind of hell."

"Sure," the doctor said. "At least a kind of purgatory. You walk on the bodies. They are all around. I can hear them cry *de profundis* and wring their hands. I hear them, poor human beasts. I can't help hearing. And my eyes are open to it. I have to cry, too. This is the human tragedy-comedy."

Wilhelm tried to capture his vision. And again the doctor looked untrustworthy to him, and he doubted him. "Well," he said, "there are also kind, ordinary, helpful people. They're—out in the country. All over. What kind of morbid stuff do you read, anyway?" The doctor's room was full of books.

"I read the best of literature, science and philosophy," Dr. Tamkin said. Wilhelm had observed that in his room even the TV aerial was set upon a pile of volumes. "Korzybski, Aristotle, Freud, W. H. Sheldon, and all the great poets. You answer me like a layman. You haven't applied your mind strictly to this."

"Very interesting," said Wilhelm. He was aware that he hadn't applied his mind strictly to anything. "You don't have to think I'm a dummy, though. I have ideas, too." A glance at the clock told him that the market would soon open. They could spare a few minutes yet. There were still more things he wanted to hear from Tamkin. He realized that Tamkin spoke faultily, but then scientific men were not always strictly literate. It was the description of the two souls that had awed him. In Tommy he saw the pretender. And even Wilky might not be himself. Might the name of his true soul be the one by which his old grandfather had called him—Velvel? The name of a soul, however, must be only that—soul. What did it look like? Does my soul look like me? Is there a soul that looks like Dad? Like Tamkin? Where does the true soul get its strength? Why does it have to love truth? Wilhelm was tormented, but tried to be oblivious to his torment. Secretly, he prayed the doctor would give him some useful advice and transform his life. "Yes, I understand you," he said. "It isn't lost on me."

"I never said you weren't intelligent, but only you just haven't made a study of it all. As a matter of fact you're a profound personality with very profound creative capacities but also disturbances. I've been concerned with you, and for some time I've been treating you."

"Without my knowing it? I haven't felt you doing anything. What do you mean? I don't think I like being treated without my knowledge. I'm of two minds. What's the matter, don't you think I'm normal?" And he really was divided in mind. That the doctor cared about him pleased him. This was what he craved, that someone should care about him, wish him well. Kindness, mercy, he wanted. But—and here he retracted his heavy shoulders in his peculiar way, drawing his hands up into his sleeves; his feet moved uneasily under the table—but he was worried, too, and even somewhat indignant. For what right had Tamkin to meddle without being asked? What kind of privileged life did this man lead? He took other people's money and speculated with it. Everybody came under his care. No one could have secrets from him.

The doctor looked at him with his deadly brown, heavy, impenetrable eyes, his naked shining head, his red hanging underlip, and said, "You have lots of guilt in you."

Wilhelm helplessly admitted, as he felt the heat rise to his wide face, "Yes, I think so too. But personally," he added, "I don't feel like a murderer. I always try to lay off. It's the others who get me. You know—make me feel oppressed. And if you don't mind, and it's all the same to you, I would rather know it when you start to treat me. And now, Tamkin, for Christ's sake, they're putting out the lunch menus already. Will you sign the check, and let's go!"

Tamkin did as he asked, and they rose. They were passing the bookkeeper's desk when he took out a substantial bundle of onionskin papers and said, "These are receipts of the transactions. Duplicates. You'd better keep them as the account is in your name and you'll need them for income taxes. And here is a copy of a poem I wrote yesterday."

"I have to leave something at the desk for my father," Wilhelm said, and he put his hotel bill in an envelope with a note. *Dear Dad, Please carry me this month, Yours, W.* He watched the clerk with his sullen pug's profile and his stiff-necked look push the envelope into his father's box.

"May I ask you really why you and your dad had words?" said Dr. Tamkin, who had hung back, waiting.

"It was about my future," said Wilhelm. He hurried down the stairs with swift steps, like a tower in motion, his hands in his trousers pockets. He was ashamed to discuss the matter. "He says there's a reason why I can't go back to my old territory, and there is. I told everybody I was going to be an officer of the corporation. And I was supposed to. It was promised. But then they welshed because of the son-in-law. I bragged and made myself look big."

"If you was humble enough, you could go back. But it doesn't make much difference. We'll make you a good living on the market."

They came into the sunshine of upper Broadway, not clear but throbbing through the dust and fumes, a false air of gas visible at eye-level as it spurted from the bursting buses. From old habit, Wilhelm turned up the collar of his jacket.

"Just a technical question," Wilhelm said. "What happens if your losses are bigger than your deposit?"

"Don't worry. They have ultra-modern electronic bookkeeping machinery, and it won't let you get in debt. It puts you out automatically. But I want you to read this poem. You haven't read it yet."

Light as a locust, a helicopter bringing mail from Newark Airport to La Guardia sprang over the city in a long leap.

The paper Wilhelm unfolded had ruled borders in red ink. He read:

Mechanism vs Functionalism
Ism vs Hism

If thee thyself couldst only see
Thy greatness that is and yet to be,
Thou would feel joy-beauty-what ecstasy.
They are at thy feet, earth-moon-sea, the trinity.

Why-forth then dost thou tarry
And partake thee only of the crust
And skim the earth's surface narry
When all creations art thy just?

Seek ye then that which art not there
In thine own glory let thyself rest.
Witness. Thy power is not bare.
Thou art King. Thou art at thy best.

Look then right before thee.
Open thine eyes and see.
At the foot of Mt. Serenity
Is thy cradle to eternity.

Utterly confused, Wilhelm said to himself explosively, what kind of mishmash, claptrap is this! What does he want from me? Damn him to hell, he might as well hit me on the head, and lay me out, kill me. What does he give me this for? What's the purpose? Is it a deliberate test? Does he want to mix me up? He's already got me mixed up completely. I was never good at riddles. Kiss those seven hundred bucks good-by, and call it one more mistake in a long line of mistakes— Oh, Mama, what a line! He stood near the shining window of a fancy fruit store, holding Tamkin's paper, rather dazed, as though a charge of photographer's flash powder had gone up in his eyes.

But he's waiting for my reaction. I have to say something to him about his poem. It really is no joke. What will I tell him? Who is this King? The poem is written *to* someone. But who? I can't even bring myself to talk. I feel too choked and strangled. With all the books he reads, how come the guy is so illiterate? And why do people just naturally assume that you'll know what they're talking about? No, I don't know, and nobody knows. The planets don't, the stars don't, infinite space doesn't. It doesn't square with Planck's Constant or anything else. So what's the good of it? Where's the need of it? What does he mean here by Mount Serenity? Could it be a figure of speech for Mount Everest? As he says people are all committing suicide, maybe those guys who climbed Everest were only trying to kill themselves, and if we want peace we should stay at the foot of the mountain. In the here-and-now. But it's also here-and-now on the slope, and on the top, where they climbed to seize the day. Surface narry is something he can't mean, I don't believe. I'm about to start foaming at the mouth. "Thy cradle . . . *Who* is resting in his cradle —in his glory? My thoughts are at an end. I feel the wall. No more. So——k it all! The money and everything. Take it away! When I have the money they eat me alive, like those piranha fish in the movie about the Brazilian jungle. It was hideous when they ate up that

Brahma bull in the river. He turned pale, just like clay, and in five minutes nothing was left except the skeleton still in one piece, floating away. When I haven't got it any more, at least they'll let me alone.

"Well, what do you think of this?" said Dr. Tamkin. He gave a special sort of wise smile, as though Wilhelm must now see what kind of man he was dealing with.

"Nice. Very nice. Have you been writing long?"

"I've been developing this line of thought for years and years. You follow it all the way?"

"I'm trying to figure out who this Thou is."

"Thou? Thou is you."

"Me! Why? This applies to *me?*"

"Why shouldn't it apply to you. You were in my mind when I composed it. Of course, the hero of the poem is sick humanity. If it would open its eyes it would be great."

"Yes, but how do I get into this?"

"The main idea of the poem is *con*struct or *de*struct. There is no ground in between. Mechanism is *de*struct. Money of course is *de*struct. When the last grave is dug, the gravedigger will have to be paid. If you could have confidence in nature you would not have to fear. It would keep you up. Creative is nature. Rapid. Lavish. Inspirational. It shapes leaves. It rolls the waters of the earth. Man is the chief of this. All creations are his just inheritance. You don't know what you've got within you. A person either creates or he destroys. There is no neutrality . . ."

"I realize you were no beginner," said Wilhelm with propriety. "I have only one criticism to make. I think 'why-forth' is wrong. You should write 'Wherefore then dost thou . . .'" And he reflected, So? I took a gamble. It'll have to be a miracle, though, to save me. My money will be gone, then it won't be able to destruct me. He can't just take and lose it, though. He's in it, too. I think he's in a bad way himself. He must be. I'm sure because, come to think of it, he sweated blood when he signed that check. But what have I let myself in for? The waters of the earth are going to roll over me.

5

Patiently, in the window of the fruit store, a man with a scoop spread crushed ice between his rows of vegetables. There were also Persian melons, lilacs, tulips with radiant black at the middle. The many street noises came back after a little while from the caves of the sky. Crossing the tide of Broadway traffic, Wilhelm was saying to himself, The reason Tamkin lectures me is that somebody has lectured him, and the reason for the poem is that he wants to give me good advice. Everybody seems to know something. Even fellows like Tamkin. Many people know what to do, but how many can do it?

He believed that he must, that he could and would recover the good things, the happy things, the easy tranquil things of life. He had made mistakes, but he could overlook these. He had been a fool, but that could be forgiven. The time wasted—must be relinquished. What else could one do about it? Things were too complex, but they might be reduced to simplicity again. Recovery was possible. First he had to get out of the city. No, first he had to pull out his money. . . .

From the carnival of the street—pushcarts, accordion and fiddle, shoeshine, begging, the dust going round like a woman on stilts—they entered the narrow crowded theater of the brokerage office. From front to back it was filled with the Broadway crowd. But how was lard doing this morning? From the rear of the hall Wilhelm tried to read the tiny figures. The German manager was looking through his binoculars. Tamkin placed himself on Wilhelm's left and covered his conspicuous bald head. "The guy'll ask me about the margin," he muttered. They passed, however, unobserved. "Look, the lard has held its place," he said.

Tamkin's eyes must be very sharp to read the figures over so many heads and at this distance—another respect in which he was unusual.

The room was always crowded. Everyone talked. Only at the front could you hear the flutter of the wheels within the board. Teletyped news items crossed the illuminated screen above.

"Lard. Now what about rye?" said Tamkin, rising on his toes. Here he was a different man, active and impatient. He parted people who stood in his way. His face turned resolute, and on either side of his mouth odd bulges formed under his mustache. Already he was pointing out to Wilhelm the appearance of a new pattern on the board. "There's something up today," he said.

"Then why'd you take so long with breakfast?" said Wilhelm.

There were no reserved seats in the room, only customary ones. Tamkin always sat in the second row, on the commodities side of the aisle. Some of his acquaintances kept their hats on the chairs for him.

"Thanks. Thanks," said Tamkin, and he told Wilhelm, "I fixed it up yesterday."

"That was a smart thought," said Wilhelm. They sat down.

With folded hands, by the wall, sat an old Chinese businessman in a seersucker coat. Smooth and fat, he wore a white Vandyke. One day Wilhelm had seen him on Riverside Drive pushing two little girls along in a baby carriage—his grandchildren. Then there were two women in their fifties, supposed to be sisters, shrewd and able moneymakers, according to Tamkin. They had never a word to say to Wilhelm. But they would chat with Tamkin. Tamkin talked to everyone.

Wilhelm sat between Mr. Rowland, who was elderly, and Mr. Rappaport, who was very old. Yesterday Rowland had told him that in the year 1908, when he was a junior at Harvard, his mother had given him twenty shares of steel for his birthday, and then he had started to read the financial news and had never practiced law but instead followed the market for the rest of his life. Now he speculated only in soy beans, of which he had made a specialty. By his conservative method, said Tamkin, he cleared two hundred a week. Small potatoes, but then he was a bachelor, retired, and didn't need money.

"Without dependents," said Tamkin. "He doesn't have the problems that you and I do."

Did Tamkin have dependents? He had everything that it was possible for a man to have—science, Greek, chemistry, poetry, and now dependents too. That beautiful girl with epilepsy, perhaps. He often said that she was a pure, marvelous, spiritual child who had no knowledge of the world. He protected her, and, if he was not lying, adored her. And if you encouraged Tamkin by believing him, or even if you refrained from questioning him, his hints became more daring. Sometimes he said that he paid for her music lessons. Sometimes he seemed to have footed the bill for the brother's camera expedition to Brazil. And he spoke of paying for the support of the orphaned child of a dead sweetheart. These hints, made dully as asides, grew by repetition into sensational claims.

"For myself, I don't need much," said Tamkin. "But a man can't live for himself and I need the money for certain important things. What do you figure you have to have, to get by?"

"Not less than fifteen grand, after taxes. That's for my wife and the two boys."

"Isn't there anybody else?" said Tamkin with a shrewdness almost cruel. But his look grew more sympathetic as Wilhelm stumbled, not willing to recall another grief.

"Well—there was. But it wasn't a money matter."

"I should hope!" said Tamkin. "If love is love, it's free. Fifteen grand, though, isn't too much for a man of your intelligence to ask out of life. Fools, hard-hearted criminals, and murderers have millions to squander. They burn up the world—oil, coal, wood, metal, and soil, and suck even the air and the sky. They consume, and they give back no benefit. A man like you, humble for life, who wants to feel and live, has trouble—not wanting," said Tamkin in his parenthetical fashion, "to exchange an ounce of soul for a pound of social power—he'll never make it without help in a world like this. But don't you worry." Wilhelm grasped at this assurance. "Just you never mind. We'll go easily beyond your figure."

Dr. Tamkin gave Wilhelm comfort. He often said that he had made as much as a thousand a week in commodities. Wilhelm had examined the receipts, but until this moment it had never occurred to him that there must be debit slips too; he had been shown only the credits.

"But fifteen grand is not an ambitious figure," Tamkin was telling him. "For that you don't have to wear yourself out on the road, dealing with narrow-minded people. A lot of them don't like Jews, either, I suppose?"

"I can't afford to notice. I'm lucky when I have my occupation. Tamkin, do you mean you can save our money?"

"Oh, did I forget to mention what I did before closing yesterday? You see, I closed out one of the lard contracts and bought a hedge of December rye. The rye is up three points already and takes some of the sting out. But lard will go up, too."

"Where? God, yes, you're right," said Wilhelm, eager, and got to his feet to look. New hope freshened his heart. "Why didn't you tell me before?"

And Tamkin, smiling like a benevolent magician, said, "You must learn to have trust. The slump in lard can't last. And just take a look at eggs. Didn't I predict they couldn't go any lower? They're rising and rising. If we had taken eggs we'd be far ahead."

"Then why didn't we take them?"

"We were just about to. I had a buying order in at .24, but the tide turned at .26¼ and we barely missed. Never mind. Lard will go back to last year's levels."

Maybe. But when? Wilhelm could not allow his hopes to grow too strong. However, for a little while he could breathe more easily. Late-morning trading was getting active. The shining numbers whirred on the board, which sounded like a huge cage of artificial birds. Lard fluctuated between two points, but rye slowly climbed.

He closed his strained, greatly earnest eyes briefly and nodded his Buddha's head, too large to suffer such uncertainties. For several moments of peace he was removed to his small yard in Roxbury.

He breathed in the sugar of the pure morning.

He heard the long phrases of the birds.

No enemy wanted his life.

Wilhelm thought, I will get out of here. I don't belong in New York any more. And he sighed like a sleeper.

Tamkin said, "Excuse me," and left his seat. He could not sit still in the room but passed back and forth between the stocks and commodities sections. He knew dozens of people and was continually engaging in discussions. Was he giving advice, gathering information, or giving it, or practicing—whatever mysterious profession he practiced? Hypnotism? Perhaps he could put people in a trance while he talked to them. What a rare, peculiar bird he was, with those pointed shoulders, that bare head, his loose nails, almost claws, and those brown, soft, deadly, heavy eyes.

He spoke of things that mattered, and as very few people did this he could take you by surprise, excite you, move you. Maybe he wished to do good, maybe give himself a lift to a higher level, maybe believe his own prophecies, maybe touch his own heart. Who could tell? He had picked up a lot of strange ideas; Wilhelm could only suspect, he could not say with certainty, that Tamkin hadn't made them his own.

Now Tamkin and he were equal partners, but Tamkin had put up only three hundred dollars. Suppose he did this not only once but five times; then an investment of fifteen hundred dollars gave him five thousand to speculate with. If he had power of attorney in every case, he could shift the money from one account to another. No, the German probably kept an eye on him. Nevertheless it was possible. Calculations like this made Wilhelm feel ill. Obviously Tamkin was a plunger. But how did he get by? He must be in his fifties. How did he support himself? Five years in Egypt; Hollywood before that; Michigan; Ohio; Chicago. A man of fifty has supported himself for at least thirty years. You could be sure that Tamkin had never worked in a factory or in an office. How did he make it? His taste in clothes was horrible, but he didn't buy cheap things. He wore corduroy or velvet shirts from Clyde's, painted neckties, striped socks. There was a slightly acid or pasty smell about his person; for a doctor, he didn't bathe much. Also, Dr. Tamkin had a good room at the Gloriana and had had it for about a year. But so was Wilhelm himself a guest, with an unpaid bill at present in his father's box. Did the beautiful girl with the skirts and belts pay him? Was he defrauding his so-called patients? So many questions impossible to answer could not be asked about an honest man. Nor perhaps about a sane man. Was Tamkin a lunatic, then? That sick Mr. Perls at breakfast had said that there was no easy way to tell the sane from the mad, and he was right about that in any big city and especially in New York—the end of the world, with its complexity and machinery, bricks and tubes, wires and stones, holes and heights. And was everybody crazy here? What sort of people did you see? Every other man spoke a language entirely his own, which he had figured out by private thinking; he had his own ideas and peculiar ways. If you wanted to talk about a glass of water, you had to start back with God creating the heavens and earth; the apple; Abraham; Moses and Jesus; Rome; the Middle Ages; gunpowder; the Revolution; back to Newton; up to Einstein; then war and Lenin and Hitler. After reviewing this and getting it all straight again you could proceed to talk about a glass of water. "I'm fainting, please get me a little water." You were lucky even then to make yourself understood. And this happened over and over and over with everyone you met. You had to translate and translate, explain and explain, back and forth, and it was the punishment of hell itself not to understand or be understood, not to know the crazy from the sane, the wise from the fools, the young from the old or the sick from the well. The fathers were no fathers and the sons no sons. You had to talk with yourself in the daytime and reason with yourself at night. Who else was there to talk to in a city like New York?

A queer look came over Wilhelm's face with its eyes turned up and his silent mouth with its high upper lip. He went several degrees further—when you are like this, dreaming that everybody is outcast, you realize that this must be one of the small matters. There is a larger body, and from this you cannot be separated. The glass of water fades out. You do not go from simple *a* and simple *b* to the great *x* and *y*, nor does it matter whether you agree about the glass but, far beneath such details, what Tamkin would call the real soul says plain and understandable things to everyone. There sons and fathers are themselves, and a glass of water is only an ornament; it makes a hoop of brightness on the cloth; it is an angel's mouth. There truth for everybody may be found, and confusion is only—only temporary, thought Wilhelm.

The idea of this larger body had been planted in him a few days ago beneath Times Square, when he had gone downtown to pick up tickets for the baseball game on Saturday (a doubleheader at the Polo Grounds). He was going through an underground corridor, a place he had always hated and hated more than ever now. On the walls between the advertisements were words in chalk: "Sin No More," and "Do Not Eat the Pig," he had particularly noticed. And in the dark tunnel, in the haste, heat, and darkness which disfigure and make freaks and fragments of nose and eyes and teeth, all of a sudden, unsought, a general love for all these imperfect and lurid-looking people burst out in Wilhelm's breast. He loved them. One and all, he passionately loved them. They were his brothers and his sisters. He was imperfect and disfigured himself, but what difference did that make if he was united with them by this blaze of love? And as he walked he began to say, "Oh my brothers—my brothers and my sisters," blessing them all as well as himself.

So what did it matter how many languages there were, or how hard it was to describe a glass of water? Or matter that a few minutes later he didn't feel anything like a brother toward the man who sold him the tickets?

On that very same afternoon he didn't hold so high an opinion of this same onrush of loving kindness. What did it come to? As they had the capacity and must use it once in a while, people were bound to have such involuntary feelings. It was only another one of those subway things. Like having a hard-on at random. But today, his day of reckoning, he consulted his memory again and thought, I must go back to that. That's the right clue and may do me the most good. Something very big. Truth, like.

The old fellow on the right, Mr. Rappaport, was nearly blind and kept asking Wilhelm, "What's the new figure on November wheat? Give me July soy beans too." When you told him he didn't say thank you. He said, "Okay," instead, or, "Check," and turned away until he needed you again. He was very old, older even than Dr. Adler, and if you believed Tamkin he had once been the Rockefeller of the chicken business and had retired with a large fortune.

Wilhelm had a queer feeling about the chicken industry, that it was sinister. On the road, he frequently passed chicken farms. Those big, rambling, wooden buildings out in the neglected fields; they were like prisons. The lights burned all night in them to cheat the poor hens into laying. Then the slaughter. Pile all the coops of the slaughtered on end, and in one week they'd go higher than Mount Everest or Mount Serenity. The blood filling the Gulf of Mexico. The chicken shit, acid, burning the earth.

How old—old this Mr. Rappaport was! Purple stains were buried in the flesh of his nose, and the cartilage of his ear was twisted like a cabbage heart. Beyond remedy by glasses, his eyes were smoky and faded.

"Read me that soy-bean figure now, boy," he said, and Wilhelm did. He thought perhaps the old man might give him a tip, or some useful advice or information about Tamkin. But no. He only wrote memoranda on a pad, and put the pad in his pocket. He let no one see what he had written. And Wilhelm thought this was the way a man who had grown rich by the murder of millions of animals, little chickens, would act. If there was a life to come he might have to answer for the killing of all those chickens. What if they all were waiting? But if there was a life to come, everybody would have to answer. But if there was a life to come, the chickens themselves would be all right.

Well! What stupid ideas he was having this morning. Phooey!

Finally old Rappaport did address a few remarks to Wilhelm. He asked him whether he had reserved his seat in the synagogue for Yom Kippur.

"No," said Wilhelm.

"Well, you better hurry up if you expect to say *Yiskor* for your parents. I never miss."

And Wilhelm thought, Yes, I suppose I should say a prayer for Mother once in a while. His mother had belonged to the Reform congregation. His father had no religion. At the cemetery Wilhelm had paid a man to say a prayer for her. He was among the tombs and he wanted to be tipped for the *El molai rachamin.* "Thou God of Mercy," Wilhelm thought that meant. *B'gan Aden*—"in Paradise." Singing, they drew it out. *B'gan Ay-den.* The broken bench beside the grave made him wish to do something. Wilhelm often prayed in his own manner. He did not go to the synagogue but he would occasionally perform certain devotions, according to his feelings. Now he reflected, In Dad's eyes I am the wrong kind of Jew. He doesn't like the way I act. Only he is the right kind of Jew. Whatever you are, it always turns out to be the wrong kind.

Mr. Rappaport grumbled and whiffed at his long cigar, and the board, like a swarm of electrical bees, whirred.

"Since you were in the chicken business, I thought you'd speculate in eggs, Mr. Rappaport." Wilhelm, with his warm, panting laugh, sought to charm the old man.

"Oh, Yeah. Loyalty, hey?" said old Rappaport. "I should stick to them. I spent a lot of time amongst chickens. I got to be an expert chicken-sexer. When the chick hatches you have to tell the boys from the girls. It's not easy. You need long, long experience. What do you think, it's a joke? A whole industry depends on it. Yes, now and then I buy a contract eggs. What have you got today?"

Wilhelm said anxiously, "Lard. Rye."

"Buy? Sell?"

"Bought."

"Uh," said the old man. Wilhelm could not determine what he meant by this. But of course you couldn't expect him to make himself any clearer. It was not in the code to give information to anyone. Sick with desire, Wilhelm waited for Mr. Rappaport to make an exception in his case. Just this once! Because it was critical. Silently, by a sort of telepathic concentration, he begged the old man to speak the single word that would save him, give him the merest sign. "Oh, please —please help," he nearly said. If Rappaport would close one eye, or lay his head to one side, or raise his finger and point to a column in the paper or to a figure on his pad. A hint! A hint!

A long perfect ash formed on the end of the cigar, the white ghost of the leaf with all its veins and its fainter pungency. It was ignored, in its beauty, by the old man. For it was beautiful. Wilhelm he ignored as well.

Then Tamkin said to him, "Wilhelm, look at the jump our rye just took."

December rye climbed three points as they tensely watched; the tumblers raced and the machine's lights buzzed.

"A point and a half more, and we can cover the lard losses," said Tamkin. He showed him his calculations on the margin of the *Times*.

"I think you should put in the selling order now. Let's get out with a small loss."

"Get out now? Nothing doing."

"Why not? Why should we wait?"

"Because," said Tamkin with a smiling, almost openly scoffing look, "you've got to keep your nerve when the market starts to go places. Now's when you can make something."

"I'd get out while the getting's good."

"No, you shouldn't lose your head like this. It's obvious to me what the mechanism is, back in the Chicago market. There's a short supply of December rye. Look, it's just gone up another quarter. We should ride it."

"I'm losing my taste for the gamble," said Wilhelm. "You can't feel safe when it goes up so fast. It's liable to come down just as quick."

Dryly, as though he were dealing with a child, Tamkin told him in a tone of tiring patience, "Now listen, Tommy. I have it diagnosed right. If you wish I should sell I can give the sell order. But this is the difference between healthiness and pathology. One is objective, doesn't change his mind every minute, enjoys the risk element. But that's not the neurotic character. The neurotic character—"

"Damn it, Tamkin!" said Wilhelm roughly. "Cut that out. I don't like it. Leave my character out of consideration. Don't pull any more of that stuff on me. I tell you I don't like it."

Tamkin therefore went no further; he backed down. "I meant," he said, softer, "that as a salesman you are basically an artist type. The seller is in the visionary sphere of the business function. And then you're an actor, too."

"No matter what type I am—" An angry and yet weak sweetness rose into Wilhelm's throat. He coughed as though he had the flu. It was twenty years since he had appeared on the screen as an extra. He blew the bagpipes in a film called *Annie Laurie.* Annie had come to warn the young Laird; he would not believe her and called the bagpipers to drown her out. He made fun of her while she wrung her hands. Wilhelm, in a kilt, barelegged, blew and blew and blew and not a sound came out. Of course all the music was recorded. He fell sick with the flu after that and still suffered sometimes from chest weakness.

"Something stuck in your throat?" said Tamkin. "I think maybe you are too disturbed to think clearly. You should try some of my 'here-and-now' mental exercises. It stops you from thinking so much about the future and the past and cuts down confusion."

"Yes, yes, yes, yes," said Wilhelm, his eyes fixed on December rye.

"Nature only knows one thing, and that's the present. Present, present, eternal present, like a big, huge, giant wave—colossal, bright and beautiful, full of life and death, climbing into the sky, standing in the seas. You must go along with the actual, the Here-and-Now, the glory—"

. . . chest weakness, Wilhelm's recollection went on. Margaret nursed him. They had had two rooms of furniture, which was later seized. She sat on the bed and read to him. He made her read for days, and she read stories, poetry, everything in the house. He felt dizzy, stifled when he tried to smoke. They had him wear a flannel vest.

> Come then, Sorrow!
> Sweetest Sorrow!
> Like an own babe I nurse thee on my breast!

Why did he remember that? Why?

"You have to pick out something that's in the actual, immediate present moment," said Tamkin. "And say to yourself here-and-now, here-and-now, here-and-now. 'Where am I?' 'Here.' 'When is it?' 'Now.' Take an object or a person. Anybody. 'Here and now I see a person.' 'Here and now I see a man.' 'Here and now I see a man sitting on a chair.' Take me, for instance. Don't let your mind wander. 'Here and now I see a man in a brown suit. Here and now I see a corduroy shirt.' You have to narrow it down, one item at a time, and not let your imagination shoot ahead. Be in the present. Grasp the hour, the moment, the instant."

Is he trying to hypnotize or con me? Wilhelm wondered. To take my mind off selling? But even if I'm back at seven hundred bucks, then where am I?

As if in prayer, his lids coming down with raised veins, frayed out, on his significant eyes, Tamkin said, "'Here and now I see a button. Here and now I see the thread that sews the button. Here and now I see the green thread.'" Inch by inch he contemplated himself in order to show Wilhelm how calm it would make him. But Wilhelm was hearing Margaret's voice as she read, somewhat unwillingly,

> Come then, Sorrow!
>
> . . . .
>
> I thought to leave thee,
> And deceive thee,
> But now of all the world I love thee best.

Then Mr. Rappaport's old hand pressed his thigh, and he said, "What's my wheat? Those damn guys are blocking the way. I can't see."

6

Rye was still ahead when they went out to lunch, and lard was holding its own.

They ate in the cafeteria with the gilded front. There was the same art inside as outside. The food looked sumptuous. Whole fishes were framed like pictures with carrots, and the salads were like terraced landscapes or like Mexican pyramids; slices of lemon and onion and radishes were like sun and moon and stars; the cream pies were about a foot thick and the cakes swollen as if sleepers had baked them in their dreams.

"What'll you have?" said Tamkin.

"Not much. I ate a big breakfast. I'll find a table. Bring me some yogurt and crackers and a cup of tea. I don't want to spend much time over lunch."

Tamkin said, "You've got to eat."

Finding an empty place at this hour was not easy. The old people idled and gossiped over their coffee. The elderly ladies were rouged and mascaraed and hennaed and used blue hair rinse and eye shadow and wore costume jewelry, and many of them were proud and stared at you with expressions that did not belong to their age. Were there no longer any respectable old ladies who knitted and cooked and looked after their grandchildren? Wilhelm's grandmother had dressed him in a sailor suit and danced him on her knee, blew on the porridge for him and said, "Admiral, you must eat." But what was the use of remembering this so late in the day?

He managed to find a table, and Dr. Tamkin came along with a tray piled with plates and cups. He had Yankee pot roast, purple cabbage, potatoes, a big slice of watermelon, and two cups of coffee. Wilhelm could not even swallow his yogurt. His chest pained him still.

At once Tamkin involved him in a lengthy discussion. Did he do it to stall Wilhelm and prevent him from selling out the rye—or to recover the ground lost when he had made Wilhelm angry by hints about the neurotic character? Or did he have no purpose except to talk?

"I think you worry a lot too much about what your wife and your father will say. Do they matter so much?"

Wilhelm replied, "A person can become tired of looking himself over and trying to fix himself up. You can spend the entire second half of your life recovering from the mistakes of the first half."

"I believe your dad told me he had some money to leave you."

"He probably does have something."

"A lot?"

"Who can tell," said Wilhelm guardedly.

"You ought to think over what you'll do with it."

"I may be too feeble to do anything by the time I get it. If I get anything."

"A thing like this you ought to plan out carefully. Invest it properly." He began to unfold schemes whereby you bought bonds, and used the bonds as security to buy something else and thereby earned twelve per cent safely on your money. Wilhelm failed to follow the details. Tamkin said, "If he made you a gift now, you wouldn't have to pay the inheritance taxes."

Bitterly, Wilhelm told him, "My father's death blots out all other considerations from his mind. He forces me to think about it, too. Then he hates me because he succeeds. When I get desperate—of course I think about money. But I don't want anything to happen to him. I certainly don't want him to die." Tamkin's brown eyes glittered shrewdly at him. "You don't believe it. Maybe it's not psychological. But on my word of honor. A joke is a joke, but I don't want to joke about stuff like this. When he dies, I'll be robbed, like. I'll have no more father."

"You love your old man?"

Wilhelm grasped at this. "Of course, of course I love him. My father. My mother—" As he said this there was a great pull at the very center of his soul. When a fish strikes the line you feel the live force in your hand. A mysterious being beneath the water, driven by hunger, has taken the hook and rushes away and fights, writhing. Wilhelm never identified what struck within him. It did not reveal itself. It got away.

And Tamkin, the confuser of the imagination, began to tell, or to fabricate, the strange history of *his* father. "He was a great singer," he said. "He left us five kids because he fell in love with an opera soprano. I never held it against him, but admired the way he followed the life-principle. I wanted to do the same. Because of unhappiness, at a certain age, the brain starts to die back." (True, true! thought Wilhelm) "Twenty years later I was doing experiments in Eastman Kodak, Rochester, and I found the old fellow. He had five more children." (False, false!) "He wept; he was ashamed. I had nothing against him. I naturally felt strange."

"My dad is something of a stranger to me, too," said Wilhelm, and he began to muse. Where is the familiar person he used to be? Or I used to be? Catherine—she won't even talk to me any more, my own sister. It may not be so much my trouble that Papa turns his back on as my confusion. It's too much. The ruins of life, and on top of that confusion—chaos and old night. Is it an easier farewell for Dad if we don't part friends? He should maybe do it angrily— "Blast you with my curse!" And why, Wilhelm further asked, should he or anybody else pity me; or why should I be pitied sooner than another fellow? It is my childish mind that thinks people are ready to give it just because you need it.

Then Wilhelm began to think about his own two sons and to wonder how he appeared to them, and what they would think of him. Right now he had an advantage through baseball. When he went to fetch them, to go to Ebbets Field, though, he was not himself. He put on a front but he felt as if he had swallowed a fistful of sand. The strange, familiar house, horribly awkward; the dog, Scissors, rolled over on his back and barked and whined. Wilhelm acted as if there were nothing irregular, but a weary heaviness came over him. On the way to Flatbush he would think up anecdotes about old Pigtown and Charlie Ebbets for the boys and reminiscences of the old stars, but it was very heavy going. They did not know how much he cared for them. No. It hurt him greatly and he blamed Margaret for turning them against him. She wanted to ruin him, while she wore the mask of kindness. Up in Roxbury he had to go and explain to the priest, who was not sympathetic. They don't care about individuals, their rules come first. Olive said she would marry him outside the Church when he was divorced. But Margaret would not let go. Olive's father was a pretty decent old guy, an osteopath, and he understood what it was all about. Finally he said, "See here, I have to advise Olive. She is asking me. I am mostly a freethinker myself, but the girl has to live in this town." And by now, Wilhelm and Olive had had a great many troubles and she was beginning to dread his days in Roxbury, she said. He trembled at offending this small, pretty, dark girl whom he adored. When she would get up late on Sunday morning she would wake him almost in tears at being late for Mass. He would try to help her hitch her garters and smooth out her slip and dress and even put on her hat with shaky hands; then he would rush her to church and drive in second gear in his forgetful way, trying to apologize and to calm her. She got out a block from church to avoid gossip. Even so she loved him, and she would have married him if he had obtained the divorce. But Margaret must have sensed this. Margaret would tell him he did not really want a divorce; he was afraid of it. He cried, "Take everything I've got, Margaret. Let me go to Reno. Don't you want to marry again?" No. She went out with other men, but took his money. She lived in order to punish him.

Dr. Tamkin told Wilhelm, "Your dad is jealous of you."

Wilhelm smiled. "Of *me?* That's rich."

"Sure. People are always jealous of a man who leaves his wife."

"Oh," said Wilhelm scornfully. "When it comes to wives he wouldn't have to envy me."

"Yes, and your wife envies you, too. She thinks, He's free and goes with young women. Is she getting old?"

"Not exactly old," said Wilhelm, whom the mention of his wife made sad. Twenty years ago, in a neat blue wool suit, in a soft hat made of the same cloth—he could plainly see her. He stooped his yellow head and looked under the hat at her clear, simple face, her living eyes moving, her straight small nose, her jaw beautifully, painfully clear in its form. It was a cool day, but he smelled the odor of pines in the sun, in the granite canyon. Just south of Santa Barbara, this was.

"She's forty-some years old," he said.

"I was married to a lush," said Tamkin. "A painful alcoholic. I couldn't take her out to dinner because she'd say she was going to the ladies' toilet and disappear into the bar. I'd ask the bartenders they shouldn't serve her. But I loved her deeply. She was the most spiritual woman of my entire experience."

"Where is she now?"

"Drowned," said Tamkin. "At Provincetown, Cape Cod. It must have been a suicide. She was that way—suicidal. I tried everything in my power to cure her. Because," said Tamkin, "my real calling is to be a healer. I get wounded. I suffer from it. I would like to escape from the sicknesses of others, but I can't. I am only on loan to myself, so to speak. I belong to humanity."

Liar! Wilhelm inwardly called him. Nasty lies. He invented a woman and killed her off and then called himself a healer, and made himself so earnest he looked like a bad-natured sheep. He's a puffed-up little bogus and humbug with smelly feet. A doctor! A doctor would wash himself. He believes he's making a terrific impression, and he practically invites you to take off your hat when he talks about himself; and he thinks he has an imagination, but he hasn't, neither is he smart.

Then what am I doing with him here, and why did I give him the seven hundred dollars? thought Wilhelm.

Oh, this was a day of reckoning. It was a day, he thought, on which, willing or not, he would take a good close look at the truth. He breathed hard and his misshapen hat came low upon his congested dark blond face. A rude look. Tamkin was a charlatan, and furthermore he was desperate. And furthermore, Wilhelm had always known this about him. But he appeared to have worked it out at the back of his mind that Tamkin for thirty or forty years had gotten through many a tight place, that he would get through this crisis too and bring him, Wilhelm, to safety also. And Wilhelm realized that he was on Tamkin's back. It made him feel that he had virtually left the ground and was riding upon the other man. He was in the air. It was for Tamkin to take the steps.

The doctor, if he was a doctor, did not look anxious. But then his face did not have much variety. Talking always about spontaneous emotion and open receptors and free impulses, he was about as expressive as a pincushion. When his hypnotic spell failed, his big underlip made him look weak-minded. Fear stared from his eyes, sometimes, so humble as to make you sorry for him. Once or twice Wilhelm had seen that look. Like a dog, he thought. Perhaps he didn't look it now, but he was very nervous. Wilhelm knew, but he could not afford to recognize this too openly. The doctor needed a little room, a little time. He should not be pressed now. So Tamkin went on, telling his tales.

Wilhelm said to himself, I am on his back—his back. I gambled seven hundred bucks, so I must take this ride. I have to go along with him. It's too late. I can't get off.

"You know," Tamkin said, "that blind old man Rappaport—he's pretty close to totally blind—is one of the most interesting personalities around here. If you could only get him to tell his true story. It's fascinating. This is what he told me. You often hear about bigamists with a secret life. But this old man never hid anything from anybody. He's a regular patriarch. Now, I'll tell you what he did. He had two whole families, separate and apart, one in Williamsburg and the other in the Bronx. The two wives knew about each other. The wife in the Bronx was younger; she's close to seventy now. When he got sore at one wife he went to live with the other one. Meanwhile he ran his chicken business in New Jersey. By one wife he had four kids, and by the other six. They're all grown, but they never have met their half-brothers and sisters and don't want to. The whole bunch of them are listed in the telephone book."

"I can't believe it," said Wilhelm.

"He told me this himself. And do you know what else? While he had his eyesight he used to read a lot, but the only books he would read were by Theodore Roosevelt. He had a set in each of the places where he lived, and he brought his kids up on those books."

"Please," said Wilhelm, "don't feed me any more of this stuff, will you? Kindly do not—"

"In telling you this," said Tamkin with one of his hypnotic subtleties, "I do have a motive. I want you to see how some people free themselves from morbid guilt feelings and follow their instincts. Innately, the female knows how to cripple by sickening a man with guilt. It is a very special *de*struct, and she sends her curse to make a fellow impotent. As if she says, 'Unless I allow it, you will never more be a man.' But men like my old dad or Mr. Rappaport answer, 'Woman, what art thou to me?' You can't do that yet. You're a halfway case. You want to follow your instinct, but you're too worried still. For instance, about your kids—"

"Now look here," said Wilhelm, stamping his feet. "One thing! Don't bring up my boys. Just lay off."

"I was only going to say that they are better off than with conflicts in the home."

"I'm deprived of my children." Wilhelm bit his lip. It was too late to turn away. The anguish struck him. "I pay and pay. I never see them. They grow up without me. She makes them like herself. She'll bring them up to be my enemies. Please let's not talk about this."

But Tamkin said, "Why do you let her make you suffer so? It defeats the original object in leaving her. Don't play her game. Now, Wilhelm, I'm trying to do you some good. I want to tell you, don't marry suffering. Some people do. They get married to it, and sleep and eat together, just as husband and wife. If they go with joy they think it's adultery."

When Wilhelm heard this he had, in spite of himself, to admit that there was a great deal in Tamkin's words. Yes, thought Wilhelm, suffering is the only kind of life they are sure they can have, and if they quit suffering they're afraid they'll have nothing. He knows it. This time the faker knows what he's talking about.

Looking at Tamkin he believed he saw all this confessed from his usually barren face. Yes, yes, he too. One hundred falsehoods, but at last one truth. Howling like a wolf from the city window. No one can bear it any more. Everyone is so full of it that at last everybody must proclaim it. It! It!

Then suddenly Wilhelm rose and said, "That's enough of this. Tamkin, let's go back to the market."

"I haven't finished my melon."

"Never mind that. You've had enough to eat. I want to go back."

Dr. Tamkin slid the two checks across the table. "Who paid yesterday? It's your turn, I think."

It was not until they were leaving the cafeteria that Wilhelm remembered definitely that he had paid yesterday too. But it wasn't worth arguing about.

Tamkin kept repeating as they walked down the street that there were many who were dedicated to suffering. But he told Wilhelm, "I'm optimistic in your case, and I have seen a world of maladjustment. There's hope for you. You don't really want to destroy yourself. You're trying hard to keep your feelings open, Wilhelm. I can see it. Seven per cent of this country is committing suicide by alcohol. Another three, maybe, narcotics. Another sixty just fading away into dust by boredom. Twenty more who have sold their souls to the Devil. Then there's a small percentage of those who want to live. That's the only significant thing in the whole world of today. Those are the only two classes of people there are. Some want to live, but the great majority don't." This fantastic Tamkin began to surpass himself. "They don't. Or else, why these wars? I'll tell you more," he said. "The love of the dying amounts to one thing; they want you to die with them. It's because they love you. Make no mistake."

True, true! thought Wilhelm, profoundly moved by these revelations. How does he know these things? How can he be such a jerk, and even perhaps an operator, a swindler, and understand so well what gives? I believe what he says. It simplifies much—everything. People are dropping like flies. I am trying to stay alive and work too hard at it. That's what's turning my brains. This working hard defeats its own end. At what point should I start over? Let me go back a ways and try once more.

Only a few hundred yards separated the cafeteria from the broker's, and within that short space Wilhelm turned again, in measurable degrees, from these wide considerations to the problems of the moment. The closer he approached to the market, the more Wilhelm had to think about money.

They passed the newsreel theater where the ragged shoeshine kids called after them. The same old bearded man with his bandaged beggar face and his tiny ragged feet and the old press clipping on his fiddle case to prove he had once been a concert violinist, pointed his bow at Wilhelm, saying, "You!" Wilhelm went by with worried eyes, bent on crossing Seventy-second Street. In full tumult the great afternoon current raced for Columbus Circle, where the mouth of midtown stood open and the skyscrapers gave back the yellow fire of the sun.

As they approached the polished stone front of the new office building, Dr. Tamkin said, "Well, isn't that old Rappaport by the door? I think he should carry a white cane, but he will never admit there's a single thing the matter with his eyes."

Mr. Rappaport did not stand well; his knees were sunk, while his pelvis only half filled his trousers. His suspenders held them, gaping.

He stopped Wilhelm with an extended hand, having somehow recognized him. In his deep voice he commanded him, "Take me to the cigar store."

"You want me—? Tamkin!" Wilhelm whispered, "You take him."

Tamkin shook his head. "He wants you. Don't refuse the old gentleman." Significantly he said in a lower voice. "This minute is another instance of the 'here-and-now.' You have to live in this very minute, and you don't want to. A man asks you for help. Don't think of the market. It won't run away. Show your respect to the old boy. Go ahead. That may be more valuable."

"Take me," said the old chicken merchant again.

Greatly annoyed, Wilhelm wrinkled his face at Tamkin. He took the old man's big but light elbow at the bone. "Well, let's step on it," he said. "Or wait—I want to have a look at the board first to see how we're doing."

But Tamkin had already started Mr. Rappaport forward. He was walking, and he scolded Wilhelm, saying, "Don't leave me standing in the middle of the sidewalk. I'm afraid to get knocked over."

"Let's get a move on. Come." Wilhelm urged him as Tamkin went into the broker's.

The traffic seemed to come down Broadway out of the sky, where the hot spokes of the sun rolled from the south. Hot, stony odors rose from the subway grating in the street.

"These teen-age hoodlums worry me. I'm ascared of these Puerto Rican kids, and these young characters who take dope," said Mr. Rappaport. "They go around all hopped up."

"Hoodlums?" said Wilhelm. "I went to the cemetery and my mother's stone bench was split. I could have broken somebody's neck for that. Which store do you go to?"

"Across Broadway. That La Magnita sign next door to the Automat."

"What's the matter with this store here on this side?"

"They don't carry my brand, that's what's the matter."

Wilhelm cursed, but checked the words.

"What are you talking?"

"Those damn taxis," said Wilhelm. "They want to run everybody down."

They entered the cool, odorous shop. Mr. Rappaport put away his large cigars with great care in various pockets while Wilhelm muttered, "Come on, you old creeper. What a poky old character! The whole world waits on him." Rappaport did not offer Wilhelm a cigar, but, holding one up, he asked, "What do you say at the size of these, huh? They're Churchill-type cigars."

He barely crawls along, thought Wilhelm. His pants are dropping off because he hasn't got enough flesh for them to stick to. He's almost blind, and covered with spots, but this old man still makes money in the market. Is loaded with dough, probably. And I bet he doesn't give his children any. Some of them must be in their fifties. This is what keeps middle-aged men as children. He's master over the dough. Think—just think! Who controls everything? Old men of this type. Without needs. They don't need therefore they have. I need, therefore I don't have. That would be too easy.

"I'm older even than Churchill," said Rappaport.

Now he wanted to talk! But if you asked him a question in the market, he couldn't be bothered to answer.

"I bet you are," said Wilhelm. "Come, let's get going."

"I was a fighter, too, like Churchill," said the old man. "When we licked Spain I went into the Navy. Yes, I was a gob that time. What did I have to lose? Nothing. After the battle of San Juan Hill, Teddy Roosevelt kicked me off the beach."

"Come, watch the curb," said Wilhelm.

"I was curious and wanted to see what went on. I didn't have no business there, but I took a boat and rowed myself to the beach. Two of our guys was dead, layin' under the American flag to keep the flies off. So I says to the guy on duty, there, who was the sentry, 'Let's have a look at these guys. I want to see what went on here,' and he says, 'Naw,' but I talked him into it. So he took off the flag and there were these two tall guys, both gentlemen, lying in their boots. They was very tall. The two of them had long mustaches. They were high-society boys. I think one of them was called Fish, from up the Hudson, a big-shot family. When I looked up, there was Teddy Roosevelt, with his hat off, and he was looking at these fellows, the only ones who got killed there. Then he says to me, 'What's the Navy want here? Have you got orders?' 'No, sir,' I says to him. 'Well, get the hell off the beach, then.'"

Old Rappaport was very proud of this memory. "Everything he said had such snap, such class. Man! I love that Teddy Roosevelt," he said, "I love him!"

Ah, what people are! He is almost not with us, and his life is nearly gone, but T. R. once yelled at him, so he loves him. I guess it is love, too. Wilhelm smiled. So maybe the rest of Tamkin's story was true, about the ten children and the wives and the telephone directory.

He said, "Come on, come on, Mr. Rappaport," and hurried the old man back by the large hollow elbow; he gripped it through the thin cotton cloth. Re-entering the brokerage office where under the lights the tumblers were speeding with the clack of drumsticks upon wooden blocks, more than ever resembling a Chinese theater, Wilhelm strained his eyes to see the board.

The lard figures were unfamiliar. That amount couldn't be lard! They must have put the figures in the wrong slot. He traced the line back to the margin. It was down to .19, and had dropped twenty points since noon. And what about the contract of rye? It had sunk back to its earlier position, and they had lost their chance to sell.

Old Mr. Rappaport said to Wilhelm, "Read me my wheat figure."

"Oh, leave me alone for a minute," he said, and positively hid his face from the old man behind one hand. He looked for Tamkin, Tamkin's bald head, or Tamkin with his gray straw and the cocoa-colored band. He couldn't see him. Where was he? The seats next to Rowland were taken by strangers. He thrust himself over the one on the aisle, Mr. Rappaport's former place, and pushed at the back of the chair until the new occupant, a red-headed man with a thin, determined face, leaned forward to get out of his way but would not surrender the seat. "Where's Tamkin?" Wilhelm asked Rowland.

"Gee, I don't know. Is anything wrong?"

"You must have seen him. He came in a while back."

"No, but I didn't."

Wilhelm fumbled out a pencil from the top pocket of his coat and began to make calculations. His very fingers were numb, and in his agitation he was afraid he made mistakes with the decimal points and went over the subtraction and multiplication like a schoolboy at an exam. His heart, accustomed to many sorts of crisis, was now in a new panic. And, as he had dreaded, he was wiped out. It was unnecessary to ask the German manager. He could see for himself that the electronic bookkeeping device must have closed him out. The manager probably had known that Tamkin wasn't to be trusted, and on that first day he might have warned him. But you couldn't expect him to interfere.

"You get hit?" said Mr. Rowland.

And Wilhelm, quite coolly, said, "Oh, it could have been worse, I guess." He put the piece of paper into his pocket with its cigarette butts and packets of pills. The lie helped him out—although, for a moment, he was afraid he would cry. But he hardened himself. The hardening effort made a violent, vertical pain go through his chest, like that caused by a pocket of air under the collar bones. To the old chicken millionaire, who by this time had become acquainted with the drop in rye and lard, he also denied that anything serious had happened. "It's just one of those temporary slumps. Nothing to be scared about," he said, and remained in possession of himself. His need to cry, like someone in a crowd, pushed and jostled and abused him from behind, and Wilhelm did not dare turn. He said to himself, I will not cry in front of these people. I'll be damned if I'll break down in front of them like a kid, even though I never expect to see them again. No! No! And yet his unshed tears rose and rose and he looked like a man about to drown. But when they talked to him, he answered very distinctly. He tried to speak proudly.

". . . going away?" he heard Rowland ask.

"What?"

"I thought you might be going away too. Tamkin said he was going to Maine this summer for his vacation."

"Oh, going away?"

Wilhelm broke off and went to look for Tamkin in the men's toilet. Across the corridor was the room where the machinery of the board was housed. It hummed and whirred like mechanical birds, and the tubes glittered in the dark. A couple of businessmen with cigarettes in their fingers were having a conversation in the lavatory. At the top of the closet door sat a gray straw hat with a cocoa-colored band. "Tamkin," said Wilhelm. He tried to identify the feet below the door. "Are you in there, Doctor Tamkin?" he said with stifled anger. "Answer me. It's Wilhelm."

The hat was taken down, the latch lifted, and a stranger came out who looked at him with annoyance.

"You waiting?" said one of the businessmen. He was warning Wilhelm that he was out of turn.

"Me? Not me," said Wilhelm. "I'm looking for a fellow."

Bitterly angry, he said to himself that Tamkin would pay him the two hundred dollars at least, his share of the original deposit. "And before he takes the train to Maine, too. Before he spends a penny on vacation—that liar! We went into this as equal partners."

7

I was the man beneath; Tamkin was on my back, and I thought I was on his. He made me carry him, too, besides Margaret. Like this they ride on me with hoofs and claws. Tear me to pieces, stamp on me and break my bones.

Once more the hoary old fiddler pointed his bow at Wilhelm as he hurried by. Wilhelm rejected his begging and denied the omen. He dodged heavily through traffic and with his quick, small steps ran up the lower stairway of the Gloriana Hotel with its dark-tinted mirrors, kind to people's defects. From the lobby he phoned Tamkin's room, and when no one answered he took the elevator up. A rouged woman in her fifties with a mink stole led three tiny dogs on a leash, high-strung creatures with prominent black eyes, like dwarf deer, and legs like twigs. This was the eccentric Estonian lady who had been moved with her pets to the twelfth floor.

She identified Wilhelm. "You are Doctor Adler's son," she said.

Formally, he nodded.

"I am a dear friend of your father."

He stood in the corner and would not meet her glance, and she thought he was snubbing her and made a mental note to speak of it to the doctor.

The linen-wagon stood at Tamkin's door, and the chamber-maid's key with its big brass tongue was in the lock.

"Has Doctor Tamkin been here?" he asked her.

"No, I haven't seen him."

Wilhelm came in, however, to look around. He examined the

photos on the desk, trying to connect the faces with the strange people in Tamkin's stories. Big, heavy volumes were stacked under the double-pronged TV aerial. *Science and Sanity,* he read, and there were several books of poetry. The *Wall Street Journal* hung in separate sheets from the bed-table under the weight of the silver water jug. A bathrobe with lightning streaks of red and white was laid across the foot of the bed with a pair of expensive batik pajamas. It was a box of a room, but from the windows you saw the river as far uptown as the bridge, as far downtown as Hoboken. What lay between was deep, azure, dirty, complex, crystal, rusty, with the red bones of new apartments rising on the bluffs of New Jersey, and huge liners in their berths, the tugs with matted beards of cordage. Even the brackish tidal river smell rose this high like the smell of mop water. From every side he heard pianos, and the voices of men and women singing scales and opera, all mixed, and the sounds of pigeons on the ledges.

Again Wilhelm took the phone. "Can you locate Doctor Tamkin in the lobby for me?" he asked. And when the operator reported that she could not, Wilhelm gave the number of his father's room, but Dr. Adler was not in either. "Well, please give me the masseur. I say the massage room. Don't you understand me? The men's health club. Yes, Max Schilper's—how am I supposed to know the name of it?"

There a strange voice said, "Toktor Adler?" It was the old Czech prizefighter with the deformed nose and ears who was attendant down there and gave out soap, sheets, and sandals. He went away. A hollow endless silence followed. Wilhelm flickered the receiver with his nails, whistled into it, but could not summon either the attendant or the operator.

The maid saw him examining the bottles of pills on Tamkin's table and seemed suspicious of him. He was running low on Phenaphen pills and was looking for something else. But he swallowed one of his own tablets and went out and rang again for the elevator. He went down to the health club. Through the steamy windows, when he emerged, he saw the reflection of the swimming pool swirling green at the bottom of the lowest stairway. He went through the locker-room curtains. Two men wrapped in towels were playing Ping-pong. They were awkward and the ball bounded high. The Negro in the toilet was shining shoes. He did not know Dr. Adler by name, and Wilhelm descended to the massage room. On the tables naked men were lying. It was not a brightly lighted place, and it was very hot, and under the white faint moons of the ceiling shone pale skins. Calendar pictures of pretty girls dressed in tiny fringes were pinned on the wall. On the first table, eyes deeply shut in heavy silent luxury lay a man with a full square beard and short legs, stocky and black-haired. He might have been an orthodox Russian. Wrapped in a sheet, waiting, the man beside him was newly shaved and red from the steambath. He had a big happy face and was dreaming. And after him was an athlete, strikingly muscled, powerful and young, with a strong white curve to his genital and a half-angry smile on his mouth. Dr. Adler was on the fourth table, and Wilhelm stood over his father's pale, slight body. His ribs were narrow and small, his belly round, white, and high. It had its own being, like something separate. His thighs were weak, the muscles of his arms had fallen, his throat was creased.

The masseur in his undershirt bent and whispered in his ear, "It's your son," and Dr. Adler opened his eyes into Wilhelm's face. At once he saw the trouble in it, and by an instantaneous reflex he removed himself from the danger of contagion, and he said serenely, "Well, have you taken my advice, Wilky?"

"Oh, Dad," said Wilhelm.

"To take a swim and get a massage?"

"Did you get my note?" said Wilhelm.

"Yes, but I'm afraid you'll have to ask somebody else, because I can't. I had no idea you were so low on funds. How did you let it happen? Didn't you lay anything aside?"

"Oh, please, Dad," said Wilhelm, almost bringing his hands together in a clasp.

"I'm sorry," said the doctor. "I really am. But I have set up a rule. I've thought about it, I believe it is a good rule, and I don't want to change it. You haven't acted wisely. What's the matter?"

"Everything. Just everything. What isn't? I did have a little, but I haven't been very smart."

"You took some gamble? You lost it? Was it Tamkin? I told you, Wilky, not to build on that Tamkin. Did you? I suspect—"

"Yes, Dad, I'm afraid I trusted him."

Dr. Adler surrendered his arm to the masseur, who was using wintergreen oil.

"Trusted! And got taken?"

"I'm afraid I kind of—" Wilhelm glanced at the masseur but he was absorbed in his work. He probably did not listen to conversations. "I did. I might as well say it. I should have listened to you."

"Well, I won't remind you how often I warned you. It must be very painful."

"Yes, Father, it is."

"I don't know how many times you have to be burned in order to learn something. The same mistakes, over and over."

"I couldn't agree with you more," said Wilhelm with a face of despair. "You're so right, Father. It's the same mistakes, and I get burned again and again. I can't seem to—I'm stupid, Dad, I just can't breathe. My chest is all up—I feel choked. I just simply can't catch my breath."

He stared at his father's nakedness. Presently he became aware that Dr. Adler was making an effort to keep his temper. He was on the verge of an explosion. Wilhelm hung his face and said, "Nobody likes bad luck, eh Dad?"

"So! It's bad luck, now. A minute ago it was stupidity."

"It is stupidity—it's some of both. It's true that I can't learn. But I—"

"I don't want to listen to the details," said his father. "And I want you to understand that I'm too old to take on new burdens. I'm just too old to do it. And people who will just wait for help—must *wait* for help. They have got to stop waiting."

"It isn't all a question of money—there are other things a father can give to a son." He lifted up his gray eyes and his nostrils grew wide with a look of suffering appeal that stirred his father even more deeply against him.

He warningly said to him, "Look out, Wilky, you're tiring my patience very much."

"I try not to. But one word from you, just a word, would go a long way. I've never asked you for very much. But you are not a kind man, Father. You don't give the little bit I beg you for."

He recognized that his father was now furiously angry. Dr. Adler started to say something, and then raised himself and gathered the sheet over him as he did so. His mouth opened, wide, dark, twisted, and he said to Wilhelm, "You want to make yourself into my cross. But I am not going to pick up a cross. I'll see you dead, Wilky, by Christ, before I let you do that to me."

"Father, listen! Listen!"

"Go away from me now. It's torture for me to look at you, you slob!" cried Dr. Adler.

Wilhelm's blood rose up madly, in anger equal to his father's, but then it sank down and left him helplessly captive to misery. He said stiffly, and with a strange sort of formality, "Okay, Dad. That'll be enough. That's about all we should say." And he stalked out heavily by the door adjacent to the swimming pool and the steam room, and labored up two long flights from the basement. Once more he took the elevator to the lobby on the mezzanine.

He inquired at the desk for Dr. Tamkin.

The clerk said, "No, I haven't seen him. But I think there's something in the box for you."

"Me? Give it here," said Wilhelm and opened a telephone message from his wife. It read, "Please phone Mrs. Wilhelm on return. Urgent."

Whenever he received an urgent message from his wife he was always thrown into a great fear for the children. He ran to the phone booth, spilled out the change from his pockets onto the little curved steel shelf under the telephone, and dialed the Digby number.

"Yes?" said his wife. Scissors barked in the parlor.

"Margaret?"

"Yes, hello." They never exchanged any other greeting. She instantly knew his voice.

"The boys all right?"

"They're out on their bicycles. Why shouldn't they be all right? Scissors, quiet!"

"Your message scared me," he said. "I wish you wouldn't make 'urgent' so common."

"I had something to tell you."

Her familiar unbending voice awakened in him a kind of hungry longing, not for Margaret but for the peace he had once known.

"You sent me a postdated check," she said. "I can't allow that. It's already five days past the first. You dated your check for the twelfth."

"Well, I have no money. I haven't got it. You can't send me to prison for that. I'll be lucky if I can raise it by the twelfth."

She answered, "You better get it, Tommy."

"Yes? What for?" he said. "Tell me. For the sake of what? To tell lies about me to everyone? You—"

She cut him off. "You know what for. I've got the boys to bring up."

Wilhelm in the narrow booth broke into a heavy sweat. He dropped his head and shrugged while with his fingers he arranged nickels, dimes, and quarters in rows. "I'm doing my best," he said. "I've had some bad luck. As a matter of fact, it's been so bad that I don't know where I am. I couldn't tell you what day of the week this is. I can't think straight. I'd better not even try. This has been one of those days, Margaret. May I never live to go through another like it. I mean that with all my heart. So I'm not going to try to do any thinking today. Tomorrow I'm going to see some guys. One is a sales manager. The other is in television. But not to act," he hastily added. "On the business end."

"That's just some more of your talk, Tommy," she said. "You ought to patch things up with Rojax Corporation. They'd take you back. You've got to stop thinking like a youngster."

"What do you mean?"

"Well," she said, measured and unbending, remorselessly unbending, "you still think like a youngster. But you can't do that any more. Every other day you want to make a new start. But in eighteen years you'll be eligible for retirement. Nobody wants to hire a new man of your age."

"I know. But listen, you don't have to sound so hard. I can't get on my knees to them. And really you don't have to sound so hard. I haven't done you so much harm."

"Tommy, I have to chase you and ask you for money that you owe us, and I hate it."

She hated also to be told that her voice was hard.

"I'm making an effort to control myself," she told him.

He could picture her, her graying bangs cut with strict fixity above her pretty, decisive face. She prided herself on being fair-minded. We could not bear, he thought, to know what we do. Even though blood is spilled. Even though the breath of life is taken from someone's nostrils. This is the way of the weak; quiet and fair. And then smash! They smash!

"Rojax take me back? I'd have to crawl back. They don't need me. After so many years I should have got stock in the firm. How can I support the three of you, and live myself, on half the territory? And why should I even try when you won't lift a finger to help? I sent you back to school, didn't I? At that time you said—"

His voice was rising. She did not like that and intercepted him. "You misunderstood me," she said.

"You must realize you're killing me. You can't be as blind as all that. Thou shalt not kill! Don't you remember that?"

She said, "You're just raving now. When you calm down it'll be different. I have great confidence in your earning ability."

"Margaret, you don't grasp the situation. You'll have to get a job."

"Absolutely not. I'm not going to have two young children running loose."

"They're not babies," Wilhelm said. "Tommy is fourteen. Paulie is going to be ten."

"Look," Margaret said in her deliberate manner. "We can't continue this conversation if you're going to yell so, Tommy. They're at a dangerous age. There are teen-aged gangs—the parents working, or the families broken up."

Once again she was reminding him that it was he who had left her. She had the bringing up of the children as her burden, while he must expect to pay the price of his freedom.

Freedom! he thought with consuming bitterness. Ashes in his mouth, not freedom. Give me my children. For they are mine too.

Can you be the woman I lived with? he started to say. Have you forgotten that we slept so long together? Must you now deal with me like this, and have no mercy?

He would be better off with Margaret again than he was today. This was what she wanted to make him feel, and she drove it home. "Are you in misery?" she was saying. "But you have deserved it." And he could not return to her any more than he could beg Rojax to take him back. If it cost him his life, he could not. Margaret had ruined him with Olive. She hit him and hit him, beat him, battered him, wanted to beat the very life out of him.

"Margaret, I want you please to reconsider about work. You have that degree now. Why did I pay your tuition?"

"Because it seemed practical. But it isn't. Growing boys need parental authority and a home."

He begged her, "Margaret, go easy on me. You ought to. I'm at the end of my rope and feel that I'm suffocating. You don't want to be responsible for a person's destruction. You've got to let up. I feel I'm about to burst." His face had expanded. He struck a blow upon the tin and wood and nails of the wall of the booth. "You've got to let me breathe. If I should keel over, what then? And it's something I can never understand about you. How you can treat someone like this whom you lived with so long. Who gave you the best of himself. Who tried. Who loved you." Merely to pronounce the word "love" made him tremble.

"Ah," she said with a sharp breath. "Now we're coming to it. How did you imagine it was going to be—big shot? Everything made smooth for you? I thought you were leading up to this."

She had not, perhaps, intended to reply as harshly as she did, but she brooded a great deal and now she could not forbear to punish him and make him feel pains like those she had to undergo.

He struck the wall again, this time with his knuckles, and he had scarcely enough air in his lungs to speak in a whisper, because his heart pushed upward with a frightful pressure. He got up and stamped his feet in the narrow enclosure.

"Haven't I always done my best?" he yelled, though his voice sounded weak and thin to his own ears. "Everything comes from me and nothing back again to me. There's no law that'll punish this, but you are committing a crime against me. Before God—and that's no joke. I mean that. Before God! Sooner or later the boys will know it."

In a firm tone, levelly, Margaret said to him, "I won't stand to be howled at. When you can speak normally and have something sensible to say I'll listen. But not to this." She hung up.

Wilhelm tried to tear the apparatus from the wall. He ground his teeth and seized the black box with insane digging fingers and made a stifled cry and pulled. Then he saw an elderly lady staring through the glass door, utterly appalled by him, and he ran from the booth, leaving a large amount of change on the shelf. He hurried down the stairs and into the street.

On Broadway it was still bright afternoon and the gassy air was almost motionless under the leaden spokes of sunlight, and sawdust footprints lay about the doorways of butcher shops and fruit stores. And the great, great crowd, the inexhaustible current of millions of every race and kind pouring out, pressing round, of every age, of every genius, possessors of every human secret, antique and future, in every face the refinement of one particular motive or essence—*I labor, I spend, I strive, I design, I love, I cling, I uphold, I give way, I envy, I long, I scorn, I die, I hide, I want.* Faster, much faster than any man could make the tally. The sidewalks were wider than any causeway; the street itself was immense, and it quaked and gleamed and it seemed to Wilhelm to throb at the last limit of endurance. And although the sunlight appeared like a broad tissue, its actual weight made him feel like a drunkard.

"I'll get a divorce if it's the last thing I do," he swore. "As for Dad— As for Dad— I'll have to sell the car for junk and pay the hotel. I'll have to go on my knees to Olive and say, 'Stand by me a while. Don't let her win. Olive!'" And he thought, I'll try to start again with Olive. In fact, I must. Olive loves me. Olive—

Beside a row of limousines near the curb he thought he saw Dr. Tamkin. Of course he had been mistaken before about the hat with the cocoa-colored band and didn't want to make the same mistake twice. But wasn't that Tamkin who was speaking so earnestly, with pointed shoulders, to someone under the canopy of the funeral parlor? For this was a huge funeral. He looked for the singular face under the dark gray, fashionable hatbrim. There were two open cars filled with flowers, and a policeman tried to keep a path open to pedestrians. Right at the canopy-pole, now wasn't that that damned Tamkin talking away with a solemn face, gesticulating with an open hand?

"Tamkin!" shouted Wilhelm, going forward. But he was pushed to the side by a policeman clutching his nightstick at both ends, like a rolling pin. Wilhelm was even farther from Tamkin now, and swore under his breath at the cop who continued to press him back, back, belly and ribs, saying, "Keep it moving there, please," his face red with impatient sweat, his brows like red fur. Wilhelm said to him haughtily, "You shouldn't push people like this."

The policeman, however, was not really to blame. He had been ordered to keep a way clear. Wilhelm was moved forward by the pressure of the crowd.

He cried, "Tamkin!"

But Tamkin was gone. Or rather, it was he himself who was carried from the street into the chapel. The pressure ended inside, where it was dark and cool. The flow of fan-driven air dried his face, which he wiped hard with his handkerchief to stop the slight salt itch. He gave a sigh when he heard the organ notes that stirred and breathed from the pipes and he saw people in the pews. Men in formal clothes and black homburgs strode softly back and forth on the cork floor, up and down the center aisle. The white of the stained glass was like mother-of-pearl, the blue of the Star of David like velvet ribbon.

Well, thought Wilhelm, if that was Tamkin outside I might as well wait for him here where it's cool. Funny, he never mentioned he had a funeral to go to today. But that's just like the guy.

But within a few minutes he had forgotten Tamkin. He stood along the wall with others and looked toward the coffin and the slow line that was moving past it, gazing at the face of the dead. Presently he too was in this line, and slowly, slowly, foot by foot, the beating of his heart anxious, thick, frightening, but somehow also rich, he neared the coffin and paused for his turn, and gazed down. He caught his breath when he looked at the corpse, and his face swelled, his eyes shone hugely with instant tears.

The dead man was gray-haired. He had two large waves of gray hair at the front. But he was not old. His face was long, and he had a bony nose, slightly, delicately twisted. His brows were raised as though he had sunk into the final thought. Now at last he was with it, after the end of all distractions, and when his flesh was no longer flesh. And by this meditative look Wilhelm was so struck that he could not go away. In spite of the tinge of horror, and then the splash of heartsickness that he felt, he could not go. He stepped out of line and remained beside the coffin; his eyes filled silently and through his still tears he studied the man as the line of visitors moved with veiled looks past the satin coffin toward the standing bank of lilies, lilacs, roses. With great stifling sorrow, almost admiration, Wilhelm nodded and nodded. On the surface, the dead man with his formal shirt and his tie and silk lapels and his powdered skin looked so proper; only a little beneath so—black, Wilhelm thought, so fallen in the eyes.

Standing a little apart, Wilhelm began to cry. He cried at first softly and from sentiment, but soon from deeper feeling. He sobbed loudly and his face grew distorted and hot, and the tears stung his skin. A man—another human creature, was what first went through his thoughts, but other and different things were torn from him. What'll I do? I'm stripped and kicked out. . . . Oh, Father, what do I ask of you? What'll I do about the kids—Tommy, Paul? My children. And Olive? My dear! Why, why, why—you must protect me against that devil who wants my life. If you want it, then kill me. Take, take it, take it from me.

Soon he was past words, past reason, coherence. He could not stop. The source of all tears had suddenly sprung open within him, black, deep, and hot, and they were pouring out and convulsed his body, bending his stubborn head, bowing his shoulders, twisting his face, crippling the very hands with which he held the handkerchief. His efforts to collect himself were useless. The great knot of ill and grief in his throat swelled upward and he gave in utterly and held his face and wept. He cried with all his heart.

He, alone of all the people in the chapel, was sobbing. No one knew who he was.

One woman said, "Is that perhaps the cousin from New Orleans they were expecting?"

"It must be somebody real close to carry on so."

"Oh my, oh my! To be mourned like that," said one man and looked at Wilhelm's heavy shaken shoulders, his clutched face and whitened fair hair, with wide, glinting, jealous eyes.

"The man's brother, maybe?"

"Oh, I doubt that very much," said another bystander. "They're not alike at all. Night and day."

The flowers and lights fused ecstatically in Wilhelm's blind, wet eyes; the heavy sea-like music came up to his ears. It poured into him where he had hidden himself in the center of a crowd by the great and happy oblivion of tears. He heard it and sank deeper than sorrow, through torn sobs and cries toward the consummation of his heart's ultimate need.

TOPICS FOR PAPERS AND DISCUSSION

1. *Thematic focus on love.* Maurice Venice said to the young Wilhelm: "You become a lover to the whole world." Tommy says: "A man is only as good as what he loves." Relate these statements to the many references to love, both positive and negative, involving Margaret, Olive, Dr. and Mrs. Adler, Tamkin, and his poem. Check the revealing reference to "one of those subway things" in Chapter Five. What evidence is there that Tommy is or is not capable of reciprocating? Relate his statements about love to scenes, including the final one, in which the theme is rendered indirectly. Examine Tommy and the quality of his love at various levels: as son, husband, father, lover, friend, etc.

2. *"Sunk though he be beneath the wat'ry floor."* Analyze the full range of possible meanings of the important motif of water and everything related to it. Discuss the motif of sinking, descending, and falling. Examine references to eyes and sight and the multiple variations on them. How are water, sinking, and eyes related? How do the motifs overlap, repeat, extend, reinforce, or even stand in contrast to each other as groups of related ideas? Analyze closely those passages in which they are united. Include crossing or the refusal to cross or touch water. Discuss watery settings used as metaphor, as in the first paragraph.

3. *Thematic polarities and doublings.* This novel is densely packed with dramatic tensions, opposing ideas, counterthemes, and doublings of characters. One of the most important is "fathers and sons." Examine this conflict in detail as it reflects theme. Consider other thematic subjects: aging and death, sickness and health, animality and humanity, communication and noncommunication, youth and age, sadism and masochism, innocence and guilt, pretense and authenticity, alienation and accommodation, wasting one's life and seizing an elusive day,

freedom and suppression, the individual and the crowd, need and denial, thinness and fatness.

4. *Suffering-loss-redemption.* Discuss this ancient pattern of initiation and/or salvation as a paradigm for Tommy's life during the few hours covered by the novel. Describe the range and function of the motifs of pain, destruction, and reward. For instance, these three may be physical, psychological, or spiritual. Recall what Tommy thinks he might be dedicated to. Relate his mistakes and those of the other characters to this pattern. Show the significance of the conversations and thoughts about hell, purgatory, and paradise. Also, consider this subject in terms of the "pretender soul" and "true soul."

5. *Success and money.* How do the principles of materialism affect Tommy and everyone within the money-oriented society of this story? Relate these broader ideas: (1) the implicit American dictum "to be is to succeed," (2) the American "dream of success" and the "nightmare of failure." Why would money not actually solve Tommy's existential crisis? Given the symbolic role of money, why is it necessary that he be wiped out in the commodities market and especially by losses in lard? What is the relationship of success, money, and Tommy's particular financial problems to Tamkin's poem and to some of Tamkin's stories?

6. *Wilhelm as antihero and hero.* Gather evidence that Tommy is a dirty slob and a resounding failure. Next list his worthwhile attributes. Then decide what are the qualities of his mind, emotions, aspirations, and relationships that might contribute to a revised opinion of him. In what complex ways does he view himself, his father, Perls, Tamkin, and the women in his life? Account for the repeated identification with toys, and the repetition of his childlike characteristics. How are his Jewishness (the "wrong kind" or "right kind") and the use of his four names significant? Examine his need to distinguish himself and his need to be liked by and to like others.

7. *Human responsibility.* Describe Tommy's concern or lack of concern for others on this day of multiple crises. What is thus revealed about his sense of responsibility to himself and others? With whom and what does he sympathize most deeply? Analyze his search for identity, his silent plea for transformation, and his quest for salvation as related to his sense of responsibility. How do the other characters, notably Dr. Adler and Tamkin, meet or evade responsibility? How does the thematic subject of responsibility color the ending? Ponder the meaning of passages in the novel that deal with universal brotherhood.

8. *Tamkin.* What is to be made of the enigmatic Tamkin who appears profoundly wise and thoroughly deceptive? Consider the physical description of him. What is the significance of his appearance precisely at this crucial point in Tommy's life? Read Carl G. Jung's essay "The Phenomenology of the Spirit in Fairy Tales" and relate it to Tamkin's

role. How does he serve as a surrogate father? Explain how he can be a spur to creative thought, even a savior, and yet find it necessary to render Tommy penniless. Does the character of Tamkin need to be more fully developed, as Bellow himself once suggested? Explain.

9. *Parallelism in characters.* The roles of Maurice Venice, Margaret Wilhelm, and Tamkin have certain similar features. For example, Tommy is tempted by them. Discuss the nature and importance of these temptations. What other aspects of character do they share which are important to Tommy's fate? Given his character, why is it necessary that the three encounters with these people end in similar ways? It should be noted that Tommy's mother tried to put a stop to the Hollywood venture, and that Dr. Adler claims prior wisdom by warning him about Margaret and Tamkin. How do these parental attempts to restrict Tommy reflect his own intuitions and actions?

10. *Minor characters.* Explain the roles of the unseen women who figure in Tommy's life. What is the relationship of 'Nita Christenberry and Olive, if any? Why is Tommy so disturbed that his father had apparently forgotten his mother's death, and that the bench by her grave had been broken? What common element do almost all the women share in their relationship with Tommy? How do the minor male characters function to reveal aspects of his character? Consider Rubin, the German manager, the old men like Perls and Rappaport, and Artie, the cousin. In addition, how is the dog Scissors important to the story?

11. *Symbolic setting and expressive structure.* What does the novel reveal about conditions of urban life, particularly New York's upper Broadway? Analyze the symbolic use of the Gloriana Hotel, its public and private rooms, above and below ground, including the movie house. Do the same for the Ansonia Hotel, the brokerage office, etc. What is significant about other places like Penn State, the talent scout's office, Southern California, Cuba, Florida? Why are many of them identified by theater imagery? Comment on the importance of Roxbury. Connect the settings and Tommy's activities to the novel's seven-part structure. Work back and forth from the pivotal fourth chapter.

12. *Digressive passages.* Discuss the thematic function of Tamkin's apparently outrageous stories about his own adventures, the affairs of his patients, and his personal life. How would you defend the inclusion of his theories about the psychology of the stock market in this group? Contrast those stories with his philosophy of life, if it can be called that. In what manner, if at all, do the stories dramatize his philosophy? What relationship do his digressions have to Tommy's problems? Examine other digressions and relate them to the central concerns of the novel.

13. *The art of allusion.* Examine the text carefully for titles of books and literary allusions to Jesus, Plato, Donne, Shakespeare, Milton, Shelley, Wilde, Yeats, and others. Explain how the original context of the

allusions sheds light on their context within *Seize the Day* itself. Determine whether each allusion reinforces the new context, whether it enlarges the situation, whether it is symbolic, whether it is analytical, or whether it serves profound thematic ends. How might each allusion function as a device of characterization and of tone? Trace the literary background of the Latin phrase *carpe diem.*

14. *The end.* The ambiguous ending provokes critical controversy. Should the ending be taken as affirmative or negative? How are many of the strands of the story focused in the final scene, including the motifs of dying and death, of water and tears, of hypocrisy and genuineness, of vain love and true love? Read Ferdinand's remarks and Ariel's song in Shakespeare's *The Tempest:* "This music crept by me on the waters" (I, ii, 391–402). How does this passage dealing with death by water and a transformation to a higher order of being provide a clue to one interpretation of the ending? Defend your own interpretation, whether it be optimistic or pessimistic.

15. *The Bellow style and voice.* Describe the Bellow style as concretely as possible. Is it an adequate instrument to convey the weighty psychological and philosophical content of Tommy's (and maybe mankind's) story? Could the style be considered labyrinthine at times? Find examples for analysis. Comment on the maze of conflicting tones and what they convey of emotions and characters. Analyze some of those passages in which Bellow's narrative voice is didactic, objective, ambiguous, or lyrical. Attempt to determine what is gained by this flexibility of voice.

Biographical Notes

PHILIP ROTH was born March 19, 1933, in Newark, New Jersey. He graduated from Bucknell University in 1954 and took a master's degree from the University of Chicago in 1955. After Army service, he taught English at the University of Chicago from 1956 to 1958. He has been a visiting instructor of writing at several universities: Iowa, Princeton, Pennsylvania, and SUNY at Stony Brook. Roth burst into prominence in 1959 with the publication of *Goodbye, Columbus and Five Short Stories,* a collection which won the National Book Award for fiction the following year. Since then he has written ten novels: *Letting Go* (1962); *When She Was Good* (1967); *Portnoy's Complaint,* which became a bestseller (1969); *Our Gang,* a political satire (1971); *The Breast,* a short novel (1972); *The Great American Novel,* a fable about baseball (1973); *My Life as a Man* (1974); *The Professor of Desire* (1977); *The Ghost Writer,* a short novel (1979); and *Zuckerman Unbound* (1981). He also wrote a book of critical commentary, *Reading Myself and Others,* which appeared in 1975. He has been instrumental in bringing distinguished Eastern European writers to the attention of an American audience by serving as General Editor of the "Writers from the Other Europe" series for Penguin Books. Roth is an accomplished writer of short fiction, and his short stories have appeared in noted collections like *Best Short Stories, O. Henry Prize Stories,* and *The New American Review.* He has published articles, reviews, and stories in such magazines as *Commentary, The New Yorker, Esquire, The New York Review of Books,* and *Harper's.* Roth received a Guggenheim Fellowship in 1960, held a Ford grant in 1962, and in 1970 he was elected a member of the National Institute of Arts and Letters. Now unmarried, he lives and writes in New York City.

CARSON (SMITH) McCULLERS was born in Columbus, Georgia, February 19, 1917. Unlike many other Southern writers, notably William Faulkner and Flannery O'Connor, she chose to live away from her native region. However, the South remained the principal setting of her fiction. As a teenager, she went to New York to pursue a career in music, and New York was to remain her home for most of her adult life. After brief attendance at Columbia University and New York University, she was married in 1937 to Reeves McCullers. (He took his life in 1953.) Although music seemed to engage her at first, she expressed an early interest in writing. Her first novel, *The Heart Is a Lonely Hunter,* was published when she was only twenty-three. She produced four more novels: *Reflections in a Golden Eye* (1941), *The Member of the Wedding* (1946), and *Clock Without Hands* (1961). *The Ballad of the Sad Café,* which appeared in 1943 in *Harper's Bazaar,* became part of a distinguished collection of stories published in 1951 under the same title. Her other works include *The Square Root of Wonderful* (1958) and a volume of children's rhymes, *Sweet as a Pickle and Clean as a Pig* (1964). McCullers also met success as a playwright, adapting her novel *The Member of the Wedding* for the Broadway stage; it won the New York Critics Award as the best play of 1950. In 1963 she assisted Edward Albee with his stage adaptation of *The Ballad of the Sad Café.* A volume of previously uncollected writings, entitled *The Mortgaged Heart,* appeared posthumously in 1971. McCullers was plagued by ill health, writing for many years handicapped by partial paralysis. She died at the age of fifty on September 29, 1967, in Nyack, New York. A slow, meticulous worker, she produced a small body of work that is limited in range, but marked by its skillful control, strength of characterization, and profound vision.

KURT VONNEGUT, JR., was born on Armistice Day, November 11, 1922, in Indianapolis, Indiana. His father and grandfather were prominent Indiana architects, and his older brother is a distinguished scientist. Vonnegut attended four universities, including Cornell where he was a student of chemistry from 1940 to 1942, and the University of Chicago where, from 1945 to 1947, he studied anthropology. During World War II he served as an infantryman in Europe. Captured in the Battle of the Bulge, he was among a group of American POW's interned in Dresden, Germany, when it was bombed by American and British planes in February, 1945. After brief stints as a news reporter in Chicago and a public relations man for General Electric in Schenectady, Vonnegut began full-time writing in 1950. Living on Cape Cod with his first wife Jane and their large family, he managed to make a living writing for the paperback market and for popular magazines like *Collier's, Cosmopolitan,* and the *Saturday Evening Post.* Vonnegut's career ascends over three decades from obscurity and mislabeling as "science fiction writer" to recognition as a youth-cult figure to overdue critical acceptance as a serious artist to continuing national stature. He has written ten novels: *Player Piano* (1952), *The Sirens of Titan* (1959), *Mother Night* (1961), *Cat's Cradle* (1963), *God Bless You, Mr. Rosewater* (1965), *Slaughterhouse-Five* (1969), *Breakfast of Champions* (1973), *Slapstick* (1976), *Jailbird* (1979). His latest book is *Palm Sunday* (1981), a fictional and journalistic pastiche. He has also written two collections of short stories, *Canary in a Cat House* (1961), and *Welcome to the Monkey House* (1968). His best known play is *Happy Birthday, Wanda June* (1968); he has also written for television. Some of his many stories, reviews, and articles were collected in *Wampeters, Foma & Granfalloons* (1974). He taught at the Writers' Workshop at the University of Iowa for two years and also later held a guest lectureship at Harvard. He was awarded a Guggenheim Fellowship to Germany in 1967, and in 1973 was elected a member of the National Institute of Arts and Letters. His second wife is the photographer Jill Krementz. He now resides in New York City.

TONI MORRISON (christened Chloe Anthony Wofford) was born in Lorain, Ohio, a port and steel-mill city on Lake Erie, on February 18, 1931, of a family of emigrants from the South. She graduated from Howard University in 1953 and took an M.A. in English from Cornell in 1955. She has been a college beauty queen, a dancer, and an actress. She taught English and humanities at Texas Southern for two years, at Howard for another seven years, and was later a guest lecturer at Yale and Bard. She worked as a textbook editor in Syracuse for a short time. As a senior editor for Random House in New York City, she has been instrumental in the publishing of esteemed fiction, history, and biography by black writers. She edited *The*

Black Book (1974), a miscellany that covers Black American life over 300 years. Her own career as a writer began in 1967. Her first novel, *The Bluest Eye,* was published in 1970. Since then, to mounting critical acclaim, three more of her novels have appeared: *Sula* (1973); *Song of Solomon* (1977), for which she won the National Book Critics Circle Award; and *Tar Baby* (1981). Her fiction is distinguished by its evocative, lyrical prose, its mythologizing of character, its strong sense of place. She relies on folklore, history, sociology, ritual, music, poetry, and supernaturalism to attain her vivid re-creations of black experience and black culture in America. She lectures widely, and has also published criticism and social commentary. She is a member of the American Academy and Institute of Arts and Letters, and an active member of the National Council on the Arts. Her marriage to Harold Morrison ended in 1964; as a single parent, she raised two sons. She lives in a four-story former boathouse on the Hudson River near Manhattan.

JERZY KOSINSKI was born in Lodz, Poland, June 14, 1933. He arrived in the United States in 1957. In Poland he was educated at the University of Lodz, and later served as an associate professor at the Polish Academy of Arts and Sciences in Warsaw. With master's degrees in both history and political science, he also studied sociology at the doctoral level for several years at Columbia University. He has taught English at Yale and Princeton and held a fellowship at the Center for Advanced Studies at Wesleyan University. His first novel, *The Painted Bird* (1965), won the French *Prix du Meilleur Livre Etranger* for the best foreign work of fiction. His next novel, *Steps* (1968), won America's National Book Award for fiction. After *Being There* (1971), he published five more novels: *The Devil Tree* (1973; revised edition, 1981), *Cockpit* (1975), *Blind Date* (1977), *Passion Play* (1979), and *Pinball* (1982). His nonfiction works include two books of literary criticism and two volumes on collective behavior: *The Future Is Ours, Comrade: Conversations with the Russians* (1960) and *No Third Path* (1962), written under the pen name of Joseph Novak. For his screen adaptation of *Being There* he won the Best Screenplay of the Year Award from both the Writers Guild of America and the British Academy of Film and Television Arts. He has held Ford and Guggenheim fellowships, and, among his many honors, he received the Award in Literature of the National Institute of Arts and Letters. His works have been translated into every major language. Of individuals he wrote (in *The New York Times*) that "the knowledge we form of ourselves is nothing but a collective image which like ubiquitous television engulfs us. One image is interchangeable with another." He adds that "we are a culture of the denial of the self," and he sees the great enemy permeating our culture to be "the collective-conformist" attitude of individuals. Kosinski lives in New York City.

MARGARET ATWOOD was born in Ottawa, Ontario, Canada, November 18, 1939. She received her B.A. from Victoria College, University of Toronto in 1961, and M.A. from Radcliffe in 1962, undertook graduate studies at Harvard in the middle Sixties, received the D.Litt. from Trent University in 1973, and an LL.D. from Queens University in 1974. Her career has been diversified: cashier, waitress, market research firm writer, film script writer, college teacher, editor, critic, novelist, poet. From 1964 to 1973, she taught English at the University of British Columbia, Sir George Williams University, York University at Toronto, and the University of Toronto where she was writer in residence. She was editor and member of the board of directors, House of Anansi Press, Toronto. Her fiction includes *The Edible Woman* (1969), *Surfacing* (1972), *Lady Oracle* (1976), and *Life Before Man* (1979). Her books of poetry are *Double Persephone* (1961), *The Circle Game* (1966), for which she won the Governor-General's Award, *The Animals in That Country* (1968), *The Journals of Susanna Moodie* (1970), *Procedures for Underground* (1970), *Power Politics* (1971), *You Are Happy* (1974), and *Selected Poems* (1976). Critics have described her poems as deceptively simple; they display an interest in myth making, and their imagery and technical control are extraordinary. Her critical study *Survival: A Thematic Guide to Canadian Literature* was published in 1972. Atwood's poetry, fiction, and critical articles have appeared in Canadian and American literary magazines and anthologies, and she has won numerous awards and prizes. The critic Melvin Mattocks draws attention to her preoccupation with "primeval isolation; a selfhood that is mystery, most of all to oneself; an animal sense of mortality." In her work "technology and social sophistication are transparent pretenses behind which man is naked, with drooling fangs and club at the ready." She has worked in Canada, the United States, England, Italy, and now lives near Alliston, Ontario.

SAUL BELLOW, the son of Russian-Jewish immigrants, was born in Lachine, Quebec, July 10, 1915, and grew up in Chicago. He attended the University of Chicago from 1933 to 1935 and graduated from Northwestern University in 1937. For a time in the 1940s, he was a member of the editorial department of *Encyclopaedia Britannica;* he also saw service as a merchant seaman during World War II. Bellow has taught at several colleges and universities, including Bard, Princeton, Minnesota, and most recently served as a professor with the Committee on Social Thought at the University of Chicago. He was made a Guggenheim Fellow in 1948 and 1955. He received the National Book Award for fiction in 1953 and 1965, a Ford Foundation grant in 1959, the International Literature Prize in 1965, and the Pulitzer Prize for fiction in 1976. He is also a member of the American Institute of Arts and Letters. Bellow's first published story appeared in 1940, and since then he has written eight novels: *Dangling Man* (1944), *The Victim* (1947), *The Adventures of Augie March* (1953), *Seize the Day* (1956), *Henderson the Rain King* (1959), *Herzog* (1964), *Mr. Sammler's Planet* (1970), and *Humboldt's Gift* (1975). Bellow has also written short stories, plays, essays, and reviews. A collection of his shorter fiction, *Mosby's Memoirs and Other Stories,* was published in 1968. Among his best-known stories are "A Father-to-Be," "Looking for Mr. Green," "A Sermon by Dr. Pep," "The Mexican General," and the recent prizewinning "A Silver Dish." The essays include "Deep Readers of the Word Beware," "Distractions of a Fiction Writer," "Facts That Put Fancy to Flight," and "The Future of Fiction." His last piece of nonfiction writing was *To Jerusalem and Back* (1976). *The Last Analysis,* a play, was produced in 1964, and in 1966 the three short plays *Out from Under, Orange Soufflé,* and *The Wen* were produced. Bellow also edited the literary journal *The Noble Savage.* He has lived most of his life in Chicago. The crowning achievement of his distinguished career occurred in 1976 when he became the eighth American to be awarded the Nobel Prize for Literature.